D1342116

ST. HELENS COMMUNITY LIBRARIES

This book is due for return on or before the last date shown. Fines are charged on overdue books. Renewal may be made by personal application, post or telephone, quoting date, author, title and book number.

1 6 OCT 2000	27 JAN 2004	-9 DEC 2009
Z19		
2 0 APR 2001	25 FEB 2004	-4 MAY 2011
1 1 MAY 2001	22 MAR 2004	
C 2.	-8 OCT 2004	Used copy
2 8 SEP 2001		CA- APR 2013
2 0 NOV 2001	-7 FEB 2008	1 2 NOV 2015
		-7 DEC 2016
2 7 JUN 2002	2 3 SEP 2008	
	N2L	1 4 NOV 2018
-8 NOV 2002	-6 OCT 2009	
B14 - AUG 2022		

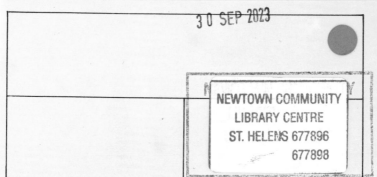

3 0 SEP 2023

T.C. BARKER

*Professor of Economic History
in the University of London*

The Glassmakers

*Pilkington: the rise of
an international company
1826-1976*

77   00865

666.1

WEIDENFELD AND NICOLSON
London

Weidenfeld and Nicolson
11 St John's Hill, London SW11.

Chapters 1-11 are based on T.C.Barker *Pilkington Brothers and the Glass Industry* published in 1960. All enquiries should be made to The Group Archives and Records Service, Pilkington Brothers Limited, St Helens, Merseyside WA10 3TT.

ISBN 0 297 76909 X

Printed in Great Britain by The Kynoch Press, Birmingham B6 7BA

'*Facts are stubborn, wilful things. You can arrange them in either logical or chronological order, but very seldom at the same time in both. Therein at once lie the difficulty and the fascination of historical composition.*'

From T. S. Ashton's inaugural lecture as Professor of Economic History in the University of London, 7 February 1946

Contents

The introduction of coal-fired furnaces for glassmaking at the beginning of the seventeenth century caused the industry to move to the coalfields. The Tyne, the chief source of coal, became the centre of the glass industry and held this position until the middle of the nineteenth century. Auxiliary furnaces were built in districts which could not be supplied easily from the north-east. Lancashire was such a district. The first coal-fired furnace was built just to the south-east of Manchester. By 1700 a furnace had been built near St Helens. Early history of plate glass, a luxury product made in London. Small-scale attempts to make this thicker glass by casting instead of by blowing. The first factory to cast plate glass on a large scale built at Ravenhead, St Helens, largely owing to the intervention of John Mackay, a local coalowner. The works' early failures and later successes. The Mackays became partners in the Eccleston Crown Glassworks, started in 1792. William Pilkington, who had set up in practice in the area as a doctor a few years before, also ran a wine and spirit business which his sons later joined.

J. W. Bell (who had come to the neighbourhood as a flint glass-maker) and five other local men formed a partnership in 1826 to make window glass, the firm being known as the St Helens Crown Glass Company. William Pilkington, Dr Pilkington's second son, was probably brought in by his brother-in-law, Peter Greenall. At first William Pilkington considered the venture merely as an investment, but he was drawn into its management when Bell became involved in a dispute with the excise authorities and the other partners, except Greenall, withdrew.

and many glassmakers were tempted to break their contracts and seek higher pay elsewhere. This happened at Pilkingtons and the firm had the misfortune of failing to bring a runaway to justice owing to a legal technicality, thereby creating the impression that their contracts were invalid. Glassmakers' contracts and their working and living conditions considered. Pilkingtons provided recreation facilities and schooling at an early date. Note on the two Pilkington partners and their families.

The firms which had taken up sheet glass before the boom of the mid-40s flourished, whereas the others grew feeble and eventually went out of business. Remarkable collapse of window glass manufacture on the Tyne. Chances, Pilkingtons and Hartleys (of Sunderland) emerged as the three leading manufacturers. Great expansion in the 1850s; extensions at St Helens and acquisition of the Eccleston factory where rolled plate glass, a new product, was made. The firm also began to make cathedral glass and branched out into the coal and chemical industries.

The removal of duties on home-produced glass was accompanied by a reduction of the tariff on imports. From 1853 cheap Belgian glass started to come into Britain in some quantity and, when Belgian exports were diverted from America during the Civil War, competition became more intense and continued to grow very rapidly. The Manufacturers' Association tried to limit this competition but there was no Belgian counterpart with which it could come to terms. The Belgians were soon sending to Britain as much window glass as Chances, Pilkingtons and Hartleys themselves made. This competition led to retrenchment. Crown glass went out of production, Siemens' regenerative gas furnaces saved fuel, and a cut in freight charges between St Helens and the Mersey reduced transport costs. Retirement of Richard and William Pilkington. They were each succeeded by two of their sons.

The second generation puts new life into the firm which became very profitable. More land was purchased next to the works and further extensions built. Rolled plate manufacture was removed there from the Eccleston factory. Pilkingtons wrested supremacy from Chances by quickly installing tank furnaces (which allowed round-the-clock working) and by venturing successfully into plate glass in a new works, built at Cowley Hill, St Helens. Pilkingtons alone among plate glass manufacturers were able to weather very intense competition in plate glass towards the end of the century because window glass was still profitable and because of lower production costs. Pilkingtons became sole producers of plate glass in Britain in 1903. With the demise of Hartleys in 1894, they and Chances, then a much smaller concern, emerged as the only surviving makers of window glass. Profits were large enough, particularly between 1882 and 1892, to make possible much reinvestment. A new plate glassworks was acquired at Maubeuge and warehouses in Canada. Rapidly-growing exports were a particular feature of these years. In 1894 Pilkingtons became a limited company, with shares confined to the family. Several members of the third generation were introduced to the Board.

threats followed in an attempt to bring Pilkington into line. A new window glassworks was started at St Helens, but soon failed and a new English plate glass factory was threatened. Pilkington agreed to follow the continentals' plate glass prices and to limit its surface grinding area but managed nevertheless to double output by installing more up-to-date grinding machinery. It also built a plate glass lehr and invested heavily in mechanisation and electrification. St Gobain's decision to take a stake in Chances (1911), however, at last caused Pilkington to collaborate more closely with the Plate Glass Convention.

13   1900–1914: NORTH AMERICAN INFLUENCES   208

Pilkington's flourishing commercial base in Canada, where more warehouses were opened across the continent to supplement those at Montreal and Toronto, brought the company into close touch with technical developments in the United States. It also caused it to take a licence for and work a new window glassmaking process in Britain and Canada in order to prevent its developers, the giant American Window Glass Co., from manufacturing in Canada. This drawn cylinder process, which replaced window glass blowers but not flatteners, committed Pilkington to a non-continuous process when continuous processes were starting to be developed. It also involved the company in a Canadian factory at Thorold which became a serious drain upon its resources. Correspondence with Austin Pilkington, who was sent to Colorado to recuperate from tuberculosis from 1909, sheds light upon these events and insights into the problems of a sales staff working far from head office.

14   1900–1914: LABOUR AND CAPITAL   229

The introduction of the new process at St Helens did not give rise to labour disputes. Trade union activity grew – the National Amalgamated Union of Labour recruited glassmakers – but the company, while discussing industrial matters more frequently than before with deputations of its own employees, many of them trade unionists, refused to recognise any trade union as such. Importance of Windle Pilkington (d.1914). New scientifically-trained recruits to management and larger office staffs needed to handle the growing business. Profits at record levels but even larger sums reinvested in the business. Reserves held in foreign securities. Casualties among the third generation of the Pilkington family, then taking charge but arrival of the future Lord Cozens-Hardy, a trained electrical engineer, whose sister had married Austin Pilkington.

15 THE FIRST WORLD WAR

Glass imports were reduced in 1915 and 1916 and reached very small proportions by 1917. Pilkington exports also fell sharply after 1914. The company's main problem was now to manufacture enough glass for the home market. More women were employed and new sources of high quality sand discovered. Part of the Cowley Hill works was devoted to munitions production, the proceeds from which were devoted to the building and equipping of an emergency orthopaedic and limb-fitting hospital at Ravenhead. Trade unions recognised and the St Helens Plate and Sheet Glass Joint Industrial Council formed.

16 THE INTERWAR YEARS: AN INTRODUCTORY SURVEY

The economic difficulties of the interwar years hit Pilkington's export markets, especially in the earlier 1920s and during the 1930s, rather than those at home, for in Britain housing demand after 1925 was greater than ever and to this was added a growing new market: the motor industry. In plate and cast glass the company performed well at home; but in sheet glass it fared badly until a modern, flat drawn process became available at the beginning of the 1930s.

17 FORWARD WITH PLATE

At the end of the war Pilkington capitalised its reserves and then raised additional capital from the family shareholders, mainly to build a new plate glass factory at Doncaster at a cost of nearly £2m. This was a badly-timed investment decision, for the factory was built in the immediate post-war period when costs were very high, and new manufacturing techniques were very soon to render it obsolete and unnecessary. Fruitful collaboration began between the company, which had been developing a continuous plate glass grinder, invented by its Experimental Engineer at Cowley Hill, F. B. Waldron, and the Ford Motor Company of Detroit, which had developed a similar machine and, more important, had managed to flow plate glass from a tank. This made it possible to reduce plate glass manufacturing costs considerably from 1924 onwards. Doncaster was more than anything a gesture of independence of the Plate Glass Convention with which Pilkington declined to come to terms after the war. Relations with the continentals were strained and, although they took a licence for the continuous grinder (on surprisingly advantageous terms), the more valuable Flow process was kept a close secret. Maubeuge was rebuilt. Death and retirement placed main responsibility for Pilkington management upon the brothers Austin and Cecil Pilkington and Lord Cozens-Hardy. With the continued proliferation of the family, many of the shareholders were not actively involved.

18 BACKWARD WITH SHEET   284

Pilkington experimented with a flat drawn process which did not succeed while its rivals, after much expenditure and effort, developed two others – the Colburn (or Libbey-Owens) and the Fourcault – successfully. The U.K. licence for the latter had gone to Sheet Glass Ltd in 1919. (Its factory at Queenborough made such losses that it was closed in 1924. It fared no better when it was re-started, under new ownership, for a few months in 1929.) Pilkington carefully monitored the progress of the former in the United States, failed to secure a share in the company formed to exploit it in Europe in 1920 and failed again in 1927 to secure the U.K. rights, having been outmanoeuvred by the Plate Glass Convention. Meanwhile, confronted with cheap, competitive flat drawn glass, Pilkington had to abandon the hand-blown product (apart from the manufacture of a special product marketed as Vita glass) and to extend its intermittent, cylinder drawn capacity. (The cylinder drawn plant at Thorold, having made large losses, had ceased production in 1924.) Pilkington was at last driven to come to terms with the Convention in 1929. St Gobain's good offices were available to Pilkington when J. B. Watt came to develop in 1930/1 the PPG flat drawn process. Sheet glass having carried plate at the end of the nineteenth century, plate (and cast glass, a steady earner) for a few years had to carry sheet.

19 REORGANISATION IN THE 1930S   320

Poor trading results and a disagreement between Austin and Cecil Pilkington led to the resignation of both of them in June 1931. An Executive Committee was then formed with Cozens-Hardy as its chairman and R.M.Weeks, a Cambridge graduate who had distinguished himself with the company and married into the family, as his closest associate on the Board. Realising that the business had long outgrown the rather haphazard administrative arrangements which dated from its partnership days, Cozens-Hardy devised a new committee structure which would involve senior executives more actively in top management. Further members of the fourth generation of the family joined the Executive during the decade but only after the most searching trials, which not all passed, and two non-share-qualified directors also joined the Executive. A management trainee scheme was started and a Personnel Department formed. Outside consultants reported, often critically, upon office arrangements and Bedaux methods were applied in the works. The accountants' office was built up. Greater emphasis was given to research and technical development. A Central Research Department was formed which at first had a particular interest in plastics.

Laminated safety glass manufacture, started before the war, increased with the growth of car production. Pilkington reached a sales agreement with Triplex in 1928 and this was soon followed by a joint company, Triplex (Northern) Ltd, to build a factory at St Helens, and by a switch from laminated to toughened glass. The latter, by increasing sales of plate glass in which the company kept ahead technically with the development of the twin grinder, gave it a short-term advantage but in the longer run it opened the way for the use of thick drawn sheet. Export sales of plate glass fell and home sales for non-motor purposes remained stationary, though this branch of manufacture remained quite profitable, unlike sheet glass where profits remained meagre despite increased output from new and more efficient PPG machines, the acquisition of Queenborough (1933), the opening of Pontypool (1938) and attempts to reach agreements with foreign manufacturers. Cast glass continued to make a steady profit and a market sharing arrangement with Chances in 1936 soon led to an agreement for a phased take-over of Pilkington's oldest rival. With this merger came an interest in glass fibres and optical glass to add to that recently acquired in Vitrolite, glass bricks and pressed ware. Abroad Pilkington disposed of Maubeuge in 1935 (part of the rationalisation of plate glass manufacture in Europe) but acquired a large stake in a number of new safety glass plants: in Canada (Duplate); with considerable reluctance but to great advantage in Australia; and in South Africa. In the Argentine Pilkington not only put down its own safety glass plant but also took the lead in establishing a window glass manufacturing concern in collaboration with St Gobain, Glaver and other major producers. Prosperity returned to the parent company in the mid- and later 1930s; but those family members who managed the business derived relatively little financial benefit from it as shareholders.

The company's 9,000 glassworks employees at St Helens in the mid-1920s, with their dependants, probably accounted for about a third of the population of the town. Although this total fell at the beginning of the 1930s during the worst of the depression, it had regained its former level by 1937. Pilkington was not a pioneer in welfare schemes but it was ahead of most other large firms. It tried, though without success, to build a garden village after the war but did manage to introduce a superannuation scheme for staff in 1918 and a pensions scheme for adult wage earners in 1925. Austin and Cecil Pilkington endowed out of their own pockets a special fund for glassmakers displaced by the new mechanical processes; but so smooth was the transition from craft to machine that the fund was growing more rapidly than the demands made upon it by the end of the seven-year endowment period. The company's relations with the trade unions were good and the Joint Industrial Council provided a good forum for discussion. Improved facilities for dental and medical inspection, a new canteen and widows' pensions were all provided in the later 1930s.

During the war Pilkington supplied much more sheet glass, for re-pairing war damage at home and for export, than it had done before 1939, and new pricing arrangements were introduced to take account of new glassmaking methods. After the war, with Sir Harry (later Lord) Pilkington as the company chairman, D.V.Phelps as chairman of the Executive and the fourth generation of the family in charge, the company managed to excel in both home and foreign markets at the same time. Pilkington's labour force abroad grew more rapidly than that at home as its manufacturing and marketing activities were extended overseas. The larger and infinitely more complex business called for further changes in administrative structure and, although the Pilkington family con-tinued to play a leading part in the management, non-family directors became increasingly important. The float process, invented by (Sir) Alastair Pilkington, a post-war recruit, was the most remarkable achievement in the whole history of flat glass and put Pilkington ahead of all its international competitors in this field. The company itself stopped making plate glass in 1967. Thicker substances of sheet glass have also been replaced by the new product. In 1976, 21 manufacturers abroad were paying float royalties to Pilkington. This vast concern finally went public in 1970.

Appendices

Tables

Photographs

The above are to be found in the Pilkington Archives Photographic Collection unless otherwise stated in the illustrations.

Drawings, Graphs, Charts and Plans

Preface

This is a substantially revised and greatly extended version of a previous book, *Pilkington Brothers and the Glass Industry*, first published in 1960 and now long out of print. Whereas the earlier history virtually ended in 1918, the subsequent 40 years or so being covered only in the broadest outline, the present volume tells in six new chapters the full story of the company's struggles, setbacks and successes between the wars, and a new epilogue outlines its quite remarkable progress since then. Although this is a work commissioned by the company, I have had *carte blanche* in writing it and responsibility for the opinions expressed in it is mine alone. I have had unrestricted access to all the Pilkington archives down to 1939, and in this book I have used Pilkington's accounts and other statistical information from the 1860s onwards much more extensively than in the earlier volume. The writing of company history has made great strides during the past 15 years, as the full-length studies of Courtaulds, ICI, The Royal Exchange Assurance and other businesses attest. As historians have become more numerate, so their powers of analysis have increased.

It is impossible to mention by name all those both at Pilkington and elsewhere from whom I have had help in the writing of this book, research upon which began in the early 1950s for the original volume, and has been continued during the past decade and particularly in the last few years. During this latter period, I have been greatly helped by Mr T.G. Woosey of the Group Accounting Department, who has extracted the statistical information from the company's accounts from 1918 onwards and has advised me on their interpretation. Mr T.R.Buxton of Group Marketing Services supplied me with the trade statistics for the same period. DATS of Warrington, in conjunction with Mr A.D.Riden of Central

Engineering, drew the maps and plans. Mrs J. Green of Flat Glass Divisional Planning drew a number of helpful graphs which, although they do not appear in the volume itself, were of considerable assistance to me in drafting chapters 17 to 21. Mrs S.F. Major read the proofs on my behalf and Mrs Brenda Hall compiled the Index. In the final stages, Mr D.B. Wood, Group Public Relations Co-ordinator, gave particularly valuable help.

Lord Pilkington, who was Chairman of the Company from 1949 to 1973, has taken a deep personal interest in this history from the very outset. He has helped me in innumerable ways, especially in explaining some of the developments since the later 1920s when he himself entered the business, and in commenting upon the interwar and epilogue chapters. For certain parts of the latter, he wrote a memorandum, now deposited in the Pilkington archives, which has not only been of use to me for my present purpose but will also be of value to those who, at some future date, may be interested in the history of the company during the period of his chairmanship. I should like to place on record that far from suggesting that anything I had written should be excised from the text, he has always fed me with more information and argument and encouraged me to be more outspoken. No company historian could hope for more sympathetic understanding and unstinted support from the head of the business about which he was writing. This encouragement and help has been continued in very full measure by Sir Alastair Pilkington FRS, his successor as Chairman; and the other directors of the company and members of the staff have also been most helpful whenever I have had occasion to consult them.

One sequel to the publication of the original volume was the setting up of a company archive in 1961. Mr A.E. Owen, the original archivist, and his successor, Mr L.J. McDonald, both helped me greatly not only by putting the existing records in order but also by locating in various parts of the Pilkington organisation both at home and abroad, and making readily available, original source material previously thought to have been lost. This has included the accounts stretching back to the mid-1860s from which the archives staff have kindly extracted the relevant statistics included in this volume. My chief debt, however, is to Miss P.A. Pemberton who succeeded Mr McDonald as archivist. She has not only provided me with enormous help during the final stages of research and writing but, a historian herself, has also served as a quite invaluable and indeed indispensable research assistant. Her recent departure to her native Australia to take up the position of Deputy Archives Officer at the Australian National University is a severe loss to the company. Other members of the archives staff have also been unfailingly helpful: Mrs D.G.Stobbs, Assistant Archivist, whose mathematical skills have proved particularly valuable, and Mrs Ann Frampton who has had the somewhat unenviable and totally unrewarding task of trying to decipher my handwriting on many occasions and has typed – and sometimes re-typed – draft chapters. The photographs for the book were collected by members of the staff, particularly, Mr G.N.Garvey.

My original interest in this subject was first aroused at the end of the 1940s when J.R.Harris and I worked together as postgraduates upon the development of the St. Helens area where we had both grown up. Professor Harris, now Professor of Economic History at the University of Birmingham, has latterly been engaged in a study of eighteenth-century coal technology, and I am particularly glad to have this opportunity of acknowledging the help I have received from him concerning the earlier history of the St Gobain works which I have used in the first chapter.

My final debt is to my wife for her patience with and understanding of an academic husband who keeps on disappearing, sometimes un-expectedly but all too often, into his study.

London School of Economics and   T.C.Barker
Political Science
October 1976

Introduction

THIS is the story of the earlier struggles and subsequent growth, during its first 150 years, of a business which now provides almost all the windows and other forms of flat glass for the buildings of Britain, the windscreens for British-made cars and a number of other glass products. Such a large market share is quite a recent development. Sales in Britain were important to foreign competitors right down to 1939; and Pilkington, for the first half of its existence, had also to struggle against other British manufacturers. Indeed, it did not even enter the luxury branch of the industry, plate glass, until it had been in existence for 50 years. Nor has its record of growth been an uninterrupted one. The years between the mid-1830s and the mid-1850s and between the 1870s and 1914 saw great progress, and the period since 1945 has been the most remarkable of all; but the third quarter of the nineteenth century and the interwar years were disappointing, and at one stage, in the later 1920s, the company was on the verge of abandoning an important part of its business altogether. How different from the years since 1945 when it was equally successful with its home and export sales, managed to diversify vigorously into new fields with optical and fibre glass, secured control of British safety glass manufacture, and, acting through subsidiary or associated companies, set up glassworks in each of the five continents. Above all, by its astonishingly rapid development of the float process – a revolutionary new method of glassmaking, made possible only by the most advanced technology – it managed, as it approached its 150th anniversary, to bring about the most important manufacturing change that flat glass has ever undergone during the whole of its history stretching back more than 2,000 years. The suggestion has often been made that family businesses lose their drive and become less successful as later generations, less dedicated and perhaps less able, take charge. Here is one notable example which clearly challenges this pessimistic generalisation. The fourth generation of the Pilkington family, which was in charge from the 1940s, managed better than ever.

When it went public in 1970, Pilkington Brothers Limited, with close on £175 m. employed in the business (of which shareholders' equity amounted to over £100 m.), was probably Britain's largest private company. But because it was private and produced a rather anonymous range of products, surprisingly little was known about it. The financial journalists were not interested, for its shares were not quoted on the stock exchanges, and the public at large knew little about it for its panes of glass could not be distinguished from those of its foreign competitors by the untutored eye. In any event, they were sold through merchants and it was they, and not the manufacturers, with whom the public usually came into contact. In earlier times this lack of limelight had suited the family directors who wanted to be allowed to manage their business undisturbed by outside interference or publicity and who set considerable store by not having to publish financial details and trading results which might place them in a less advantageous position in any negotiations with competitors abroad. The fact that the business throughout these years was conducted from a relatively small town in south-west Lancashire (population about 5,000 in 1826, just under 100,000 in 1911 and little larger subsequently) also helped to keep it out of the public eye. Since we shall have occasion to refer to St Helens quite frequently in these pages, a plan of the place is included in chapter one to assist readers unfamiliar with the area.

This book publishes for the first time the facts and figures of Pilkington's progress and seeks to explain the company's success. It also tries to relate this success to other developments, both at home and abroad, in the glass industry. Since Pilkington and British flat glass have become synonymous during the present century, the opportunity has been taken to provide, at least in outline, the earlier history of the other businesses which later became part of the Pilkington group. The first chapter is devoted entirely to setting the scene, to indicating the background, earlier growth and structure of the industry and the state of the glassmaker's art when the original Pilkington brothers first became involved in the industry. Later ones take account of their rivals' demise – the proud but backward-looking manufacturers of the north-east, for instance – and, when Pilkington became sole British producer, of the activities of its main foreign competitors, particularly in Belgium, France and the United States. The course of international glassmaking diplomacy and the bargaining counters used in negotiations with these great foreign glassmaking powers, are no less revealing and instructive than are the manufacturing and selling problems which confronted the St Helens business at various stages in its existence.

Demographic and financial matters are also of critical importance to our story. As families have become smaller during the past 100 years, a trend which began in the better-off sections of society, there have been fewer sons available to run family businesses as they grew in size and complexity. Fortunately the two Pilkington founders had enough sons between them while families were still large – 12 of 18 infants survived infancy – to provide a wide choice of successors, and the increasing numbers of subsequent male offspring as the branches multiplied were able to provide a wide field of candidates for top management later on, even though each individual branch became less prolific. In-laws were also admitted to the Board and so were a few carefully-chosen and highly experienced senior executives. But the Pilkington family remained very definitely in control. It also managed to furnish the capital needed for expansion. This usually came from ploughed-back profits, though the family was called upon to dig deeply into its pockets to finance developments after the First World War; and during the 1960s, as taxation became heavier and expansion more rapid, the company depended more on loans and overdrafts. That the family shareholders were prepared to have their capital tied up in the company for so long, knowing that they could sell their shares only to other family shareholders and at artificially low prices, was as important a factor in the survival and success of the business as was the enterprise shown by the much smaller number of family members who were actually managing it. The distinction which arose in the present century between the Pilkingtons who were directors of the company and the other, more numerous, members of the family, who might be active enough elsewhere but were passive so far as the glass industry was concerned, confining their role to that of investor, is another important thread running through the later part of our story. Little has been written about how family businesses actually worked in practice. This book aims to give at least a preliminary glimpse of some of the problems involved.

There are various ways of measuring Pilkington's achievement over the 150 years: from a capital employed of about £10,000 to one of over £400 m.; from a small number of male employees at St. Helens to 32,000 men and women throughout the world; from a small output of relatively expensive crown glass to a huge output of various sorts of flat glass produced at far lower real cost. (A single eight-hour shift on a float line in 1976 produced more glass than did Pilkington's original crown glass

furnace in a whole year.) This book aims to explain how this remarkable record of growth was achieved under the leadership of a small number of unusually able and dedicated men drawn from four generations of the same family, loyally supported by a growing workforce who, though they might occasionally grumble at their lot and even, at astonishingly long intervals, go on strike, nevertheless had a sense of working for good employers in a sound business to which they, and sometimes their children and grandchildren, really developed a sense of belonging.

Chapter 1

The Historical Background

'The chief circumstance which seems to determine the seats of the glass manufacture is the neighbourhood of coal, of which very large quantities are necessary, but the facilities for obtaining other materials, such as sand ... have also in some cases had an important influence.'
– From a Parliamentary Report of 1865

BEFORE the coming of canals and railways made it easier to transport fuel – it has been said that to carry coal overland for ten miles usually doubled or trebled its price[1] – furnace industries had to be sited either in the midst of, or with easy access to, forests or coalfields. It paid the glassmaker to build his furnace where fuel was cheap and then to transport to it the smaller weights of sand, alkali, clay and other materials he required. In the early days when people were not particularly troubled if their window glass was somewhat discoloured, the level of impurity of all these materials did not matter much. Local supplies could be used. Sand from a brook or river was good enough for the Wealden glassmakers, wood and bracken yielded satisfactory alkali and the pots were made from local clay.[2] Later, when brilliant, colourless glass was demanded and sand with a much lower iron oxide content had to be sought, glassmakers still found it paid to carry their sand to their coal, even though long distances were sometimes involved. When the works at Ravenhead near St Helens were opened in the later eighteenth century, for instance, white sand was brought all round the coast from Lynn in Norfolk.[3] This sand was also being used at that time by Newcastle glassmakers.[4] It was, therefore, the availability of fuel rather than sand which chiefly determined the location of glassmaking.

Clearly, the transition from wood to coal, as the fuel employed to stoke the glass furnaces, was a development of crucial importance so far as the siting of the industry was concerned. During the reign of Queen Elizabeth I, increasing demands were made upon the country's supplies of wood, particularly by the iron smelters who were rapidly extending the scale of their operations. Fuel prices rose and by 1581 they were declared to have

grown 'very great and unreasonable'.[5] This trend of events caused the owners of furnaces to look for an alternative fuel. They began to investigate the possibility of firing with coal, which could be obtained cheaply in coal-mining areas and in those parts of the country which had good communication by water with those areas.[6] Since the requirements of the iron smelters were far greater than those of the early glassmakers, research into coal as a fuel was chiefly concerned with devising a means of smelting iron. By the early seventeenth century attempts were made to separate the coal, with all its impurities, from the iron ore by using the reverberatory principle of furnace design. In this type of furnace the fuel and the ore are kept quite apart, the flames being made to strike back from the arched roof of the furnace upon the materials to be smelted.[7] These early experiments failed so far as iron was concerned;[8] but the reverberatory furnace that was developed by Thomas Percival[9] was found to meet the glass-maker's needs. Using certain types of coal, and placing a cover over his pots, he could melt his materials without filling the molten glass with impurities. He was not slow to apply with at least a measure of success the principle which the iron smelter had been unable to use. By the early months of 1612 'green glass for windows' – no doubt an apt description – was being imperfectly made at a coal-fired furnace in Southwark.[10]

In its ultimate form the new furnace and glasshouse design differed in several respects from its predecessors.[11] A long, underground tunnel fed fresh air from outside the glasshouse to the grate in the centre of the furnace. As may be seen from Plate 1 facing page 48, the furnace itself was built around this central grate in the shape of an inverted funnel. Halfway down the neck of the funnel was built a curved dome (or crown), which reflected the flame from the fire down again on to the pots which were ranged round the waist of the furnace on a circular course of brickwork. The pots were often covered (or caped) as a protection against soot, smoke and black drops which fell from the crown. The smoke and hot air escaped *via* flues close to the outer wall and through the chimney at the top. A furnace of this type could be erected in the centre of a square building with its chimney piercing the roof. In the case of British window glass manufacture, however, it was more usual to construct the outer building of the same shape as the furnace itself, allowing the glassmaker just enough room between the furnace and the wall to blow and manœuvre his cylinders or tables. To what extent the pioneers were themselves able to develop the cone-shaped glasshouse which later became the most outstanding physical feature of the industry, is open to debate. It was certainly in use by 1700.[12]

But any uncertainty about the details of design ought not to be allowed

to detract from the fundamental importance of the innovation itself. Although a group of men who held an earlier furnace patent (but not the group who were eventually credited with having produced a working model) agreed that they had gained some assistance from the results of unsuccessful experiments which had been conducted in France,[13] the new furnace seems to have been a wholly English development. At all events, the glass produced from coal-fired furnaces was a matter which a French visitor saw fit to comment upon in 1738, and across the Channel the glasshouse *à l'anglaise*[14] was confined to bottleworks, apart from some notable experiments with coal-fired furnaces in the middle of the eighteenth century to which we shall have occasion to refer presently.

Although the English appear to have possessed a distinct advantage in furnace design, they still relied for the greater part on skilled, foreign craftsmen to work the molten glass – or metal, as it was called – which their furnaces heated. In the early seventeenth century when coal-fired furnaces were introduced, foreign names loomed very large among the makers of window glass.

It is now evident that the British tradition of glassmaking, dating from medieval times, continued into the sixteenth century; but it is also clear that considerable imports were needed to satisfy the growing demands from house builders.[15] When these imports were interrupted by the disruption of trade with Antwerp, the foreign glassmakers came to England and laid the foundations of a more efficient industry which not only conserved fuel but produced glass of a better quality. Jean Carré, an Antwerp merchant, together with Becku, another merchant, secured a patent to manufacture window glass in England in 1567, and we hear of the arrival of Norman and Lorraine glassmakers, the Bungars, Henseys, Tytterys and Tyzacks, about the same time.[16] Despite some difficulties with the immigrant craftsmen, who refused to train native Englishmen as the patent had stipulated, the industry developed well in the thickly-wooded land of the Weald which had long been the scene of glassmaking on a smaller scale.[17] The invasion of foreign workmen, however, aroused the hostility of the English and the depredations in their native woodlands served as a popular battle-cry against the newcomers.[18] It was an unfair line of attack: the glassmakers used only the branches of trees, which grew again,[19] and their glasshouses were very few in number compared with the host of ironworks which were responsible for the bulk of the damage. In 1589 there were said to be only 14 or 15 glass furnaces of all kinds in the whole of England[20] and a little later only eight were making broad or spread glass, a crude form of cylinder glass then in general use for window panes.[21] Nevertheless the foreign glassmakers seem to have been

elbowed out of their early centre of operations around Wisborough Green in Sussex. We find them at Buckholt, near Winchester and on the North Staffordshire–Shropshire border in the middle of the 1580s.[22] At the end of the century they were also working in the Nailsworth district and the Forest of Dean.[23] Here they continued to blow glass at their little furnaces fired with wood, an extraordinary and rather nomadic race of people.

With the appearance of the new furnace, employing a cheaper and more plentiful kind of fuel, the days of wood firing were numbered. The end came more swiftly than even the most pessimistic would have ventured to forecast. On 23 May 1615, King James I passed the death sentence on furnaces using wood. Anxious, as he pointed out, to preserve the forests, he decreed that in future glass was to be made in coal-fired furnaces alone.[24] The control of the furnace was already in the hands of those who held Letters Patent for its use.[25] By the royal proclamation of 1615, the patentees were given monopolistic control not only of the furnaces but of the industry as well.

The history of glassmaking in England between 1615 and the outbreak of the Civil War is dominated by one man: Sir Robert Mansfield or, as he came to be known, Sir Robert Mansell.[26] One of the furnace patentees, he soon bought out the other partners and thus gained absolute authority over the entire glass industry of the country. He was a courtier and a sailor, holding after 1618 the office of Vice-Admiral of England. He had no previous knowledge of glassmaking. Indeed, his venture into the industry surprised the King who characteristically observed that it was unusual for one who had gained such a reputation for prowess at sea to tamper with fire, since fire and water were two contrary elements.[27] But, despite Mansell's frequent absences on naval service prior to 1621, he took his new responsibility very seriously. The glass made at the furnace in Southwark in 1612 had been 'uneven and full of spots',[28] and obviously much had to be done before glassmaking by the new method was perfected; Mansell spent upwards of £30,000 before he was able to obtain consistently satisfactory results from coal-firing.[29] Under his direction the manufacture of window glass was eventually settled in a part of the country which was to remain the chief centre of production for nearly 250 years.

At first his works were situated in London where he used Scottish coal brought down the coast by sea. This was relatively free from sulphur and therefore less liable to discolour the glass. As a contemporary put it, Scottish coal was 'the best flamer and consumeth away into white ashes, as having in it more unctiousnesse than sulpharousnesse'.[30] But it was

extremely expensive and Mansell was, therefore, obliged to seek sites for his furnaces elsewhere in order to have access to other sources of coal.[31] He first tried the Isle of Purbeck in Dorset, but 'the coal proved altogether unuseful', so he erected furnaces at Milford Haven in Pembrokeshire some distance to the west of the Mansell estates at Margam. There he enjoyed no greater success; the coal did not prove serviceable nor was 'the transportation of glass possible to be had'. Next he moved to a site near the Trent but manufacture in Nottinghamshire was no more economic than it had been elsewhere.[32] Finally, 'for his last refuge, contrary to all mens opinions', he set up furnaces at Newcastle-upon-Tyne at a cost of some £2,000.[33] Here, at last, he succeeded.

The Northumberland and Durham coalfield was the first in England to be intensively exploited. It was very advantageously situated, for the rich measures extended to the coast and the coal could be easily removed by sea. Shipments from Newcastle to London (the chief market in Britain), as well as to the continent and elsewhere, grew at an unprecedented rate, from some 35,000 tons a year in the 1560s to 400,000 tons in 1625.[34] Nowhere in the country could coal be had in such abundance or perhaps so cheaply as at Newcastle when Mansell came to site his window glass furnaces there about 1618.[35] Of his sources of sand and alkali for these works, we know little beyond the fact that 'ashes and materials for glass' were shipped from London.[36] We do know, however, that clay was the only requirement which he had difficulty in obtaining. At first he had to bring it 'at an infinite charge' from Stourbridge and, later, from the continent. Eventually he found suitable deposits in Northumberland.[37]

This, then, was the genesis of the glass industry in the north-east, which soon became the great centre for the manufacture of English window glass. By 1624, between three and four thousand cases of glass were reaching London from Newcastle every year.[38] When the Scots invaded the north in 1640 and seized the Newcastle glasshouses, three furnaces were at work and 1,200 cases of glass waited to be shipped.[39] After the Long Parliament put an end to Mansell's monopoly,[40] others thought it worthwhile to venture into the trade. In the middle of the 1640s, for instance, Edmund Harris, a London merchant, erected two new glasshouses on the Tyne at Newcastle not far from the Ouseburn, where Mansell's furnaces still stood.[41] 'On the North side of the River,' wrote William Gray in 1649, 'is Ewes Burne, over which is a wood Bridge, which goeth down to a place called the Glass-Houses, where plaine Glasse for windowes are made, which serveth most parts of the Kingdom.'[42] From this original nucleus, the industry spread out along Tyneside. Glass was being made at South Shields by 1650,[43] outside the Close Gate, to the west of

Newcastle, by 1684,[44] and at Howden Pans by 1698.[45] In the latter part of the century Stourbridge achieved some prominence for its window glass, but that branch of the industry did not take such firm root there.[46] In 1736 Newcastle still continued to provide the glass that was 'most in use in England'.[47]

Early in the eighteenth century, the Cooksons, a Penrith family, first became associated with glassmaking on the Tyne. When Isaac Cookson died in 1743, he was stated to be 'one of the most considerable Glass Manufacturers in those parts'.[48] A hundred years later Isaac Cookson and Company, who owned extensive works both at South Shields and in Newcastle, paid £61,500 a year in excise duty, a greater amount than was paid by any other firm and just under one-tenth of the total sum paid for all the glasshouses in England. By that time, the glassmakers of the north-east contributed £204,000 in duty to the Exchequer annually, about twice as much as any other district in the country.[49] Although these excise returns can be misleading – the different branches of the industry paid different rates of duty – nevertheless they serve our purpose if we use them as a rough guide. There is certainly justification for the claim, made by the glassmakers of the Tyne and Wear in 1833, that they manufactured more window glass than all the other houses in Britain put together.[50] But by that time they were facing a serious challenge: manufacturers elsewhere were rapidly gaining upon them. Of particular significance was the remarkable growth of the industry in south-west Lancashire.

Although Newcastle was well placed for the operation of coal-fired furnaces, it was by no means the ideal centre for distributing fragile finished wares throughout the country. Lying close to the north-eastern corner of England, the Tyne was easily reached by collier from London or from anywhere along the east coast. Some of these vessels also plied round the coasts of Kent, to Sussex and beyond. They therefore provided a regular means of conveying glass to those parts of England which lay within easy reach of the North Sea or the English Channel. But the western half of England and the Midlands lay beyond the area that could be easily supplied. To meet the needs of what he called these 'most remote places of the kingdom from London', Mansell erected nine other furnaces to manufacture window glass 'for the ease of the subjects' charge in carriage and avoiding hazard of breaking and to the end that all the subjects might be served alike'.[51]

The north-west of England, the part of the country farthest removed by sea from Newcastle, was certainly a region which was likely to require at

least one of these auxiliary furnaces to supply the local demand. Glass-making was no new industry in that part of the country. It had been carried on at Wilderspool in Roman times,[52] and in Delamere Forest in the Middle Ages.[53] Various references to glaziers and glassmen seem to indicate that there was quite a brisk trade in glass in the north-west immediately prior to the Proclamation of 1615.[54] But unfortunately these are indefinite terms which may refer to those who were actually engaged in the manu-facture of glass or, as seems more likely, only to dealers in glassware. We have, however, one example of the term glassman almost certainly used to mean glassmaker. It occurs among entries in the Ormskirk Parish Register[55] on 10 December 1600:

A stranger slayne by one of the glassmen beinge A Frenchman then workinge at Bycarstaff.

The exact site of the wood-fired furnace at which he worked was dis-covered in January 1968 by Ruth Hurst Vose, then Deputy Curator of the Pilkington Glass Museum, at Glass Hey Field on Bickerstaffe Hall Farm. She took charge of archaeological excavations there later in the year, and again in 1969. Specimens of glass crucible and charcoal were collected and analysed.[56] One other field name, Glasshouse Close near Carr Mill Dam to the north-east of St Helens, suggests that wood-fired furnaces may have been worked there too, but no written or other evidence has yet come to light.

The parish registers of Stockport and its vicinity mention glassmakers between 1605 and 1653. It was already supposed that the men worked at a place called Glasshouse Fold, in the valley of the river Tame, at Haughton Green, a few miles to the south-east of Manchester.[57] Whether the furnace was wood-fired at first, as the earlier date would indicate, is not known; but a second and larger dig undertaken by Mrs Vose and Miss Freda Burke, between 1969 and 1973, has shown beyond doubt that this was one of Mansell's nine auxiliary works, the earliest coal-fired furnace yet to be discovered.[58]

Why was this furnace not located in south-west Lancashire where vast quantities of sand were available as well as coal? The Shirdley Hill sand, a deposit some ten feet thick which is to be found a little below the surface over a considerable area to the north of present-day St Helens, is admirably suited for glassmaking on account of its low iron oxide content. Indeed, it is one of the very few places in the whole country where such high grade sand and coal occur together.[59] Why, then, was the south-eastern corner of the county preferred, which lacked this appreciable advantage?

The answer seems to be twofold. As we have noticed, the early glass-makers were not very particular about the quality of their product – and

they had a virtual monopoly in the area which they supplied. They could therefore use any sand, no matter how discoloured it made the glass. Provided they could find deposits of sand in sufficient quantity, close to their source of fuel, they seem to have been quite satisfied. No doubt the sand of the Stockport neighbourhood was good enough for their rough and ready purposes.

Secondly, with transport charges so high, geographical location was immensely important. It was essential to site glasshouses at places from where as many glaziers as possible could be supplied. A furnace at Stockport lay in the heart of a relatively highly-populated district. South-west Lancashire, on the other hand, was not yet the busy centre of commercial activity that it was later to become. Liverpool was little more than a small fishing port enjoying a limited trade with Ireland and with a sparsely-populated hinterland. There was no great demand for glass thereabouts nor any export trade to justify the erection of an auxiliary furnace in that part of the county. It was not until the first half of the eighteenth century, when Liverpool rose to rival, and later to surpass, Bristol as the leading port on the English west coast, that we hear much about glassmaking on or near Merseyside.

The industry grew with the market. This was partly a local market: as more houses, factories, warehouses, shops and buildings of all kinds were built, more window glass was required. Much of the glass, however, was loaded on ships at Liverpool to be carried away, some round the coast, some over the sea. By 1770, more than 250 tons of glass of all kinds were being shipped from the port per annum.[60] Almost half a century later, in 1812, one manufacturer of window and flint glass (that is, tableware and the like) was sending more than two-thirds of his output to America.[61] There is no reason to believe that other proprietors of glassworks in the vicinity of Merseyside were any less fortunate in securing orders from the United States which only possessed three or four window glass factories in 1800 and did not begin to develop this branch of the industry until after 1812.[62]

The rise of the glass industry in south-west Lancashire occurred, therefore, at roughly the same time as the development of Liverpool itself. Two glasshouses are mentioned in Houghton's list of 1696, one described as 'near Leverpool', and the other at Warrington.[63] The first Liverpool glasshouse seems to date from 1715, when it was leased to Josiah Poole, and a second was in operation by 1729.[64] There was a marked increase in the amount of glassmaking activity in the port from about 1750.[65] The Warrington glasshouse seems to have been the property, from about 1650, of a Huguenot family which took the English name of Leaf. In 1688 they

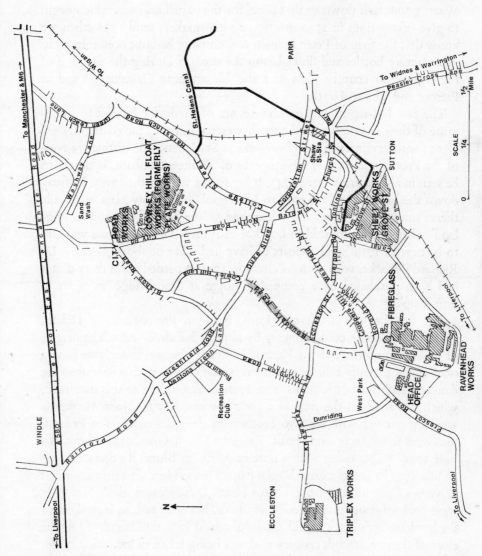

Plan 1 Pilkington Works and Head Office in St Helens in 1976

leased property in Sutton, to the south of St Helens, which included a building already used as a glasshouse, no doubt the one referred to by Houghton as 'near Leverpool'. This appears to have been situated at what is now known as Glasshouse Farm near Eltonhead Hall. A member of the Leaf family could still be described in 1730 as 'of the Glasshouse in Sutton, gentleman'.[66] Glassmaking does not seem to have been carried on in Warrington itself down to that time, for the parish registers which begin to give occupations in 1730 mention no glassmakers until 1758 when we know that the firm of Peter Seaman & Company had just been formed to manufacture bottles and flint glass in the town.[67] During the first half of the eighteenth century glass was also blown near Ormskirk,[68] and at Prescot and Thatto Heath.

The two last-mentioned glasshouses are of particular interest to us because of their situation near the south-western limits of the coalfield: they were the forerunners of the glassworks at St Helens. The distinctive cone of the Prescot glasshouse, the property of Thomas Cobham, is clearly to be seen in an old print dated 1743. It lay to the west of the town, halfway down the hill, just off the road to Liverpool.[69] Window glass was made there: some of the panes were described as 'the best of that sort in England' when they were sold in London in 1734.[70] The glasshouse was said to be new in 1719[71] and appears to have had a life of about 30 years. Dr Richard Pococke, who visited Prescot in 1751, recorded in his diary that it had been purchased by a competing house at Stourbridge 'in order to shut it up'.[72]

The bottleworks at Thatto Heath, between Prescot and St Helens, outlived its Prescot contemporary by about a hundred years. The origins of glassmaking in and about Thatto Heath are obscure, though we have a clear and apparently reliable statement which fixed within a year or so the date at which the bottleworks were opened. According to this statement, which was made at the time of a poor law case in 1745, John Hensey, a working partner with his two brothers in the glass concern at Prescot, removed from there and 'built Thattow Heath Glasshouse' about the year 1721.[73] This tallies with a note in Nicholas Blundell's diary that on 22 July 1721 he bought some bottles from Thatto Heath.[74] From the point of view of glassmaking, the Thatto Heath location was ideal. Not only were coal, sand and clay[75] readily available, but rock salt, an ingredient of the bottlemaker's batch, could also be obtained without difficulty.[76] At the close of the seventeenth century coal was being taken in increasing quantity from the south-western fringe of the Lancashire coalfield to feed the furnaces at the Cheshire saltworks. It would not have been difficult to return with a load of rock salt. This was, indeed, the beginning of the coal

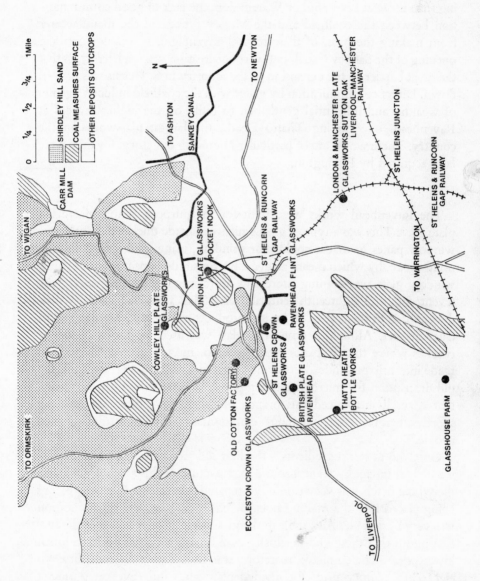

Plan 2 Geology of the St Helens area

and salt connection which eventually gave rise to the Merseyside chemical industry of which glassmaking became part.[77]

Although sites close to the collieries and within easy reach of the precious deposits of Shirdley Hill sand were obviously more suitable for glassmaking than those at Liverpool or Warrington, the lack of good communication between the coalfield and the Mersey prevented the manufacturer from making the most of these natural advantages. It was not until the opening of the Sankey Canal – a Liverpool creation – in the later 1750s that the great barrier to the expansion of the industry in St Helens was broken down. Direct communication by water with the coalfield induced a group of wealthy and influential gentlemen to build on the higher ground at Ravenhead, overlooking Thatto Heath, the largest glassworks in the country. These works are of particular interest to our story, for they were later acquired by Pilkington.

The Ravenhead works were built for the purpose of manufacturing plate glass. This was a type of glass which was made thicker than ordinary window panes so that it could bear grinding, using sand, and polishing, using rouge, by which means an even, lustrous finish was imparted. While window glass was coming more and more into general use during the seventeenth and eighteenth centuries, plate glass remained a luxury product and, as in the case of all luxury products in England, London was its chief market. Although some plate glass was used for the windows of coaches where thicker panes were required, most of it was silvered and made into mirrors. Indeed, its name seems to have been derived from the old description for mirrors: looking glass plates. It was under that name that Mansell introduced this branch of the manufacture into England shortly before 1621, finding employment for upwards of 500 people.[78]

Only the purest ingredients – the best soda and lime, and thoroughly washed white sand – went into the manufacture of this kind of glass, and the whole batch was very carefully prepared and calcined (fritted) before being placed into the melting pots. Being thick glass, any discolouration was very noticeable. Any spots in the glass itself or unevenness of the surface meant that these glasses, chiefly used for mirrors, would fetch much lower prices. The emphasis, therefore, was always upon high quality. An eighteenth century price list divided plate glass into five categories: a fine watery colour, the best; a reddish colour, 'much coveted by pale-faced people'; a greenish colour, a yellowish colour and a blackish colour, the last being 'worst of all'. 'But,' added the compilers, 'even all these, when ground down, will do for Coach-glass and many other unsilvered purposes. . .'[79]

Until the end of the seventeenth century, although plate glass was made with much purer materials than window glass, the glassmaker manipulated his molten glass, or metal, in much the same way when he was making both varieties. In both cases he blew the glass into a cylinder which he slit along its length and then flattened out into a pane. This method had serious disadvantages, chief of which was that it imposed a strict limit upon the size: the cylinder could not be blown more than 50 inches long without a loss of thickness which would make grinding impossible.[80] This disadvantage could, however, be overcome if the metal, instead of being made into a pane *via* a cylinder, was run straight on to a flat table, rolled out, and then annealed (cooled at a slow, controlled rate). The resulting plate of glass would not be transparent, since both surfaces would be marred, but this defect could be removed by the usual finishing processes of grinding and polishing.

The French were the first to make plate by casting, though just who was responsible for this important development is far from clear. Both Bernard Perrot of Orléans and Louis Lucas de Nehou, an official at the Tourlaville glassworks near Cherbourg, where plate glass was already being made, lay claim to the honour.[81] What is undisputed is that several Frenchmen of note, acting through one Abraham Thévart, were in December 1688 granted Letters Patent which gave them a monopoly of glass manufacture by the casting process for the French home market, and, later, for export as well. The concern had a chequered career and had to be reconstructed in 1702. Thereafter manufacture was concentrated in two main works, at Tourlaville and at St Gobain in Picardy. It was at the latter that the process was finally developed with success.[82] By 1725 output probably reached about 700 tons annually, by 1750 about 850 tons, and after 1760 upwards of 1,150 tons.

In theory, the casting process was so much more straightforward than the complicated method of making a flat piece of glass by way of a cylinder, that it seems curious that plate glass was not made in this way long before the end of the seventeenth century. In practice, however, casting, grinding and polishing required a very large capital outlay, a strong deterrent to even the wealthier investors. Instead of the customary small glasshouse, a large casting hall was needed, complete with an extensive melting furnace in the centre, a number of sizeable annealing ovens round the walls, a casting table upwards of ten feet long and six feet wide, and cuvettes (or cisterns) in which the metal could be transferred from the furnace to the casting table, together with a crane to carry them. Then there were all the workpeople's houses to be provided, the machinery required for grinding and polishing, and the warehouse accommodation. Above all, a large sum of money was permanently tied up in materials and stock, each plate of glass being an expensive – and fragile – item. All these factors made the manufacture of this kind of glass a most costly and risky venture. It is not surprising that St Gobain lacked a serious English rival for 80 years.

That is not to say that the English never made any attempt to compete with the French in the early days, particularly in wartime when imports of French manufactures were restricted. In 1691 Robert Hookes and Christopher Dodsworth (the former described as a gentleman and the latter as a merchant) obtained a patent which, among other things, included 'the Art of Casting Glasse and particularly Looking Glasse Plates much larger than ever was Blowne in England or any Forreigne Parts'.[83] On 5 October of that year a number of men who were interested in the glass trade, Dodsworth prominent among them, presented a petition to Parliament that they should be incorporated into the Company of Glass Makers with powers to raise stock and purchase land.[84] The proposal that Hookes and Dodsworth should be the first wardens of this Company makes it reasonably certain that this was an attempt to raise capital to erect the necessary large-scale plant for casting. The fate of this project is uncertain. No Bill passed through Parliament and no English St Gobain came into being. Yet the patentees and other glasshouse proprietors do seem to have banded together. In June 1692, they were advertising for sale 'all sorts of exquisite Looking-Glass plates, Coach-Glasses, Sash and other lustrous Glass for Windows and other Uses'.[85] Nine years later, in 1701, large looking-glass plates, six feet long and six feet wide, 'the like never made in England before', were being sold at the Vauxhall glasshouse in London.[86] Not long afterwards an interchange of broadsides between two competing London firms called forth the extravagant assertion that:

The Trade of Looking-Glass-Plates is so considerably improv'd that they serve not only for Furniture and Ornament in Her Majesty's Dominions at Home, but are likewise in great Esteem in Foreign Parts; the Venetians themselves buying these Plates and preferring them before their own.[87]

Even if we accept this boast at a mere fraction of its face value, we are still left with the impression of considerable recent progress in this branch of the industry.

How long plate glass continued to be cast in England is far from clear, but it is certain that the process was completely abandoned and had to be revived later in the eighteenth century. One proprietor, a descendant of two of the petitioners of 1691, confessed in 1773 that he had destroyed his apparatus for casting 'long since'.[88] The Vauxhall glasshouse, so proud of its large looking-glass plates in 1701, made none of them 70 years later. The proprietor had 'a sufficient trade in the less sizes' and 'did not choose to run so great a risk' as the casting process involved. Several merchants testified that no large plates of glass could be obtained from English glass firms; all their supplies came from St Gobain.

By the later eighteenth century the demand was great and rising fast, as it became more and more the fashion for the well-to-do to specify large windows for their houses. By 1773 it was estimated that between £60,000 and £100,000 worth of plate glass was imported from France every year. One merchant alone handled £10,000 worth annually. He thought that most of it was smuggled into the country and alleged that 'a kind of trading company' had been formed for that purpose. There was obviously money in this branch of the glass business, and as the demand continued to grow, a large-scale manufactory on the lines of St Gobain became a much more attractive economic proposition than it had been in 1691.

The whole matter came to a head in the early 1770s when a company, known as the British Cast Plate Glass Manufacturers, was formed. Its origins are obscure for none of the records relating to its formation has survived. But we are able to piece together local knowledge and information from other sources. Since the proprietors needed to raise about £50,000 in order to finance the project, like the men of 1691 they deemed it advisable to seek an Act which would grant them incorporation and limited liability.[89] The *Journals of the House of Commons* are therefore a useful source of information about the promotion of the concern.

A Frenchman, Philip Besnard, who claimed to have been engaged in the casting of plate glass at St Gobain for 15 years, appeared before the Commons' Committee as a technical expert. According to him, a large factory for the casting of glass would succeed in England because all the raw materials required, with the exception of barilla, the source of soda,[90] were obtainable in the country. The cost of production would be lower than in France because English fuel (coal) was cheaper. The factory could be built and equipped, he thought, for £12,000 and the entire outlay would be in the region of £50,000.

We now know more about the background of the promotion of this British plate glass concern thanks to Professor Harris's recent researches in the French Archives which have led to the discovery of *inter alia* a 600-page 'Essai Historique sur la fabrication des Glaces' by Delaunay Deslandes, director of the St Gobain Works from 1750.[91] Under his enterprising management great improvements were made and manufacturing capacity was extended. Most significantly he planned a fifth working hall in 1762 to use either wood or coal. In fact coal does not seem to have been tried till 1768; but it was certainly being used in 1770 and 1771, and at one point a second working hall was also burning it. In due course the greater availability of wood from nearby forests and its relative cheapness caused St Gobain to abandon coal; but the moral of Deslandes' success in making plate glass from a coal-fired furnace was not lost on the English who had come to accept their superiority over the French in coal furnace technology and, as has been seen, had been making other types of glass in such furnaces since the early seventeenth century. There is a suggestion that the promoters of the British plate glass concern tried to secure the services of Deslandes himself to help them get started, and Lord Mansfield and another English peer (whose name Deslandes unfortunately had forgotten when he came to write his 'Essai Historique') certainly visited St Gobain at that time. According to Deslandes, Besnard was an unsatisfactory workman who had been dismissed from St Gobain and from another French glassworks before he turned up in England posing as an authority on the casting of plate glass using coal.

Cheap coal was seen as the main justification for promoting the British plate glass factory. One of the petitioners for the Bill, John Mackay, was certainly responsible for causing the works to be sited at Ravenhead where he owned coal mines. He was a Scot who had reached Lancashire *via* London. He was still living in Holborn when, in May 1761, he took out a patent for a new method of making salt, with Jonathan Greenall of Parr near St Helens.[92] His interest in salt drew him northwards to the St Helens district from where the saltworks derived their supplies of coal. After leasing coal mines in Parr in 1763, he started to exploit those measures which lay below Ravenhead and Thatto Heath a few years later,[93] raising part of the capital by mortgaging the estate to Charles Woodcock of Brentford Butts for £2,500, and to Thomas Lawrence of St Clement Danes, Samuel Pococke of Haybourne, Berkshire, and Alexander Mackintosh of Lombard Street, London, for a further £2,000.[94] Mackay was selling coal from his Ravenhead Colliery by mid-1771.[95]

Like the other local coal proprietors, he looked to the Cheshire saltfield, and to the works and the export trade of Liverpool for the bulk of his sales. But he also saw that if he could attract a large furnace industry to settle on his newly-acquired estate, he would create a considerable local market for the output of his collieries. We know, from the terms of agreement which he signed with a copper smelting firm (later induced by him to establish furnaces on his land), that he went to great lengths to make his terms acceptable: the low price and high grade of coal and other attractive features were all carefully specified.[96] If Mackay went to such pains to attract a furnace industry in 1779–80, he would certainly have gone to even greater trouble to make his sites attractive six or seven years earlier when his collieries had been only recently opened.

Besnard told the Commons that he had arrived in England in the autumn of 1771, just about the time that Mackay's second colliery came into production. Unfortunately there is no clue to enable us to solve the mystery of how Mackay became concerned at this critical juncture with Besnard and the group of men who eventually promoted the British Cast Plate Glass Manufacturers. The prime mover among them was later identified as Admiral Philip Affleck, a naval man with East India connections.[97] We know that after going north Mackay still maintained connections with the capital: his mortgages to Londoners leave that point in no doubt. We do not know how strong these connections were, but the fact that a later mortgagee of Ravenhead was none other than the famous actor David Garrick is significant.[98]

Probably these London friends helped him to make out an appealing case for Ravenhead as the best site for the proposed works. He certainly needed all the support he could get, for proximity to Liverpool and the American trade was not, in this branch of the glass industry, a bargaining counter: the chief market for plate glass was London, 200 miles away, and if any oversea market was to be sought, it was much more likely to be in the east than in the west.[99]

Perhaps the prospect of canal communication with London was an added incentive: Pickford's boats were eventually to carry Ravenhead glass to the company's warehouse near Blackfriars Bridge. But this link by inland waterway was not completed till 1805, though water carriage to London *via* the Trent and Mersey to the Humber, and then by sea to London, was possible after 1777; and by canal to Oxford, and then by the river Thames, after 1790. Even so, this only placed Ravenhead on an equal footing with the Newcastle area which, as the main glassmaking centre, was a much more logical place for the new works. It is not without relevance that a rival group of promoters headed by the Duke of Northumberland did try to establish a plate glassworks there in the early 1770s;[100] but there was no room at that stage for two such costly enterprises.

The new company obtained incorporation for 21 years by an Act of Parliament passed in April 1773.[101] This permitted the proprietors to raise a joint stock of £40,000 in £500 shares and empowered them to raise an additional £20,000 with the consent of three-quarters of the shareholders. The foundations of the great casting hall at Ravenhead, 113 yards long and 50 yards wide, were laid in 1773. A correspondent writing from Warrington on 7 May of that year noted in his letter that 'the great plate glass manufactory which is to be established in this county is begun and they hope to be ready to work in 28 months'.[102] Glass was in fact cast there three years later.[103]

The first 50 years of the company's history fall into two sharply-contrasted phases: miserable failure was followed by brilliant success, the turning point being the year 1792 when Robert Sherbourne was appointed to manage the works.

The company was spared further expert advice from Besnard: he deserted to the rival, but unsuccessful, north-eastern venture. The introduction of the new process was left to a number of other men from St Gobain,[104] a drain which caused the St Gobain company to adopt counter-measures to put a stop to further desertions. The original superintendent appears to have been Jean Baptiste François Graux who, after his arrival in Britain, added to his name the suffix de la Bruyère. He had been born at St Gobain in 1739 and died at Ravenhead, 5 December 1787. According to his epitaph, 'he was the first who brought to perfection [in Britain] . . . the cast plate glass manufacture'.[105] The company certainly put a high value upon his skill at first. By an agreement dated 25 March 1776, he was to be paid £800 during the following 12 months and £500 per year for each of the seven years after that, with accommodation and fuel free. He was described in the document as 'a person well skilled in the method and process of making, casting and finishing Plate and other Glass of the best quality and of the largest Dimensions and also in the construction of buildings and works suitable and necessary for that purpose having for several years been employed in a Manufactory of a similar nature in France'.[106] Deslandes' verdict upon him, however, was that he was 'absolutely without any kind of knowledge or talent',[107] and events at Ravenhead seem to confirm this unfavourable opinion. In the 11 years from 1776 to the time of his death, only 452 tons of saleable glass were produced from 1,385 tons of metal.[108] The art of coal firing was not yet fully understood at Ravenhead – it was not until Sherbourne's time, for instance, that caped pots were successfully introduced to protect the metal from the large number of black drops which fell from the furnace roof – and the factory even seems to have had to burn wood to produce good glass. Other technical difficulties were encountered, too, before manufacture became really profitable.[109]

In its attempts to overcome these problems, the company was not without the most expert advice then available. Alexander Black, its secretary, was a brother of Joseph Black, Professor of Chemistry at Edinburgh University from 1766 to 1797 and a scholar of European stature. He was prevailed upon on many occasions to make analytical tests for Ravenhead and was consulted not only upon the materials which went into its glassmaking mixture and the temperature at which its furnaces were to be operated but also upon the actual construction of those furnaces. He knew about the latter because of a close friendship with the manager of Leith bottleworks, and he did his best to persuade the Ravenhead manager to learn from Leith's experience with coal-firing; but without success. 'It is a pity,' he wrote to his brother in March 1783, 'that La Bruyère & Geddes do not become better acquainted'.[110]

The company's difficulties were considerably aggravated by the workings of the excise, another problem which the French glassmakers never had to face in their own country.[111] The tax was levied by weight upon the metal in the pot, an allowance being made for wastage. It was found that, for blown glass of all kinds, an allowance of a quarter of the metal and four inches at the bottom of the pot was sufficient compensation for metal lost in the course of manufacture. But in the case of glass that was cast, even had the process been efficiently worked, the wastage, was far greater, nearer to a half than a quarter. To make matters worse, in 1777, only a year after the Ravenhead works went into production, the excise rate was doubled as a war measure.[112] The proprietors appealed to the Commissioners of Excise to increase the allowance from a quarter to a half, but the Commissioners refused on the justifiable grounds that the losses were really due to 'the inexperience and improper management of the workmen'.[113] In vain the proprietors sought to reverse this decision, urging, with equal justification, that 'the extraordinary waste of metal and materials is unavoidable and peculiar to the manufactory'.[114] The Excise Commissioners would not relent and, as the American war lingered disastrously on and a severe trade depression was experienced, the company saw its burden of debt grow heavier and heavier. In the four years 1780–3, they paid out £44,000 (a quarter of which went in duty) and sold glass worth only £40,000. These sales consisted almost entirely of unpolished plates, £28,000 worth being sold in London and £11,000 worth directly from Ravenhead. Only £1,000 worth of finished glass was sold throughout these four years, all of it in London.[115] This showed not only that there was gross inefficiency in casting, but also that the finishing process, the lucrative part of the operation, had hardly been embarked upon. This was indeed far from perfection – so far, in fact, that on 18 May 1784 the company, having spent in all more than £100,000, decided that all casting was to be stopped in order to avoid careering further into debt. The great works at Ravenhead lay idle, apart from the *blowing* of smaller plates, and was still idle a year later.[116]

Once again the Excise Commissioners were importuned for relief. On this occasion the manufacturers urged a new method of levying the duty, upon the finished or squared plates. This request was eventually granted, in 1787.[117] Although the company's troubles with the excise were by no means over – the excise officers interpreted 'squared' to mean at right angles and broke every plate that was not so cast[118] – there were some signs of improvements in technique and of a greater volume of business. Between 1787 and 1792, for instance, the wastage was reduced from 200 per cent to 100 per cent; almost as much saleable glass – 405 tons – was produced in these five and a half years as in the previous 11.[119] Of equal significance was the company's decision to grind and polish more of its rough cast glass instead of selling the plate unpolished to others in the trade and handing over to them the profit of this lucrative finishing process. Moreover it was agreed to install the latest steam machinery for this purpose: correspondence was opened with Boulton and Watt in 1786 for the purchase of one of their engines and this was at work at Ravenhead in 1789.[120] Ravenhead, however, was still but a pale reflection of St Gobain. A mere 80 tons of glass a year would have looked almost insignificant beside St Gobain's comparatively huge annual output of more than 1,000 tons. It was not until Robert Sherbourne took over the management in 1792, that the manufacture of cast plate glass on the English side of the Channel really began in earnest.

Sherbourne inherited the results of many years of inefficiency and mismanagement when, as the proprietors later recalled, the records were full of 'the failure of expensive experiments' and 'the misconduct of managers'.[121] As we have seen, the company was deeply involved in debt. The original capital of £40,000 had been spent long before, and loans had been raised totalling a further £60,000. In 1794 the 21 year charter of incorporation expired and creditors were clamouring for payment. A statement published about that time drew attention to the depressing effects of the outbreak of war and the impending loss of limited liability.[122] The company petitioned Parliament for a new Act of Incorporation but, although this passed the Commons in May 1794,[123] it failed to reach the Statute Book. The shareholders were at the mercy of their creditors, and decided at a general meeting on 9 August to sell all their property at once before they lost their privilege of limited liability. But at this eleventh hour Thomas Oakes of Upper Wimpole Street, by arrangement with the proprietors, stepped in and bought the entire business for £105,000.[124] Oakes and the proprietors continued to run the concern as a private company until 1798 when a second attempt to secure reincorporation met with success. The new company included some of the old names: Philip Affleck, Thomas Dundas, Robert Sherbourne, John and Henry Grant and

Alexander Aubert. Its title was changed by dropping the word 'cast'. It was hereafter known merely as the British Plate Glass Manufacturers.[125]

While these changes in the structure of the company were taking place in London, Sherbourne was busy transforming the works at Ravenhead. He was well fitted for the task since he had an intimate knowledge of the works and all its processes. He had helped to lay the foundations of the casting hall in 1773 and had, indeed, been brought up at Ravenhead.[126] Moreover, he was, as a grateful committee later observed, 'on a different footing from a common manager',[127] for he possessed three £500 shares.[128]

His origins have, until recently, been a mystery: but now we know, as a result of the researches of Miss P.A.Pemberton while Pilkington Archivist, that he was the illegitimate son of Admiral the Honourable Sir Robert Digby, one of the earliest shareholders and a promoter of the unsuccessful Bill of 1794.[129] This explains his close association with Ravenhead from the outset and his special status.

Sherbourne's first action was to install a cuvette furnace which produced results 'so flattering as to encourage the Committee to go to the expense of additional Buildings etc. for the purpose of completing the plan he had recommended, the object of which was to double the then produce of glass'.[130] The depressed economic condition of the country and the financial troubles of the company prevented this target being reached before 1801; the average weight of glass squared annually between 1794 and 1801 was 130 tons, an increase in production of five-eighths.[131] But most striking was the reduction of waste from 100 per cent to less than 25 per cent. The company persuaded the Excise Commissioners to change the method of levying duty back again to the weight of metal in the pot and on this measure had been granted an allowance for wastage of $33\frac{1}{3}$ per cent.[132] They were, therefore, recouping some of their previous losses at the expense of the excise. At the same time, Sherbourne found ways of saving money in other directions: for example, emery was bought as stone and prepared at the works instead of being purchased in a prepared state; and some local sand was used in place of that from Lynn.[133] In 1809 the committee recorded thankfully in the minutes: 'the business of the manufactory being now brought to such a state of perfection . . . goes on like clock-work'.[134]

All these improvements and economies turned the Ravenhead Works from a heavy liability into a valuable asset. Output soared. Profits rose from £15,000 on sales totalling £46,000 in 1801, to £20,000 on £52,000 in the following year, and £30,000 on £85,000 in 1811. Five per cent dividends reached shareholders with regularity: four of them in each of the two years 1807 and 1808, and five in 1809, a rate that was still being paid in the four years 1812–15. Nor did these large distributions prevent capital from being ploughed back on extensions and improvements to plant and further land purchases in the vicinity of the factory. The minutes abound with eulogies of the energetic manager at Ravenhead to whose efforts all this prosperity was due. His salary was raised from £500 a year to £700 in 1809 and to £1,000 in 1815. When he retired in 1829, he was voted an annuity of £500.[135]

The Ravenhead Works were added to the list of those industrial wonders which so attracted eighteenth-century Englishmen. It was a sight not to be missed and was prominently featured in the itineraries of any travellers who visited south-west Lancashire, though few of these sightseers could get permission to go round the works themselves: even proprietors had to obtain a special order from the committee in London before they could pass through the gates.[136] Most visitors had to be content to look down on the vast building from higher ground outside the walls.

It is hard to realise, in view of Ravenhead's relative insignificance in recent years – it was eventually closed in 1976 – that the reputation of glassmaking in the St Helens district originally depended upon this one factory alone. The huge polished plates – surely a rival to delicately designed tableware as the best advertisement for glass – made Ravenhead famous throughout the country, drew attention to the local advantages of the neighbourhood as a glassmaking centre, and associated the district with glassmaking in the public mind. In the end even St Gobain was suitably impressed. A visitor with interests in the French concern who inspected the factory after the end of the Napoleonic War commented particularly on the quality of the grinding and polishing. 'They take care to show in this workshop,' he ruefully observed, 'a French plate compared with the polish of an English plate, the first is dull, the other of a fine brilliance.'[137]

Many years were to pass, however, before St Helens became as well-known for its ordinary window panes as it was for its expensive plates of glass. The real origin of the window branch of the industry was in a sense an offshoot of Ravenhead: three members of the first partnership to make window glass in the neighbourhood were members of the Mackay family.

John Mackay died in 1783, leaving his entire fortune to his daughter, Millicent, as his only son, John, had died before him. As we have seen, Mackay was particularly concerned in the formation of the British Cast Plate Glass Manufacturers and his interest in the factory, close to his home at Ravenhead House, did not flag: indeed, it seems to have been considerably greater than that of a mere shareholder or fuel supplier. He provided cottages for the employees at the new works,[138] and a collector of land tax went so far as to describe the works in his return in 1781 as belonging to 'John Mackay and Co.'[139] George Mackay, of unknown relationship to John Mackay, though certainly a brother of Angus Mackay, another proprietor of 1773, was book-keeper at Ravenhead in 1785 and was still there five years later.[140] Clearly, the name of Mackay seems to have been particularly connected with the early period of inefficient administration at the works. We may perhaps be justified in surmising, therefore, that the appointment of Sherbourne in 1792 bore some relation to the eclipse of George Mackay as book-keeper. If this was the case, it may go far to explain why, in April of that year, a new firm called Mackay, West & Company made its appearance in the district as manufacturers of window glass.[141] The original partners in this concern, besides the brothers George and Angus Mackay, were Alexander Mackay (another brother who was a Major-General in the army), James Campbell, and Thomas and William West. (Thomas West was the leading proprietor of the Thatto Heath Bottleworks which, since 1785, had been trading as Thomas West and Company.)[142] Mackay, West & Company's factory, newly-opened in April 1792, was situated in Eccleston, to the west of St Helens but soon part of the town, at the corner of what came to be known as Boundary Road and Eccleston Street. This was within half a mile or so of the Ravenhead plate glassworks.

By the end of the eighteenth century window glass made on the cylinder principle, the method particularly associated with the Lorraine glassmakers, had gone out of favour in Britain and had been largely replaced for domestic glazing by glass made in a completely different way. This was known as crown glass, and sometimes as Normandy glass. Instead of the metal being blown into a cylinder, it was formed into the shape of a small pear by blowing, heating and rolling on a polished metal surface (known as marver)[143] until it formed a sphere. The part of the sphere from the blowpipe was then flattened and an iron rod, called a punty,[144] was sealed to the centre of this flattened surface. The blowpipe was broken off and the piece (as the mass of glass was now called) was re-heated at a flashing furnace. As the piece began to soften, it was rapidly twirled round on the punty. By the effect of centrifugal force, the glass was gradually opened out – or flashed[145] – into a flat, circular plate which could extend up to 60 inches in diameter, according to the extent of rotation and amount of metal which the gatherer had originally collected on the end of the blowpipe. This was known as a table of crown glass. The great

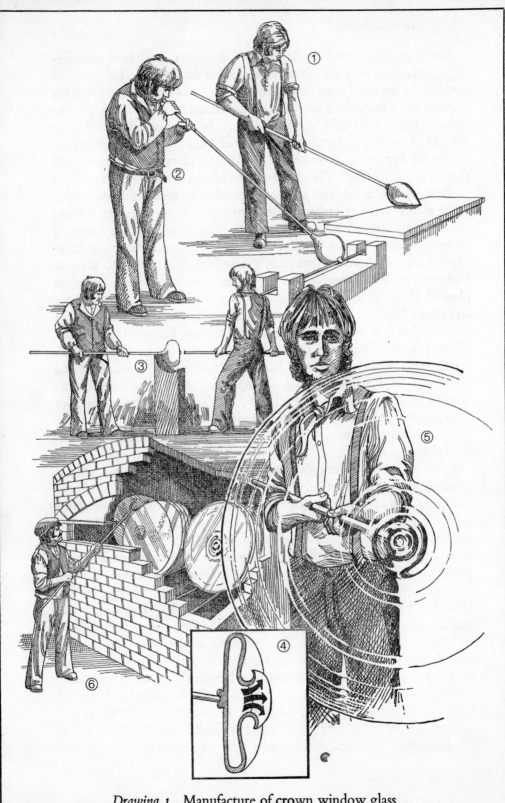

Drawing 1 Manufacture of **cro**wn window glass

advantage of this method of manufacture was that the glass never came into contact with any surface while it was still in a malleable state. As a result, it was remarkable for its polish and lustrous appearance. On the other hand, only small panes could be cut from the circular table, and the central 'bull's eye' (where the punty was attached) and the selvage at the rim were wasted.

No doubt it was the superior quality of crown glass which accounted for its growing popularity during the eighteenth century. Cylinder glass – usually called broad glass or (more descriptively) green glass – was a much cheaper article in all senses of the word. Crown glass[146] had, as we have seen, been introduced by Normandy glassmakers in the 1560s[147] but does not seem to have been manufactured in England uninterruptedly, for in 1679 a certain Henry Richards went to Normandy 'solely to learn the art . . . of making Normandy or "crown glass" and, so he claimed, brought that invention into England'.[148] According to Houghton's list of 1696, five houses in and around London were making this type of glass,[149] and during the eighteenth century the process spread to the provinces. On the eve and at the beginning of the Revolutionary War, (see graph 1 over the page) output exceeded 90,000 cwt a year. By 1800, as shown in graph 2 the days of broad glass, with an output of 20,000 cwt and tumbling, were definitely numbered. In 1833 only one firm still made it.[150]

It was crown glass, therefore, that Mackay, West and Company began to manufacture in 1792. Their factory, known as the Eccleston Crown Glassworks, remained the only one in the St Helens district making window glass until the 1820s.

In 1822, John William Bell, whose origins are not known, took over a disused iron foundry situated a little way to the east of the Ravenhead terminus of the Sankey Canal, and began to make flint glass there.[151] He was also conversant with the manufacture of crown glass and in 1826 he became the technical expert among a group of men who formed a partnership to set up the second window glass factory in the district. This was the partnership which William Pilkington, and later his brother, Richard, joined.

Fig. 1 The molten glass, gathered on the end of a blowpipe was formed into a pear shape by rolling on a marver, a polished iron slab. Fig. 2 By reheating, rotating and blowing, a globe was formed. Fig. 3 When the globe was of sufficient size, a punty or solid iron rod, was attached to it opposite the blowing iron which was then cracked off. Fig. 4 The globe on the punty was reheated then rotated at considerable speed so that centrifugal force acting on the edge of the opening caused the metal (molten glass) to be flung outwards, forming a flat disc or 'table'. This operation is known as 'flashing'. Fig. 5 The completed table with the bull's eye or bullion in the centre where the punty was attached. Fig. 6 The completed tables were piled in a kiln for annealing.

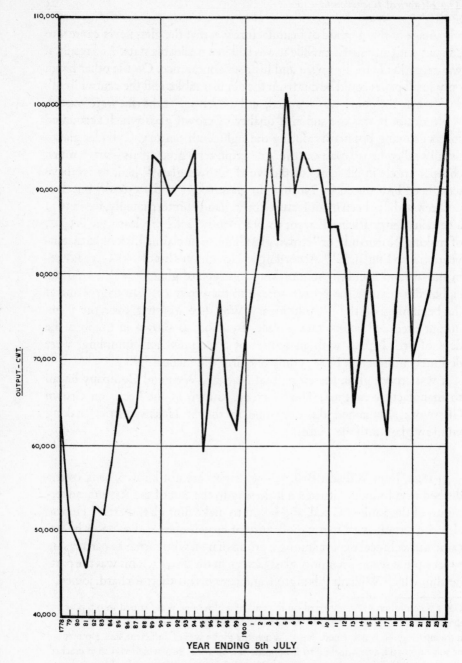

OUTPUT OF CROWN GLASS (ENGLAND AND WALES)
1778-1824

Graph I *Source:* Excise Returns

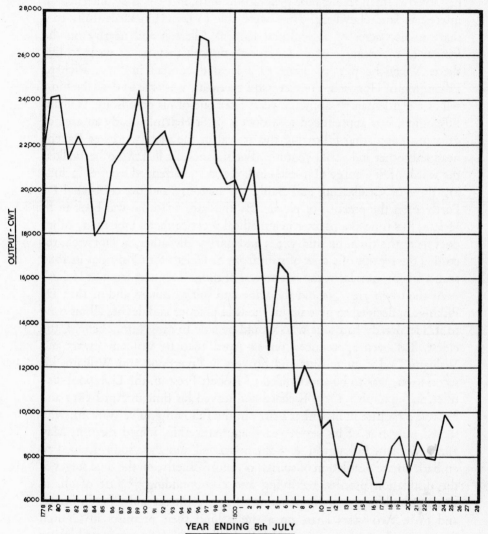

YEAR ENDING 5th JULY

OUTPUT OF BROAD GLASS (ENGLAND AND WALES)
1778-1825

Graph 2 *Source:* Excise Returns

This branch of the Pilkington family came from Horwich near Bolton, 22 miles from St Helens and in the foothills of the Pennines. There they had lived as small farmers for generations until, in 1759, they inherited an interest in land elsewhere. They were able to lay claim successfully to a share of 600 acres of agricultural land at Allerton and nearby on the fringes of the rising port of Liverpool, though they never went to live there. When he put his name to a legal document in 1761, Richard Pilkington of Horwich, the successful claimant, was able to describe himself as a gentleman.[152] Some 20 years later one of his grandsons, William Pilkington, was apprenticed to a doctor in St Helens, already an area of growing population following the arrival of the plate works at Ravenhead and other industrial ventures. For six months in 1785-6 he walked the wards of St George's Hospital in London and attended lectures including those of Cruikshank and Baillie on anatomy and the celebrated Dr Fordyce on the practice of physic. By the later 1780s he was back in St Helens, this time as a partner in a medical practice there. Like many other doctors at the time, he sold wines and spirits. His father, in Horwich, recorded the receipt of a cask of rum from St Helens for Christmas in 1789 and, a few months later, the safe arrival of more 'Licquors from St Hellin'.

As the town grew, so did the wine and spirit business and in 1813 Dr Pilkington decided to give up his medical practice and devote all his time to it. He already had sons who would be able to assist him. Richard, the eldest, had been apprenticed on 28 April 1810 to William Ewart and William Taylor, merchants and brokers in Liverpool, and William, his second son, was to be apprenticed to Robert Preston, the Liverpool distiller, in September 1815. Richard had served his time in April 1817 and became a partner in his father's firm in the following July. William, who served only five of his seven years' apprenticeship, joined them in May 1820. William Pilkington & Sons flourished and they soon decided to embark on the distillation of spirits; or, more exactly, on the final stages of the distillation process, rectifying and compounding,[153] first of all, in 1823, in buildings near the junction of Bridge Street and Church Street, and then, two years later, on a site behind their premises in Church Street, where the business could be more conveniently conducted.[154] By September 1825, William Pilkington was able to write that their orders were already 'very considerable and likely to be still greater in consequence of the intended reduction of the duties', a reference to the halving of the English spirit duties which came into force at the beginning of the next month.[155] The wine and spirit business was evidently doing very well when William Pilkington was prevailed upon to take a share in the new window glass works which were to be built in the town.

Chapter 2

An Unpromising Start

THE middle of the 1820s was a most opportune time to start window glass manufacture. Between 1822–5 building activity almost doubled, an unprecedented boom (see graph 3 over page). The demand for glass was further stimulated by the halving of the window tax in 1823 and an increase in the number of tax-free windows from six to seven two years later.* Crown glass output in England and Wales reached a peak 50 per cent above the average of the previous decade. While demand on such a scale could not be expected to persist, the need to house the rapidly-growing population was raising it to higher levels.

This market was growing with particular rapidity in the north-west of England and, although most of the houses built there – as in other parts of the country – had fewer than seven or eight windows, Lancashire and Yorkshire could boast considerable numbers of larger residences which exceeded the tax-free quota. In 1829, for instance, over 19,000 houses were taxed in Lancashire and some 20,000 in Yorkshire, each considerably more than in any other county with the exception of Middlesex and Surrey.[1] Business premises, which were being put up in large numbers in the industrial areas, were exempt from window tax altogether and usually went in for glazing on quite an extensive scale. Clearly, close proximity to a rapidly-growing market, as well as access to cheap coal and plentiful supplies of raw materials, was an important factor in locating this branch of the glass industry at St Helens.

While the building boom of 1822–5 lasted, the cost of putting up new glassworks was excessive. By waiting until 1826, when the boom had

* For a discussion of taxation, see pp. 75–79.

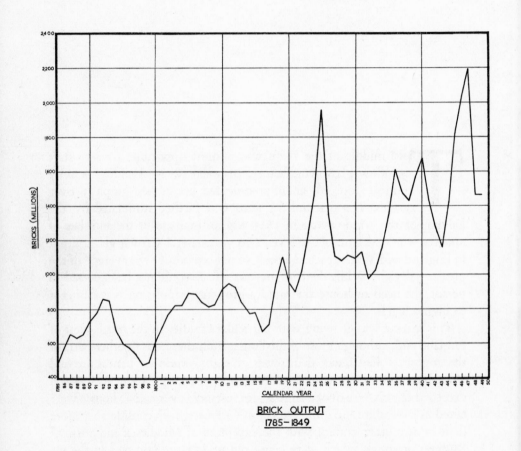

BRICK OUTPUT
1785–1849

Graph 3   *Source:* H.A.Shannon, 'Bricks – A Trade Index, 1785-1849', *Economica*, 1934

broken and prices had fallen, the would-be manufacturer employed his capital to better advantage. This was particularly true in the neighbourhood of St Helens, where the recession in trade was especially marked; in May 1826, the very month that the St Helens Crown Glass Company came into being, the proprietors of the British Plate Glass Company decided to vote 100 guineas to a relief fund, 'their works at Ravenhead being in the distressed district'.[2] Unfortunately we do not know if the founders' decision to build the factory when they did was a rational piece of decision making or whether it just happened that the boom had burst by the time they came to act. If so, they were very fortunate in their timing.

In its origin the St Helens Crown Glass Company was intended to be the combined product of the technical knowledge and ability of John William Bell and capital from three of the richest and most influential local families: the Bromilows, the Greenalls and the Pilkingtons. There were six proprietors altogether and the company's stock was divided into 11 shares. Two shares were held by Bell himself and one by a Thomas Bell whose relationship to J.W.Bell is not known. Thomas Bell was also described as a glassmaker, though he was not conversant with the manufacture of crown glass. The remaining eight shares were divided equally between four local men who knew nothing whatsoever of glassmaking. Of these, John Barnes was the only solicitor in the town, and James Bromilow was the second son of William Bromilow of Merton Bank, the foremost local coal proprietor.[3] The remaining two partners interest us most of all. They were Peter Greenall and William Pilkington.

Peter Greenall, born in 1796, a younger son of Edward Greenall of Wilderspool, came to St Helens in 1818 to take charge of their St Helens Brewery. Three years later, on 6 March 1821, he married Dr Pilkington's second daughter, Eleanor.

Their marriage testifies to the position and prestige of the Pilkington family in St Helens even before its members went into glassmaking. The Greenalls, who had been in a most lucrative line of business for more than sixty years, had already amassed a sizeable fortune. They had wisely invested much of their wealth in land and property which appreciated in value as the town grew. By the 1820s they possessed many acres of land in Eccleston and Windle townships and were by far the largest owners of house and cottage property in St Helens itself. Rent day at their Fleece Inn was a major collecting operation. They were undoubtedly of the class that contemporaries liked to describe as 'great people'. That Peter Greenall should have married Eleanor Pilkington shows very clearly that by this time the Pilkingtons, in addition to being in a business often allied to that of brewing, were of a similar family status. Eleanor Pilkington had a marriage dowry of £1,000.[4] Five years later, in 1826, when her father, then aged 61, decided to retire, he went to live at Windle Hall which, with its large surrounding estate, he rented from Sir John Gerard for £300 a year.[5] He died in 1831 leaving a fortune of £20,000.[6] Like the Greenalls, the Pilkingtons, too, had risen rapidly in the world in the space of two generations.

Peter Greenall was a man of great resource and capability. In the course of a very active life he engaged in many industrial ventures besides managing the St Helens Brewery, and in 1841 he was elected one of the Members of Parliament for Wigan.[7] Already, by the early 1820s, he showed the first distinct signs of speculative acumen outside the routine round of brewery affairs. In 1824 he started to supply the town with water – an unusual service for a brewer – and in the same year he became leading promoter of the first St Helens Building Society. This was formed to run up cottages, mainly on Greenall land. The success of this excursion into building, with which Barnes was also prominently connected and all the other partners in the glass concern were associated in a smaller way, may have led to their advancing capital for glassworks on land nearby in the hope of even greater returns. Certain it is that during 1827 the Building Society was to advance £400 to each of the six partners on the security of their interest in the glassworks.[8] £2,400 was just over one-fifth of the total capital of the firm at that time, a considerable proportion of the initial outlay.

We do not know whose idea the glassworks was in the first place, though, presumably, as J. W. Bell was the technical expert and in the trade, he must be our most likely choice. He certainly bought the necessary land on behalf of the others at the end of March 1826,[9] near his own flint glass-works (see plans pp 11 and 108). It was a quite narrow rectangular strip of freehold land about two and a half statute acres in extent, stretching from the corner of present-day Watson Street and Grove Street southwards. Grove Street, which then ran on to the Ravenhead Copper Works, formed the larger, western side of the rectangle and a road which cut across from Grove Street eastwards to the Bells' Ravenhead Flint Glassworks, formed its southern boundary. For this valuable industrial site, advantageously placed near to the Canal, the turnpike road to Liverpool and the Ravenhead Colliery, Bell paid £764 15s 0d. Seven weeks later, in the middle of May, the other partners confirmed that he had acquired the land on behalf of the company[10] and articles of co-partnership were drafted.[11] This draft would appear to confirm the view, already suggested by his purchase of the land, that Bell was the prime mover in the whole enterprise.

Although Bromilow was named as the general book-keeper and cash-keeper (for which he was to receive £250 a year), Bell, the manager (also to be paid £250 a year), was to be responsible for

attending to the Workmen, the manufacturing of the Crown Glass and all things incident thereto. And also in the travelling department to effect Sales of Crown Glass when manufactured and purchasing Articles used in the Manufacturing of Crown Glass on the best possible terms...

Moreover, he was not expected to give the new firm his undivided attention for he was to be allowed to devote a reasonable part of his time to his neighbouring flint glassworks. While acting as works manager and chief salesman and at the same time keeping an eye on his other concern, he was also to

teach and instruct ... the said Peter Greenall, James Bromilow, Thomas Bell and John Barnes in the different operations respecting the mixing of metal, manufacturing of crown glass and all other things incident thereto ... [Greenall, Bell and Barnes were not] to attend to ... the management ... further than ... from time to time shall be convenient or agreeable to themselves.

Two points emerge quite clearly from this allocation of responsibilities. The first is that J. W. Bell was charged with a whole host of duties which, even granted that the works were to start on a small scale, would tax the strength and ability of any one man. No doubt he hoped to delegate some of these jobs to others, but there was a limit to the extent of such delegation, particularly in the early stages of a new concern. The partners were expecting too much from one person.

Secondly, the draft articles do not mention William Pilkington at all. This may, of course, only have been an oversight which was eventually corrected in the final copy. In support of this view is the fact that his name appears in the purchase deed of 16 May, two days *before* the date of the draft articles. Yet the complete omission of one of the partners' names is curious, suggesting that William Pilkington was, in fact, brought into the company some time after the others. There is a later hint of this; it appears in William Pilkington's obituary notice which, published in identical words in the *St Helens Newspaper* and the *St Helens Standard*, bears all the marks of being both well-informed and accurate. According to this source, the works were promoted by Greenall, Bell, Bromilow and Barnes and 'to these names that of Mr Pilkington was added'.[12] If William Pilkington was in fact introduced to the partnership at a later stage than its other members, it seems reasonable to suggest he may have been

C

introduced by his brother-in-law, Peter Greenall, whose name, significantly, appeared first in order upon the draft deed.

The glasshouse, a single cone 120 feet high with an internal diameter of 66 feet, possibly modelled upon one of the cones at Dumbarton,[13] was built during the summer, autumn and winter of 1826 at a cost of about £8,500.[14] Tables of crown glass were blown and flashed[15] there for the first time on 14 February 1827.[16] It was later claimed that James Kenmore, a native of Northumberland who came to St Helens from Scotland, made the first piece of glass at the works,[17] but we do not know the names of any of the other workmen concerned, 40 to 45 in number.[18] The earliest surviving list of employees refers only to the year 1849 and the first list of occupants of the company's cottages is dated 1835.[19]

The partners were no sooner in a position to embark upon full-scale production than they ran into serious difficulties. Bell was never given a chance to show whether he was equal to the multitude of responsibilities he had assumed. In the spring of 1827 yet another worry was loaded upon his already grossly overburdened shoulders: he became involved in a tedious battle with the Commissioners of Excise in connection with his flint glassworks.[20]

Bell had been in the habit of removing some coloured metal from the bottom of one of his pots after working. This he did in the presence of an excise officer who made allowance for this glass, charging for it only when it became part of the new metal. This practice had been permitted up to April 1827, but in that month the officers suddenly insisted that the metal was dutiable as soon as it was removed, on the grounds that it might be slipped into the pots again after gauging, unknown to the officer. Moreover they accused Bell of 'contriving and fraudulently intending craftily to deceive and defraud' them since 5 July 1825, when a new set of regulations had come into effect, and they required that he should pay duty on all the cullet he had removed since that date. This involved the payment of some £243. Bell resisted the claim and took the matter to law. After lengthy (and, no doubt, costly) preliminaries, the case came on for trial in the Exchequer Court in London on 16 February 1828, with Bell and Barnes, his solicitor, in attendance. The jury decided by 11 to one in favour of Bell. They did not believe that he had been guilty of any attempt to defraud. But the Commissioners, with a principle at stake, were unwilling to let the matter drop. They demanded a re-trial and this was heard at the end of November in the same year, 1828. Again Bell secured a verdict in his favour and again the Commissioners refused to dismiss the matter. Discussions concerning a third trial were still taking place in May 1830.

These proceedings must have taken up much of Bell's time from early in 1827, precisely when the new crown glassworks required his closest attention. The two trials and the legal business associated with them could not have been undertaken without incurring considerable expense. It is not surprising to discover, therefore, that both J. W. and Thomas Bell had to sell their shares in the crown glass company. At the end of December 1827, when the first case was pending, J. W. Bell parted with a half of his two-elevenths' share for £1,000 to Greenall, Bromilow and Pilkington, who divided it equally among them.[21] Five months later, the first trial over and the second in prospect, he was obliged to sell his remaining eleventh share and Thomas Bell also sold his eleventh. Peter Greenall and William Pilkington each acquired one-third of these two-elevenths and James Bromilow and John Barnes each took up one-sixth.[22] The Bells withdrew from the partnership on 15 April 1828.[23] J. W. Bell continued to manage his flint glassworks until 1838 when he was killed in an accident.[24]

The loss of Bell, to whom so much responsibility for the success of the works had been entrusted, was a most severe blow to the young firm; to some observers, it must have looked like a knock-out. But the partners were too far committed to the enterprise to accept elimination lightly. Already a large sum of money had been invested and more had to be put in every day. An eleventh share in December 1827 was worth £1,000 and the two-elevenths which the Bells transferred at the beginning of May 1828, fetched £2,485. This suggests that, within the space of five months, the partners had increased their total investment from £11,000 to more than £13,500. By the beginning of 1829 it exceeded £18,000. (An eleventh share was then worth £1,640.) This was then a vast sum to have put into a firm which lacked an expert manager. The four remaining proprietors, Peter Greenall, William Pilkington, James Bromilow and John Barnes, must have experienced some restless nights with their new investment at such risk.

In this crisis William Pilkington was prevailed upon to take an active part in the firm's affairs.[25] No doubt he had already been schooled in the techniques of glassmaking (as the draft articles of co-partnership had laid down) and had the opportunity to get to know some of the details of its day-to-day working before the Bells retired from the partnership in April 1828. His readiness to assimilate these details and his previous business training fitted him well for his new task. All his energies were to be needed.

William Pilkington, then in his later 20s, had already shown himself in the wine and spirit business to be a very able, hard-working and forceful personality. He discovered that Bromilow had not been keeping the accounts properly, having failed to credit the firm with a sum of £500 which was received, or to make allowance for trade discounts totalling more than £1,200.[26] Such a state of affairs could not be tolerated and, as James Bromilow's brother put it, with a lawyer's tact, 'differences' arose between the two men.[27] James Bromilow left the partnership in February 1829, and John Barnes went with him.[28] William Pilkington, acting on behalf of himself and his elder brother Richard,[29] bought their five shares for £8,200. He now held eight of the eleven shares in the company, his brother-in-law, Peter Greenall, possessing the other three.

£8,200 was a considerable sum of money to advance in addition to the capital already invested. It can hardly have been a coincidence that this money was put into the glass concern at a time when the family wine and spirit business was yielding particularly handsome dividends. A general cash book of William Pilkington & Sons has survived which gives details of their income and expenditure from October 1828.[30] It shows that in the last three months of 1828, expenditure totalled £7,098 and income £8,251. In the following year £24,162 was expended as against £31,951 received. Even if we make due allowance for sundries – discounts and the like – the wine and spirit business was still making a clear annual profit of around £5,000. We do not know what Richard and William Pilkington's share in this happened to be, but there can be little doubt that these large and timely profits made it easier for William Pilkington to acquire control of the glass business. Even so he had to borrow £500 at 4½ per cent from Thomas Astbury in January 1829, and £4,000 from the executors of Sir William Gerard in the following April. Yet it may be said with some justification that the reduction of the spirit duty played its part, if not in the Pilkingtons' initial venture into glassmaking, then in enabling them to secure control of the company in order to save it from total collapse and failure.

Although Peter Greenall did not join his brothers-in-law in buying out Bromilow and Barnes, and although he never, so far as we know, took an active part in the firm's management, it would be a mistake to dismiss him merely as a sleeping partner. His name lent further credit worthiness to the concern and, even though he held only a minority of the shares, the firm was known as Greenall & Pilkingtons and not vice versa. An excise officer in 1833 even returned it as 'Peter Greenall and Co'. Moreover, the Greenall family had an interest in the leading bank of the neighbourhood, Parr's at Warrington, then known as Parr, Lyon and Greenall. Peter Greenall's brother, John, was a partner in this banking house and Peter Greenall himself may have been intimately connected with its affairs.[31] He certainly had considerable influence there and this probably made it easier for the glass firm to be granted a very large overdraft as we shall see presently. Clearly, Peter Greenall was a great source of strength to the glass firm even though its management was not his particular province. But from February 1829, so far as the day-to-day control of the company's business affairs was concerned, the St Helens Crown Glass Company was already Pilkington in fact, if not yet in name.

The years which immediately followed the retirement of the Bells must have been a period of uninterrupted anxiety for William Pilkington and his brother Richard. By purchasing Bromilow's and Barnes' shares, they were taking an enormous personal risk. This meant that, with his earlier investments, William Pilkington, acting on behalf of himself and his elder brother, had paid into the concern more than £13,000 in the space of three years. And since this was a partnership and not a limited company, they and Greenall stood liable for the whole of the business's debts, not merely the sum they had invested.

It was a prospect which called for a good deal of confidence and courage from men, who, three years before, had known nothing of the glass trade. In the north-east were entrepreneurs whose firms went back generations, the goliaths of the trade. In Lancashire itself, within a radius of less than twenty miles from St Helens and competing in the same markets were the crown glassworks in Warrington and Liverpool, also long-established. And from Greenall & Pilkingtons itself, smoke was to be seen pouring out menacingly from the cones up the hill, a quarter of a mile away, belonging to Mackay, West and Company's Eccleston Crown Glassworks, almost 40 years old.

Or compare the Pilkingtons' background with that of the Chances, who were to be their chief business rivals for so many years.[32] Robert Lucas Chance, who bought the single-cone factory at Spon Lane, Smethwick, in 1824, had already spent much of his life in the glass trade. His father, William Chance, a Birmingham hardware merchant, and his uncle, John Robert Lucas, were both partners in glassworks at Nailsea,[33] and young Robert Lucas Chance had been sent there to gain experience before setting up as a glass merchant on his own account in London. By the time he acquired the Smethwick works, he had a thorough knowledge of the trade and knew everyone who mattered in it. In 1828, the year in which Greenall & Pilkingtons lost Bell, their only technical expert, John Hartley, one of the great authorities on crown glass in his day, was brought up from Nailsea to act as managing partner at Smethwick, by then a three-furnace concern. Robert Lucas Chance continued to superintend his glass merchant's business in London.

As William Pilkington surveyed the scene – one in which glass production at the end of the 1820s had not fallen as much as housebuilding, if the brick index is taken as a guide – he could have found little to encourage him. But, as so often happens when a dominating personality is concerned, fortune took his side even before building activity revived again. The workings of the excise, which had caused the departure of the Bells, now led to the elimination of Pilkingtons' most immediate competitor. It was the turn of the proprietors of the Eccleston Crown Glassworks to become caught up in the tax collector's toils.

Chapter 3

The Collapse of a Competitor and the Struggle for Survival

AT a time when the duty on crown glass was twice as great as the prime cost of production,[1] there was a grave temptation for manufacturers to add to their incomes by defrauding the excise authorities. We have the informed testimony of Robert Lucas Chance that when the duty was paid on metal gauged in the pots prior to 1815, frauds were 'enormous'.[2] Later, when the tax was charged upon the panes of glass in the kiln, there was a considerable tightening up of the regulations and few manufacturers thought it worth their while to cheat the Government in order to gain an advantage over their competitors. But William West, the managing partner of Mackay, West and Company, was a notorious exception.

His misdeeds were discovered towards the end of 1828 when an observant Acting Examiner of Excise visited the Eccleston Crown Glassworks and noticed various irregularities which aroused his suspicions.[3] He kept a close watch for several weeks and discovered that it was West's custom to bribe the excise officer on duty – a practice which West even tried to adopt in the case of the Acting Examiner himself when he knew that his offence had been detected. It was estimated that 600 pieces of glass were being fraudulently removed from the kiln every week. Sometimes John Garthwaite, the officer, connived with West by lending him the keys of the excise lock which fastened the door of the kiln. On other occasions (as the excise solicitor later asserted) when 'Garthwaite for fear of a discovery could not conveniently leave the keys', they used a secret way into the kiln.

The entrance front of the lear underneath the grated doors was ... so constructed that defendants could, by the removal of a few bricks, take any quantity of glass privately from the lear at their pleasure.

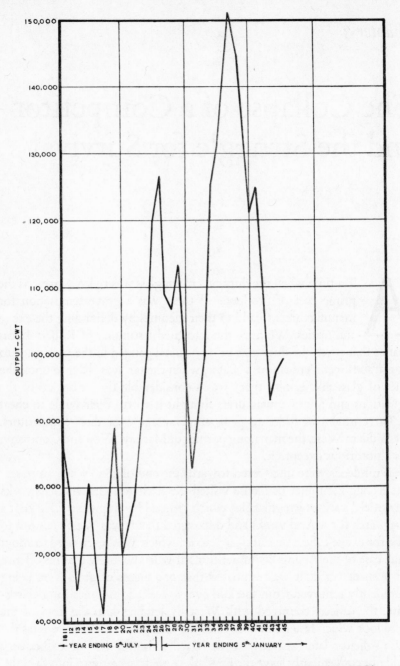

OUTPUT OF CROWN GLASS (ENGLAND AND WALES)
1811-1845

[Entries from 1826 refer to previous year, e.g. year ended 5 January 1827 = 1826]

Graph 4   *Source:* Excise Returns

West was brought before the Collector at Prescot and charged with these offences. He wriggled and squirmed and did his utmost to explain away the accusations, admitting only to giving £5 to the officer not, he was careful to point out, as a bribe, 'but as an act of charity as he had been informed that he was in distress'. His explanations were not accepted: Mr Carr, the Solicitor of Excise, proceeded to file an information in the Exchequer for the recovery of penalties for breach of the excise laws amounting to nearly £20,000.

This news caused consternation among the three other partners in the firm – James Underhill West, brother of the culprit, and Thomas Holt and George Mackay. They sent the offending partner post-haste to London to see Mr Carr, in a last-minute attempt to compromise the information. But West, though well versed in the ways of influencing lesser officials in the excise service, made the very worst impression upon the department's solicitor who, we learn, 'expressed a determination never again to have any intercourse with him'. Thereupon the partners, having taken advice from William Huskisson, MP for Liverpool and a member of the Government, optimistically offered to pay £100 as a compromise; and, when this act of somewhat limited generosity was rejected by Their Lordships, they raised the figure to £1,000. When this more substantial gesture also proved of no avail, it was decided, in March 1829, to send the firm's books for the Commissioner's inspection, this being the only condition under which there was any hope of compromising the case and thereby avoiding a public trial.

At this juncture there occurred a split among the partners, a result of the fraud, which was eventually to prove more disastrous to the firm than the detection of the fraud itself. West was resolutely opposed to permitting the books to be sent to London, for he knew that by doing this the full enormity of the offence (to which he alone among the partners was privy) would become known. This time it was his turn to take alarm. He hurried down to London to put his own case and by doing so jeopardized the chances of reaching a private settlement out of court. The other partners were most indignant at this display of independence and a definite schism appeared between West and his fellow proprietors.

The other partners continued to seek a compromise. They sent a memorial to the Commissioners of the Treasury on 13 November 1829, admitting the frauds, but pointing out that none of them had been in the habit of attending the works, 'which have been wholly under the care of the Superintendent', West. They offered to settle for £2,000 and there is good reason to believe that this offer would have been rejected outright had Carr still been in charge of the case for the Crown.[4] According to the firm's

books, the defalcation even for the previous four years amounted to
£4,500. The illegal removals of glass had been occurring before that, but
West had been careful to mutilate the books so that the exact amount was a
matter for conjecture. Carr favoured payment in full; but he died while
the negotiations were proceeding and his successor, Dehany, was more
lenient. The Commissioners of Excise agreed to settle for £5,000 and this
was paid in January 1830.[5]

The forfeiture of this considerable sum of money at a time of bad trade,
and the apparent lack of confidence among the proprietors, completely
disrupted the partnership. In January 1830, the works were advertised for
sale by private treaty[6] but did not find a purchaser. Shortly afterwards
they were leased by Mackay, West and Company to a new firm, West
and Bromilow; James Bromilow, fresh from two years' bad bookkeeping
at St Helens Crown Glassworks, having gone into partnership with the
tax evader, William West. Although up to this time Mackay, West and
Company appear to have managed to keep their misdeeds quiet, West and
his other partners do not seem to have straightened out their differences,
and in 1831 West's brother, James Underhill West, sent a circular to their
old customers, which, though concerned with old debts owing to them,
presented their new tenants, West and Bromilow, in a most unfavourable
light. Although we no longer possess a copy of this circular, we know
that it was directly responsible for causing many customers to switch their
orders from the Eccleston concern to Greenall & Pilkingtons. This is
made abundantly clear from a letter which William West wrote to his
brother on 19 May 1831:

Whatever hostility you have shewn towards me I have said little of it, but
when I contemplate the hasty steps you took in sending off the Circulars, I must,
as I said in a former letter, charitably suppose that you could not be aware of the
consequences to the Firm of West and Bromilow; indeed, I little calculated on
the issue, nor can I now tell myself where the mischief will end; to give you
some idea, however, I will just tell you what occurred to me in Manchester. I
went round as usual. The first I called on was Mr Occleshaw. He had given an
order for fifty crates and several thousand feet of glass were cutting here for him.
The whole was countermanded and transferred to [the] St Helens [Crown Glass
Company]. Next Jos. Elleray who not only countermanded his order for 20
crates but returned four crates and insisted on a receipt in full of all demands.
Thence I went to Mr Winder, on whom Elleray had waited to know whether he
has a letter similar to the one he held in his hand. Mr Winder replied No, but
the consequence was that when I asked Mr Winder for the confirmation of the
order for 50 crates, he said he had given it to another house for that under the

circumstances he knew not how to act. . . I thence crossed over into Salford where our best customer William Harrison recalled his order and gave it to the St Helens house; his next door neighbour did the same, Mr Livingstone the same. . . In a word here is a sample of what we may expect throughout the country. An alarm is given which will take months to quiet and such is the distress caused by it, what with glass being returned and orders countermanded, I am almost distracted. . .[7]

For the Eccleston works the situation went from bad to worse and West must have become even more harassed as the months passed. He tried to recoup his losses by again attempting to defraud the excise, but was again detected.[8] The differences between Mackay, West and Company and West and Bromilow soon ripened into open dispute, and the whole matter was sent for arbitration in June 1833.[9] The firm of West and Bromilow was tottering. In 1834 it fell. The works were advertised for sale by auction on 24 June 1834, on which day West signed a promise to vacate the premises by 24 December.[10] There were no satisfactory bids, however, and West appears to have contrived to remain in possession for another two years. It was not until October 1836 that he finally left the works. At a dinner on that occasion his workmen presented him with a silver cup which (in the words of the inscription on it) was 'to mark their respect and gratitude towards him for the uniform kindness evinced and practised by him towards them'.[11] In January 1837 he sold his share in Mackay, West and Company,[12] and a few months later filed his petition of bankruptcy.[13] Thereafter the Eccleston Crown Glassworks appear to have been idle until 1846 when they found a new owner.[14]

While Mackay, West's misfortunes were of most direct assistance to Greenall & Pilkingtons, troubles at other glass factories elsewhere probably helped William Pilkington to secure some of their orders as well. Chance & Hartleys went through a crisis in 1831, possibly because of a heavy loss in a patent speculation which had nothing at all to do with the glass industry. William Chance, Robert Lucas Chance's brother who had inherited the family hardware business, came to the rescue. The crisis was surmounted, but Robert Lucas Chance was obliged to remove his home from London to Birmingham in order to give his Smethwick works proper supervision.[15]

The crisis at Smethwick was short and transient: that at the large and important glassworks at Dumbarton was longer drawn out and ended in the total collapse of the concern. This three-furnace crown factory, dating from the 1780s, was among the largest in Britain with an output not far short of one-third of that of all England's crown glassworks put together.

Controlled by the Dixon family, it was part of a larger Clydeside coal, glass, bottle and brewing complex with a capital of almost £100,000. (John Hartley, the Chances' partner at Smethwick, had worked there earlier in the century.) As may be seen from the excise returns (graph 5), Scottish crown glass manufacture never reached the high peak that the English glass industry did in the middle of the 1820s; and at the end of the decade production fell much more sharply than in England, from nearly 32,000 cwt in 1827 to 14,000 cwt in 1830 and less than 10,000 cwt in 1831. In that year, Jacob Dixon, the strong man in the business, died and the management became divided. Production ceased during 1832 and, although the works were started again by other proprietors at the close of the 1830s, they did not enjoy any real success and were closed for good in 1850.[16]

The elimination of this large and powerful concern was probably of no less relevance to the survival of Greenall & Pilkingtons than was the collapse of their rival in St Helens itself. It was from Dumbarton, too, as we shall see, that the St Helens company itself gained many of its skilled glassmakers when it expanded its own productive capacity a few years later.

Window glassmaking already possessed an effective manufacturers' association by this time. Production was undertaken by a comparatively small number of firms, each of which had relatively large amounts of capital at stake, not only fixed capital in furnaces and other buildings, but also working capital in stocks of glass upon which high duties had already been paid. There was, therefore, a strong incentive for manufacturers to get together to regulate the market (particularly when prices were falling and competition intensifying) in an attempt to defend their sizeable investments; and, since there were only a few units of production, a manufacturers' association was not difficult to organize.

Restrictive practices in the industry can be traced back to the beginning of the seventeenth century when the London glaziers complained that two manufacturers, named Bungar and Bennett, had secured control of all the Sussex glasshouses. Prices were kept high and, added the irate glaziers,

If at any time we paid less, it was when another man set up a furnace. And then they would advance their size and fall their price ... though it were (by their own protestation) to their loss £200, of purpose to overthrow the party, which in short time they effected. By which their policy they brought the market to their own desires and so sunk their size and raised their price as before they had done ...[17]

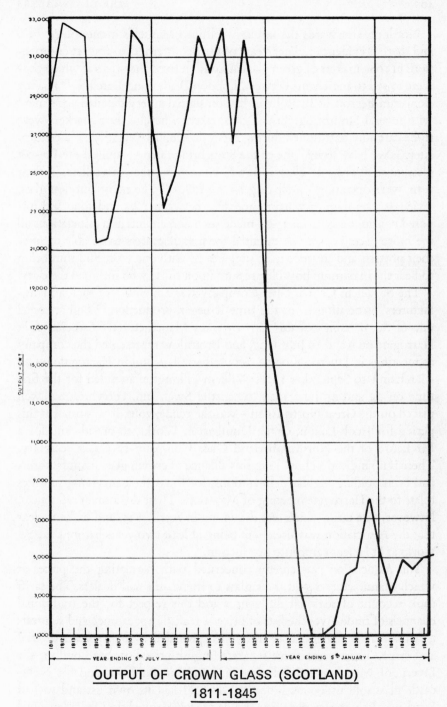

OUTPUT OF CROWN GLASS (SCOTLAND)
1811-1845

[Entries from 1826 refer to previous year, e.g. year ended 5 January 1827 = 1826]
Graph 5 *Source:* Excise Returns

Not long afterwards the industry fell into Mansell's monopolistic grip and there is evidence in later years of further attempts to restrict competition: in 1684 makers of green glass in London fixed the prices at which they were to sell to merchants between London Bridge and Ratcliffe;[18] in 1703 Benjamin Perrott of Bristol and his son signed a very detailed agreement with several Stourbridge broad glassmakers whereby their markets were to be carefully partitioned during the following 11 years;[19] half a century later, as we have seen,[20] one of the Stourbridge firms acquired the Prescot glasshouse in order to close it down. In London, the glass sellers, in their turn, were operating a price ring by the 1780s.[21] The excise duty on glass, levied as a temporary wartime measure between 1695 and 1699 and imposed continuously from 1746, made such agreements and associations all the more necessary; it was essential for manufacturers to be able to utter their protests and advance their suggestions with one voice and thus bring to bear the maximum possible pressure upon those who imposed the duty.

The St Helens Crown Glass Company was a member of such a manufacturers' association from the time it began production.[22] Bell attended one of the meetings of this Crown Glass Manufacturers' Association at Harrogate on 9 and 10 July 1827, and Bromilow represented the company at meetings in Liverpool on 28 September 1827, and in Harrogate on 28 March and 19 September 1828. William Pilkington attended for the first time on 24 and 25 June 1829, when the Swan Inn, Ferrybridge – well placed on the Great North Road – was the rendezvous. It was usual at this period for Jacob Dixon, of the Dumbarton Works, to preside and for a Mr Lamb of the Northumberland Glass Company to act as secretary. There is no indication how long this alliance of crown glass manufacturers had been holding regular deliberations, for the earliest surviving minutes relate to the Harrogate meeting of May 1827. These do contain references, however, to a tariff which was drawn up in April 1825, and make it clear that the Association was already in being at least two years before the new works at St Helens came into production.

The Association was chiefly concerned with regulating the prices at which manufacturers sold their glass to merchants and dealers. The tariff took account of regional differences and this respect for the traditional channels of trade gives the lists of prices a realistic appearance and suggests that these arrangements may have been preceded by many years of trial and error. There were three separate English price lists: for London; for Liverpool, Manchester, Leeds, Sheffield and Birmingham; and for Newcastle glass sold to 'country dealers'. Ireland had its own list and so had Scotland. The crown glass was divided into five qualities: firsts (an ideal which was never realized at either the St Helens or Spon Lane works), seconds, thirds, fourths and CC, the last being described as 'the worst glass ever made'.[23] The chief difference between the three English lists was not in the basic price but in the size of the crates and the amount of discount which was allowed. For the London market, for Scotland and for 'glaziers on the West' supplied by Newcastle, the imaginary firsts were quoted in crates of 12 tables, seconds in crates of 15, and thirds, fourths and CC in crates of 18. Elsewhere, however, all qualities were packed in 12-table crates, though the inferior qualities could be obtained in crates of 15 or 18 if so preferred. The basic price of the glass sold to English dealers ranged from about 15s a table of four-to-five feet diameter for firsts to about 10s a table for fourths and 9s 6d a table for CC. But the actual price quoted varied according to the size of crate and the amount of discount. In London, where a discount of only 5 per cent was allowed for payment within three months and 45 days, 12 tables of firsts were listed at £9 10s 0d and 18 tables of fourths fetched £9 9s 0d. The Newcastle rates were almost identical (as might be expected, the Newcastle factories being the traditional suppliers of the London market) but $7\frac{1}{2}$ per cent was allowed for prompt payment or 5 per cent within six months. A larger discount was allowed in the other English price zone (Liverpool, Manchester, Leeds, Sheffield and Birmingham): 15 per cent for payment within three months and 10 per cent for payment within six months. In this case, however the basic price was correspondingly higher per table: a 12-table crate of firsts cost £10 15s 0d (25s more than in London) and fourths in a crate of the same size cost £7 8s 0d. The inferior quality of glass which was disposed of in Ireland was sold much more cheaply. For that market there were only four categories: A, B, C and CC. A crate of the first cost only £4 10s 0d and of the last £2 10s 0d, 5 per cent discount being allowed upon bills paid within three months. The following is an indication of the prices in force during the St Helens Crown Glass Company's first years:

London				
	1st	12 tables	£9 10s 0d	
	2nd	15 tables	£9 18s 0d	Discount 5% if bill
	3rd	18 tables	£10 2s 0d	paid within 3 months
	4th	18 tables	£9 9s 0d	and 45 days.
	CC	18 tables	£8 12s 6d	

Liverpool, Manchester, Leeds, Sheffield, Birmingham

	1st	12 tables	£10 15s 0d	
	2nd	12 tables	£8 15s 0d	Discount 15% if bill
	3rd	12 tables	£7 17s 0d	paid within 3 months
	4th	12 tables	£7 8s 0d	and 10% within 6 months.
	CC	12 tables	£6 18s 0d	

Newcastle	1st	12 tables	£9 10s 0d	
	2nd	12 tables	£8 0s 0d	Discount 7½% for immediate
	3rd	12 tables	£6 18s 0d	payment or 5% if bill
	4th	12 tables	£6 9s 0d	paid within 6 months.
	CC	12 tables	£5 18s 0d	

Scotland and 'Glaziers on the West' from Newcastle

	1st	12 tables	£9 15s 0d	
	2nd	15 tables	£10 5s 0d	Discount 7½% for immediate
	3rd	18 tables	£10 11s 0d	payment or 5% if bill
	4th	18 tables	£9 18s 0d	paid within 6 months.
	CC	18 tables	£9 3s 0d	

Ireland	A	12 tables	£4 10s 0d	
	B	12 tables	£3 10s 0d	Discount 5% if bill
	C	12 tables	£2 15s 0d	paid within 3 months.
	CC	12 tables	£2 10s 0d	

The formal minutes of these manufacturers' meetings, handwritten at first, lithographed from 1836 and printed from 1841, contain only the results of each conference and are concerned almost entirely with alterations in prices. Although the contents of the minutes were not to be divulged, as each manufacturer sent out his price list they soon became common knowledge among the merchants. The minutes, therefore, contained very little of what we might call secret information. That is not to say, however, that the manufacturers did not discuss matters not mentioned in the minutes. It would be surprising if their conversations did not cover most of the topics of interest and range over the current trends in their industry. We have evidence that in later years most of the real business was transacted privately over dinner on the night before the formal, minuted meeting. This practice may have had a long history.

It is difficult to say with certainty what degree of success was achieved by the Association. We cannot discover whether the manufacturers honoured the resolutions which they passed or whether they were tempted to steal a march on one another by allowing higher discounts, selling thirds for the price of fourths or employing some other stratagem to sell lower than the fixed price. It is difficult to imagine complete harmony among rival manufacturers competing in a limited market. Disobedience to the rules could always be excused on the grounds that one was only repaying a rival in his own coin. Thus, despite several resolutions of the Association not to employ workmen unable to produce a note of

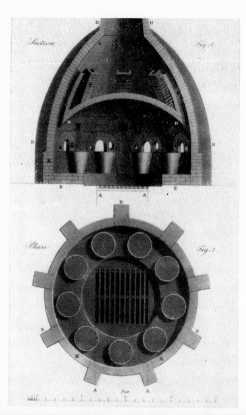

1 A COAL-FIRED GLASS FURNACE.
Fresh air was fed in to the grate
(A–A) from outside the glasshouse
via an underground tunnel. The
flames from the fire made upon the
grate reverberated down from the
dome (D–D). (From *Pantalogia,
A New Cyclopaedia*, 1813.)

2 CASTING PLATE AT RAVENHEAD
c1800. (After Joseph Wright of
Derby, Pilkington Glass Museum.)

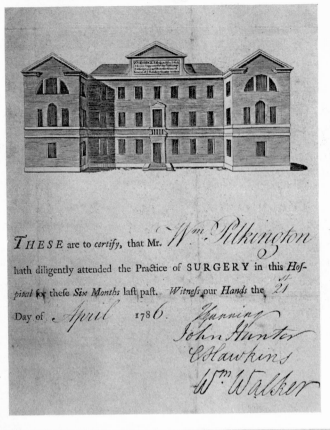

THESE are to *certify*, that Mr. *Wm Pilkington* hath diligently attended the Practice of SURGERY in this *Hospital* for these *Six Months* last past. *Witness* our *Hands* the *21* Day of *April* 178*6*.

Manning
John Hunter
C Hawkins
Wm Walker

3 DR PILKINGTON'S ATTENDANCE CERTIFICATE FROM ST GEORGE'S HOSPITAL, LONDON 1786.

4 WINDLE HALL, ST HELENS. Home of the Pilkington family since 1826. (Sketch by Captain William Latham reproduced by permission of Manchester Central Library.)

Sketch of Windle Hall, near St. Helens, Lancashire. Late the Residence of John Gerard Esqr Taken by Wm Latham April 4th 1824.

5 Peter Greenall
1796–1845
(Portrait by Spindler at St Helens Town Hall.)

6 William Pilkington
1800–1872

7 Richard Pilkington
1795–1869

8 THE ST HELENS CROWN GLASS WORKS. Artist's impression of Greenall & Pilkingtons in the 1830s.

9 EXTERIOR OF FIRST GLASSHOUSE, finally demolished 1931.

discharge from their previous master, William Pilkington had no qualms in writing to his brother, Richard:

As the Bristol house has a good name for well-annealed glass, it would be desirable to engage Grimes, and as you are perhaps not aware that they made overtures to Kenmore, we need not have any scruples on that head.[24]

Nevertheless, so far as the agreed prices were concerned, the league of manufacturers possessed machinery which encouraged the reporting of attempts to undercut. On the complaint of two constituent firms, the secretary was obliged to summon within six weeks a full meeting of manufacturers to consider the charges and to seek redress. During the interval between the protest and the meeting, the other houses were permitted to sell at prices even lower than those charged by the allegedly offending party. Despite these strong incentives to report those who deviated from the agreed lists, the minutes of the Association contain no hint of any such complaints until 1836.[25] But the evidence is somewhat inconclusive, for there is a large gap in the minutes: at neither Pilkington nor Chance is there any record of a general meeting of manufacturers being held between 16 September 1830, when they met in Buxton, and 26 October 1835, when they met in Newcastle.[26] This may mean either that prices were maintained without consultation during these five years, or that meetings were held and the minutes have not survived, or that the Association had ceased to exist. On the one hand, William Pilkington reported from London in 1831 that 'the price ... is low and squares shockingly so',[27] which suggests that price-fixing had been suspended; yet, on the other, when the minutes are resumed in 1835, they reveal every sign of continuity, which suggests that price-fixing had never been abandoned. On the whole, the slender evidence that we have during this period when demand was rising rapidly seems to point to an unbroken tradition of agreement and organisation rather than to an interregnum of what contemporaries chose to call 'fighting trade'.

If this was, in fact, the case, it follows that competition within the trade was confined to the quality rather than to the price of the glass which each house produced. The more manufacturers were precluded from seeking orders by promising lower prices, the more they were obliged instead to prove to their customers that the goods which they offered were of better quality – for which the agreement permitted higher prices to be charged. In order to manufacture the necessary high-grade glass, each house sought to collect together the most skilled body of glassmakers that could be found, and each manufacturer was constantly badgering his managers and men to provide him with glass of a higher quality than that of his rivals.

This emphasis on quality was the recurring theme in the letters which William Pilkington wrote home to his brother as he travelled round the country for orders. In April 1831, he was in London seeking to establish personal contacts in the capital, particularly with the wealthy, glass-selling house of Hayward and Chater to whom the St Helens Company's glass had been sent since the beginning of 1828.[28] He bewailed the fact that the glass which the firm had sent to London previously was 'very indifferent' and went on:

the flashing of it is downright bad, and tell both Charles and Spanton that if we cannot have our work flashed as well as other houses, I will discharge both, if you have not done it by one already, and if James Wood does not give it us less bent out of the kiln, I will serve him the same. I am surprised, too, that Roger should say such glass was good. If he does not inform us when the work is bad and be more decided I shall be very angry with him. In consequence of the flashing being so bad and the tables so bent, there is not a crate but what has four, five, or six tables broken. Tell Robert Morgan to make his crates wider at the bottom so that they be not pinched and broken.[29]

A week later, still in London, he returned to the charge:

I should wish you to tell Robt. Morgan to get as many 18 table crates made as possible. Let them be a little wider at the bottom – four slips on each side – and made as strong as possible. Let Roger re-assort all glass of bad or poor colour as well as bad make, pack the worse into tables with no mark but simply 18 on the end of the crate; the better qualities of the same, as also better colour, pack into 18 table crates and mark them 18 CC. He must also pack the best glass of our present make into 18 for the London market. I hope that every exertion will be used at present to send good work, it makes glass appear 10 p. cent better. Tell Blanshard that I have seen glass from Richardsons[30] without any rim or selvage at all – and some Birmingham glass with very little indeed. I am not overstating facts. I could not have believed it had I not seen it. As therefore it is possible to be done, *we must if possible do the same* – and without it we need not attempt to send glass here. There will be one advantage in selling here (if we can sell it in safe hands and which I trust we shall) that as credit is shorter, we may curtail our accounts in other quarters. I have done better than I expected in getting orders but I repeat that they are all given as trial orders and our future will depend on our present execution; in fact, if the glass is good I believe I could here sell all our make.[31]

This persistent chivying is a constant feature of William Pilkington's correspondence at this time. But his criticisms were always more than mere reprimands. He always followed caustic comments by detailed remedies. On one occasion, for instance, when he learnt that there had been trouble with the furnace, he was most indignant:

I find that the furnace broke out on Monday. Now what childish nonsense that is! They have scarcely a circumstance of that sort ever happening at Spon Lane. Then why with us? Our founders and teasers are surely old enough and have had experience enough. Then why should it happen? Let Peter take the charge of it to one period – and then the skimmer. But first ask Roger as to the right division of the time and then let a penalty be the consequence of such results in future. But if the manager says that the furnace is good when the founder leaves it, the teaser must be punished – or why give them plus at all? I was quite out of patience to hear the *cool, quiet, amiable* proposition of going four rounds this week, thereby (with number four *slightly* running) incur the risk of breaking a pot, hurry the furnace, change the mixture and waste material – all forsooth rather than a penalty should be inflicted.[32]

If William Pilkington was insistent that the firm's glass was to be of good quality and that the works were to be efficiently conducted, he was equally concerned with the art of selling. Here he was able to draw upon his earlier training and experience in the wine and spirit business. He realized that direct contact with his customers was the key to success. As he remarked to his brother:

I feel... assured of the necessity of personal interviews and regular visits to our connexions. It not only pleases them but affords them an opportunity of stating their views and wishes *in a conference*, which cannot be communicated in a letter. It also – which is an important matter – keeps that tie stronger and closer between you and them than either could or would be prudent to entrust to a traveller – "ecce signum" – and none but who would rather do business with a principal than a clerk.[33]

He put these principles into practice and during the early years did all the travelling for the firm himself. These journeys often involved considerable discomfort and sometimes even danger. In 1834 when he was on his way in a small 100-ton steamer from Liverpool to Holyhead *en route* to Ireland, a violent storm sprang up, prolonging the rough passage by ten hours. Another vessel which had made the same voyage at the same time sank after she had been towed into Holyhead harbour.[34] The overland journeys were made by stage coach in these early days, often in the open. In the later '30s, the railways, slowly laying the foundation of a network of lines, made travel easier but paid little attention to the comfort of passengers. In 1838, for instance, when William Pilkington caught the train home from Birmingham, he had to be at the station by six in the morning. 'The trains from Birmingham,' he grumbled, not without justification, 'are at such untimely hours.'[35]

Messages to his brother give us occasional glimpses of his travels about the country making new openings, gaining customers' confidence and securing regular orders. His first visit to London, in 1831, was followed by many others. He became friendly with the Chater family, into which his eldest daughter was to marry.[36] Already, on 15 September 1834, he was able to write home:

Mr Chater is still all kindness. He wants us to dine today in a quiet way and he has made a party of his family and friends to meet us tomorrow. He kept the last brace of birds until they were spoiled in the hope that we should return in time to eat them. To give you some idea of the extent of their, or rather his business – he received £10,000 in part payment of one contract last week.[37]

Also in 1834 he referred to export orders, wrote about his visit to glass merchants in the West Country and described the pleading antics of hordes of beggars which he witnessed as he journeyed from place to place in search of customers in Ireland. Later, he wrote from Birmingham, Glasgow and Edinburgh. These long journeys, regularly undertaken, must have been a very severe strain. He was not a man to reveal his feelings but on one occasion, having read a depressing letter from home, he confessed that it had vexed him considerably. He confided to his brother:

After having had a solitary long day's ride with my thoughts continually bent on home and its concerns, a letter ought to be a relief and a pleasure, but I really felt inclined to put off opening yours, feeling low and fatigued... Mr Chance carries a book on his journeys to rest his mind from thinking about matters at home when he cannot do any good by thinking only...[38]

The rapid expansion of output at the works, however, bears testimony to the success of William Pilkington's salesmanship as well as to the quality of the glass which he sold.[39] In 1828 an average of 742 tables were manufactured every week. In the following year, when William Pilkington first assumed control, output fell slightly to 722 tables a week but in 1830 it rose again to 758. Then followed five years of steady, uninterrupted progress. In 1831, the year of the Mackay, West circulars, and the year of William Pilkington's first visit to London, glass was produced at the rate of 945 tables a week. This rapid increase was sustained in the following two years when the rate rose to 1,215 and 1,483 tables a week respectively. The building cycle was swinging upwards again, particularly in the textile districts.[40]

Business was so brisk that the partners decided, in 1834, to expand productive capacity by building a second glasshouse. This came into use in October of that year.[41] Output in 1835 was twice what it had been two years before. The building cycle was reaching a new peak and the output of window glass from English factories was one-third greater than during the boom of the mid-1820s, though if Scottish production is also taken into account, the two peaks were roughly of the same magnitude. Greenall & Pilkingtons seized the opportunity to build a third furnace. Production in 1836 exceeded 5,000 tables per week.[42] These were years of considerable growth and many more skilled glassmakers had to be found. Many of them seem to have been recruited from those who found themselves unemployed when the Dumbarton works were closed.

TABLE 1
PILKINGTON PRODUCTION 1828–36

Year	No. of tables		Annual Weight (cwt)
	per week	in the year	
1828	742	38,566	3,419
1829	722	37,560	3,229
1830	758	39,399	3,322
1831	945	49,152	4,193
1832	1,215	63,161	5,226
1833	1,483	77,136	6,350
1834	1,939	100,813	8,328
1835	3,092	160,804	13,662
1836	5,095	264,921	21,525

The extension of the factory and the increased working capital which had to be raised to finance larger purchases of raw materials put a considerable strain on the partners' resources. By 1834 they had advanced £24,300 and there was an overdraft at the bank of £9,661. Turnover continued to grow, and £5,500 was needed to build the third furnace.

All this time the Pilkington brothers had maintained their interest in the wine and spirit business of William Pilkington & Sons, though inevitably they played an ever-decreasing part in its management. Perhaps this may explain to some extent why it became less successful as the glass firm grew and flourished. Another reason was a repeal of the duty on beer in 1830 which exercised as decisive an effect on sales, though in the opposite direction, as the reduction of the spirit duty had done four years earlier. In 1826 the scales had been tipped in favour of the distiller and rectifier. Now they were redressed in favour of the brewer. William Pilkington &

Sons' profits fell from £7,107 in 1830 to £5,160 in 1831; £4,872 in 1832, £3,496 in 1833, £3,131 in 1834 and £2,210 in 1835.[43] As the sales of the glassworks had grown, those of the wine and spirit business had dwindled. In 1836, Richard and William Pilkington's younger brother, Thomas, who was a partner in William Pilkington & Sons, grew restive and decided on retirement.[44] (Thomas – not to be confused with William Pilkington's son of the same name, who was a partner in Pilkington Brothers from the mid-nineteenth century – turned out to be the black sheep of the family. He was a source of embarrassment to his brothers and, when he died at Leyland in 1880, their sons were concerned about the welfare of 'the two children' who 'in the natural course . . . would go to the workhouse'.)[45] It was Thomas's withdrawal from William Pilkington & Sons rather than the fall in profits that seems to have been the major cause of his elder brothers' decision to sell the business, for the rapidly-growing glass business was now taking up all their time.

William Pilkington confessed that they would have continued to manage the wine and spirit business, which brought in 'from 14 to 17 hundred p. annum besides keeping our two families', had the glass business not grown to such immense proportions:

> If we could have given up the Glass Works [he wrote] we should, but from the great outlay of Capital, in building, etc., we should find it next to impossible. You are also aware that this is a step we at one time never contemplated but from the circumstances of our Brother Thomas giving up active business and the glass trade growing too heavy for one person to manage to advantage, we thought it better to give up one than verify the old adage of having too many irons in the fire and letting some burn.[46]

Accordingly, the rectifying plant was sold and the premises rented as a shop from the beginning of 1837 for £250 a year.[47] This meant that William Pilkington, his wife Eliza Charlotte (whom he had married in 1824)[48] and his already large family had to find a new home. They removed to Millbrook House in Eccleston, then in the country outside St Helens, once the residence of Dr Adam Clarke, the Methodist biblical scholar, and at that time unoccupied. William Pilkington leased this property from his brothers-in-law, the Greenalls, for a term of 14 years, at an annual rent of £30.[49]

The year 1836 marked a turning point both for Greenall & Pilkingtons and for the glass trade in general. For the former, it ended the first phase of their efforts to obtain a secure foothold in the industry. Their works were still in the early stages of growth, but they were increasing their turnover quite impressively and by 1836 seem to have gained about one-seventh of the total production of window glass in England and Wales. They did well to establish themselves when trade was good; after 1836 it entered a period of depression and the Manufacturers' Association decided to set limits upon output as well as upon prices. Had Greenall & Pilkingtons not been so successful in their quest for orders while business was brisk, their quota would have been smaller and their lot would have been all the harder in the following years of depression and restriction.

The later 1830s were also a critical period for the glass industry from another point of view. They saw the beginnings of technical change in an industry which had depended for so long upon human skill alone. The introduction of machinery into first one and then another department of glassmaking confronted manufacturers with a new challenge. It was a challenge that was taken up by the newer firms rather than by the older goliaths. It was one of those pebbles in the hands of the younger businesses which was, within the space of twenty years, to prove the giants' undoing.

Chapter 4

The Introduction of a New Technique

DURING the eighteenth and early nineteenth centuries, as has been noticed, crown glass slowly drove off the British market the crude form of cylinder glass, known as broad, or green, glass. Unlike broad glass, crown glass never came into contact with any surface while it was still in a malleable state. The resultant polished, lustrous appearance gave it an obvious advantage even though, since it had to be cut out of large circles, it could only be obtained in quite small-sized panes.[1] On the continent of Europe, however, crown glass went out of fashion during the eighteenth century because manufacturers there began to employ a much improved method of making cylinder glass, from which much larger panes could be cut.[2] Previously, the cylinder had been slit, when still hot, by means of a cold iron and clumsily opened out (or spread) on an iron plate at the mouth of the furnace.[3] By the improved method, the cylinder was allowed to cool down before being slit from end to end

---

Fig. 1 The molten glass, gathered on a blowpipe was blown into an open wooden block or mould which dictated the ultimate diameter of the cylinder. Water sprinkled on the wood prevented the glass from scratching and the wood from burning. Fig. 2 After reheating at the 'glory hole', blowing and rotating, the molten metal formed a flat bottomed hollow vessel. Fig. 3 The glass was then alternately reheated and swung over a swing hole or trench so that a cylinder was formed. The diameter of the cylinder was kept constant by blowing. Fig. 4 When the cylinder had cooled, a longitudinal cut was made on the inner surface. The cutting tool was a diamond guided by a wooden ruler. Fig. 5 The split cylinder was placed in a flattening kiln where, after reheating, it opened and flattened onto a flat sheet of glass or lagre. A polissoir, a wood block on the end of a rod, soaked in water, was used to iron out any irregularities. The sheet of glass was then placed in an annealing kiln.

Drawing 2 Manufacture of blown cylinder sheet glass

with an iron or diamond,[4] the ends having been trimmed. It was then reheated in a special kiln – known as a flattening kiln – to a temperature at which it could be opened out upon a piece of polished glass, called a lagre, with little damage to its surface.

There were various attempts to introduce this improved form of cylinder glass on to the British market before it was successfully launched in the 1830s. As early as 1758 the Excise Commissioners were aware of the manufacture in England of an improved form of broad glass 'appearing to be of a quality and colour greatly superior to common Green Glass and of as good colour as some Crown Glass and being judged to be Crown Glass by several Glass-makers and Glaziers'.[5] In 1777 when the excise duty on glass was doubled, special provision was made for 'Glass now called German Sheet Glass': it was taxed at twice the rate levied on broad, and at the same rate as crown.[6] At the beginning of the following year, the Society for the Encouragement of Arts, Manufactures and Commerce awarded a prize to George Ensell of Amblecote, near Stourbridge, for some sheet glass which he had manufactured, all of it in panes over 30 inches by 26 inches.[7] Shortly afterwards, in July 1780, the firm of Honeyborne and Ensell advertised in the *Birmingham Gazette* that they were making sheet, as well as crown, at their factory near Stourbridge.[8] This venture appears to have been short-lived; but there are various scraps of later evidence to show that manufacturers went on trying to make an improved product. Robert Lucas Chance's uncle, John Robert Lucas, for instance, the partner in Nailsea glassworks, took out a patent in 1805 for 'An Improvement in the Art or Method of Making, Spreading or Flattening Sheet Glass, Plate Glass or any other Spread Glass requiring a polished surface'.[9] The Tyneside glassmakers attempted to develop a market for sheet glass some time after this but did not succeed.[10]

Two explanations are usually advanced for Britain's clinging to crown glass manufacture when a better process was available. The first is that, by the later eighteenth century, crown glass with its lustrous finish had become so firmly established and so highly esteemed that no alternative which lacked such a finish could be made to appeal to the customer. The second is that, since the production of sheet glass involved a new type of skill, it could only be introduced if workmen, trained abroad, were brought over here at great expense to start the new process and if new kilns were built. It is hard to believe in either of these explanations as the main reason for the tardy arrival of sheet glass, though they may have been quite important secondary ones. One would expect, rather, to trace Britain's slowness in adopting this innovation in some way to the workings of the excise duty on glass, for this was the only fundamental point of difference between the industry in Britain and that on the continent of Europe.

Here there is, in fact, a much more plausible explanation to be found. The duty on window glass was levied by weight[11] but the glass was sold by size and quality. With the duty so high – twice the prime cost of production – the manufacturer had every incentive to make his panes very thin so that they would weigh as little as possible. He then paid the minimum possible duty and yet received roughly the same market price since the size was not affected at all and the quality very little. Because it was made by a centrifugal process, crown glass could be made thinner than sheet. It was easier to spin out a thin table than to blow a thin cylinder. Indeed the higher rates of duty imposed during the Napoleonic Wars and not subsequently reduced did, in fact, cause crown glass to be made very much thinner than it had previously been. The window glass manufacturers who, in 1830, urged a revision of the excise duties and cited the very small increase in the total output of window glass by weight since the early 1790s, had to agree that this was attributable in part to 'the skill of the manufacturer having diminished the weight of glass relative to the surface'.[12] It was suggested in 1835 that sheet glass was usually about 40 per cent thicker than crown.[13] Even if this were a slight over-estimate, and if we make due allowance for the greater wastage in crown glass manufacture, the balance would still be tipped strongly against sheet glass, particularly in the early days of its manufacture, so long as the rate of duty remained high. When the considerable initial capital expenditure (in securing labour and building plant) and the public prejudice against any window glass without a bright surface are also taken into account, it is hardly surprising that would-be pioneers became discouraged. The initial obstacles were great and ultimate success far from certain.

We have already seen, however, that the operation of the glass excise duty was quite unpredictable in its effects. Here again it sprang one of its surprises. Paradoxically, the workings of the duty, which had done so much to discourage the introduction of sheet glass manufacture, eventually made it an economic proposition.

Since 1813 an additional drawback (or rebate of duty) of one-third had been granted on squares of window glass when exported: £4 18s od per cwt on panes of glass on which £3 13s 6d had been paid.[14] The intention of this rebate was to compensate crown glass manufacturers – that being the only kind of window glass then exported – for the wastage in cutting the square panes out of the circular tables. The excise authorities, however, put sheet glass in just the same category as crown and any sheet glass which was exported could also claim the rebate, even though there was no wastage in cutting panes out of the flattened cylinders. What was a compensation to the exporter of crown became a bounty for anyone who chose to send abroad panes of sheet.

This, William Chance (R.L.Chance's brother), the Birmingham hardware merchant with important American connections, decided to do. Having come to the rescue of the Spon Lane business in 1831, he was determined to inject new life into it by introducing the manufacture of sheet glass, chiefly for export, counting on a welcome little subsidy from public funds to assist him in this praiseworthy and patriotic venture. As the firm frankly confessed when the Excise Commissioners asked how, in 16 months, Chances had paid £24,451 in duty and drawn back £25,061 – an estimated gain of some £1,250, allowing for home sales:[15]

This[bounty] was taken into consideration by them as a set-off against the overwhelming expense that was necessarily attendant on the establishment of a new branch of the manufacture; and it was not to be supposed that a Law of Twenty Years standing would be abrogated for the simple purpose of suspending a new manufacture until the duty should be taken off and this under an enlightened Government which would be naturally anxious that a source of National Wealth, so scientific and so important, should meet with all the fostering encouragement it deserved.[16]

The Excise Collector at Stourbridge reported in May 1832 that William Chance had sent *James* Hartley (aged 20) to a factory near Paris where he gained 'such a competent knowledge of the manufacture he has no fear but he can superintend and carry on a similar one in this country with the assistance of workmen from the Continent'. Accordingly, William Chance had ordered that one of the crown houses be converted for the purpose and these alterations were then proceeding under the direction of John Hartley and James, his son.[17] In gaining knowledge of the sheet glass process and in recruiting workmen, Chance & Hartleys were greatly assisted by Georges Bontemps, whose factory at Choisy-le-Roi was almost certainly that referred to by the Excise Collector. Bontemps had visited England in 1828 and R.L.Chance, together with John Hartley, had gone to see Bontemps' factory in 1830.[18]

Sheet glass was first blown at Spon Lane in August 1832.[19] North America was its principal destination. The firm had a depot in New York, with George Chance (R.L.Chance's brother) in charge. By October 1835, this market was described in the Board minutes as 'one of the greatest importance to our manufacture'.[20] In 1835 the excise authorities, at last alive to the bounty which they were unwittingly giving, reduced the drawback from £4 18s od to £4 4s od per cwt, and in 1838 this was further

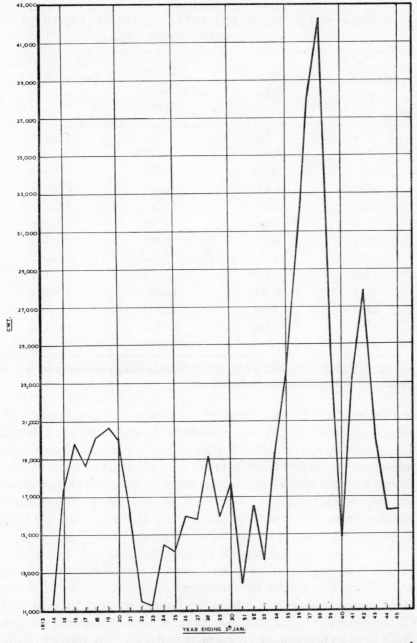

EXPORTS OF CROWN & SHEET GLASS (ENGLAND & SCOTLAND)

1813 - 1844

[Entries refer to previous year, e.g. year ended 5 January 1814 = 1813]
Graph 6   *Source:* Excise Returns

TABLE 2

BRITISH SHEET GLASS EXPORTED AND RETAINED FOR
HOME CONSUMPTION, 1832–44

Calendar year	Exports cwt	Home consumption cwt	For comparison: Total production of Crown Glass cwt
1832	692	179	103,030
1833	4,422	Nil	125,562
1834	5,343	Nil	131,365
1835	6,135	4,248	144,210
1836	8,498	Nil	155,431
1837	5,449	707	150,399
1838	4,412	2,262	140,879
1839	4,787	5,170	126,755
1840	8,156	7,914	128,113
1841	8,766	11,298	116,895
1842	7,662	17,117	97,495
1843	7,520	21,634	102,222
1844	7,703	23,857	104,340

Sources: Parliamentary Returns, 1839 [419] XLVI; 1844 [414] XXXII; 1845 [169] XLVI;
statistics at Library of HM Customs and Excise.

reduced to £4.[21] By then, however, the new process was firmly established and some of the glass was beginning to be sold on the home market.
The great demand for window glass during the building boom of the
mid-1830s had enabled Chances to sell over 4,000 cwt at home in 1835,
though for some reason – possibly the boom in America – all their output
was shipped abroad in the following year, even though Britain's own
building boom rose to even greater heights. Home sales did not really
begin until after 1837. This may be seen from the table above.

The continued increase in home sales of sheet glass at the beginning of
the 1840s, during one of the worst depression periods in British history,
was chiefly due to the resourcefulness of James Timmins Chance,
R.L.Chance's nephew. He entered the business in 1838, straight from
Cambridge where he had read mathematics and had been seventh wrangler
in his year, an interesting early example of the graduate entering British
industry.[22] Without any previous technical training, he proceeded to add
a refinement to the sheet glass process which improved the finished product considerably and made it a much more attractive selling line.

Glassmakers in France had already tried to remove the dull appearance of sheet glass by smoothing and polishing it, using techniques similar to those employed in the manufacture of plate glass, but these experiments had been unsuccessful. In 1836 two Birmingham men, Robert Griffiths, a machine maker, and John Gold, a glass cutter, took out a patent for improvements in machinery 'for grinding, smoothing and polishing plate glass, window glass, marble, slate and stone and also glass vessels, glass spangles and drops'.[23] R.L. Chance bought a half interest in this somewhat all-embracing patent[24] and used it as a prototype to be adapted to his own particular needs. It was at this juncture that J.T. Chance entered the business. Within the space of a few months he felt justified in taking out a patent of his own.

The patent specification, dated October 1838,[25] sets out quite clearly the difficulties associated with the polishing of sheet glass as well as the manner in which they were overcome. The excise duty on the thicker plate glass was levied at a higher rate than that upon window glass. A maximum thickness had therefore to be fixed for window glass to prevent its being ground and polished and exported as plate glass at a higher rate of drawback. One-ninth of an inch was the stipulated maximum.[26] Smoothing and polishing at this thickness was an extremely tricky operation, only possible if the flexible characteristic of this thinner glass could be turned to good account in order to preserve it from breaking under the strain. Chance's patent depended on bedding the glass to be polished, not upon plaster of Paris as was the prevailing practice for plate glass, but upon a foundation of damp leather. As the patent specification put it:

The glass, when laid on this level or plane surface, will seldom, if ever, lie flatly, so as to touch at all parts upon the table, but as the glass is flexible to a considerable extent, and may be readily bended, it is capable of being pressed down close to the damp bed or table by commencing pressure at the one edge, and passing over the other, in a somewhat similar manner to the action used in pasting a sheet of paper on to a level surface.

Two sheets of glass, each bedded upon this impressionable leather base, were rubbed one upon the other, with emery powder or burnt copperas (rouge) – the smoothing and polishing materials – placed between them.

The newly-patented idea took time to develop. 'My new process,' wrote J.T. Chance on 2 July 1839, 'as far as it extends at present answers perfectly: but we have determined not to make any regular sales until we can ensure a large supply.'[27] Among his earliest customers was Joseph Paxton who, in 1839, glazed the conservatory at Chatsworth with what a rather bewildered newspaper reporter described as 'patent flattened crown glass'.

This, it was observed, was 'much thicker than the common crown glass ... and the panes may be made 40 inches long at the same cost per foot as ordinary sized panes'.[28] In the following year, 1840, J.T.Chance was able to tell the makers about the successful trial of the first seven smoothing machines. He went on to ask when he was to receive 'the last pair of eight polishing machines so as to finish the first division'.[29] In making these preparations, the pioneer of the Midlands depended to a large extent on the skill and resources of Lancashire. Wren & Bennett of Manchester built all his machinery. A.B.Goss of Ormskirk was approached for a supply of felt[30] and enquiries were made at a St Helens chemical works to see if the proprietors would provide the necessary polishing powder.[31] Chances appear to have begun to market their new product towards the end of 1840. The firm later claimed for their product, soon generally known as patent plate, a greater hardness of surface than cast plate itself possessed and therefore greater resistance to scratching when being cleaned.[32]

Once a growing home demand for cylinder glass began to emerge, other concerns started to take an interest in its manufacture. Among them was the new firm of James & John Hartley. Although they had gone into partnership with the Chances after their father's death in December 1833, they soon became restive and in November 1836 the partnership was dissolved.[33] They moved to the north-east and established the Wear Glassworks at Sunderland in 1837. There they began to experiment with cylinder glass in the following year.[34] Cooksons, the old-established Tyneside firm, also began to take an interest in it, as did Greenall & Pilkingtons. At a manufacturers' meeting in August 1841, it was decided that Greenall & Pilkingtons, Cooksons, and Hartleys should all be given a sheet glass quota, but the production of none of these firms was to exceed half that of Spon Lane.

Greenall & Pilkingtons chose a good time to enter this promising field. A market had been created without any trouble or expense on their part and glassmakers skilled in this particular type of manufacture were by then to be found in England. The market, though small, continued to grow during the early 1840s, unlike that for crown which fell as building activity languished. It was a shrewd – or fortunate – move to begin manufacture during a depression when money was relatively cheap and there was the prospect of a few years moderate growth in which to overcome teething troubles before the next building boom arrived.

Abraham Hartley – a distant relative of James and John – who came to St Helens from Spon Lane to work for Greenall & Pilkingtons in 1835, later recalled that the first sheet glassmakers to be employed there were some Belgians who had previously worked at Spon Lane and then in

Sunderland. He went on to describe how they came to St Helens and how others learned the tricks of their trade:

One day a Belgian whom I had known at Chances, named Legget – nay, I don't know how the name is spelt – called on me and asked what sort of masters I had. I told him and he came to terms, I suppose, with them for he started blowing sheets soon after. Then others came along and they worked away amongst us. Certainly they tried to keep their operations as secret as they could, but they each had to have a gatherer and the gatherers saw how the thing was done. It was all a question of knack... Gradually our men picked it up and they and the Belgians used to work side by side at the blowing... One or two of them were big, powerful chaps; and they were rather objects of curiosity when they walked the streets. They only spoke English indifferently well; most of their leisure time they spent playing bagatelle at the Peel Arms in Westfield Street... They gradually got scattered; one went to Liverpool where he started business in the public line; two of them died and are buried in Windleshaw.[35]

The census enumerators' books show that a glassmaker named Jean Baptiste Leguay, aged 33, was in June 1841 living in St Helens. Two other foreign glassmakers, Daniel Schmidt and Louis Dartes, lived close by.[36] Alphonse Demanet, described on the tombstone as 'Directeur de la Verrerie Francaise' at Pilkingtons, who was born in Namur on 19 February 1812, died in St Helens on 7 April 1845, and was buried at the old Roman Catholic cemetery at Windleshaw as Hartley stated.[37]

Early in 1842, Greenall & Pilkingtons acquired a vacant two-storey cotton mill, not far from their factory, in which to erect their smoothing and polishing equipment. (The site was not far from present-day Kirkland Street.) There was no difficulty in securing a lease, for the owner was Peter Greenall himself. On 4 March 1842, the three partners (now described as crown and sheet glass manufacturers) agreed to rent the building for £131 10s 0d a year, the first payment to be made six months after the firm should 'commence polishing German Sheet Glass at or upon the aforesaid premises'. Exactly how sheet glass was polished there must remain something of a mystery, for Greenall & Pilkingtons never took out a licence from J. T. Chance to use his patented process. On 14 September 1842, the holder of the patent wrote to Wren and Bennett:

You are probably aware that two glass manufacturers, Cooksons and Pilkingtons, are now grinding and polishing German Sheet glass, *in what manner* I am quite in the dark.[38]

By March of the following year, he seems to have made up his mind on the matter. The Board of Chances resolved:

D

That J.T.Chance write to Mr Pilkington to inform him that we are satisfied that he is invading our patent in his mode of grinding and polishing glass.[39]

Greenall & Pilkingtons appear to have started off by trying to adapt to their needs the unpatented smoothing and polishing methods then used in the manufacture of plate glass. This used plaster of Paris as a bed for the glass. J.T.Chance himself thought that plaster of Paris might be able to serve the purpose and, in September 1842, he wrote to Wren & Bennett, telling them to hold up any further work on the machinery he had ordered from them until it was known whether these experiments were a success.[40] Two months earlier Hartleys had written from Sunderland to the British Plate Glass Company to enquire whether their sheet glass could be finished at Ravenhead; but this request was refused.[41] These experiments with plaster of Paris do not appear to have met with any success; a few years later J.T.Chance could say dogmatically that 'People may grind [sic] this glass upon the principle of cast plate glass as much as they please, for it will prove a failure.'[42] Nevertheless, when, through their solicitor, Greenall & Pilkingtons replied to Chance's letter, they assured him they were grinding German sheet glass 'embedded solid in Plaster of Paris'. 'In fact,' they added, 'the process is in every respect precisely the same as that in use in grinding, smoothing and polishing Plate glass in this country long before the patent was taken out'. Chance was at liberty to come to St Helens to see for himself if he cared to do so.[43] He did not take up the invitation, nor did he persist with his idea of prosecution.[44]

Whatever method of polishing sheet glass may have been carried on in the early days at St Helens it was certainly improved subsequently by Henry Deacon. This new arrival was a young man in his early twenties who was later to achieve a considerable reputation as a manufacturing chemist at Widnes. He had been apprenticed to the London engineering firm of Galloway & Son. When they went out of business, his indentures had been transferred to Nasmyth & Gaskell, at whose Bridgewater Foundry at Patricroft he is said to have been intimately concerned with designing the famous Steam Hammer.[45] We do not know how Greenall & Pilkingtons came to hear of him. Possibly Nasmyth & Gaskell had the contract for installing the polishing benches and Deacon was sent to help. If so, he may have decided to stay in St Helens some time in 1843 when he had reached the age of 21 and, presumably, completed his apprenticeship.

The first definite evidence that Deacon was interesting himself in processing glass is contained in a statutory declaration that he had 'invented Improvements in Apparatus for Grinding and Smoothing Plate Glass, Crown Glass and Sheet Glass'.[46] The declaration itself was undated, but it was written on a piece of paper bearing a legal stamp dated 17 December 1844. Having reserved the right to this invention, he described it in greater detail in the specification of a patent taken out in May of the following year.[47] He continued to lay the sheets of glass either on plaster of Paris 'in the usual mode ... or, when sufficiently true ... on a wet cloth supported on a piece of felt of about half an inch thick'. In essence this was the same as Chance's patent, the only difference being the substitution of wet cloth upon felt for wet leather as the all-important impressionable surface. (Pilkingtons were still using wet cloth for this purpose 20 years later.[48]) The detailed enumeration of the speeds at which the machinery was to run with different grades of emery and a device for allowing 'the more perfect spreading of the raw emery or other abrading material' did not disguise the fact that Deacon may have succeeded in getting round Chance's patent by a comparatively minor change. In this respect James Hartley kept him company: in July 1843, Hartley had taken out a patent for polishing sheet glass in which he employed india-rubber in place of leather.[49]

From polishing sheet glass, Deacon turned his attention to designing flattening kilns.[50] Here again he was concerned with only minor improvements, scarcely comparable with those continental developments in kiln construction which J.T.Chance introduced into England in 1842.[51] Deacon realised the importance of preserving a good surface to the lagre, the piece of glass that was placed over the stone in the flattening kiln to give the flattened cylinder an even surface. By the method then in use, the lagre and sheet, still hot from flattening, were both loaded on to a small carriage and pushed from the flattening kiln into the annealing kiln, where the sheet was unloaded by means of a fourchette and piled by the side of other sheets to be slowly cooled. While the lagre was removed from the flattening kiln, dust fell on to the flattening stone which, on the return of the lagre, raised (in Deacon's own words) 'bumps and cockles, only too faithfully copied by the sheets afterwards flattened upon it'. By Deacon's patent, the flattening stone was no longer left exposed to the dust. He placed a series of wheels in the floor itself, each wheel protruding very slightly, so that the flattening stone *and* the lagre with the flattened sheet upon it could all be pushed through into the annealing kiln. He also devised a method, using counterbalancing weights, by which the door between the two kilns could be opened with the least exertion. At the end of 1845 William Pilkington was able to describe the firm's flattening kilns as 'the best kilns of the day'; they were sufficiently unusual to cause an employee to abscond with a model of them which he tried to sell to a rival.[52]

The successful introduction of cylinder glass to the British market in the late 'thirties and early 'forties was a development of great importance to the industry. Crown glass had survived so long unchallenged in Britain chiefly because of the excise laws. In 1845, when the excise duty was removed, those firms which had already managed to establish cylinder glass departments, had an enormous advantage over their competitors who had clung to crown glass alone. The technical changes which had taken place were to have profound economic consequences. We must now retrace our steps, therefore, and look at the late 'thirties and the 'forties from the window of the counting house rather than from the heat of the furnace or the dust of the polishing bench.

Chapter 5

Growth During a Depression

THE building boom of the mid-1830s, which had been particularly marked in the Lancashire textile districts, reached its peak in 1836. In 1837 and 1838 building activity slackened. It rose again in 1839 and 1840, only to fall more sharply in 1841 and 1842 to a trough in 1843. From then onwards there was a renewal of activity and the boom which developed in the middle of the 1840s reached a higher level than that of ten years earlier and was higher even than that of 1825 as will be seen from graph 3 on page 30.

Output of window glass reflected the movement of the building cycle, though the recovery of 1839 and 1840 – attributed chiefly to railway building[1] – found no echo in home demand for glass. Output of crown glass continued to be reduced until, at the depth of the depression, it was 30 per cent lower than it had been at the height of the boom (see Table 3 on next page). By contrast, as we have seen, output of sheet glass showed steady growth throughout these years. Home sales exceeded exports regularly after 1841, and by 1844 nearly 30 per cent as much sheet as crown glass was being made in Britain. This was despite the operation of the excise laws which favoured the thinner crown glass. The repeal of the glass duties in 1845 removed this handicap and gave manufacturers of sheet glass a real advantage. The firms which clung to crown glass alone were not able to withstand for long the unfettered competition from the new technique.

Greenall & Pilkingtons, having greatly increased the capacity of their works to meet the heavy demands of the mid-1830s, were soon obliged to retrench. They could have had very little return on their new furnaces, for the shrinking market soon left them with surplus capacity. On 30 November 1838, William Pilkington wrote home:

TABLE 3

BUILDING ACTIVITY AND WINDOW GLASS OUTPUT, 1836–46

Calendar Year	Brick Output (million bricks)	Crown Glass		Sheet Glass	
		retained at home (cwt)	exported (cwt)	retained at home (cwt)	exported (cwt)
1836	1,606	125,779	29,652	nil	8,498
1837	1,478	113,562	36,837	707	5,449
1838	1,427	120,465	20,414	2,262	4,412
1839	1,569	116,671	10,084	5,170	4,787
1840	1,678	112,797	15,316	7,914	8,156
1841	1,424	97,793	19,102	11,298	8,766
1842	1,272	85,126	12,369	17,117	7,662
1843	1,159	93,481	8,741	21,634	7,520
1844	1,421	95,709	8,631	23,857	7,703
1845	1,821	Excise duty removed			
1846	2,040				

Sources: H.A. Shannon, 'Bricks – a Trade Index, 1785–1849', *Economica*, 1934; Parliamentary Returns, 1839 [419], XLVI; 1844 [414], XXXII; 1845 [169] XLVI; statistics at Library of H.M. Customs and Excise.

... As the demand for glass, both in Ireland and England, will fall off, we must immediately give notice to more hands to go, which as we have already commenced, must be followed up – and notice must be given too, to the customers to reduce their accounts as much as possible.

Again on 8 December:

I am glad that you go on discharging hands. I told Peter Benson that his wages should remain as they were but I did not say that we would never give him notice. Of course he must have notice, and can if he chooses ... If you think proper to give him 22/– I have no objections, but it is come to something if we cannot discharge a workman who is of value only in his own estimation.[2]

Meanwhile the manufacturers were making their own plans to meet the coming depression through their Association.[3] Richard and William Pilkington were present at a well-attended meeting held at the Adelphi Hotel in Liverpool on 10, 11 and 12 October 1838, at which a proposal was made to restrict the total British output of crown glass to 1,500,000 tables a year. Each firm's quota was to be based upon the proportion that its output had borne to the total production of the country during the four years 1834–7. Thus, for example, a company that produced one-thirtieth of the total product of British factories during those four years would be permitted to make one-thirtieth of 1,500,000 tables of crown glass during the first year in which the restriction was in force. The necessary details of each firm's output were to be ascertained from the returns of excise duty, and Richard Shortridge, a member of the Association, was delegated to inspect these returns. Provision was made for a system of fines in order to penalise those concerns which had exceeded their quota. At the outset, each firm was to pay into a central fund the same number of shillings as its allotted weekly quota of tables of glass. From these payments each stood to lose one shilling for every excess table produced. There were, however, arrangements to wipe out such fines if output subsequently fell below the allocation to such an extent that the prescribed limit was not exceeded over three consecutive quota periods.

This stinting of crown glass output was a scheme which favoured the larger, well-established house at the expense of the smaller, growing firm. The latter's production was bound to be more heavily curtailed by a quota based on a four-yearly average than was the output of the older firms, whose rate of growth had not been so rapid. It is not surprising, therefore, to discover that the whole plan of limiting output was devised by the men of the north-east. Nichol, of the Newcastle Broad and Crown Glass Company, originated it. Shortridge, chief proprietor of the South Tyne Glass Company at South Shields, supervised it, and a bank in South Shields held the forfeit fund.

These proposals aroused strong opposition; so much so that the men of the north-east had to agree to delay their introduction. Two months after the Liverpool meeting William Pilkington still believed that restriction would not be applied. On 8 December for instance, he wrote to his brother:

I would take no notice of the restriction if it be carried. It will soon be broken up before any penalty can be required.

Ten days later, having seen three of the manufacturers of the north-east, Shortridge, Ridley and Nichol, two of them prime movers in the scheme, he wrote again:

The restriction is their sole panacea and their object is to keep us out of the market and prevent us upstarts from growing greater. I contend that if the restriction is not carried, the prices may remain as at present ... I am convinced that we must discharge more hands and just make for our demand which the present rate of plus[4] enables us to do at less cost, for again, if the restriction were carried it would not long exist . . . I think that there is very little hope of the Gentn. in the North either agreeing among themselves or with us. Therefore we must cultivate as good an acquaintance as possible with our neighbours, Messrs Chance and the Bristol house. In that case, too, restricted make is at an end.[5]

But at the beginning of the new year there was a complete change in William Pilkington's attitude to the restriction policy, probably occasioned in part by a worsening of the economic situation and in part by concessions he gained as a result of hard bargaining with the promoters of the policy. Although the four-year quota was retained, there were two changes in the scheme as it had been originally proposed at Liverpool. The quota was no longer related to a national total; each house was to make ten per cent less than it had *itself* made during the four-year period. This was a definite gain to the rising concerns. It was also decided that any house could by arrangement transfer part of its allotted make to another firm. Further flexibility was gained when three of the north-eastern companies – the Newcastle Broad and Crown Glass Company, the North Tyne Glass Company and Isaac Cookson and Company – agreed to amalgamate their quantities with the Bristol house (Lucas Coathupes and Company) and Greenall & Pilkingtons. Thus, three months after William Pilkington had declared himself irreconcilably opposed to the proposals put forward by the establishment figures in the north-east, we find him supporting them, having obviously struck a bargain which was to his firm's advantage.

Nevertheless, his forecast that this attempt at regulating output would fail was soon realised. The refusal of one of the Association's members to agree to a further ten per cent reduction in output, which was decided by the Association in August 1839, caused the whole scheme of regulation to be dropped after it had been in force for only about one year. When market conditions deteriorated still further, however, the Association was driven to attempt another quota – this time successfully – in August 1841. Again, the quota involved a ten per cent reduction, but on this occasion it was upon the output of each firm in 1839 and 1840. Chances' sheet glass quota was cut by almost ten per cent; but, as we have seen, Cooksons, Hartleys, and Greenall & Pilkingtons were then each allowed to make half as much sheet glass as Chances. This was a generous quota when Chances' lead in this field is taken into account. The other concerns appear to have been quite content to forgo this opportunity of making the increasingly popular product. Indeed, it was agreed that they should not start to make it during the term the quota was in force, it being understood that the four firms who had an allowance would supply them at a discount. This interesting – and for all the abstaining firms, suicidal – clause deserves quotation:

> In consideration that such Crown Glass Manufacturers as are not now Manu-
> facturers of German Sheet agree not to commence the manufacture of it, Messrs
> Chance, Cookson, the St Helens Compy. and Hartley, agree to allow the other
> Crown Glass Manufacturers not less than five per cent on the net price charged
> to London first-class dealers for the Sheet Glass they may purchase by way of
> Commission and Guarantee; and they also undertake to supply them with
> whatever quantity of Sheet Glass they may require in the ordinary way of trade
> so long as the regulations are in force.[6]

Cooksons never took enthusiastically to sheet glass. In April 1842, they even went so far as to sacrifice one-third of their total allocation to Chances in exchange for an addition to their own crown glass quota. (The amounts involved – 2,000 cwt of sheet glass for 1,250 cwt of crown glass – are a further indication of the greater weight of the former in proportion to surface area.) It was clearly not the men of the north-east but Chances, Hartleys, and Greenall & Pilkingtons who were taking full advantage of the new technical developments in the industry. By 1841, therefore, the restriction policy, at first so carefully devised to prevent the 'upstarts from growing greater', was having precisely the opposite effect.

Greenall & Pilkingtons' production figures during these years reveal to what extent William Pilkington had succeeded in turning the restriction to his firm's advantage. The amount allocated under the first short-lived quota is not known. As it was in force only for a few months, it could have had little effect. In fact, during the whole of that year, 1839, Greenall & Pilkingtons' production was at the same level as it had been in 1835, when demand was strong. The firm's second quota was in the region of 11,250 cwt of crown glass and 6,450 cwt of sheet glass. As will be seen from Table 4 on page 74, the allocation of crown glass was not quite taken up in 1841 and 1842, but it was reached in 1843 and exceeded in 1844. The firm's share of the total national output of crown glass rose during these years from one-twelfth to one-tenth. The production of sheet glass, in its infancy so far as Greenall & Pilkingtons were concerned, fell short of the quota by one-third in 1842 and by one-seventh in 1843, but in 1844 it came much closer to the permitted amount. Taking crown and sheet glass together, the firm's total production of window glass steadily increased from 1840, right through the trough of the depression.

Greenall & Pilkingtons' policy of taking calculated risks, which led them to build two additional glasshouses in the mid-30s when trade was

D*

TABLE 4
GREENALL & PILKINGTONS' OUTPUT OF GLASS, 1838–44

Calendar Year	Crown Glass			Sheet Glass	
	Tables	Weight cwt	Quota cwt	Weight cwt	Quota cwt
1838	145,132	11,697	No quota		
1839	167,286	13,579	Not known		
1840	140,872	11,970	No quota		
1841	68,680*	5,241*	5,609*	1,970*	3,214*
1842	135,646	10,350	11,249	4,380	6,445
1843	141,419	11,250	11,249	5,590	6,445
1844	144,625	11,385	11,249	6,655	7,070

*Half year only
Source: Two lists of production figures drawn up by William Pilkington about 1840 and about 1844.[7]

brisk and to embark upon the new technique of manufacture in 1841 when it was slack, yielded encouraging results even before the building cycle started to swing upwards once more. But heavy expenditure of capital was involved, and, as the years passed, the firm's overdraft at the bank grew larger. As early as September 1834, when William Pilkington had just returned from a visit to the continent, he admitted that this debt was his major worry. 'My principal uneasiness at being absent,' he wrote, 'is that the world may say that I am spending time and money abroad that ought to be spent elsewhere. If we were out of debt, I would not mind'.[8] At that time the overdraft at Parr's Bank in Warrington was just under £10,000. By the end of 1835 it had reached £13,410 and a year later it had risen to £17,292. When trade deteriorated towards the end of 1838, there are signs that the bank began to grow restive about the size of this overdraft and William Pilkington for a time gave Warrington a wide berth in order to avoid his bankers. On one occasion, in November 1838, he told them that he had no time to call and, relating this to his brother, he added: 'any excuse, you will say, is better than none'. He did not wish anything to be mentioned 'about our account as we will endeavour to reduce it by changing our system as much as we are able and will try afterwards not to increase it but to decrease it as much as possible after the latter end of March [1839]'. In May 1840, £6,000 was raised on mortgage at 5 per cent from Thomas Brooke of Norton Priory in Cheshire, and some of this may have been used to reduce the bank overdraft.[9] The beginnings of sheet glass manufacture in the following year, however, certainly caused it to be increased and in 1842 it stood at £20,000. In that year a three-elevenths share in the partnership was valued at £7,000, making the entire partnership capital worth a little more than £25,660. When the £6,000 mortgage is taken into account, the overdraft at the bank was not quite covered by the estimated value of the shares. That the bank permitted the overdraft to be increased under these circumstances at a time when trade was depressed, makes it quite clear that Greenall & Pilkingtons were able to take advantage of the Greenall interest in Parr's Bank.[10] Without this private influence, it seems highly unlikely that the additional capital would have been forthcoming for the all-important venture into sheet glass manufacture. Greenall support at this juncture was of critical importance, especially in the light of banking instability and the increasing number of business bankruptcies elsewhere in Lancashire at this time.[11]

It is difficult to explain why Peter Greenall, having exercised such a decisive influence, should have chosen to withdraw from the partnership shortly afterwards. Perhaps his election, in 1841, as one of the Members of Parliament for the Borough of Wigan may have had some bearing on the matter. He was certainly still on the best of terms with his brothers-in-law, and the conditions under which the partnership was dissolved make it quite clear that Greenall did not need the money and had no intention of embarrassing the firm by demanding its immediate repayment. According to the agreement, signed on 1 February 1842,[12] Richard and William Pilkington were to repay him his share, then worth £7,000, over seven years in 28 quarterly instalments of £250. The partnership of Greenall & Pilkingtons was not formally dissolved, therefore, until 1849. By that time, however, Peter Greenall was but a legal fiction. He died from a stroke while on a visit to William Pilkington at Millbrook House on 18 September 1845.[13] The official notice announcing the dissolution of the partnership, which eventually appeared in the *London Gazette* in 1849, stated that it was dissolved as from the date of Peter Greenall's death.

The mid-1840s saw a big increase in demand for window glass. Subsequent writers have tended to explain this solely in terms of the removal of the excise duty, without reference either to the growth in building activity or to the effects of the window tax, a completely separate form of taxation. A discussion of the effects upon the glass industry of both the excise duty and the window tax is therefore necessary at this point.

Until the nineteenth century windows were considered a luxury and, as such, suitable objects of this twofold taxation. It was not until the pioneers of sanitary reform began to campaign for light and airy houses that the inhabitants of the British Isles began to take the view that windows were a necessity, and to consider removing the taxes from them. Both the glass excise duty and the window tax had first been imposed during the 1690s as a means of raising supplies for the wars of William III. The tax on glass was dropped in 1699 and not levied again until 1746, but that on windows was retained. From the middle of the eighteenth century both were greatly increased, as the public expenditure of the day dictated.[14]

Glass manufacturers showed more opposition to the window tax than they did to the excise duty. According to them, the excise duty might be a cause of irritation – the activities of the excisemen in the factories and the rules and regulations for levying the duty were constant causes of complaint – but it did not limit demand to the extent that the window tax did. This was the theme on which manufacturers constantly harped. R.L. Chance, for instance, was asked by the Commissioners of Excise Enquiry:

You are of the opinion that the tax on windows is much more injurious to consumption than the duty on window glass?

He replied:

Most assuredly. I think that is obvious from the style of building here and on the Continent. If you go to Hamburg and the northern, or to France and the southern, parts of Europe, the windows are double to what they are here.[15]

It seems unlikely that the excise duty, heavy though it was, had much effect upon demand. Just after its repeal, in 1845, *The Economist* noted that the tax on glass had raised the selling price to as much as three times its untaxed cost; but even at that price the cost of putting windows in a building was not greater than that of the same quantity of plain brickwork.[16] Window glass firms had not much to gain from repeal. On the other hand, in the short run they had much to lose. Manufacturers held large stocks of glass on which duty had been paid and were afraid lest they should have to bear the loss involved when the duties were removed. More important, they realised that the repeal would lead to loss of protection against glass imported from abroad.[17] While the excise duties were high, hardly any foreign glass came into the country;[18] but when the duties went, the selling prices of both British and foreign glass would grow closer to each other. As Chances noticed in 1833:

one of the effects of the repeal of the glass duties would be that the cheap Green Glass of Belgium would come into Great Britain in large quantities unless a considerable duty by weight was laid upon it, and as the best quality of sheet glass would also come in, it would behove us in case of such repeal to do all we can with [the] Government to lay on not only a duty by weight but by value also.[19]

Chances were then beginning to profit from the excise drawback, as we have seen. It is significant that, once their sheet glass was well launched on the market and the advantage of the drawback had been removed, they began to change their tune and were soon whole-hearted advocates of repeal, unlike the crown manufacturers who went on supporting the duty because it favoured their thinner panes. 'Take off the Excise duty,' Chances begged the authorities in 1842, 'and give us three or four years to shake off the effects of having been trammell'd by it for half a century [*sic*] and we shall be able to meet all the manufacturers in the world.'[20]

How important was the window tax in limiting demand? It was levied only on inhabited houses. Factories, warehouses and offices, rapidly increasing in number, were exempt. It did not, therefore, have any effect at all upon the considerable industrial and commercial demand for window glass. As early as 1780 we hear of a factory with 300 windows and upwards,[21] and when Peter Drinkwater was building his factory in Manchester in 1789, he wrote to Boulton and Watt:

I wish you to block up no more of my intended windows than you can help by either the width or the height of your brickwork or roof, for to give the building (I mean the factory part) its greatest possible convenience, it should have a continuous series of windows – one and a pier introduced in the distance of every 8 or 9 foot or thereabouts.[22]

Glass manufacturers, particularly those in the north, must have sent a considerable proportion of their output to glaze business premises such as these.

Inhabited houses, however, were subjected to an increasingly heavy window tax. From the middle of the eighteenth century they had been

TABLE 5
INCREASES IN WINDOW TAX, 1766–1808

	1766	1784	1802	1803	1808
House with 7 windows	1s 2d	7s 2d	14s 6d	18s 6d	20s 0d
House with 8 windows	4s 0d	12s 0d	21s 0d	30s 0d	33s 0d
House with 9 windows	6s 0d	16s 6d	27s 0d	38s 0d	42s 0d
House with 10 windows and rising scale up to	8s 4d	21s 4d	34s 0d	50s 0d	56s 0d
House with 180 windows ..	£18	£20	£61	£83	£93

taxed on a sliding scale, at first starting with ten windows (1747), then with eight (1762) and finally with seven (1766). This tax was paid by the occupier, not the landlord. In subsequent years the rate per window was greatly increased, as may be seen from Table 5, page 77.

The high wartime level of taxation continued until 1823 when the rates were halved. In 1825 the seventh window was exempted. This was still the position in the 1840s.

We know, from the tax returns, that the overwhelming majority of houses in Britain in the later years of the tax possessed fewer than eight windows and therefore paid no duty. Out of 2,750,000 houses in England, Wales and Scotland in 1830, for instance, only 380,000 had eight windows or more.[23] By the middle of the 1840s, this figure had only increased to around 450,000[24] out of a total of over 3,000,000. But how many of these homes would have had more than seven windows except for the tax? Unfortunately we are only now starting to embark upon serious study of housing standards at this time[25] and cannot answer this question with any certainty. It is arguable that most of the cottage property in which the majority of the population lived consisted of one room upstairs and one down. If these dwellings had a window at each end on each floor, they would have had only four windows altogether. It would be a mistake, therefore, to run away with the idea that, but for the window tax, demand would automatically have been far greater. Obviously the better-off section of the population who lived in bigger houses made do with fewer windows than they would otherwise have had; it was in the bigger houses that windows were blocked up. To this extent the window tax undoubtedly did limit the total demand for glass. But it can be argued that in the majority of cases housing standards exercised an even greater influence by keeping the number of windows below even the tax-free maximum.[26]

The excise duty on glass was repealed on 5 April 1845, a sacrifice to the Treasury of £650,000 a year. To this total the manufacturers of window glass had contributed £450,000, the balance coming from other branches of the glass industry. This was less than a quarter of the revenue from the window tax.[27] It is not surprising, therefore, that, despite the industry's views, and despite the growing public outcry on health grounds, the window tax survived for several years longer. The repeal of the excise duty was carried through with considerable regard to the manufacturers' interests; their fears of being left with duty-paid glass on their hands were not realised. Any glass made after 15 February 1845 was not dutiable, provided it was stored until the date of repeal, and duty could still be drawn back on glass exported up to 15 June. On all other glass which had not been disposed of by that time, manufacturers could recover three-quarters of the duty they had originally paid.[28]

The immediate effect of repealing the duty was to cut the manufacturer's prices by more than half. The following list of one 'extensive' firm (not identified) indicates the fall in crown glass prices:

TABLE 6

	PRICES BEFORE REPEAL			PRICES AFTER REPEAL		
Per 12 tables	Gross	Discount	Nett	Gross	Discount	Nett
Best	£9 4s 0d	36s 5d	£7 7s 7d	£4 0s 0d	4s 0d	£3 16s 0d
Seconds	£8 4s 0d	32s 5d	£6 11s 7d	£3 0s 0d	3s 0d	£2 17s 0d
Thirds	£7 14s 0d	30s 5d	£6 3s 7d	£2 14s 0d	2s 8d	£2 11s 4d
Fourths	£7 10s 0d	30s 0d	£6 0s 0d	£2 10s 0d	2s 6d	£2 7s 6d

Source: The Economist, 19 July 1845.

Manufacturers were clearly not reducing the gross price by the full amount of the duty and, by reducing the rate of discount from four shillings to one shilling in the pound, they were pocketing even more of the balance. This they were able to do because of the insistent demand for glass at that time. The building cycle was moving sharply upwards as a new boom developed. Moreover, orders, which had been held up for weeks so that glass could be had at the new price, poured in from all parts of the country, particularly from Lancashire and Yorkshire.[29] Very heavy orders also arrived from London. This was attributed to the Building Act which imposed more stringent regulations upon houses begun in the London area after 1 January 1845.[30] There had been a rush to start building before that date so as to avoid conforming to the new regulations.[31] As a result, an unduly large number of houses were ready for glazing about the time when the excise duty was removed. There arose what one window glass manufacturer described as 'a famine of sheet and sheet plate in London'.[32]

The extent of this sudden huge demand took even the manufacturers themselves by surprise. 'None in our branch,' wrote one of them at the beginning of 1846, 'had any notion that the demand would have been so extraordinary as it has proved ... The extra make, since the repeal, could not be less than fifty per cent.' This great boom caused speculators to venture their capital in what appeared to be a most promising industry. The manufacturer just quoted went on to report the starting of no fewer than five new factories and five more 'under way'.[33]

Growth at such a pace brought about an acute shortage of skilled labour. For Pilkingtons, a serious crisis arose because of an attempt to challenge the validity of the firm's contracts with its employees when the labour shortage made it extremely difficult to secure new men. Months of legal haggling ensued before these contracts were finally declared to be binding and during these months some glassmakers, assuming that they were free to leave the firm's employment at their pleasure, left the works when their services were most urgently required. Before considering the rationalisation which took place in the industry in the wake of the excise duty's repeal, it is necessary, therefore, to interrupt the story in order to see how the labour crisis arose at Pilkingtons and, at the same time, to learn something about the wages and working conditions there at that period.

Chapter 6

A Labour Crisis

B Y the middle of the nineteenth century each window glass factory employed several hundred people. Remarkably few of these were themselves skilled glassmakers or even assistants to glassmakers. Numbers of employees worked at a wide variety of tasks outside the glasshouses. Many hands were needed in the cutting rooms and warehouses, for instance, sorting, cutting, packing and loading the finished product; in the polishing rooms transforming sheet into patent plate glass; in the joiners' shop putting the crates together and in the pot rooms making pots. Of those who actually did work at the furnaces, many were juveniles serving their apprenticeship. They were assistants to the fully-trained glassmakers, and performed such menial tasks as wiping blowpipes before the metal (molten glass) was gathered from the pots, holding a shovel to shield the gatherer's face from the intense heat, or carrying the cooled cylinders from the splitters to the flatteners. Eventually these boys, if employed in crown glass manufacture, graduated to punty sticking – the process of sealing the piece to the pontil or punty on which the piece was twirled into a circular table – and to gathering the metal.[1] Some became skilled blowers, flashers of crown glass, or flatteners of sheet, while others piled the glass into kilns to be annealed.

Very few of those who worked at a glass factory, therefore, had the right to call themselves glassmakers. At Pilkingtons, where about 500 were employed in 1845, there were only four blowers and four gatherers to each of the three houses.[2] If we add the flashers, flatteners and pilers, the firm probably employed altogether about 50 fully-skilled glassmakers, ten per cent of the total number in its service.

In 1845, just before the repeal of the excise duty, there were 14 factories in Britain engaged in the manufacture of window glass.[3] Some of them were larger and some smaller than the St Helens works. If we may assume that Greenall & Pilkingtons represented the average size of concern (an assumption that will certainly not lead to any underestimation of the total) there were at that time probably about 700 skilled window glassmakers in the whole of Britain; of these fewer than 200 were blowers, the key men upon whom the whole industry depended. Moreover, only a minority could blow the long cylinders needed for the manufacture of sheet glass; there were perhaps fewer than 50 sheet glass blowers in the country when the excise duty was repealed.

It was always the policy of the few skilled workmen to keep their practical knowledge of the various glassmaking processes within their own families, fathers passing on the closely-guarded secrets of the trade to their sons. They sought to maintain an aristocracy of skill by barring all strangers from entering their ranks. Immediately after the repeal of the excise duty, for instance, when they joined together to form the Crown Glass Makers' Society – the first trade union in the industry of which we have any evidence – one of the rules laid down that 'any Glass Makers not becoming members of this Society, his or their sons shall not go forward in our business'. A special allowance of one pound a week was to be paid to any member who was discharged from his employment 'because he will not teach any person who is not a Glass Maker's son'.[4] Such an exclusion policy, which harked back to the days when the industry was more static and when glassmaking was the jealously-guarded preserve of but a few families, could still be enforced to some extent. In a list of Pilkington Brothers' employees, drawn up in 1849,[5] the same names recur frequently, particularly among the higher-paid workmen of the glasshouses; in several cases fathers and sons still worked together. But as the firm grew in size and importance, the existing glassmaking families could no longer provide all the skilled labour required; new blood had to be introduced from outside. Often the partners selected recruits from families already known to them. Frederick Vose, for instance, the son of William Pilkington's cook, was trained as a glassmaker.[6] In 1836, Thomas Gerard, a son of the Greenalls' head brewer, began to serve his time[7] and when the national census was taken in 1841, James Oldfield and James Appleton, who were living on brewery property in Hall Street, were also described as apprentice glassmakers.

Local recruitment was a satisfactory method of obtaining a gradual supply of skilled labour over a period of time by way of seven-year apprenticeships; but it was quite useless as a means of meeting a sudden emergency, such as arose in 1845, when fully-trained men were required immediately. The supply of sheet glass blowers and flatteners was so strictly limited in Britain that every firm had to send scouts to the continent in search of additional hands. Pilkingtons sent on this errand William Pilkington's eldest son, William, who had only just entered the business in the previous year at the age of 17.[8] In July 1845, he was reported to be trying to recruit men from St Gobain.[9] These foreign workmen could only be persuaded to leave home and come to England by the offer of fantastically high wages and special concessions. Charles Singré, for instance, a sheet glass blower from Choisy-le-Roi near Paris, one of the men who signed a two-year contract with Pilkingtons, was to receive £6 10s od per week and to be provided with a house and all the fuel he should require without any payment. Moreover, £240 was advanced to him as a loan (to be stopped out of his wages) and his fare was paid not only from Paris to St Helens but also back again to Paris after two years when he had fulfilled his contract.[10] Georges Bontemps, Singré's employer at Choisy-le-Roi, reporting this defection to Robert Lucas Chance, noted that the £240 (6,000 francs) was to pay off a loan on a house that Singré was building there. 'Though he be a good workman,' Bontemps added, 'I do not regret him as he is never contented . . . I do not believe that he will last long.'[11]

Such huge earnings had an unsettling effect upon the British glassmakers who worked alongside these fortunate newcomers. They found themselves contracted to perform the same skilled tasks for about a quarter of the foreigners' wages, and it was not long before they started to exploit their scarcity value by demanding more pay and additional concessions. 'We have exchanged the excise for a much severer taskmaster . . . our own men,' wrote the proprietor of one English house early in 1846.[12]

The terms of service, moreover, gave the continental glassmakers an advantage over their British counterparts. In France and Belgium glassmakers served their masters for the life of a furnace, a period which they called a campaign.[13] They were thus obliged to serve only for short periods at a time and were, in consequence, freer to change masters than were the British glassmakers who usually contracted to serve their employers for seven years at a time. The Englishmen could not go away to another firm in search of higher wages unless their contracts happened to run out. In 1845 this was an unlikely eventuality, for most manufacturers had taken the wise precaution of binding their men anew just before the excise duty was removed. Some of the more adventurous spirits, however, were tempted to defy their masters and run the risk of imprisonment in order to better themselves financially. The sudden departure of one of their men, Richard Pemberton, led Pilkingtons into a series of legal actions which sharpened still further a labour crisis that was already dangerously acute.

Pemberton came of a Scottish glassmaking family. His father, John Pemberton, who had blown glass for Greenall & Pilkingtons for at least 12 years, was manager of one of the glasshouses in which his son worked.[14] Soon after the repeal of the excise duty, James Christie, who had re-started the Dumbarton Crown Glassworks some years previously,[15] offered Richard Pemberton the position of manager in one of his glasshouses. Pilkingtons agreed to release him from a contract he had signed on 4 March 1845, on condition that he provided a proficient substitute. This he was unable to do; but, rather than lose an opportunity of promotion, he decided to risk leaving St Helens without finding a replacement. He set off for Dumbarton on 18 June 1845.

Pilkingtons demanded £100 compensation from Christie. When, after two months, there were no signs either of this compensation or of the runaway's returning, they exercised their legal right, under the Master and Servant Law, of obtaining a magistrate's warrant for his arrest.[16] A police officer brought Pemberton back from Dumbarton at the beginning of September and placed him in prison pending his appearance before the justices, who had the power to impose a sentence of up to three months' imprisonment with hard labour should the case be proved. The prisoner, however, obtained the legal services of that remarkably able and wily lawyer, William Prouting Roberts, who was rapidly gaining a reputation for his agile defence of trade unionists, particularly in the mining industry. It seems that one of Pemberton's fellow-glassmakers named Lyon, who was the first to visit him in prison when he arrived from Dumbarton, and whom William Pilkington had noted was 'collier bred', was responsible for suggesting that Roberts be called in.

When the case came before the justices at Prescot on 6 September 1845, Roberts was in characteristically aggressive form. He made a fierce onslaught upon the validity of the firm's contracts and this radical display was eagerly listened to by a crowd of Pilkingtons' employees who thronged the court room. Roberts's tirading defence failed to impress the magistrates however, and Pemberton was sentenced to a month's imprisonment with hard labour. Here the matter might, and probably would, have rested had Roberts not been defence counsel. On 19 September (when the prisoner had already served only about half of his sentence) he applied to Mr Baron Platt, the judge, in London, for a writ of *habeas corpus* to transfer Pemberton to the capital and for a writ of *certiorari* directed to Samuel Taylor, requiring Taylor, who had presided over the court at Prescot, to return the record of Pemberton's conviction. This application was successful, and on 25 September the learned judge, after two and a half hours' consideration of this record, reached the conclusion that the magistrate had not shown

sufficient cause for the detention of the prisoner. He therefore ordered
Pemberton's discharge.

Although Roberts's success resulted solely from a legal technicality,
Pilkingtons' employees, recalling Roberts's scathing remarks about the
firm's contracts, immediately jumped to the conclusion that the release of
the prisoner meant that all the contracts had been proved null and void.
This, they thought, freed them to seek employment elsewhere, just as
Pemberton had done, without fear of any legal action being taken against
them. This interpretation of the judge's decision was vigorously fostered
by Roberts himself who, true to his radical colours, paid regular visits to St
Helens to harangue the men. Other employers, taking advantage of Pilkingtons' difficulties, sent agents to lure workmen away by offers of higher
wages. Despite a full explanation of the facts which Richard and William
Pilkington issued in the form of a public address on 7 October,[17] the
proprietors of other companies had some success in persuading a few of
Pilkingtons' most valuable men to desert. The first of these enticers, somewhat fallen in the world but nevertheless morally unchanged by his descent,
was none other than William West, the author of the gigantic excise frauds
at the Eccleston Crown Glassworks some 20 years before. He subsequently
became manager of the Birmingham Plate Glassworks. This factory had
recently formed crown and sheet glass departments and was desperate for
labour.[18] On 14 October William Pilkington reported upon the position
to his solicitors:

On Sunday Roberts held a large meeting on Green Bank as usual and yesterday and today several of our workmen have absconded and gone to that pattern
of purity W.A.A.West, who is now ready and for want of them was obliged to
lade his first found of metal because they were not there to blow it and this
morning I have received a most Jesuitical letter from him . . . It was hinted to me
some time ago – say three or four months – that these men had formed an engagement with Mr West and that so soon as he was ready, they would leave us.
As they were under contracts and some of our steadiest and, as I believed, best
men I disbelieved it but of course could only await the results . . . Lyon, who has
gone to Mr West with the others . . . no doubt encouraged him [Pemberton] to
resist [imprisonment] and arranged the plan of employing Roberts not to get
Pemberton off merely but to break through their agreements to enable them to
go to Mr West. This they have now done . . . We learn today that Richard
Pemberton is [again] working for the Dumbarton Company along with two
others of our men who have absconded . . . Now I would rather fight the masters than the men who have no reason nor money but strong sympathies for
each other . . . In case we are obliged to stop a house, which at present we are on

the verge of doing, this would not only be strong ground for damages but also strong proof of the necessity of making very stringent agreements as there is not a surplus of hands and if our men choose to leave and give us a month's or even three months' notice our capital is at a stand and our warehouse apprentices and others of no use whom we must under any circumstances pay; and what is worse we are obliged to keep up our fires to protect our pots and to preserve our furnaces.

A few days later a further item of depressing news reached William Pilkington's desk. He had sought counsel's opinion on the best way of regaining Pemberton's services and was informed that the period of imprisonment purged the offence and no further action was likely to succeed. This news caused him to write again to his solicitors:

> If a man enters into a contract for seven years and receives £15 binding money[19] he may the day after refuse to work and if we venture to take him before a magistrate and get him committed very much to our loss and inconvenience, it would appear that he not on; purges himself from the crime but is absolved from his contract on his liberation . . . he receives £15 from us as the price of a month's incarceration.

William Pilkington went on to observe that 'none of the truants' had returned from Birmingham, and Christie's emissaries were at that moment 'regaling our workmen and sowing dissatisfaction as much as possible among them'.

The months of September and October 1845, when the labour crisis reached its peak, must have been a period of great anxiety for the proprietors, comparable with some of the worst worries of earlier years. At a time when the demand for glass had reached unprecedented heights, the firm was faced with the prospect of closing one of its houses and was able to keep going by maintaining only three sets of men at work at each furnace instead of four. And with new companies about to start, all of them clamouring for men, the labour shortage promised to grow worse rather than better.

On top of all this worry came the unexpected death, before his fiftieth birthday, of Peter Greenall on 18 September 1845, as we have seen. It was a loss felt particularly keenly by his brothers-in-law. Small wonder that by the end of October William Pilkington, annoyed with himself for being 'so distracted and tired', found himself under doctor's orders.

But Pilkingtons still had one means of redress. As William Pilkington made clear in his letter of 14 October which has been quoted, they could always sue competing firms for damages arising from the loss of their hired servants. It is true that, had these competing firms refused to dis-charge Pilkingtons' bound employees, there would have been an inevitable time-lag before the matter could be settled in the courts and this delay might have had serious short-term consequences. But as events turned out, the mere threat of such an action was quite sufficient to frighten both West and Christie into discharging the runaways, who, having expressed their regrets, began to work for their former masters once again.

William Pilkington seized the opportunity offered by the pardoning of the first group of runaways to enter into negotiations with the men's representatives in order to bring about more cordial labour relations and put an end to the reign of uncertainty and indiscipline. He proposed to introduce new contracts, to be valid for three and a half years. The men, however, insisted on the seven years then customary, for as we shall see, the contract involved a minimum wage clause and trade was bound to go slack again before long. Six years was eventually decided upon as a compromise. These contracts would, of course, be accompanied by bind-ing fees or premiums. In the past such premiums had amounted only to a few pounds but, owing to the dearth of skilled labour after the repeal of the excise duty, employers had been obliged to pay up to £15. It was the payment of this lump sum, the 'golden bait' as William Pilkington termed it, that sweetened the negotiations and brought the men to terms. They on their side agreed not to employ any longer the services of W.P. Roberts as their legal adviser and consented to a clause in the new contracts whereby their masters were empowered to suspend workmen for up to a week at a time in cases of disobedience or non-attendance without just cause. These new contracts were signed on 19 November.

On the whole, these agreements secured the Pilkington labour force. But there was still some reneging. Letters from the firm's solicitors con-tinued to reach West and Christie, warning them that legal action would be taken if certain men were not discharged. After some prevarication on the part of the pirate employers, the men usually returned. The proprietor of Dumbarton, in particular, was a past master at holding out as long as he could: 'Christie's plausibility,' William Pilkington thought, 'would over-match W.A.A.West's Jesuitism.'

In November 1845, the plausible Christie even managed to obtain tech-nical information from one of the runaways. William Pilkington explained to his solicitors how Frederick Vose, his cook's son, who had been 'almost nursed' by the Pilkington family and had been trained as a glassmaker at their works, was involved in the theft:

This scamp has been privately instructing one Garralty in the art of flattening sheet glass contrary to our expressed directions but it was done stealthily and during night. This Garralty was not a hired servant and therefore left us about a fortnight ago to go to Dumbarton and returned the latter end of last week and Mr F.Vose is now missing and has we believe absconded along with him. But this is not the worst – between them, we are informed, they have made and taken away with them a model of our flattening kilns which are the best kilns of the day and have thus obtained an engagement at Dumbarton.

Ten days later, however, William Pilkington was able to report:

Vose is back and has made peace with us, which I am sorry to say is too easily done nowadays . . . Frederick Vose admits that Garralty has carried the model of our kilns to Dumbarton.

The sequel to these events came in July 1846, when Pilkingtons appealed – successfully – against Mr Baron Platt's judgment in the Pemberton case. This meant that Christie was at last obliged to discharge Pemberton from his service. An abject and apologetic letter from this, the first of the runaways, dated 20 July 1846, ends the whole unfortunate chapter which had started with his release from prison almost ten months earlier:

If I did wrong in entering an agreement with Mr Christie, it was from the advice I got from my lawyer [Roberts] who assured me that your agreement was not a binding one and that my being discharged from prison was sufficient to show that you had no further claim upon me . . . I have no wish to have any expenses incurred on my account and I have no objection to return to your service, if you will allow me to work here a reasonable time to get arrangements made so that I could leave with my wife and family. I have a large family and my wife has not yet recovered from her late confinement and in my present situation I have not the means to remove either myself or family; one of my sons is an apprentice to Mr Christie and he is too young to be left without a proper person in charge of him.

If you favour me with a discharge upon paying a sum of money, I would be obliged by your naming the amount and if at all reasonable I think I would be able to raise the money: and if you would be kind enough to oblige me in this way, it might perhaps be best for both you and myself. In the event of your not being inclined to make an arrangement of this nature, I must throw myself on your generosity and request you to allow Mr Christie to employ me until I can make enough to remove with my family, which at present it is entirely out of my power to do, and I do not suppose that you would be inclined to advance me any money.

William Pilkington's reply was kindly and lenient. He had, he said, 'no vindictive feelings in the matter,' and would be willing to accept £50 for Pemberton's discharge payable over two years, or £40 to be paid at once. This was quite a generous offer, for when Pemberton's own father had gone to work at St Helens, Greenall & Pilkingtons had been obliged to pay £150 to his master in lieu of the seven months that his contract was still due to run.

These contracts, signed during the turbulent months of 1845, together with one or two others of earlier date and wages sheets for two weeks in 1849, provide us with details of glassmakers' pay at that time. To them may be added evidence from other sources about hours and conditions of work, home life and leisure occupations.

So long as the materials used in glass manufacture were prepared in pots, there could be no continuous production. The pots, once emptied, had to be recharged and the contents heated up to the correct viscosity for working. The duration of this period of preparation determined the glassmaker's timetable. A complete charging, melting and cooling cycle usually took 24 hours. The working itself then took rather less than half that time, usually about ten hours. This meant that even at the maximum rate of production the glassmakers were bound to have about 24 hours off at the end of each ten-hour shift. They started at 6 a.m. on Monday morning and worked a ten-hour shift until Monday afternoon, began the second shift about 4 p.m. on Tuesday, the third at 2 a.m. on Thursday, and the fourth about noon on Friday, finishing work for the week late on Friday night. This left them with Saturday and Sunday completely free. (See Table 23, page 177.)

These hours, of course, were very approximate, for the teazer (or furnaceman) could never guarantee that the metal would be ready precisely at any prearranged time, nor could the glassmakers be absolutely sure of emptying their pots within ten hours. The timetable could not be a rigid one: when the men left the works, they were on call. One of the apprentices, summoned beforehand by the furnaceman to sweep up and prepare for the next shift, was sent round to call the glassmakers when all was ready.[20] A 12-year-old boy named Gaskell, one of Pilkingtons' apprentices, has left this brief account of how they, in their turn, were called by the furnaceman:

We are about ten hours on and twenty-four off, that is the journey; but we boys always get called about three hours before we start with the men, for we have to sweep up and get ready for them before they come. We could do it all in an hour if we liked but we like to play in that time. We are called at all times night and day. The 'teazer' or furnace man goes round the town and calls every boy in the house when the furnace in that house has heated the metal in the pots enough to start working in about three hours. He comes to the door at home and knocks and calls 'Gaskell', and then, if it's night, my father looks out of the window and the teazer says, 'Number —— called'; that is the number of the house. So I get out of bed and go off.[21]

Four blowers and four gatherers made a set, as we have noticed. Only three pairs made glass at any one time, thus allowing the fourth an opportunity to rest. These rest periods were essential, for the work was extremely hot and exacting and the glasshouses themselves dark and ill-ventilated. (Conditions must have been particularly arduous when only three pairs were at work during the labour crisis of 1845.) In order to stimulate the draught through the furnaces via the underground flues, the actual cones were built to exclude draughts of air from other sources. Very little air was permitted to penetrate the glasshouse in the normal way except through such openings as were absolutely necessary to allow the men to move in and out of the building and to permit the raw materials and finished products to be carried in and out. This meant that there was very little light apart from the bright glare from the molten glass. The heat close to the openings into the furnace was unbearable for any length of time and the men only went near when they were actually engaged in one or other of the processes of manufacture. Each glassmaker was, therefore, constantly moving to and fro in the firelit gloom. Around him scurried his band of assistants, fetching and carrying. Heat, bustle and dexterity, as one observant visitor remarked, were the characteristic features of the old pot furnaces.[22]

The men were invariably paid by the set and at piece rates. In the manufacture of crown glass, 1,200 'good and merchantable' tables were deemed to constitute a week's work for each set of four blowers and gatherers. According to William Pilkington, writing in April 1846, 'at a low average a set would and do make 1,600 [tables]'. These additional 400 or so tables were paid for at a higher rate – 'plus' as it was called. When John Pemberton, manager of one of the crown houses, contracted in 1833 to serve Greenall & Pilkingtons as a blower, the firm agreed to pay him 27s 6d for his contribution to the set's production of 1,200 tables 'with plus as usual'. From two later agreements of October 1839 and March 1845,[23] 'plus as usual' appears to have meant a rate of 30s 0d for a further 1,200 tables or 2s 6d per 100 tables. James Pye, signatory to the first of these two agreements, was to receive 27s 6d for the basic 1,200 tables if he served as a piler, 26s 0d if as a blower, piece warmer or flasher, 21s 0d if as a gatherer or kiln assistant or 18s 0d if as a punty sticker, 'plus' being 30s 0d as a piler, blower, piece warmer or flasher, 25s 0d as a gatherer or kiln assistant and 21s 0d as a punty sticker. James Oldfield who signed the agreement of March 1845, was only to receive 26s 0d for the first 1,200 tables if he worked as a piler and 15s 0d if as a punty sticker but otherwise the rates had not changed since 1839. The greatly increased demand for labour in subsequent months led to an advance in wages. By 15 August 1845, when Thomas Cutter contracted to serve Pilkingtons,[24] the basic rate had been raised by 4s 0d for all tasks except that of punty sticking which remained at 15s 0d. This advance brought the basic rate up to the 'plus' rate for all but the lowest ranks.

At these rates, and under the boom conditions of that time, the highest paid glassmaker could earn about 40s 0d a week if he was the member of a set which made 1,600 tables. Gatherers could make about 33s 0d and punty stickers about 22s 0d. No doubt during the boom of 1845–7 glassmakers were, in fact, making that much 'plus', though we do not know what arrangements were made when only three pairs constituted a team; but the wages lists for the weeks ending 12 and 19 May 1849[25] – the only ones which survive – show what earnings were like when trade was slack. In the first of these two weeks, for instance, two sets of blowers made £1 12s 0½d and £1 11s 3d and in the second they made £1 17s 8½d and £1 11s 10½d respectively. William Blanshard, superintendent of all the crown houses, earned more than this, £2 17s 9d per week, and the other glassmakers and their assistants earned proportionately less, the apprentices receiving only a few shillings.

The makers of sheet glass were paid at a much higher rate. Like Singré, whom we have already noticed, the other foreign workmen had to be given exceptionally high wages and these influenced the rate paid to the British sheet glassmakers. Henry Dodds, one of the runaways, had agreed in May 1845, to make, weekly, 425 cylinders 40 in. by 30 in., of a thickness thirteen ounces to the foot, or proportionately fewer cylinders of larger size and greater weight, for 53s 8d.[26] This, his basic weekly wage, is to be compared with the crown glassmaker's of 30s 0d. But it was only the actual blowers in the sheet houses who benefited in this way. The gatherers were given the same rate as if they had been working in a crown house, as another agreement of 19 November makes clear.[27] The wages lists for the two weeks of May 1849 confirm that although the few key men in the sheet houses were earning large sums of money, gatherers were no better off than their counterparts in the crown houses, and there was a far larger proportion of low-paid juveniles fetching and carrying for the sheet than for the crown glassmakers. This meant not only that more menial labour was required but also that the sheet glasshouses had already become the main training centres at the works. M.Hypolite, who appears to have been Demanet's successor as the firm's superintendent of sheet glass manufacture, was paid £4 4s 0d a week and the other foreign workmen earned between £3 and £4. One of them, who had his son helping him, reached £4 3s 0d. The British sheet glass blowers earned between £2 and £3.

The highest paid employee of all was Henry Deacon who, in 1847, was described as the firm's Chemist and Engineer.[28] In 1849, when he was only in his twenty-seventh year, he was earning £5 18s 6d a week, considerably more than young William Pilkington who earned £4 4s 0d, and very much more than the £2 6s 0d received by James Varley, the firm's cashier who had 11 years' service behind him. Among others who were employed in departments away from the glasshouses, several were earning as much as the more highly paid glassmakers, particularly those in the joiners' shop where the departmental manager, Thomas Colquitt, received £3 5s 0d. At the other end of the scale were some of the boys in the cutting room (who sometimes earned so little as 3s 0d), and the smoothers and polishers: the women, girls and 'red lads' – so called because they worked with rouge.

These rates of pay placed the skilled glassmaker in the forefront of the artisan class. Estimates of earnings are hard to arrive at, but, for the sake of comparison, ironfounders, generally agreed to be among the highest paid workpeople at that time, were then earning up to £2 per week and skilled engineers sometimes received a little more than that. The general run of skilled craftsmen, such as carpenters, builders and stonemasons, usually earned round about 30s 0d.

The glassmaker also received various concessions which were not enjoyed by other artisans. He received an allowance for house rent and firing. This was a legacy of former days before accommodation was available and the master had to house his own servants. In their early days, Greenall & Pilkingtons built a row of 37 cottages adjoining their works. But by the 1840s this was no longer necessary and £10 a year was therefore granted to each man as a living-out allowance instead.

The glassmaker's contract also contained a clause giving him a guaranteed minimum wage. In the event of work being interrupted because of furnace trouble, lack of fuel (owing to a coal strike) or other unforeseen cause, he was to be given half pay. He received no accident or sick pay but the glassmakers themselves, as has been seen, had their own association which served also as a friendly society, and there were many other friendly societies in the district.[29]

Pilkingtons also made provision for leisure-time activities from the later 1840s. The recreation section dates from 1847.[30] Cricket appears to have been the main interest of members at the outset, and two of William Pilkington's sons were keen players.[31] In the course of time, as membership grew, other activities were arranged. By the early 1860s there was a bowling green and a skittle alley attached to Pilkingtons' cricket field close to the old cotton factory which they acquired (see page 65), and William Pilkington spoke of a new building in course of erection where members would have 'billiards and draughts and other games . . . conveniences for washing and a refreshment bar for tea and coffee and light drinks'.[32] The recreation section was probably responsible for organising works outings during the summer, and dances in the winter. In July 1850, a party from the works went to Runcorn and Halton,[33] possibly the first of the annual one-day excursions. In January of the previous year the firm had held an all-night ball, also described as an annual event. This lasted from 8.30 at night until 7 o'clock the next morning.[34]

About this time Pilkingtons engaged a schoolmaster to teach the three Rs to the boys and lads in their employment up to the age of 17. They had to attend classes for an hour or two either in their own time after work or by arrangement with managers and foremen during the daytime.[35] They paid no fees but were fined one penny for every absence without good reason. At first, it would seem, attendance was rather erratic. Fines sometimes reached 30s 0d per week. But a later teacher, Edward Johnson, achieved better results and was able to boast that

They used to duck all who went to school but now they 'rundle' any who don't; that is, put him in a ring of them, each of whom pulls his hair.

He went on to tell how some of the boys were so tired after their day's work that they fell asleep and had to be sent home. The 'red lads', coming straight from the polishing benches, made everything they touched, the forms and the books, red too.[36] Perhaps some of these tell-tale marks were also to be found on books in the works library. This had been built up from the proceeds of some of the fines levied on the men as penalties for indiscipline.[37]

Glassmakers as a class are said to have been 'in general a very decent set of fellows but . . . given to drinking'.[38] To some extent the nature of their work obliged them to consume large amounts of liquid, and, in days before an unpolluted water supply was readily available, beer – untaxed and very cheap – was the usual beverage. While they were at work, glassmakers used to send out their apprentices to fetch jugs of beer, and a commission which investigated the employment of children in the 1860s reported that 'running out for men's drink is a very common errand'.[39] Some employers paid their men a special beer allowance in addition to their wages. At the Eccleston Crown Glassworks, for instance, two glassmakers brought an action against their masters for failing to give them their weekly beer money.[40] Pilkingtons' contracts contain no such clauses; yet there is plenty of evidence to show that the men drank heavily. But as opinion hardened against drinking, particularly within working hours, the practice came to be forbidden. The men, therefore, stole away across the canal to the Navigation Inn or to one or other of the numerous hostelries nearby in Liverpool Road and Greenbank. William Windle Pilkington, Richard Pilkington's eldest son, who was not only to take charge of the works but also to become a strict Congregationalist, determined to put an end to drinking in working hours and waged a constant campaign against this long-established habit. His angry visits to the Navigation Inn are often recalled by descendants of the glassmakers of his day. But drinking persisted. Deprived of their jugs of beer inside the factory and forbidden to go drinking outside during working hours, the men often preferred to take time off altogether and venture further afield. An employee of the firm from 1871 to 1926 spent much of his time during his last years as a sick visitor searching out men who had been neglecting their work, usually because of their heavy drinking bouts.[41]

The glassmaker of a century ago, then, whose labour was highly skilled and physically exacting and whose hours were irregular and unsettled, had several advantages over his fellow artisans. He inherited a tradition of privilege. He had a living-out allowance. His wages were high and were guaranteed in case of interruptions at the factory. He worked only about 40 hours a week, and, though a certain amount of night work cut into such leisure time as he had during the week, he enjoyed a longer week-end than most other workpeople who at that time finished for the week late on Saturday afternoon or even on Saturday evening. These were the privileged minority on the payroll. Further down the list came other employees, such as carpenters and glass cutters, who were paid at skilled rates. At the bottom there was the residuum of poorly paid unskilled, and juveniles.

This is, perhaps, an appropriate point at which to discuss the growth of the Pilkington family and the entry of the second generation into the business.

In 1824 William Pilkington married Eliza Charlotte Boyes, who was then living with her widowed mother at Parr Hall, near St Helens.[42] The pedigree on pages 96–7 gives details of their 14 children, born between 1825 and 1849. 12 of them survived infancy and six of the survivors were sons. Richard Pilkington, William's elder brother, did not marry until 1838. His bride was Ann Evans, a daughter of Richard Evans of Haydock, one of the most successful coal proprietors in Lancashire. All of their six children were boys.

That both partners had six sons from whom to choose their successors – in the event each chose two – relieved them of any worries about the succession for at least the next generation. Indeed, the chief problem appears to have been not whom to choose to enter the firm but rather what to do with those for whom there was no partnership share.

As we have already noticed, William Pilkington's eldest son, William (later called Sutton or Roby after his places of residence to distinguish him from his cousin), entered the business in 1844 and subsequently became a partner. The second son, Richard, was trained as a mechanical engineer. He seems to have been associated with the firm for some time, but, certainly from 1864 and possibly from an earlier date, he severed his connection and took his skill elsewhere.[43] The third son, Thomas, went into the business in 1853 and later became a partner. The fourth son, George, who had been to the Royal College of Chemistry,[44] was works chemist for a time but later became a chemical manufacturer on his own account in Widnes, together with the sixth son, Leonard. The fifth son, Harold, was given a legal training and eventually became Town Clerk of St Helens.

Of Richard Pilkington's sons, the two eldest went into the business. William (who was always known as William Windle) was sent to Bruce Castle, Tottenham, a remarkable school in its day, developed by Rowland Hill of penny post fame, which provided pupils with a choice in their courses and a degree of self-government.[45] He joined the firm in 1857 at the age of 18. His younger brother, Richard, arrived in 1858 or 1859. None of Richard Pilkington's other sons went into the works. Edward, Alfred, Charles and Lawrence joined their uncles, Joseph and Josiah Evans, in the Clifton and Kearsley Colliery Company near Manchester. It is from them that the Manchester branch of the Pilkington family is descended. Margaret Pilkington (1891–1974), a Slade student who became a prominent patron of the arts in the city and honorary director of Whitworth Art Gallery from 1935 to 1959, was Lawrence Pilkington's daughter.[46]

All Richard Pilkington's sons were baptised at the St Helens Congregational Church. William Pilkington, however, had his children baptised there only up to 1838. In that year a new Anglican place of worship, Christ Church, Eccleston, was opened quite close to Millbrook House, where he had recently gone to live. He started to attend service there and

CHART 1

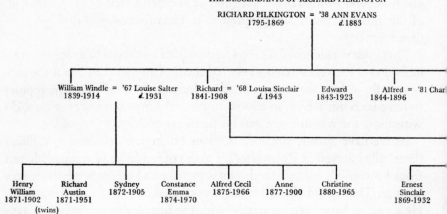

THE DESCENDANTS OF RICHARD PILKINGTON

RICHARD PILKINGTON = '38 ANN EVANS
1795-1869   d. 1883

William Windle = '67 Louise Salter	Richard = '68 Louisa Sinclair	Edward	Alfred = '81 Char
1839-1914 d. 1931	1841-1908 d. 1943	1843-1923	1844-1896

Henry William 1871-1902	Richard Austin 1871-1951	Sydney 1872-1905	Constance Emma 1874-1970	Alfred Cecil 1875-1966	Anne 1877-1900	Christine 1880-1965	Ernest Sinclair 1869-1932
(twins)							

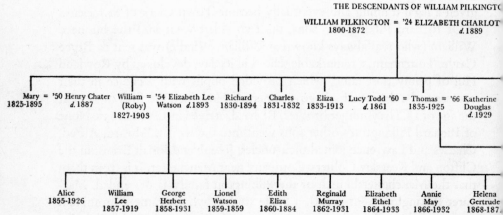

THE DESCENDANTS OF WILLIAM PILKINGTO

WILLIAM PILKINGTON = '24 ELIZABETH CHARLOT
1800-1872   d. 1889

Mary = '50 Henry Chater	William = '54 Elizabeth Lee	Richard	Charles	Eliza	Lucy Todd '60 = Thomas = '66 Katherine
1825-1895 d. 1887	(Roby) Watson d. 1893	1830-1894	1831-1832	1833-1913	d. 1861 1835-1925 Douglas
	1827-1903				d. 1929

Alice 1855-1926	William Lee 1857-1919	George Herbert 1858-1931	Lionel Watson 1859-1859	Edith Eliza 1860-1884	Reginald Murray 1862-1931	Elizabeth Ethel 1864-1933	Annie May 1866-1932	Helena Gertrude 1868-187

les = '84 .Mabel Fielden   Lawrence = '90 Mary Stevenson
-18   *d.* 1941   1855-1941   *d.* 1942

Charles Raymond 1875-1938	William Norman 1877-1935	Edith Mary 1878-1950	Margaret Evelyn 1879-1955	Guy Reginald 1881-1970

2

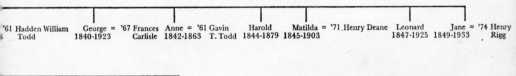

'61 Hadden William   George = '67 Frances   Anne = '61 Gavin   Harold   Matilda = '71 .Henry Deane   Leonard   Jane = '74 Henry
Todd   1840-1923   Carlisle   1842-1863   T. Todd   1844-1879   1845-1903   1847-1925   1849-1933   Rigg

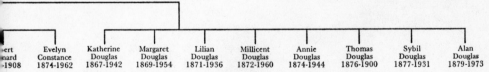

ert nard -1908	Evelyn Constance 1874-1962	Katherine Douglas 1867-1942	Margaret Douglas 1869-1954	Lilian Douglas 1871-1936	Millicent Douglas 1872-1960	Annie Douglas 1874-1944	Thomas Douglas 1876-1900	Sybil Douglas 1877-1931	Alan Douglas 1879-1973

E

became one of the first churchwardens. It was left to Richard Pilkington to maintain the nonconformist traditions of the family. Throughout his life he was one of the Congregational Church's most active members. Up to the time of his marriage, in 1838, he was for many years superintendent of the boys' Sunday School.[47] In those days the classes met at 8.30 in the morning and Richard Pilkington used to make the journey on foot from his home at Windle Hall to the school in College Lane two miles away. After morning school, he went to church, had lunch in town and was at his desk again when the afternoon school began at 1.30.

Richard Pilkington's deep religious sense, and quiet, contemplative – almost retiring – nature mark him out as a man of a very different temperament from his more active younger brother. 'You underrate yourself and your abilities sadly too much,' chided William Pilkington, brimful of justified self-confidence, in a letter he wrote in 1834. Richard Pilkington does not seem to have taken very kindly to the hurly-burly of business and it was left to his brother, more a man of the world, to rescue the infant glass concern from failure and nurse it to success. This success was chiefly the product of William Pilkington's flair for salesmanship. As the search for orders took him away from the works for long periods at a stretch, it was essential that the partner who stayed at home should be someone in whom he could have complete trust, a man who did not possess a fiery temper and was not likely to lose his head in a crisis. Richard Pilkington does not seem to have been the type of man who could himself have achieved great things in business; but he was the ideal business associate.

Chapter 7

The Removal of British Competitors

THE repeal of the glass excise duty in 1845, by removing the fiscal advantages bestowed upon crown glass manufacturers, placed Chances, Pilkingtons, Hartleys and (to a smaller extent) Cooksons, who had already started to make sheet glass, in a stronger competitive position than those firms which made crown glass alone. During the great building boom of the mid-1840s, and, in particular, immediately after the repeal of the duty when there was a huge pent-up demand for glass at the lower price, glass manufacturers could sell all they made, whether it was crown or sheet. The prosperity of the industry at that time was such that many optimists were decoyed into entering it. According to James Hartley, the number of firms grew from '13 or 14' immediately before the repeal to 24 in 1846–7.[1] Then prices fell. Many firms, particularly the newcomers, were driven out of business. From a total of 24 concerns, the number fell, by 1852, to ten, and, by 1856, to seven.[2] Thus, within ten years of the repeal, the number of firms making window glass had been halved.

The failure, before 1850, of two window glass factories within ten miles of St Helens removed much of Pilkingtons' local competition. Clare & Brownes at Warrington had apparently stopped production during the previous depression, in 1842, and do not appear to have reopened subsequently.[3] The Liverpool Union Crown Glass Company, which had belatedly added a sheet glass furnace to its two crown houses at Old Swan, ceased manufacture at the close of 1847 after a loss of £3,743 on the year's working.[4] This concern, which had been formed in 1836, with 2,500 £20 shares, to take over the existing Liverpool Crown Glass Company and had, in the later 1840s, 55 shareholders, mostly local men,[5]

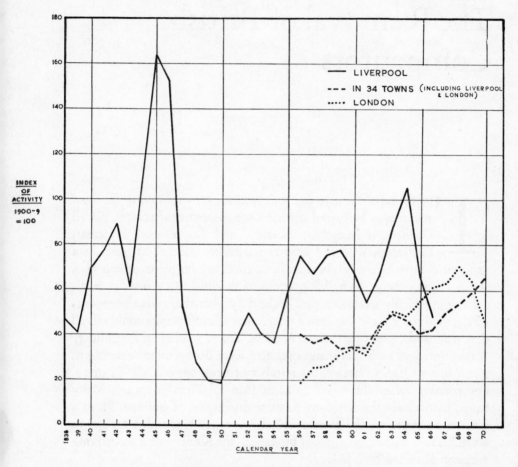

INDEX OF HOUSEBUILDING

__1838-1870__

Graph 7   *Source:* B. Weber 'A New Index of Residential Construction, 1838-1950', *Scottish Journal of Political Economy*, June 1955

was finally dissolved in December 1849. The premises were eventually sold in 1851 and acquired by Chances and Pilkingtons who disposed of them for purposes other than glassmaking.

Crippling losses on the scale of those sustained by this Liverpool concern were also experienced by the old goliaths on the Tyne, which, one might say, almost had a vested interest in the excise duties. It was, perhaps, a sign of the times that Isaac Cookson, who had inherited the large glass business which his family had built up at South Shields and Newcastle over a period of more than 100 years,[6] took the opportunity to sell out in 1845, immediately after the duty had been removed. It was bought by a new firm trading under the name of Cookson's manager, R. W. Swinburne, and including among its partners two famous names from the railway world, the go-getting George Hudson and George Stephenson, then in the closing years of his life.[7] Later in the same year Richard Shortridge, chief proprietor of the South Tyne Glass Company, also retired; he had been in the business for 40 years.[8]

Those Tyne glass firms which continued to manufacture only crown glass found it impossible to compete when prices fell. The business with which Sir Matthew White Ridley had been particularly associated – still called the Newcastle Broad and Crown Glass Company even though broad glass had not been made there for many years – began to run into difficulties in 1847. £20 had to be raised on each of the 36 shares in the concern. At the end of 1848 the 'extremely unprofitable state of the glass trade and the failing health of the managing partners' caused the works to be put up for sale. The partners were paid off gradually between 1849 and 1855.[9] The works never again made window glass.

The other firms on the Tyne also stopped making window glass, though Swinburnes at South Shields,[10] who had inherited a sheet glass department from the days when the factory belonged to Cooksons, had a longer lease of life than the rest. *The Newcastle Guardian*, in April 1849, reported that the Tyne glass industry was 'reaching the climax of its decline';[11] and *The Builder* later noted, on 11 May 1850:

The Crown Glass Trade on the Tyne is said to be now completely paralysed, only three out of twenty houses [furnaces] being in operation and even those not fully employed.

By 1863 no window glass of any kind was being made on the Tyne; the South Shields works were then making only plate glass.[12]

A satisfactory explanation of the sudden collapse, within a decade, of an industry which had flourished on the Tyne and provided most of Britain's glass for nearly 250 years, must await a regional study of the north-east in

the nineteenth century. It is necessary to know, for instance, whether
capital previously invested in window glass manufacture was attracted
away by other, more lucrative, avenues of investment. Or was it merely
removed by elderly proprietors who, having stubbornly clung to out-
dated methods, were in a position to retire when these methods no longer
brought in profits? Why were their businesses not purchased by men with
more up-to-date ideas? Although, as we shall see, factories elsewhere, when
they came on the market, were acquired by the surviving window glass
manufacturers in order to close them down, there is no evidence of this
having happened on the river Tyne. Were there, in fact, serious disadvantages in costs of raw materials and transport which made the north-
east *suddenly* so unattractive? If so, why was window glass manufacture
carried on so successfully on the Wear right to the last decade of the nineteenth century? In 1863 James Hartley and Co. were said to be making as
much window glass as all the factories on the Tyne had previously produced.[13] Can Hartley's prosperity at Sunderland be explained, as an
obituary suggested,[14] solely in terms of the one patent which is dealt with
in the next section of this chapter? These are all questions to which a careful consideration of the local records may provide clear answers. For the
present we can do no more than raise the questions and return to the
story of the surviving concerns who profited considerably from the
collapse of these old giants.

James Hartley's patent for rough (or rolled) plate glass, which he took
out in 1847, not only gave rise to a lucrative branch of window glass
manufacture but also led to closer collaboration among the leading firms.

There was at that time a rapidly growing need, particularly from the
railway companies, for a type of glass which would be suitable for sky-
lights and for the roofing of railway stations, then being built in large
numbers. And, apart from the growing industrial and commercial demand, new local authorities were starting to build covered market halls.
Greenhouses, too, were requiring more glass in this, the age of Paxton.
Such glass needed to be strong and cheap. So long as it was translucent,
it mattered little or not whether it was also transparent. Hartley devised
a very simple means of meeting this need. His patent was remarkable for
its brevity: it ran to only a small page of print. The patentee noted that
rough plate glass was at that time made by ladling the metal from the pots
into a cuvette, or cistern, re-heating it, pouring it on to a casting table
and rolling it out flat. He proposed to dispense with the cuvette, and ladle
the metal direct from the furnace to the casting table where it was to be

rolled out in the usual manner but into smaller plates. The roller which was applied after the second ladleful had been poured onto the table, uniting it with the first, could, if required, impress a pattern. As Hartley put it in his patent:

The several ladlesful do not require to be poured at the same time but may be added towards the end of the preceding quantity and that is the manner of producing long sheets which are comparatively narrow.

Hartley thus managed to patent what looked very like the unpatented plate glass process with the omission of only one stage. Rolled plate glass, however, was to become one of the mainstays of window glass manufacturers. It has, perhaps on account of its lack of technical sophistication, received less attention from historians than it deserves.

Despite its simplicity, the newly patented process took time to develop, for the Wear Glassworks were then in very low financial water and according to J.J.Kayll, who worked for Hartleys from 1840 and became a partner in 1848, James Hartley had, for a period in 1847–8, to take a salary elsewhere as manager of the Birmingham Plate Glassworks.[15] So when it came to tendering for the Great Exhibition building, Chances were able to put in their 16 oz sheet glass at a lower price and secured the contract. (That they could, within the space of a few months, produce nearly a million square feet of sheet glass in panes 49 in. by 10 in. in addition to their other orders,[16] is clear proof of Spon Lane's supremacy at this time.) Hartley did not consider that his rolled plate glass was 'fairly on the market' until the beginning of 1852[17] and it is not until 1854 that we hear of great expanses of railway station roof, such as Lime Street, Liverpool 374 ft × 155½ ft, and New Street, Birmingham 840 ft × 212 ft, being glazed with the new product.[18] Besides making the glass himself, Hartley also licensed Chances and Pilkingtons to make it for an annual fee of £500 per furnace. This he only did reluctantly for, as he was quick to point out to Pilkingtons:

I have no desire to license the patent to any one, it is no advantage to me to receive £500 a year from a House, I am out of pocket by what you and Messrs Chance pay me, as compared to what I should be if you did not make rolled glass but it is not good policy for a patentee to grasp too much, but to be satisfied with a fair amount of reasonable compensation, hence my satisfaction with our present agreement.[19]

The simplicity of the process tempted unlicensed manufacturers – including Chances for a time[20] – to make rolled plate. Richard Hadland was another maker who tried to produce it without a licence. Indeed, according to Kayll, it was not until Hadland challenged the patent that Hartley took it at all seriously and gained faith in it – and then only when prodded and helped by Kayll himself.[21]

During the boom of 1845–6, Hadland, who was previously connected with the Liverpool Union Crown Glass Company at Old Swan,[22] purchased for a little over £4,000 the Eccleston Crown Glassworks,[23] which had been at a standstill since West had gone out of business. Much of the capital appears to have been advanced by William Stock, a Liverpool glass merchant, to whom the factory was mortgaged in February 1847 for £6,333.[24] In 1850–1 it was extended and its rateable value was increased from £291 to £445.[25] Hadland tried to make rolled plate glass soon after his arrival but failed because he used two rollers instead of one. He began experimenting again in 1849, however, and eventually had some success, for early in 1852 Hartley charged him with infringing the patent. A major point in his case was that Hadland had taken into his service Hartley's nephew who had a detailed knowledge of the patented process.[26] Hadland lost the case and this defeat led to his bankruptcy. In the spring of 1852, Chances toyed with the idea either of acquiring the Eccleston works by compounding with Hadland's creditors for five shillings in the pound or of purchasing them in concert with Pilkingtons; but, while Chances were hesitating, Pilkingtons stepped in and themselves bought the works – then equipped with four furnaces – for £13,500.[27] They continued to make rolled plate glass there under licence from Hartley.[28]

At the close of 1854, Hartley proposed to grant licences to other firms. This Chances and Pilkingtons vigorously opposed. They entered into negotiations with Hartley and the three finally agreed that no other firm should be licensed to use the process without their joint consent, and that Chances, Pilkingtons and Hartleys should together be responsible for the defence of the patent. This arrangement succeeded in keeping out all British competition[29] and, for the duration of the patent, confined to the three firms a highly saleable product which, on account of its lower price, was not to attract the same competition from abroad as sheet and plate glass.

The alliance led to further collaboration between the three firms, this time to bring other parts of the window glass industry more closely under their control. With the downfall of the factories in the north-east, they had already come to dominate the manufacturers' association, which continued to hold meetings.[30] Independently, they had taken the opportunity, when competing firms ran into difficulties, of buying out these competitors lest their factories should, at some later date and under new ownership, become serious rivals. At the beginning of 1848, for instance, Chances bought a window glassworks at Bagot Street, Aston, Birmingham; R.L. Chance feared that they would be 'the means of keeping prices low for many a long year'.[31] A few years later, as we have seen, Pilkingtons acquired the Eccleston works. In 1855, Hartleys were considering buying the Tyne and Tees works at Stockton, if they had not already done so, and, in June of that year, William Pilkington, in a letter to Chances, makes it clear that Pilkingtons and Chances had between them acquired the Old Swan Glassworks after they had been put up for sale in 1851. 'Would you in such a case,' he wrote, 'contribute in the same way as we do with the Old Swan Works already, that is *pro rata* so long as the remainder of the works continue silent?'[32] The factory in question was at Newton-le-Willows, only a few miles from St Helens. It was this particular purchase which led Chances, Pilkington and Hartleys, together with three smaller concerns, to share the cost not only of this acquisition but also of the earlier closures.

The Newton works, built in 1832, had started to make glass in the following year.[33] They eventually passed into the hands of William Stock, the Liverpool glass merchant whom we have already mentioned, and he appears to have been in partnership in this particular venture with one Robert Gardner, whom William Pilkington described as a 'thoroughly go-ahead Manchester man'.[34] The new proprietors extended the works which, by the close of 1854, consisted of two crown houses and one sheet house, capable of producing 7,000 tables of crown and 4,000 pieces of sheet glass per week.[35] This company was obviously a most serious rival to Chances, Pilkingtons and Hartleys, the more so as Gardner was reported by William Pilkington to have imbibed the sound economic doctrine that 'the more he makes, the cheaper he gets it'. William Pilkington also conveyed the sad news that Gardner had 'a strong antagonistic feeling against the Glass Trade and its members, which he says he will "purge" if he stays in it'.[36]

Fine words; but Gardner lacked the knowledge to fight on his own. As he himself admitted, he was 'as ignorant of the Glass trade as the pen I now write with',[37] and he therefore had to rely heavily on his partner, Stock. By 1855, however, the two proprietors were drifting apart. Stock was putting up another works at West Leigh, not far away, and Gardner confessed that he had lost all confidence in him. It was under these circumstances that William Pilkington urged his fellow manufacturers to buy out 'the most *formidable enemy* that we have ever encountered'.[38] On 4 July 1855, it was agreed between Pilkington and Gardner that £12,000 should be paid for the works plus an additional £2,500 for the furnaces, all materials apart from finished glass to be taken at a valuation.[39] A week later representatives of Chances, Pilkingtons and Hartleys met at the Great Western Hotel in London and agreed to bear joint responsibility not only for the purchase of the Newton factory but also for the Tyne and Tees, Old Swan and Bagot Street works, the whole scheme depending upon the successful accomplishment of the Newton agreement of 4 July. They invited three of the other window glass firms – Swinburne at South Shields, the Wearmouth Glass Company and the Nailsea Glass Company (Bristol) – to join them. The contributions make it clear that by this time Pilkingtons had caught up with Chances in window glass-making capacity and that the two firms were leaders of this branch of the industry in Britain. Each of them possessed nine glasshouses, while Hartley had six, Swinburne four, and the Wearmouth and Nailsea companies two each.[40]

Little time was lost. Two days after the London meeting, Swinburne and Matteson (of the Wearmouth Company) agreed to collaborate in the plan[41] and on the following day James Varley, Pilkingtons' book-keeper, wired Chances with the news:

Newton is shut up. We have possession. Our own manager has charge of the Furnaces six p.m.

There were hitches in valuing the materials at the works and these caused James Hartley to complain bitterly against William Pilkington who, he believed, was temporising for his own ends.[42] But when all the facts were explained to him, he agreed that Gardner's solicitors were at fault.[43] Unfortunately our documents cease at this point and we have no evidence of when the whole matter was finally settled. But it is certain that the Newton factory, though it manufactured bottles, never made any more window glass and from this we may infer that the manufacturers' agreement was eventually carried through. Stock's new works at West Leigh, however – to be known as the Lancashire Glass Works, Plank Lane, Leigh – went into production. They were still listed as makers of crown, sheet and (rolled) plate glass in the 1880s.[44]

Chances, Pilkingtons and Hartleys again acted in concert in 1860, this time to close down a factory belonging to Joshua Bower and Co. of Hunslet, near Leeds.[45] Bowers agreed not to make any crown, sheet, rolled plate glass or other window glass anywhere in Lancashire, York-shire, Northumberland, Durham or the Midlands for 14 years in considera-tion of a payment of £1,000 a year. They also received £3,204 for their stock and the three purchasers promised to honour all the agreements Bowers had made with their workmen and to fulfil all the contracts with their customers.[46]

The ending of window glass manufacture at Hunslet was soon followed by an attempt to launch another manufacturing concern not far away at Castleford, in much the same way as the Leigh works had followed the closure at Newton. This venture, however, does not appear to have got beyond the issue of a prospectus. It claimed that window glass could, 'without doubt', be made at Castleford 20 per cent more cheaply than at Birmingham, and 15 per cent more cheaply than at St Helens. In addition to this alleged cost advantage, profits in that branch of the glass industry were, they asserted, 'unequalled by any other manufacture in the kingdom ... The present manufacturers, about five or six in number, have practically become "One Firm" and thus established a great monopoly.'[47]

The road to success was not to be so easy as the writers of this prospectus imply. The three largest firms were still making 75 per cent of all Britain's window glass;[48] but, as shall be seen in the next chapter, they had to struggle hard, for Belgian competition was becoming greater. There could be no question of monopoly so long as cheap Belgian glass flooded the British market. Before considering the effects of this growing competition from abroad, however, we must discuss the expansion of Pilkingtons' works at St Helens during the years following the repeal of the excise duty.

The two plans of the Grove Street factory (Plans 3 and 4 on pages 108-9), from deeds of 1840 and 1856, provide a useful commentary on the firm's development between those two dates. In 1840 the works, still confined to the original rectangle of freehold land on the eastern side of Grove Street, consisted of three glasshouses, three cutting rooms with pot rooms over them, a mixing room, a warehouse and joiners' shop (both in one building), a saw mill, a crate shop, a masons' shop, a clay mill, a clay room, brick kilns, a smithy and a timber yard. About one-third of the site was occupied by two parallel rows of cottages, 37 in all, stretching from the timber yard southwards to the road leading from Grove Street to the Bells' Ravenhead Flint Glassworks. There were in the area of the works itself three more cottages and the manager's house. The lodge and office were both accommodated in a small space at the end of the mixing room building.

So many additions and alterations were made between 1840 and 1856 that within those 16 years the whole appearance of the works was transformed almost beyond recognition. The first house had been turned over from crown to sheet glass manufacture and several blowing furnaces and flattening kilns had been added. The second and third houses were still

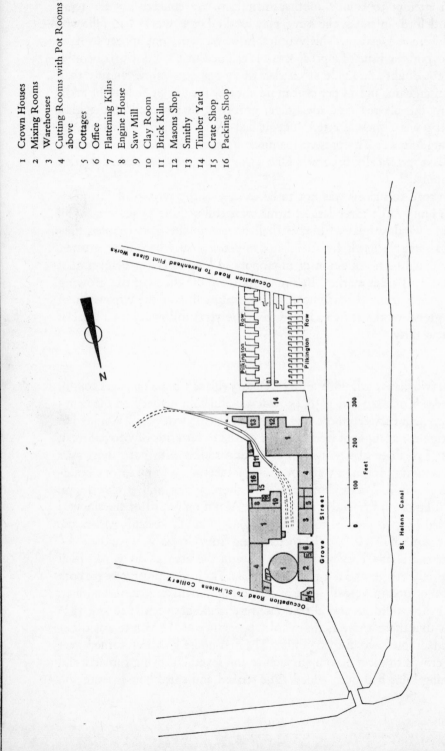

1   Crown Houses
2   Mixing Rooms
3   Warehouses
4   Cutting Rooms with Pot Rooms
    above
5   Cottages
6   Office
7   Flattening Kilns
8   Engine House
9   Saw Mill
10 Clay Room
11 Brick Kiln
12 Masons Shop
13 Smithy
14 Timber Yard
15 Crate Shop
16 Packing Shop

Plan 3 Greenall & Pilkingtons in 1840

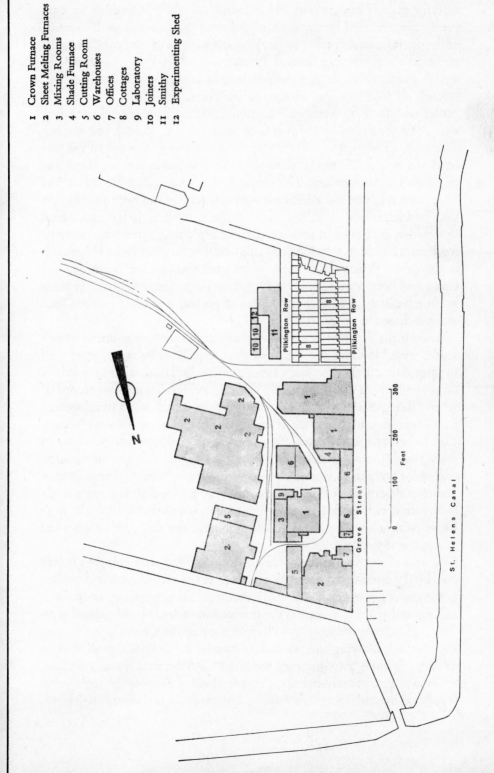

1 Crown Furnace
2 Sheet Melting Furnaces
3 Mixing Rooms
4 Shade Furnace
5 Cutting Room
6 Warehouses
7 Offices
8 Cottages
9 Laboratory
10 Joiners
11 Smithy
12 Experimenting Shed

Plan 4 Pilkingtons in 1856

used for making crown glass and a fourth, adjoining the third on land previously occupied by the timber yard, was also devoted to this branch of the manufacture. Further ground had been acquired immediately to the east of these glasshouses (behind them if viewed from Grove Street), an area as extensive as the original purchase of 1826. On this site had been erected, in two compact groups of buildings, five sheet furnaces, together with their attendant blowing and flattening furnaces and annealing kilns. The joiners' shop (with timber yard behind), smithy and turning shop were all housed in a single U-shaped building to the east of the two rows of cottages. There was also a shed in this building where experimental work was undertaken. The original warehouse in Grove Street had been trebled in size and additional warehouse space had been provided in two buildings behind it. In place of the combined lodge and office, squeezed in at one end of the mixing room building, more spacious counting houses had been put up at one side of the main gates and a lodge built at the other. A few small plots of land between Grove Street and the Canal had been acquired in the 1830s and 1840s, presumably to provide loading facilities. A further large piece of ground bordering on the Canal was purchased in 1854.

Among the furnaces in the new group of buildings was one at which shades were blown. These pieces of glass, usually bell-shaped, were used to keep dust off articles which needed to be displayed, such as goods in shop windows or clocks in family drawing rooms. There is no record of when Pilkingtons entered this branch of trade, which was a development from sheet glass manufacture. It was certainly sometime between January 1845 (when one set of production figures ends without any reference to shades) and January 1848 (when the next set begins with the information that about 800 shades were then being made every week). Henry Deacon has left a description of how shades up to 16 inches diameter were made from cylinders,[49] while larger-sized and square- or oval-shaped shades were blown in moulds. The mould sheds adjoining the shade house are to be seen in the 1856 plan.

Several of the pots in the shade house were filled with coloured metal, used by the ornamental department, which in the early days was described as the staining room.[50] It eventually encompassed enamelling, embossing, etching and staining as well as the production of leaded and painted windows. This department seems to have come into existence about the same time as shade blowing and was the creation of Ralph Edmundson who, in 1849, was earning two guineas a week. By 1850 the firm was in a position to issue a handsomely-produced *Trade Book of Patterns for Ornamental Window Glass with Designs for Church, Hall, Staircase and Memorial Windows,* the designs being by Frank Howard, described in the *Trade Book* as 'a well-known and celebrated artist'.[51] He designed the Pilkington entry for the Great Exhibition, a painted window nine feet by five feet entitled 'St George casting out the great red dragon'. He also designed a Pilkington window which was installed in Liverpool Parish Church in January 1853.[52]

Much of the expansion during this period occurred after 1851. The removal of the tax on windows on 1 April of that year, the upswing of the building cycle, and that great advertisement for glass, the Crystal Palace, all helped to stimulate demand. Four warehouses were opened in provincial centres: at Bristol (already in existence by 1851), Birmingham (1857), Leeds (1863) and Sheffield (1867).[53]

Growing orders, both at home and from abroad, led to the firm's output being increased from 80 tons a week in 1851 to 150 tons a week at the beginning of 1854. Pilkingtons were then employing 1,350 hands and paying out £1,050 in wages every week, a remarkable jump from the £360 or so they were paying per week in the middle of 1849 to under 450 employees.[54] Despite the growing popularity and economic advantages of sheet glass, it is interesting to notice that, even at this date, its total production had not yet overhauled that of crown at St Helens, as may be seen from the firm's weekly production figures:

TABLE 7
WEEKLY PRODUCTION AT PILKINGTON BROTHERS
AT THE BEGINNING OF 1854

Crown	12,400 tables	161,200 lb
Sheet and Patent Plate	9,800 pieces	132,300 lb
Rolled Plate	15,000 ft	45,000 lb
Shades and Miscellaneous	3,500 items	10,500 lb

Source: Lecture by R.B.Edmundson, published in *The Builder*, 8 April 1854.

As there was much more waste with crown glass than with sheet, Pilkingtons were probably already making more *saleable* sheet glass. There were then four crown and four sheet furnaces. A fifth sheet furnace, then under construction, must have tipped the balance much further when it came into use. This ninth furnace, as we have noticed, gave Pilkingtons parity with Chances and half as much capacity again as Hartleys.

As Pilkingtons extended the scale of their operations, they required an increasing supply of coal and raw materials, particularly sand and alkali.

Coal was needed in very large amounts, several tons being necessary to produce each ton of glass. In 1851, for instance, when Pilkingtons were making 80 tons of glass every week, the various furnaces at the works were devouring no less than 650 tons of coal, a ratio of eight to one. Backward integration into coalmining held out certain cost advantages when glassmaking was being undertaken on a fairly large scale. Above all, it offered the prospect of ensuring supplies during coal strikes.

During the later months of 1843 the colliers of the Lancashire coalfield had organised themselves into a powerful trade union, and in January 1844 the St Helens men – but not their fellow workers elsewhere on the coalfield – went on strike. For two or three weeks the factories in the St Helens neighbourhood were able to keep open by drawing on their accumulated stocks, but as the strike dragged on these stocks became depleted almost to the point of exhaustion. Some firms sent for coal to the collieries on the southern fringe of the Wigan coalfield: others began to prospect for coal themselves. Frederick Fincham, the resourceful and energetic manager of the Ravenhead Plate Glassworks, began to open out some old disused workings within his company's grounds.[55] Pilkingtons followed his example and began to look for their own source of coal. On 19 February they engaged Robert Whyte, a skilled mining engineer, to select a suitable site in the town and there sink a pit for the firm's use.[56]

After one or two trial bores for coal on land to the north of Duke Street, Whyte began, in June 1844, to prospect further along the Ormskirk road about 200 yards beyond Four Lane Ends (later known as the Lingholme) on the north side of the road. This land had the added recommendation that it belonged to Peter Greenall.[57] Boring on this occasion was successful and, although the colliers had long since resumed work and the men showed no signs of a further turn-out, Pilkingtons decided that they ought to continue with plans for getting their own coal. In September 1844 Whyte began to sink an engine pit at the Green Lane Colliery (as it came to be called), and the winding of coal from the Little Delf mine, a seam just under three feet thick, started in February 1845. The workings soon became extensive. During the six years between the colliery's opening and the end of 1850 the Little Delf measures were worked from under a total area of more than 12 statute acres of land. By that date all the coal that could be worked economically from this particular pit had been dug and the colliery was closed. A new pit, sunk further to the south, in Eccleston township, was at work by September 1854.[58] Robert Whyte remained colliery agent to the company until 1856 when he emigrated to Australia.[59] The following year, Pilkingtons purchased from John Clare and the executors of Thomas Haddock the remains of the extinct St Helens

Colliery, close to their glassworks on the south-east side, which Clare, Haddock & Company had operated until 1844.[60] By this time Pilkingtons were selling coal to other firms and to the general public as well as using it to stoke the furnaces and heat the kilns at their glassworks. Although the colliery appeared in the accounts as part of the glass concern, it was as Pilkington Brothers, coal proprietors, and not as Pilkington Brothers, glass manufacturers, that the firm made the St Helens Colliery one of the largest and most profitable concerns in the district.

Sand, relatively free from iron oxide and therefore suitable for window glass manufacture, was also available locally. In 1834 excise officers in various parts of the country were asked by the Treasury to send in information about glass manufacturers' sources of sand. The sand available in Eccleston, near St Helens, was singled out for particular mention. It was of a good quality, almost in the same category as that from Alum Bay (Isle of Wight) or Lynn, and could be had locally for 12s 6d a ton delivered.[61] Although Pilkingtons did, in 1869, order a trial cargo of foreign sand, this did not produce any better window glass than the local variety. They therefore continued to draw all their supplies from deposits which lay just under the surface soil to the north and west of St Helens.[62] In 1881 they built their own sand wash at Rainford.

Alkali was also obtainable from local sources. The rise of the firm coincided with the growth of the Leblanc process and there was never any shortage of soda or saltcake, particularly at St Helens where several new chemical works were sited. The local alkali manufacturers were able to supply soda or saltcake of good quality (relatively free from iron) in sufficient quantity and at a reasonable price. Pilkingtons, therefore, preferred to buy from them rather than to go to the trouble and expense of erecting plant to manufacture these products on their own account. Moreover, glassmakers during the 1830s and 1840s were learning how to use more of the cheaper saltcake (sodium sulphate) in place of the dearer soda ash (sodium carbonate). Already by 1837 Greenall & Pilkingtons were purchasing saltcake from the nearby works of S. & W.T.Clough. By the late 1840s the firm was using saltcake almost entirely,[63] and was being supplied by several alkali makers: Morley & Speakman in Parr, Gamble at Gerard's Bridge, and, especially, Muspratt at Earlestown. Their saltcake was of a satisfactory quality for glassmaking and it was only after J.C.Gamble had patented a new process, employing iron retorts in place of brick furnaces,[64] that William Pilkington had any reason to complain. When, early in 1845, he was asked to support the development of Longmaid's process, whereby saltcake was to be manufactured by calcining together salt and pyrites, he replied:

Salt cake made by this Process being very and, indeed, altogether free from Iron, is so peculiarly adapted for Glass making that unless we can procure some made either upon this or the old plan in contradistinction to Mr Gamble's patent, we must, though very unwillingly, put up chambers and manufacture our own salt cake.[65]

But Pilkingtons were not driven to become manufacturing chemists just yet. Saltcake sufficiently free from iron continued to reach the glassworks from the local alkali factories and by canal from Earlestown. At the beginning of the 1850s, however, just at the time when output of glass increased and the firm's saltcake requirements took a sharp upward turn, Muspratt was obliged to close his works at Earlestown, and Pilkingtons were, consequently, thrown into greater dependence upon other manufacturers. This caused William Pilkington once more to contemplate setting himself up as a manufacturing chemist and he actually entered into a partnership for the purpose. His associate in this venture was Henry Deacon, the young man whom we have already encountered as the firm's highly-paid Chemist and Engineer.

Deacon left Pilkingtons at the beginning of July 1851, when he was just 29 years of age. Although he was then earning the remarkable salary of £7 a week – 14s 0d more than William Pilkington's eldest son – he no doubt saw that he could advance himself little further as an employee. Partnerships in the firm were obviously reserved for members of the family. If he was to maintain his very rapid rate of progress, he had to become a manufacturer in his own right. The chemical industry held out the brightest prospect and Widnes then had cost advantages over St Helens because of an increase in freight rates on all materials, apart from coal, passing along the canal which linked the two places.[66] It therefore paid chemical manufacturers to transport St Helens coal south rather than bring vast quantities of salt, limestone and pyrites at greater cost up to the coalfield. It used to be thought that Deacon spent his first couple of years in Widnes as manager of a small chemical works;[67] but more recent investigation has suggested he may have gone there at Pilkingtons' instigation to find out about experiments which William Gossage was then carrying out on a new method of making soda ash.[68] Gossage's experiments did not succeed; but Deacon nevertheless persuaded William Pilkington to go into partnership with him, each partner advancing £3,000 to build a Leblanc alkali works on the north bank of the Canal almost opposite to Hutchinson's pioneer plant. Pilkington and Deacon signed a 1,000-year lease for the land on 1 October 1853.[69]

In the following year the partners made arrangements to install equipment for the production on a commercial scale of soda ash [*sic*] suitable for glassmaking, employing newly-patented processes.[70] Although this step was almost certainly undertaken at Deacon's suggestion, William Pilkington advanced the capital to buy the necessary equipment, £580 in all. The experiments yielded no quick results, however, and William Pilkington, the business man, grew more and more impatient with Deacon, the chemist. By the middle of 1855 Pilkington decided to withdraw altogether. Another of Deacon's former employers, Holbrook Gaskell, was persuaded to take his place and the deed for the dissolution of the partnership was signed on 15 June 1855. It was then agreed that Holbrook Gaskell should pay William Pilkington the £3,000 that he had invested in the partnership. The outstanding £580 was to be repaid over a number of years, either by providing Pilkingtons' glassworks with high grade soda ash suitable for glassmaking at 5 per cent below the invoice price if the plant eventually yielded such a product, or, if it did not, in annual payments of £100. (We do not know which method was finally adopted.) Although the partnership was dissolved without any outward show of ill-feeling, William Pilkington was not sorry to escape from this business relationship. As he confided to his solicitors:

> I cannot tell or express to you how much pleased and relieved I shall be to get rid of such an unsociable, selfish and arrogant fellow as he is.[71]

Almost ten years were to elapse before William Pilkington again ventured into alkali manufacture at Widnes. On this occasion he chose as his partners his two younger sons, George (b. 1840) who had had a formal training at the Royal College of Chemistry and was already chemist at the glassworks,[72] and Leonard (b. 1847). The Mersey Chemical Works of William Pilkington & Sons, a short distance up the Canal from Gaskell-Deacons, was in course of erection when the Alkali Inspector drew up his First Report for the year 1864,[73] and on 9 March 1865, William (Roby) and William Windle Pilkington were expecting that the arrival of the first deliveries of saltcake from these works would effect a great improvement in the quality of the firm's glass, an expectation that was soon realized.[74] As with Pilkingtons' colliery, the Mersey Chemical Works, though originally built chiefly to serve the requirements of the glassworks, were soon supplying other customers as well. By 1870 the alkali factory employed between 100 and 150 men and manufactured 2,000 tons of bleaching powder and 120 tons of nitrate of soda annually, in addition to producing soda and saltcake[75]. Unlike the colliery, its finances were always kept separate from those of the glassworks. It was later absorbed into the United Alkali Co. Ltd, and later still became part of ICI Ltd.

The elimination of most of their British competitors, and their own ventures into coalmining and chemical manufacture, assisted Pilkingtons greatly when, unprotected by tariffs, they came to be confronted by a growing tide of cheap, imported glass. This foreign, and chiefly Belgian, competition, was far more severe than anything British manufacturers had ever experienced amongst themselves.

Chapter 8

Competition from Belgium and Consolidation at St Helens

BELGIUM did not emerge as a major window glass producing country until the second quarter of the nineteenth century. In 1823 only ten small factories were engaged in this branch of manufacture in that part of the kingdom of the Netherlands which was to become, after 1830, the independent state of Belgium, and they could only muster 66 glassmaking pots among them. By 1834 the number of factories had increased to 21 and their combined capacity to 224 pots. By 1847, although the number of factories had not increased, their average size had grown; there were then 272 pots in use altogether.[1] Almost all of this glass was exported. Concentrated in the Charleroi area in the south of the country, where the necessary raw materials were to hand, the industry was able to take advantage of good communications to the coast; from there the crates of window glass could be shipped cheaply to all parts of the world. During the 1840s exports of this glass from Belgium averaged just over 8,000,000 kilograms per year[2] – just under 160,000 cwt. This was an amount exceeding the whole output of British factories during the early 1840s and not far short of their peak in the boom of the mid-1830s.

The Belgian manufacturers exploited to the full the natural cost advantages which they enjoyed and so were able to undersell the home producers in other countries, especially in the more common grades of sheet glass for which there was the largest market. Although coal was not particularly cheap in Belgium, and was certainly more expensive than in England, other costs were lower. Most contemporaries emphasised labour as the factor of production which gave the Belgians a particular advantage. In 1841, for instance, R.L.Chance found that glass blowers there made 50 per cent more glass in a week than their British counterparts and received less than half a British glassmaker's wage. Chance believed that the Belgians were 'such formidable rivals from their economy and activity that unless we manufacture on the best principles, we can never sell our extra quantities abroad to a profit. . .'[3] This was written when sheet glass manufacture was still in its infancy in Britain; but, 20 years later, a British consular report from Brussels, dealing with the progress of Belgian industry generally, had this to say about the cost of labour:

The characteristics of the Belgian workmen are steadiness and perseverance, combined with great intelligence in working after models; their habits are not so expensive as those of English artificers; their diet is more humble – they consume less meat, and their bread is seldom purely wheaten or white in quality . . . beer and spirits are both lower in price than in England. They seldom use tea and the chicory root constitutes a very economical and wholesome substitute for coffee. Instead of coals and open grates, closed stoves and artificial fuel, made of mere dust of coal and clay worked into lumps, are universally in use. The system of schools for infants from two to seven years, and from seven to twelve years, is very general and affords great facilities – the children being cared for – to both their parents to occupy themselves in daily service and by combined industry to ameliorate the condition of the family.[4]

Unfortunately no detailed estimates of costs of production in particular

TABLE 8

BONTEMPS' COMPARISON OF THE COST OF
MANUFACTURING 1,000 kg OF WINDOW GLASS IN
BELGIUM AND ENGLAND

	Belgium Francs Centimes		England Francs Centimes	
Furnace and pots	–	76	–	98
Frit materials	4	82	5	90
Fuel	5	10	2	55
Labour (melting)	–	81	–	88
(blowing)	4	60	5	40
Flattening	2	40	2	60
Warehousing	–	74	–	90
'Emballage' [Packing]	2	46	2	59
Carpentry and forge work	–	37	–	40
Rents and taxes	–	73	–	89
Management: general expenses	1	50	2	00
	24	29	25	09

Source: Georges Bontemps, *Guide du Verrier* (Paris 1868), 405, 408.

Belgian factories are available to enable us to verify whether cheaper labour did, in fact, give Belgian glass manufacturers their great advantage over manufacturers in other countries. The only relevant information, published by Bontemps in the later 1860s (Table 8), shows that, while the Belgians certainly benefited from cheap labour, they gained less advantage from this than the British from cheaper coal. Their success was really due to economies in all departments for which cheap labour may have been only partly responsible.

British glass manufacturers began to complain about Belgian competition even before reduction of the import duties permitted Belgian glass to obtain a market in Britain itself. Already, in 1837, they were complaining of being undersold in all parts of the world by French, Belgian and German firms.[5] In 1841 they returned to the charge, arguing that they were 'in fact nearly shut out from all except in our own Colonies where we have hitherto had protection'.[6] Chances pointed to the loss of the Indian market 'by the partial application there of the principles of free trade'.[7] The trade figures confirm that re-exports of Belgian glass from Britain grew rapidly in the 1840s and, by 1845, were running at nearly the same level as the exports of British glass:

TABLE 9
RE-EXPORTS OF WINDOW GLASS (ALMOST WHOLLY BELGIAN) AND EXPORTS OF BRITISH WINDOW GLASS
1842–9 (cwt)

Year	Imports	Retained for Home Use	Re-exported	British Exports
1842	2,104	106	1,998	20,031
1843	3,349	137	3,166	16,261
1844	7,451	240	7,147	16,286
1845	22,455	8,374	12,790	14,788
1846	44,811	9,882	32,716	20,345
1847	35,117	4,693	30,831	29,084
1848	31,037	6,888	25,883	19,708
1849	25,576	7,712	17,916	17,255

Source: Parliamentary Papers, 1843 [173] XXX, 1844 [200] XLV, 1845 [169] XLVI, 1846 [214] XLIV, 1847 [361] LIX, 1847/8 [305] LVIII, 1849 [534] L; *Economist*, 11 February, 1850.

From 1842 to 1844 most of these re-exports went to the territory of the East India Company, as Chances had indicated. In 1845, however, Belgian glass began to be exported to British North America (Canada) which was then the British manufacturers' best export market. In 1846 twice as much Belgian as British window glass crossed the North Atlantic to Canada; but in subsequent years re-exports to Canada resumed more modest proportions and the territories of the East India Company again became the chief destination. Presumably British merchants handled this re-export trade as well as Belgian sales in Britain itself.

These shipments of Belgian glass to Britain represented but a small fraction of Belgium's total exports. Her glass was sent to all parts of the world by other routes. Over twice as much was exported to the United States as to Britain, and America was, throughout the 1850s, by far the largest of Belgium's customers. Holland took as much Belgian glass as did Britain (presumably for re-export) and Hamburg and the Turkish Empire were also markets of consequence.

TABLE 10
BELGIAN EXPORTS OF WINDOW GLASS, 1850–2
('000 kilograms)

	1850	1851	1852
To Britain	1,813	1,980	1,866
United States	3,429	5,213	4,949
Holland	1,507	1,920	1,848
Hamburg	1,048	1,337	1,662
Turkish Empire	1,230	1,085	1,215
Total	11,672	14,681	16,444

Source: Tableau Générale du Commerce avec les Pays Etrangers (Statistique de la Belgique) for the years concerned.
Details for subsequent years will be found in Appendix 4.

By this time the progressive reduction of British import duties was enabling the Belgians to sell more of their glass to the British home market instead of re-exporting it. Before 1845, imported Belgian glass had had to bear a prohibitive customs duty of 30s 0d per cwt in addition to the excise duty. With the removal of the excise duty, the customs duty was reduced to 14s 0d per cwt. It was further reduced in 1846 to 7s 0d, in 1848 to 3s 6d, in 1853 to 2s 6d and in 1855 to 1s 6d. From April 1857 all glass was allowed to enter the country duty-free.[8] The reduction of 1853 and the abolition of the duty in 1857, coinciding as they did with a period of rising prices on the British market, were both accompanied by large increases in the amount of Belgian glass sold to British customers. Retained imports were, in 1853–6, double what they had been in 1850–2, and, after 1857, they doubled again. Re-exports, having dwindled to negligible propor-

TABLE 11

WINDOW GLASS (ALMOST WHOLLY BELGIAN) RETAINED
FOR HOME CONSUMPTION AND RE-EXPORTED
1850–60 (cwt)

	Retained in Britain	Re-exported	British Exports
1850	9,406	11,604	15,518
1851	10,696	2,059	16,460
1852	13,170	3,197	22,162
1853	23,350	5,485	39,159
1854	27,127	3,012	35,514
1855	25,816	1,126	21,473
1856	27,787	2,399	28,522
1857	39,631	16,429	32,000
1858	61,927	33,655	26,008
1859	67,591	51,715	27,697
1860	75,088	25,116	33,408

Source: British Trade and Navigation Returns

tions in the middle of the decade, resumed their former scale after 1857.
Within a decade the sale of Belgian glass in Britain had grown to formidable proportions. Moreover, the capture of a large share of this market had
been achieved without the diversion of exports from elsewhere: Belgian
exports to Britain continued to run at about one-sixth of the total, still
considerably below those to the United States. After the outbreak of the

TABLE 12

WINDOW GLASS (ALMOST WHOLLY BELGIAN) RETAINED
FOR HOME CONSUMPTION AND RE-EXPORTED
1861–70 (cwt)

	Retained in Britain	Re-exported	British Exports
1861	90,244	11,959	35,732
1862	117,145	25,425	49,171
1863	135,762	46,223	62,674
1864	173,726	62,881	58,010
1865	226,214	37,842	50,608
1866	Total retained and re-exported 272,392		59,171
1867	237,737	47,957	64,431
1868	320,786	81,908	73,301
1869	328,156	71,381	92,111
1870	369,874	53,183	76,654

Source: British Trade and Navigation Returns

American Civil War in April 1861, however, Belgian shipments to the
United States fell off while those to Britain continued to increase. Britain
became, and remained for the next 20 years, the chief market for Belgium's huge and still growing output.[9] Between the plateau of the
mid-1850s and 1870 sales of Belgian window glass in Britain increased
nearly fifteenfold, from some 25,000 cwt to 370,000 cwt.

From the middle of the 1850s prices fell during most years, recovering
slightly on occasion in response to building demand, but always losing
any slight gain by a much greater fall. In 1858, when Belgian glass first
reached the British market on a really large scale, the price was more than
20 per cent higher than it became at the end of the 1860s. And this was
just the beginning of a secular fall which was to continue until the eve of
the First World War.

By the middle of the 1860s the three great glassmaking firms in Britain
– Chances, Pilkingtons and Hartleys – were together making about
340,000 cwt of glass per annum.[10] Before 1870 sales of Belgian glass had
almost certainly exceeded British sales and there was no sign of imports
ceasing to grow. The Manufacturers' Association, having succeeded in
curbing competition at home, was now confronted with other, and much
more powerful, competitors who were unwilling to come to terms.
Attempts were indeed made to open negotiations with the Belgians. The
Board minutes at Pilkingtons for 4 August 1865 record that, on the previous day, George Gwilliam, the permanent secretary of the Association,[11]
had called 'in reference to the Belgian houses being induced to accept a
fixed minimum for the lowest qualities, say 1½d for 15 oz we agreeing not
to go below 1⅝d'. Gwilliam then intended 'to see the London representative of the Foreign houses and work through them'. Six weeks later he
called again at St Helens to report on a visit to Charleroi where he had met
the Belgians. He believed that a price-fixing bargain could be struck with
them and advised that a deputation of English manufacturers should 'meet
the Belgian houses, interchange ideas and do much good mutually'.[12] We
know that by the beginning of 1866 the British were seriously entertaining
the idea of visiting Belgium during the summer,[13] but there is no evidence
to show whether they actually went or, if they did, what was the upshot of
their negotiations. If any agreement was reached, it was certainly short-
lived, and did not halt the downward trend of prices. Ten years later
R.L.Chance could write to Richard Pilkington:

There is unfortunately no Association of window glass manufacturers in
Belgium and no understanding of any kind amongst them ... I fear that
Gwilliam would do no good by going amongst them.[14]

Powerless when confronted with foreign competition, the Association had to be content with continuing its policy of driving out of business the occasional new competitor at home. When glassworks at Stourbridge fell into Hartleys' hands in 1867, it was agreed that Chances and Pilkingtons should each bear two-fifths of the cost and Hartleys the remainder.[15] The Nailsea works near Bristol ceased production soon after this. They had been leased in 1862 by Samuel Bowen of West Bromwich – who had already filed his bankruptcy once – and John Powis of London. This firm began to sell rolled plate glass – a branch in which, because of its lower production cost, Belgian competition was not severe[16] – at prices below those of the Association. They gained a considerable number of large orders immediately, including one for 100,000 feet for glazing the roof of London Road Station in Manchester.[17] The Association's machinery went into action and the other manufacturers cut their prices so that they undersold even Bowen & Powis. Within a year of the Association's intervention, there were negotiations afoot for James Hartley to purchase the works, William (Roby) Pilkington and R.L. Chance acting as arbitrators.[18] Bowen failed again in 1869, this time for about £30,000,[19] and, the lease having been surrendered, Hartleys sought to dispose of the property. Chances bought it for £14,000, made glass there for a short time during the boom of the early 1870s, and then closed it down for good because the local coal supplies proved unsatisfactory.[20]

Against the real competitors, however, the only course was for each firm to improve its efficiency. The 1860s saw the beginning of a new phase of technical improvement.

By this time Pilkingtons were in a much better position to keep abreast of technical development than they had been 20 years earlier. The founders of the firm owed their success chiefly to expert salesmanship and constant vigilance in office and factory. They laid no claim to being technical men and were certainly not of an inventive turn of mind in the same way as was J.T. Chance or James Hartley. In the 1840s Pilkingtons had been obliged to call in Henry Deacon to take charge of this side of their business and it was Deacon, and not either of the partners, who addressed learned societies on the mysteries of glassmaking. The position was different, however, with the second generation: among the sons of the founders were two very capable engineers. William Pilkington's second son, Richard (b. 1830), became a mechanical engineer and, though he did not become a partner, he was certainly interested in the mechanical side of glassmaking for a time. He was, from 1854, a member of the Institution of Mechanical

Engineers and, in 1863, delivered a paper to that body 'On the Processes and Mechanical Appliances in the Manufacture of Polished Sheet Glass'.[21] By then, however, he was living away from St Helens and does not seem subsequently to have taken an active interest in glass manufacture.[22] It was left to his younger cousin, Richard Pilkington's eldest son, William Windle (b. 1839), who soon showed an aptitude for technical matters, to take control of this side of the firm's activities. Windle Pilkington served a long apprenticeship during the 1860s. Soon after that, as we shall see in the next chapter, his determined advocacy of the newly-patented tank furnaces, which allowed continuous working to take place for 24 hours a day, tipped the balance decisively in Pilkingtons' favour.

He did not possess an original or imaginative mind of the sort which produces major new inventions; but he was quick to spot potentially valuable improvements made by others and he himself made a considerable contribution to reducing unit costs by devising ways of improving existing glassmaking techniques. In the middle of the 1860s, for instance, he turned his attention to developing a better method of making patent plate glass. Richard Pilkington, junior, had told the Institution of Mechanical Engineers in 1863 that it took about nine hours to polish each side of a sheet of glass, largely because much of the initial work had to be done by hand. The new benches, made at the Haigh Foundry near Wigan in 1866, reduced this time by half with a saving of $1\frac{1}{4}$d on every foot of glass produced. And it was reported that the quality was 'superior to Chances'.[23]

The most important innovation of this period, however, and the one which, more than any other, pointed the way to future development, was undoubtedly the Siemens Regenerative Gas Furnace. During the 1850s Frederick Siemens had invented and his brother, William, had 'matured',[24] a coal-fired furnace which was constructed in such a way that the flames and resulting hot products of combustion were made to travel alternately in opposite directions, thereby producing a regenerative effect and extracting most of the heat before the air was eventually allowed to escape up the chimney. This resulted in a considerable saving of fuel which William Siemens optimistically claimed amounted to as much as 79 per cent in the case of one of the early prototypes.[25] Serious practical difficulties arose, however, when an attempt was made to apply the regenerative principle to larger furnaces. It was found impossible to use solid fuel.[26] The brothers Siemens, therefore, started to experiment with gas-firing and in 1861 they took out a patent for a gas-fired regenerative furnace suitable for glassmaking.[27]

The gas-fired furnace possessed a two-fold attraction for the glass manufacturer. It saved fuel and it prevented impurities from the coal from coming into contact with and discolouring the glass. In 1861 Siemens furnaces were erected at the flint glassworks belonging to Lloyd & Summerfield at Birmingham, and at Chances. The following year one of the new furnaces was being built at the British Plate Glassworks, Ravenhead.[28] Once again Chances were quicker off the mark than Pilkingtons. It was not until January 1863, almost two years after the pots had first been set in the Siemens gas-fired furnace at Smethwick, that Pilkingtons first began to consider the matter seriously.[29] William (Roby) Pilkington consulted John Crossley of the Ravenhead Works who already had some experience of the new furnaces there.[30] Crossley agreed to superintend the erection of a Siemens furnace at Pilkingtons, and on 26 March 1863 Pilkingtons decided to write to Siemens for terms. Siemens' offer of £100 for the drawings and a levy of 5s 0d on each ton of glass produced was accepted by the firm and one of the Siemens brothers came to St Helens in May to talk the matter over. The furnace was lit for the first time on 2 November. Three weeks later the quality of glass from the gas furnace was declared to be 'decidedly the best' and after a month's operation Windle Pilkington considered that 'the saving upon coal alone will almost pay Siemens' royalty . . . of 5s 0d per ton on thirty tons per week'. On 11 April 1864, the new furnace was declared to be 'a decided success commercially' and on 5 May the Board discussed the possibility of installing a gas furnace in the first house

instead of the present one which makes wretched metal. The house is the only one where the furnace could be put in without altering it. On the other hand the blowing house, etc., would cause great alteration, taking up the present warehouse and rebuilding one upon the site of the late No. 2 house – altogether involving a great outlay.

The following week it was decided to build this second furnace 'with all speed in order to meet the demand in Autumn . . . but not to enlarge the blowing place or build the new warehouse till the new furnace has been fully tried'. Pots were set in this furnace on 14 August, the flattening kilns were then put in hand, and the warehouse was erected subsequently.

On the whole, although there were certainly the usual teething troubles, Pilkingtons appear to have found the new Siemens furnaces very satisfactory, particularly after they had substituted slack for coal in the gas producers. William (Roby) Pilkington reported to the Board on 8 June 1865, that

a producer with slack burns $\frac{1}{2}$ less fuel than if worked with coal but does a third less work. There is no doubt that the gas furnace to be used to any advantage should be worked with slack and not coal.

Chances, on the other hand, do not appear to have found the new furnaces so economical. J.H.Chance confided to William (Roby) Pilkington on 28 July 1864:

How does your gas furnace answer? We don't find any saving – fuel is more.

And on 24 October 1865:

How do your gas furnaces go on? Ours remain much the same.[31]

Although Chances were first in the field, they were not so successful in developing gas-firing and – most important – making it pay.

The emphasis at this time was wholly upon cost-reducing innovation rather than upon expansion, which had been the chief feature in the years before the mid-1850s. In 1865 Pilkingtons operated the same number of furnaces as they had done ten years before,[32] and Henry Chance's statement that his own firm, together with Pilkingtons and Hartleys, were making only 340,000 cwt of glass confirms that Pilkingtons could not themselves have been making more than the 150 tons per week – or 156,000 cwt per year – which was their reported production in 1854.[33] The additional demand was obviously being satisfied by Belgian imports. The most the British firms could do, apparently, was to consolidate their position in order to prevent their market from actually shrinking.

With technical changes and economy came the final extinction of crown glass. In 1865 Pilkingtons were still making crown glass at three of their nine furnaces.[34] Two years later the number had been reduced to two. Chances were then making 4,000 tables per week and Pilkingtons 3,600.[35] Soon after this Pilkingtons re-equipped these two furnaces. The last crown house was closed in July 1872.[36]

At a time when economy was the universal watchword, a reduction of a sixth in transport charges to and from the Mersey – and, moreover, the fixing of this reduced rate by Act of Parliament – was a concession of considerable value. The amalgamation of the St Helens Canal and Railway Companies in 1845 had created a transport monopoly, and rates had been advanced since 1845, from 8d to 1s per ton on the canal and from 1s to 2s per ton on the railway. When, in 1864, the London & North Western Railway presented a Bill to Parliament to take over the St Helens Canal and Railway, all the transport users brought pressure to bear to secure a reduction in the rates. By their persistence in committee, they obliged the London & North Western to insert into the Bill a clause fixing the rate to Widnes at 10d per ton on the canal and 1s 8d on the railway.[37] The St Helens and Widnes Traders Association, created in 1864, has successfully defended these concessions ever since.[38]

The second generation of the firm became partners in the 1850s and 1860s. As we have seen, William Pilkington's eldest son, William (Roby) had started work in 1844 at the age of 17. Five years later he was employed in the cutting rooms at four guineas a week. He had become a partner by June 1853, for he was so described in the licence taken out by Pilkingtons for Hartley's rolled plate process. His younger brother, Thomas, who joined the business in 1853, went onto the commercial side. They were joined in the later 1850s by the two sons of Richard Pilkington: William Windle went into the works and Richard joined his cousin Thomas on the sales side. Richard, the youngest of the four, came of age in January 1862. They were all members of a newly-formed Board which held its first meeting on 8 January of that year but a subsequent agreement[39] shows that the two most recent arrivals did not have a financial stake in the business until a few years later. In the year to 30 June 1865 the two seniors each held a 5/12 share and William Pilkington's two sons 1/12 each. The balance between the two branches of the family was then re-dressed. William Windle received his 1/12 in 1865-6 and his younger brother Richard in 1866-7, each senior partner's share being reduced to 9/24 and then 4/12.

Board meetings were held at first on each alternate Thursday but after three meetings it was decided to meet weekly instead. A regular routine was soon worked out, each department being considered in turn. Symptomatic of the new and more methodical régime was the decision to fix the partners' holidays. On 4 January 1866,

some system being thought expedient for regulating the absence of partners, it was resolved that each be allowed a full month (31 days) of absence during the year; that exceptional days be unnoticed, but that if anyone be absent for a continuous number of days such as a week, it shall be taken into consideration against the yearly holiday. . .'

The early minutes of the Board show that the two senior partners, both in their sixties, were content to exercise a general surveillance over the firm's affairs and leave all the active management to their sons, particularly to William (Roby), who had such an advantage over the others both in age and experience. The seniors finally handed over control in 1865.[40] Richard Pilkington, who reached the age of 70 that year, continued to live at the family home, Windle Hall, but his brother, William, removed from Eccleston Hall in 1869 and went to live at Downing Hall, near Holywell in Flintshire. At the age of 69 he had finally retired from business: his removal from St Helens was an admission of the fact. He was still hale and strong and in a farewell message to the firm's employees in

February 1869, expressed the hope that they would all be as fit as he was when they reached his age.[41] On 10 September he was able to report to his brother from Downing that he had enjoyed an excellent day's shooting and could not remember ever having shot better, but was obliged to confess:

> I can no longer do what I once could and am painfully reminded of the infirmities of old age, by over-exertion.

This was one of the last letters in the long correspondence that had passed between the two brothers over a period of 50 years or more. Richard Pilkington died at Windle Hall at the end of December 1869. William Pilkington lived on in Flintshire for almost three years longer. He died on 12 September 1872.[42] Neither of them left a very large personal fortune. Richard Pilkington's will was proved at under £50,000 and his brother's at under £100,000.

The founders of the firm, without any specialised knowledge of glassmaking but with a thorough training in business methods, had saved a small glassworks from bankruptcy and guided it successfully through years of competition when most other window glass firms had gone to the wall. Their sons, recapturing some of the boldness and persistence of earlier years, were soon to turn it into by far the largest glassmaking concern in the country.

Chapter 9

Expansion Once More

THE four partners of the second generation were men of purpose and determination. They are reputed to have possessed to a marked degree all the sternness and strictness particularly associated with Victorian industrialists, and there is clear evidence of these characteristics throughout the Board's minute books. They ruled their business like autocrats, though there are indications that the despotism was not without its moments of benevolence. Efficiency was their watchword: little escaped their hawk-eyed vigilance. Yet it was not efficiency of a penny-pinching kind. Their aim was to run existing plant as efficiently as possible; not to make bigger profits for themselves but to provide resources for further development so that they could diversify, innovate and hold their own in a growingly competitive world. They were always willing to spend money – often very large sums of money – on improvements which seemed at all promising. They experimented with electric light so early as 1880, for instance, and installed a telephone to their colliery in the same year. Windle Pilkington, the technical expert among the partners, was tireless in his advocacy of new and more up-to-date plant. His zeal for spending often led to heated discussions. Tradition has it that the four were often not of one mind and decisions were frequently reached only after periods of considerable tension. This interplay of strong personalities does not appear openly in the minutes; but they do contain hints of what had passed orally before pen was put to paper. In June 1868, for instance:

Building operations. T[homas] P. alluded to the great outlay going on. W.W[indle] P. stated that Rolled Plate kilns built by G.Harris were abt finished at a cost of abt £50 a piece. That the 1st House job will be ended in another three weeks after which the only things in prospect are our new flat kilns and the mixing room job also Tank furnaces.

And in April 1869:

Resolved that it is essential that W.W.P. get a young fellow to act as draughts-man and lieutenant in concentrating the work and bringing it in such form to him, leaving him more free to direct his attention to particular points without being required here, there and everywhere as at present. W.W.P. will look out for such a man accordingly.

Despite – or perhaps because of – internal differences of opinion, the four partners formed an effective team. They all appear to have been men of considerable ability, lived for their business and invested heavily in it. The last quarter of the nineteenth century saw generally falling prices and profits in the world as a whole, and British glass manufacturers suffered particularly because of the growing intensity of Belgian competition. Business men as a class were loud in their complaints about the difficulties of these years. It is a measure of Pilkingtons' success that they were able to thrive and grow rapidly amid these difficulties. As we shall see presently, between 1873 and 1894 the nominal value of the partners' investment increased sevenfold.

The Board ruled their domain through a number of picked men, known as managers. Each glasshouse had its own manager and there were also head managers who supervised departments. Soon after the second genera-tion assumed complete control they became preoccupied with the poor quality of much of the glass that was then being produced. This caused them to look into the efficiency of their labour force – with results which will be discussed in the next chapter which deals with labour relations. They also brought in two men from outside who were to be of con-siderable service to them.

John J. Wenham was engaged in 1869 to take charge of the two outposts, the rolled plate department, which was located in the buildings of the former Eccleston Crown Glassworks, and the patent plate department which was then still located in the old cotton mill. He came from Richard Evans and Company, the Haydock coal proprietors, where he was then earning £2 per week. Pilkingtons came to rely heavily upon him, his salary was steadily increased, and, at the beginning of 1883, he reached a rate of £800 a year with the promise of £1,000 12 months later. His status after over 20 years' service did not, however, prevent the partners from reprimanding him for having taken a month's holiday without permission. His pay was stopped for the period in question and an explanation sought.[1]

Douglas Herman, the other new recruit, became the firm's chemist. George Pilkington had left in the middle of the 1860s, when he set up in business on his own, and the firm had not been able to find a satisfactory replacement for him. In 1870, however, it was decided to enquire at the Royal College of Chemistry, where George Pilkington had been trained, for 'a German if possible'. Herman was strongly recommended by the College as 'a young Englishman though of German extraction . . . a clever young fellow of original thought'. He started at £150 a year and reached £1,000 at the end of 1892, having proved his worth to the firm not only in locating and supervising the supply of sand and dealing with all kinds of chemical problems but also, as we shall see, in introducing Pilkingtons into business activity on the continent.[2]

Wenham's influence was soon felt. Within a few months of his arrival he was recommending the transfer of manufacture from the two outposts to the main works which, he estimated, would save £700 a year. No action was taken at the time but, two years later, in 1871, the Board were obliged to consider removing rolled plate from Eccleston because they wanted to expand this branch, the demand for this sort of glass having become 'excessive'. The Eccleston factory, however, was 'a tumble down place', quite unsuitable for extension; on the other hand, there were obvious advantages in building anew at Grove Street on vacant land immediately to the east of the existing sheet glass factory. The estimated cost of putting up two houses on this site was, however, on Wenham's estimate, about £10,000 and the Board 'discussed at length the policy of such an outlay, T.P. laying stress upon its so much exceeding what was first contemplated'. The expenditure was sanctioned, however, and the first new rolled plate house at Grove Street was in production in May 1872. A second house was put in hand almost at once, together with a warehouse. Some of the bricks from the dismantled Eccleston cone were used in this extension.[3]

In 1872, when rolled plate glass began to be made at Grove Street, the main sheet works there were benefiting from two recent innovations and were on the eve of a major technical advance. The first innovation, the Bievez lehr,* enabled sheets, rapidly cooled by being raised successively

---

* Professor Turner has shown that the word 'lehr', certainly *not* of German origin, was first used in the United States between 1890 and 1900 and later came to replace the older spellings of the word: leer, lier and lear. (W.E.S.Turner, 'That Curious Word "Lehr"', *J.S.G.T.*, xxxiii, No. 154, October 1949.) The first reference to a 'lehr' in the Pilkington Board minutes does not occur until after 1900 but since the word is now universally used in this form, it has been decided to use it throughout this book.

on iron bars and so kept apart, to be annealed in 25 to 30 minutes as against seven or eight hours in the piling kilns. A promising pilot model of the lehr was working at Pilkingtons in May 1869, and, after a visit to see other prototypes in action at Valenciennes in the following month, Windle Pilkington made certain improvements to this model. In its improved form the lehr was a great success and, in March 1870, Pilkingtons secured the exclusive British rights to the patent for £200 a year.[4] The other innovation was an appliance to assist glassmakers in blowing the heaviest of cylinders. It had been invented by Windle Pilkington, assisted by Wenham, and was patented in 1871. Four such machines were in use by the beginning of the following year.[5]

The major advance was the coming of tank furnaces. The advantages of tanks over pots had long been obvious. To feed in raw materials at one end of a tank, melt them as they passed along, and then cool the molten glass to the correct consistency for working by the time it reached the other end, would allow window glass manufacture to become an uninterrupted process. The 24-hour interval while the metal was prepared, inevitable with the existing pot furnaces, could then be avoided and time, fuel and labour saved. The economic benefits were such that a number of inventors in Britain and on the continent of Europe had already tried to develop a satisfactory type of glassmaking tank.

One of the earliest English experimenters was a Birmingham furnace maker called Richardson who carried out trials in 1836–8.[6] He and his successors had all failed, however, because they were unable, using coal as a fuel, to obtain the necessary constant temperature. A French inventor named Pocheron, of Souvigny near Tours, seems to have been the first person to develop a tank furnace capable of making poorer quality glass suitable for bottlemaking. He took out a patent in 1866 and a number of bottlemakers took out licences. Among them was John Cannington, who became a partner in a bottleworks in St Helens about that time. An action for infringement which he brought at the end of 1869 against another local bottle manufacturer, gave James Hartley the opportunity to testify that by then tank furnaces could produce glass which was good enough for making rough plate as well as bottles. (The economics of the matter, however, he did not go into.)[7] In 1868, Pilkingtons tried to make a 'cistern furnace' of the same design as Cannington was using and the next year the firm made another unsuccessful attempt, this time at Eccleston, but very poor glass was produced and the experiment had again to be abandoned.[8] It was left to the brothers Siemens, who, as we have seen, had already developed gas-firing for pot furnaces, to go on to apply gas-firing successfully to tanks. Their experiments at glassworks in Dresden soon reached a stage at which they felt justified in taking out patents. These were dated 1870 and 1872.[9]

Siemens' patent of 1870 reveals that they only took slowly to the un-qualified use of tanks. They were then still considering the possibility of rather fancifully-designed pots as alternatives. In both pots and tanks, according to this first patent, the melting vessels were to be divided into three compartments, for preliminary melting, for further melting, and for working. The materials, when melted, were to pass *over* a barrier erected in the pot or tank, into the second compartment, where they were raised to a higher temperature. The hotter metal was then passed *underneath* the next partition into the working section.[10] In the 1872 patents, however, the use of pots had been forgotten. So, too, had the idea of fixed clay barriers, for it had been found in the interval that these soon became unserviceable. In a provisional specification, dated 18 July 1872, the stationary partitions in the tank were to be

replaced by a number of movable rings made of fire-clay or other suitable re-fractory material which are introduced, by preference, at the working end of the tank and which, floating on the molten glass metal cover the whole of its surface, or nearly so, up to the point where the solid material is introduced. As these rings are gradually dissolved or worn away, they are replaced by fresh rings . . .

The floor and sides of the tank were to be provided with special cooling flues. In the final patent, taken out a few months later, floating bridges made of fire-clay were to be placed transversely across the tank to prevent any imperfectly melted or impure material from reaching the working section.

Pilkingtons were quick to employ Siemens' important new discovery. From the end of May until the beginning of July 1872, Windle Pilkington missed five successive Board meetings. The minutes record that he was in Switzerland. He had, in fact, also gone farther afield. On his return, at a Board meeting held on 10 July, it was decided 'to put a Continuous Tank in the cylinder place next to the flattening kilns upon the principles of the one that W.W.P. has seen working at Dresden'. At the following week's meeting – on the very day that Siemens registered the provisional specifica-tion of the patent in London – it was agreed that Windle Pilkington and William (Roby) Pilkington should 'meet Siemens in London on Monday next to discuss suggestions made to W.P. as to rings and divisions in furnace'.

Nine months elapsed before the tank was ready to be worked. Blowing began on 14 April 1873, and an enthusiastic entry in the minutes on the 17th records that 'the metal at first was slightly seedy from the cullet but has continued to improve and at the present moment is beating any pot furnace on the ground . . . Consider that we ought to seriously discuss the advisability of getting the patent secured to us by Siemens for our especial use and will see Siemens if all be well next week'. This is followed by three months' silence, without a word about the tank or about negotiations with Siemens. It is not until 21 July that the next reference occurs and not until 14 August that the tank began to make glass 'for the second time'. Evidently, soon after 17 April, something happened to the first attempt which suddenly quenched the partners' initial enthusiasm. They were obviously still not very happy about the tank's prospects even after it had been re-lit and had performed successfully for over a month. On 18 September they noted: 'Working so far very satisfactory', but ordered that plans for making further tanks should be so made 'that if tanks failed, pot furnaces (to blow over) could be put up instead'.

What went wrong at the first attempt? James Taylor, then a young man working in the laboratory, has given us the answer. He later recalled that the tank

only worked one week before the bottom was eaten through; the metal leaked and set the place on fire. Nothing further was heard of this experiment for several months . . .[11]

That a second attempt was made was due to the persistence of Windle Pilkington alone. This was explained soon afterwards by one of Pilkingtons' men:

The first tank failing at the end of the first week, Messrs Pilkington decided to abandon them, but after several Board Meetings and Mr Windle Pilkington stating that if they would not make another attempt, he would secure a piece of ground himself and erect one on his own account, they then gave way and agreed to another trial when he succeeded . . .[12]

In fact, at the second attempt, the tank ran non-stop for 97 days. In the original version the side walls and crown of the furnace had been built on top of the refractories holding the molten metal. When the refractories wore out, they collapsed. At the second attempt they were independently supported.[13]

Having built one successful tank, Pilkingtons began to substitute tanks for pots at a rapid rate. A second tank was in use by February 1874. By the end of August 1876, there were nine tank furnaces in operation and the ground was being cleared for a tenth.[14] By February 1877, there were ten such furnaces, an eleventh was being built and two others were described as 'in hand'.[15] In May 1877, 12 tanks were at work and more were being built.[16] The scale on which the patent was being operated was so large that the Siemens brothers agreed to receive royalties at a lower rate than the four shillings per ton of finished glass which they usually charged, itself much lower than the five shillings royalty on their pot furnaces.[17] In February 1877 William Siemens admitted to Henry Chance that 'with regard to royalty . . . Pilkingtons had a preferential arrangement', but he refused to divulge its nature.[18]

The earliest tanks were built with one wide bridge and rings on both sides of it[19] but in 1878 Windle Pilkington ordered that the rings be placed in the gathering end only, for they were thought to do 'a great deal of harm in the form of Knots and String'.[20] There is very little detail about these tanks among Pilkington's papers, but Chances, anxious to find out all they could about their rival's progress, kept a record of statements made by anyone who came to them from St Helens. Early in 1877, Thomas May, a furnace builder at Canningtons, the bottlemakers, who appears to have had an intimate knowledge of the Pilkington furnaces, gave them the information that Pilkingtons were building their tanks longer and narrower than they had done at first. They were at that time using tanks nine feet wide and 36 feet long whereas formerly their tanks had been 12 feet wide and rather shorter in length. These held

2' 6" of melted glass when the tank is new. When the sides are worn thin, less glass is put in lest the sides should burst. The sides require renewal every 3 or 4 months. If they last 4 months it is good working.

The bottom of the tank needed renewing every ten or 11 months. In each case these renewals took about three weeks. May therefore calculated that the furnace could work for 42 weeks in the year.[21] Another informant, who had been a furnaceman at Pilkingtons, told Chances that Pilkingtons' tanks were fed by four producers which consumed about six tons of slack in 12 hours. At first one large flue was used 'for all the tanks and producers and one chimney', but they found the tanks overrunning each other and went back to separate producers and a chimney to each tank.[22] Yet another informant, who signed himself E.J.F., provided a plan of a Pilkington tank, revealing its main details.[23] There were two gathering and four blowing holes. The men worked in three eight-hour shifts, each blower making between 75 and 90 cylinders per shift.[24] Two men looked after the furnace during the day and two during the night.[25]

The lack of details about these early tanks among Pilkingtons' archives is partly explained by the manner in which they were built. Having obtained the original drawings from Siemens, Windle Pilkington made his own modifications and improvements as he went on. These he carried in his own head and did not commit to paper in the first instance. In 1890 S. E. Baddeley, who had just started to work in the drawing office – which then included only one other person – was told to measure up a small melting tank, newly repaired, and to make a drawing of it. He was struck by the unusual procedure of drawing the tank after, and not before, its erection. He made a search of the office for drawings but could find none. He then tackled the foreman bricklayer who informed him that he merely cleared the ground on which the tank was to be built. Windle Pilkington would then come round and trace the outlines with the side of his foot. Informal meetings took place between them afterwards as the work progressed. As the foreman bricklayer put it: 'Mr Windle can do owt'.

The tendency all the time was towards increase in the size of tanks. In 1880 a tank was built with four gathering and eight blowing holes, twice the capacity of the type of furnace which was being used in 1876, at which only four blowers could be employed. After the firm acquired land to the north of Watson Street in 1884 and 1885,[26] three larger tank furnaces were erected there with 12 blowing holes each. By that date there were, in all, 13 smaller tanks for making sheet glass and three larger ones.

The installation of continuous tank furnaces on this scale resulted in a considerable increase in sheet glass production. The largest recorded weekly output before the introduction of tanks was 350,000 sq. ft. The weekly average throughout the year 1877 was just over 500,000 sq. ft and throughout 1887 was just over 900,000 sq. ft. The 1,250,000 mark was passed in the early 1890s and, by the end of the century, production exceeded 1,600,000 sq. ft per week.

With their success in making good glass out of tanks from the outset, Pilkingtons did not need first to make an inferior quality for rolled plate, but went straight for sheet. The first rolled plate tank did not, in fact come into service until June 1878[27] and was soon followed by several more. In 1889 Windle Pilkington began to experiment there with tunnel type lehrs, presumably along the lines of the Tondeur and rod lehrs which had been used in America since earlier in the decade.[28] While the pilot model was being built at St Helens, he worked every day (according to an eye-witness) 'with just his trousers on'. Like the first tank furnace, the lehr was a failure: it blew up. The original aim was to develop a lehr suitable for annealing *cast* plate glass. This was not then achieved but, in 1891, a lehr was being used successfully for *rolled* plate manufacture and others followed.[29]

Output of rolled plate glass grew at a pace comparable with that of sheet, although the increase was not so regular year by year. The annual make rose from 2,750,000 sq. ft to more than 6,000,000 sq. ft in 1884, and then, after some ten years of arrested development, the upward course was continued, output reaching 10,000,000 sq. ft in 1898. In this field Chances maintained a technical ascendancy and this may explain to some extent the interruption in the growth of output at St Helens. In the late 'eighties George and Edward Chance successfully developed a machine, patented in 1884 by Frederick Mason and John Conqueror, whereby the molten glass was poured down an inclined plane and passed between a pair of iron rollers. In 1890 Edward Chance perfected the machine by adding a second pair of rollers, one of this second pair impressing a pattern where required. The manufacture of rolled plate glass became 'of the very first importance' to Chances[30] and the royalties from other companies – including St Gobain – which operated it under licence were considerable. That Windle Pilkington was actively engaged in developing a rolled plate machine at St Helens is evident from the patents he took out in 1891 and in 1899. Pilkingtons also began, in 1895, to make wired glass, using an American patent,[31] and developed this product to great advantage, though Chances were particularly successful with their figured rolled and cathedral.*

By 1870 Pilkingtons were not making much profit out of their Ornamental department, for competition from the small outside firms was fierce. In 1872, special one-off orders were handed over to William Gardner, one of their employees, to handle as a separate concern in part of the Eccleston works, now no longer needed for glassmaking. The firm, however, continued to make standard stained and enamelled designs itself, together with coloured glass. The manufacture of shades, too, was still carried on in a separate shade house. Among the products of the latter were glass cells, required by the infant electrical industry. The first cells were moulded by Pilkingtons in the early 1890s. Corrugated sheet glass was also made by moulding.[32]

All these developments, and particularly the increase in capacity for making sheet and rolled plate glass, called for more ground on which to build additional plant and warehouses. Fortunately Pilkingtons were able to acquire land in the immediate vicinity of their existing works. In the

---

* The term 'cathedral glass' first appears in the early 1840s to describe lightly tinted sheet glass with a slightly textured surface, used mainly in stained glass work. With the coming of rolled glasses, 'cathedral' was applied to those with an indeterminate textured surface 'figured' or 'patterned' being used for rolled glasses with more specific and definite designs (Arctic, Muranese, Flemish etc.). In the twentieth century, the term has also been used in trade names for particular rolled glasses (eg 'Rimpled Cathedral'). The textured surface was a deliberate attempt to imitate the blemishes which gave luminosity to medieval stained glass.

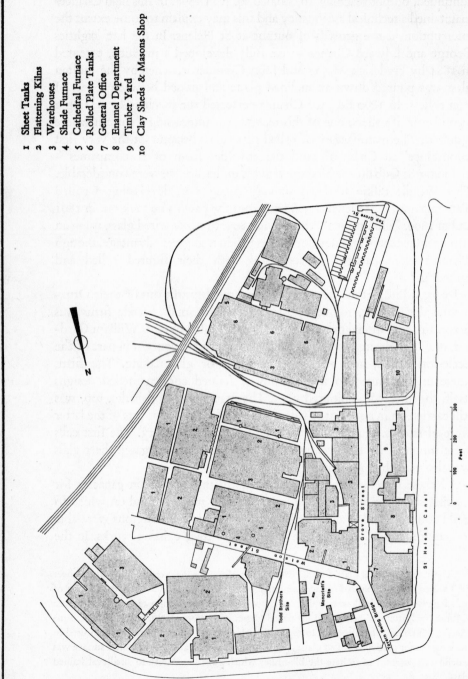

1 Sheet Tanks
2 Flattening Kilns
3 Warehouses
4 Shade Furnace
5 Cathedral Furnace
6 Rolled Plate Tanks
7 General Office
8 Enamel Department
9 Timber Yard
10 Clay Sheds & Masons Shop

Plan 5 Pilkington Brothers' Sheet and Rolled Works in 1892

1870s they bought a number of small factories which lay to the south and east of their own, including the property which had formerly been the Bells' flint glassworks. By the end of the decade they owned the whole of the large triangle bounded by the canal on the west, Watson Street on the north and the Ravenhead branch railway on the south. To this was added land to the north of Watson Street in the mid-1880s – the Jubilee Side as it came to be called.[33] Apart from the Greenbank site, which was acquired later, these have remained the limits of Sheet Works to the present day. Plan 5 shows the extent of the works in 1892.

This impressive phase of growth had been started off during the boom of the early 1870s when, for a few years, British manufacturers were able to obtain better prices for their glass because their Belgian rivals were temporarily handicapped by a coal shortage and high fuel costs.[34] The rising wave of Belgian glass, which had been so marked in the period before 1870, was temporarily stemmed for a few years: the official British returns show that total imports remained at around 420,000 cwt from 1870–2, rising to just over 450,000 cwt in 1873. Retained imports stayed at about 370,000 cwt during these four years.[35] The price of imported glass rose, and in 1873 it was more than 30 per cent higher than it had been in 1870. At the same time Pilkingtons, as colliery proprietors, also shared in the quite phenomenal demand for coal which was a feature of these years.

Siemens' tank furnace was developed just when the economic climate was favourable for its adoption. Pilkingtons seized their opportunity and, by moving quickly and by introducing tanks on a large scale, they obtained preferential rates of royalty. Chances, on the other hand, were content to sit back and collect information. After much pondering, they came to the conclusion that tanks could not produce a sufficiently high percentage of good quality glass to make them a worthwhile investment. This was a major error of judgment – and it was not rectified until 1892.[36] As Walter Lucas Chance later conceded:

It was the adoption of the tank system for making sheet glass by their St Helens competitors ... that finally deprived them of the predominant position which they had hitherto held.[37]

There were other reasons, too: Chances' purchase of the Nailsea works in 1870 turned out to be a mistake, and their venture into plate glass manufacture – to be considered later in this chapter – was a costly failure.[38]

By the end of the 1870s there are clear indications that Pilkingtons had already reached the position at which they could take a more independent attitude towards Chances and Hartleys. Lucas Chance, junior, wrote to Sunderland on 14 January 1878:

I . . . can quite understand your feelings of irritation at the treatment we are receiving at the hands of Pilkington Brothers and if I thought it advisable to consult my own feelings only, I should fall in with your views and say, dissolve the Association. But we cannot always allow our feelings to rule us and I am inclined to think that it will be better to swallow the annoyance and retain the Association than stand upon our dignity and throw it over. There is no doubt that it has been a substantial benefit to us in the past, checking the downward tendency of the time and putting us right when we were getting all abroad. What it has done in the past, it is competent to repeat in the future; although at present it certainly does not show symptoms of producing much fruit.'[39]

Later in the same month he wrote to the Secretary of the Association:

As regards Sheet and Rolled prices, you will have to be careful what you say to Mr Richard, as from what William told me when we last met, neither Richard nor Tom (I think Tom but may have been Will. Windle) care about the Assocn. and would rather be free to do as they like but if you find Mr Richard in a humour to listen to what you have to say, you can tell him that we are dissatisfied with the evasive and offensive manner in which their people reply to our enquiries.[40]

Richard Pilkington may have been in a humour to listen to Gwilliam, but he was apparently in no mood to co-operate, as Lucas Chance reported to Sunderland a few days later:

Mr Richard's conversation with Mr Gwilliam is not of a reassuring character – but he speaks very much as he acts – independently of us all and of all arrangements. I have occasion to be in London on February 7th and will write to William Pilkington and ask him if he can meet me there. I will then explain to him that an Association cannot exist without a free exchange of communications about prices and reports of underselling.[41]

Some rather forthright correspondence also passed from St Helens to Spon Lane about this time. Richard Pilkington wrote to Chances that he was 'startled and horrified' that they were sending out crates of coarse glass. 'If you do this,' the letter went on in schoolmasterly fashion, 'you will soon knock the bottom out of everything in the sheet glass trade. You ought not to allow more coarse metal to be blown than can easily be got rid of in your export orders: such I think you know has always been my idea of proper manufacturing. I hope you will not go and throw away any of your money and take ours along with it.'[42]

This correspondence took place when the building cycle was again beginning to move downwards over most of the country, though activity in London lagged behind that of other towns (p.143) and only peaked in 1881. This may explain the improvement in import prices in the early 1880s; but, after this, building activity fell off, and until the later 1890s there was a continuous fall in prices, interrupted only by a very slight rally in 1891-2. A steep rise in imports soon caused them to fall once more.

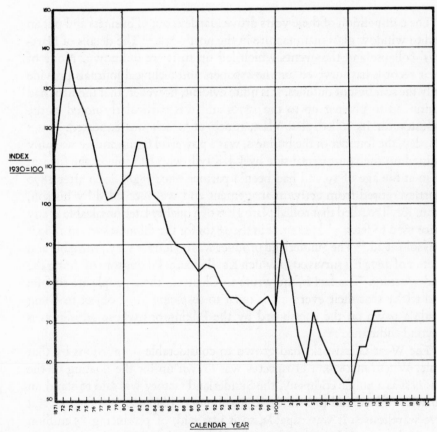

CALENDAR YEAR

INDEX OF PRICE OF WINDOW GLASS

1871-1914

Graph 8 *Source:* K.Maiwald, 'An Index of Building Costs in the United Kingdom, 1845–1938', *Economic History Review*, December 1954

TABLE 13
RETAINED IMPORTS OF WINDOW GLASS, 1889–95 ('000 cwt)

1889	670
1890	789
1891	795
1892	947
1893	881
1894	1,061
1895	987

Source: Trade and Navigation Returns

The competition of these years drove Hartleys out of business and put an end to window glass manufacture in the north-east.[43] The details of Hartleys' collapse and the events which led up to it are unknown. None of their records has survived and newspapers and technical journals provide only the scantiest of outlines. It is quite evident, however, that the firm had continued to prosper up to the 1870s and was particularly noted in the industry for its rolled plate glass, much of which was exported. James Hartley, the founder of the business, was a powerful figure and he was ably assisted on the commercial side by J. J. Kayll, who had joined the firm in 1840 at the age of 19 and had been a partner since 1848. Soon after 1870 Hartley retired from active management and was succeeded by his son, John. Kayll recalled that rolled plate glass of a quality later unsaleable at any price used to fetch 4½d per sq. ft in the 1850s for the thinnest sort; in 1880 it was sold at 2d.[44] The Sunderland product was no longer very profitable and a letter of 1874 has survived in which Kayll accuses Pilkingtons of doing the undercutting. 'The fact is,' he wrote to Chances, 'these people are so false and tricky that their every act is open to suspicion ... I object to being made a pawn on the chessboard by the Pilkingtons whose selfishness is beyond endurance'.[45]

The Wear Glassworks had grown to considerable proportions by that time. When, in 1879, a prospectus was drawn up for the floating of the business as a public company, the Sunderland factory was said to stand on 10 acres of land and to include 10 glasshouses, a Siemens gas furnace and five warehouses. It was capable, so it was said, of producing 15 million square feet of window glass per year. The firm also occupied a 10-acre site at Stourbridge on which stood workshops, packing rooms and offices. It claimed to be the largest maker in England of coloured glass, much in demand at the time for the manufacture of stained glass windows. The intention was to capitalise the business at £150,000. The partners were

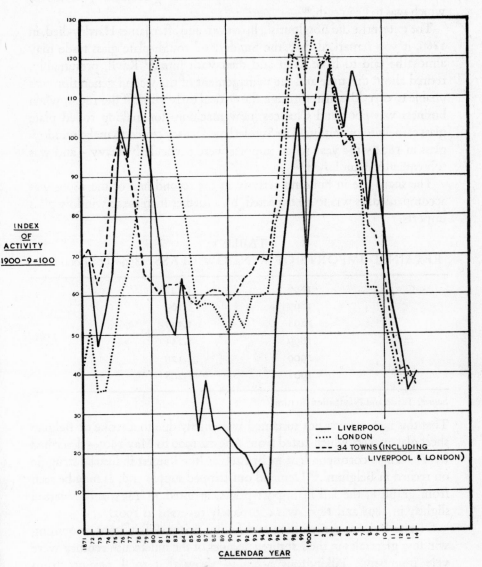

INDEX OF ACTIVITY 1900-9 = 100

CALENDAR YEAR

LIVERPOOL
LONDON
34 TOWNS (INCLUDING LIVERPOOL & LONDON)

INDEX OF HOUSEBUILDING
1871 - 1914

Graph 9 *Source:* B.Weber, 'A New Index of Residential Construction, 1838-1950,' *Scottish Journal of Political Economy*, June 1955.

prepared to sell out to the new company for £110,000, £60,000 of which was to be in cash.[46]

The enterprise did not flourish, however, and after James Hartley died, in 1886, it was remarked that 'the Sunderland rough-plate glass trade may almost be said to have lived and died with him'.[47] Kayll, presumably, retired about this time and the management of the second generation was unable to carry the firm through the critical early years of the 1890s, when business was poor and Chances' new machines for making rolled plate glass came into operation. The Sunderland factory ceased to make window glass in 1894 – the year when imports were particularly heavy – and was subsequently demolished.[48]

The sharp rise in building activity in the second half of the 1890s was accompanied, as was to be expected, by a further increase in window glass imports.

TABLE 14

RETAINED IMPORTS OF WINDOW GLASS, 1896–1901 ('000 cwt)

1896	1,142
1897	1,169
1898	1,347
1899	1,253
1900	1,129
1901	1,208

Source: Trade and Navigation Returns

That this increase was not sustained was chiefly due to a strike of Belgian sheet glassmakers which lasted from August 1900 to May 1901 – described by *The Times* correspondent in Brussels as 'the longest industrial struggle on record in Belgium'.[49] Demand outstripped supply and, as may be seen from graph 8, the fall in import prices, arrested in 1895 and reversed slightly in 1898 and 1899, was completely reversed in 1901.

Despite Belgian competition and falling prices, Pilkingtons' mounting window glass sales in the last three decades of the nineteenth century were very impressive. Pilkingtons' accounts show that total receipts from this source grew from about £150,000 at the end of the 1860s to £250,000 in the later 1870s. There was then a very marked acceleration to £300,000 in 1881/2 (explained by a rise in price as well as by greater output) and an even more remarkable advance to £400,000 in 1888/9 and to close on £500,000 in 1891/2, more noteworthy because it was achieved against a downswing in building activity in Britain and a sharp fall in prices down to 1890, followed by a comparatively minor recovery during 1891/2.

Sheet glass sales, which grew from £86,000 to £401,000 between 1866/7 and 1891/2 account for almost the whole of this success. In 1867 they contributed four-sevenths of the total receipts of the window glass factory: by 1892, four-fifths. Rolled plate sales did well in the 1870s and early 1880s (£18,000 in 1869/70; £89,000 in 1883/4) but then settled down around £60,000 to £70,000 until 1895. Between 1895 and 1901, however, sales doubled and those of cathedral glass, another product of the rolled plate department, which rarely brought in more than £10,000 per year before 1894, were earning over £30,000 by 1899. This is no doubt explained, to some extent, by the technical improvements in this branch of glass manufacture, to which reference has already been made, as well as to the increased market demand.

All these activities brought in substantial profits, as will be seen later in this chapter when we come to consider the financial success of the business during these years. These profits from window glass were, from the mid-1870s, needed to sustain a plate glassworks which Pilkingtons opened. In this branch of manufacture foreign competition was to prove much fiercer and profits much less predictable.

The particular problems of making plate glass by the casting process were considered in chapter one in connexion with the beginnings of the Ravenhead works at the end of the eighteenth century. Great amounts of both fixed and working capital were required. A large casting hall had to be built and equipped, and machinery provided for grinding and polishing; stocks and warehousing were also expensive items with such an expensive product. From the start manufacture was confined to a few large joint-stock companies.

On the continent of Europe the long-established St Gobain Company owned four of the seven factories in France and operated the only two plate glassworks of importance in Germany.[50] It was said that St Gobain 'virtually controlled the manufacture of plate glass on the continent of Europe, and, to a large extent, its production and prices throughout the world'.[51] Plate glass manufacture in Belgium began much later than in France or England. The first factory had been built at Sainte-Marie-d'Oignies (Hainaut) in 1840. A second, at Floreffe (Namur), opened in the mid-1850s, was followed by others at Roux (1869), Courcelles (1870) and Auvelais (1875).[52] By 1880, they were controlled by a syndicate which also operated two of the three French factories outside the St Gobain empire.

In England the various plate glass factories continued to be operated by independent concerns, though it seems likely that, by the 1850s and 1860s, a certain amount of discussion was taking place among them. Of the companies formed in the first half of the nineteenth century – some five in number – two had built their works in the St Helens area, the other three were located on the Tyne, on the Thames[53] and in the Birmingham area. Of the two St Helens factories, one, at Pocket Nook, was owned by the Union Plate Glass Company and the other, at Sutton Oak, by the London and Manchester Plate Glass Company.[54] By the later 1860s, these two factories and the pioneer at Ravenhead which had been considerably extended about twenty years before[55] were said to be responsible for two-thirds of Britain's output.[56] Ravenhead had by then overreached itself, however, and in 1868 the factory was taken over by the London and Manchester company on a 99-year lease at a rent of £6,200 per year.[57] Ten years later it was claimed that the works at Ravenhead and Sutton Oak were producing more than half the total plate glass output in the kingdom.[58]

In 1873 Chances and Pilkingtons, who had both been previously bound by the rolled plate agreement not to make this kind of glass,[59] decided to take it up. The strong upswing of this particular trade cycle, marked by a great boom in iron and coal, brought great prosperity to Pilkingtons even though the housebuilding index shows a fall in 1873 (Graph 9). Net profit reached just over £50,000 in 1871/2 and over £93,000 in 1872/3. This represented a return on capital (£150,503) of 62¼ per cent in the latter year.[60] The Board's first minuted discussion concerning entry into plate glass occurred on 13 February 1873:

Plate Works. Discussed the question of site and general question at considerable length. W.P. and W.W.P. went last Saturday over a site near Blackbrook [two miles to the east of St Helens] which seemed very likely and we decided at once to make further inquiry as undoubtedly this is the time to go into that Trade.

They eventually decided on a site, not at Blackbrook, but close to Gerard's Bridge, about a mile from their existing works (see p. 9). The elevated position, on a slope at Cowley Hill, was a particularly suitable one. The grinding process left much waste sand, and this could be disposed of more easily from the grinding shed when it was situated at a little height. The extent of the site – over 120 acres – left plenty of lower-lying space in the immediate vicinity for lodging this sand. The railway from St Helens to Rainford, which passed by, provided good rail communication (see pp. 150–1).

Pilkingtons discovered from Gwilliam, the secretary of the window glass manufacturers' association, that H.C.Lockhart, manager of the Birmingham Plate Glassworks, was likely to be interested in taking charge of their own new venture. The Birmingham Company was then the property of two men who were anxious for 'some Capitalists to come forward' and buy them out. (The London and Manchester Company had been interested and Chances were, in fact, soon to take over.) With financial control of the Birmingham works hanging in the balance, Pilkingtons were probably justified in their conclusion that Lockhart's position was 'evidently not a permanent one'. He was persuaded to come to St Helens with the offer of a five-year agreement rising to £1,500 per year, and started to superintend building at Cowley Hill on 1 October 1873.[61]

The factory took about three years to build, the partners keeping a watchful eye on the cost. In April 1875, for instance, finding that George Harris the builder had apparently 'put a heavy profit upon the work and other extras', they decided to take such work into their own hands whenever they could 'and at the same time to overhaul his contract throughout as closely as possible'.[62] The factory consisted at first of a large casting hall with three 30-pot furnaces in the centre and annealing kilns along each side. Adjoining the casting hall were a matching room, a grinding shed, smoothing and polishing rooms and a warehouse. At the end of March 1876, Lockhart was instructed to start recruiting the necessary labour, 'the wages to be based on the Sutton rates [London and Manchester Plate Glass Company], but men not to be taken from Sutton'. (Pilkingtons seem to have been on very good terms with the Congregationalist William Blinkhorn, manager of the Sutton factory.) Much of the specialised labour which was taken on at Cowley Hill came, as Lockhart had done, from Birmingham. When Chances wrote to all the other plate glass concerns complaining of this poaching, Blinkhorn sent them an unhelpful reply and passed the news on to Pilkingtons.[63] In order to accommodate the newcomers, cottages owned by Pilkingtons were 'overhauled', others were bought, and yet others were specially built.[64]

The building and equipping of the new works involved the partnership in considerable new investment at a time when it was also putting down tank furnaces at its existing window glass factory. The total capital employed, according to the accounts, grew from £150,503 in June 1873 to £303,136 in June 1876. Fortunately window glass profits remained high in these three years – £78,838, £76,464 and £85,530 making £240,832 altogether – more than enough to provide the extra £153,000 required. One branch of the family, William (Roby) and Thomas, wanted to take the opportunity to turn the business into a limited company and to borrow some of the capital. (Thomas, it will be recalled, had complained about the cost of the new rolled plate factory; presumably he was eager to have more profits distributed to the partners and fewer put

THE GLASSMAKERS

back into the business. He had six young children to support by 1876 and his brother ten, some of whom had reached marriageable age.) The other branch, William Windle and Richard, would not contemplate incorporation under any circumstances and, although they too had young families – William Windle had five children and Richard four – favoured taking out only a fixed sum every year in order to support the family, thus enabling the whole business expansion to be financed from profits. The difference of opinion on this crucial issue almost caused the dissolution of the partnership.

Although the minutes maintain a discreet silence on the matter, a letter from Richard Pilkington to his mother, undated but from internal evidence written at the end of December 1875, reveals the extent of the crisis. It is worth quoting in full, for it conveys the tense atmosphere of the occasion. Business is not without its drama and family ties do not prevent quarrels. Nor, apparently, were some lady members of the Pilkington family kept in ignorance of what was going on when the family finances were concerned. This is a side of business history about which more needs to be known but on which the evidence is usually unavailable.

My dear Mama,

It would be wrong not to write to you, to tell you of what passed here.

On the day I saw you I went in Liverpool and saw Hawkins [partner in the legal firm, Forshaw and Hawkins]. Pears, their [William and Thomas's] lawyer,[65] had come down to Liverpool on purpose to try and settle.

I ought perhaps, as you are so very much interested and this is the completion of what has been a two month struggle, to tell you how the end has come. On Saturday we told Cousin Will that he could not go to Vienna unless he signed. He said, 'If you pay my courier I will stay.' We said, 'No. Your courier is your own affair and we will not'.

On Saturday we had a consultation in Hawkins' office which resulted in him writing to Pears to say such was the utmost we could do and the matter must be settled. On Monday I saw both Cousins and they were then told that if I sent to London with Hawkins to see Pears, it must be settled one way or the other. In the afternoon of Monday Tom received a telegram from Pears saying he would be down and they must meet him in L'pool and bring their Cousin (that was me). We went in. Hawkins saw Pears. They conceded everything but the Plate Glass Clause. Will and I saw Hawkins on Tuesday and agreed with him that all must go up to London and settle. We met at the Westminster Palace at 4. We began at 4.30, Pears, Hawkins and we four. We sat for 3 hours. Pears was very stiff about the Plate Glass Clause, so was Tom most obstinate. We were also stiff. They went out of the room at nearly 8 o'clock, came back, said they would not consent. Hawkins buttoned his coat and said, 'Then there's the other alternative', meaning dissolution. I then broke in and reproached them with not meeting us. They then agreed to the clause with no alteration, which Hawkins had suggested before they left the room.

Hawkins and Sinclair drew up the clause in an agreement. We went to the Palace Hotel this morning. Pears came in first. Hawkins and he read it through. Then the Cousins came in and at last Pears said, 'I think it's alright. I must explain to my clients.' We went out and waited a long time. We began to fear they were again trying to strike the clause or remodel it, taking the strength out of it, but we now think Cousin Will and Pears were convincing Tom. At last we were called back. Then Hawkins and Pears talked and we agreed to some verbal alteration, which was fair and practically left the clause as we previously had it. We then signed. We got everything we asked for and in addition the plate glass clause which, if they had agreed to our propositions in the first instance, would not have been put in. Their trying to force the Limited Company on us has done them no good but made them consent to this Plate Glass Clause. The battle, I believe, is now over and *won*. Tom was very obstinate but, we believe, made to see that he must give way.

With best love

    Your affec. son
      Richard Pilkington

better say nothing to aunt except that everything has been settled most amicably as we wished it.

Cousin Will met us several times during the discussion very fairly. Tom stuck most obstinately to his point of a recognized power to borrow. We would not concede this.[66]

The new partnership agreement, dated 29 December 1875, was deemed to date from the firm's financial year beginning 1 July 1873 when the investment in plate glass began. During the 21-year period between then and 1894 only £12,000 was to be divided among the partners annually (£3,000 each) and the rest ploughed back into the business. Each partner was to devote his whole time to it and was to receive £20 a week for doing so.[67] (This sum was doubled after the plate works were opened) Although £5,000 a year was then a handsome income, it would have been very much higher if William (Roby) and Thomas had had their way. Here some historians may perceive the continuing influence of religion upon the spread of capitalism. William Windle and Richard came from the branch which had remained staunchly nonconformist. They remained pillars of the Congregational Church in St Helens to which their father had

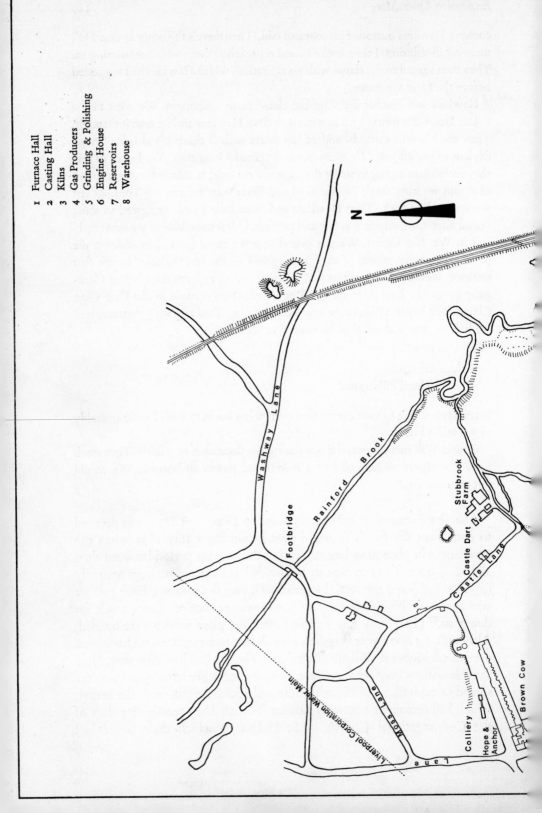

1 Furnace Hall
2 Casting Hall
3 Kilns
4 Gas Producers
5 Grinding & Polishing
6 Engine House
7 Reservoirs
8 Warehouse

Washway Lane

Rainford Brook

Footbridge

Liverpool Corporation Water Main

Noss Lane

Castle Lane

Castle Dart

Stubbrook Farm

Colliery

Hope & Anchor

Brown Cow

N

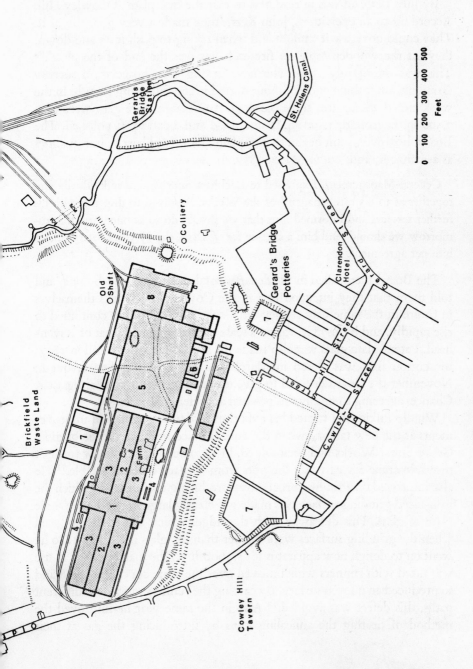

Plan 6 Pilkington Brothers' Plate Works in 1876

Brickfield
Waste Land

Cowley Hill Tavern

Old Shaft

Colliery

Gerards Bridge Station

Gerard's Bridge Potteries

St. Helens Canal

Clarendon Hotel

Hill Street

Cowley Street

Abbey Street

Gerard Street

0 100 200 300 400 500

Feet

devoted so much of his time.[68] What is beyond dispute is that it was the younger partners who got their way in the end. In 1875 William (Roby) was nearly 50 and Thomas 40. William Windle and Richard were in their mid-30s.

By July 1876, all was in readiness to cast the first plate at Cowley Hill. According to an eyewitness, John Kerr, 'they made a very poor job of it. They could not stow it straight and when trying to push it up and down, they set the wooden table on fire and that was the end of the plate'.[69] This was on 14 July 1876. The next casting was, however, a success. Grinding, smoothing and polishing started in the following month. In the week ended 26 August, some 9,000 sq. ft of rough plate glass were cast, 7,500 sq. ft ground, 4,500 sq. ft smoothed and 2,000 sq. ft polished. The Board, however, soon began to complain about Lockhart's poor qualities as a manager, and, on 20 March 1877, matters came to a head:

General Management. Expressed to Lockhart our opinions individually and together as to his mismanagem^t of the Works. Resolved to dispense with his further services and informed him that we should do so at once, and that to-morrow we should send him a cheque for £2,250, the 1½ years' salary due to him per agreement.

The Board then called in the departmental managers, one by one, and told them that they intended to run the Cowley Hill works themselves in future in the same way as they did Grove Street. Output continued to rise rapidly, and by 1878 it was on a scale comparable with that of Raven-head. Patent plate glass was also made for a time at Cowley Hill in 1877: the cotton mill was closed in March and the men transferred, but in November the Board decided to give up making patent plate altogether, Chances agreeing to supply this product at preferential rates.[70]

Windle Pilkington turned his attention to devising technical improve-ments at the new factory when the tank furnace problems at the original Grove Street Works had been solved. In 1879 he invented a new form of movable crane for carrying the pots from furnace to casting table.[71] He also improved the grinding process by introducing machinery in which the iron-faced grinding surface was made sufficiently large to cover the whole plate of glass. This did away with the ridges which had been produced when the grinding surfaces were smaller than the glass itself.[72] In 1880 he went on to design new apparatus for smoothing. The machine then in use was fitted with runners which moved over the same curvilinear path and so produced an uneven surface. By causing the runners to traverse different paths, this defect was avoided.[73] Also in the same year he improved the method of heating the annealing kilns by introducing the gas at their crown and thus providing a more uniform heat throughout.[74] A patent which he took out in 1886 envisaged the use of an overhead gantry for transporting the pots to the casting table, a clear advance upon the device he had patented in 1879. [75]

A diary kept from 1885 by J.H.Dickinson reveals how closely the partners watched technical changes elsewhere in the industry at this time. There are many entries concerning visits to Liverpool to consult J.T.King, who advised them on matters of patent law. Pilkingtons, for instance, decided to try out three foreign grinding discs which had been seen working near Charleroi to see if they were an improvement on the fixed tables then in use.[76] Two years later they opted for the more complicated machinery patented in Britain in 1888 by a Belgian, Melchior Malevez.[77] His circular discs, instead of grinding and polishing in two separate processes as the earlier foreign discs had done, enabled the glass to be ground, smoothed and polished on the same movable table. (For technical details, see Appendix 6.)

On 14 October 1889, Malevez himself visited the works and had conferences with Richard and Windle Pilkington, J.T.King and Douglas Herman. On 17 and 18 October the four men were in London conferring with Malevez and his agents, and soon afterwards Pilkingtons acquired the patent rights.[78] The long process of installing Malevez machinery was begun at Cowley Hill during the summer of 1890,[79] and the new equipment, four polishers and six grinders, powered at first by steam engines, shafting and rope drives, was in use by the end of the year. It proved more expensive than the old method at first, but, by February 1893, was starting to pay its way. By November 1893, the old method had been entirely superseded. While the Malevez equipment was being installed at Cowley Hill, Windle Pilkington, as we have noticed (page 136), was trying to develop a lehr which would anneal plate glass, but his attempt had to be abandoned on account of the great expense involved.[80] Pilkingtons were not to have a continuous lehr at Cowley Hill for another ten years. Tanks could not be used for making plate glass and it was not until after the First World War that a satisfactory equivalent was devised to replace pot furnaces.

The weekly production figures (Table 15 p.154) show how Pilkingtons succeeded in making an increased quantity of polished plate from their rough cast. Their sales of plate glass rose from £104,000 in 1878/9 to £214,000 in 1887/8, generally in proportion to polished plate production. Profitability, however, was erratic, as we shall see when we come to examine the firm's financial progress later in this chapter. But Pilkingtons' relative success at Cowley Hill was in striking contrast to Chances, utter failure at Birmingham. The Birmingham works had to be closed for 15 months while costly new plant was installed, and when this came into operation, late in 1875, the glass produced was of poor quality and there was a high proportion of breakages. In 1876 the factory ran at a loss of £20,000. With prices falling, it was decided to stop production altogether in July 1877. Glass was never cast there again and the works were eventually disposed of in 1889. The venture was later described by the historian of Chances as 'disastrous'.[81]

TABLE 15

AVERAGE WEEKLY PRODUCTION OF PLATE GLASS
AT THE COWLEY HILL WORKS (SQ. FT) 1876-88

		Cast	Ground	Smoothed	Polished
Month of December	1876	21,000	18,000	16,000	14,000
January–December	1877	32,750	22,100	20,810	20,730
,,	1878	48,600	32,120	28,410	28,100
,,	1879	59,400	43,600	38,100	37,550
,,	1880	69,000	51,900	46,400	45,000
,,	1881	77,700	56,900	50,900	49,000
,,	1884	76,700	67,300	63,800	61,000
,,	1885	78,400	71,500	68,500	65,600
,,	1886	78,800	70,600	67,300	65,000
,,	1888	83,100	75,800	73,000	70,900

While Pilkingtons were establishing themselves as producers of plate glass and increasing their sales, more and more of this type of glass was also being imported from the continent. The market was growing quickly. Greater competition in business generally and particularly in retail trade – the growth of department stores and multiple shops, for instance – was accompanied by more attractive displays of goods and, to show these off to best advantage, plate glass windows became the fashion. Large mirrors also gained a larger market; plate glass in this form was an essential feature of the late Victorian gin palace, for example. The market for plate glass, in fact, was growing in the last quarter of the nineteenth century in much the same way as the market for window glass had grown 25 years before. Foreign manufacturers made every effort to cater for this growing demand – and, by cutting retail prices, to stimulate it – in much the same way as they had done, and were still doing, with window glass.

As the graph on the next page shows, imports grew quite rapidly between 1873 and 1878. They did not move upwards again until after 1887 when they rose more steeply than they had done in the 1870s. The figures in Table

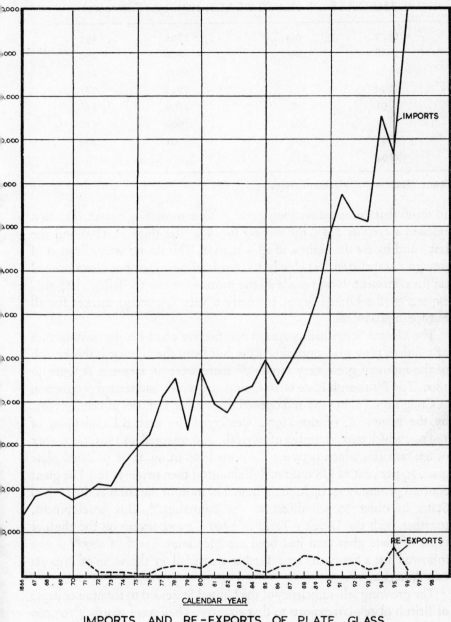

CALENDAR YEAR

IMPORTS AND RE-EXPORTS OF PLATE GLASS.

1866-1896

Graph 10 *Source:* British Trade and Navigation Returns

TABLE 16

IMPORTS OF PLATE GLASS, 1887–1901 ('000 CWT)

1887	99	1895	193
1888	109	1896	259
1889	128	1897	252
1890	156	1898	281
1891	176	1899	246
1892	164	1900	316
1893	162	1901	464
1894	211		

Source: Trade and Navigation Returns

16 show that competition then grew in four mounting waves. The first reached a crest in 1891, the second in 1894, the third in 1896 and the last – and by far the highest of all – in 1901. This strong intensification of foreign competition was chiefly the result of new factories being opened on the continent. It was made all the more severe by the fall in plate glass exports to the United States, formerly a very important market for all European producers.

The United States had possessed no effective plant for the manufacture of polished plate glass until the 1870s, but from then onwards this branch of the industry grew very rapidly;[82] there were 16 factories at work in 1890. The Pittsburgh Plate Glass Company, which had started production at Creighton, Pa. in 1883 and opened three other factories in Pennsylvania by the beginning of the 1890s, weathered the financial difficulties of 1893–5, which sank a number of its rivals, and emerged, in 1895, the owner of ten factories which between them made 20 m. sq. ft of polished plate glass, 80 per cent of US output.[83] (Pilkington then made $3\frac{1}{2}$ m.) The giant concern promptly set up jobbing houses in most of the cities of the United States in order to sell direct to the consumer.[84] This development, together with the Dingley Tariff of 1897 – more severe on the cheaper types of plate glass than had been the McKinley Tariff of 1890[85] – was followed for a few years by a further sharp fall in the value of imports into America.

The growing self-sufficiency of the United States led to the utter collapse of British plate glass exports to that country. They were worth £107,000 per year in 1880–4, £89,000 in 1885–9, £18,000 in 1890–4, and a mere £3,000 in 1895–9. Competition elsewhere was intensified and total British plate glass exports to all foreign markets slumped from £251,000 per year in 1885–9 to £93,000 in 1895–9.[86] Belgium, the United States' chief

TABLE 17

AMERICAN IMPORTS OF CAST PLATE GLASS, 1890–1900

('000 DOLLARS)

Year	Polished but unsilvered	Polished and silvered
1890	931	250
1891	1,351	183
1892	888	119
1893	830	154
1894	450	75
1895	684	16
1896	773	34
1897	285	22
1898	162	·5
1899	233	·4
1900	226	12

Source: US Treasury, Bureau of Statistics cited in US Census Reports, 1900, vol. IX, 985

supplier, also suffered severely, and this caused the Belgians to ship more to Britain than they would otherwise have done. According to the official Belgian returns, plate glass exports to the United States were worth 7½ million francs in 1890 and only 1½ million francs in 1898; in the same period, Belgian shipments to Britain rose from 5 to 15 million francs.[87] The British manufacturer not only lost an important transatlantic market as a result of the growth of the American industry, but also had to contend with much heavier Belgian competition at home.

One British company after another collapsed. The Tyne Plate Glass Company failed in 1891, having lost the whole of its capital of £89,000.[88] The Union Plate Glass Company Ltd, which owned the Pocket Nook works at St Helens, began to install Malevez machinery at the end of 1891 but closed its factory at the beginning of the following year. Production of plate glass apparently re-started, but seems to have stopped for good in 1897.[89] The London and Manchester Company, capable of making 65,000 sq. ft of glass per week at its Sutton Oak works and a further 26,000 sq. ft at Ravenhead, also introduced Malevez machinery; but this did not prevent their losing nearly £83,000 in the two years ending August 1893, and £60,000 in the following year. The Sutton works were closed for a period and the lease of Ravenhead surrendered.

While cheap foreign glass was either destroying or crippling all the other English plate glass concerns, Pilkington, by contrast, were extending their Cowley Hill factory. A new casting hall was built in 1896–7 and other extensions made between 1893 and 1897. Kilns of a new type were installed, capable of annealing glass in three, instead of four, days. Electrical 'transporters' were ordered in 1893 and 'electric casting machinery' for the new casting hall a few years later; Pilkingtons was one of the early firms to use electricity as a source of power.[90] At first, they had to employ handymen as electricians, such a division of labour being then a novelty. Among the wiremen early in the present century was a young man called Walter Citrine.

Both the Ravenhead and Sutton Oak works came to life again for a time in the mid-1890s, the former controlled by their owners, the British Plate Glass Co. Ltd, and the latter operated by a new limited company which took its predecessor's name. But the much fiercer foreign competition at the turn of the century soon drove them both out of business for good. Pilkington acquired their property. They bought Ravenhead from the British Plate Glass Co. Ltd in 1901 for £93,000, and, when they had 'knocked off the "fancy" things made there',[91] these works were used to supplement the capacity of Cowley Hill. The Sutton Oak works of the London and Manchester Plate Glass Co. Ltd, reported to be losing £200 per week towards the end of 1902, stopped production in June 1903.[92] The factory fell into Pilkington's hands for £82,000 in July 1905.[93] It was used only for warehousing, being disposed of later for purposes other than glassmaking.

Edward Ford, son of one of the founders of the Pittsburgh Company, visited St Helens on 21 April 1893. The entry in his diary for that day indicates the extent to which Pilkingtons had come to depend on the Malevez machines, and Ford's verdict on their Cowley Hill works was very favourable. It also gives us a rare glimpse of Windle Pilkington.

This morning we took the 9 o'clock train from our station, to St Helens, to see Messrs Pilkington. Took cab and drove to their office. Sent in our cards, were shown into the waiting room, when in about 20 minutes in came Col. William Windle Pilkington, who shook hands and received us very well, but although very polite and pleasant, I thought he looked as though he would rather we had not come. But after talking a half hour, he seemed rather to enjoy our visit and, as I thought, softened, when finally he said, 'Well, I suppose you gentlemen would like to visit our Works. My two Brothers [sic] are away, and, as you know, we are very strict in this matter. I hardly know what to say to you. I don't like to turn you away, and at the same time I don't want the responsibility of admitting you.' After talking awhile longer, he said, 'Well, I will go and consult two of the Younger members of the Firm who are in the office', and out he went.

In a short time he returned smiling and said, 'Well, I will have to take the responsibility all myself, so, if you like, we will start.' He called his carriage, which he says he always keeps at the Works for running from one works to the other. We all three got in. He made us take the back seat. He took the front, and gave the order to drive to the Plate Works, over a mile distant. He conducted us personally all through; first to the Casting, where we saw two or three pots cast, thence to the Grinding, Polishing and Ware Rooms, where they have a very large stock of Finished Plate. These Works are being entirely remodeled i.e. the machinery. They believe in the best, and, as he said, 'paid dearly for it. But it was much more economy to do it now than to bugger along for a time longer and, in the meantime, allow their competitors to pass them.' So they paid Mallevez [*sic*] $100,000 for his Patent, for England and America . . .

They have 12 Mallevez Machines (Polishers) running, each producing 4,000 sq. ft *per week*, and are putting on eight more, which will give them 20 polishers, and from which they expect to get 80,000 feet of glass *per week* . . . Mr P. seemed very anxious to sell us the sole right to the Mallevez Patent in America, he claiming it to be *the Key* to the business in England, and whoever bought the American right would find it the same in America.

The Pilkington Brothers are the most enterprising Plate Glass men, and are the most progressive we have met in Europe, and I think they are in the lead.[94]

Technical progress at Cowley Hill goes far to explain why Pilkingtons survived in plate glass manufacture when all their longer-established British rivals succumbed; but it is by no means the whole explanation. Despite their technical progressiveness, even Pilkingtons were making losses approaching £50,000 per year on their plate glass in the years 1893 and 1894. It was the profit on their other products, notably sheet glass, and a rising income from rents due to the partners from the works and other properties, which kept their whole business profitable.

Capital invested at Cowley Hill was much less remunerative in this period than that invested in the original works at Grove Street where sheet, rolled plate and other varieties of window glass were made. As will be seen from Table 18, in the 18 years between 1876/7 and 1893/4, Cowley Hill made losses in eight, totalling (in round figures) £141,000, and profits for the remaining ten totalling £281,000. Grove Street, on the other hand was consistently profitable, in seven years to the tune of about £100,000 or more, and brought in a total net profit over the period of £1,347,000. The fact, however, that £171,000 of the £281,000 profit at Cowley Hill was made in the three years 1887/8, 1888/9 and 1889/90, when the new grinding and polishing machinery was coming into use,

TABLE 18
PILKINGTON BROTHERS, NET PROFIT 1867/8-1893/4

Year to 30 June	Sutton Sheet Works, Grove Street	Cowley Hill Plate Works	Rents – Works and Properties	Interest and Investment (or loans)	Income Tax, Colliery Etc.	Total Net Profit
	£	£	£	£	£	£
1868						22,513
1869						5,618
1870						3,741
1871						11,328
1872						50,044
1873						93,667
1874						78,838
1875						76,464
1876						85,530
1877	39,393	−6,388	14,109	—	−1,100	46,014
1878	19,240	−11,158	16,159	—	226	24,467
1879	19,265	1,312	17,026	—	−558	37,045
1880	56,596	−4,450	16,145	—	−551	67,740
1881	36,250	−4,886	17,062	—	−572	57,626
1882	66,083	19,110	19,050	—	−770	103,473
1883	85,926	29,740	26,303	−2,305	−8,000	131,664
1884	96,010	14,073	26,514	234	−11,235	125,596
1885	98,558	13,611	26,351	2,164	−10,000	130,684
1886	62,078	11,800	26,540	2,249	−12,017	90,650
1887	73,243	21,004	26,861	3,298	−18,183	106,223
1888	98,332	51,674	26,231	3,744	−18,087	161,894
1889	98,464	63,756	26,318	4,289	−20,648	172,179
1890	129,674	55,488	26,840	4,880	−14,959	201,923
1891	120,681	−1,799	27,498	6,319	−16,169	136,530
1892	115,283	−15,598	27,620	7,513	−18,687	116,131
1893	83,689	−47,947	28,004	8,448	−23,396	48,798
1894	48,373	−48,359	28,169	9,756	−16,429	21,510

Source: Pilkington Accounts

was a promising sign. The subsequent heavy losses in plate during the
early 1890s was due to the unusually severe competition from abroad,
particularly Belgium, caused by the switch of their exports from America
to a duty-free British market at a time when house-building was slack.

TABLE 19
PROFIT ON PILKINGTON SUTTON (SHEET) GLASS WORKS, GROVE STREET AND COWLEY HILL (PLATE) GLASS WORKS, 1894/5–1900/1

Year ended 30 June	£ Grove Street	£ Cowley Hill
1895	54,536	−4,579
1896	99,962	49,197
1897	114,493	53,235
1898	168,974	35,747
1899	199,689	25,793
1900	237,705	41,147
1901	275,892	54,303

Source: Pilkington Accounts

There was a strong suggestion that Cowley Hill would perform better when the building cycle began to move up again, and this is what happened during the building boom which reached a peak in 1899 and remained active for the next few years.

The extent of Pilkington's* progress is to be judged by a comparison of their manufacturing costs at Cowley Hill with those at Ravenhead after it fell into Pilkington's hands in 1901. Between 1895 and 1903, during which time a further £100,000 was invested at Cowley Hill, costs there per foot were reduced from 9·17d to 7·36d.[95] At Ravenhead – where according to the Pilkington Board, kilns were 'wrong and out of date and everything else'[96] – the cost of production in 1902 was as high as 11·75d and in 1903 12·73d.[97]

The meagre total profits of Chance Brothers & Co. Ltd, details of which have become available following Pilkington's much more recent acquisition of that business, also indicate the degree to which Pilkington had forged ahead. Chances made overall losses of £100 in 1892, £80 in 1893, £6,187 in 1894 and £2,321 in 1895. The company then became profitable again to the extent of £10,000 in 1896; but even during the building boom around 1900 it was only making £20,000 to £25,000 net profit per year. On this however, it was able to pay its shareholders a tax-free dividend of 9 or 10 per cent.[98] Having failed in plate glass and fallen behind in sheet (because of its reluctance to put down tanks), it was now a far smaller concern than Pilkington and had come to depend chiefly upon its rolled plate manufacture, on which it had contrived to keep ahead of the times technically.

* For the singular use of the name from the 1890s, see note p.483.

G

Edward Chance's improvement of the machine for making rolled plate glass (see page 137) brought his company into closer touch with the St Gobain company in France. In July 1892 Chances licensed their newly-patented double-rolled machine to that company but restricted sales of glass made upon it to the continent of Europe and the French colonies.[99] This association between Chances and St Gobain was soon to grow as we shall see. Soon after this Pilkingtons, too, became interested in glassmaking in France and in a much more direct way. They obtained a controlling interest in a small plate glass factory there.

This factory was brought to Pilkingtons' notice by their chemist, Douglas Herman. At the end of 1890 he had received an invitation to invest 'in a new works about to be erected near the Belgian frontier at Maubeuge in France', which he passed on to the Board. The partners followed up the prospectus of the company, a French concern with head office in Paris, and decided to invest in it. By the beginning of 1892 they had put over £26,000 into the undertaking, which then consisted of one 16-pot furnace and five grinding and four polishing machines. The venture, as was to be expected, lost money at first but then began to return a modest profit. While the partners were, as usual, loud in their complaints of inefficient management and, in 1898, were wondering whether to sell the works, they eventually decided against such a course. Maubeuge provided a return on capital, it was a source of information about what was happening on the continent, and it was to prove a valuable diplomatic asset.[100]

It was at Herman's suggestion, too, that Pilkington became interested in a Belgian sandfield in order to safeguard their supplies of silver sand, of which their annual consumption was about 13,000 tons by 1900. At the end of that year Herman drew the Board's attention to the recently-formed Anglo-Belgian Silver Sand Company which owned property at Moll, 28 miles north-east of Louvain. By 1903 Pilkington had invested £7,000 in the concern and had lent it a further £11,000 on mortgage. The company passed into Pilkington's hands completely in 1907.[101]

Pilkington's increased efficiency in manufacturing was matched by an enterprising sales policy at home and, particularly, abroad. The growing volume of business made the existing office accommodation too small and a new head office was opened in 1887. It was designed by J. Medland and Henry Taylor, Manchester architects who specialised in churches. Its central feature was a lofty, rectangular, single-storey general office with a dome-like roof, a clerestory and massive pillars. Orders were processed by busy clerks working at long tables on the floor beneath. Smaller offices, occupied by senior staff, opened off at one end, and another set from a balcony immediately above. Leading from one of the longer sides of this hall, through heavy oak doors, were the rather dark and austere, though spacious and panelled, offices of the partners. Through a diamond pane of glass in each of these doors, the family heads of the business could be seen at work by their employees. Their comings and goings, as they entered or left their sanctums by way of the general office, were known to all.[102]

New warehouses were also needed at St Helens. (Compare Plans on pp. 109 and 138.) Elsewhere, new warehouses were added to the four existing ones (Birmingham, Bristol, Leeds and Sheffield) at Glasgow (1868), Bradford (1872), Newcastle (1880) and Nottingham (1885).[103] In London Pilkingtons continued to sell for a long time only direct to glass merchants and, though they had an office at 26 Bridge Street, Blackfriars, there was no London warehouse until 1889. The firm's general warehousing policy came under review at a meeting of the Board on 2 July 1874:

Discussed at length the policy of our warehouse system and whether it is advisable to enlarge their spheres and add lead or any other branches to glass or whether it would be better to contract their range and reduce them to a simple office like our London one. Admitted that when our glass wanted first introducing to the market then a secured outlet like a whouse was a *good* thing but when our make is in the market and is liked and sought, the expediency of a whouse is naturally altered.

No action was then taken but, a year later, when the Birmingham warehouse had shown a small net loss, it was decided that

the orders from the country should be sent as much as possible, in fact entirely, direct to the works, keeping the whouse as much as possible as a store for the use of the town and in the town to stop retail and deal as exclusively as possible with the 1st and 2nd class men only.

The Bristol warehouse, too, was to be used 'as much as possible as a town store'. Glasgow was put on the same footing in 1876, all the books of the three warehouses being then sent to the works.[104]

Although Pilkington glass was no doubt being exported by merchants in London and elsewhere from the early days, the firm does not seem to have been involved in much direct exporting itself until the last quarter of the century. The earliest surviving evidence of an agency abroad is a letter of attorney, dated 6 April 1836 and signed by Peter Greenall, giving Charles Cremer Tropolet, a merchant of Halifax, Nova Scotia, authority to recover debts from Edward Lawson, another Halifax merchant – not a very promising beginning.[105] By the middle of the century Pilkingtons were in correspondence with a potential agent in Australia. This was William Nash of South Geelong, to whose letter asking for this post Pilkingtons replied on 11 September 1857. Nash had previously been connected with

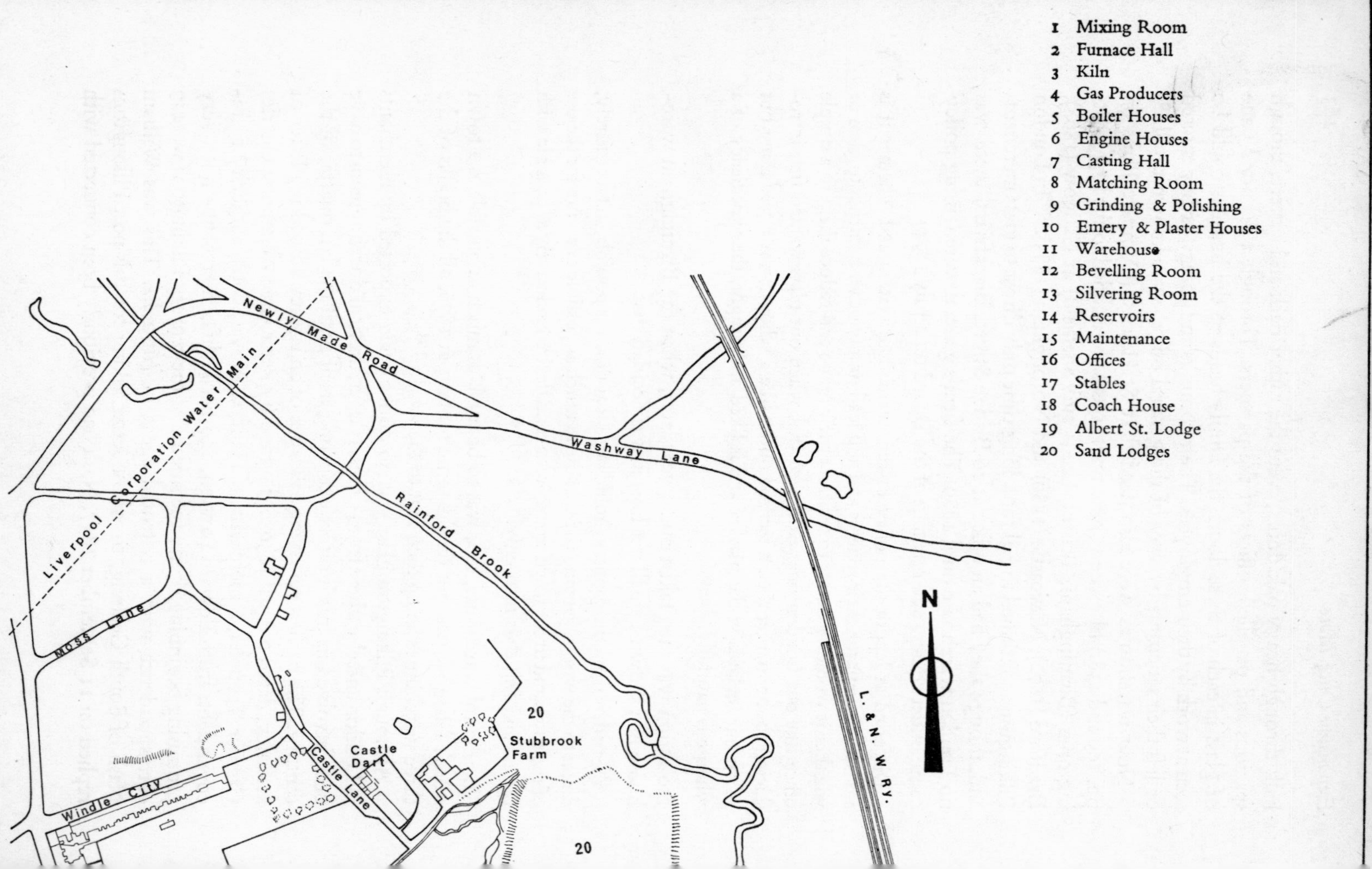

1 Mixing Room
2 Furnace Hall
3 Kiln
4 Gas Producers
5 Boiler Houses
6 Engine Houses
7 Casting Hall
8 Matching Room
9 Grinding & Polishing
10 Emery & Plaster Houses
11 Warehouse
12 Bevelling Room
13 Silvering Room
14 Reservoirs
15 Maintenance
16 Offices
17 Stables
18 Coach House
19 Albert St. Lodge
20 Sand Lodges

N

L. & N. W. Ry.

Washway Lane

Rainford Brook

Newly Made Road

Liverpool Corporation Water Main

Stubbrook Farm

Castle Dart

Castle Lane

Windle CITY

20

Plan 7 Pilkington Brothers' Plate Works in 1892

the glass trade in Britain for, after promising to send him the best glass they could at the lowest price, the letter goes on:

There have been many changes in the Glass trade since you left the old country and prices at present are considerably on the increase.

Your brother John still carries on business as before but he now does very little business with us. We presume he does not do much in glass or we should hear from him oftener than we do.

Trusting you will succeed in establishing a good business and expecting to hear from you as promised . . .

In the following year invoices were sent to Nash for crown and sheet glass shipped out to him; but as no further correspondence has survived, we do not know how long these shipments were continued.[106]

Any direct trading Pilkingtons may have attempted abroad in these earlier years amounted to very little compared to Chances' activities, for they benefited from the start from William Chance's American connexion as a Birmingham merchant and they had their own depot in New York. Chances' established position in North America was still recognised by Pilkingtons in the 1860s. In 1868, for instance, when Pilkingtons heard that a person competent to act for them happened to be going to America, they got in touch with him 'relative to our doing a trade with Boston'. They gave him the address of a merchant house there which bought plate glass from Ravenhead but added: 'We fear they are Chances' agents'.[107] In 1873, while the Belgian manufacturers were temporarily handicapped by a fuel shortage, Pilkingtons sent one of their travellers, Scott, to America for four months and, in the following year, John Salmond, who had previously been employed at their warehouse in Birmingham and at their London office, was sent right across the United States to make business contacts. He did not, however, consider the American market sufficiently promising to justify his remaining there as Pilkingtons' agent, and he returned home to become manager, and later proprietor, of James Hetley and Co., the London glass merchants.

The real beginnings of Pilkingtons' export trade overseas were in 1879 when Richard Pilkington went to America from March until May and the firm engaged John Thorpe (1853–1927), who had previously worked for the Wearmouth Company, 'to travel through the States and Colonies'. Unfortunately we have no record of how Thorpe covered his extensive assignment, soon made even larger by his being sent to the East. He visited Japan in 1882. In 1890 he went to Montreal where, in 1892, Pilkingtons opened a warehouse in rented premises in Busby Lane so that the supply of glass could be maintained during the winter when the St

Lawrence was frozen. By the following year it carried stocks worth $100,000.[108] A second Canadian warehouse was opened in 1893 in Toronto. By 1895, Pilkington had £45,000 of their capital tied up in Canada. The dominion was to become an important export market and as we shall see in chapter 13, the firm was to open a chain of warehouses across the whole continent. From 1890 Thorpe, based on Montreal, used to go to the States once a month. This continued until 1904 when he moved permanently to New York.

Meanwhile, from the 1880s, orders also came in on some scale from South America, one in 1888 for £2,900 worth of sheet glass and 70,000 sq. ft of rolled plate being so large that it had to be given special consideration by the Board.[109] Sales in Australia were handled from 1895 by Richard W.Hill. Formerly Pilkington's Birmingham, and then their London agent, he was sent there for health reasons and acted as the company's agent, working on commission. He was succeeded in 1904 by the redoubtable Harold Mees, previously a clerk in the Sheffield warehouse who was also sent to Australia for the good of his health – he was a suspected TB case. Confronted with the considerable task of covering the whole of that great continent from Melbourne, his health picked up remarkably and he made a very good living out of the commission he was able to earn. (In 1910 he was put on the salaried staff.) In New Zealand, A.G.D.Willcocks, of Adderley Willcocks & Co., worked in Pilkingtons' interest from about 1900. He is said to have owned a farm at Nelson, on the north coast of the South Island from which he sallied forth on a stately progress of the country once a year to receive orders. South Africa was served in a more regular fashion, by J.R. and R.H.Pritchard, general commission agents, Cape Town, from 1882 onwards. In the Middle East, where there was a demand for patterned and figured glasses which Pilkingtons could not dispose of elsewhere, there was an agency in Egypt from 1892. Jules Levy served as Pilkingtons' agent in Alexandria from 1902.

Much of Pilkingtons' trade with the continent seems to have been handled by H. and E.Lion of Hamburg. Selling in northern Europe against Belgian competition was particularly difficult. As H.Lion pointed out – rather obviously, perhaps – while he was on a visit to St Helens in 1878, 'he could sell large quantities of sheet, rolled, and plate in Holland, Norway, Sweden, Denmark and Russia if we could meet the foreign prices'. In 1882 and 1883, Adams, one of Pilkingtons' representatives, visited Holland, Spain and Italy and, from then onwards, separate agencies came to be formed in those countries. By 1894, in addition to an office in Hamburg, Pilkington had depots in Paris and Naples. Italy seems to have provided quite a flourishing market at that time if one may judge from the number of agencies – in Palermo, Bari, Rome and Turin, as well as in Naples itself.[110]

All these efforts to supplement the exports of merchants in London and elsewhere by sales of their own direct to the countries concerned, were of crucial importance to Pilkingtons during these years. Their export department grew rapidly; by the end of the 1880s, the work had to be divided into two sections. One dealt with the European countries (apart from France) and such Middle East and Far East trade as did not pass through the hands of export merchants. The other handled sales to France, North and South America, and British possessions abroad. The effect of all this sales promotion in distant parts of the world may be seen clearly from the figures of home and foreign sales from 1877 to 1887.

TABLE 20
PILKINGTONS' SALES, HOME AND FOREIGN, 1877–87

Year	Plate Home £	Plate Export £	Sheet Home £	Sheet Export £	Rolled Plate Home £	Rolled Plate Export £	Total Home £	Total Export £
1877	68,887	6,056	201,095	11,041	41,798	2,125	311,780	19,222
1878	93,531	8,138	182,244	6,693	38,239	2,178	314,014	17,009
1879	108,953	27,268	161,862	17,073	37,455	7,260	308,270	51,601
1880	117,477	39,660	172,450	39,655	40,442	7,585	330,369	86,900
1881	119,210	48,642	190,913	42,171	45,789	9,205	355,912	100,018
1882	144,227	60,272	192,339	52,816	56,661	13,954	393,227	127,042
1883	142,326	65,110	222,791	56,068	70,364	18,496	435,481	139,674
1884	139,026	82,015	232,282	53,006	73,936	12,954	445,244	147,975
1885	128,375	87,231	214,989	47,361	62,766	14,697	406,130	149,289
1886	121,365	88,175	195,555	71,160	60,781	15,954	377,701	175,289
1887	121,588	140,240	202,851	78,116	64,020	22,290	388,429	204,646

Source: Statement on loose sheet in Board minutes, 1881–91. PA PB139

Confronted by increased difficulty in selling plate and sheet glass on the home market, Pilkingtons developed outlets overseas where they were still able to find new customers. We do not know the relative profitability of their home and foreign sales nor do we know what happened after 1887; but it would seem reasonably safe to assert, on the basis of these figures, that Pilkingtons owed the prosperity as much to growing profits from exports as to lower production costs. The greater volume of glass handled by their shipping office at Drury Buildings, Liverpool, made an essential contribution to the profitability of the business.

In the middle of 1872, just before the firm embarked upon large-scale expenditure – building the plate works and extending the sheet works – it was decided to call in an outside accountant 'to put the accounts upon the best commercial footing'. They engaged Arthur W. and Reginald A. Wenham, partners in the London firm of Wenham, Angus and Company. The Wenhams presented twice-yearly balance sheets from 1874 and began to undertake a continuous audit ten years later. From the account books, which have come to light since the first edition of this book appeared in 1960, it is possible to relate, year by year, the firm's growing capital assets – fixed capital in the form of buildings, machinery and equipment, and

TABLE 21

PILKINGTON BROTHERS CAPITAL, NET PROFIT AND RESIDUE, 1873/4–1893/4

Year ended 30 June	Partners' Capital	£ Increase Over Previous Year	Net Profit	% of Capital	Residue not ploughed back into the business
1874	173,834	23,331	78,838	45¼	55,507
1875	240,672	66,838	76,464	31¾	9,626
1876	303,136	62,464	85,530	28	23,066
1877	376,666	73,530	46,014	12¼	−27,516
1878	367,664	−9,002	24,467	6½	15,465
1879	381,429	13,765	37,045	9¾	23,280
1880	399,963	18,539	67,740	16¾	49,201
1881	448,448	48,485	57,626	12¾	9,141
1882	572,291	123,843	103,473	18	−20,370
1883	683,447	111,156	131,664	19¼	20,508
1884	784,778	101,331	125,596	16	24,265
1885	837,462	52,684	130,684	15¼	78,000
1886	916,115	78,653	90,650	9½	11,997
1887	970,223	54,223	106,223	11	52,000
1888	1,029,018	58,680	161,884	15¾	103,211
1889	1,149,197	120,179	172,179	15	52,000
1890	1,259,121	109,824	201,923	16	91,999
1891	1,311,682	52,531	136,530	10½	83,999
1892	1,389,782	78,130	116,131	8½	38,001
1893	1,420,580	30,798	48,798	3½	18,000
1894	1,426,091	5,511	21,510	1½	15,999

Source: Pilkington Accounts

G*

working capital tied up in raw materials and stocks – to net profits already given in Table 18. From this it is possible to see just how much of these profits were ploughed back into the business during the life of the 21-year partnership agreement from 1873 to 1894.

The extent of the firm's progress under the leadership of the second generation is obvious. The eightfold expansion indicated by the capital figure is, in fact, an underestimate for prices fell by about 30 per cent during these years. The so-called 'great depression' of 1875–96 was a period of great prosperity for enterprising businesses prepared to meet the greater competition rather than be beaten down by it. And all this growth was self-financed. Profits were high enough to permit a massive ploughing back in order to renew obsolescent buildings and equipment (the accountants made no separate provision for depreciation at this time) and to allow for innovation and expansion.

At the same time, the residue available for tax-free distribution in equal amounts for the four partners, was for many years well above the £12,000 total to which they agreed to limit these dividends when they drew up their partnership agreement. Down to the year ended June 1882 this residue was not particularly large, bearing in mind the two years in which the partners had to pay in about £48,000 when investment outran current profits. For this nine-year period the total residue was £137,400 or £15,267 per year. What happened was that the four partners kept a capital account, out of which they paid themselves the stipulated £3,000 each, the remainder being left to cover the years like the two mentioned when it was necessary to call upon revenue. After 1882, however, the position changed. Despite ploughing back at an ever higher rate, the residue grew larger. At this point the partners began paying bonuses into their cash accounts. These started in 1883/4 when they received an additional £1,000 (i.e. the total distribution was £16,000, not £12,000). In 1884/5, a very good year, they *each* received a bonus of £16,500. The next year was a poor one and there was no bonus, but then the bonuses began again:

> 1886/7 £10,000 *each*
> 1887/8 £22,000 *each*
> 1888/9 £10,000 *each*
> 1889/90 £20,000 *each*
> 1890/1 £18,000 *each*
> 1891/2 £6,000 *each*
> 1892/3 £1,500 *each*
> 1893/4 £2,500 *each*

Source: PA PB280 Private ledgers

The plain truth was that in those halcyon years Pilkingtons were making far more profit than they could economically use within their business without even more rapid expansion. Hence not only the bonuses but also the willingness to contemplate warehouses in Canada and the stake in Maubeuge.

A clause in the 1875 agreement permitted any partner to give the whole or part of his interest to his sons when they reached the age of 21. For taking part in the management of the firm, the sons were to share the salary of their fathers. In accordance with this clause, in 1885 William (Roby) Pilkington, the senior member, then aged 68, introduced his two sons, William Lee Pilkington and George Herbert Pilkington, each of them being given one-tenth of his share. In July 1894, when the 21-year term had expired, Pilkingtons were transformed into a limited company under the Companies Act of 1862. Although in law the private limited company did not come into existence until a later Act of 1907, in fact a number of undertakings became private companies before that time merely by not offering any shares to the public.[111] This was the course followed by Pilkingtons who informed their clients in a circular letter that 'the change is simply made for family reasons; no shares are offered to the public and no alteration whatever is made in the management of the business'.[112] The ordinary share capital was divided into 8,000 ordinary shares of £100 and the rest of the existing capital was divided into £600,000-worth of 5 per cent debenture stock. The Companies Act required that there be a minimum of seven members. The four senior partners therefore took the opportunity to introduce four other sons, Henry William Pilkington and Richard Austin Pilkington (twin sons of Windle Pilkington), and Ernest Sinclair Pilkington and Arthur Richard Pilkington (sons of Richard Pilkington). The senior partners were each allotted 2,000 ordinary shares and £150,000 of debenture stock to be divided, if desired, with their sons. The allocation of the shares was as follows:[113]

William (Roby) Pilkington	1,600 ordinary shares and	£120,000 of debentures
Thomas Pilkington	2,000	£150,000
William Windle Pilkington	1,960	£150,000
Richard Pilkington	1,960	£150,000
William Lee Pilkington	200	£15,000
George Herbert Pilkington	200	£15,000
Henry William Pilkington	20	nil
Richard Austin Pilkington	20	nil
Ernest Sinclair Pilkington	20	nil
Arthur Richard Pilkington	20	nil

It will be noticed that, not only was the family management increased to handle the growing business, but also the descendants of the founder Richard's branch came to predominate in the management, though they did not gain a larger financial stake. This was because Thomas's elder son, Thomas Douglas, did not become a director (he was subsequently killed in the Boer War) and his younger son did not enter the firm until 1903.

From 1894 until after the First World War the large profit of the company from the works and colliery, from rents of property and interest on investments, continued to be sufficient in themselves to provide all the capital needed after the directors and shareholders had taken their due: 5 per cent interest on debenture stock, 5 per cent dividend and an annual bonus. When all these payments had been made and much ploughed back into the concern, there still remained a surplus to be invested as company savings, chiefly in foreign rails, government bonds and public utilities. These rose from £85,000 in the year 1896–7 to £355,000 in 1902–3. Shares in the Maubeuge factory by then accounted for about £30,000 of these totals.

TABLE 22

DISPOSAL OF PROFIT IN THE YEARS ENDED 30 JUNE
1896–1903

Year ended 30 June	Profit	Directors' salaries, fees and expenses	Income tax	Debenture interest and dividend	Bonus on shares	Balance retained in company for development
1896	£186,343	£18,880	£1,768		£10,000	£85,695
1897	209,125	17,801	965		30,000	90,359
1898	248,870	17,654	2,549		50,000	108,667
1899	267,439	16,128	2,808	£70,000 paid annually	60,000	118,503
1900	334,497	16,827	5,769		120,000	121,901
1901	394,746	15,760	12,344		120,000	176,642
1902	295,197	17,010	13,582		90,000	104,605
1903	196,197	17,274	14,286		40,000	54,637

Source: Pilkington Accounts

While foreign competition had driven most other British manufacturers out of business, Pilkingtons had got nicely into its stride.

Chapter 10

Labour Relations and Welfare Services in the Later Years of the Nineteenth Century

A FTER the labour troubles of the mid-1840s, Pilkingtons went for many years without any further disputes. But, with foreign competition growing more severe and glass prices falling, it was inevitable that some attempt should be made to cut labour costs and this led to further collisions between Pilkingtons and their employees. These occurred, however, during the 1870s and were dealt with so firmly – some would say ruthlessly – that, when trade unionism in the country as a whole became more militant towards the end of the century, the movement found little or no response among those employed at the Grove Street factory.

An entry in the Board minutes on 8 January 1863 calls 'a fair blower's average about 35s crown and 45s sheet...' Although this was approximately the same rate as the English blowers had been receiving 15 years before, it represented a fall in real wages, for the cost of living had moved upwards in the interval. These were the highest paid men. At the other end of the scale, boys starting work at Pilkingtons earned only 2s 6d per week. One of them was James Sexton, who was later to become well-known as a trade union leader. He worked at Pilkingtons for four years before running off to sea.[1]

At the end of the 1860s complaints about the quality of Pilkington glass were increasingly reported to the works and there was evidently some slackness on the part of the glasshouse managers. In the year ended 30 June 1869 net profit fell to £5,618. (The year before it had been £22,513.) Two of the partners returned from a visit to Belgium in June 1869 more than ever convinced that their blowers and flatteners – the skilled workmen upon whom the firm was completely dependent for the size and quality of its product – were not working so efficiently as they had done in the past. The Board thereupon

carpeted all the managers and explained to them what had been seen in Belgium lately by W.P. and W.W.P., how far faster the men worked from one end to the other and hence our inability to compete with them; further, that we work now much more slowly than we used to do.[2]

In an effort to raise standards, a bonus was offered to those who produced a high proportion of number one quality glass.

At the same time a reduction was made in the number of people employed outside the glasshouses and the wages of the rest were reduced. Despite this cut, the economy-minded Thomas Pilkington could still complain, in the following March, that wages were 'excessive in almost all departments connected with the Yard'. More men were laid off and others demoted. At least one of them refused the new terms which were offered:

Told T. Glover that we had decided to put him to the trowel again when he at once replied that he had been expecting it as the work and reduced staff wouldn't warrant his remaining in his present position; but though he should be willing at any time to take the trowel to work *piece work* for us, he should decline to take it otherwise. This, of course, settled the matter and he goes.[3]

Attention was now given to the wages of the glassmakers themselves. What appears to have been a new standard was introduced for calculating wage rates: 100 pieces of 15 oz. to the sq. ft and sized 50″ × 35″, safely delivered to the warehouse. This was a man's average production per shift. Heavier weights per sq. ft were based on 46″ × 34″ and were counted as more than one piece at the standard rate. 26 oz. glass sized 46″ × 34″, for instance, was to count as two pieces for wage purposes. There were also bonuses for larger sizes. Blowers were divided into three categories according to their skill and experience. The best were to be paid at a rate of 14s per 100 standard pieces (56s per week of four shifts at the average output), the second grade 13s (52s) and the third 11s (44s). Flatteners were also divided into two classes and were to receive 8s or 7s per 100. Gatherers were to be paid 6s 8d per 100.

As we have no information about wage rates for the 1850s and 1860s, nor any lists of earnings, it is not possible to estimate the effect of these changes. The rates were, in fact, increased slightly after they had been tried out, the 11s basic for third-class blowers being put up to 11s 6d and the others advanced by 6d per shift bringing their basic weekly total to 46s, 54s and 58s respectively. Windle Pilkington estimated that, with this addition, the new rates would not cut any earnings by more than 15 per cent, and most would be reduced very much less than that. The men claimed the cuts would *average* 23 per cent. Of significance, perhaps, were the inducements to blow larger sizes, the decision to pay only for pieces safely delivered to the warehouse, and, above all, the division of these skilled employees into different categories.

The new conditions provoked the most protracted strike in Pilkingtons' history, far longer than the much publicised seven-week unofficial stoppage in 1970. The sheet glass blowers stopped work on 19 April 1870, and the other glassmakers had to be laid off. The firm maintained a token output, using younger managers and apprentices, for over six months. When the strike eventually ended, on 5 November, the men came back on their masters' terms. Towards the close of the following month the Board was able to record 'a great improvement in the character of the glass altogether now'.[4]

A Sheet Glassmakers' Association was formed in 1870. We know of its existence from a Book of Rules, printed in 1874, which refers to its having been formed four years previously.[5] Presumably it had been established to resist the wage cuts and had managed to survive the strike. During the four years of its existence, the Rules noted,

beneficial changes in our social position have been achieved; for is it not our duty to do the best we possibly can to provide comfortable homes for ourselves and our families: and it is our duty by Divine Command, to assist each other and make the best possible use of the talents which God has given us.

There had, indeed, been improvements in sheet glassmakers' pay. In 1872, when high fuel prices had put up the cost of living and, at the same time, the demand for glass was strong, Pilkingtons advanced the basic rate from 11s 6d to 12s 6d. A further increase of ten per cent was given the following. October, plus a bonus of ten per cent on all pieces above 400 per week. By 1874, the Sheet Glassmakers' Association had branches at Sunderland and Spon Lane as well as St Helens and was proposing to open bank accounts in the town for a surplus fund of £1,000. The three branches were to contribute to it equally.[6]

The office staff were not forgotten at this time, for they, of course, did not share in the glassmakers' increases nor did they receive pay for overtime. They then numbered only 36 all told; but among them £200 was distributed. This caused the recipients to send a letter of thanks to their employers. In it they wrote of Pilkingtons' consideration for them:

Your thoughtfulness and liberality in the present trying times of high prices, felt by all classes of the community, comes with double force to your servants who have thereby been enabled to look calmly on what were previously our difficulties; which, added to your general kindness to us in the past, tends to confirm our conviction of the interest taken in our welfare by yourselves.[7]

The office staff was still very small in the early 1870s; and there do not appear then to have been more than 200 sheet glassmakers (blowers, flatteners and gatherers) and there were probably not more than another 50 skilled men at work in the rolled plate factory and other glassmaking departments. Yet, in 1876, 1,500 people were employed altogether at Grove Street.[8] The ratio of glassmakers to others, at one to six, was perhaps somewhat greater than it had been in the 1840s; yet the overwhelming majority of Pilkingtons' employees still worked outside the glasshouses. No lists of earnings for this period have survived, so we do not know how these employees fared. The Board minutes refer, at one extreme, to sorters earning about 30s per week, and, at the other, to apprentices receiving just a few shillings. All these people, who did not actually make glass, were working a $55\frac{1}{2}$-hour week in the early 1870s: from Monday to Friday 6 a.m. to 5.30 p.m. and on Saturday from 6 a.m. to 12 noon, with intervals for meals.[9] For them, and for the glassmakers, there were three days' holiday in the year: Christmas Day, Good Friday and the Friday of Newton Race Week in June. (This last holiday was changed to Whit Monday about 1880.) August Bank Holiday – a half-holiday at first – was taken from 1882. Departmental managers sometimes had a week's holiday with pay, but the partners did not encourage this. When, for instance, one manager, who earned £5 10s 0d per week, was away and his work was done by a deputy who was paid £3, the Board decided to subtract the difference between the two wages from his holiday pay and added:

Last year paid him in full, but holydays are becoming more the fashion and it behoves us to check the tendency.[10]

So long as pot furnaces were used, glassmakers had to work altogether four, 10-hour shifts per week, followed in each case by 24 hours off while the pots were being recharged. With the coming of tanks during the 1870s, work could continue uninterruptedly throughout the week and the week-end rest, though preserved, was shortened. Under the old intermittent system the glassmakers' shifts had been as shown in Table 23. All these times had been approximate, however, as there was no certainty when the pots would be ready for working or precisely how long

TABLE 23
GLASSMAKERS' SHIFTS USING POT FURNACES

	Glassmakers at work	Glass being prepared for working
Monday	6 am–4 pm	4 pm–4 pm (Tuesday)
Tuesday	4 pm–	
Wednesday	2 am	2 am–2 am (Thursday)
Thursday	2 am–12 noon	12 noon–12 noon (Friday)
Friday	12 noon–10 pm	

it would take the glassmakers to blow all the molten glass into cylinders. Under the new tank system working hours were fixed. There were three eight-hour shifts per day for six days a week.[11] Unfortunately, we do not know just how these shifts were arranged at first. Presumably blowing began late on Sunday night – at say 10 pm – and the shifts then ran from 10–6, 6–2 and 2–10 for the next six days. So, when Saturday half-holidays were becoming general, Pilkingtons' glassmakers were having to work on Saturdays which previously they had had free. On the other hand, they gained the advantage of shorter shifts at the same time each day for a whole week instead of having to do one night shift in the middle of a number of shifts at different times of day. They worked longer hours altogether – 48 instead of about 40 – but their basic output, on which their pay depended, went up from 400 to between 450 and 540 cylinders.[12] The new arrangements do not seem to have been unfavourably received by the glassmakers at first.

Trouble came, however, in the later 1870s, a bad time for the British economy as a whole, and a period when the building cycle over most of the country was turning downwards. Pilkingtons' profits, £85,530 in the year ended 30 June 1876, dropped to £24,466 two years later. The ten per cent bonus over 400 pieces was cut in May 1875 and a ten per cent reduction in the wages themselves in November 1877 was followed by a second ten per cent cut from March 1878.[13] This the St Helens branch of the Sheet Glassmakers' Association resisted. It demanded an increase and, when this demand was turned down, a strike began on 9 August.[14] This was only a partial stoppage, however, for 32 blowers, eight flatteners and ten gatherers refused to support the strike. It was never really effective and it eventually petered out in the middle of November, the men again returning on their masters' terms. As they came in, they were obliged to sign six-month contracts. This would appear to have been a shorter term than had obtained before the strike; it was certainly very much shorter than the six to seven years common in the middle of the century. These new contracts were arranged so that they expired at different dates, which meant that only a small section could, in future, strike at any one time without breaking their agreements. In 1879, as the contracts came up for renewal, the men were re-bound at a lower rate of pay, Sheet Works profits still remaining low. At the beginning of the year, when the Board considered the new rates, they decided that they should be 'the lowest that can possibly be gone to'. In fact, the basic rate for third-class blowers was reduced to 10s, 1s 6d less than it had been after the 1870 strike. The contracts also included a clause which made glassmakers liable to fines of up to 10s for each day's absence without good cause. There was also another clause obliging all hand blowers to average, over six shifts per week, 100 feet per hour, the average being reduced to 90 feet during the hot months of June, July and August. When the non-strikers came to be bound at these new low rates, they were granted a bonus for life of £5 per year, subject to their being 'steady and sober' and behaving to the firm's satisfaction. There were no more strikes at Grove Street after this, nor is anything more heard about the Sheet Glassmakers' Association.[15]

Pilkingtons soon saw that they had gone too far in cutting wages. Several of their men left for America and, although some are said to have returned from the United States 'disgusted', a ten per cent advance was agreed to in April 1880, because 'the American makers were trying to seduce [the others] into going over there ... Some advance here might cause them to turn a deaf ear to the temptation'. In July, when Chances cut wages by ten per cent, Pilkingtons refused to follow suit because of rumours that 'a lot of our men are going to America as soon as they light up there again'. (The American glassworks were closed from May to July because of the hot weather.) The ten per cent cut was considered again on two occasions during the following 12 months, but no action was taken.[16]

The American glassmakers soon became concerned about the effects of this influx of foreign labour. In 1884 St Helens became the centre of a determined effort to organize the British glassmakers, instigated by the American Knights of Labor.[17] One of the Knights' branches – or Local Assemblies as they were called – had its headquarters in the glassmaking centre of Pittsburgh. This was Local Assembly number 300. It was, in fact, more than a local branch, for it enrolled window glass workers throughout America. L.A. 300 decided to reduce the number of skilled glass workers from Europe who were entering American factories at wages below the current rates. In 1880, two of their members, James L.Michels and John Fetters, were sent to Europe

... for the purpose of making an investigation into the condition of the window glass workers in Europe, and, if possible, to ascertain why so many window glass workers come to America under contract for less than current wages, and, if possible, to have the European workers form a union and establish a closer communication between America and the old country, in order to protect the interests of all window glass workers.

This mission does not appear to have had any success in Britain, but its activities may, perhaps, have had some bearing upon the formation in August 1882, of the Belgian *Union Verrière*.[18] In the following year this union sent money to help strikers in the United States, and the year after that, 1884, the Americans, in their turn, helped the Belgians to strike successfully for higher wages.[19] This *liaison* led, in June 1884, to a conference at Charleroi, attended by Isaac Cline and Henry Burtt, President and Secretary of L.A. 300, to found a Universal Federation of Glass Workers. Later in the same month, Cline, Burtt and representatives from France, Belgium and Italy, appeared at St Helens. Their conference, held at the White Lion Inn and attended by some 300 people, was, in fact, the first Universal Convention. It was addressed by Cline, Oscar Falleur and Chery Desguin of the *Union Verrière*, F. Barr of the French association of glassmakers, and delegates from Sunderland and Spon Lane.[20] At a further meeting, held on a Sunday morning a few days later, the visitors are said to have attracted an audience more than twice as large.[21] The local chairman, named Rigby, was an employee of Pilkingtons. They promptly dismissed him and when a union deputation waited upon Windle Pilkington to ask why, he (according to the Board minutes) 'gave them some good advice and told them that we were determined to oppose it in any way that it interfered with us'.[22]

In the following November, A.G.Denny, another member of L.A. 300, came over to consolidate the work of Cline and Burtt. L.A. 3,504 was formed as the Knights' Local Assembly for British window glass workers, with headquarters at Sunderland, and a 'preceptory', or branch, at St Helens. The branch appears to have had a certain limited success in enrolling members. In February 1885, for instance, 20 were enrolled at the society's club house, the Sefton Arms Hotel.[23] In that month, too, its secretary, Joseph Norbury, an ex-miner who had just left Pilkingtons after three-and-a-half years' service with the firm, was prominent in an attempt to form a local Trades Council. Also among the trade unions interested in setting up this body was a Plate Glass Workers' Society, which had recently been largely responsible for a strike at the Pocket Nook works.[24] The St Helens branch of L.A. 3,504 survived for a few years longer. The Universal Convention was again held in the town in 1886 and 1888. On the latter occasion, Pilkingtons asked the Chief Constable to keep close watch both upon these meetings and upon the firm's two factories.[25] But, despite these efforts to rally Pilkingtons' men, the union made no headway at St Helens. Norbury, the branch secretary, turned out to be an alcoholic and became an increasing liability; and Pilkingtons themselves would have no truck at all with the union. *The American Glassworker*, in its issue of 11 September 1885, had contrasted the 'tyrannical vigilance of the Pilkingtons' with the attitude of 'the Chance Brothers and Messrs Hartley', who 'have at different times treated our committee with great kindness'. At the end of March 1887, the secretary of L.A. 3,504 reported to the head of the Knights in America that, whereas they were 'in good organized condition' at certain factories, at St Helens 'what with the tyrannical disposition of the capitalist and the general depressed condition of the men (through that curse Drink) we are not able to make any progress whatever ... Messrs Pilkington Bros are continually discharging our members for no other reason than that they belong to our Society'. His successor as secretary, writing to Beatrice Potter in 1891 (shortly before she married Sidney Webb), attributed the failure at St Helens to Pilkingtons' staggered contract system.

The intention of all this trade union activity had been to recruit the highly skilled and relatively well-paid sheet glassmakers. At the end of the 1880s came the spread of New Unionism among the unskilled. In 1889 the United Plate Glass Society started to enrol plate glassmakers, for the greater part unskilled men. By June of that year they claimed to have 800 members but only 100 of these were said to belong to the Cowley Hill works.[26] The plate glass business was enjoying an unusual spell of profitability and the union pressed for better wages. The Pocket Nook, London & Manchester, and Ravenhead works were brought to a stop in 1890.[27] Perhaps as a result of this activity more support was gained among Pilkingtons' employees. On 21 June they stopped work at Cowley Hill on the grounds that their wages were being gradually reduced. The strike dragged on until 5 November but in the end the strikers had to return on their masters' terms.[28] While the great factory lay idle, the Board took the opportunity to press ahead with installing the Malevez machinery,[29] and when the strike was over they were able to claim a rebate of one-third on the St Helens town rates on account of the 20-week stoppage.[30]

While this strike was in progress, an attempt was made to organise the labourers at Sheet Works, much on the lines of the Chemical and Copper Workers' Union which had just been formed at St Helens. In October 1890 there were said to be 800 members.[31] In the following year a Sheet

Glass Flatteners' Society is mentioned for the first time.[32] To what extent these developments indicated any real spread of trade unionism at Grove Street is far from clear. There are certainly signs that the first eager enthusiasm was not sustained. When one of Pilkington's sheet glass blowers was asked in 1895 whether the workers were organised in any way, he replied in the negative.[33]

The firm's recreational activities continued to grow with the increasing number of employees. A new sports ground was opened at City Road in the mid-'70s when the adjacent Cowley Hill factory came into use. Meanwhile, as urban St Helens gradually spread outwards, the original home of the Recreation Club had to retreat before the ever-advancing builders. The first ground in the vicinity of the cotton factory had to be given up in 1877 when the firm surrendered its lease, and a new field was taken in Boundary Road. When this was acquired by the Corporation and became part of Queen's Recreation Ground, the Club removed to its present home in Ruskin Drive, opened in 1901.[34]

Until the 1880s cricket stood unchallenged as the most popular outdoor sport and it continued to have a wide appeal. In 1893, for which year a fixture book survives, the club was able to send three teams into the field every Saturday. Two of them used the Boundary Road ground and the third played at City Road. By this time, however, the summer game had a winter counterpart which enjoyed an even larger following. The rugby section was formed in 1879, and in 1884 the 'Recs' (as the team came to be known) joined the West Lancashire and Border Town Rugby Union. From then onwards the teams that came to play at Boundary Road – particularly the fierce rivals from Wigan – drew large crowds.[35]

In 1891 a club was formed for those employees who wished to ride that new-fangled creation, the bicycle. The firm bought a number of cycles at cost price and sold them to members of the club who paid in weekly instalments.[36]

The oldest of Pilkingtons' welfare services, the school, continued to give part-time education to the apprentices. The schoolmaster for 21 years up to within a month of his death in 1887 was Edward Fidler, who taught his often unruly pupils in premises at Eccleston Street.[37] When Pilkingtons gave up their Eccleston Street property, the school was removed to the old mill, close to the Grove Street works.[38] From 1876 Fidler had an un-certificated assistant, Walter Tittensor, who continued to teach after Henry Edward Lea, who did have a teacher's certificate, succeeded Fidler as schoolmaster. Classes grew, standards rose and a second assistant, Alfred W. Harris, also certificated, was appointed in 1890. Five years later, however, 20 per cent of the part-timers were still under 12 years of age. The school appears to have been taken over by the St Helens Local Education Authority from 1 May 1903.[39]

During the winter the Recreation Section sponsored various lectures, an early form of adult education. A coffee room at Sheet Works was agreed upon by the Board at the end of 1874 and a dining room in 1888. The Navigation Inn, acquired by Pilkingtons in 1890 and later converted into a staff café and recreation rooms, served as an excellent centre for such purposes. Early in this century a works canteen was opened in a building opposite the General Office in Grove Street.[40]

The firm's medical services date from 1882. Although there had previously been arrangements between Pilkingtons and various doctors in the town for medical attention in case of accidents at the works, the employees had been obliged to rely on one or other of the town's numerous friendly societies for assistance in case of illness. Towards the end of 1881, the glassblowers, who already ran such a sickness and burial society among themselves, asked if they might hold meetings at the works instead of at a public house. Pilkingtons agreed but asked them to consider extending their club to all the other employees at Grove Street. Within a short time J.H.Dickinson, representing the firm, was negotiating with local doctors to attend nearly 1,200 employees and their wives and families. Pilkingtons, who had previously paid £40 a year to doctors for attending accident cases, now gave £50 to the club instead. They were soon contributing £100 to keep it solvent. By 1884 there were complaints – they have a distinctly modern ring – that 'yard men' who belonged to the firm's club and to another one outside, were taking every opportunity to be ill, for then they 'really got more money than if they had been at their work'. The Board commented: 'Much more sickness now than before the Club existed. No doubt some rascality exists.' By the end of the 1880s the club's income exceeded £2,000 a year. Local doctors continued to be employed until 1905 when the club appointed a doctor of its own. These arrangements did not apply to the Cowley Hill works where Pilkingtons continued to pay for medical attention in cases of accident and the men had their own contributory accident fund.[41]

Pilkingtons had no pensions scheme in operation until the inter-war years. Yet they often granted small pensions to their employees, and sometimes also to widows of employees. These grants, however, were by no means an automatic reward for long service. On one occasion, for instance, the Board noted than an elderly employee had

been applying for assistance in shape of a pension and has written saying that he has been 50 years with the Firm, etc. Don't think him entitled to anything; been a regular black sheep.[42]

But Pilkingtons did continue to employ him for several years longer on lighter work, instructing the younger blowers.

Topics such as wages, working conditions and labour relations excite as strong feelings in the minds of readers of history as they do in readers of present-day newspapers. It is difficult for an historian to comment with proper detachment. How could a firm that was doing so well in many of these years take such a hard line with its employees?

First and foremost, it must be emphasised that Pilkingtons were operating in a very tough competitive situation. They had to struggle to sell their glass against fierce competition from countries where labour conditions were considerably inferior to those at St Helens. In Belgium, for instance, there was no week-end break at all. That the partners drove their employees – and themselves – so hard at this time, must explain to some extent why Pilkingtons were the only British window and plate glass manufacturers to survive the struggle (apart from Chances, who were operating on an altogether smaller scale and mainly in rolled plate glass). As Pilkingtons told their men a few years before the end of the century:

We have put forth immense energy in placing agencies, travellers and warehouses to intercept and take orders; and while others have either gone back or shut up, we have kept you at full work. While large works at St Helens have been out and men getting nothing, you have been at work.[43]

In any case, how much of the profit could have been paid out to the employees without weakening the firm – bearing in mind that it was from these profits that further family investment was to be forthcoming after the First World War? If £15,000 had been paid out in any one year at the end of the nineteenth century to the 2,000 employees at Grove Street and the 1,000 at Cowley Hill, it would have raised each man's pay only by 2s per week, ten per cent or less of the wages of all but juveniles and very much less than that in the case of the skilled glassmakers who could often earn between £2 and £3 a week, a princely wage in those days. Ordinary St Helens folk certainly looked upon them as very well off indeed.[44]

It is worth noting, perhaps, that while manufacturing costs at Grove Street as a whole were reduced in relation to sales revenue, this desirable objective was not achieved by cutting the total wage bill. This continued

TABLE 24

RELATIONSHIP OF WAGES AND TOTAL MANUFACTURING
COSTS TO SALES REVENUE AT GROVE STREET AND
COWLEY HILL, IN THE LATER NINETEENTH CENTURY

Total Sales Revenue		Wages		Manufacturing Charges*	
	£	£	%	£	%
(i) Grove Street					
1865/6	145,691	47,166	32·4	94,975	65·0
1869/70	152,426	58,358	38·3	115,046	75·4
1875/6	246,913	86,702	35·1	171,978	69·6
1880/1	260,650	92,419	35·5	164,617	63·1
1885/6	338,957	123,982	36·6	207,064	61·1
1890/1	471,906	150,465	31·9	274,214	58·1
1893/4	372,830	128,409	34·4	240,586	64·5
(ii) Cowley Hill					
1876/7	56,060	26,712	47·6	50,767	90·6
1880/1	153,818	58,391	38·0	121,815	79·2
1885/6	198,453	74,518	37·5	146,310	73·7
1890/1	166,196	59,566	35·8	135,797	81·7
1893/4	166,842	61,876	37·0	163,591	98·0

* less transport costs

Source: Pilkington Accounts

to bear roughly the same relationship to revenue throughout this period. This was also true of wages (though not of total manufacturing costs) at Cowley Hill when the unusually high initial costs had been brought down.

The régime at Pilkingtons at the end of the nineteenth century must have seemed hard to many who lived through it, despite the general fall in the cost of living – though not so hard as it would appear to those who look back from the higher living standards of the present day. It must have been extremely irritating at times; on one occasion, for instance, the partners even went so far as to forbid domino-playing at the recreation club on the grounds that 'dominoes have a gambling tendency.'[45] On the other hand, in terms of welfare provision, small though this may seem in modern terms, Pilkingtons were among the industrial leaders of the day; and the family had already gained a reputation for unostentatious help to employees and their dependants in particular need.

Chapter 11

Colliery Affairs

PILKINGTONS' coalmining activities, unlike their venture into the chemical industry, came under the direct control of the Board at Grove Street. The St Helens Colliery was an integral part of Pilkington Brothers, and William (Roby) Pilkington was responsible for its management. It is appropriate, therefore, that we should devote a brief chapter to events at the Pilkingtons' colliery from the later 1850s, when they began to work the coal measure in the immediate vicinity of the works.

Although coal was certainly being wound at the St Helens Colliery in 1861,[1] complimentary remarks from a mines inspector on 'the very judicious way in which the coal had so far been opened out' make it clear that some of the seams were still being prepared for working two years later, in 1863.[2] Perhaps Pilkingtons' decision at the beginning of the latter year to join the South Lancashire Coal Association may be taken as a sign that their mining activities had by then reached a scale when affiliation to that body had become desirable.[3]

As the workings became more extensive, official approval regarding their safety turned to censure. Complaints were made about their ventilation. At the end of 1863 an inspector asserted that the mines contained gas and 'could not be efficiently worked as at present'. He suggested that the remedy would be 'either a reconstruction of the air courses or sinking a new shaft'.[4] The Board favoured the latter, and it was decided to sink a new pit to the southward, not far from the main entrance of the Ravenhead plate glassworks. From there it would be possible to get the higher quality Rushy Park and Little Delf coals as well as to improve the ventilation system in their existing workings by means of an underground tunnel.

Work on the new pit began early in 1864. On 17 March the shaft was 24 yards down.[5] McGill, the manager, acquired a steam engine from Chorley for £120 to pump out the water which flooded in as the men continued boring and sinking deeper into the ground. By September a winding engine had also been bought.[6] By May the following year, 1865, £7,000 had already been spent on the new pit and there was a year's work ahead before the Rushy Park mine could be reached. A further £3,100 was spent during these next 12 months.[7] The Little Delf mine, which lay a short distance below the Rushy Park seam, was entered early in 1867.[8] Meanwhile the ventilation tunnel was being cut. The Board minutes of 20 December 1866, include the note: 'Doing well in the Tunnel at Ravenhead pit: expect to get it through in one month's time.' This, however, was an optimistic estimate for it was not until 9 May 1867 that the Board could record: 'Connected tunnel with Little Delf from New pit at Ravenhead May 1st'. Further work had still to be done; the minutes of 17 May, for instance, mention the driving of a tunnel to connect the Rushy Park and Little Delf seams. It was not until the end of the year that the 40 workmen were entertained to a spread at one of the local hostelries, the customary conclusion to such an operation.[9] The new colliery was named after Princess Alexandra who had paid a visit to the nearby Ravenhead works in 1865.[10]

At the beginning of 1866 Pilkingtons engaged a new colliery manager at a salary of £200 a year in place of McGill. This was Francis France, then a young man in his middle twenties. He came from the Mains Colliery, Wigan, with the highest recommendations,[11] and was soon said to be doing very well. Roby Pilkington thought it was 'a fortunate thing our getting him as many laxities had crept in down below'.[12] France continued in charge of the firm's colliery affairs until his death, 37 years later.[13]

He was joined soon after his arrival by William Hopton, who had previously managed the nearby Croppers Hill Colliery, which had recently closed. Hopton, an older man who had made a careful study of underground ventilation over a number of years, set about improving the flow of air in the workings even before the new tunnel was completed. He remained with Pilkingtons until 1870.[14] In an autobiographical volume, published years later, he recalled that when he went to the St Helens Colliery

the ventilation ... was very bad. Only 19,000 ft of air per minute passed through the workings and the mine gave off much explosive gas. The lamps in several parts were unsafe to work with, and the inspector found it necessary to stop some part of the mine. Gas came out of the workings now and then and filled the safety lamps hundreds of yards along the main pony roads. As soon as possible, however, I changed the up-cast shaft and split the ventilating current in parts; this increased the air from 19,000 to 40,000 feet per minute. The men then felt more safe and when I left the colliery [four years later] over five hundred miners presented me with a gold watch.[15]

Events soon brought about a merger between the St Helens and the Ravenhead Colliery.[16] The latter was situated immediately to the south of the glassworks between the original pits of the St Helens Colliery and the newly-opened Alexandra Pit. The two concerns collaborated to maintain pumping engines at the disused Gerard's Bridge Colliery in order to keep their own coals dry,[17] but came into dispute over the right to work a certain seam.[18] Such a collision was inevitable when two companies were working in such a confined area. A merger was most desirable. In this matter Pilkington Brothers were in a much stronger position to take the initiative than were Bromilow, Haddock & Co. Ltd,[19] the proprietors of the Ravenhead Colliery. Roby Pilkington, lord of the manor of Sutton from 1860, had acquired extensive coalmines in that township from the heirs of the Bold family.[20] This allowed considerable extension of the St Helens Colliery's workings to the southward. The 14-acre piece of ground, leased by the firm in 1872, was available for surface extensions if required. In contrast, the Ravenhead company was running into financial difficulties. It sustained losses on the year's working in 1869, 1870 and 1871[21] but was, presumably, saved by the great coalmining boom that developed after that.

The depression following the boom, however, hastened the amalgamation. By the beginning of 1876 the *Colliery Guardian's* Liverpool correspondent reported 'the coal trade almost stagnant . . . prices drooping [*sic*] and, with a reduction offered, no more business resulting . . . A reduction in wages must come and even with that, short time during the summer appears inevitable'.[22] As summer approached – on 27 April to be exact – there was an extraordinary meeting of the members of the Ravenhead Colliery Co. Ltd to consent to the sale of their shares to a representative of the St Helens Collieries Co. Ltd, a company in process of formation which was to take over both concerns. The Ravenhead shareholders were to receive three £50 shares in the new company for each of their existing £100 shares, together with £10,950 in 5 per cent debentures.[23] The St Helens Collieries Co. Ltd was registered on 12 July with a share capital of £500,000.[24] On the following day the directors of the new company held their first meeting. In addition to the four

Pilkington partners, there were present: David Bromilow, H.J.Bromilow
and James Haddock – the sons of William Bromilow and Thomas
Haddock, founders of Bromilow, Haddock & Co. – and David Gamble,
the chemical manufacturer, who had become a director of the Ravenhead
Colliery some time after his marriage to James Haddock's sister, Elizabeth.
The minutes show that the old Ravenhead directors only attended
meetings for two years. After 1878 only members of the Pilkington
family were actively concerned with this large coalmining business.

Pilkingtons' fuel requirements were, by the 1870s, very considerable.
In 1872, for instance, they burned about 75,000 tons at the Grove Street
works. With later extensions there and the new factory at Cowley Hill,
the glassworks' demand must have increased greatly from then onwards.
Output from the two collieries could easily meet it. In 1880 the St Helens
Colliery produced over 91,000 tons in six months and the Ravenhead
nearly 112,000. The latter continued to make a loss, but the former
remained profitable; and this was after Pilkingtons had obtained coal for
their glassworks at preferential rates.[25]

At their second meeting, on 20 July 1876, the directors resolved that
Pilkingtons should be supplied with fuel at the lowest prices in each
month. On 3 August coal cost the firm 8s a ton, blend 7s and slack –
used in the Siemens gas producers – only 4s 4d. The price for slack was
5d a ton less than that quoted to Bibby's Copper Works, even closer to
the collieries than Pilkingtons. The advantage of this cheap fuel becomes
even more evident in a minute recorded on 10 November 1876:

> Messrs Chance Bros. of Birmingham would not take any more of our coal
> at the price quoted . . . 10s 9d per ton delivered in our wagons.

Cheap fuel was not the least of Pilkingtons' assets.

It was customary for the coal proprietors of the St Helens district to
operate a brickworks in conjunction with their collieries, the clay brought
up from underground being well suited for brickmaking. The directors
of the Ravenhead Colliery Co. Ltd, for instance, decided in 1872 to start
such a brickworks and 'to mix the stuff from the Pits with field clay'.[26]
Pilkingtons had a brickworks before this: it is referred to in the Board
minutes in 1865.[27] Two years later Thomas Pilkington was urging 'that
we should make the most of the present opportunity to get rid of the
machine and works altogether, being neither worth our time nor
trouble',[28] but a new manager, Isaac Whitehead, was engaged[29] and the
brickworks appears thereafter to have become a more profitable concern.
Its original location, according to an old employee, George Blake, who
remembered it in the early 1870s, was 'near Groves's Colliery, between

the dam and Sherdley Road'. It was, however, a very modest under-taking, employing only 33 people altogether at the time of the colliery merger. Pilkingtons' colliery alone was then employing 748 men.[30] Their share in the new St Helens Collieries continued to bring in a small, but useful, income to the glass firm.

Chapter 12

1900–1914:
European Influences

THE twentieth century ushered in an era of closer international relationships and more intense technical effort within the glass industry. From 1900 onwards, outright competition between manufacturers in different parts of Europe began to give way to agreements and understandings. In plate glass manufacture so much capital was by this time invested – and so much new capital had constantly to be found in order to keep up to date – that unrestricted price-cutting to capture new markets was no longer a profitable exercise. In the window glass branch, much more labour intensive, the skilled workmen were becoming more politically and industrially active. Growing labour costs (or the threat of them) encouraged inventors both in America and Europe to press on more purposefully to find some means of making glass by machine instead of having to rely upon this growingly restive army of blowers and flatteners, now much more vocal in their demands for higher wages and better living conditions, and beginning to secure political support for their cause.

In Belgium, where window glass manufacture was heavily concentrated in the Charleroi area – there were 21 factories there, all but two of them under separate individual ownership[1] – the *Union Verrière* was responsible for two prolonged strikes within the space of four years. The first, in 1900–1901, lasting for ten months, has already been mentioned (p. 144). The second, in 1904, dragged on for nearly a year. It ended on 1 June 1905 with the men being obliged to return to work on their masters' terms.[2] The resulting shortage of glass put up prices and encouraged the opening of four more factories in Belgium, away from the main glassmaking area and the *Union Verrière's* main stronghold.[3]

Overproduction soon resulted and the Belgian window glass manufacturers, who relied for 95 per cent of their sales upon the more unpredictable foreign markets, many of them overseas, were in real trouble
again.

After the 1900–1901 strike the American Window Glass Manufacturers
Association, which controlled most of the United States' production,
sent a representative to try to persuade the Belgians to set up a similar
organization and offered to put up a third of the capital.[4] The attitude
of the Belgian workmen, reported *The Times* correspondent, was 'largely
responsible for the readiness with which Belgian manufacturers have
responded to the advances made by the trust'.[5] But, the strike over, the
self-reliant Belgians preferred to continue as before – until the next
prolonged stoppage in 1904–1905. After the collapse of the boom which
followed it and the failure of several firms, closer collaboration was
again canvassed. As a British consular report pointed out, the majority
of raw material suppliers joined forces to 'fix more or less regular prices,
while the manufacturers are to a certain extent the victims of circumstance
in the state of workmen's organizations . . . It is estimated in some
quarters that unless the window glass makers take a decisive step towards
co-operation, the present situation of low prices and small returns will
continue for a considerable period before the previous prosperity of the
industry can be re-established.'[6] Already, in May 1906, the possibility of
forming an association to regulate sales and prices was being considered,[7]
but the only outcome appears to have been a syndicate, formed at the
end of 1906, to regulate exports to the increasingly important markets of
the East and to Canada.[8] This step does not seem to have been then
accompanied by understandings relating to other markets, and prices in
Britain continued to fall until 1909, as may be seen from graph 8 on p. 141.
In that year, however, there was a 15 per cent increase in wages in
Belgium[9] and the price of Belgian glass was put up. British prices also
began to rise after this, and in 1913 were one-third higher than they had
been four years before.

Table 25 shows the extent to which the profitability of Pilkington's
window glass depended upon these events in Belgium. Good prices and
profits in the early years of the century are to be explained as much by
the Belgians' difficulties at that time, which affected world prices since
they were such major exporters, as by the high level of building activity
in Britain. The effect of the second strike in 1904–1905 is also reflected
in the higher profits of that and the succeeding year. They then slumped
as Belgian competition worldwide became fiercer again. Rising prices
after 1910, however, did not bring greater profit until the two years

TABLE 25
RETAINED IMPORTS OF WINDOW GLASS AND
PILKINGTON WINDOW GLASS SALES FOOTAGE AND PROFIT,
1900/1901–1913/1914

Year Ended 30 June	Retained Imports of Window Glass* '000 sq. ft	Pilkington Sales Footage '000 sq. ft	Pilkington Window Glass Profit £
1901	90,600	85,670	275,892
1902	105,450	73,831	236,187
1903	101,625	82,137	163,127
1904	79,350	86,577	139,392
1905	91,800	90,660	185,400
1906	103,050	87,728	182,536
1907	96,225	87,136	142,176
1908	91,275	85,758	88,999
1909	88,575	84,942	79,282
1910	90,150	89,132	85,368
1911	90,375	94,268	76,289
1912	99,075	96,528	80,339
1913	92,250	95,995	149,636
1914	56,175	92,895	158,420

Source: Trade and Navigation Returns; Pilkington Accounts.

*Calendar year. For purpose of comparison this column has been translated from weight, in which it appears in the Customs returns, to volume at the rate of 75 sq. ft per cwt.

immediately before the war. More important than anything else is the fact that sales of Belgian window glass in Britain, having gone on rising insistently and menacingly from the middle of the nineteenth century, stopped doing so after 1900. The volume was nevertheless immense and in excess of Pilkington's total output, only about 50 per cent of which was sold on the home market. Thus, although the total of Belgian window glass had stopped rising, the Belgians were selling half as much again as Pilkington in Britain.

These years saw further consolidation and reorganisation at Pilkington's window glassworks which, in 1904, a Belgian writer was able to describe as 'la plus puissant . . . du monde entier'.[10] The extensions at Grove Street were made possible by the closing of the Ravenhead spur of the canal, permitted by Act of Parliament in 1898. (Compare Plans 5 and 9.) The construction of Canal Street on part of the site enabled the firm to make out a good case for closing that part of Grove Street which ran through the works; the two streets ran parallel to each other and there was no need for both. The filling in of the canal also gave access across Canal Street to Greenbank, and between 1899 and 1902 Pilkington made some fifty purchases of property in the Greenbank area. The timber yard was removed to this new site. The vacated timber yard and the closed section of Grove Street left room for the erection of a fourth warehouse and more tank furnaces; there were 23 altogether by this time. Some of the pot and block makers, who had previously occupied 12 pot rooms at the otherwise disused Eccleston Street factory, moved down to Grove Street in 1899 and others went to Cowley Hill. The people of St Helens were no longer regaled with the sight of large glassmaking pots being carried through the town on specially-constructed chariot-like vehicles.

About one-sixth of Pilkington's window glass footage consisted of rolled plate and it was an attempt to control the market for this production which first brought the company into closer touch with the continental manufacturers. Rolled plate was the branch in which Chances excelled and, as has been seen (p. 137), they had licensed their double roll machine to St Gobain. This led to meetings with Lucien Delloye (1856–1938) who had become general manager of the glassmaking side of the St Gobain business in 1903. An engineering graduate who had gone into the company in 1881, Delloye had already distinguished himself by making improvements to its grinding and polishing machinery.[11] He was, reported E. F. Chance after the first meeting with him in July 1903, 'a very gentlemanly, good looking, quiet, capable man and is probably one of the most capable glass works engineers of the day . . .'[12] They discussed the possibility of dividing up the rolled plate market territorially. The idea soon became a reality.

In 1904 the St Gobain Co., together with nine other rolled plate glass manufacturers in France, Belgium and what is now East and West Germany and Czechoslovakia, formed the *Convention Internationale des Verres Spéciaux* to control output on the continent. On 27 October 1904 they signed in Brussels a five-year agreement with the three British producers of this kind of glass: Chances, Pilkington, and the Glasgow [Rolled] Plate Glass Co., which owned a very small factory with a four-pot furnace on the Forth-Clyde Canal at Firhill, opened in 1872. The continentals contracted to sell all their rolled plate glass on the U.K. market *via* the three British companies. Indemnities were to be paid by

H

the British if less than a certain quota of foreign glass was sold per year and they also agreed to market patterned and cathedral glass at fixed prices, again with penalties if sales fell below certain footages. The Europeans agreed to provide returns of their despatches of glass to Britain and the two parties promised not to open factories in each other's territories.[13]

A number of the signatories to this agreement were plate glass companies, and in several of them, in other countries besides France, St Gobain either had a share interest or outright control.[14] It was no doubt under St Gobain's lead that they formed in 1904 a Plate Glass Convention, the *Convention Internationale des Glaceries,* in an attempt to control the continental market. Pilkington, however, now sole producer in the United Kingdom, was not prepared to sign this agreement, though it was willing to adopt the Convention's prices and it received notification whenever these were altered.[15]

This loose alliance was an uneasy one, however, and marked by a singular lack of trust. The same was true, too, of the Rolled Plate Convention, for there was no love lost between Pilkington and Chances, and matters were not improved when K. A. Macaulay of Chances happened to pick up a packet of papers belonging to Pilkington at the end of a joint meeting – he claimed it was an accident – and discovered that the St Helens company was selling below the agreed rate to two London merchants.[16]

Pilkington's interest in Maubeuge was another bone of contention so far as St Gobain was concerned. Delloye told E. F. Chance that they were 'spoiling prices (Pol[ishe]d Plate) with their small make on the Continent where they can't be doing any good to themselves or anyone else'.[17] St Gobain was always threatening to start a plate glassworks in Britain in retaliation. It was reported to be interested in the former London & Manchester Plate Glass Company's idle works when they were about to be put up for auction in May 1905. Before Pilkington managed to acquire them through nominees, for £82,000, a shrewd observer at Chances noted that St Gobain's aim may have been 'merely to push Pilkingtons into buying them thinking that they will permanently close them and that in doing so they will be burdened in their competition with this large outlay in the shape of Capital'.[18]

Soon after this, at the beginning of 1906, Pilkington had more immediate cause for concern when a new glassworks began to be built just south of St Helens, not far from the old London & Manchester. Although the business masqueraded as Turner & Co., Turner was a glass merchant and rumour had it that he was backed by foreign capital and expertise.

The name of a continental engineer, Emile Gobbe, was, in particular, associated with the venture. In so far as the aim was to produce rolled plate glass, this was a matter for the Rolled Plate Convention and all the British adherents to it. Pilkington accordingly alerted Chances to what was happening and promised to make further enquiries.[19] Chances, in their turn, were in touch with both the Glasgow works and with Delloye, who agreed to find out what he could from continental sources.[20] When Chances had one of their frequent meetings with Delloye early in March, they were told that Gobbe was not involved and that, in any case, that engineer was 'very theoretical' and had 'more book knowledge than practical works experience'. Despret, however, another of the continental leaders, made the point that Gobbe was very much concerned with Fourcault's experiments to draw sheet glass (to be considered further in due course) and felt that his idea might be to install the Fourcault process at St Helens.[21] But, in any event, both Chances' informants were in no doubt that the works were intended for the manufacture of sheet glass – and that did not come within the Rolled Plate Convention's purview. The British were not so sure, and Austin Pilkington pointed out that, since the continentals were 'sometimes apt to interpret an agreement according to the letter rather than the spirit of the law', what was needed was an additional clause in the agreement with the Convention preventing the latter from taking a financial interest in any new rolled plate works in the United Kingdom or providing any technical assistance in its construction.[22]

It soon became clear that the intention was to make both sheet and rolled plate glass at the new works, and Despret confirmed that Gobbe, and his assistant, Dethier, were designing the furnaces.[23] It was not until 1 December 1906, however, that Turner & Co. informed potential customers that they were in a position to quote for sheet glass and were in the process of putting down plant to make rolled varieties too.[24] The latter took time, and it was not until early April 1907 that Richard Pilkington approached Chances about drawing up contingency plans for when this new glass came on to the market. Representatives of the two companies met in Liverpool on 6 June, by which time Turner & Co., having recruited one of Pilkington's men to take charge, were starting to light their second furnace.[25] The parties agreed to meet the new competition as and when it appeared and to act in the closest collaboration so as not to upset the general price structure.

By August, however, the threat had already passed away. Richard Pilkington reported to Chances that a hole had been knocked in the side of the sheet tank and the crown had tumbled in. And the rolled plate tank had 'really made nothing'. Instead of three shifts per day they had managed only one. 'The whole place is idle – nothing being done except a few cutters trying to re-sort their coarse.' 'It really is remarkable what a thorough mess they have succeeded in making of the whole thing,' Chances' managing director commented.[26] It only remained for Pilkington to purchase the factory, which they eventually did (though again, not in their own name), for £20,000 in April 1909. It was then disposed of for about £12,000 for use as an ironworks, and Chances contributed £1,500 to the costs.[27] The associates were fortunate in being confronted by such a weak challenge; but they were quite prepared to act effectively had the challenge been stronger.

This combined operation did not, however, bring Pilkington and Chances any closer together nor did it make Pilkington any more popular with the continental manufacturers. St Gobain, in particular, was convinced that the St Helens company was prepared to undercut Plate Glass Convention prices if this would win an order. Yet Pilkington continued to take notice of Convention arrangements while not whole-heartedly going along with them. In November 1906, for instance, when the Convention factories took the further step of reducing their output, Pilkington refused to give any such undertaking but was prepared to promise not to re-open the London & Manchester works nor to extend its works at Cowley Hill, Ravenhead or Maubeuge apart from replacing old plant with new. But this still gave a considerable scope for increasing output by putting in more efficient machinery, and St Gobain felt that this was not honouring the spirit of the undertaking. Pilkington, for its part, had refused to sign the Convention in the first place precisely so that it could retain this freedom of manoeuvre.

St Gobain's intense dislike of Pilkington at this time, and its threat, if need be, to start a plate glassworks in England, were frequent topics of conversation at meetings between Chances' representatives and Delloye. Some of the notes taken by the former deserve quotation:[28]

13 December 1905: Delloye obviously thinks he cd give P. Bros a good knock in Plate, as being able to make better and probably cheaper article. He has great distrust of P. Bros and now has reason to suppose they are doing the Convention. Referring especially to some particular orders which P. Bros regularly take from St Gobain Co.

4 October 1907: Plate Works in England. Cost would be about 20/- per metre needing a capital of £300,000 up. St Gobain Co. Wks produce at St Gobain 1,300,000 metres per annum and P. Bros about 1,000,000 m. per annum. No difficulty as to technical management also St Gobain Co. have agents all over the world . . . He thinks such works wd keep P. Bros in better order and that if there was a fight, no profit might be made for some time but I [E.F.Chance] have no doubt that if their Plate Convention ended 31 December 1909 or at a later period, they wd probably go in for some such scheme.

6 March 1908: Mr D. is very sick with P. Bros who are at their usual games in Italy, invoicing large sizes in Plate (which, of course, would command high prices) at improper rates by selling the pane as if it had actually been divided up and cut up in small sizes . . . He is red hot upon plate wks in England, though it is not at all certain if the St Gobain Co. would be free to erect same if their plate convention continues for another 5 years after end 1909, but he rather fancies he could overcome this apparently by using our name . . . He now advocates a works, say 150,000 sq. metres and £20,000 for working capital, and he prefers the East Coast such as Sunderland or Newcastle to Widnes which he thinks too near to St Helens. Referring to the proposed capital of £300,000 which had been referred to at my [E.F.Chance's] last interview, I said I did not think our Co. wd care about taking up a large portion of this; but of course if they had actually decided to come to England, there were other possibilities such as general amalgamation.

26 March 1908: Plate situation is entirely changed. Trade very bad indeed; practically no orders from America; whereas sales had been 20 per cent below production [from the Convention works], they were now 50 per cent and 60 per cent below.

P. Bros not members of Convention. They refused to join. RP had said, however, that they would observe the conditions as to not increasing make and as to keeping prices. RP said he pledged his word they could do this, though they could not enter formal agreement. They broke their pledges in both respects. D. was content to wink at this (though he took care to let P. Bros know he was aware of the facts) as long as trade was good; now he can stand it no longer when every order is of consequence . . . D. intends to meet Windle P. as soon as he can and have it out with him. If he can come to satisfactory terms, he will prefer to do, and not start works in England. If compelled to start works in England, he cannot now do so with us alone; he will have to bring in some Belgian manufacturers in order to come to terms with the Convention . . . He wd not go public, nor have any preference shares . . . They would regard works in England as mainly to control P. Bros and not as a profit making concern . . . They would fight at first for all they were worth, and take all men they could from P. Bros.

In this new age of industrial diplomacy, Delloye was acting as the mouthpiece of the continental plate glassmaking powers. To threaten violence to another nation in order to gain concessions was that well-known ploy of traditional international diplomacy known as sabre-rattling. By talking to his English ally in this aggressive way, Delloye was no doubt expecting that the information confided would in due course reach his adversary and make him more amenable to the normal processes of negotiation. The adversary, however, had greatly strengthened his position during the previous decade by emerging as sole British producer and by acquiring the remaining plate glassworks which might have given the continentals a relatively inexpensive foothold of the sort that Pilkington itself had managed to get at Maubeuge in France. To have expended £300,000 in building a completely new factory with the prospect – on Delloye's own admission – of a hard fight and no profit for years, would have been a desperate throw indeed. Yet nobody could deny St Gobain's enthusiasm for empire building; and the process had gathered pace in recent years. The French giant had owned Stolberg Plate Glassworks near Aachen since 1857, acquired Mannheim-Waldhof in 1858, built Pisa (designed by Delloye) in 1888, purchased an interest in Bilin (Bohemia) and built Franière (Belgium) both in 1896, acquired an interest in Altwasser (Silesia) in 1898, a controlling interest in Sas van Gent (Holland) in 1904 and a connection with Herzogenrath (also near Aachen) in the same year.[29]

As it happened, this diplomatic offensive had its effect upon Windle Pilkington who emerged as Pilkington's chief negotiator after his brother Richard died in March 1908. He saw the need to be more conciliatory in view of the continentals' increased difficulties. Belgian exports of plate glass, at 90 per cent of total production,[30] were almost as high a proportion as their exports of window glass.

The short, sharp collapse of the American market following the financial crisis there in October 1907 had hit the continentals as hard as Delloye had claimed. His overtures to Windle Pilkington bore quick results. On 2 July, at a meeting at the Euston Hotel in London, Pilkington admitted that it had already cut its output by 20,000 sq. ft per week and promised to reduce it by a further 23,000 sq. ft. Delloye had proposed that in future Pilkington and the Convention members should limit their output by operating only a fixed area of grinding surface. Pilkington agreed to stop 11 polishing tables and a corresponding number of grinding benches. It also agreed not to increase its output so long as the Convention's production remained under 50 per cent of capacity.[31]

Here, however, Pilkington pulled off a diplomatic *coup*. The grinding and polishing machinery that was removed – including all the machines at Ravenhead – was already obsolete. New higher-speed equipment, with far greater output from the same grinding surface area, had just been installed.[32] Pilkington production fell hardly at all in 1908–1909, as we shall see. This was the culmination of years of investment and improvement at Cowley Hill which Pilkington saw as its best defence against threats and pressure from abroad.

The company invested altogether the very large sum of £620,000 at Cowley Hill between 1903–1904 and 1913–1914. A very important innovation was the substitution of a lehr, which worked continuously, in place of the intermittent kilns. In the United States, where plate glass lehrs had first been used in the form of five preliminary ovens and an enclosed runway 30 ft long forming a temperature gradient, the time taken by the annealing process was greatly reduced.[33] Cecil Pilkington, who had joined the company in 1897 after being educated at Shrewsbury and Oxford, where he read Natural Sciences, first saw one of these lehrs on a visit to the United States in 1901 with his father, Windle. According to his later recollection of the event, the train in which they were travelling happened to stop at a place on the Allegheny River, 16 miles up from Pittsburgh, and there they saw 'a lot of interesting activity' at a works by the line. They got out and Windle 'walked up to the people and said "What's all this?" The man who developed the lehr was called Hyden Kamp. Windle asked him "Can I have it?" Hyden Kamp was very pleased to give it to him as he had been unable to sell it in the States. There was apparently no patent . . . !' So interested was Cecil in the new discovery that he failed to catch the train to Pittsburgh with his father and, not having any money on him, had to walk the 16 miles back.[34]

When he returned to England, Cecil Pilkington began to work on a pilot plant at the recently-acquired Ravenhead works, using a tray lehr for these experiments. He was assisted by Leonard Lackland, a Liverpool graduate. With the aid of an electrical recording pyrometer, one of the first to be used in Britain, he was able to regulate the temperature fall in the tunnel with sufficient accuracy to produce properly annealed glass. The pilot plant at Ravenhead having served its purpose, in 1904 a large Cruickshank rod-type lehr was built at Cowley Hill amid great secrecy.[35] This reduced the time of annealing from four days to four or five hours. The original lehr was subsequently modified and others built. By 1907 there were three in operation. Before 1914 thermo-couples and resistance pyrometers had been introduced.[36]

Technical improvements were also made in the other stages of plate glass manufacture, notably in the grinding machinery as has been noted. The replacement programme embarked upon at the end of 1905 and costing £100,000, involved a large amount of electrification.[37] The old 22 ft diameter grinding tables were replaced, in February and July

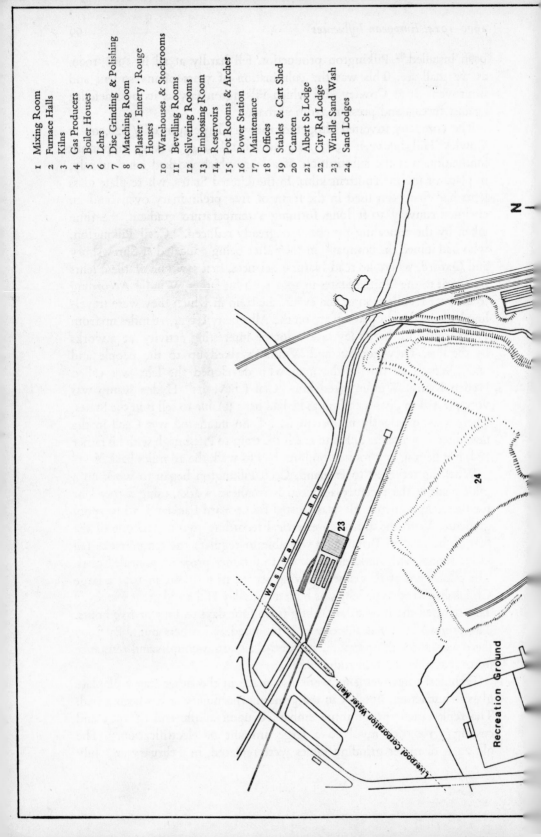

1 Mixing Room
2 Furnace Halls
3 Kilns
4 Gas Producers
5 Boiler Houses
6 Lehrs
7 Disc Grinding & Polishing
8 Matching Room
9 Plaster · Emery · Rouge Houses
10 Warehouses & Stockrooms
11 Bevelling Rooms
12 Silvering Rooms
13 Embossing Room
14 Reservoirs
15 Pot Rooms & Arches
16 Power Station
17 Maintenance
18 Offices
19 Stables & Cart Shed
20 Canteen
21 Albert St Lodge
22 City Rd Lodge
23 Windle Sand Wash
24 Sand Lodges

N

Washway Lane

Liverpool Corporation Water Main

Recreation Ground

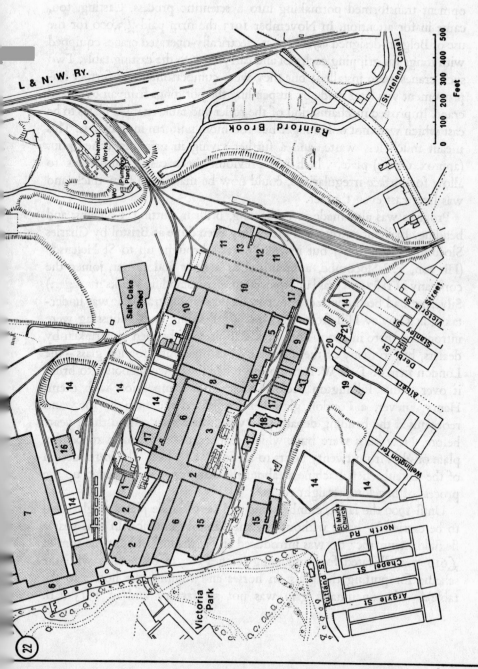

Plan 8 Pilkington Brothers Ltd Plate Works in 1914

1907, January 1908, June 1910 and February 1912,[38] by five new sets of tables of 35 ft, each driven by its own electric motor, and the footage was thereby increased from 380 to 963 per table. The pot capacity of furnaces was increased from sixteen to twenty. Potmaking itself was improved. French clays, imported via Maubeuge, began to be used about 1905, and from 1907 Edwin Hopkinson's systematic research and development transformed potmaking into a scientific process. Casting, too, came in for attention. In November 1913 the firm paid £3,000 for the use of Belgian-designed *défourneuses*, electrically-operated cranes equipped with tongs for gripping each pot and carrying it to the casting table. Two such cranes were installed; but they were cumbersome, and further improvement was later made by suspending the pot tongs from an overhead crane. Improved mechanisation of the roller and table enabled plates to be cast which were not only longer but also more uniform in thickness. This meant much less waste, and a further saving in grinding time. $\frac{1}{4}$ in. (approx. 6 mm) plate, which had previously been cast 12 mm thick to allow for surface irregularities, could now be made 10·6 mm thick and was later cast even thinner.

Progress was also made in embossing, brilliant cutting, bevelling and bending. Brilliant cutting had previously been done at Bristol by Charles Slocombe (1829–1905) but in 1881 he was brought up to St Helens.[39] (His son, F.E. Slocombe, apprenticed as a fitter and turner, joined the company in 1887 and was later to become an outstanding works manager.) Silvering had been contracted out to Dodd and Oultram but was undertaken at Cowley Hill from 1885–1886.[40] Bending and embossing were introduced there in 1900. This work had previously been undertaken by dealers, but so many of them were by this time using foreign glass – the London firm of T. & W. Farmiloe even had their own schooner to bring it over – that Pilkington decided to go into competition with them. Henry Enever, a London glass bender, joined the firm in 1902 and reorganised the bending department which had been started three years before. New kilns were built which reduced the time taken to bend a plate of glass from twenty hours to an hour and a half. The introduction of the Offenbacher machine at about the same time also speeded up the process of bevelling straight edges.[41]

Until 1909 the large, cumbersome and very fragile plates of glass had to be carried by hand without any mechanical assistance. In that year a flexible pneumatic grip was introduced and at the end of 1911 the sum of £619 was allocated for purchasing 'cranes etc. in connexion with the scheme for putting the glass on horses and running the horses to the table'.[42] The pneumatic grip was not satisfactory and in 1913 F.B.

Waldron, who had been educated at University College, Sheffield, and had joined Pilkington in 1911 as head of the drawing office at Cowley Hill, invented sucker pads, exhausted by a vacuum pump and suspended from an overhead crane. St Gobain held a patent for a similar, but inferior, device – it was never used in England – but they agreed, for a small consideration, not to interfere with what was being done at Cowley Hill.[43] The talented Waldron, soon to become Experimental Engineer, was to play an important part in the technical development of the plate glass industry between the wars, as we shall see.

Most of the machinery for the cranes, as well as for the grinding and polishing, was worked by electricity. The old power station with its gas engines could not meet the increasing demand, and it was decided to install a completely new 4,500 kW generating set. After three weeks of frantic activity and much last-minute anxiety, it was finished in time to be started up on 8 July 1913, by King George V. This, the first royal visit to the company, was a recognition of its growing national status.

That Pilkington gained greatly from these innovations and from the Convention's efforts to maintain prices and stint output, is clear from Table 26. Unit costs fell impressively at Cowley Hill, where most of the plate glass was made, though Ravenhead made a surprisingly useful contribution to the total profit. The sharp fall in costs there in 1908–1909 was, of course, due to the stopping of grinding and polishing under the 1908 arrangement with the Convention. The rough cast made at Ravenhead was transferred to Cowley Hill for finishing. (This is also reflected in Ravenhead's lower profit in 1908–1909 despite greater output, in contrast to the considerably higher profit that year at Cowley Hill.) Because it was also processed at Cowley Hill, Ravenhead rough cast appears also in the former's output figures. And because of this double counting there was not such a sharp production leap at Cowley Hill in 1908–1909 as the table seems to suggest; rather a slight falling back in accordance with Pilkington's promises to the Convention. But from then onwards production forged ahead quickly to a new, and much higher, plateau.

The late nineteenth century pattern of lower and more hard-won profit in plate than in window glass continued until 1905–1906. But from then onwards, as may be seen by comparison with the window glass statistics in Table 25, plate glass entered a distinctly more prosperous period. Indeed, plate glass profits rose as those on window glass fell. The two were about equal in 1906–1907, but from then onwards – even in 1912–1913 and 1913–1914 when window glass recovered its

TABLE 26
IMPORTS OF PLATE GLASS AND PILKINGTON MANUFACTURING COSTS AND PROFITS AT COWLEY HILL AND RAVENHEAD
1901/1902–1913/14

Year Ended 30 June	Imports* '000 cwt	Imports* '000 sq. ft	Cowley Hill Footage made sq. ft	Cowley Hill Profit	Ravenhead Footage made sq. ft	Ravenhead Profit	Plate Glass Production (d. per foot) (i) Cowley Hill	Plate Glass Production (d. per foot) (ii) Ravenhead
1902	413	14,455	4,962,223	£14,000	1,082,174	−£16,616	11·62	15·46
1903	415	15,785	5,159,496	−£4,477	1,387,948	−£16,308	10·44	14·05
1904	478	16,730	5,308,045	£6,899	1,450,210	£3,147	10·22	11·97
1905	420	14,700	5,522,453	−£5,432	1,676,721	£35,708	9·59	9·83
1906	390	13,650	6,282,328	£38,531	2,044,734	£40,040	9·39	9·77
1907	406	14,210	7,022,198	£88,331	2,422,908	£56,433	8·15	9·42
1908	328	11,480	8,524,394	£97,588	2,238,551	£53,288	7·68	9·24
1909	331	11,585	10,320,843	£126,351	2,430,832	£48,585	7·25	5·72
1910	308	10,780	11,828,663	£170,801	2,456,688	£46,741	7·31	5·15
1911	332	11,620	13,925,992	£195,802	2,397,030	£56,276	6·46	5·38
1912	352	12,320	12,309,611	£137,321	2,199,726	£61,551	6·77	4·50
1913	443	15,505	14,093,125	£147,606	2,779,238	£65,198	6·87	4·29
1914	213	7,450	14,341,277	£145,786	2,583,300	£49,352	7·67	5·08

Source: Trade and Navigation Returns; Pilkington Accounts.

Note: The import footage figures have been calculated on the basis of 700 sq. ft to the ton of ¼ in. plate glass.

*Import figures are for the calendar years stated.

former profitability – plate took the lead. The decision to diversify, taken in the early 1870s, was now justifying itself and Pilkington's heavy investment and shrewd diplomacy in more recent times were paying off.

The years immediately before the war saw the sequel to Delloye's much-threatened invasion of the British plate glass industry. St Gobain did land in England, but not to make plate glass. Its invasion was, indeed, little more than a carefully-timed excursion: the purchase of 250 shares in Chance Brothers, with whom it had made a new agreement in 1909 concerning their double roll machines.

Chances had, in 1907, bought the small Glasgow [Rolled] Plate Glassworks, which manufactured mainly figured and cathedral glass, in order to prevent them (so they said) from falling into Pilkington's hands. The vendors, Brogan and Malloch, were kept on as managers until 1911.[44] At the beginning of that year, E.F. Chance told Delloye that they wanted to expand the factory and asked him whether St Gobain would collaborate with them in this 'as possibly having some bearing upon future developments and co-operation'.[45] Delloye showed an interest, but preferred to provide capital for Spon Lane as well, his company having had, Chance noted, a very successful year and being well off for cash.[46] Negotiations were protracted – among other matters, G.F. Chance was concerned with what Delloye would think about their cost of administration and scale of salaries 'probably out of proportion according to French ideas' – and agreement was not finally reached until 2 July 1911. By it St Gobain paid £22,500 for the 250 £100 shares it bought and promised to meet three-quarters of the cost (up to £50,000) of Chances' investment on extensions. The Director General of St Gobain was to have a seat on the Chance Board, and both companies were to exchange information about processes of common interest and to have free use of each other's patents and designs.[47]

The timing of the agreement was just right, for Delloye had reached the point at which he needed to exert more pressure on Pilkington. At the end of 1911 he had broached to Pilkington the idea of its supplying the Plate Glass Convention, which had been extended in 1909 for a further five years, with carefully certified statistics of its output, sales and stocks. Pilkington, on its side, wanted the Convention's clearance for building a lehr at Maubeuge.[48] A meeting was arranged, to be held in London towards the end of July; but Delloye had to cancel this because, he wrote to Pilkington on 24 July, a crisis had blown up which threatened the very being of the Convention. So serious was it, indeed, that he had decided to put off his annual holiday and invited the Pilkington directors to meet him in London on 2 August. Apparently some of the Belgian members of the Convention were stepping out of line, and it had been decided to form an export agency which would handle the export sales for all the plate glass made at 'a good many' of the works. This agency would guarantee that the Convention's prices were kept and would also avoid duplication of its selling outlets abroad. The most important part of Delloye's letter of invitation to the London meeting, however, came at the end, when he imparted the news that St Gobain had bought 'a certain number of shares' (no details) in Chances. 'The advantage resulting for the English group from a fixed and lasting alliance between one of the English manufacturers and an important Continental Company,' he added 'will not escape you'.[49]

Delloye's diplomacy succeeded. At the meeting on 2 August Pilkington agreed to supply the Convention with the required statistics every three months, certified by its chartered accountants. This new arrangement, however, was to be conditional upon prior consultation by the Convention when price changes in markets governed by the English tariff were concerned, and upon the setting up of the new selling organisation.[50] In acknowledging Pilkington's written confirmation of these terms, Delloye, having referred to 'the annoying situation of the Belgian companies', underlined their implications. 'It is quite clear,' he wrote, 'that if an exceptional crisis were to occur and if we were obliged to reduce our output below the present figure, you on your part would have to take account of the situation'.[51]

During the latter part of 1912, the Convention succeeded in bringing the errant continental manufacturers back into the fold. *The Times* Brussels correspondent, reporting at the beginning of December that the Convention was to be renewed for another ten years when it ran out in August 1914, noted that all the continental works were involved apart from those at Courcelles in Belgium, controlled by the Pittsburgh Plate Glass Company, which had, nevertheless, agreed to adhere to it, in the same way as Pilkington had. The selling agency, to be known as the *Union Internationale et Commerciale des Glaceries*, was to be backed with a capital of 2,000,000 francs (£80,000).[52] Pilkington was later informed that it was to come into being on 1 April 1913.[53]

From then until the outbreak of war the working of the new arrangements caused little comment in the correspondence between St Helens and the continent so far as the British price list was concerned. The English company, which had mistakenly read L. Delloye's signature as

T. Delloye in the first place, continued to address the chief executive at St Gobain as such. (It remained in ignorance of Delloye's Christian name until the middle of the 1920s.) Chief attention was centred upon events in Germany where the leading bottlemaking combine diversified into plate glass. Its new factory in Westphalia, Spiegelglasfabrik Reisholz, came into use in October 1913. In April 1914 it was said to be working day and night.[54] No doubt it continued, but not for long, to supply markets outside the central European *bloc*. The invasion of France and Belgium, and the destruction or capture of many of the leading plate glassworks on or near the Belgian and French frontiers, including Maubeuge, put an end to the Convention so far as the British were concerned in August 1914, the very month when it was to enter into a renewed ten years of existence.

Chapter 13

1900–1914:
North American Influences

I N the early years of the present century Pilkington depended to an unusual extent on sales abroad. In terms of footage, exports just before 1914 exceeded sales to the home market in plate and cathedral glass, though not in sheet and other forms of rolled glass.

TABLE 27
AVERAGE ANNUAL FOOTAGE OF HOME AND EXPORT SALES,
1910–13
'000 sq. ft

	Home Sales	Exports
Plate	5,741	6,740
Sheet	43,957	33,206
Rolled	11,387	5,418
Cathedral (Ravenhead)	2,112	3,835

Source: Pilkington Accounts; Pilkington Central Statistics Department

Among Pilkington's export markets, Canada was the richest prize, and the company already had 200 people working there in 1904.[1] Moreover, this Canadian commercial base brought it into closer touch with the early mechanisation of window glass manufacture in the United States; and this, in its turn, had very important consequences for the development of the company at St Helens itself.

Pilkington opened warehouses in Vancouver (1903), Winnipeg (1906),

BLOWN CYLINDER MANUFACTURE IN THE LATE NINETEENTH/EARLY TWENTIETH CENTURY

20 Glassblower using 'bicycle' apparatus and compressed air.

21 Cylinders being split for flattening.

THE DRAWN CYLINDER
PROCESS AT SHEET WORKS.

24 *Right* Filling
reversible pot by ladle
from tank.

25 *Left* The start of the draw.

26 *Right* Finished
cylinder being lowered
onto a cheval prior to
being cut and split.

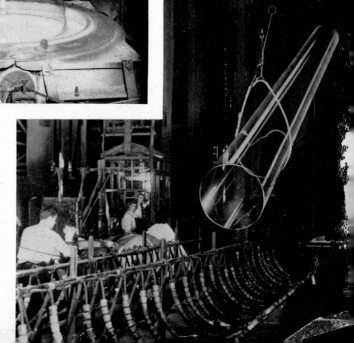

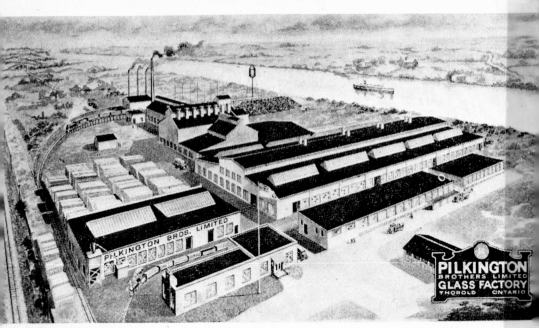

THOROLD, CANADA

27 The sheet and rolled factory (an artist's impression).

28 Windle Village, separated from the factory site by the main line of the Canadian National Railway.

and Calgary (1912) to supplement those at Montreal and Toronto. As may be seen from Table 28, the volume of Pilkington glass sold in Canada rose impressively until 1906/7, after which a high level of imports was maintained but profits fell for a few years. Canada was Pilkington's most important oversea market for glass, the company's warehouses alone – that is to say, excluding direct sales to Canadian importers – taking about one-tenth of total Pilkington output of all kinds of glass in the early years of the century and over 15 per cent in 1910. Of this, plate glass seems to have accounted for about half by value in the early 1890s, falling to about a quarter by 1906.[2] Although much more foreign (European and American) glass was sold in the dominion than Pilkington

TABLE 28

TOTAL FOOTAGE OF GLASS OF ALL KINDS SOLD THROUGH AND PROFIT FROM PILKINGTON CANADIAN WAREHOUSES

1895/6–1913/14

Year Ended 30 June	Footage Sold sq. ft	Profit $
1896	3,842,408	27,778
1897	3,918,122	5,876
1898	5,569,475	35,319
1899	6,370,976	70,965
1900	5,947,192	98,015
1901	6,037,694	95,516
1902	7,738,466	122,520
1903	7,737,404	101,113
1904	10,066,752	103,484
1905	10,968,159	109,174
1906	13,823,041	185,857
1907	15,255,674	190,278
1908	14,168,501	147,539
1909	14,319,151	120,139
1910	17,534,073	143,204
1911	14,795,616	99,385
1912	16,582,544	124,764
1913	15,283,232	232,181
1914	6,337,832	116,476

Source: Pilkington Accounts; Return to the Executive Committee, 18 January 1933

supplied, Canada nevertheless became an increasingly important market which brought in a profit both from manufacture and from sale.*

The size and profitability of these sales depended to a large extent upon Canada not possessing its own flat glass industry. Under these circumstances the tariff was relatively low, 15 per cent. When, however, some American promoters proposed to build a window glass factory, one of their first actions was to try to obtain tariff protection for the venture. Much more significant, in the longer run, was the fact that the new works proposed to employ a completely new mechanical process.

Real economies in glass manufacture were to be gained only by transforming it from an intermittent to a continuous process. This involved the substitution of machines for hand labour. In plate glass, some headway had been made, as has been seen, by the installation of electrically operated cranes to avoid the manhandling of the heavy glass plates from one part of the works to another, and by the introduction of lehrs and larger and faster grinding benches. But the melting process itself still had to be carried on intermittently in pot furnaces because tanks could not then produce molten metal good enough for this high quality product. Moreover, despite improvement, the grinding and polishing was still very inefficient. Each piece of rough plate glass, when annealed, had to be transported to a separate table and embedded in plaster of Paris to withstand the weight of the grinding and polishing heads. This embedding operation, known as swimming the plate, was an extraordinary affair, carried out by a gang of 12 hefty men who stood on the upper surface of the glass, and by a rhythmic movement of their feet, legs and bodies, moved the plate about until the surface plaster oozed from underneath and the glass and plaster became an unbroken surface. One side was then ground and polished. This completed, the plate of glass was then lifted from the plaster bed, freed from any plaster adhering to it, covered with a special thick cloth known as bench cloth, and then relaid on the table for the other side to be processed. In 1914 plate glass manufacture was obviously still highly intermittent; big changes were not to come about until after the First World War.

With window glass the prospects for continuous production were

*In South America, where the company had had a particularly resourceful commission agent, Thomas Holt, a warehouse was put in hand in Buenos Aires in 1907.[3] Samuel Platt was sent from the Leeds depot to take charge of it, and he stayed there until returning to become London agent in 1914. The venture lost money at first but was profitable from 1910/11; in 1912/13 it sold over 2¼ m. sq. ft. of glass and earned a profit of over £6,500.[4] In Europe a depot in Rome was added in this period to those in Paris and Naples.

better, for the raw materials were already melted continuously in tank furnaces. The first stage of manufacture, at any rate, was continuous. Mechanisation was applied initially, as we have seen, to the coarsest variety of window glass, rolled plate, when, in the 1880s, the molten glass was poured down an inclined plane and through a pair of iron rollers. Sheet glass, however, the staple which found its way into most window frames, was still made by hand-blowing into cylinders which were split longitudinally, flattened and annealed. As has been seen (p. 132) an appliance had been introduced to help with the blowing of the heaviest cylinders; but in 1887 there was only one such machine per tank and by 1900 only two. It was not until George Hyde, the works manager, with the assistance of Joseph Wilson, a fitter, had developed a lighter machine – known as the bicycle – that machine blowing became general and larger cylinders could be made.[5] (Plate 20). This was as far as mechanisation had gone at Grove Street by 1906.

Pilkington then had no organised team of engineers and scientists whose task it was to develop new processes. The company preferred instead to take licences of other people's inventions, as was the case, for instance, with the Siemens tank furnace or the Malevez machines. The main production director, Windle Pilkington, and his son, Cecil, with his Oxford degree in Natural Sciences, were primarily concerned with improving existing arrangements, not with making major technical discoveries. Science graduates were only just beginning to come into the company, and they, like most science graduates entering industry at the time, confined their attention to the routine testing, analysing, and sampling of materials.[6]

The Manchester Chemistry School, in particular, maintained the links with industry first forged by Sir Henry Roscoe, Professor of Chemistry there from 1857 to 1885.[7] One of its able graduates was Robert Francis Taylor (b. 1882; educated at Hulme and Manchester Grammar Schools) who took a First and then went on to Berlin University. He worked for the Pilkington Tile and Pottery Company – a business near Manchester in which Windle Pilkington's Clifton colliery-owning brothers were interested* – before coming to St Helens in 1905. E. B. LeMare (b. 1880), who followed him two years later, had a similar background: Hulme Grammar School and a Manchester Chemistry degree (an MSc taken in

---

*One of them, Lawrence Pilkington, was a close friend of the science-trained businessman and electrical engineer, Edward Hopkinson (10th Wrangler in the Mathematical Tripos at Cambridge in 1881), the younger brother of the more famous John Hopkinson, F.R.S. (1849–1898), who was, for a time, superintendent of Chances' lighthouse department, and of (Sir) Alfred Hopkinson, then Vice-Chancellor of Manchester University.[8]

1903), though he had subsequently gone to work in America. It was Windle Pilkington's Clifton contacts again who found this promising candidate, 'evidently a very clever man and very highly recommended', who wanted to get back to a job in England.[9] He was appointed at £200 a year and started work at the potmaking plant at Cowley Hill.

The important inventors in the glass industry were to be found at this time on the continent and in the United States. In Belgium Emile Fourcault was trying to draw a ribbon of glass out of the working end of a tank and upwards through a vertical lehr. An idea very like this had been patented in 1857 by an English engineer, William Clark,[10] but he had failed to make it work. (Fourcault believed he would have succeeded had tanks then been available.)[11] It was the Fourcault process with which Gobbe was associated and which was rumoured in 1906 to be destined for Turner's works. The rumour may have had a grain of truth in it, for relations between Pilkington and Fourcault were somewhat strained at that time.

Pilkington had been in touch with Fourcault since 1903 when the company had heard that his machine was drawing a sheet 16 inches wide and 20 feet long; but there were many defects in the glass. Windle Pilkington and his son, Austin, visited Charleroi towards the end of 1903 and, as a result of the visit, the Pilkington Board

agreed to pay £8,000 for the machine for rolled plate, cathedral, fluted, and other kinds of glass except sheet glass and polished glass for the British Empire. In return for our taking this risk we are to have a royalty of half the rate compared to any other manufacturer in England. Germany, France and Belgium – outside these countries we pay the lowest royalty charged. As to the making of sheet, we have the option for 12 months. They asked £40,000 for the whole thing, but kept off sheet as much as possible. Austin will go over again before agreement finally drawn up . . .

Something must have happened soon after this which caused Pilkington to have second thoughts about the proposed agreement. At the end of the following April, Fourcault wrote asking Pilkington to make up its mind before 1 May. The company evidently did not sign any contract but, early in 1905, when Fourcault was said to be making 'something like 5,000 ft per day' and the process was claimed to be 'a success for thin plate as well as sheet', negotiations were re-opened. On this occasion, however, Fourcault was distinctly unfriendly. According to the Pilkington Board minutes, he 'had said they were rid of a very bad contract when we refused their offer'. Again, nothing seems to have come of the talks and Fourcault's efforts to develop his process continued for years after this before the machine could be relied upon to produce saleable glass. In 1907, for instance, the Pilkington Board noted that he was 'having a lot of trouble. His best run is 98 hours'.[12] Development was certainly very slow, but in the more favourable economic climate of 1912 he managed to form a new company, La Société des Verriers de Dampremy, to back his efforts. Delloye told Pilkington in October 1913 that, though still short of cash, Fourcault had raised enough to build a new tank; but his machine was still working only very slowly. Although it turned out 300,000 sq. metres of saleable glass in two years just before the war started,[13] it was not to become of serious commercial interest until the 1920s.

The flat drawn process, which cut out both hand-blowing and flattening, had proved too difficult to develop into a money-making proposition before 1914, though considerable progress was made with its development. In America, too, a flat drawn process invented by Irving W. Colburn was encountering similar difficulties.* An intermediate process was, however, successful. This was what was known as the drawn cylinder process, a method which obviated hand-blowing but not flattening; and it did not even blow glass continuously. It was only a halfway house, a partial solution to the problem.

By this process, a flanged metal disc (or 'pipe') on the end of a large blowpipe was dipped into molten glass in a specially constructed pot which was filled from a tank before each drawing with sufficient glass to make one cylinder. As this bait was slowly raised between guiding shafts, it drew up the glass with it. Compressed air, passed through the blowpipe, was blown in at such a rate as would maintain the diameter constant. By this method, a cylinder of glass could be drawn 25 ft long and 24 in. diameter. Later types of machine were able to manufacture cylinders of more than 40 ft by 30 in. (By comparison, hand blown cylinders were usually about 5 ft by 12 in.) These machines only blew the glass; afterwards the giant cylinders had to be cut up into smaller lengths, flattened in the usual way and then annealed.

John H. Lubbers, the inventor, was an American who had been a glass

---

*The Colburn Machine Glass Company was formed in America in 1906 to develop Colburn's invention. By this system a ribbon of glass was carried upwards from the tank for a short distance and then, while still soft, bent over a roller and passed into a horizontal lehr. Experiments at Franklin (Pa) were later continued at a window glass tank at Reynoldsville (Pa) but the ribbon of glass kept breaking and was of very poor quality. Work stopped after 42 days when the money ran out. The company failed in 1911 but, with the help of M. J. Owens, the patents were acquired by the Toledo Glass Company and the process further developed. It started to become commercially viable after 1917.[14]

flattener. He began experiments in the early 1890s and subsequently took out several patents. He succeeded in interesting the American Window Glass Company, a vast company capitalised at $17,000,000 and owning plant representing over 70 per cent of all the window glassmaking capacity of the United States,[15] and they financed his research. In 1903 the American Window Glass Machine Company was incorporated as a subsidiary to acquire Lubbers' patents and develop the process for commercial use. Pilkington was already in touch with the promoters of the new machine in June 1903 but, as a result of independent advice from someone who had just returned from America, they decided not to proceed with negotiations until Lubbers, whom their informant described as 'a clever man but generally drunk', had developed his process further.[16] After two years' work, some glass was being produced which could compete with that blown by hand.[17] But Windle Pilkington, who went to America to see the process in operation, returned of the opinion that the glass produced was not yet of good enough quality for the British market.[18] While this was no doubt true – in 1905, forwarding samples of the glass, John Thorpe noted that it was very brittle[19] – Pilkington had to take notice of the new process because the American Window Glass Machine Company announced its intention of putting up a factory in Canada at a town called Cayuga, almost due south of Hamilton on the Niagara Peninsula. The news appeared in the *National Glass Budget* on 2 September 1905 and was sent to St Helens by Thorpe three days later.[20] In November a traveller was despatched from Toronto to spy out the land.[21]

The Window Glass Machine Company of Canada Limited, which was formed in 1905 with a capital of $40,000, wholly owned by its American parent,[22] reached an agreement with Cayuga local authority whereby it received a 14-acre site tax-free for the following 30 years, and, moreover, the town agreed to pay the cost of a siding to the nearby Grand Trunk Railway. The company, on its side, promised to build a factory which would find employment for 30 men at the outset and 100 later on.[23] Building of the new factory started early in July 1906 and by the end of the year $20,000 had been advanced.[24] By the middle of February 1907, three machines had been installed and tanks and lehr erected.[25]

Meanwhile the promoters were seeking an increase in the tariff, and this brought to a head differences among the Canadian dealers, most of whom sold hardware and paint as well as glass.[26] Much correspondence passed between Austin Pilkington and Donald Macmaster, of Macmaster, Hickson and Campbell, Montreal lawyers, about the presentation of the Pilkington case to the Canadian Tariff Commission, and Austin

Pilkington himself went to Canada soon after Easter 1906 to help prepare this. Many Canadian dealers had by then rallied to Pilkington's support. They signed a petition against any tariff increase.[27] The Pilkington petition itself, dated 26 October 1906, stressed that the company was already operating in the Canadian market in keen competition with Belgian manufacturers; that the small imperial preference introduced in 1897, which induced it to invest more heavily in Canada, did not offset the Belgians' native advantages; and that Canadian dealers could buy f.o.b. Liverpool rather than from Pilkington's warehouses if they cared to do so.[28] In the end the Americans did not get their higher tariff and the prospects for their factory grew less attractive. When, in 1907, an amendment to the English patent law required a patent to be worked within three years if it was to be valid in Britain,[29] the two parties were given further encouragement to move closer together. By then, according to an historian of the American glass industry, machine production 'had reached a state of near perfection' and American glass prices had been cut in order to drive the hand blowers out of business.[30] Pilkington was well aware of these developments for, as Windle Pilkington told the company's glassmakers, it had

kept a watch upon what was going on and had the glass over to look at it . . . They [the Americans] had either to work the patent here themselves or let someone else do so, and they approached us first, informing us that they were negotiating with several other people. At their invitation Mr Cecil went over to see the process, and on his return we settled that if we could come to terms (which would prevent their upsetting the glass trade here) it was the best thing to do. This was not easy as they had no interest in the glass trade here and their one idea was to get their process worked as widely as possible.[31]

The Board minutes give further details of these negotiations, though not of the agreement that was eventually reached. The report of Cecil Pilkington, to which his father referred, was given to the other directors on 24 November 1908. It resulted in a telegram being sent to J. Thorpe, Pilkington's agent in New York, which read:

Go Pittsburgh. Tell American Window Glass Co. we are prepared to consider proposition. Get terms exclusive and non-exclusive rights.

A draft agreement was drawn up on 2 February 1909, and at the Board meeting on 2 April Cecil Pilkington and Edward Cozens-Hardy were authorised 'to proceed to the U.S.A. and finally to settle and conclude

the negotiations and arrangements with the Window Glass Machine
Company and American Window Glass Company, with full power to
make such variations in the agreement of 2 February 1909, as they may
think desirable . . .' The formal agreement was signed by the two directors
on 22 April and a licence was granted to Pilkington five days later giving
it the right to work the drawn cylinder process not only in Britain but
also in Canada.[32]

This was a momentous decision, for it committed the company to
considerable expenditure upon a machine which was not continuous at
a time when, on the continent and in America, flat drawn continuous
processes were being developed which, before long, would mechanize
window glass manufacture completely and make the drawn cylinder
apparatus obsolete. Pilkington's interests in Canada had started a chain
of events leading to a premature investment which was to make the really
important move into flat drawn glass all the more difficult later on.
Indeed, as we shall see, the delay almost caused the company to abandon
sheet glass manufacture altogether at the end of the 1920s.

Pilkington lost little time in setting up an experimental machine at
St Helens. This was built in the rolled plate department at Grove Street
under the supervision of R.F.Taylor. It was ready to begin drawing in
October 1909.[33] Several improvements were made to the American
model by Windle Pilkington,[34] notably the replacement of the block
tap, employed for regulating the inflow of compressed air, by a needle
valve. Eight machines were brought into commercial operation on 2 May
1910, and others were started in April 1912. There was no question, at
this stage, of the machine-made glass driving the hand-blown product
off the market, because the quality of the former was poor – Eastern
Quality as it was called. As the manager of an American hand-operated
plant put it: 'The machines make more poor glass . . . but they make so
much more glass that they can pick out a great deal of good glass and
sort it very carefully.'[35] Production rose from 320,601 sq. ft in 1909/10
to about 6,500,000 sq. ft in the following year (about one-fifteenth of
Pilkington's total window glass output). It doubled in 1912/13, and in
the year just before the war nearly 15,000,000 sq. ft of drawn cylinder
glass were produced (about one-seventh of total production).

Pilkington's agreement with the American Window Glass Machine
Company involved it in helping the Americans to exploit the new process

outside the United States as well as in making it itself in Britain and Canada. Licensing outside Britain, Canada and the United States was to be achieved by a joint concern, the Empire Machine Company, with a capital of $306,000, 40 per cent paid up, in which the Americans held two-thirds of the shares, and the British the rest. With the strong selling point that Pilkington had faith in the machine and was installing it at St Helens, the directors set about finding possible licensees in Europe. They approached Delloye for France and Louis Lambert and Paul Noblet for Belgium. (Lambert also had glassmaking interests in Russia.) Delloye's answer, delivered from customary olympian heights, showed that he, at least, thoroughly understood that drawn cylinder glass was only an interim solution:

We have, in fact, directly or indirectly, interests in several countries on the continent in window glass works . . . I am, moreover, pretty well informed as to the position of the window glass industry in the United States, and I know the principle of the processes at present being applied. It is certain that as regards production the American Window Glass Company have got a good start, *but it is possible that other processes may soon assume a certain importance.* In a word, for reasons which vary somewhat as between one country and another, it seems very difficult to consider at this moment the acquisition of the patents of the American Window Glass, as this company have almost surely very high pretensions, and the profits to be looked for in works of average importance are not sufficient to justify very considerable expenses of installation while paying for expensive licences . . .[36]

In May of the following year, however, Delloye did go so far as to send a German engineer, Adolphe Engels, and a foreman from Aniche, Oscar Destatte, to America to see the process.[37]

The Belgians moved much more quickly, though with no greater ultimate effect. They were in America by the end of August 1909 and took an option on a non-exclusive licence which had to be taken up by 1 November.[38] By then they had reached the conclusion that the risks in introducing the new machine were too great and that there was not enough hope of profit. They had obviously given much thought to the matter and their conclusions, despite the bad contemporary translation, are worth quoting:

. . . We have to introduce in this country a new patent and are in this way compelled to make all the expensive experiments . . . Despite the fact that you agree to help us to some extent by sending us trained workmen, it will be highly difficult for us to give them all the easiness they are in the habit of having in their works; we will further have to train all the necessary workmen that they may undertake the management of the machines when your people leave us, and during all the time of this training our people, on account of their not being up to the work, will no doubt cause us heavy losses . . .

We will have to face a very hard struggle with the working people. They are strongly united in Belgium, and almost all of them are included in a mighty union which is possessed of a large lot of money and it is able to prevent that its members should work in any firm which should blow glass by means of machinery . . .

Workmen, as soon as they will see that machinery is a danger for themselves, will accept, just as they did in the U.S.A., a lowering of their wages in order to face the mechanical process, and they will make the very best out of their skill and exert themselves in order to turn out first-class make [so] that the glass produced according to the old process should be preferred by the consumers . . . Glass turned out according to old methods . . . will be of good make . . . buyers . . . will grow untrustful in as much as mechanical glass is concerned and the latter will only pull through by means of low selling rates so that, also in these quarters, we will lose all the profit of our endeavours during a good deal of time.

We take it that we have begun to work by means of machinery and that after some time we have succeeded in pulling through all the obstacles we have mentioned in this letter. What will now happen? Our opponents who, up to this moment will have turned out glass according to old processes, as soon as they will be aware that we have succeeded and that old methods must be given up . . . will apply to you. You did not agree to claim from them a price different from ours. They will consequently get from you licences at prices equal to ours and, taking advantage of our experience, they will fit their works with machines without any of the risks we have had to reckon with. They can even afford, by means of higher wages, to carry off the people we will have trained at our own expense and will in this way be able to compete with us on the spot . . . Such a competition is so much more to be feared by us [than] that our opponents will not have to bear – as we shall – the losses at the beginning.[39]

Other Belgian sheet glassworks were soon in touch with America, too – 'all these Belgian manufacturers are more or less related', St Helens told Pittsburgh[40] – but without any apparent result. Meanwhile, at Dampremy in Belgium itself, Fourcault was soon to embark upon the final stages in the development of his flat drawn process.

Lack of early success with licensing caused relations between Pilkington and the Americans to become somewhat strained. The development of the process had been so costly that it had driven American Window Glass into the hands of a creditors' committee, prominent among whom were the bankers. Pilkington's main contacts in the Window Glass Machine Company were M. K. McMullin, President of McMullin's Bank, Pittsburgh, and T. H. Given, President of The Farmers' Bank there, in which building the company had its offices.[41] The American financial crisis of 1907 had not helped matters and, reported the *National Glass Budget* on 30 April 1910, 'both companies [the parent and the machine company] have been and now are at the mercy of creditors'. Further measures were then being taken to renegotiate the debt.[42]

There were soon two other areas of contention between St Helens and Pittsburgh besides the failure to secure early licences. One concerned the ownership of Pilkington's improvements to the machine and the other the working of the process in Canada. Both were dealt with in a supplementary agreement, dated December 1912.[43] By it, Pilkington agreed to grant the Empire Machine Company an exclusive licence for all its improvements to the machine, free of royalty in all countries apart from Britain and Canada. (In the U.S.A. the licence was to be held by the parent, the American Window Glass Machine Company.) It also agreed to communicate to the Empire Machine Company details of any future improvements 'before publishing the same or taking any steps which would impair the right to obtain patents upon said improvements in other countries', and at the same time supplying details of the countries to which it proposed to apply for patents. In Canada it agreed to work the process often enough to secure its protection under Canadian patent law.

Without a higher protective tariff, and with its sponsoring parent already heavily in debt, the Window Glass Machine Company of Canada Limited had achieved little at Cayuga. Its $20,000 capital – or even the full $40,000 – would not go far. F. Baylis, then Pilkington's representative at Toronto, visited Cayuga in February 1907 and was obligingly shown over the factory by the engineer there, a young man thirty years old who was formerly at the Inchore Works near Dublin and who had later worked for Harland and Wolfe, Belfast. Three machines had been installed, and the tanks and lehrs erected within a wooden building; but they could not begin making glass until the ground got softer, for the gas main laid across the river had been fractured by the ice.[44]

The Cayuga works do not seem to have been operated commercially. The minute books of the Window Glass Machine Company of Canada Limited[45] record purely formal meetings until 1909 when Pilkington acquired it (and Cayuga works) as part of its agreement with the Americans. Pilkington was not anxious to work the process in Canada either, for to start it up on a commercial scale at such a distance from home was a risky venture, the success of which was doubtful in the absence of a higher tariff which would, of course, hit Pilkington's own lucrative exports. It was better to let the factory stand idle for as long as possible, sure in the knowledge that nobody else could work the process in Canada without infringing Pilkington's patent rights.[46] This was the position until 1911 when the suggestion was made that the patent might not be safeguarded unless the machine was occasionally heated up and made to produce specimens of glass. Donald Macmaster, the Montreal lawyer, was consulted and as a result of his advice the Pilkington Board decided, on 8 June 1911, that the process should be worked in Canada twice a year.[47] Pilkington wrote to Pittsburgh asking for natural gas to be made available, noting that 'it to some extent appears to be on the premises at the present time as we understand the watchman was seen to cook [sic] his tea on a gas jet in one of the pipe heaters'.[48] R.F. Taylor was despatched on the *Empress of Ireland* on 5 October to see to this demonstration working, McMullin being asked to supply an engineer to be in overall charge as Taylor was 'not used to handling American labour or to the ways of Canada'.[49] On his arrival, however, Taylor was told that the Patent Office had granted a year's extension and that the machine did not, in fact, need to be worked until later in 1912. He therefore visited McMullin and spent some time at the A.W.G. factories in America.

We happen to know a great deal about Canadian ways at this time, at least in the glass trade, because one of Pilkington's directors went to live in North America and his correspondence, which has come to light since the first version of this book appeared, makes a rich addition to the more routine exchange of letters between the Canadian head office at Montreal and St Helens. The director was Austin Pilkington who was taken ill with TB in 1907. His twin brother, Henry William, apparently fit and strong – he had distinguished himself as an athlete and a rowing man at Oxford – had previously fallen ill with lung trouble and had died in December 1902. Austin Pilkington's illness was also serious and spells in sanatoria near Whitby and in the New Forest did not prevent him from becoming steadily worse, though he was able to go into the office for odd days in July, September and October 1908 and in April and May 1909.[50] The illness became so bad that he could hardly speak and then only with the greatest difficulty. It was decided as a last desperate resort that he should go to Colorado where the air was particularly dry and thin. Accordingly he and his family (including the present Lord Pilkington, then a boy of four) moved there in the autumn of 1909, the family living first in the Acacia Hotel, Colorado Springs, while he was in a sanitorium. He then rented a property there called Council Bluffs and finally built himself a house, which he named Windle Springs, at Palmer Lake, some distance to the north, on the road to Denver. There he recovered. 'The climate is *wonderful*,' he wrote, not long after their arrival, to Baylis, now Pilkington's chief Canadian agent and located in Montreal. 'I had to take it easy till now, but was out again today. The air is so electrical that when I take off my coat it crackles'. Shortly after this he sent out a letter from the rented house headed: Austin Bluffs, Colorado Springs.[51]

From the time of his arrival in Colorado, Austin Pilkington took quite a close, and certainly an increasing, interest in events in Canada, and to some extent in the United States as well. Baylis was determined and outspoken. He did not take kindly to being treated in the same way as were Pilkington agents in the United Kingdom. His monthly returns to St Helens – giving the most recent sales statistics available and comparing them with the same month a year previously, commenting on the competition and assessing prospects for the near future – are carefully and clearly written, but not without an undertone of dissatisfaction at having to refer everything to the Export Department – which he usually called the Works – for decision. He had, for instance, to obtain permission even to buy a new typewriter.[52]

The selling price of Pilkington glass in Canada was fixed at St Helens by deciding the maximum discount which would be allowed. Baylis was repeatedly writing to the Works to complain that this did not give him enough room for manoeuvre in the battle for a larger share of the market. He was particularly bitter about not being able to cut his prices in the spring of 1910 – the starting price when the St Lawrence became navigable after the winter determined prices for the ensuing season – in order to meet increased Belgian competition which, he believed, explained the fall in the volume of Pilkington's business in that year. As he later wrote to Austin Pilkington:

The business has undoubtedly been lost to us through the Works persistently refusing to grant even one point better on the orders which were submitted to them. They went into the matter with their eyes open; representations were made to them by me and the other representatives here without the least effect, and now, when the bulk of the business is gone and the orders placed with our opponents, they wire me . . . 'Are very disappointed with your sheet orders'.[53]

Austin Pilkington agreed that since 1893 the margin between Pilkington and Belgian prices had been widening. St Helens had finally 'overstrained the loyalty of our customers. There had been warnings enough from Montreal and from here, and the lesson is now, I hope, learnt'.[54]

Complaints of a different sort were sent from Canada to St Helens when the price was right and the customers were clamouring for glass which could not be supplied in the quantities required. Production from the works was then not sufficient for the needs of the Canadian market. Stocks had to be run down dangerously low and orders not fulfilled. Austin Pilkington emphasised that the company's interests would best be served by encouraging sales through its warehouses and discouraging those by individual importers. He advocated giving different discounts to the different warehouses according to local conditions; 'preserving our normal supplies for good warehouse customers'; 'declining . . . small import orders from men who order nothing else'; and selling to those who patronised the Belgians 'only when we have a surplus which we may want to place'.[55]

In an attempt to shorten the lines of communication and to lower the tension with St Helens, Austin Pilkington assumed more responsibility for Canada from August 1911.[56] Baylis sometimes went to Colorado, and Austin Pilkington stopped in eastern Canada on his way to and from England, which he visited during the summer of 1912. He explained that Head Office monitored the Belgians' production and estimated their likely exports to all parts of the world. With Baylis's monthly reports, St Helens was, therefore, in a better position to decide Canadian prices than was Baylis himself. In any case, it was important for an agent to encourage his sales force really to exert itself and sell glass at a good price, not himself to be bullied by them to get St Helens to lower prices in order to make their job easier. When, early in 1912, prices were advanced, Austin Pilkington wrote to Baylis:

There is great strength in the market, and if the travellers welcome this, as they should do, . . . the increase in price will help them get orders. If there were more of this spirit shown in the travellers' reports, it would be better. They seem far too responsive, to my mind, to tales about competitors' prices. You have reported fully to England what these prices are, and we know in England just how the Belgian works are situated, and we are not alarmed about the position . . .

The trade in Canada generally watches our attitude with regard to prices, and if they think they can see a difference of opinion between the Works and the Agencies, or the Agencies and the Travellers, or your travellers and yourself – they will at once think that they have only to work on the travellers sufficiently to obtain lower prices. You now know the position in Europe, and the amount of orders which we shall now obtain depends upon the willingness of the travellers to play up.[57]

Baylis's handling of the travellers was another cause of disagreement. A demand from the Export Department to explain why they did not report to him daily and why their reports were often so brief, caused him to explode, for it revealed a lack of understanding of the distances to be covered:

You may not be aware of the facts that travellers are required to board trains at 2 or 3 o'clock in the morning and arrive at their destinations at 10 or 11 in the morning, and work a town and get out of it the same night. Even if they stay in that town, it is more than likely that they will not have any inclination to write any reports after they have done their business, because in the smaller places a good portion of the business is done after business hours, and travellers should be allowed time for a reasonable recreation and rest. In some of the places that are visited, there are no proper facilities for writing reports.

You speak of the material in the reports being of meagre character; but it is not always that travellers have got any special circumstances to report and, if they have not, we see no reason for these reports being made unduly lengthy.

We trust you will pardon us for saying so, but our experience is that very few travellers' reports are commented upon by you. We do not think that during the whole of this year, when travellers were constantly reporting upon the conditions they met with in regard to their inability to obtain orders for reasons explained, that you once specially mentioned any of these reports or stated that they were having your attention or otherwise . . .[58]

This brought the polite, if rather curt, retort from H.L.Kimmins in the Export Department that 'while very few of your travellers' reports may have been commented upon by us, they have all been carefully read and the various Departments here duly notified'.[59] These efforts to assert central authority must have been galling to the man struggling with reality on the spot.

Austin Pilkington also had his problems at Vancouver, which reported independently to St Helens. There the agent was Arthur Granville

Thynne (1867–1948), a distant relative of the Marquess of Bath. (His grandfather, a canon and sub-dean of Westminster, was a younger son of the second Marquess. His father, also a clergyman, became Rector of Kilhampton in north Cornwall.) Austin Pilkington took the view that 'one of the most important things for an Agent to maintain is a spirit of loyalty and cheerfulness in his staff'.[60] This Thynne was not doing. Baylis was consulted. 'Don't the staff like Mr Thynne, or why is it? It cannot continue like this'.[61] Matters soon came to a head. Thynne was sent to New Zealand as Pilkington's first full-time agent to replace the general commission agent, A.G.D. Willcocks.[62] In New Zealand Thynne would have no staff at all to upset.

Exports to New Zealand had grown impressively since 1908 when the import duties on glass had been removed. Those of plate glass from the United Kingdom (all made by Pilkington) had shot up from 319,000 sq. ft a year in the six years 1902–7 to 692,000 sq. ft a year in the following six years. The comparable figures for window glass (most made by Pilkington) were 1,833,000 sq. ft and 2,134,000 sq. ft. This meant that in the six years 1908–1913 New Zealand was taking about 5 per cent of Pilkington's plate glass and about 2 per cent of its window glass. Such vast quantities of plate glass were not to be shipped to New Zealand again until during and after the Second World War.

Thynne, however, was not to profit from this pre-1914 bonanza. He had only just arrived in Wellington when he wrote to Austin Pilkington to say that he would have to leave again:

I am sorry to say that I do not think I shall be able to stay in New Zealand, principally on account of my wife's health; she has been ill ever since we arrived in Wellington and in the hospital for the last two weeks. I am taking her to Christchurch tomorrow and hope the climate there will suit her better. The doctor says she will not be able to live in Wellington on account of the high winds here (it blows a gale here 5 days out of 6) and it is necessary for whoever looks after the business in N.Z. to make headquarters here.

As to the business, I am sure that it could be worked up all right although it will be uphill work for a while as Willcocks was at loggerheads with most of our customers. I think the best plan would be to appoint a local man agent, who knows the business and customers . . .[63]

Austin Pilkington did not take Thynne's advice, but instead made it his business to see him when they were both visiting St Helens in the following June. Thynne's connexion with the company was then terminated and Frank William Butcher, originally St Helens-trained and then in charge at Winnipeg, was offered the New Zealand agency[64]. Powers of attorney were granted him on 9 September 1912. He soon moved the agency to Auckland and continued to serve Pilkington there until his sudden death in 1929. Meanwhile Thynne returned to Canada and set up in insurance. Pilkington authorised J.E.Harrison, his successor at Vancouver, to insure half its new Calgary warehouse through him.[65]

By 1912 the Americans were putting increased pressure upon Pilkington to work the drawn cylinder process in Canada. This pressure was applied in two ways: by threatening to work the process themselves there – such threats were made when they met R.F.Taylor later in 1911[66] – and by selling their American-made glass in Canada in direct competition with Pilkington glass imported from England. Macmaster's opinion had made it clear that Pilkington possessed exclusive rights to the working of the machine in Canada, but it was clearly doubtful how long it would be possible to proceed with the charade of demonstration working. American imports were a much more serious threat, however, for they were concentrated at first in the Winnipeg area where they not only undercut Pilkington on price but also had a six-week advantage in delivery times.[67] Competition in other regions was to be expected and here the Americans had an ally in W.R.Hobbs, a merchant trading as Consolidated Plate Glass Co. and a keen speculator who is even said to have had an interest in the ill-fated Turner works at St Helens.[68] By the autumn of 1912 American competition was reported in Ontario.[69] In November Austin Pilkington, writing to his father, sounded a note of real anxiety as he surveyed the position with the practised eye of the sales director:

The Americans have, particularly since June, made very great inroads into our connection for sheet, rolled and wired from Toronto as far west as Regina, and a decided inroad in the Provinces of Quebec and Alberta.

They will now be faced by an unprecedented demand in the United States, and they have already raised their prices to such an extent that the Canadian dealers will not be able to replace supplies at such figures. They have, however, spoiled the buyers from the point of view of quick delivery, and of the general willingness of the manufacturers to cater to them.

I have made careful enquiries on this point, and feel decidedly that in view of the *great* development in *Canada*, we must take the opportunity of stepping into the breach promptly, or else expect to see someone else do so. The trade cannot be supplied entirely by importation as heretofore.

If we do start, we have an excellent prospect of keeping the tariff as it is, and of getting from the railway companies protective commodity rates against Pittsburgh . . . I am assured by Henderson that the C.P.R. will certainly grant us protection in the matter of rates, and [i.e. but] if the Americans start here, they will get the protection not only against the U.S., *but also against England*.[70]

By early in 1913 Pilkington's directors were persuaded that they needed to work the process commercially in Canada in such a way as to interfere as little as possible with imports from Britain. A small works located within reach of the Middle West – and the main seat of American competition – was considered first of all: Sarnia, at the southern end of Lake Huron, was suggested in February 1912. But by April they were also considering the claims of a site on the New Welland Ship Canal, on the Niagara Peninsula but to the south-west of Hamilton (not, as Cayuga was, due south of it and away from navigable water). By November the possibilities had been narrowed down either to Windsor, Ont., just opposite Detroit, or to Thorold on the Welland Canal. Thorold was the eventual choice and Austin Pilkington, who had been actively involved in site prospecting, was soon dealing with the purchase of the land. This was completed in May 1913.[71] On the site was to be built not only a factory but also houses for the factory manager and warehouse manager and 13 other double and 12 single houses, together with a recreation hall, a store and a school. The little community was named Windle Village after the company's chairman.[72]

R.F.Taylor, who had been concerned with the drawn cylinder process at St Helens and the exhibition working at Cayuga in 1912, carried out the detailed research which had finally narrowed down the choice of possible sites. He was given charge of the installation of the plant. The plans were sent out from St Helens, but many unexpected problems arose as a result of having to work so far from the technical base. Taylor was reduced to sending weekly photographs of building operations, taken at first on a small Kodak camera.[73] The tank came into use in May 1914 and rolled plate glass was made from it.[74] The drawn cylinder machines proved much more troublesome. A month after the outbreak of war Taylor had little to report that gave any cause for encouragement:

Things are improving slightly but there is not that change which we look for daily and which so far has not come. Every time we try some alteration and some new idea, we look for this change and feel sure we have reached the correct solution but so far it has always been a disappointment . . . If we cannot get things straight soon, I don't see how we can go on because at present we are losing money heavily . . . Besides losing money we are disappointing customers, which is quite as bad . . .[75]

The plant lost $250,000 in 1915. Cecil Pilkington, writing from St Helens, conceded that to have tried to combine drawn cylinder with rolled plate was a mistake; but he could still not understand why Thorold's breakage losses were between 12 and 18 per cent while those at St Helens had been brought down to $2\frac{1}{2}$ per cent. 'It is a great disadvantage to be at such a distance off from the plant,' he lamented. 'Whenever we ask how much fuel is being used, or what the flatteners are doing per hour, your returns of output, they seem so far behind, particularly in questions of cost, that we are unable to give as good considerations to the questions at issue as if the rough general estimate was furnished each week'.[76]

Despite the wartime interruption of Belgian competition, Pilkington could not make Thorold pay until 1918, when virtually no glass was being exported from Britain – by which time the factory had lost $664,000, or over £130,000, on its operations.[77] And by the end of 1915 over £220,000 had already been invested there (to be compared with £725,000 in the whole of the Grove Street window glass factory at St Helens). The drawn cylinder process, a temporary expedient which was to lead Pilkington into future trouble at St Helens, was an obvious failure in Canada. America had pressured and frightened Pilkington into taking what turned out to be a rash investment decision.

The addition of manufacturing to Pilkington's Canadian commercial activities – the warehouses and stock there were worth over £400,000 in 1914 – led to an overhaul of the management structure so that Canadian-made glass, when it appeared on the market, could be phased in smoothly with that made at St Helens.[78] It was realised that the Montreal agent could no longer be responsible for running Montreal, overseeing the other warehouses and attending to Thorold sales as well. It was, therefore, decided to open a new central office in Toronto, in charge of a general manager, William Stuart Tunnock (1877–1947), educated at Glasgow High School, the son of Pilkington's Scottish agent, who had gone into the Glasgow warehouse at fourteen as an office boy. He had succeeded his father as agent when a young man and was, after a brief spell in Head Office at St Helens, sent to Canada to take over temporarily from the outspoken Baylis (who left Pilkington's service) and to train as his successor James Eustace Harrison (1878–1949) who had been apprenticed at Head Office in 1891 and had been at the Nottingham depot for a year as a traveller before going to Vancouver as agent. Tunnock lost no time in encouraging the various agents to exercise more control over their travellers[79] and to establish better relations between Canada and St Helens. 'I think that in some ways the most important result of your stay in Canada,' Austin Pilkington wrote to him, 'will be the establishing of an understanding between St Helens and Canada which has been much wanted; not merely an understanding but a decided friendship. I also think that the relations between Harrison and the agents will, unless there is a serious fault on their part, be of a much more friendly nature than has been the case before with the Montreal agent'.[80] Harrison proved an apt pupil and richly fulfilled all the hopes placed in him. He served Pilkington in Canada for over 30 years, until 1945.

The dismissal of the watchman at Cayuga and the disposal of that phantom factory closed this chapter of Pilkington's activities in Canada, much as the rumour of the factory's impending arrival had opened it nine years before by arousing the company's serious interest in drawn cylinder glass. On 19 October 1914 the manager of the Canadian Bank of Commerce at Cayuga was informed that, because of the war, the Window Glass Machine Company of Canada found itself without funds and was going out of business. The land was to be handed back to the local authority, together with the wooden buildings which stood upon it.[81]

Chapter 14

1900–1914:
Labour and Capital

T HE labour troubles, which the Belgian glass manufacturers prophesied would flare up if the new drawn cylinder machines were introduced into their country, did not occur at St Helens. Pilkington's glassmakers, though by this time becoming subjected to greater union and political influences, were prepared to accept mechanical change.

As may be seen from Table 25 (page 192), the sales volume of Pilkington window glass held up very well from 1902/3 down to the war. While sales may not be directly equated with actual production year by year – glass was put into stock when sales flagged and taken out again when it was brisk – they do nevertheless present a picture of this period as one in which there was usually little shortage of work for glassmakers. Even when the machines were introduced in the year 1909/10, these threatened the jobs of blowers and gatherers only; the splitters and flatteners, and all the other ancillary workers, were employed as before. Moreover, machine production at first was very small: negligible in the first year and only 6,500,000 sq. ft in 1910/11, a year in which total output was 5,000,000 sq. ft greater than the year before. It was in the three pre-war years that the total volume of glass blown by hand fell, but then apparently by only about 10 per cent. And if this fall in demand for the services of skilled blowers and gatherers was not covered by normal wastage, there were jobs on the machines which any displaced men could do. In America, for instance, where the new machines employed a greater, though less skilled, labour force than the hand process,[1] they still employed a man (whom they called a blower) to operate the drawing and blowing motors, and another to place the cap on the glass to be drawn.[2]

We do not know what dispositions Pilkington made at this time; but we shall see that the company showed much concern for its skilled glassmakers when displacement did occur in the 1920s. It would seem unlikely that it behaved differently before 1914.

Fear of machine competition and the redundancy or lower wages which might result was, however, a much more powerful cause of labour discontent, and it was not the least of Pilkington's achievements that these fears were allayed, particularly as trade unions were becoming more active and the climate of political opinion was encouraging workers to bring greater pressure to bear upon management. St Helens was then still in the midst of a coalmining district. Trade unionism and labour politics were growing in the town, led by Thomas Glover, the local miners' leader. So early as 1890 Windle Pilkington, an active member of the borough council, had lost his seat for a time, defeated by a leader of the bottlemakers' trade union.[3] Radical fervour increased as Labour gained stronger representation on the council. By June 1904, a local trade union leader confidently remarked: 'There is a great awakening of Labour in this and other towns; we are learning to be trade unionists not only at our lodge rooms, but at the Ballot Box'.[4]

Trade union activity had been intensified by the selection of a Labour candidate for the borough seat. This had been held, since its creation in 1885, by William (Roby) Pilkington's son-in-law, (Sir) Henry Seton-Karr (Conservative). He had spoken on several occasions against certain concessions sought by the miners' union, and so had Richard Pilkington, who, since 1899, had been M.P. for the neighbouring Newton constituency. The miners were keen to assert their electoral strength in St Helens – and get their own back on the Pilkington influence – by securing the Labour Representation Committee (L.R.C.) nomination for the seat. Representatives of the sheet glassmakers' union were among those who attended meetings leading up to Thomas Glover's selection as candidate.[5] According to Alan Wild, who has consulted the National Amalgamated Union of Labour and L.R.C. records as well as those belonging to Pilkington, the campaign to elect Glover associated Pilkington's skilled blowers and flatteners increasingly closely with the NAUL and made them much more vocal than they had previously been. The glass cutters, too, were prominent NAUL members, some of them having joined in 1902; but the flatteners stood aside with a union of their own. At an NAUL meeting in the town, held on a Sunday morning in June 1904, 'quite 700 glass and other workers' attended and gave the speakers a good hearing.[6]

In January 1906 Glover was returned triumphantly to Parliament.

Within a few weeks, Pilkington's glassmakers held a meeting to press for the restoration of wages, cut in 1903, to their former level. Over 500 blowers and gatherers (out of a possible total of perhaps 750) were then said to belong to the union, and the flatteners were also reported to be strongly organised.[7] Although Pilkington refused to recognise any trade union, it was nevertheless prepared to negotiate with known trade unionists provided they were Pilkington employees. Members of the Board had long received deputations by prior appointment, and this procedure was used to deal with the series of resolutions passed at the glassmakers' meeting which had been held at the Co-operative Hall in St Helens on 17 March 1906.

The resolutions were duly presented to Windle and W. Lee Pilkington by six blowers (Robert Groves, Joseph Hankinson, William Carson, John Twist, Richard Pierce and Arnold Wilcock) and six gatherers (Joseph Case, William Bate, Hamlet Lawrenson, Jesse Varley, William Barrow and John Simpson). The deputation then withdrew to give the directors time to digest the document. Some weeks later, having decided to grant the blowers (but not the gatherers) the five per cent increase they sought, and having also decided not to alter the existing arrangement of staggered contracts, dating from 1879, along with certain other matters, the two directors summoned the deputation to meet them and a third colleague, Cecil Pilkington, on 10 May. The personnel was then somewhat changed. The six blowers, described in the Glassmakers Deputation Book as union men, came back again, but they were accompanied by three other blowers (non-union men): Fred Pownall, Levi Whittle and Joseph Fillingham. And only three of the union gatherers returned – with two non-unionists: William Appleton junior and Robert Greenall. A question was asked about what was known as the 'B' contract list. The directors had agreed that the men should only be demoted to this in cases of what was described as 'inattention to work', not in cases of sickness, and should have a right to appeal to a director within a fortnight. The minutes of the meeting continue:

John Twist asked whether 'we can have a voice in the question of men being put on the "B" list'. Mr Windle told him 'NO'.

The union men asked if Mr W. W. Pilkington would attend a meeting of the men at the Gymnasium on Saturday evening, May 12th 1906, to explain the Firm's proposals to them, as they thought this would give the men greater satisfaction. Mr W. W. Pilkington having expressed his willingness to do this, the deputation withdrew.[8]

The flatteners were also offered a five per cent rise on the following day when their representatives (William Frodsham, Ernest Edwards, Edward Johnson, Thomas Taylor, Richard Martin and Henry Ashall, none of them defined as either union or non-union men) waited upon W. Lee Pilkington and J. Seddon, the flattening manager. Windle Pilkington spoke, as he had promised to do, to the mass meeting on the Saturday night; but this was not the end of the matter, for the blowers and gatherers had been told by their union not to sign any new contracts until another meeting had been held a week later. Those present then agreed to the company's terms by a large majority.[9]

Deputations became quite common from 1906 onwards and proved a forum for persuasion on both sides, Windle Pilkington, on one occasion, in 1907, reminding his hearers that 'in America where they had introduced machines, they did away with blowers and gatherers'.[10] The minutes suggest that some of these meetings may have provided real opportunities for the airing of genuine grievances and, moreover, that these were looked into. Yet on pay and union recognition the company refused to yield to pressure. When in 1911, for instance, a representative from the rolled plate department asked about a letter sent to the company by Tom Williamson, the union organiser, he was told that 'such a letter was not from a workman and it had been put on the fire'.[11]

Time, however, was on Tom Williamson's side. Although membership of the three branches of the NAUL which recruited Pilkington employees fell from the peak it had reached in 1906, it started to pick up again from 1912. In the fourth quarter of 1913, the St Helens glassmakers were said to be joining the union 'in a promising manner'.[12]

The absence of industrial unrest at Pilkington's during the years before 1914, when the spread of new political ideas and the introduction of the new machines gave it every encouragement, cannot be explained just in terms of heartless and repressive capitalists ruthlessly enforcing upon their skilled glassmakers the staggered contract system. On the crest of left-wing enthusiasm in 1906, many Pilkington employees were organised and could have pressed their claims much harder than they did had they wished to do so. There are clearly other factors to be taken into account.

By 1906 many Pilkington employees had been working for the company for years; some had followed their fathers, and a few even their fathers and grandfathers, into 'Pilks' as they all called it. It was seen to be a good company to work for in that it was highly successful and always expanding at a time when all but one of its competitors in Britain – many of them in St Helens itself – had gone out of business. At Pilks jobs were secure and, for the skilled men, pay was high. The management, which insisted on strict discipline from employees, also drove itself hard and saw to it that capital was available for reinvestment on a generous scale in the most modern equipment. Management was as efficient as it expected labour, and indeed the whole business, to be. The fall-off in trade union membership between 1906 and 1913 was not the result of Pilkington threats but rather because former trade union supporters had evidently lost confidence in the movement and preferred to negotiate on a company basis for the time being.

Above all, much is to be explained by the personality of the senior production director, Windle Pilkington. He was known to the glass-makers and respected by them because he knew more about the practical side of glassmaking than any of them did. He knew the problems on the factory floor, and the men understood that he knew. How many other 'bosses' would be invited to explain his point of view to a meeting of the men as he had been during the crucial 1906 trial of strength? He emerges as the outstanding partner of the second generation. He was actively engaged at the works almost right up to his death in March 1914, at the age of 74. In his 56 years in the business, he was responsible for making Pilkington one of the most technically advanced glass firms in the world. Though he took out in all more than 50 patents, he was not, as we have seen, an inventor but rather a successful developer and im-prover. To him alone must go the credit for Pilkingtons' early develop-ment of tank furnaces; and from this innovation was derived the firm's advantage in sheet glass manufacture which helped it to weather the crisis at the turn of the century when the competition in plate glass became much fiercer. Windle Pilkington, together with his brother, Richard (d. 1908), also played a very active part in local affairs. After nearly thirty years' service, he became a Lieutenant-Colonel in the Volunteers in 1888 and, on his retirement in 1902, was succeeded by his brother. Between them they established Pilkington's link with the volunteer forces which later became a tradition; the close connexion between certain of the directors and employees of the company was continued with the Territorial Army. Both brothers became mayors of St Helens (in Richard Pilkington's case for three years) and were rewarded for their services to local government by being made aldermen and freemen. Richard Pilkington was M.P. for the Newton Division from 1899 to 1906. Windle Pilkington was a pillar of the local Congregational Church, as his father had been before him. He was well known for his benevolence. As a young man he helped to found a Ragged School in the town, and was later an enthusiastic supporter of the YMCA, the St Helens Hospital and the St Helens District Nursing Association.

I*

The two second generation partners from the other branch of the family – William Pilkington's sons – were older than their cousins. Thomas played no part in the active management of the company at this period, for he retired at the end of 1898 and went to live at Holm Lacy in Herefordshire. The death of his eldest son in the Boer War caused him great grief and made him change all his plans. He sold up and divided his time between a shooting estate in Caithness and London, from where he later removed to Bournemouth. He outlived the other three and died, at the ripe old age of 90, in 1925.

William (Roby) Pilkington (b. 1827) did play an active part in local affairs until his death in 1903. He intervened effectively in the negotiations which led up to the incorporation of St Helens in 1868, but then his interest turned to politics generally rather than to local government as such. He was a very keen Conservative and was chairman of the local Conservative Association from its beginnings in 1868. He refused to stand, in 1885, as parliamentary candidate for the newly-formed borough seat, but supported the candidacy of his son-in-law, Henry Seton-Karr. Among the Salisbury Papers at Christ Church, Oxford, are two letters, dated 1889 and 1892, from Seton-Karr to Lord Salisbury, the Prime Minister, urging Roby Pilkington's claim to a baronetcy. This claim was made partly on the grounds that 'no glass manufacturer had yet been honoured with a baronetcy, though representatives of nearly all the other great mercantile firms had been so honoured', and partly because it was to Roby Pilkington's support that the Conservative Club of St Helens 'owed its existence and present financial soundness'. 'Peerages', Seton-Karr added, 'have often been given for smaller services than his'. He was at pains to stress that these approaches were entirely unsolicited by his father-in-law, 'who is the last man to advocate his own merits'. Confirmation of this was contained in a third letter, which followed soon after the second. This informed Lord Salisbury that 'for urgent family reasons' – which are not disclosed – his father-in-law would decline the honour even if it were offered.[13]

The continued growth of the business called for a larger office staff. In 1909 additional office accommodation was approved.[14] Within the expanding office, much specialisation was taking place. The order department, for instance, was separated from the ledger work.[15] A careful system of costing was gradually evolved and at the beginning of 1913 a central cost department (one man, T. B. Steane, in charge of two clerks) was set up, equipped with a Hollerith machine. Here the company had been quick off the mark, for, according to Hollerith, it was their second oldest customer. Care was taken, however, that the three people working in the new department did not compare notes with those who had access to the sales figures. Profits were a private matter for the attention of the directors alone. A small, discreet circle of trusted retainers were also privy to these secrets. They prepared the necessary documents and, having been instructed to do so by the directors, took action on these and other confidential matters.

On the sales side, greater emphasis was laid upon the standardisation of qualities. When one new employee went to work as a cutter at Cowley Hill in 1902, he found that

the men working at the various tables had not (officially) the remotest idea what quality of glass each was turning out, there then being no such policy of standardization of quality. Each sorter and cutter had his own ideas of quality and worked to them in his own way.[16]

Such a haphazard method of working was replaced by stricter control, which must have given greater satisfaction to customers. So, too, did the practice, introduced early in the present century, of sending specialists from the works – not the office – to attend to complaints.

The early years of the twentieth century also witnessed the three sounds which have become so familiar in the modern office: the clatter of typewriters, the ringing of telephone bells and the chatter of girls' voices, none of which was often heard prior to 1900. At the beginning of 1907, Pilkingtons decided to employ 'two typewriting girls'.[17] This number was soon increased and by 1912 the firm was turning more and more to this new source of labour. A Board minute passed in the autumn of 1912 has a distinctly modern flavour about it:

Telephone. Partners not to be unreasonably troubled. Someone of good education needed in telephone room to take confidential and partners' [sic] messages. Question of having a girl for this was discussed – also of employing more girls generally and of using them for the night work.

The company also acquired in these years some very talented men who were to rise to top managerial positions. Two of them, indeed, became members of the Pilkington family by marriage.

The first to do so was Edward Herbert Cozens-Hardy (b. 1873, educated at Rugby) whose sister, Hope, had married Austin Pilkington in 1903. They were children of Sir Herbert Hardy Cozens-Hardy of

Letheringsett Hall, Holt, Norfolk, then a Lord Justice of Appeal, shortly to be made Master of the Rolls and, in 1914, to be created the first Baron Cozens-Hardy. The family seat has had the rather doubtful distinction of being described by Sir John Betjeman, the Poet Laureate, as 'a half-seen mausoleum in the oak trees on the hill'. Of more immediate importance was the fact that Edward Cozens-Hardy had entered the infant electrical engineering industry *via* a pupilage with Brush and had then set himself up as an electrical engineering consultant in partnership with Mervyn O'Gorman. (O'Gorman was another unusually able man; a graduate in Classics and Science from University College, Dublin, he had then taken a graduate course in electrical engineering at City & Guilds, London. He was, after 1909, to play a leading part in the development of British aviation as superintendent of the Royal Aeronautical Establishment, Farnborough.)[18] Cozens-Hardy was consulted by Pilkington in connexion with the electrification at Cowley Hill. He joined the Board in October 1908 after his brother-in-law had become ill – he was never a salaried manager – and was very much involved in developments on the manufacturing side.

The other arrival who eventually became a member of the family – by marriage in 1922 – was Ronald Morce Weeks (b. 1890; educated at Charterhouse and Gonville and Caius College, Cambridge where he read Natural Sciences). He had captained the university football team and came to Pilkington in 1911 with the strongest recommendations from the Cambridge University Appointments Board which had started to provide promising graduates to various business concerns, notably Brunner, Mond in Cheshire.[19] Weeks soon left for the war, was mentioned in despatches and won the D.S.O., M.C. and Bar before returning to play a leading managerial role at St Helens until 1939. He distinguished himself once more in the Second World War and became eventually chairman of Vickers and other companies and the first Baron Weeks of Ryton.

The years just before 1914 also saw an injection of talent from Scotland. Tunnock has already been mentioned. Three other young men of ability came from Allan Glen's School, Glasgow. James Rutherford Kerr, Pilkington's medical officer, was the eldest son of Dr J.G.Kerr, the school's distinguished headmaster. This established the connexion in the first place. The next ex-Allan Glen pupil to come to the town was Patrick Mackintosh Hogg who originally applied, in 1912, for a post at the St Helens electricity works. He did not get it, but Cozens-Hardy, one of the interviewers, offered him a job with Pilkington instead, for the company was then building a new electrical generating plant, as

TABLE 29
DISPOSAL OF PROFIT IN THE YEARS ENDED 30 JUNE 1904–14

Year ended 30 June	Profit	Directors' salaries fees and expenses	Income Tax	Debenture interest £30,000 and Ordinary dividend £40,000	Bonus on shares	Balance retained in company for development
1904	£172,564	£16,980	£13,123	£70,000	Nil	£72,461
1905	£225,218	£16,297	£11,960	£70,000	£60,000	£96,961
1906	£319,808	£17,100	£8,157	£70,000	£60,000	£164,551
1907	£341,963	£18,105	£8,941	£70,000	£20,000	£224,917
1908	£306,223	£17,287	£12,241	£70,000	£30,000	£176,695
1909	£256,992	£13,956	£13,955	£70,000	£10,000	£149,081
1910	£322,960	£15,557	£17,442	£70,000	£40,000	£179,961
1911	£375,492	£16,403	£15,202	£70,000	£60,000	£213,887
1912	£331,926	£17,220	£13,773	£70,000	£70,000	£160,933
1913	£432,685	£18,313	£18,195	£70,000	£110,000	£216,177
1914	£400,026	£15,896	£19,512	£70,000	£40,000	£254,618

Source: Pilkington Accounts

we have seen. He brought down another electrical engineer in 1914. This was James Meikle (1890–1972) who had gone on to the Royal Technical College, Glasgow after leaving Allan Glen and was then trained at an electricity works before arriving at St Helens. The third of the trio was James Bonar Watt (b. 1896), who had acted as the headmaster's secretary during the year before he came to St Helens. Both Meikle and Watt were ultimately to become production directors.

Table 29 shows that the business became more profitable than ever during this period.

In the 11 years 1903/4 to 1913/14, Pilkington made an average annual profit of nearly £320,000, compared to £267,000 in the previous eight years. But less was distributed in bonuses to shareholders (£45,455 compared to £65,000) and more was retained for development (£173,658 instead of £107,626). Much of this investment was at the factories, particularly at Cowley Hill, the value of which grew from £603,000 in 1904 to £1,178,000 in 1914. Grove Street grew from £450,000 to £714,000; and in the latter year Ravenhead, then used mainly for making cathedral glass, was valued at £119,000, Thorold at £151,000 (and growing fast) and Pilkington's other properties at £193,000. The company was also financially very strong, having put away about £350,000 in investments by the end of 1914. These were placed almost entirely in a wide range of foreign securities.

TABLE 30
PILKINGTON INVESTMENT PORTFOLIO, 31 December 1914

Algoma Central Terminals Limited – £5,000
Argentine Government – £9,000
Argentine Great Western Railway – £6,000
Associated Portland Cement Manufacturers (1900) Limited – £4,000
Atchison, Topeka and Santa Fé Railway Company – £5,000
Atlantic and St Lawrence Railway Company – £8,000
Bahia Blanca and North Western Railway Company – £5,000
Baltimore and Ohio Railroad Company – £10,000
United States of Brazil – £5,000
Brazil Railway – £19,000
British South Africa Company – £5,000
British Columbia Electric Railway Company Limited – £5,000
Buenos Aires Port and City Tramways Company Limited – £2,000

Buffalo and Lake Huron Railway – £21,000
Calcutta Electric Supply Corporation Limited – £3,000
Canada Atlantic Railroad – £7,000
Canada Cement Company Limited – £5,000
Chilean Northern Railway Company – £10,000
Chinese Government – £5,000
Cunard Steam Ship Company – £10,000
Elder, Dempster & Company Limited – £15,000
Grand Trunk Pacific Railway – £19,000
Grand Trunk Railway of Canada – £5,000
Grand Central Railway Company Limited – £6,000
City of Helsingfors – £10,000
Illinois Central Railway Company Limited – £15,000
Jardin Botanico Companhia Ferro Carril De – £5,000
Lamport & Holt Limited – £5,000
London General Omnibus Company Limited – £5,000
Manaos Harbour – £9,000
Manila Railway Company (1906) Limited – £5,000
Northern Pacific Railroad – £6,000
Ontario and Quebec Railway – £12,000
Oregon and Washington Railroad and Navigation Company – £5,000
Premier Investment Company – £6,000
State of Rio de Janeiro – £5,007
City of Rio de Janeiro – £4,000
Rio de Janeiro Tramways Light and Power Company Limited – £10,000
St Lawrence and Ottawa Railway – £2,000
St Louis Iron Mountain and Southern Railway – £9,000
St Paul, Minneapolis and Manitoba Railway – £7,000
Sao Paulo Electric Company Limited – £5,000
Shawinigan Water and Power Company Limited – £3,000
Sorocabana Railway Company Limited – £9,000
Southern Pacific Railroad – £12,000
United Railways of Havana and Regla Warehouse Company – £4,000

At that date the company had also invested £94,000 in three per cent war loan, and it had over £150,000 in other business commitments connected, in one way or another, with glassmaking: £55,000 in Richard Evans and Co., the Haydock coal proprietors; £52,000 in the Empire Machine Co.; £35,000 in Maubeuge; £9,000 in Dorstener Glashütte A.G.; and one or two other small sums elsewhere.

It is difficult to allocate to Pilkington its precise place in the hierarchy
of British industrial companies at this time for, being privately owned,
its shares were not quoted on the stock exchange nor was its nominal
capital adjusted, by the issue of additional shares, to keep pace with
reinvestment of profit. When the private company was formed in 1894,
the nominal capital of £1·4m did reflect the value of the business as
shown in the accounts. By reinvestment this total had grown by 1905 to
£2·556m, which would place Pilkington 35th on Professor Payne's
list of the 52 largest British industrial companies in that year – above
Brunner Mond (£2·299m), Huntley and Palmer (£2·4m) and Bovril
(£2·5m); but behind Lever Brothers (£4m), Armstrong Whitworth
(£5·3m), United Alkali (£8·5m) and the industrial leader, Imperial
Tobacco (£17·5m).[20] The Pilkington figure, however, represented
capital actually invested in the business, unwatered in any way. For a
fairer comparison, it ought perhaps to be moved somewhat higher up
the list; but how much farther is pure guesswork. What is quite certain
is that the second generation had built up the business to a size and
importance that had brought it to the forefront of British industry. And
it was growing fast in these pre-war years. By 1914 the capital employed
had risen to £4·2m.

The four Pilkingtons of the second generation reaped the reward of
their success. Richard Pilkington left £692,858 gross; Windle Pilkington
£589,785; and Thomas Pilkington £688,578. Only William (Roby)
Pilkington left less than this – £107,658. Presumably he had transferred
most of his fortune to his sons before his death. He had already begun
to do this in 1885, as we have seen (p. 171).[21]

The second generation was physically tough, escaped accidents and
lived long. This was not true of their sons. As we have seen, Thomas's
eldest son, Thomas Douglas, was killed in the Boer War, and Windle's
eldest son, Austin's twin, Henry William, died two years later, at the end
of 1902. The two sons of William (Roby), William Lee and George
Herbert, retired from active management at the beginning of 1907,
aged 60 and 59 respectively, though both were brought back from their
retirement during the war. Then Austin fell ill in 1907 and was later
sent to Canada to recuperate. There were other candidates available,
though they were not always of their parents' calibre: William Norman,
for instance (b. 1877; educated at Clifton and Trinity College, Cambridge,
where he captained the university rugby team) who came in as a replacement for his brother, Ernest Sinclair, who had gone off to the Boer War
and decided not to return to the business. Thomas's second son, Alan
Douglas (b. 1879; educated at Eton and Oxford where he read History

29 Munitions manufacture at Cowley Hill Works.

30 Pilkington Special Orthopaedic Hospital, Ravenhead, built from munitions profits. A view of the Electro Room.

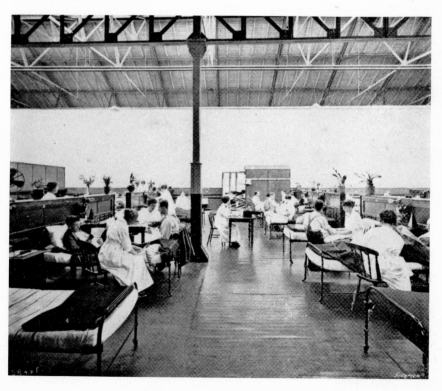

DONCASTER 1919
31 Investigation of the proposed site was made by directors and senior managers.
Left to right: R.M.Weeks, W.N.Pilkington, R.A.Pilkington, unidentified,
Hon. E.H. Cozens-Hardy, F.E.Slocombe.

32 A.R.PILKINGTON (1871–1921)

33 A.C.PILKINGTON (1875–1966)

34 ECCLESTON GRANGE. Home of R.A.Pilkington and subsequently used as the Central Analytical Laboratory.

35 KIRK SANDALL VILLAGE, DONCASTER. Part of the village built by Pilkington near the Doncaster Works.

HEAD OFFICE, ST HELENS

36 External view across the canal c1900.

37 Internal view of General Office 1926.

WORK AND LEISURE

38 A glassblowing team from No. 13 sheet tank c1900.

39 The recreation grounds at Ruskin Drive, St Helens c1926.

EARLY TRANSPORT

40 Turn of the century horse and cart for local glass deliveries.

41 'The largest plate' leaving Doncaster Works for the Wembley Exhibition, 1924.

WAREHOUSES OVERSEAS – MONTREAL AND PARIS

42 *Right* The first overseas depot Busby Lane, Montreal, Canada (1890), photograph taken c1913

43 *Below* Glaces de Maubeuge Paris depot, 52–4 Boulevard de la Villette, Paris XIX, 1923.

RIO DE JANEIRO DEPOT 1923   44 Exterior 45 Interior.

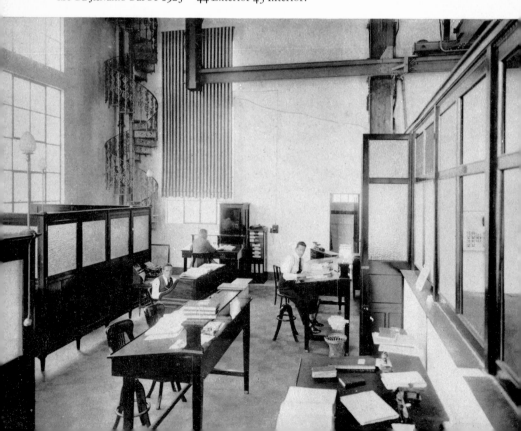

at New College) also came in in place of his brother soon after 1900 and was on the Board by 1904. Edward Cozens-Hardy, as we have seen, followed him in 1908. George Herbert's son, Geoffrey Langton (b. 1885; educated at Eton and Magdalen) joined the company in 1909, in the same year as a third son of Richard, Guy Reginald (b. 1881; educated at Clifton and Trinity College, Cambridge, who had previously worked at Sutton Manor Collieries). Both went on to the Board in the following year.

Even so, the Board was still slightly smaller than it had been in 1894 when the partnership had become a private company and when the business was considerably smaller. In 1913 the family management consisted of: William Windle, the surviving member of the second generation and by then a patriarchal figure but in the last year of his life; his sons, Richard Austin, Alfred Cecil and their brother-in-law, Edward Herbert Cozens-Hardy; Richard's sons, Arthur Richard (to be chairman from 1914 but soon destined to be another casualty of the third generation: his health broke down after the war and he died in 1921 at the age of 50), William Norman and Guy Reginald; Thomas's son, Alan Douglas (another casualty: he retired from active management in 1920, aged 41); and William (Roby's) grandson, Geoffrey Langton.

When the size and complexity of this £4m. business is taken into account – it was then employing about 9,400 people, operating on two continents and selling throughout the world – these top managers, unschooled for business, had been recruited in an astonishingly casual way and some had been brought in as substitutes. The company's setbacks in the 1920s must be attributed to some extent to this. Indeed, it did not begin to recover until the arrival of the fourth generation.

Chapter 15

The First World War

ITH the coming of war, several Pilkington directors left for the Front. William Norman, already a Major in the Prince of Wales Volunteers, served with distinction and was awarded the D.S.O. and Bar. His brother, Guy Reginald, was also mobilised with the Territorials in 1914 and also won the D.S.O. Geoffrey Langton, who had joined the Lancashire Hussars in 1911, served in England and Egypt until 1916, when he transferred to the Royal Flying Corps. Even more remarkable, Austin Pilkington, now fully recovered from his illness, joined up in March 1916, aged 45. He served in England between then and August 1917 when he was transferred to the Territorial Army Reserve and returned to the company. William Lee and George Herbert returned to active management at the outbreak of war. As we have seen, Arthur Richard had succeeded Windle to the chairmanship earlier in 1914.

The war reduced, and then interrupted altogether, the deluge of foreign glass. Window glass imports in 1915 and 1916 were only a third of what they had been just before 1914, as may be seen from Table 31.

Plate glass imports, surprisingly buoyant in 1915, fell sharply the next year. The *Union Internationale*, the continentals' plate glass selling agency, continued in existence during the war, having moved its headquarters first to Rotterdam and then to The Hague. For a time its secretary was even allowed a special pass by the Germans in order to visit Brussels.[1] Much of the sheet glass imported was still coming from Belgium even in 1916. A message passed on by Pilkington's Paris office in July of that year claimed that 'large quantities' were being sent to England by various routes, the British Government allowing 75 per cent of the invoice to be

TABLE 31

TOTAL AND RETAINED IMPORTS OF PLATE AND WINDOW GLASS
1914–18

Year	PLATE GLASS				WINDOW GLASS			
	Total Imports		Retained Imports		Total Imports		Retained Imports	
	'000 cwt	'000 sq. ft	'000 cwt	'000 sq. ft	'000 cwt	'000 sq. ft	'000 cwt	'000 sq. ft
1910–13 (Annual Average)	359						1,239	
1914	213	6,400	212	6,355	754	56,588	749	56,188
1915	250	7,499	246	7,378	470	35,280	461	34,602
1916	135	4,059	129	3,875	480	36,103	439	32,923
1917	9	255	8	243	114	8,581	95	7,090
1918	—	—	—	—	16	1,201	6	482

Source: Trade and Navigation Returns

paid.[2] This state of affairs did not continue much longer, however. A later report, in September 1916, spoke of the Germans having prohibited almost all glass exports[3] and in March 1917 the Belgian sheet glassworks were said to have been closed by their orders, large unsold stocks having been accumulated.[4] By 1917 and 1918, when hostilities – and the blockade – were intensified, all glass imports fell to negligible proportions.

A buyers' had been turned into a sellers' market. Pilkington's difficulties now lay in making, not selling, its glass. Sources of high quality sand, needed for plate glass, had to be found and developed within Britain to replace supplies which had previously come from Belgium. A drive to recruit new labour, the employment of women on a larger scale, and much overtime were all needed to overcome the severe manpower shortage occasioned by the demands of the armed forces and munitions factories. Pilkington's very close connexion with the Territorial Army resulted in the immediate mobilisation of hundreds of its employees. Part of the Cowley Hill works was turned into a shell factory and the profit from making these munitions was devoted to building and equipping an emergency hospital at Ravenhead. This had its origins in an offer which the Board had made in August 1915 to build and equip such an institution. Dr J.R.Kerr, Pilkington's medical officer, who was posted to France in the following month, gained valuable experience as Chirurgien-Chef at Yvetot. He also had the opportunity of studying what was being done at various military centres of physiotherapy, especially under Dr Jean Camus at the Grand Palais, Paris. He returned to England in 1916 and was put in charge of the new Pilkington hospital which was devoted mainly to orthopaedic and limb-fitting work. It received its first intake of servicemen in January 1917.

Soon after that Dr Kerr's father, the distinguished headmaster of Allan Glen's, who had also been to Yvetot, retired from the school and came to St Helens as the hospital's lay superintendent. By 1920, in which year Dr Kerr received a C.B.E. for his services, £85,296 had been spent on the venture by the company, largely financed by the £72,998 profit it had made from munitions production. The hospital continued in existence until 1925 by which time the demand for the treatment of war wounded had virtually disappeared.[5]

The war had two other results for Pilkington which were of a more lasting nature. First of all it caused the collapse of the company's export sales, so extensive before 1914. By 1918, as may be seen from Table 32, plate glass exports had fallen to less than one-tenth of their pre-war total, and those of window glass to less than one-sixth. The great old pre-war markets in Canada and the other white dominions had suffered

TABLE 32
PILKINGTON EXPORT SALES, 1914–18

Year	(a) Plate	(b) Sheet	'000 sq. ft (c) Rolled	(d) Cathedral	Total Window Glass (b+c+d)
Annual Average					
1910–13	6,740	33,206	5,418	3,835	42,459
1914	5,722	28,784	3,292	3,180	35,256
1915	4,432	16,008	1,858	2,043	19,909
1916	3,846	12,373	1,749	2,303	16,425
1917	2,859	8,648	2,064	1,936	12,648
1918	586	4,586	939	1,293	6,818

Source: Pilkington Central Statistics Department

even more than these dismal totals would suggest, for in 1918 much less plate glass was being shipped to them than to India and Japan. Similarly, of the sheet glass exports in 1918, 1,500,000 sq. ft went to India and over 1,800,000 sq. ft to France. Canada received only 29,000 sq. ft, Australia 43,000 and New Zealand 38,000, though South Africa did a little better with 212,000 sq. ft.[6] United States manufacturers, in particular, had moved into these markets, especially in South America and Canada, though in the latter many sales had been through Pilkington outlets. The Americans' total plate glass output had been increased to 70,000,000 sq. ft in 1917.[7] Table 33, based upon a summary of the position compiled by Pilkington after the war, indicates the extent of their penetration. Clearly a struggle lay ahead to regain these old markets which the Belgians would not be slow in joining.

The other significant, and lasting, event of the war was Pilkington's eventual recognition of the National Amalgamated Union of Labour and other trade unions to which its employees now belonged. This important change, however, did not come until the war was nearly over. So late as March 1916, Lee Pilkington was still resolutely refusing to end the staggered contracts.[8] By 1916, however, the industrial climate was beginning to change nationally. A Ministry of Labour was formed at the end of that year with a trade unionist in charge. Trade union leaders were co-operating with the government in the war effort but local militants were taking an independent line of their own. The acute labour shortage placed organised labour in a much more powerful

TABLE 33
PILKINGTON AND AMERICAN SALES OF PLATE GLASS IN
CERTAIN EXPORT MARKETS, 1914-17

'000 sq. ft

Year		Canada	Australasia	South Africa	India China Japan	South America
1914	P	1,277	1,166	352	1,136	551
	A	438	14			53
1915	P	359	931	354	1,687	519
	A	1,477	1,220	12	319	946
1916	P	145	838	363	1,521	373
	A	2,204	1,111	12	353	619
1917	P	47	308	220	1,256	542
	A	2,308	775	13	463	754

Source: PA PB 97/97 TD10, Pilkington to T.R.Willis (Paris), 22 March 1919

bargaining position than it had been before the war, and trade union membership in the country as a whole grew from just over 4 millions in 1914 to 5½ millions three years later. The need for better industrial relations, emphasised by widespread strikes, came to be generally accepted, and the Whitley Committee on the Relations of Employers and Employed in its first report, published in July 1917, proposed joint industrial councils at national, district and works level.

The new national climate influenced industrial relations even at St Helens. The Board minutes record, rather laconically, on 14 February 1917:

National Union of Labour. Williamson. Think it very desirable to have a private interview with Sir George Askwith [the Chief Industrial Commissioner and a well-known conciliator].

The spring of 1917 saw a wave of strikes and there were 60,000 people on strike in Lancashire in May. August and September saw stronger demands at Pilkington for union recognition and abolition of staggered contracts, backed up by strike threats.[9] In October Williamson, the District Delegate of the Union, paid an official visit at the company's invitation. According to the Board minute of 11 October 1917:

T. Williamson called as arranged and A.R.P., A.C.P. and E.H.C.H. met him. A.R.P. told him that with regard to his letter we were arranging to see our men next week and if we find that they want a change in the method of discussing questions with them, we want to go into the matter and let him know what we are prepared to do. Williamson said in reply that he could not raise any objection to that.

There was no doubt what the outcome of this consultation would be. Shortly afterwards Pilkington told its employees that the company had agreed to recognise the union. Williamson commented:

We have for years been trying to get recognition from Messrs Pilkington Bros . . . and just recently after several mass meetings and their men becoming completely organised, we have been able to obtain recognition of the union and its officials. This is a great success not only for ourselves but for the rest of the unions in St Helens.[10]

The Electricians' Trade Union was recognised in February 1918[11] and in that month Cozens-Hardy visited the Ministry of Labour to tell them that Pilkington was willing to set up a Joint Industrial Council but that there could be no question of the company joining with other branches of the glass industry, such as the bottlemakers, because it normally had no connexion with them.[12] The St Helens Plate and Sheet Glass Joint Industrial Council, confined wholly to Pilkington, was formed on 3 August 1918 and accepted the status of a District Council under the Glass Industry National Committee on 5 November.[13]

Peace, which was soon to bring unprecedented difficulties for the company and, within little more than a decade, the end of skilled glass-blowing, was then less than a week away.

Chapter 16

The Interwar Years: An Introductory Survey

A FTER the First World War our story becomes more intricate as the business grew larger and its activities more involved. Great strides were made in glass technology with the advent of commercially successful continuous manufacturing processes. Industrial diplomacy with the leading glassmaking powers on the continent and in America assumed greater importance. New factories were built, or acquired, in Britain. The greater scale of Pilkington's activities made it impossible to run the company any longer as if it were still a partnership. Long overdue structural changes at last occurred in 1931, new faces appeared at the Board, and the new *régime*, with the Pilkington family still proudly in command as well as in possession, set about transforming the old firm into a modern international company. A committee structure was set up, outside consultants called in, administrative arrangements overhauled, a trainee scheme started, and the fourth generation of the family, now coming into the business, subjected to very rigorous selection procedures. Research and development was taken much more seriously. A technical committee was formed and, soon afterwards, a Central Research Department. Pilkington was also drawn again, rather reluctantly after its disastrous experiences at Thorold, into manufacturing operations even farther away, in Australia, South Africa and South America.

So far as the home market was concerned, prospects were good for glass manufacturers. Their main customers were builders and builders' merchants, and the building industry flourished from the early 1920s onwards as it had never done before, thanks to subsidised council housing, cheap money, the spread of building societies and the growth of

.middle-class home ownership. Housebuilding in Britain was hardly affected, as were many other industries, by the world depression of the early 1930s and, moreover, since houses were now expected to be brighter and airier, more glass was put into them. At the same time, glass manufacturers were gaining new custom from the young and vigorous motor industry which also grew rapidly, also weathered the depression well and also required more glass per unit. The saloon cars of the 1930s, even the smaller ones which then became popular, required more than windscreens, which was all that the open tourers had been fitted with formerly.

The rising housing demand of these years is readily seen by comparing the index of housebuilding between 1915 and 1940, graphed on the next page, with the comparable graph for 1871–1914 (p. 143). In the former period, two housebuilding peaks, in the mid-1870s and about 1900, were separated by a wide trough. At the first of these peaks, in 1876, 131,000 houses were built; at the second, a twin peak in 1898-9 and 1902-3, over 150,000 houses a year were put up. That total was exceeded in 1925 and never fell below it until the Second World War. From 1932 it climbed again as steeply as it had done in the mid-1920s, reaching new heights, above 350,000, in each of the years 1935–8.[1] The glaziers were kept busy. So were the glassmakers.

The rise in demand from the motor industry was even more spectacular. The total number of cars licensed in Britain grew from a mere 110,000 in 1919 to close on 2,000,000 in 1938; of commercial vehicles from 62,000 to 495,000; and of buses, coaches and taxis from 44,000 to 88,000.[2] Most of this market was supplied by British motor manufacturers who were also able to develop a bustling export trade. Production of cars, 71,000 in 1923, climbed every year, apart from 1930 and 1931 when the setback was only minor, to a peak of 390,000 in 1937. Similarly, commercial vehicle production increased, with a small drop in 1932 and 1933, from 29,000 vehicles in 1923 to 118,000 in 1937. In that year, according to the Society of Motor Manufacturers and Traders' estimate, the industry used 1,830,000 sq. ft of glass for windscreens, 7,260,000 sq. ft for side and back windows (technically known as body lights) and 620,000 sq. ft for other purposes;[3] 44 per cent of Pilkington's home sales of plate glass were used in motor vehicles. Moreover, as we shall see, the spread of safety glass, compulsory for windscreens from the beginning of 1932, required further processing beyond grinding and polishing.

While the high, and growing, level of building activity and the rapidly developing car industry ensured an increasing demand for glass at home, the export position was not so encouraging. Here the world depression of the early 1930s hit primary producers very hard. As the

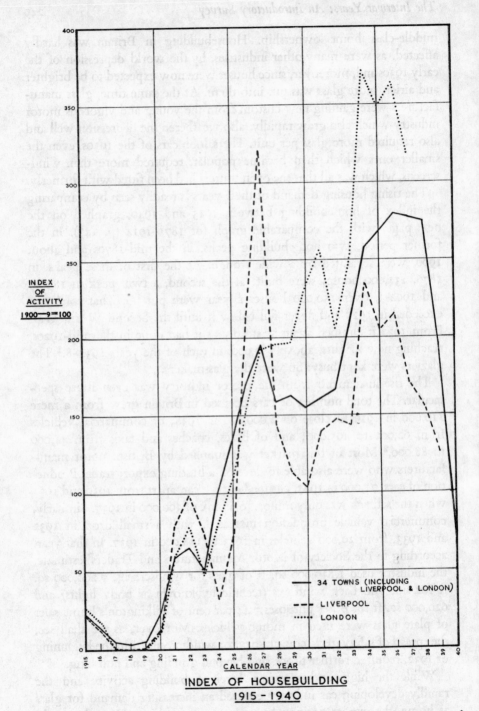

INDEX
OF
ACTIVITY
1900—9=100

34 TOWNS (INCLUDING
LIVERPOOL & LONDON)
--- LIVERPOOL
... LONDON

CALENDAR YEAR

INDEX OF HOUSEBUILDING
1915-1940

Graph 11 *Source:* B.Weber, 'A new index of Residential Construction, 1838-1950'. *Scottish Journal of Political Economy*, June 1955

price they could obtain for their food and raw material exports fell, they tended to produce more in an effort to maintain their incomes. This caused prices and purchasing power to fall even further. They could no longer afford to import the same volume of manufactures, the price of which had not fallen so much. The level of glass exports in the 1930s was usually far below that of the previous decade.

As we shall see when we come to examine the economics of its various manufacturing operations, Pilkington was able to sell an increasing footage of its plate glass very profitably throughout this period. Output exceeded pre-war production from 1923 onwards. Sales both at home

TABLE 34

PILKINGTON PLATE GLASS SALES FOOTAGE
AND PLATE GLASS IMPORTS INTO THE U.K.

1919-39

Year	Home Sales	'000 sq. ft Exports	Total Sales	Imports
1919	6,627	2,520	9,147	2,260
1920	6,440	3,458	9,898	6,924
1921	5,667	3,112	8,779	4,379
1922	6,076	5,704	11,780	6,408
1923	7,625	8,590	16,213	6,918
1924	8,689	8,830	17,519	7,260
1925	10,334	11,166	21,500	6,922
1926	9,849	11,843	21,692	6,913
1927	11,201	11,906	23,107	8,139
1928	12,847	11,991	24,838	9,381
1929	14,852	10,638	25,490	10,351
1930	13,111	9,609	22,720	7,966
1931	12,264	7,440	19,704	10,926
1932	10,525	5,563	16,088	8,888
1933	12,572	5,157	17,729	9,187
1934	15,449	5,841	21,290	10,087
1935	17,434	5,552	22,986	14,559
1936	18,337	5,663	24,000	15,535
1937	19,088	6,139	25,227	15,835
1938	13,949	4,470	18,419	11,548
1939	11,823	4,778	16,601	7,331

Source: Pilkington Central Statistical Department; Trade and Navigation Returns

TABLE 35

PILKINGTON CAST GLASS SALES FOOTAGE AND CAST GLASS IMPORTS INTO THE U.K.

1919–39

'000 sq. ft

Year	ROLLED			WIRED			FIGURED AND CATHEDRAL			Total Cast Glass Sales (i)+(ii)+(iii)	Cast Glass Imports*
	Home Sales	Exports	Total (i)	Home Sales	Exports	Total (ii)	Home Sales	Exports	Total (iii)		
1919										10,692	1,500
1920										11,631	2,000
1921										7,729	1,700
1922	7,237	1,833	9,070	2,732	1,650	4,382	3,966	4,105	8,071	21,523	2,300
1923	7,982	2,551	10,533	3,374	1,865	5,239	4,695	4,534	9,229	25,001	2,700
1924	8,023	2,664	10,687	3,847	1,923	5,770	5,604	4,612	10,216	26,673	3,400
1925	9,075	2,123	11,198	4,628	2,014	6,642	6,886	5,425	12,311	30,151	4,400
1926	8,865	2,416	11,281	4,893	2,369	7,262	7,268	6,141	13,409	31,952	4,400
1927	9,382	2,005	11,387	5,474	2,778	8,252	7,462	6,282	13,744	33,383	5,000
1928	10,005	1,981	12,036	7,209	3,321	10,620	7,173	7,157	14,330	36,986	6,100
1929	9,202	2,177	11,379	6,951	3,505	10,456	7,654	7,551	15,205	37,058	7,100
1930	8,743	2,143	10,886	6,977	2,369	9,346	7,479	5,633	13,112	33,344	6,200
1931	6,916	1,633	8,549	5,646	1,547	7,193	7,511	4,105	11,616	27,358	7,000
1932	6,816	814	7,630	4,908	1,132	6,040	7,727	2,919	10,646	24,316	6,000
1933	6,697	1,022	7,719	4,873	1,537	6,410	9,059	3,434	12,493	26,622	5,790
1934	7,889	1,158	9,047	6,924	1,808	8,732	10,730	2,931	13,661	31,440	10,393
1935	8,928	1,388	10,316	7,259	1,903	9,162	11,249	2,799	14,648	34,126	10,689
1936	10,446	1,066	11,512	8,883	1,515	10,398	11,955	3,036	14,991	36,901	10,087
1937	10,880	1,467	12,347	10,486	2,010	12,496	11,506	2,764	14,270	39,113	7,400
1938	8,871	1,124	9,995	12,214	1,568	13,782	11,991	2,546	14,537	38,314	6,873
1939	6,998	881	7,869	14,900	2,224	17,124	10,325	2,347	12,672	37,635	4,708

Source: Pilkington Central Statistical Department; Trade and Navigation Returns.

Note: Until 1933 sheet and cast glass were added together in the trade statistics. I am grateful to Mr T.R. Buxton for this disaggregation of the two between 1919 and 1932 based upon a study of the pattern of glass imports and of Pilkington sales in those years.

and abroad did well in the later 1920s; but then exports fell quite sharply to a much lower level, while the volume of home sales, after holding up well during the worst of the depression, moved upwards until 1937. They then fell back again, in keeping with the general downturn in economic activity in the country. It should be noted that, despite technical progress in this branch of the industry and falling production costs, the price at which Pilkington sold its plate glass did not stop a large volume of imports coming in even after – indeed particularly after – a modest tariff had been imposed upon them at the beginning of the 1930s. Imports in most years were two-thirds or more of Pilkington's home sales though for most of the 1920s the former were well below the pre-war level.

The company also did well in the various forms of rolled (or cast) glasses which continued to be sound, if not spectacular, revenue earners. Here imports were not so severe, though their volume became notably larger for a few years in the mid-1930s. As with plate glass, the footage of exports in the 1930s was well below that of the 1920s. The more sophisticated forms of the product – wired, figured and cathedral – gained a larger share of the market, ordinary rolled glass itself failing to sell at home and abroad in the better years of the 1930s any more than it had done in the better years of the 1920s. Figured glasses of various patterns were used to glaze the bathrooms and lavatories with which most of the new houses of the period were now being equipped.

Pilkington's sheet glass performed abominably badly in the 1920s because of the malign effects of the intermittent, drawn cylinder process, now in competition with the continuous Fourcault and Colburn machines which had been developed to the point at which they could produce increasing quantities of saleable glass. Exports fell away even in the favourable later 1920s, and the company's sheet glass also proved quite incapable of taking advantage of the growing building demand in the home market, all of which was snatched away by foreign importers. Recovery came after 1930 with a new, continuous flat drawn process, acquired in the nick of time. Pilkington gained almost 50 per cent of the home market in 1933 but, even so, was unable to make as much of the ensuing high level of building activity as the foreigners. Not until 1938 and 1939, when other glass sales fell, did Pilkington sheet really excel itself and dramatically increase its market share. Another unusual feature was that Pilkington's sheet glass exports were higher from 1933 onwards, and particularly from 1937, than they had been in the 1920s; but that was only a further reflection of their weakness before 1930.

Plate glass, embarked upon half a century after the original window glass firm had been established, and carried by sheet glass in the later nineteenth century, had become increasingly important to Pilkington in the years just before 1914. Now, between the wars, it became, for a time, absolutely essential to the company's survival.

TABLE 36

PILKINGTON SHEET GLASS SALES FOOTAGE
AND SHEET GLASS IMPORTS INTO THE U.K.

1919–39

Year	Home Sales	'000 sq. ft Exports	Total Sales	Imports*
1910–1913	43,957	33,206	77,163	92,962
1919	54,298	11,857	66,155	19,207
1920	51,801	12,178	63,979	34,601
1921	46,096	7,063	53,159	30,551
1922	36,720	16,445	53,161	48,784
1923	40,157	18,565	58,222	45,292
1924	43,560	16,491	60,051	51,246
1925	44,517	15,562	60,079	66,393
1926	38,377	11,404	49,781	84,215
1927	38,485	10,157	48,622	88,405
1928	37,564	8,181	45,745	83,615
1929	39,298	10,072	49,370	88,786
1930	37,946	6,281	44,227	93,155
1931	34,304	2,841	37,145	101,156
1932	48,406	3,670	50,076	84,214
1933	70,483	10,164	80,647	71,944
1934	75,581	11,258	86,839	88,885
1935	75,744	13,946	89,690	90,093
1936	73,001	15,852	88,853	99,549
1937	84,977	20,687	105,664	94,881
1938	88,571	24,167	110,738	78,639
1939	100,526	26,875	127,201	47,923

Source: Pilkington Central Statistical Department; Trade and Navigation Returns
*See note to Table 25, p. 192

Chapter 17

Forward with Plate

T HE end of the war was followed by a comparatively short period of feverish business activity throughout the British economy made possible by the speedy removal of wartime controls. Those who could afford to do so – and there were many, both individuals and companies, who now found themselves with accumulated profits to spend – fell over themselves to replace worn-out equipment or to replenish depleted stocks. The release of this huge, pent-up demand, coming at the same time as the eight-hour day and higher labour costs,[1] pushed up prices. Already twice its pre-war level in 1918, the price index rose to three times that figure before the boom broke later in 1920.

Many companies, anxious to lay claim to a larger market share in the brave new world, took the opportunity of the favourable economic climate to raise new capital. This, together with the considerable reserves which they had managed to build up, enabled them to embark upon considerable programmes of expansion. The sums involved were often very large. Courtaulds, for instance, increased their share capital from £2 m. to £4 m. in 1919 and to £12 m. in 1920.[2] Lever Brothers increased the capital employed in their business from £17½ m. in 1918 to £26¼ m. in 1919 and £47¼ m. in 1920.[3] Pilkington's expansion was more modest. Unable, as a private limited company, to appeal to the public at large for funds, it relied initially on the capitalisation of its reserves. These had grown during the war from £2,300,000 to just over £4,126,000 and rose a little further to £4,175,000 by June 1919. They were reduced later that year by over £2,500,000 to £1,657,000. At the same time, the share capital was increased from £810,000 to £2,430,000. (An extra £10,000 had been added in 1916 to the original issue of 1894 and the denomination of shares had then been reduced from £100 to £10. The difference between the total realised from the reserves and the £1,620,000 added to the share value is explained mainly by the larger volume of working capital needed immediately after the war.) At the end of 1919, then, shareholders' funds stood at £2,430,000 plus the £600,000 5 per cent debentures of 1894, and a further £1,657,000 in reserve, £4,687,000 in all. The increase in ordinary share capital did little more than take account of the company's greater value resulting from the ploughing back of profits over the 25 years since its formation.

Completely new money was needed in 1920 in order to finance further growth. Family shareholders now had to dig deeply into their pockets. The ordinary capital was increased by a further £680,000 to £3,080,000 and 3,000 £10 'A' shares were issued in the name of Norman Pilkington. In May 1920 there was also an issue of 6½ per cent 'B' debenture stock at £95 per cent to the face value of £298,250, redeemable in May 1925. These new debentures are of particular interest, for the company offered them not only to members of the family (including women members) but also to other people connected with the business, including senior staff. Some of the latter, it is relevant to note, were in a position to invest what were, in those days, considerable sums. W. Blackledge, J. H. Bridge, H. L. Kimmins, Dr J. R. Kerr, T. Railton and F. E. Slocombe each put in £1,000; F. B. Waldron £800; H. H. Gleave £600; W. H. Lackland £500 (and L. Lackland £300); Harry Teale and James Meikle also contributed £500 each, and others put in smaller amounts. This was not a move towards profit sharing of the sort already embarked upon by Chance Brothers,[4] but it did nevertheless give others the opportunity to invest on the same advantageous terms as members of the Pilkington family, particularly when the Bank rate fell to 5 per cent towards the end of 1921 and then went lower than that. Even when these debentures were renegotiated in 1925 at 5¾ per cent, they were still a good investment. In all, employees and other subscribers, some of whom were distantly related to the family, provided £43,440, the family itself taking up stock worth £254,810. Together with the extra £710,000 in ordinary shares, this meant that the Pilkington family found additional resources to the face value of £965,000 during that single year, 1920. Considerable sacrifice was needed from individual shareholders to make the money available. Indeed, £55,500 was still outstanding at the end of the year, nearly £40,000 of it on the new debentures. With this additional capital and rising reserves, total shareholders' funds exceeded £6 m. by the end of 1920.

By this time there was a division between ownership and management, for with each generation more members of the family had to be sup-

ported. In 1894, as we have seen (p. 171), the four senior members engaged
in actual management divided the shares and debentures equally among
themselves, allocated a portion of them, if they wished, to sons in the business, and were responsible for the care of their particular branch of the
family. There was, therefore, not only identity between shareholding and
management but also equality between the four branches of the family. By
the end of the First World War, all this had changed. Now members of
the family not involved in the business, and their wives, held debentures,
high rates of death duty had led to the formation of a number of family
trusts, and individual need had brought about transfers of shares from one
branch of the family to the three others. After Alan Douglas Pilkington's
retirement from active management in 1920, those in active management,
italicised in Table 37, held only about one-third of the ordinary shares,
and this was reduced to little more than a quarter after Arthur Pilkington's
untimely death in 1921. Lee Pilkington had died in 1919 and George Herbert Pilkington retired, for the second time. This left Geoffrey Pilkington,
the first arrival from the fourth generation, who had only 5,000 shares, as
the sole descendant of the founder William Pilkington then at work in the
company. Although there was no doubt that the managing directors were
in charge of the business, there were now absentee owners who were quite
prepared to appear at shareholders' meetings and to blame management
if results were poorer than expected.

Apart from the issue of a further 8,200 shares early in 1921, bringing the
total (excluding the 3,000 'A' shares) to 316,200, the issued share capital
remained unchanged throughout the rest of the interwar period. All further expansion was financed, as we shall see, by outside loans or by
ploughed-back profit.

The demands on the family shareholders ceased after 1920; but this new
capital, together with their existing shares, could not be readily sold if they
wanted to raise cash for their own purposes. They could sell shares only to
other shareholder members of the family. Consequently the value of the
shares bore no relationship to the price at which they could have been
sold on the open market had the company been a public one. As Lord
Pilkington later recalled to the author: 'Virtually the shares were not
saleable and the price was deliberately kept low [it was fixed at each
shareholders' meeting according to the dividend then paid] as a recognition of this and also to discourage shareholders (who had, of course, to
offer to other shareholders) from doing so, since almost all were in some
way short of money following the effort to raise new capital'.

There were further transfers of shares within the family during the
1920s. The joint holdings in the 1920 list represented family trusts, and

K

TABLE 37

HOLDERS OF ORDINARY SHARES ON 31 DECEMBER 1920

Descendants of William Pilkington		Descendants of Richard Pilkington	
Thomas Pilkington's Branch	William (Roby) Pilkington's Branch	William Windle Pilkington's Branch	Richard Pilkington's Branch
Thomas 36,000	Exors. Albert Leonard (1871–1908) 21,456	Exors. William Windle (1839–1914) 16,000	*Arthur Richard* (1871–1921) 21,500
Alan Douglas 32,000	Reginald Murray 21,472	*Richard Austin* 22,200	*William Norman* 16,400
	George Herbert 16,472	*Alfred Cecil* 28,800	*Guy Reginald* 5,300
	Exors. William Lee (1857–1919) 11,700	Mrs R.A.P. and Alfred Cecil jointly 5,000	Ernest Sinclair 18,800 Lionel Edward 15,750
	Geoffrey Langton 5,000		
	Reginald Murray and George Herbert jointly 3,900	*E.H. Cozens-Hardy* 8,000	William Norman and Lionel Edward jointly 2,250
68,000	80,000	80,000	80,000

Source: Pilkington Accounts

more of these were soon formed. By 1930 William Windle's branch, either in their own names or through family trusts controlled by them, had acquired a much larger proportion of the ordinary shares than they had held in 1920, 106,906 instead of 80,000. The proportion held by Richard's branch had grown much more modestly, from 80,000 to 85,420, and that of Cozens-Hardy had actually fallen, from 8,000 to 5,000. Cozens-Hardy had been obliged to sell these 3,000 shares in 1922 in order to reduce his overdraft at the bank. 'My overdraft has increased,' he wrote to Austin Pilkington on 24 May 1922, 'whilst at the same time the prospects of surplus income for wiping it out have vanished into the dim future . . .'[5]

In general, however, this represented a large switch in ownership from the other two branches to those then actively involved in management; and in this process Austin Pilkington's holding was increased from 27,200 to 37,092 and Cecil Pilkington's from 28,800 to 41,641 shares, 33,504 of which he held in his own name. Although William (Roby)'s branch held fewer shares, Geoffrey Pilkington – until 1930 still the only member of it on the Board – increased his personal holding from 5,000 to 11,200 shares.

If the relationship of management and ownership was different after the war, so, too, was the composition of the company's investment port-folio. No longer were large sums invested overseas. Instead these funds, under the pressure of wartime, had been repatriated and deposited much more insularly in high-yielding, short-dated British Treasury Bills: £540,000 out of a total portfolio of £776,000 at the end of 1920. Another £50,000 had been put into Canadian, French, Italian and Belgian govern-ment short-dated stock. Trade investment in Richard Evans, The Empire Machine Company, Dorstener Glashütte and Maubeuge remained, nominally at any rate, as before, £151,000 in all.[6] This left only about £30,000 in public utilities abroad. Gone were the rosy imperial days when the profits from British glass were invested in developing countries both in the British Empire and elsewhere for purposes other than glassmaking.

In the 1920s – a challenging decade full of new opportunities and pro-blems as indicated in the previous chapter – the holders of ordinary shares and debentures were expecting a great deal from the six of their number upon whom the direction of the company came to depend for a time between Arthur Pilkington's death in January 1921 and the arrival of rein-forcements from the fourth generation of the family. There had not been so few Pilkingtons in the business since the 1880s when it was much smaller and easier to run. Upon the decisions of these six men depended one of the country's major industries: its sole producer of plate glass and by far its largest manufacturer of window glass, too. In the glass industry, it was a commercial power of world class, a great exporter with bases in many parts of the globe and works in Canada and France. Pilkington's only competitors, Chance Brothers, had been outpaced years before and was no longer in the same league: its share capital had been raised after the war to a mere £300,000.

The two senior directors were Austin Pilkington, 50 years old when he succeeded unexpectedly to the chairmanship in 1921, and his brother Cecil, four years his junior. Both had very acute brains and great re-serves of energy, Austin being exceptionally active. Those who worked with him testify that he was complete master of the commercial side of the business in all its aspects and was personally known to almost every im-portant customer. He had learned the trade thoroughly under the careful direction of his uncle Richard, and when, as we have seen, he had to retire to Colorado for health reasons, he never lost touch with what was going on and was soon closely involved in the important Canadian developments. Cecil Pilkington complemented him, a master of the technical side of the business: his father, Windle, had seen to that. He had an immense practical knowledge of the chemistry of glass and of glassmaking processes. He knew, and understood, those employed in the factories. He would work right through the night, leading his team of engineers, when this was necessary.

Austin, the new chairman, was a much more enigmatic figure. Tall, thin and ascetic, he had no regard at all for his personal appearance and was often to be seen walking about St Helens in a dirty old raincoat and battered hat. He was very much a non-conformist in the old tradition, not given to outward show – indeed going out of his way to avoid it – dedicated to work and with a scrupulous sense of honesty. Like his father, grandfather and great grandfather before him, he was a pillar of the St Helens Congregational Church, giving it his time as well as his money, and – also like his father – taking particular interest in educational matters in the town, becoming chairman of the local education committee in the same year as he became chairman of the company. He was also particularly interested in the work of the YMCA and the London Missionary Society, of both of which he later became a very successful national treasurer for many years. He had, however, two weaknesses. He was unpredictable, a defect which revealed itself in the taking of trivial decisions as well as of more important ones. Those travelling with him on business never knew whether he would buy a first or a third class ticket and, especially when travelling abroad, what sort of hotel room he would take; he was even known to sleep on the floor for half price. Much more serious was his other weakness, an inability to delegate responsibility, a grave drawback given a situation where the few family leaders needed all the help they could get from the very capable lieutenants who were at hand. He was the sort of a man – and so was Cecil – who walked about with important documents stuffed into his pockets. Outside his office door were often to be found queues of senior managers waiting to report to him and they often felt it diplomatic to queue even when they had little or nothing to say. 'They also serve who stand and wait' was a much-quoted slogan during his term of office.

To some extent this reluctance to delegate arose from the atmosphere of secrecy which pervaded the business in those days. In the works, glassmaking was still largely a craft or mystery, and secrecy went with this know-how. In the office, there was much that had to remain secret, too, for profits and the earnings of the various shareholders were entirely the family's concern. Even the Cost Department, as has been noticed, was for-

bidden to compare notes with Sales. The company's registered office
was in Liverpool, well separated from the head office at St Helens. Coded
telegrams were used, usually to abbreviate longer descriptions and save
money but sometimes to conceal private information. Given this close-
ness, there were limits to how far responsibility could be delegated to those
outside the family, beyond a few faithful retainers who could be trusted to
keep their mouths shut and, in any case, had no right to comment on what
they knew, let alone assist in the determination of policy. Only two non-
Pilkingtons were regularly involved in decision taking: W. S. Tunnock,
whom we have already encountered in Canada just before the war and
who became company secretary in August 1920[7] and R. M. Weeks whose
arrival in St Helens in 1911 and subsequent distinguished war service have
also been mentioned. In 1920 Major Weeks, as he was usually known, was
appointed works manager at Cowley Hill. He was then just 30 years old.
He and Tunnock were both made sub-directors in 1920[8] and in this capacity attended board meetings. They held no ordinary shares at that time
and, indeed, had not been among the original contributors to the $6\frac{1}{2}$ per
cent debentures. They soon made amends however, Tunnock taking
4,000 (and his wife a further 300) and Weeks 1,500. Tunnock was very
much Austin Pilkington's right hand man and said to be naturally obse-
quious towards his superiors. Weeks, a person of a very different calibre,
was heavily involved with day-to-day matters at Cowley Hill and plate
glass generally. He acted as Cozens-Hardy's lieutenant. The most senior
managers, such as the company's Accountant or its solicitors, or the Home
or Export Sales Manager, were consulted on matters which expressly
concerned them; but their function was essentially an advisory one.

With Austin and Cecil very definitely in charge, the other directors do
not seem to have played a great part in affairs either. Cozens-Hardy –
Lord Cozens-Hardy after his succession to the barony in 1924 – was
mainly concerned with Cowley Hill and with negotiations abroad.
Norman – Major Norman after the war – though next senior to Austin
and Cecil, seems to have been abler at accumulating shares than in the art
of management.* Guy (another Major) and Geoffrey, who had both been

*Norman Pilkington is remembered by historians of air travel as the first farepaying
passenger to fly from London to Paris after the First World War. He had missed the Paris
night boat train on 14 July 1919 but, seeing in the *Evening Standard* that civil flying between
the two capitals had just been authorised by the governments concerned, he telephoned
Hendon and booked a flight for the following day. The plane took off at 7.30 a.m. next
morning and reached Le Bourget 2h 45 min. later. The plane was a converted wartime bom-
ber and the passenger wore Sidcot suit, flying helmet and goggles. Regular civil air services
did not start until 25 August. The whole story was later recalled by the pilot, Capt. H. Shaw,
in 'The First London-Paris Service', *The Aeroplane*, 14 July 1944.

only five years in the business before going off to the war, were still relatively inexperienced in the early 1920s. As the first arrival from the fourth generation, Geoffrey, though able, at that time tended to be over-shadowed by the others.

Pilkington directors were all expected to live in or very close to St Helens and to keep regular office hours. A book was kept in which their absences were recorded, together with the reason, even if it was illness or absence on business.[9] They lived quietly in impressive, but not ostenta-tious, detached houses standing in their own grounds – gardening was a favourite Pilkington pastime – but did not do much entertaining. Austin Pilkington, for instance, continued to live during his chairmanship (and indeed until 1945) at Eccleston Grange, a house on the main road to Pres-cot, just inside the St Helens borough boundary. They had a great sense of having succeeded to a family inheritance which it was their duty to preserve and develop, and this they believed that they, by upbringing and training, were particularly fitted to do. They were a chosen people, a race of men set apart, the sons, grandsons and great grandsons of men who had themselves built up a business which had survived and flourished when all but one of its British rivals had collapsed. This remarkable success had been achieved by lives of dedication which, in turn, demanded a readiness to work at least as hard as any of their employees in a smoky industrial town and in a damp, bronchitic, rheumatic climate. It had, moreover, involved leadership in the local community as well as in the business, something which happened less and less in larger places when the better-off moved out into increasingly remote suburbs and beyond. Austin Pilkington's services have already been noticed. He was the only in-dependent member of the St Helens Town Council for about 21 years and a local JP for about 50. Guy and Norman Pilkington also served in the territorials, in which both later became Colonels, on the local Council and on the Bench. Cozens-Hardy's family background automatically pointed him in that direction, too. These were not people who took afternoons off for their own pleasure or retired to some quiet retreat in the country when-ever they got the chance. Nor did they have houses in London. Indeed, although it had the use of British Vitrolite's office in Albemarle Street from 1932, the company had no West End office of its own until 1938 when it took a short lease of premises on the third floor of Westminster Bank Chambers, 63/65 Piccadilly at £700 per year. Until then important con-ferences had to be held in the sitting rooms of London hotels. Not until January 1950 did Pilkington move into its present imposing headquarters at Selwyn House, Cleveland Row, St James's.[10]

Outside St Helens Pilkington was a relatively little-known name until quite recent times. The company did not sell a product which, like a motor car, announced its maker to the world at large. It sold not to the general public but to the trade. It had little need to advertise at all. Sales promotion, unless new sorts of glass were being marketed, consisted of persuading merchants, photographic dry plate firms or accumulator battery makers to buy Pilkington glass rather than that of foreign suppliers. Nor was the name often mentioned in the newspapers because, having no profits to announce or shares to sell, it had little or no financial news value. Most people who had heard of St Helens as a manufacturing town knew about it at that time for its much-publicised Beecham's Pills, not for its glass. The directors rarely spoke about business matters in public, or wrote about them, for they believed that the less anybody knew about what was their private family concern, and especially about trade secrets, the better. Between the wars none of the directors engaged in national politics – the lead given in the second generation by Richard, who went into Parliament, was not followed up – nor did they play any significant part at that time in national organisations such as the Federation of British Industries. Nor did they achieve a wider reputation for non-business reasons, as, for instance, did the imaginative chairman of Courtaulds, Samuel Courtauld IV, by his vision in collecting French Impressionist paintings, making them available to the public, and creating the Courtauld Institute of Art in the University of London; or the chairman of Rowntree, Seebohm Rowntree, by his writings on social questions and the researches he undertook for Lloyd George.[11] This was not the Pilkington style at all.

They preferred to pursue their private interests and carry out their public services in the local community. They took particular pleasure in being able to grow splendid specimens of bearded irises or roses. They were at home at the company's Recreation Club at Ruskin Drive. Yet the next day, or even the same night, they might be taking the train to Paris or the boat to America, to combine visits to their branches abroad with a little business diplomacy, collecting a little information here or meeting a foreign glassmaker there. Austin Pilkington, in particular, led a very restless life. As more company histories appear, we see that capitalism has many faces. It is all too easy to see very ambitious, thrusting and not always very scrupulous men like Harry McGowan of ICI as the typical captain of industry.[12] The Pilkington story shows that business success was also achieved in less ostentatious, more attractive – and much more widely acceptable – ways.

Much of the capital raised after the war was needed for the building of a new plate glassworks. This was put up not at St Helens but at Kirk Sandall, four miles east of Doncaster on a canal which gave direct water access to the Humber. The site was an open one – a 'green field site' in modern parlance – which allowed the factory to be well laid out, with room for expansion; and since there was no nearby accommodation, a new village had to be built for those who worked there.

The venture was under consideration by the Board at the beginning of 1919. In January of that year it was decided to visit possible sites.[13] On 10 April what was described as the East Coast Scheme – a works with three furnaces and a lehr – was definitely decided upon. Consideration of fuel and labour costs and freight rates definitely ruled out Sunderland, Hull and Goole. Further enquiry was made concerning Newark, Doncaster and Crowle 'and any other positions in the Trent Valley where big barges can be used'.[14] By the end of August, Doncaster had been chosen, contractors were being discussed and the Sheffield and South Yorkshire Navigation was approached about dock facilities.[15]

The timing of the scheme was unfortunate, for costs, already high, went higher still in the following year, and there were many delays in construction. It was not until August 1921 that casting began. Grinding and polishing started in March 1922, but glassmaking was not in full swing until the end of that year.[16] The works had cost by then nearly £1,900,000. (For comparison, the larger factory at Cowley Hill, built in less expensive times, was valued in the accounts at just under £1,300,000; and it was capable of three times Doncaster's output.) This heavy capital outlay, and the onset of deflation, obliged the company to negotiate a loan of up to £450,000 from the Bank of England in February 1921 on the security of its debentures. This was increased to £750,000 in August. £669,000 had been drawn by the middle of 1922.[17]

Why was this costly investment decision – by far the largest made by the company in the interwar years – taken at that time and why was the new factory located so far away from St Helens in the fields of south-east Yorkshire? The generally accepted explanation is that it was intended to give a better supply of plate glass in the eastern side of England and was well sited to receive high quality Belgian sand by water. The proximity to south Yorkshire coal and Derbyshire limestone were further advantages. No doubt at that time scope was limited for expansion on the site of the existing works at Cowley Hill given no change in plate glass technology, and in 1919 no such change was in prospect. But there were other suitable locations in and around St Helens. Indeed, the old Ravenhead works had surplus capacity and land nearby for expansion. The casting of glass had been stopped there during the war (the finishing processes had been given up in 1908/9 as we have seen) and it seems hard to believe this factory could not have been renovated and re-equipped for less than £2,000,000. This would have enabled management to be concentrated at St Helens, so avoiding tedious cross-country journeys. Costs of transporting glass from St Helens across the Pennines were not excessive; and in any case other, cheaper categories of Pilkington glass, in which the transport cost element was higher, continued to make the journey without being priced out of easterly markets. The real clue to the Doncaster decision is not to be found in such insular explanations but in the context of international glassmaking politics.

Pilkington's experience of working with the continentals immediately before the war had then convinced the directors that the wisest course was to make an ally of Delloye and St Gobain. It is true that Delloye had been responsible for much huffing and puffing, not to mention bluffing, before Pilkington came to terms with the Convention; but, having been subsequently more closely involved in negotiations with him, the company came to feel that he was more likely to make sensible, long-term plans than the Belgians who, it believed, were always keen to go for quick momentary gain. In any case, St Gobain, with its works in many countries, catered mainly for the home markets of those countries, whereas the Belgians were excessively dependent upon exports elsewhere, including Britain. 'They are an international company with more works in Germany than anywhere else,' remarked Austin Pilkington about St Gobain after the war, 'and we are not misled by the fact that the Co. is nominally a French one.'[18] Accordingly, Pilkington continued to maintain regular contact with Delloye during the war, either by direct correspondence or through the Paris office of its Maubeuge works. As the fighting went on, Delloye became more openly anti-German and pro-Pilkington, stressing the value of their working together. 'Certainly after the war we shall go through a crisis,' he wrote in March 1916, 'for in many industries there is a natural desire for development to oust the Germans ... I am very interested in the feelers which are beginning to be made with a view to a certain grouping of the allied countries ...'[19] 'M. Delloye considers that the friendly tie uniting you is stronger than any syndicate,' T. R. Willis, then in charge of Pilkington's Paris office, reported home in July 1917.[20] He 'cannot foresee the possibility of having any dealings [with Germany] after the war,' he reported a few months later. '... It is his wish, in view of the German group he will have to combat, that you join officially his group,

K*

and he added that to strengthen the competitive power of this group, it would be well that the members have no trade secrets among themselves . . .'[21]

All these flourishes of friendship were understandable in the light of wartime emotion and they also had a more solid basis in the fact that little damage had been done to the rival Belgian works whereas those in northern France – including Maubeuge – had been plundered and destroyed, though others had been, or were being, built well away from the fighting. The St Gobain works, Delloye told Austin Pilkington immediately after the war, had been 'totally devastated'.[22] For the Frenchman, closer links with the English at that time made not only political and sentimental, but also commercial sense. Delloye, however, was merely the general manager and not a member of the Board. Whether his directors shared his views, we do not know.

Austin Pilkington, at his own request, visited Delloye in Paris with Cozens-Hardy in October 1918, for the first of a number of discussions which took place between them over the following months. The two companies had worked amicably in the Italian market, and they saw no reason why they should not do so elsewhere in Europe at the expense, if possible, of the Belgians. In order to smooth the way, it was proposed that St Gobain should take a minority interest (one-third was later specified) in Maubeuge. This factory was to be rebuilt, it was hoped, on a slightly bigger scale 'in such a way as to secure the St Gobain and Maubeuge Companies a larger control of the Belgian situation'.[23] Of even more immediate importance, there was also talk, at the first meeting in October 1918, of the continentals putting up a plate glass plant in England. Delloye thought that the best idea would be for this to be done jointly, with Pilkington holding a majority interest and with interchangeability of technical information. The conversation, as recorded (probably by Cozens-Hardy who was a good minuter of such discussions) went on:

P.B.:   We had never contemplated forming a joint company with the Belgians who were different from the French.
Delloye: Well, of course, they will build in England.
R.A.P.: That would be practically war. We should be very sorry for that.
Delloye: Yes and we all lose much money.[24]

The last thing Pilkington wanted was a foreign plate glassworks on British soil, and if the company were to have a stake in it, this would only cause it to become more closely entangled with the Convention, which would limit its freedom to compete for the home market and, perhaps, for its existing markets overseas as well. Indeed, just before the war, in

July 1914, the Board had already started to consider the possibility of building a factory on or near the east coast.[25] The Belgians' reported plans – which themselves may have had a pre-war origin – caused it to return quickly to the idea and to act upon it before the Belgians had time to move. The Belgians had taken what Pilkington regarded as an aggressive attitude. Pilkington, in return, decided on a course of action which would not only thwart the foreigners' plans but would also, if need be, place the company in a stronger position to compete with the Belgians in certain European markets. If Belgian sand could be imported to Doncaster by water, English plate glass could just as well be exported by the same route and out into the North Sea, in much the same way as the Belgians shipped their glass by canal from their inland works.

The Belgians, of course, saw the whole production and sales position in Britain in a very different light. They regarded Britain, with some reason, as a long and well established market to which they now had as much right as Pilkington. Moreover, for them the 1914 renewal of the Convention was still binding and due to run its full course until 1924. The signatories of 1914 were still members. The office of the Union Internationale had, as we have seen, been operating in neutral Holland throughout the war and was now back in Brussels. It is true that the Convention and the Union were formally dissolved at the end of March 1919 but this, as Delloye was at pains to explain, was only to get rid of the Germans.[26] Three separate selling groups, one for the Belgians, one for the French and one for the Germans, had immediately replaced the Union and the Convention then became a confederation of the three national groups.[27]

There is later evidence that in 1913, when the Convention's August 1914–1924 arrangements were worked out, Pilkington had agreed to an output quota which allowed the other Convention factories together to produce 4·45 times as much plate glass as Cowley Hill.[28] The company took the view that, if this undertaking was not rendered null and void by the outbreak of war, it was certainly broken by the continentals' new selling arrangements which came into force at the beginning of April 1919. These enabled Delloye to work more independently of the Belgians and more closely with Pilkington, a point he stressed at another meeting in Paris in March 1919. He reported that the Belgians 'regarded Pilkington as an enemy' and were concerned about their loss of foreign markets. 'It is important,' commented Cozens-Hardy, 'that D. and ourselves should have a definite policy, taking a long view and not the Belgian short view.'[29] Meanwhile plans for Doncaster were going ahead.

Delloye knew nothing about them until, in the late summer of 1919, he heard rumours of the purchase of the site. He sent an indignant letter to

Pilkington on 20 September. If Maubeuge was to be increased in size and a new factory put down in England, 'a period of peace is not to be thought of'.[30] Arthur Pilkington calmly replied that Pilkington could no longer agree to limit the output of its English works and politely observed that 'the eventuality of a state of anarchy such as you fear can largely be met by the maintenance of frank and friendly relations which we have enjoyed and which we hope will continue'.[31] At a meeting with Delloye in London at the end of October at which the Pilkington directors turned up in force – Arthur, Cecil, Norman, Austin and Cozens-Hardy were all there – Pilkington refused to budge from this position. The company now proposed to install four furnaces, three grinders and three polishers at Doncaster (five of the latter were actually put in) and to increase its total plate glass output by 30 or 40 per cent.[32] In the following month a letter arrived from the Convention, brought by special messenger, demanding that Pilkington adhere to the 1913 agreement. Arthur Pilkington confirmed once again that entirely new international circumstances made it quite impossible to renew the former relationship or to enter into fresh agreements for the English market.[33]

Relations between Pilkington and St Gobain were a little chilly for a time[34] but then improved once more, for Delloye found the going difficult with the Belgians. They 'had the idea that the making of plate glass was a prescriptive Belgian right'.[35] A St Gobain share in Maubeuge was again under discussion. It was still very much a sellers' market in 1919 and 1920, and Maubeuge and Doncaster were not yet producing glass. Even the Belgians were happy; in 1920 they managed to ship abroad 83 per cent as much glass of all kinds by weight as they had done in 1912, which had been a good year for them.[36] The collapse of the market in 1921, however, changed the climate of opinion altogether. 'The severe relapse in trade,' Pilkington confessed to Delloye, 'has come much more quickly than was anticipated'. This made the offer of a third share in Maubeuge less attractive and the company admitted that it would not now be surprised if the St Gobain Board no longer wished to take up any shares.[37] In the following October, Delloye was told that Maubeuge had started to grind and polish,[38] and in June 1923 that a second grinder and third polisher had been installed. It then had an output of 250,000 to 300,000 sq. metres per year, 90 per cent of which was sold in France itself. Pilkington, by now not so keen on this particular diplomatic asset and in need of the money, offered the factory and its associated Paris warehouse to St Gobain for a million pounds. Delloye, however, felt that the price was excessive, pointing out that the factory had been rebuilt immediately after the war when costs were very high.[39] The short spell of wartime and post-war amity was over, and although the two parties kept in touch, it was now usually through Captain F.C. Gordon, who had taken charge of the Maubeuge company's Paris office and warehouse.

Given that the Doncaster factory should be seen as part of Pilkington's bid for independence of the Convention, into which they had been drawn, little by little and most reluctantly, before the war, was the decision to build it in the period of post-war inflation justified? How serious was the Belgian threat to manufacture in England? In March 1919, five months after Delloye had given his warnings, he thought that the danger had receded.[40] This, of course, was before they had heard of Pilkington's unilateral declaration of independence. Whether the Belgians might have been encouraged to move later if Pilkington had not forestalled them, is problematical. On the face of things, it seems more likely that in 1919 and 1920 they were so preoccupied with getting their businesses re-started and returning to their pre-war markets that they had neither time nor resources to contemplate a new factory in England. In any case, transport costs by water from Belgium into duty-free Britain were very low. What was the advantage of having to grapple with the uncertainties of manufacturing in a foreign country, an operation to which they, unlike St Gobain, were unaccustomed? Their plate glass exports to England in 1920 (Table 34, p. 251) were already considerable, more, in fact, than Pilkington sold in the home market in that year.

One is left with the impression that at the end of the war Pilkington's directors, by fear of an unlikely eventuality, were stampeded into making an investment decision which, if left for a year or two, would have been much less costly. And if the decision had not been taken until 1922, it would have been a very different one, for by then important new plate glassmaking techniques were being developed. Not the least misfortune of Doncaster was that the plant there was obsolescent almost as soon as it came into use.

While Pilkington's continental links were involving the company in costly capital investment, its transatlantic connection, in association with important development work at Cowley Hill, brought it major technical advantages which, in turn, were to provide real leverage in future negotiations with the continentals.

The train of events was set in motion by Frederick Barnes Waldron, who, as has been seen (p. 203), joined Pilkington as head of the Cowley Hill drawing office in 1911, an appointment he had secured in response to an advertisement. He showed his ability not only in inventing sucker pads but also in developing a sloping lehr in collaboration with Cozens-Hardy. The two of them took out a joint patent and assigned the invention to the company. In February 1916 Waldron left to do war work with Dunlops in Birmingham; but in September 1917 he wrote to Cozens-Hardy outlining an idea for further improvement of plate glass grinding and polishing.

Despite the speeding up of these finishing processes, which, as has been noticed, was a feature of the period since the later 1880s, they were still intermittent. Each rough cast rectangular plate had to be laboriously embedded in plaster of Paris, together with other smaller pieces of glass to fill the corners, on a large circular table which was then revolved under two or more surfacing wheels, technically known as runners.[41] The process was intermittent not only because of the time taken to embed the plate of glass on the table but also because different grades of sand had to be used, starting with coarse and ending with fine, and the surface had to be washed after each grade. Then emery was employed for smoothing – the removal of the pitting caused by the sand. After that the glass had to be taken to the polishing apparatus. And after that it had to be turned over and re-embedded so that the whole process could be repeated with the other side.

Waldron's proposal was to pass the rough cast rectangular plates of glass, one by one, on a slowly-travelling bed, consisting of *rectangular* tables coupled up in succession, under a series of runners in line, each with its own supply of abrasive or polishing medium. Several runners might use the same grade of sand; but between those using one grade and those another, a squeegee and water channel would wash off the used material, each set of runners being completely boxed off from the next. The glass still needed to be bedded on the tables but, Waldron claimed, a simple mechanical appliance could be used for this. Having passed through the machine once, the table was to be uncoupled, returned to the starting point, the plate of glass turned over and re-embedded before beginning its second journey through the machine.[42] The waste involved in fitting rectangles or squares of glass on to circular discs would be avoided, and labour and production time saved.

Cozens-Hardy was impressed and was authorised to offer Waldron the post of Experimental Engineer and Head of the Drawing Office, Cowley Hill, at a salary of £1,000 a year. He was also to receive certain specified payments if the continuous grinding and polishing machine became a commercial success.[43] He returned to Pilkington's employment in February 1918 and on 31 July 1919 filed an application for the patenting of his invention.[44] Although he was also responsible for designing the new plant at Doncaster and Maubeuge,[45] he managed to begin experiments in January 1920 assisted by John Harris Griffin. Six runners were used, starting with different grades of sand and ending with emery powder. Greater priority was given to this work in February 1921 when more skilled men were allocated to it, and in the following month polishing heads were added to the experimental line, making it 117 feet long altogether.[46]

At this time Pilkington happened to be in communication with an American plate glass concern which helped it to learn more about important developments in the United States. This was the Edward Ford Glass Co. of Rossford, Ohio, whose principal had formed such a favourable opinion of the Cowley Hill works after his visit to Europe a quarter of a century before.[47] In 1919 the two companies had agreed upon visits to each other's factories to inspect production machinery, but not experimental work, the idea being that they would then make offers for particular pieces of apparatus which might be of help to them. E. B. LeMare had inspected Rossford in July 1919 in company with Austin Pilkington[48] and as a result two pieces of apparatus had been requested. 'The unfortunate part about the business' R. F. Taylor* had drily remarked as he forwarded the plans to St Helens, free of charge, 'is that you have selected the two appliances which were not originated by Ford but are standard to the plate glass factories in this country.'[49] The Edward Ford company did rather better. It received, also without charge, the drawings of Pilkington's sucker pads.[50] The goodwill so created, however, was to pay dividends, for, a couple of years later, when Pilkington heard of a much richer prize, it was able to enlist Rossford's help. This was no less than a successful attempt to flow plate glass continuously out of a tank as well as subsequently to grind and polish the product in windscreen lengths under a series of grinding heads. News of this appeared in the American publication *The Glassworker* on 3 December 1921, quoting *Ford News*, the house journal of the Ford Motor Company of Detroit.

At the end of the war Ford was already world famous as the first company to mass produce the motor car. It had managed to produce over 700,000 Model Ts in a single year and output was soon to reach more than double that figure. The windscreens of those days required only narrow pieces of glass – quite small compared to the great pieces of plate glass needed to glaze large windows – and in the early days of the American

---

*R. F. Taylor, now a very experienced glassmaking technologist, had succeeded Thorpe as Pilkington's American representative in 1917. He operated from just across the frontier, at Niagara Falls, where he could keep in close touch with Pilkington's Canadian headquarters, then located at St Catherine's, Ontario. He was recalled to St Helens at the end of 1921.

motor industry, these could be had for as little as 22 cents per sq. ft; they were the offcuts which had no sale elsewhere.[51] But as motor output grew and as saloon models became more popular, there was no longer enough of this cheap glass available. The price rose to 90 cents and more because the large plates had to be specially cut for the purpose. Henry Ford, who in any case believed that his company should be independent of outside suppliers, decided to build his own glassworks and gave the task to C. W. Avery, a Michigan University graduate who had been Edsel Ford's tutor in manual training at Detroit University School before becoming a full-time Ford employee. It was he who had been chiefly responsible for creating Ford's precisely-timed production line just before the war.[52]

Neither Avery nor Fred Brown, a former fireman on the Canadian Pacific Railway who happened at the time to be in charge of windscreen assembly and was drafted as Avery's assistant, knew anything about glass or glassmaking. So Avery sent Brown to the local library to 'read up on glass'.[53] He was accompanied by the Assistant Superintendent of the Highland Park plant, W. C. Klann, who spent a year on the project. It is upon Klann's subsequent recollection and that of Avery himself that we have to rely for the description of how the process was developed.*
According to Klann:

We sent for a little crucible to Germany. It was about a month before we got the crucible back and it only held about a pint. It was about an inch thick. We got some burners and put it [sic] underneath the heat and mixed our sand and our glass and lead and arsenic and everything else. We mixed it all and it came out a piece of black glass as black as a telephone . . .

Then we sent to England for a crucible . . . It held about four pounds of glass, enough to make a piece of glass about one foot square. With that we made our first white glass . . .

These experiments began, apparently, in 1919.[54] When they had been completed, Avery, keen to make glass continuously and not by the intermittent, pot method, decided to build a furnace about 12 feet long and,

*The Oral History Section of Ford Archives, which was responsible for the interviews with Klann in 1953, reveals the influence of Professor Allan Nevins, Ford's historian, a world pioneer of oral history. Thomas Appleton, a member of the Pilkington staff who undertook preliminary research for the earlier version of the present book, carried out similar interviews with elderly Pilkington employees in 1946/7 using shorthand and, without realising it, became one of the earliest practitioners of oral history in this country. Being himself well aware of the main events, he asked relevant questions. The summaries of these interviews, unfortunately often heavily edited, have proved a useful source of information for this book.

behind it, a pit, ten feet deep, into which he attempted to pour the ribbon of glass. After eight months' work, however, they still, according to Klann, 'couldn't use the glass no how'.[55]

This seems to take us to January 1921 when a certain Edward Donner, who had been hired to make the tank work, was dismissed. In an indignant letter to Henry Ford, he claimed that the seven months he had been given since the glass was ready for working on 1 June 1920 was not long enough to expect him to achieve results. He had already made poor glass of sheet quality, and sent samples to show that improvement was on the way. Avery, he complained, was too 'wrapped up in the development of the plate machine which contains some of his personal ideas'.[56] If Avery's own recollections are to be relied upon, however, it was he who was thinking soundly and along the right lines. He carried out tank tests with colouring matter. These showed that, while some of the glass was delivered after 20 days' melting in the tank, some of it also passed through the furnace in 36 hours. As he later explained the problem:

This was due to the more liquid state of the higher temperature glass on the surface. In making plate glass by the old pot method, a variation in materials from one pot to the other as high as ten per cent was not serious. In the tank furnace, however, a portion of today's batch would probably come through tomorrow with a portion of last week's batch. If the two batches varied in chemical composition, we would have several different kinds of glass in the same sheet, each with its different coefficient of expansion, resulting in exceedingly high breakage both in the annealing furnace and under the grinding and polishing wheels, especially the latter.[57]

By the time work on the project was temporarily stopped in January 1921, $1,500,000 (over £320,000) had been spent and Avery expected the worst when he went to Ford for more money. 'If this experiment works', he urged, 'we will save many times the money we have spent'. To which Henry Ford replied: 'What do you mean – *if* it works? It *must* work. Forget the money you have spent and go back and make it work'.[58]

Although the evidence at this point is a little conflicting, it is clear that glassmaking experts were called in. Ford's chief engineer had previously acted as consultant to the Edward Ford Plate Glass Co. – there was no other relationship between the two Fords – when its last grinding tables had been installed, and it was through him that Rossford's help was obtained.[59] With this advice, it soon became quite possible to flow a ribbon of glass wide enough for windscreens and of a quality satisfactory enough for the inexacting demands of the motor trade. The narrow plates were then sent to Rossford for grinding and polishing.[60] Meanwhile the Ford

Motor Company was developing its own grinding and polishing process on a continuous belt under a series of heads on principles similar to Waldron's at St Helens. This came into operation in July 1921, but had been preceded by prolonged experiments with a single grinding table and head. The early machine could still process only half the tank's output, however, even in April 1922.[61]

The Glassworker article of 3 December 1921 took Pilkington by surprise. J.E. Harrison, in charge in Canada, could still get no evidence that Ford was making its own windscreens even in March 1922; and Ford was certainly then still buying glass in quantity from outside suppliers.[62] Pilkington was, naturally, anxious about the Waldron patents, but the company was in no particular hurry to send representatives to Detroit. Having discovered that its Rossford friends were, by a stroke of luck, the one glass concern in the United States best able to help, Austin Pilkington wrote, on 14 March 1922, to George R. Ford to enquire whether assistance might be available under their existing exchange arrangements:

We have seen an account in The Glassworker of a Continuous Grinding and Polishing Machine, stated to be used for Ford Motor Screens, and we understand that you are concerned in it.

This is of special interest to us, as we have been working on these lines for the last few years.

We do not know to what extent you may deem it desirable to exchange information on the subject, but we should like to have the opportunity of talking this over, which we think would be to our mutual advantage.

He then went on to mention that R.F. Taylor and 'one of our Engineers' (Waldron himself, no less) were about to cross the Atlantic and would like to call upon him.[63]

Taylor and Waldron duly called at Rossford but did not receive very encouraging reports of Ford's glassmaking efforts.[64] The rough cast which had reached Rossford for grinding and polishing was very poor. Nevertheless D.H. Goodwillie, the Works Engineer, telephoned Detroit and arranged for his two visitors to see the Ford plant for themselves. This they did on the afternoon of 5 April and Avery himself showed them over. Everything was very open – even the composition of the glassmaking mixture was posted prominently on the front of the furnace[65] – and Avery was only too pleased to show off what he had been able to achieve without a single glass specialist ever having been employed on the job, a claim that was strictly true but misleading in that it suggested he had received no advice at all from the glass industry. Numbers of people had already been shown the plant, including American glassmakers and a representative from St Gobain. 'In fact', Waldron wrote when he got back, 'it would appear that the apparatus has been developed by picking the suggestions of these people . . .'[66]

The two Pilkington men were very impressed by what they saw. 'It is generally a workmanlike job', commented Waldron, 'clean, neat and orderly . . . The product is commercially satisfactory for the Ford car'. At the time of the visit the glass from the furnace, though subject to ream (a non-homogeneous layer in the glass) was good enough for its purpose and the grinding and polishing machinery could handle one million of the two million sq. ft of rough cast produced by the tank. This had a capacity of 300 tons and delivered 15 tons of glass per day, 25 in. wide and $\frac{3}{8}$ in. thick, at the rate of 33 in. per minute. The glass flowed out through a hole in the end of the tank, the top of which was $2\frac{1}{2}$ to 4 in. below the level of the metal. There were two fireclay gates to the hole, one of which was used as a shut-off valve and the other as a regulator.

The rolling apparatus consisted of a table made of a series of platens carried on a chain with a cast iron, water-cooled roller above, followed by an ordinary roller and then by a pair of them at the mouth of the lehr. The ribbon of glass was carried down the 435-foot lehr on parallel rollers and cut off to windscreen length when it emerged at the other end. Each rough cast windscreen was laid in plaster of Paris on a table 3 ft 6 in. wide and 7 ft long running on six wheels on an ordinary rail track. A heavy link chain provided the drive and a spring clip on each side was provided to couple the tables together. The train of tables moved down one side of the building under 36 grinding and smoothing heads, reducing the thickness of the glass from $\frac{3}{8}$ in. to $\frac{1}{4}$ in.[67] and back along the other side under 30 polishers – the whole railway was 400 ft long – at a speed of 18 to 21 in. per minute. The glass was then turned over for the other side to be processed. Particularly efficient smoothing compensated to some extent for poor polishing. The whole plant bore the distinctive Ford stamp not only in its continuous belt layout but also in the Ford equipment used. As Waldron noted: 'All the grinding and polishing heads are made of back axles of Ford tractors, the bevel drive on the standard car for raising and lowering and the steering wheel for operating it.'

Although it was much easier to manufacture windscreens, which did not require high quality glass and could be more readily ground and polished in small sizes, than to make large panes of glass, which were much more likely to break under the grinders, Taylor and Waldron were quick to see the possibilities of adaptation from the small to the larger scale; and the improvement in the quality of glass from the tank was evidently a task for glassmakers. The two Pilkington visitors compli-

mented Avery on his achievement, unlike his other visitors who seem
to have concentrated upon the shortcomings of the plant. Pilkington,
Taylor later claimed, was the first glassmaking concern to take Ford
seriously. Avery, on his side, as he, too, later recalled, was apprehensive
about the Waldron patents, the validity of which Taylor and Waldron
had checked with a patent lawyer in Detroit at the time of their visit.[68]
Partly because of the Ford principle of openness and partly because he
wanted to be left a clear field to develop further his grinding and polishing
machinery – plans were already in hand to double its capacity – Avery
raised no objection to Pilkington using any of his ideas for full-scale plate
glass production.[69]

Pilkington lost no time in applying experimentally at St Helens the
knowledge acquired in Detroit. On 2 May 1922 it was decided to lengthen
the experimental grinding and polishing machine[70] and on 8 May the
Board decided that tank experiments should be undertaken to flow a
ribbon of glass roughly 72 in. wide; Waldron was to be responsible for
the drawings and machinery, and LeMare, in consultation with Railton,
for the day-to-day supervision of the experiments themselves. With
tanks Pilkington had a great advantage over most of its plate glass rivals in
that it also made window glass and was, therefore, quite familiar with
tank furnaces. The experiments, in fact, took place initially at a sheet glass
tank at Sheet Works without a lehr. They went well – flows of up to
25 hours were achieved[71] – and on 10 October the Board authorised the
expenditure of £10,000 on a continuous casting plant in the rolled plate
department with a very long lehr.[72] It also gave instructions for preparations to be made for the installation of the new process at Cowley Hill.

The time had obviously arrived to tell the Ford Motor Company what
was happening, and on 28 November Austin Pilkington, Taylor and
Tunnock met Avery in Detroit. The agreement then reached to exchange technical assistance and know-how was confirmed in writing by
Austin Pilkington to Edsel Ford the following day:

Referring to our recent conversations with your Mr Avery, we will place at
your disposal, for the manufacture of glass for use in your industries, all our
experience, knowledge and inventions, both present and future, whether
patented or not, in connection with the manufacture of plate glass by continuous
process. In return, you are to place at our disposal all your experience, knowledge
and inventions, both present and future, whether patented or not, for the manufacture of plate glass in our factories.

It is understood that upon request of either party the other shall use all
reasonable precaution against the disclosure of any special information . . .[73]

Blueprints of the Waldron continuous grinder were sent to Detroit the following month,[74] and Griffin went there for most of March 1923 to help improve the quality of Ford's rough cast glass. (He was put up at the Statler Hotel.) 'The tank, rolls and lehr have been working extremely well during the 18 days I have been here,' he reported. 'Ream is almost negligible.'[75] When he left, Avery wrote to Austin Pilkington acknowledging that he had 'made some suggestions which we are preparing to follow in an experimental way. We have faith that they will help us reduce the cost of manufacturing.'[76] Cecil Pilkington subsequently answered specific technical queries by post[77] and himself visited Detroit, along with Taylor and Tunnock, at the end of 1923.

Meanwhile very satisfactory progress was made at St Helens. The Waldron grinder, now 226 ft long and capable of processing glass 60 in. wide, went into commercial production at Cowley Hill on 9 April 1923, though much development work still remained to be done. The introduction of the plate glass tank was even more rapid, for the directors only decided in February 1923 on a timetable for production trials at Grove Street. If these were successful, the decision to go ahead at Cowley Hill could not be made before early in May. In fact, everything went particularly smoothly and glass flowed from the first tank there on 25 October.[78] It passed through double rollers and not, as with the original Ford machine, over platens. Apart from its continuity, the great advantage of the Flow process, as it came to be called, was that it produced rough glass 8·6 mm thick for grinding down to the required 6·4 mm ($\frac{1}{4}$ in.), whereas thicker plates of 10·6 mm had had to be made by the older casting method. The saving in energy on grinding the thinner product was very considerable. The quality at the outset, however, was poor, and it was fortunate that, as part of the deal reached at Detroit, it had been arranged that Pilkington should supply Ford with some of the glass it needed over and above what the Detroit glassmaking plant could produce. The first order, taken on 29 November 1922, for 20,000 windscreens, was followed by large contracts for over 1,100,000 sq. ft of plate glass to be delivered between March 1923 and March 1924 and a further 1,360,000 sq. ft in the following 12 months.[79] This was over 6 per cent of Pilkington plate glass production at that time. Much of it was made on the new machinery, which could produce glass adequate for the purpose. The rest of its early output not taken by Ford went to Woolworths for divisions in their counter fitments.[80] By the time the second contract had been completed, however, the machinery had been greatly improved. The original grinder stopped production on 17 November 1923 and an improved and longer version, also for 60 in. glass, came into service on 16 March 1924. The grinder and polisher was then adapted for wider glass. The first 100 in. machine, 544 ft long, replaced the existing one in April 1927 and a second, 651 ft long, was added in September 1928. (The degree of sophistication reached by this time may be judged from the fact that when the Board authorised this last machine, it was to be equipped with four oscillating grinders followed by 11 fixed grinder heads, 16 polishers and seven travelling polisher heads at a total cost of £85,966.)[81] Doncaster also had to be brought up to date. A tank was started there at the end of 1926 and a 100 in. grinder and polisher in December 1929. In return for assigning his invention to the company, Waldron in July 1924 received a lump sum payment of £5,000 in addition to £4,000 already paid to him in final settlement of all his claims on the invention.[82] Having developed the process from an imperfect method of making narrow windscreen glass to full plate glass quality and size, Pilkington, feeling unable to divulge these further secrets to Ford lest they should fall into the hands of rival glass manufacturers, terminated its agreement with Detroit on 24 November 1925.[83] For Pilkington, in particular, it had been an extraordinarily fruitful period of collaboration. Plate glass manufacture had been made much more efficient and Pilkington had gained a lead over its international rivals.

These rivals, however, had not been inactive. St Gobain had been concerned with the development of the Bicheroux process, the last word in casting technique. And, so early as December 1922, news had come from Rossford that the Pittsburgh Plate Glass Company was to build a new plant at Creighton, Pa., in which the glass was to be made in tanks and ground and polished by a continuous process; but PPG experiments until that time had achieved little apart from destroying three tanks.[84] Taylor reported further on this in the following year: the experimental tank, producing a 72 in. ribbon, was making better progress than it had previously done, though in July 1923 they still did not possess a complete machine for grinding and polishing. The new plant at Creighton was still being built.[85] Two years later Edward Ford's works manager, who had recently been to Creighton, told Pilkington that the PPG were 'making rapid progress with their tank programme' and putting up another unit to make glass 130 in. wide, which would include a continuous grinder and polisher.[86]

Continuous grinding and polishing, but not the Flow process, were also attracting attention on the continent in the early 1920s. Here Pilkington's main source of information was Charles Heuze of the Belgian machine-making concern, Ateliers Heuze Malevez et Simon at Auvelais, with whom Pilkington had had a long-standing association since the

1880s through the Malevez grinding tables. Heuze was known to be working on a continuous grinder and polisher.[87] He himself told Pilkington in March 1922 that the continentals were divided on whether or not to support such a venture, for their output quotas were based upon the grinding surfaces of existing machines. There was, however, a faction which was prepared to experiment in spite of the Convention's rules,[88] and in December 1922 H.M.S. wrote to say that it had re-started trials on a continuous grinder and polisher at a factory at Boussois, just outside Maubeuge. It had originally begun to build this not long before the war. The machine 'of large dimensions' was said to be giving excellent results and negotiations were about to start to license it to the Convention works.[89] Pilkington quickly came to terms with H.M.S. On 15 February 1923, before the Waldron machine went into commercial production at Cowley Hill, the two concerns agreed to pool their inventions, and future improvements to them, and to share the income equally. H.M.S. was to have the sole licence to manufacture and sell the machine on the continent, and Pilkington was to have the right to use it free from royalty in the United Kingdom, the Commonwealth and at its own Maubeuge works. Applications from outside Europe were to be dealt with by mutual agreement but, so far as the United States was concerned, H.M.S. was not to make any arrangements to sell the machine which would in any way prevent Pilkington's friends there from using it.[90] When Delloye visited Cowley Hill early in April 1923 to see the new 60 in. machine just before it went into commercial production, he was favourably impressed. He enquired about the possibility of the Convention taking out a licence for what came to be known on the Continent as a *Douci-Poli Continu* and was referred to Heuze.[91] Agreement with the Convention was reached in July 1923 and the contract signed on 25 January 1924.[92]

The Convention was licensed to work the Heuze-Pilkington grinder on the continent, Pilkington's rights at Maubeuge having been specified, for a fee of six million Belgian francs payable in three instalments during 1924. For the first two years of operation a royalty was payable equal to one-third of the savings over the old process, and for the remaining 13 years of the agreement, equal to one-half. H.M.S. was to supply the machines on a cost plus 20 per cent basis. They were eventually installed at Auvelais, Chantereine, Herzogenrath, Boussois, Franière and Moustier.[93] Meanwhile in America continuous grinding and polishing machines were developed by others besides the Ford Motor Company; but these did not operate on the same principles as the Heuze-Pilkington machine and were, therefore, not covered by its patents. Libbey-Owens, for instance, had its own equipment. By 1927, however, Heuze could claim that the latest

100 in. version of the Heuze-Pilkington machine was capable of processing glass of larger size and better quality than any of its rivals.[94] Licensing negotiations started that year with the National Plate Glass Company, Detroit, and the Edward Ford Glass Company, Rossford. R. M. Weeks negotiated a licence for two machines with the former during a visit to America in December 1927, and Cecil Pilkington reached a similar agreement with the latter in June 1928. A new licence was needed in June 1930 when the Edward Ford Glass Company merged with Libbey-Owens to form Libbey-Owens-Ford.[95]

Although the continuous grinder gave Pilkington a technical ascendancy and greater standing in the eyes of the other glassmaking powers, the income from licence fees and royalties was small. Pilkington's half share of the six million Belgian francs produced only £32,676 at the rate of exchange prevailing in 1924[96] and presumably the continentals were able to claim that the machine did not yield any saving over the old process, for they paid no royalties. Income from America down to the end of 1930 brought in about the same figure: £10,273 from the National Plate Glass Company and £20,208 from the Edward Ford Glass Company, Libbey-Owens and Libbey-Owens-Ford. £63,000 from all sources was a disappointing return for such considerable effort and achievement. It is more readily understood, however, in the light of the machine's relatively slow utilisation even by Pilkington. It made no major contribution to the company's output until the first 100 in. machine came into service in 1927, as may be seen from Table 38. As was to be expected with a new development, production costs were high at first. It was not until the middle of 1926 that the glass made by the new machine was produced more cheaply than on the old tables. The cost of both fell quite impressively after that, and the new grinders gained a clear advantage from the later months of 1928.

Tanks in fact replaced pots much more rapidly than continuous grinding replaced the disc method, as Table 38 also shows. Here Pilkington obtained a real advantage. The flow process, by producing a more even and smoother rough cast glass, greatly reduced the amount of grinding required. The company was at great pains to keep this secret. The arrangement with Heuze helped, for by referring would-be licensees of the Heuze-Pilkington machine to Belgium, prying eyes were kept away from St Helens and the successful plate glass tanks there.

The increase in value of the Cowley Hill factory does not suggest that these developments of the 1920s involved expenditure on the pre-war scale. It rose from £1,285,000 to £1,410,000 in 1924, and then slowly over the next four years, which saw the installation of the first 100 in.

OUTPUT, COST AND PROFIT OF PLATE GLASS AT COWLEY HILL BY THE OLD AND NEW PROCESSES IN THE 1920s

Period to	OLD PROCESS			CONTINUOUS PROCESS			Sales Proceeds (less package, freight, etc.) £'000	Manufacturing Cost £'000	Manufacturing Profit £'000
	Production '000 sq. ft Rough Cast (A) (Pot)	Polished (B) (Disc)	Polished Cost per (C) sq. ft (d)	Production '000 sq. ft Rough Cast (A) (Tank)	Polished (B) (continuous)	Polished Cost per (C) sq. ft (d)			
1920 June	7,586	5,331	9·123				666	415	251
Dec	7,819	5,386	10·819				856	493	363
1921 June	5,451	3,962	11·317				568	397	171
Dec	7,918	5,451	8·660				594	409	185
1922 June	7,731	5,360	7·227				572	324	248
1923 March	12,567	8,080	6·713				950	461	489
Sept	8,463	6,116	6·043	1,102	98	29·387	677	352	325
1924 March	7,507	6,276	6·080	3,380	80	21·000	651	362	289
Sept	6,457	6,719	5·751	6,207	316	12·911	726	390	336
1925 March	3,526	6,758	5·682	9,048	301	10·365	739	350	382
Sept	2,822	6,764	5·784	9,821	390	8·000	687	343	344
1926 March	1,966	7,606	5·080	15,810	603	5·572	710	355	355
Sept	208	7,598	5·591	13,074	733	5·566	636	346	290
1927 March	474	7,487	5·321	15,740	731	5·253	599	374	225
Sept	732	4,178	5·051	11,007	1,199	4·604	541	301	240
1928 March	318	6,331	4·890	13,080	1,412	4·419	433	283	150
Sept	544	6,370	4·747	12,895	1,415	4·719	446	272	174
1929 March	253	6,807	4·442	13,610	3,083	3·737	516	283	233
Sept	537	6,561	4·426	17,852	3,708	3·172	603	315	288
1930 March	83	4,250	4·461	12,918	3,880	3·588	427	246	181
Sept	182	2,948	4·966	12,572	5,263	3·602	424	259	165
1931 March	331	2,287	5·772	12,837	4,971	4·152	338	267	71

Source: Pilkington Accounts

(A) Glass made
(B) Finished glass into warehouse
(C) Unit cost of grinding and polishing process

TABLE 39

OUTPUT, COST AND PROFIT OF PLATE GLASS AT DONCASTER IN THE 1920s

Period to	OLD PROCESS Production '000 sq. ft Rough Cast (A) (Pot)	Polished (B) (Disc)	Polished Cost per (C) sq. ft (d)	CONTINUOUS PROCESS Production '000 sq. ft Rough Cast (A) (Tank)	Polished (B) (continuous)	Polished Cost per (C) sq. ft (d)	Sales Proceeds (less package, freight, etc.) £'000	Manufacturing Cost £'000	Manufacturing Profit £'000
1922 June	941	885	12·575				76	82	[Loss]—6
1923 March	3,655	2,213	8·285				254	154	100
Sept	3,147	2,055	10·824				227	152	75
1924 March	2,973	2,402	10·610				225	166	59
Sept	3,081	2,520	9·812				225	163	62
1925 March	3,029	2,788	9·322				242	166	76
Sept	2,672	3,049	7·146				247	145	102
1926 March	2,512	3,288	6·847				228	142	86
Sept	1,751	3,361	6·659				230	136	94
1927 March	1,644	3,406	8·484	2,416			252	198	54
Sept	81	3,693	6·606	5,240			216	155	61
1928 March	705	3,468	6·875	4,712			215	163	52
Sept	696	3,348	6·343	4,533			188	149	39
1929 March	661	3,773	6·171	5,256			220	159	61
Sept	657	3,693	6·299	5,182			218	161	57
1930 March	641	2,609	4·610	4,403	1,331	3·967	217	121	96
Sept	788	1,188	5·656	3,421	2,438	3·445	210	124	89
1931 March	586	920	7·043	5,250	2,532	3·697	198	133	59

Source: Pilkington Accounts
(A) Glass made
(B) Finished glass into warehouse
(C) Unit cost of grinding and polishing process

grinder, to £1,468,000 in March 1928. There was then quite a burst of investment, bringing the total to nearly £1,700,000 by September 1929 – the second 100 in. grinder would explain much of this – and to £1,726,000 in March 1930. Even then, however, this was over £100,000 less than had been spent at Doncaster by 1922.

Cowley Hill remained impressively profitable throughout the decade as Table 38 shows. Even in the bleak year of 1921, before these technical improvements had been made, it contributed a manufacturing profit of over £350,000. The improvements in casting and in grinding and polishing brought costs down in the second half of the decade, but more intense competition brought down prices too. Profits were lower after 1926 – and with the innovations – than they had been in the immediately preceding years.

The much more modest contribution of Doncaster in terms of both output and profit is to be seen from Table 39. While costs there fell before 1926, they did not continue to fall in the way that they did at Cowley Hill, and they were always higher than at the older works. Tank production, however, took over quickly in 1927 from the recently-installed pot furnaces, and grinding and polishing costs fell quite dramatically after a continuous grinder was installed there at the end of the decade. But, taken as a whole, the contrast between the performance at the two works, the one often producing only a quarter of the return on capital of the other, is most striking. And, with further technical change in the plate glass industry at hand, Pilkington soon had to bring in other products to keep Doncaster busy.

Chapter 18

Backward with Sheet

IN 1918 the two continuous processes for making sheet glass, the Belgian Fourcault and the American Colburn, were about to come into more widespread commercial use. The most obvious difference between them was that the former drew the ribbon of glass vertically upwards through a tower lehr whereas the latter was annealed horizontally: its ribbon had to be drawn up from the tank for only a short distance to the point where it was of the right temperature and consistency to be turned through an angle of 90° round a roller and into the lehr. The technical difficulties in producing good quality glass by either of these methods were immense. Reasonably flat, parallel surfaces, necessary for distortion-free glass, were hard to achieve; and the mixture required to produce glass of a consistency capable of being drawn out of the tank without 'waisting' (loss of ribbon width), also produced window panes which did not weather well. But the owners of the new processes, already benefiting from great economies in skilled labour, believed that these imperfections could be eliminated gradually by further development. In due course this faith was justified.

During the war little work had been possible on the Fourcault process, though the Belgian factory at Dampremy remained in production. In America, however, the other method had been energetically developed by the Toledo Glass Company, which had acquired the Colburn patents in 1912 for $15,000.[1] E.D.Libbey, Michael J.Owens and their associates in Toledo Glass, who were then exploiting the Owens bottlemaking machine so successfully, were determined, by stealing a technical march on all the existing window glass concerns, to make as impressive an entry into the flat glass branch of the industry as they had into international bottlemaking. Experimental work at Toledo had, in 1916, reached the stage at which a production unit could be embarked upon. The Libbey-Owens Sheet Glass Company was incorporated in May of that year with an authorised capital of $6,000,000, $4,500,000 of which went straight into the coffers of Toledo Glass for the patents and the experimental plant. With the remaining $1,500,000, the new company built a modern factory at Kanawha City, a suburb of Charleston, West Virginia. There it proudly showed off to would-be licensees from abroad what had by then been re-christened the Libbey-Owens process.[2]

The Libbey-Owens Company was anxious to show all, or at least to appear to do so. When Austin Pilkington called at Toledo in November 1918, apparently by invitation, he was urged to go to Charleston to see the plant for himself.[3] Accordingly he, R. F. Taylor and Thomas Railton visited the new factory on 4 and 5 December. It was, R. F. Taylor reported at the time, 'clearly intended as a show place . . . well located and excellently designed'.[4] It required not more than 15 men to work four of the six tanks then operating, together with their accompanying machines and 200 ft lehrs. They were drawing glass 63 in. wide, two working on 16 oz glass at 50 in. per minute, another 24 oz at 35 in. and the fourth 39 oz at 26 in. Output was reduced, however, by much breakage. The quality, too, was poor, rather worse than what was known in the trade as English fourths, because of waviness and devitrification. As a member of the party noted *à propos* the latter: 'one of the fundamental difficulties which has been encountered in all attempts to draw flat glass has not been overcome.'[5] Austin Pilkington wrote a polite letter of thanks to E. D. Libbey and returned home.[6]

Taylor, the company's US representative left behind in Buffalo, soon became very conscious of the burden of responsibility which lay upon his shoulders in keeping his principals informed about the development of the new machine. 'There is no doubt that there is something doing,' he wrote at the beginning of March 1919, 'and everyone that one meets immediately starts talking Charleston.' He had not changed his mind about the basic weakness of the process, but 'the possibilities are so tremendous that we cannot afford to pass over them lightly, and the more opinions we have the better'. Could Cecil Pilkington, the technical director, come out to see the plant?[7] This he did in July 1919, and Austin Pilkington and Taylor went with him on this second visit. Nobody could accuse the company of not taking the new process seriously.

Certain improvements had been made since the earlier inspection. There was less devitrification and less breakage, and the quality of the heavier glass was decidedly better. Larger sizes were being cut; but it was impossible to judge whether these were permanent improvements, whether, that is to say, the process was really under control or whether it just happened to be in the midst of a better run.[8] In an attempt to discover more, Pilkington subsequently asked for cases of glass to be sent for inspection made up of consecutive sheets as they came from the lehr.[9] Meanwhile, a few days after the Charleston visit, Cecil Pilkington and Taylor went on to Pittsburgh and called on Monro of the American Window Glass Company with whom they had a common interest as users of the drawn cylinder process. Together they scrutinised the Colburn patents very carefully.[10] The views of the A.W.G. became very important at this juncture: their interest in cylinder glass naturally predisposed them against flat drawn. As Taylor observed:

I cannot help but feel that Mr Monro always takes the point of view that the benefit of the doubt should never go to Colburn whereas I consider that we ought rather to do just the opposite. If the Libbey-Owens Co. discover the final step which leads to success, then the prior patents would be greatly strengthened and would have to be very broadly interpreted, and Colburn recognised as a pioneer. Although it is not necessary for us to assume that they will do so, I do not think that we should ignore the possibilities and consequences if they do.[11]

The A.W.G. had its experts at Charleston for some time during the latter part of 1919; but before the year was out they had presented a very unfavourable report to their directors, a fact which was promptly relayed by Taylor to St Helens.[12]

Pilkington, heavily committed to the drawn cylinder process at St Helens and in Canada, and about to become involved in costly investment in the new plate glassworks at Doncaster, was not anxious to question the discouraging evidence of its own visits, particularly when this was backed up by the verdict of America's leading window glassmaking concern. Nor did the company pursue the Fourcault process either. In June 1919 it was invited to send a representative to Dampremy and a letter survives in which it claimed that Fourcault's British patents had lapsed because of non-payment of fees in 1915. In these circumstances the Board did not want to compromise itself, for 'we cannot undertake to forget what we may see, or pledge not to make use of methods open to public use'. Fourcault had given an assurance, however, that the plant could be inspected without any secrets being divulged. It was, therefore, proposed that Geoffrey Pilkington should visit the works 'on the understanding (in writing) that if we do not come to terms with you for securing the benefit of your experience, no question shall be raised in the future if we should happen to make use of the features which we may see in your plant'.[13] The visit took place in June 1919, but Pilkington did not come to terms partly because it believed that Fourcault's patent position was weak and partly because other similar processes were being developed, particularly the Rowart patent which we shall mention in due course.[14]

If the existing glassmakers were reluctant to work the new processes, their owners were determined to find other possible licensees while the post-war demand for glass was at its height and market conditions most favourable. The British Window Glass Company was formed in 1919, with a capital of £450,000, for the exploitation in Britain of the Four-cault process. Clarence Hatry, the company promoter, was its chairman. (He was destined to achieve national fame in 1928 when his business empire collapsed and he himself was sent to prison for recording non-existent securities.) In 1920 British Window Glass became part of British Glass Industries Limited, a predominantly bottlemaking combine of which Hatry was president. A factory was built at Queenborough on the Isle of Sheppey, but it was not a success and glass production there ceased, for the time being, in 1924.

Libbey-Owens, no strangers to international licensing, having assigned the Japanese rights to the American-Japan Sheet Glass Company set up in February 1919,[15] sent their vice-president, Arthur E. Fowle, and their secretary, Charles-Adolphe Schmettau, to Europe a year later. Reporting this to St Helens on 18 February 1920, Taylor also noted that Libbey-Owens shares had risen appreciably on receipt of the news.[16] The two Libbey-Owens emissaries talked to Delloye in Paris, but not until Pilkington's representatives had spoken to him at a meeting hastily convened in Boulogne. A very unfavourable report from Taylor, who had just paid yet another visit to Charleston, was put in his hands. This emphasised that Libbey-Owens still could not control the quality of their product. While Taylor was at the factory, one of the machines started to produce some of the worst glass he had ever seen and nobody knew what to do about it. 'It appears to me,' he added, 'that the greater value of the A.W.G. drawn cylinder product, due to superior quality, far more than compensates for the extra cost of their process.'[17]

Delloye, who had previously been quite favourably disposed towards Libbey-Owens on account of the shortage of glassmaking capacity in Europe on the one hand, and the need to keep the process out of other people's grasp on the other, now took a much stiffer line with the Americans. He proposed that an experimental factory should be built in France to test it. If it worked successfully, St Gobain would form a company, which it would control, and would also take the European rights.

Factories would be put up in France and Italy, and perhaps also in Spain and Belgium. If the terms were reasonable, Pilkington was prepared to take a share in this St Gobain subsidiary in return for exclusive use of the machine in Britain. Delloye was obviously quite convinced that if St Gobain did not take up the European rights, nobody else would.[18] Here he was mistaken. Early in November 1920 a Belgian group which included the Banque Mutuelle Mobilière et Immobilière, representing the Solvay chemical interest, the Société Générale de Belgique and the Banque de Bruxelles, joined together to buy the European rights and to exploit the process in Belgium themselves.[19]

The Compagnie Internationale pour la Fabrication Mécanique du Verre was formed in April 1921 with a capital of 60,000,000 BF. In this company, apart from the financial institutions already mentioned, the Société Financière de Transports et d'Enterprises Industrielles also had a stake, as did Fernand Lambert and a group of sheet glass concerns. The American Libbey-Owens parent held all the preference and special shares and a small slab of ordinaries as well. A Belgian factory, built at Moll, came into production at the end of April 1923, operating two 84 in. machines. Four more were soon added.[20] A note in Pilkington's files shows that somebody from the company who knew all about Charleston found reason to pass by the new factory within a few weeks of its starting. He observed that it was built more substantially than was customary in Europe, along the lines of the Charleston works. 'It would be impossible to get any information round the plant,' he reported, 'but information might be obtained at any time from Moll . . . Monsieur Walter Emsens is evidently in close touch with their operations, and as he appears to be very friendly to us, it should always be possible to obtain up-to-date information from him, and a visit to that district regarding sand is always a plausible excuse . . .'[21]

Of more immediate concern to Pilkington was the formation, in November 1920, of the Canadian Libbey-Owens Sheet Glass Company to build a factory on a 10-acre site at Hamilton, Ontario. John W. Hobbs, managing director of the Consolidated Plate Glass Company, one of the leading glass merchants in Canada, was to become its general manager and Ralph King of the Dominion Glass Company, Toronto, which controlled other important sales outlets, was also on the board.[22] Two machines were in operation before the end of 1921; but the quality of the glass was poor and could not compete with the imported product. In March 1923 production ceased.[23] Libbey-Owens was no more successful in Canada than Fourcault in England. There were still, even at this date, some grounds for believing Munro's assertion, made in June 1922, that the Libbey-Owens process remained 'an uncompleted experiment'.[24] Nevertheless, by standing aloof from both Fourcault and Libbey-Owens because neither was yet producing enough satisfactory glass, Pilkington placed itself in a very exposed and vulnerable position should either, or both, be further improved.

Commitment to the cylinder method and investment in Doncaster no doubt explain to some extent why the company did not take out a licence and try to improve the machine itself. There was also a further explanation: Pilkington had decided to do exactly this with yet another invention.

This was the Rowart-Francq process, experiments upon which had been carried out at Auvelais in Belgium before the war. Originally the idea was to draw the ribbon of glass through a horizontal slit from the tank and downwards through a series of rollers.[25] Whether or not Eugène Rowart was still experimenting along these lines in 1919 when Pilkington first became interested in his work, is not clear. (A patent he took out in Belgium in July 1921, and subsequently in Britain, shows that by then he was drawing the ribbon upwards and using a new method.[26]) Cecil Pilkington told Taylor early in November 1919 that Pilkington had taken an option on the process but warned him not to pay attention to any exaggerated statements he might hear concerning what had been paid for it.[27]

Exactly when experiments on this method started at St Helens is not clear; but Cecil Pilkington was certainly working on it later in 1922, for he wrote to his brother in America in November of that year to tell him that the glass had been kept straighter and flatter in the latest experiments than had ever been achieved before; but flatness was still one of the problems confronting the experimenters, the others being devitrification and maintenance of ribbon width.[28] The experiments were considered promising enough for Cecil and Austin Pilkington to meet Rowart in Brussels in May 1923 to discuss world rights. Later that month the Board voted 150,000 BF (about £2,000) for an option to purchase for 300,000 BF within three years the rights to the patent in all parts of the world not covered by the previous agreement dated November 1919.[29] Further development work does not seem to have been so encouraging however, for in April 1924 Cecil Pilkington was having to fight hard to persuade the Board not to abandon it.[30] He seems to have succeeded in securing more money on that occasion; but foreign competition became more severe and imports rose rapidly, as may be seen from Table 36 on page 254. Although Cecil Pilkington later claimed that he was on the verge of success when prevented from undertaking further experimental work,[31] it is by no means

1 Drawn Cylinder Tank & Drawing Towers
2 Sheet Tank Houses
3 Flattening Kilns
4 Rolled Plate Tank & Lehr (Continuous)
5 Rolled Plate Tanks & Lehr (Casting)
6 Warehouses
7 Office
8 Head Office
9 Canteen
10 Staff Rooms
11 Surgery
12 Offices
13 Laboratory
14 Overhead Crane
15 Fitting Shop
16 Smithy
17 Masons Shed
18 Clay Sheds
19 Timber Yard
20 Box & Crate Making Shop
21 Boilers
22 Gas Producers
23 Wagon Shop

Plan 9 Pilkington Brothers Ltd Sheet and Rolled Works in 1927

certain that this was the case. For all practical purposes, Pilkington had backed the wrong process.

Despite all this justified concern over mechanisation, Pilkington was still producing most of its sheet glass by hand blowing and continued to do so until 1926. The company's hope was to retain the quality end of the market until such time as a flat drawn machine had proved itself capable of making good glass in stock sizes. When in 1921, for instance, the Board decided that it was time pre-war quality was being produced once more, it noted: 'Nothing short of pre-war standard would enable us to hold our position in the industry and to keep the men in employment'.[32] Hand blowing, however, was relatively costly and, as window glass prices tumbled in the early 1920s, profit margins shrank. A major cause of difficulty was the devaluation of the Belgian franc – from 57 to the £ in 1922 to 80 in the early part of 1923 (and eventually down to 162 in 1931) – which gave the Belgians a considerable price advantage in British and other markets. Drawn cylinder glass, though inferior and fetching a lower price than the hand-blown product, was much cheaper to produce and Pilkington was having considerable success in making its plant at St Helens more efficient. The time arrived, in the middle of the 1920s, when hand-blown glass was made at a loss but drawn cylinder remained profitable.

Austin Pilkington told the Joint Industrial Council, in June 1926, that prices had fallen since the post-war peak to a point only 50 per cent higher than in 1914 and some other costs, such as management and warehouse wages and freight charges, were over twice as high. Hand-blown glass was being sold at a loss of $\frac{1}{2}$d per sq. ft, almost a quarter of the production cost.[33] This turn for the worse had come about quite quickly as prices, having rallied a little in 1923–4, had fallen again in 1925 and then continued downwards, as may be seen from graph 12. The loss on hand-blown glass wiped out almost entirely the profit on drawn cylinder, and soon, as we shall see later in this chapter, regular losses were being returned on sheet glass as a whole.

Fortunately for Pilkington, these losses were offset by profits from other branches of the industry. Plate glass was doing well. Cathedral glass justified the continued existence of the Ravenhead works now that all plate glass manufacture had been moved elsewhere. From 1919 a range of miscellaneous items was made there too, such as glass shades, and cells for train lighting, batteries and wireless accumulators, the latter much in demand during the 1920s: public broadcasting had arrived in 1922–3 but so far few mains sets. And at Grove Street itself profits on rolled and

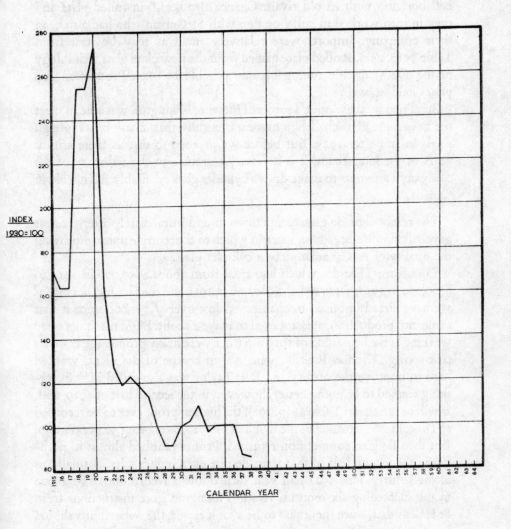

INDEX OF PRICE OF WINDOW GLASS

1915–1938

Graph 12. *Source:* K. Maiwald, 'An Index of Building Costs in the United Kingdom, 1845–1938' *Economic History Review*, December 1954

wired glass alone more than covered the manufacturing losses on sheet after 1926 (see pp. 295, 304). After the war Pilkington worked in collaboration with its old rivals, Chance Brothers,* in rolled plate and they in turn worked in collaboration with St Gobain who had a stake in their company. Imports were relatively small as may be seen from Table 35 (p. 252). Rolled plate gained from the new plate glass technology of the 1920s: double rolling became possible in 1925. Production and prices held up well.

Sustained by these other sources of income, Pilkington was able to meet the new sheet glass challenge more successfully than many of its foreign rivals in and after 1925. But before we proceed to discuss these critical years of the later 1920s, it is necessary to return to the sad story of the company's attempts to make drawn cylinder glass profitably at Thorold in Canada.

The removal of Belgian competition in and immediately after the war gave Pilkington a breathing space in which to concentrate upon improving the quality of its Canadian drawn cylinder glass.

Sales from Thorold, which had risen from about $150,000 in 1915 to $500,000 in 1917, were worth $900,000 in 1918 and the factory, having, as we have already noticed in chapter 13, lost over £130,000 since it first came into production, at last started to make a profit. Eight machines were working at the beginning of 1919 but there were many production troubles that spring. Thomas Railton, who was in charge of the plant, worked hard to improve the quality and R.F. Taylor was also called in.[35] Everything seemed to be going better, however, in the second half of 1919, and, as will be seen from Table 41 (p. 298), the highest profit ever to be recorded at Thorold was returned in the first half of 1920, sales being 50 per cent up. But then Belgian competition returned. Profits vanished almost to nothing in the second half of that year, despite even higher sales. A small loss in the January–June 1921 half year turned into a record one of $190,000 in the succeeding six months. Austin Pilkington gave instructions from St Helens that, since there was to be a tank repair, the opportunity should be taken to review the position before production started again. As he explained to J.E. Harrison, the general manager in Canada:

*Pilkington and Chance discussed possibilities of amalgamation on various occasions between 1917 and 1920. E.F. Chance feared lest the younger Chance generation would lack capital to continue the business. A deal with Pilkington would prevent Chance shares being hawked about, which he considered the worst possible prospect. St Gobain's shareholding, however, stood in the way and some of Chance's other directors were not so keen on the idea as E.F. Chance himself. By April 1920, however, even he was noting Pilkington's 'decided tendency to expand and develop perhaps beyond their powers' and the possibilities of amalgamation seem to have been shelved for the time being.[34]

TABLE 40
PILKINGTON ROLLED AND WIRED GLASS OUTPUT, NET SALES PROCEEDS AND MANUFACTURING PROFIT, AND RAVENHEAD MANUFACTURING PROFIT, 1918–1931

Half Year Ended	Output ('000 sq. ft)	Net Sales Proceeds (£'000)	Manufacturing Profit (£'000)	Ravenhead Manufacturing Profit per year (£'000)
June 1918	7,198	127	76	
December	7,543	153	90	80
June 1919	8,469	161	93	
December	8,866	187	103	45
June 1920	10,558	270	149	
December	11,207	304	156	149
June 1921	6,962	144	36	
December	7,973	172	76	50
June 1922	4,777	114	56	
June 1922– March 1923	10,136	202	114	97*
September 1923	6,734	134	69	
March 1924	8,593	161	57	107
September	8,605	139	59	
March 1925	8,184	164	71	82
September	8,442	155	59	
March 1926	9,327	175	73	115
September	8,885	177	71	
March 1927	9,752	212	42	89
September	8,013	209	56	
March 1928	9,892	264	118	76
September	10,511	251	114	
March 1929	11,090	246	98	104
September	10,779	259	125	
March 1930	9,367	237	98	88
September	9,683	186	58	
March 1931	10,670	148	25	32

Source: Pilkington Accounts

*15 months January 1922 to March 1923.

We have been engaged upon a campaign to very greatly extend the sale of Thorold Glass as the Canadian Brand of Window Glass. The quality has been very much improved and you have been selling it more widely. This may mean that you have been selling it at a lower price than you would have been doing had we been only selling more normal quantities to our regular customers, who generally pay a rather higher price than many of your newer customers . . .[36]

The difficulty was that Pilkington's once very profitable Canadian warehouses were then also losing money, and Libbey-Owens were starting to produce flat drawn glass at Hamilton, as we have seen.

If the serious loss at Thorold had been offset by better results at the warehouses, now that we have taken the Thorold situation in hand, [Austin Pilkington wrote again in September, having consulted the company's accountants] we should not need to be as seriously concerned. We know that you have very adverse conditions to contend with owing to the very low prices of Belgian Sheet which affect you particularly in Montreal. At the same time, our Auditor points out that with a prolonged period of more or less decreased trade in front of us, it would not be satisfactory for so large a section of the business to be unproductive.[37]

It was decided to set up a subsidiary, Pilkington Brothers (Canada) Limited, with J.E. Harrison in charge, to take over all the company's Canadian operations; but there was to be no question of starting up Thorold until the following spring.[38]

Austin Pilkington was himself in North America in November 1922 and was quite optimistic about prospects in Canada. He wrote to his brother, Cecil:

1. The Canadian business is going to be all right. Our system of organisation was good but it is now out of keeping with the trend of Canadian business. The formation of the Can. Coy and the removal of the books to Canada, and the system of monthly statement set up by Menzies for the guidance of the agents are going to be a great improvement.

2. The nature of the supervision from England as well as the management in Canada will have to be reviewed. Tunnock, JEH and I are agreed, I think, upon what is needed.

3. *Thorold*. The factory is in good shape ... There is no hardship among the men. They are better off than they would be at home as food and housing are so cheap. None are unemployed [sic]. The village is a brighter place, or would be, at least, if the factory were going. The question of whether we can work it when ready is one on which we find it difficult to speak definitely.

It is a question with many bearings dependent partly upon the price which we can get, the effect upon the L[ibbey] – O[wens] and upon the position at St Helens ... I can only say that the more I see and hear of the relative position of the A[merican]W[indow Glass] Coy and the LO, that now, for the sake of St Helens and Thorold, *we ought to be able to start up* if there is any further price improvement in Belgium.[39]

The factory was not immediately restarted, however; but the situation changed when warehouses made a good profit in 1922 and a record one in 1923. At the beginning of 1924 there was once again correspondence about the quality of glass being made at Thorold, then under the management of F. B. Gerard; it was up to standard, and the colour was getting a little better. Quality was causing concern in March, however, and in the following month a flattening manager was sent out from St Helens.[40] But losses rose to alarming proportions, warehouse profits were less rosy, and the factory had to be closed, this time for good. By the beginning of November 1924 Gerard had left to become general manager of a cement works.[41]

The factory stood idle until July 1926 when it was decided to sell it. A great deal of equipment had already been disposed of, and at the end of the year the furnace and flattening kilns were being sold for scrap.[42] Attempts to sell the 84-acre site, however, and the factory buildings, covering 25 of those acres and providing a floor area of 190,000 sq. ft, came to nothing. It was still one of Pilkington (Canada)'s liabilities when a representative of the company visited it in 1931. He decided to economise by stopping payment to the fire brigade but 'to keep a limited supply of hoses handy to enable the residents to cope with a fire until such a time as the Thorold brigades were on the scene'. The workmen's houses in Windle Village by then 'had more the appearance of Limehouse than a model village'.[43] Soon after this, however, a purchaser was found who was prepared to pay $225,000.[44] In January 1932 the Canadian agents were all informed that the factory and the village had been sold to Welland Securities Limited.[45]

Thorold's performance from 1918 is set out in Table 41.

The manufacturing profits of the early post-war years had been wiped out by the middle of 1922. The total net operating loss after 1918 added up ultimately to more than $1,000,000, about as much as the surplus earned by the warehouses from 1918 until 1924 when the factory went out of production. This almost equal off-setting of factory loss by warehouse profit had also been a characteristic of Thorold's earlier years, between 1913, when investment began, and 1918.[46] For a decade, therefore, the factory had effectively eaten up all the profit which Pilkington

L*

TABLE 41

PERFORMANCE OF THOROLD DRAWN CYLINDER SHEET GLASSWORKS, 1918–1925
EXPORTS OF PILKINGTON SHEET AND PLATE GLASS TO CANADA, 1918–1930
AND TRADING RESULTS OF CANADIAN WAREHOUSES, 1918–1930

Half Year Ended	Thorold Works Sheet Glass Sales $	Profit/Loss $	Calendar Year	Pilkington Exports to Canada				Trading results of Canadian Warehouses $
				Sheet Glass '000 sq ft	% of total exports	Plate Glass '000 sq ft	% of total exports	
June 1918	464,369	65,977	1918	30	0·66	140	6·30	243,421
Dec 1918	458,500	64,589	1919	124	1·05	47	1·85	321,234
June 1919	498,713	21,607	1920	641	5·25	406	11·73	18,064
Dec 1919	491,811	77,440	1921	672	9·51	395	12·68	−26,650
June 1920	789,221	83,318	1922	7,016	42·66	1,018	17·84	105,641
Dec 1920	820,776	1,464	1923	4,329	23·31	1,045	12·16	370,304
June 1921	316,332	−261	1924	2,012	12·20	1,010	11·44	189,024
Dec 1921	339,953	−190,284	1925	5,327	34·03	1,360	11·92	81,118
June 1922	158,181	−116,227						
Jan 1923 (7 months)	11,432	−149,894						
July 1923	138,122	−174,302						
Jan 1924	374,947	−137,077						
July 1924	272,235	−222,766						
Jan 1925	25,398*	−56,338						
July 1925	5,066*	−53,537						
Jan 1926	−38*	−83,401						
Year Ended								
Jan 1927		−89,230	1926	3,701	32·45	1,926	16·20	109,698
Jan 1928		−3,050	1927	2,837	27·92	2,092	17·55	2,503
Jan 1929		13,610	1928	2,076	25·37	1,549	9·85	172,883
			1929	2,420	24·02	1,508	10·95	249,579
			1930	1,563	24·88	1,340	10·87	71,975

Source: Pilkington Central Statistical Department; PA PB257 return to the Executive Committee 18 January 1932.

Source: PA PB236 and PB237, Thorold Works and Pilkingtons Brothers (Canada) Ltd Final Accounts

had come to expect from its Canadian sales organisation. Nor is that the whole story, for, apart from the loss of the capital invested in the factory itself and its accompanying village, sales of unprofitable glass made at Thorold deprived Pilkington of manufacturing profit on sheet glass from St Helens which would otherwise have been sold in Canada.

The sheet glass export figures in Table 41 show that Thorold helped by supplying the Canadian market for a short time in and immediately after 1918; but Pilkington's reduced exports to Canada in 1923, pending the restarting of Thorold and, particularly in 1924, were a direct result of its competition. And the big increase in exports in 1925 were a direct result of the factory's closing. The whole venture turned out to be such a costly mistake that for some years it caused the company to recoil instinctively from any suggestion of any other manufacturing commitments overseas.

Canada continued for the rest of the interwar period to remain by far the most valuable export market for Pilkington sheet glass, especially from 1933 onwards. It was also an important market for its more profitable plate glass. At the head office of Pilkington Brothers (Canada) Limited – moved back to Toronto in 1927, to 17 Mercer Street – J.E.Harrison, its managing director, was kept fully informed about glassmaking developments in Europe. In return, he continued to supply St Helens with similar news from the United States. When, at the end of 1932, his salary was increased to $10,000 a year,[47] he became one of the company's highest paid executives.

By 1924, when the costs of hand-blown glass were rising both absolutely and relatively to the machine-made product (see p. 303), Pilkington increased its output of drawn cylinder. In October of that year the Board decided that it needed to go farther in this direction, for most of the output was still hand-blown and only the better qualities, obviously far superior to any machine-made glass, could be sold at a profit.[48] The company was clearly confronted with the choice of either making more machine glass or surrendering a greater share of its home and foreign markets to its Belgian rivals – and at worst going out of sheet glass altogether.

With hindsight, it is evident that Pilkington should not have been in too great a hurry to put in more drawn cylinder machines; and it might be thought that its recent experiences at Thorold would have caused it to think twice about doing this. Yet it must be remembered that neither the Libbey-Owens nor the Fourcault processes had yet proved themselves completely, and even if either of them did, it was anybody's guess which would be the winner. Even so late as 1927 the American Bureau of Labor

Statistics, which was carrying out careful costings, could still not say which of the two processes would finally prevail in the industry.[49] And on the side of quality, Pilkington, always well enough aware of the deficiencies of the two machine methods, was critical. *Some* good glass could be made by each of them[50] but most of what was produced was subject to mechanical defects. The drawing of the Fourcault ribbon from the tank made it lined and fluted. The Libbey-Owens had a slight bow in it as a result of being drawn through the 90° angle; it was, therefore, liable to distortion. More serious, perhaps, were the chemical problems which beset the Fourcault product. As Pilkington salesmen were told, again as late as 1927:

All Fourcault glass made of this softer mixture is liable to decomposition. This defect is shown in the first instance in what is known as 'stain', which may either be a cloudiness of the surface which will not come off or even an iridescent appearance. The glass later becomes cloudy or semi-obscured. The defect shows itself much more where the glass has to be transported to tropical countries and quantities of glass have been returned to Belgium on account of that defect. It also shows itself occasionally, but not as often, in European countries, including England. Various attempts have been made to get over this difficulty by dipping the glass in acid etc. but so far without success.[51]

Flat drawn glass may have been cheaper to make, but it was still an inferior and uncertain product: and experience gained by Cecil Pilkington's struggles to work Rowart's patents convinced the company that it was not likely to be an obvious success for some time to come.

Above all, there was a fundamental difference between the demands of Pilkington's main market at home and markets abroad. Elsewhere glass could be sold already cut and in small sizes. Any better parts of the ribbon could, therefore, be cut out of larger sheets and sold at a higher price, the poorer parts being disposed of more cheaply. In Britain, however, glass was usually sold in full-size sheets, to be cut up by others. The larger the sheet and the higher the quality, the greater its worth per sq. ft.[52] The drawn cylinder process had been developed by the mid-1920s to the point at which it could produce a good proportion of stock sizes of consistent quality, but the flat drawn processes could not yet do this so often.

In October and November 1924, therefore, it was decided to increase the drawn cylinder capacity by putting down on disused colliery land south-east of the Grove Street works, at an estimated cost of £175,000, a new large unit, larger than the existing plant and with mechanical ladling from the tank – an innovation – together with ten new flattening kilns.

Even, then, however, there was some discussion of the 'suitability or adaptability of the buildings and site in the event of Fourcault or Libbey-Owens Flat Drawn Process being installed at any time'.[53] Pilkington did not, however, expect any rapid development of either process. Yet no sooner had the new extension been embarked upon – it was to be known as the No. 6 tank – than news began to reach St Helens that the Libbey-Owens process had been considerably improved. A well-informed visitor from the United States in August 1925, for instance, told how in his country it was gaining popularity for quality and flatness.[54] In 1926, out of 530 m. sq. ft of sheet glass produced there by hand-blowing and by machine, Libbey-Owens accounted for 152 m., already half as much as was made by the drawn cylinder process. In Belgium, Fourcault was the leader. Of 566 m. sq. ft of sheet glass made in that country in 1927, 280 m. were produced on Fourcault machines, 119 m. by Libbey-Owens and 167 m. by hand.[55] By May of that year, as J. E. Harrison reported, even the American Window Glass Company, the origin and stronghold of drawn cylinder, was convinced that flat drawn 'was the glass of the future and it was little use continuing to try to convince buyers that cylinder glass was the best'.[56] It was against this background that Pilkington's new, but already obsolescent, No. 6 drawn cylinder tank came into use.

For Pilkington, a plate as well as a sheet glass manufacturer, this successful flat drawn development posed a double threat. So long as sheet glass could be produced by blowing, there was a limit to its thickness and a clear line of demarcation could be maintained between sheet glass and plate. But by using flat drawn machines, glass of much heavier substances could be manufactured. Moreover, continuous grinding and polishing, of the sort which had just been developed for plate glass, could be used to grind and polish this thick drawn sheet and the resulting product, inferior to plate but much less costly, could be used to invade the plate glass market. Libbey-Owens had started to experiment along these lines in the United States in 1924, and Pilkington was told later in 1925 that considerable progress was being made. At the beginning of 1927 Delloye described it as 'good enough and very dangerous'.[57]

Fourcault manufacturers, however, were not encouraged to compete in the plate glass market, for in 1925 a group of Belgian plate glassmakers, in return for creating a separate company, the S.A. des Glaceries Réunis with a capital of 10 m. BF to assist the further development of the Fourcault machine, extracted an undertaking that, for at least five years, no Fourcault licensee would make glass more than 4 mm thick.[58] So the division between plate and sheet glass was maintained so far as the major machine producers in Europe were concerned; but the prohibition did not, of course, extend to the rival Libbey-Owens process. In England, however, Pilkington obtained an assurance from the glass merchants it supplied that they would not substitute thick drawn sheet when polished plate was specified nor offer it to customers for purposes for which polished plate would previously have been used.[59]

With the threat of thick drawn sheet to the plate glass trade postponed for the time being, Pilkington concentrated upon the immediate problem arising from the sudden increase in competition in sheet glass itself. Tables 42 and 43 bring out the significance of the years 1925-7 when hand-blowing was largely abandoned and replaced by the additional drawn cylinder capacity. Yet so rapidly had foreign flat drawn competition grown that even this did not prevent profit from quickly turning into loss. All in all, output was quite well maintained, the fall in the March-September half year of 1926 being explained by the protracted coal stoppage rather than the short General Strike. Even though Pilkington imported coal from the United States, production suffered and the company had to buy some foreign glass to supply its home and Canadian customers.[60]

The company kept its employees informed of the position through the Joint Industrial Council which in March 1926 was told that the two tanks for hand blowing which had already been closed would have to be followed by two others, leaving only one in operation.[61] In May 1926 working was extended until 4 o'clock on Saturday afternoons. Two years later, week-end working was begun, but on a shift system which did not involve a longer working week.[62] As may be seen from Table 42, drawn cylinder costs rose in the half year ended March 1927 with the running in of the new machines at No. 6 tank, but were then reduced to levels lower than before. This reflected the skill of Joseph Gaskell, the Sheet Works engineer, who had himself been responsible for overseeing the installation of the new plant. Forty years old in 1927, he had just been put on a new, ten-year contract at a salary rising from £1,200 per annum to £1,400 in and after 1930.

An effort was made at this time to give hand blowing another lease of life by the launching of a special glass of very low iron oxide content which would allow more ultra-violet light to pass through it, and, by transmitting more of the sun's rays, prove more beneficial to health. Chance Brothers, who were solely reliant on hand blowing for their sheet glass output, were first to take it up. They told St Gobain in October 1926 that they had acquired the process.[63] In March 1927 they were discussing with Pilkington the best means of launching it as a joint Chance-Pilkington sales venture. On 20 October 1927 the two companies reached an agreement with the inventor of what was to be called Vita glass, Francis Everard

TABLE 42
PILKINGTON SHEET GLASS OUTPUT AND COST
1918–1931

| Half Year Ended | Output '000 sq. ft | | | Cost (d. per sq. ft) | |
	Hand-Blown	Drawn Cylinder	Total	Hand-Blown	Drawn Cylinder
June 1918	20,964	5,253	26,217	1·718	1·564
December	20,518	6,851	27,369	2·030	1·494
June 1919	24,618	7,216	31,834	2·089	1·702
December	25,091	8,041	33,132	2·492	2·034
June 1920	26,858	10,070	36,928	2·831	2·399
December	24,064	9,921	33,985	3·391	2·707
June 1921	17,401	7,966	25,367	3·454	3·048
December	19,824	7,152	26,976	2·830	2·592
June 1922	26,196	10,242	36,438	2·088	1·546
June 1922– March 1923	38,820	13,390	52,210	1·883	1·647
September 1923	24,464	9,941	34,408	2·012	1·695
March 1924	24,027	16,216	40,243	2·128	1·731
September	21,613	16,486	38,099	2·308	1·768
March 1925	23,313	18,193	41,506	2·112	1·665
September	22,568	15,123	37,691	2·226	1·875
March 1926	19,853	17,740	37,593	2·161	1·697
September	13,334	14,521	27,846	2·223	1·793
March 1927	7,576	25,239	32,815	2·806	1·975
September	5,003	28,683	33,641	2·658	1·721
March 1928	6,069	24,492	30,561	2·134	1·717
September	4,042	24,304	28,346	2·788	1·624
March 1929	3,703	28,866	32,569	2·257	1·487
September	25	28,564	28,589	3·909	1·516
March 1930	—	30,235	30,235	—	1·523
September	—	36,327	36,327	—	1·605
March 1931	—	20,733	20,733	—	2·038

Source: Pilkington Accounts

TABLE 43
PILKINGTON SHEET GLASS GROSS SALES PROCEEDS AND MANUFACTURING PROFIT
1918–1931
(£'000)

Half Year Ended	Gross Sales Proceeds	Manufacturing Profit
June 1918	455	209
December	484	205
June 1919	596	235
December	567	141
June 1920	695	179
December	769	230
June 1921	409	−79
December	460	43
June 1922	428	90
June 1922–March 1923	630	88
September	451	81
March 1924	488	81
September	458	51
March 1925	503	68
September	429	6
March 1926	420	7
September	337	5
March 1927	311	−28
September	307	−32
March 1928	286	−10
September	246	−26
March 1929	301	6
September	293	26
March 1930	301	15
September	253	−18
March 1931	228	−9

Source: Pilkington Accounts

Lamplough, a former Fellow of Trinity College, Cambridge and then director of Chances' research department. (Lamplough had originally been started on this line of research by Professor Leonard Hill and the authorities at the London Zoological Gardens.)[64] A marketing board was set up, and Pilkington was persuaded to inch a little further into advertising and public relations. It had, it is true, reached an advertising agreement with W. S. Crawford in March 1924, but this was on a special service fee basis and cost only £250 per year.[65] Now, in February 1928, the Board considered a proposal from Pritchard & Partners involving £25,000 per year plus £10,000 for propaganda staff and a further £3,000 for two other people.[66] John Gloag, the author, was in charge of the creative work from the outset. When, shortly afterwards, Pritchard Wood & Partners was given all Pilkington's advertising, he became the director responsible for this and remained in overall charge until his retirement in 1962.

Vita glass, however, was not a success. Sales expectations at the beginning of 1929 were below production targets.[67] At the end of 1929 Geoffrey Pilkington was put in charge – he was then also performing a valuable service in establishing contacts with architects to encourage them to include more glass in their building designs – but in the following May losses were said to be increasing.[68] Production at Pilkington's Vita tank, however, continued in 1930 and 1931, by the end of which year twelve months' stocks were said to have been accumulated.[69] Not until the beginning of 1937, however, were stocks exhausted and the Vita glass publicity campaign finally dropped.[70]

Pilkington's efforts in the later 1920s to struggle along in sheet glass by using old methods and new publicity could be no more than an attempt to buy time and maintain a share of the market until a licence for a flat drawn process could be acquired. International glassmaking diplomacy again became imperative.

This new round of diplomatic activity began in the middle of 1926 when Pilkington heard that the continental Plate Glass Convention was to open a depot in Leeds. Austin Pilkington informed Delloye that he considered this 'a distinctly aggressive step, prejudicial to our interests' and added: 'We regret that it necessarily affects the friendly relations and co-operation which has existed between us and the St Gobain Company for many years' – by which he meant that Maubeuge would again compete as hard as possible with St Gobain in the French home market.[71] Yet the French, like the British, were already suffering from the undervaluing of the Belgian franc[72]. The Belgians were to be the main gainers from the

new Leeds depot, but here was retribution (an aggressive Maubeuge)
falling upon St Gobain. This was the signal for the beginning of another
round of meetings in France between Pilkington directors and Delloye.
The first of these, on 5 January 1927, was described by the deputation from
St Helens as 'courteous but not cordial'.[73]

These meetings in Paris, which ranged again over familiar topics such
as the building of Doncaster and the extension of Maubeuge, and also
over less familiar ones such as Pilkington's depot at Rio de Janeiro in
Brazil (opened in 1923), were soon broadened out to include Belgian
representatives, notably DeLongueville, of whom Austin Pilkington then
had a very poor opinion. In a letter to Harrison in Canada, he described
him as 'a vain and obstinate man and one who seems less qualified to
work an agreement with people than to find opportunities of quarrelling
with them'.[74] The Libbey-Owens threat soon came into these discussions,
for the continentals were as concerned about it as Pilkington, particularly
since the powerful Solvay chemical group had strengthened its shareholding by the acquisition of E.D.Libbey's interest. Emmanuel Janssen,
managing director of the Mutuelle Solvay Bank, was chairman of the
Compagnie Internationale pour la Fabrication Mécanique du Verre,
which controlled the Libbey-Owens interests in Europe. No doubt the
continentals, by now busily trying to reach a plate glass output agreement
on pre-war lines with Pilkington, were suitably impressed when at a
meeting in April 1927 Pilkington told them that it had been approached
by an interested third party to open negotiations with Libbey-Owens
and 'by coincidence' had just seen their representative.[75]

The interested third party was, in fact, Imperial Chemical Industries
which had close links with Solvay. It was the Solvay ammonia soda process
which Brunner Mond had been originally formed to exploit in the 1870s;
Solvay et Cie had a stake of about 20 per cent in the British process from
the time it was turned into a limited company in 1881; and when Brunner
Mond became part of ICI in 1926, Solvay emerged as much the largest
shareholder in the newly formed enterprise, with a seat on the Board.[76]
'In general,' ICI's historian has pointed out, 'for as long as the founders
of ICI could remember – and longer – the heavy chemical industry and
the explosive industry had been run, very successfully, within world-wide
systems of diplomacy designed to regulate markets, to share trade, in all
ways to seek agreement rather than conflict both at home and abroad.
Brunner Mond's affairs were governed by their agreements with Solvay et
Cie . . .'[77] It is not surprising that Solvay approached ICI first of all to
enquire whether they wanted to work the Libbey-Owens process in
Britain.

ICI did not wish to annoy one of their major customers; nor did they wish to see their sales decline because the customer continued to work an obsolescent, if not obsolete, process. On 14 March 1927, therefore, one of the ICI directors, B.E.Todhunter, wrote to inform Pilkington that, while his company had been very impressed with the Belgian Libbey-Owens works at Moll, where 12 machines were then fully employed, they felt that Pilkington 'would be in a much better position . . . to handle a proposition of this kind'. The first meeting between Pilkington and Schmettau of the Compagnie Internationale followed at the Hotel Scribe in Paris at the end of April.[78]

Schmettau first proposed that the Compagnie Internationale and Pilkington should form a joint subsidiary to exploit the process in Britain but Pilkington turned this down flat in favour of a licensing arrangement and payment of royalties. At a second meeting, held at the Euston Hotel, London early in May, Schmettau reported that his company was prepared to consider this but wanted a joint selling company to handle both the product of the British factory and exports from Moll. Pilkington turned down this idea, too, though it was prepared to consider some joint selling arrangement covering prices, qualities and sales quotas from the two works in various markets, including Britain. The way was now prepared for a critical series of meetings which took place in Belgium on 17, 18 and 20 June at which Poncelet, the Belgian company's general manager, recently back from the United States, was also present. The Pilkington deputation was a strong one, consisting of Austin, Cecil and Geoffrey Pilkington, Cozens-Hardy and R.F.Taylor. Pilkington was offered a 20-year licence for two machines for £30,000 in cash and a 2½ per cent royalty. The two-machine plant would cost £150,000 to £200,000 and, on an estimated output of 400,000 sq. ft per week, royalties would work out at about £3,000 per year. (This output, however – 20 m. sq. ft per year – was only about one-third of Pilkington's normal sheet glass production; one machine would be needed, it was said, to supply Canada alone. There were already 12 at Moll as we have just seen. Presumably the idea was to put down additional machines at St Helens when the first two had been proved.) The Libbey-Owens representatives were also aiming at a 40 per cent share of Belgian sheet glass exports to Britain, the remaining 60 per cent going to the Fourcault makers. The importance of the occasion was then emphasised by a call upon Janssen at the Banque Mutuelle and, on the following day, by a visit to Moll. There the Pilkington representatives found glass of remarkably uniform quality being produced, although the heavier glass was better than the thinner and there was marking of the under surface noticeable on the production of all machines. The

Belgians were told by the Pilkington experts that the glass was not yet suitable for the British market – it had, in fact, only been launched there earlier in that year, Poncelet admitted – and Pilkington would have great difficulty in disposing of any quantity of it at home. To this the Belgians suggested a visit to Germany to see how well the process had succeeded in that country only a month after starting production. Before leaving, the party again visited Janssen. He applied some last-minute diplomatic pressure by letting drop that his company was also negotiating with the Fourcault Union and were the very next day to see Delloye, too, about a licence for France. The Pilkington representatives, for their part, refused to be rushed. They thought this was a bluff and preferred to accept the invitation to see the German works first.[79]

In the event, they misjudged the situation and dismissed too readily the possibility of the Compagnie Internationale reaching agreement with Libbey-Owens' rivals. Pilkington's visit to Belgium in fact took place at a time of intense diplomatic activity among the continentals. The high cost of Fourcault licences and rate of royalty in a period of fierce competition between old methods and new, and between rival mechanical processes, had put a number of Belgian manufacturers, then switching from hand to machine blowing, into the hands of their bankers. The latter, in their turn, had insisted that the Fourcault makers should rationalise their activities instead of competing so fiercely among themselves. On 8 June 1927, only a few days before the Pilkington deputation had reached Belgium, an agency had been formed, the Comptoir Générale Belge pour la Vente des Verres Mécaniques Fourcault, to handle the sales from all the Fourcault factories (apart from the one at Lodelinsart which refused to join) and to purchase raw materials in bulk on behalf of them all. Their glass was to be marketed under the trade name COBEF.[80] A campaign to curb competition among the continental glassmakers was under way, initiated and strongly supported by the banks. There were already links between the Fourcault makers and the plate glass branch of the industry through Glaceries Réunis. The banker Janssen's visit to Delloye at that particular juncture was no mere threat.

The negotiations between these two men soon included Convention representatives in much the same way as those between Delloye and Pilkington had done earlier in the year. The main aim was to limit Libbey-Owens' output of polished thick drawn sheet glass, as Glaceries Réunis had done in the case of Fourcault. An agreement was eventually reached that this output should be fixed at its existing level for the following 30 years, rising and falling as the output of the Convention makers rose and fell. Equally significantly, the agreement also included certain (unpublished) arrangements concerning the manufacture of all thicknesses of sheet glass outside Belgium and Holland.[81] Janssen subsequently wrote to Sir Alfred Mond, ICI's chairman, that this meant Libbey-Owens 'having to give up the idea of doing anything in England'. 'I had allowed Messrs Pilkington to draw this inference when I saw them,' Janssen also noted, 'but unfortunately they did not seem to believe that our negotiations with the Convention would materialise.'[82]

Meanwhile the negotiations which had been progressing favourably in Paris between Pilkington and the Convention had been interrupted rather abruptly on 24 June 1927 – a few days after the Belgian visit – on the grounds that a price war had broken out in America which had implications for Belgium because the Courcelles works were American (Pittsburgh Plate Glass) owned.[83] And when the next meeting with Schmettau and Poncelet was held, at the Euston Hotel on 31 August 1927, the Pilkington representatives were astounded to learn that the Libbey-Owens American parent was now insisting on a joint subsidiary once again and would not contemplate a licence. The talks had suddenly returned to their starting point.

The notes of the meeting refer to 'considerable heated discussion'.[84] Cozens-Hardy is said to have lost his temper, which he rarely did; but, given the continental negotiations then in train, it seems unlikely that this in any way affected the outcome. There was further correspondence between St Helens and Brussels and one more meeting, on 28 October at the Euston Hotel, at which Pilkington relented to the extent of discussing a joint company provided the Belgians had no say in its management.[85] But it was too late. Pilkington, now increasingly weak and vulnerable in sheet glass, had been shut out from the main centre of activity in this branch of the industry. Yet the directors did not seem to know at the time that this was happening. Immediately after the August meeting, indeed, Cozens-Hardy wrote to Cecil Pilkington that he would not be surprised if it were 'a try-on by the American lot in the hope of getting information as to our plate manufacture'.[86] Cecil felt that something was wrong, but did not quite know what: 'We are only one part of a curious drama, I think,' he confided to his brother. 'It is interesting and the position of the ICI needs watching perhaps.'[87]

In fact, ICI continued to be a helpful intermediary when, at the beginning of 1928, Pilkington wanted to discover from Brussels what had gone wrong with the Libbey-Owens negotiations. St Helens was then considering the possibility of applying for a compulsory licence to work the process.

We have very fully considered the whole position as regards the Libbey-Owens

Patents, [Austin Pilkington wrote to Todhunter at the beginning of July 1928] with special reference to the fact that apparently the owners of the British patents by arrangement with foreign manufacturers have put themselves in the position of being unable to grant licences in this country. We hold – and we have fortified ourselves in this view with the opinion of leading patent counsel – that it is quite against the principle of the patent laws that the owners of the British L/O patents should refuse to license their use in this country and so compel the British manufacturers to submit to the unrestricted competition of glass made in Belgium by the patent processes.[88]

The patient Todhunter saw Cozens-Hardy later that month and wrote to E.J.Solvay in Brussels on his behalf, though noting in the course of the letter that he did not think it was any use his continuing any longer to serve as a post office.[89]

Meanwhile the Board at St Helens could do no more than pass solemn resolutions that it was imperative for the company to get hold of a flat drawn machine.[90] In March 1928 Cecil Pilkington was asking Heuze, the Belgian engineer, if he could arrange a visit to one of the Fourcault plants abroad,[91] but the opportunity passed when, in the following month, F.P.Jones, for many years chairman of Canada Cement Limited and manager of the Canadian Steel Trust, formed Sheet Glass Limited to open the Queenborough factory and work once more its Fourcault plant which had remained idle since 1924. Another notable Canadian, Lord Beaverbrook, was also involved.[92] The factory was making glass during the first half of 1929 but the losses were so great that it was then closed down until October 1932.

Valuable time was being lost. Already, in November 1927, the company had decided to buy Belgian Fourcault glass for supplying its Canadian and South American customers.[93] In November 1928 the possibility was envisaged of having to manufacture abroad in order to supply export needs.[94] At the beginning of 1929 it was agreed that the home depots could not be run on imported sheet glass and, much more alarming, 'it would be impossible to drop out of the sheet trade without incurring danger to our other trade . . .'[95]

Weakness was, however, far from being entirely on one side. The continentals, too, did not escape the effects of the new machinery even though they may have been operating it. The Fourcault Comptoir had not worked well because it had made the mistake of invoicing customers direct instead of letting the major export merchants (many in London) do so. The merchants retaliated by passing customers' orders to Libbey-Owens and elsewhere.[96] The banks found themselves having to pump more money into glassworks and exporting businesses in an effort to take rationalisation further and so to achieve a measure of stability. In March 1929 the Société des Brevets Fourcault was merged with three plate glass companies (Nationales Belges, Saint-Roch and Germania) to form the Société de Participations Verrières (Sopaverre), and two months later this new body, together with certain exporters, the Banque de Bruxelles and the Crédit Anversois, formed the Mutuelle de l'Industrie Verrière.[97]

Pilkington in the meantime used Maubeuge to bring pressure on St Gobain and St Gobain to bring pressure to bear on the Convention itself in the hope that it would amend its agreement with the Libbey-Owens Compagnie Internationale so far as the working of the process in Britain was concerned. Cecil Pilkington noted with relish in August 1928 that Pilkington's French factory had produced yet another record footage.[98] In order to exert similar pressure on the Belgians, Pilkington went so far as to buy a factory site at Grimberghen and to register a glassmaking company, S.A. Industrielle de Grimberghen, thus threatening to move right into enemy territory. Pilkington's continental competitors knew of this move by early in January 1929.[99]

In any case, the Convention was not so self-assured as it had been in 1927 owing to its difficulties in the United States market and to more independent policies pursued in Belgium by the American-owned Courcelles factory. All these developments led to a reopening of negotiations with Pilkington. By autumn of 1928, Pilkington and Delloye were in correspondence about the possibility of an agreement being reached between St Helens and the Convention on the basis of plate glass sales arrangements in the various main world markets. Delloye suggested that there should be three groups: continental national markets; the United States market; and markets elsewhere. Pilkington accepted these suggestions.[100] The talks, broken off in the middle of 1927, were resumed. At this point Pilkington was prepared to divulge its plate glass sales figures, which it had not done in the previous round of negotiations.

These show that Pilkington's plate glass sales had risen much faster than the Convention's during the 1920s and underline once again the extent of the company's achievement in this branch of the industry, discussed in the previous chapter. The Convention/Pilkington allocations in the 1913 agreement had been 81·64 m. sq. ft (Convention) to 18·335 m. sq. ft (Pilkington, excluding Maubeuge), a ratio of 4·45 : 1.[101] If another 1·25 m. sq. ft are added for Maubeuge this would bring down the ratio to 4·17 : 1.[102] The figures for 1925–7 are given in Table 44.

Negotiations between Pilkington and the Convention were long, detailed and complicated. They dragged on into the middle of 1929. The ten-year agreement, dated 1 June 1929, divided the world market for plate glass into four main groups:

Group 1 (a) France and the French colonies

     (b) Germany and the Saar; Italy, Tripoli and Cyrenaica; Czechoslavakia; Austria and Hungary

  2   Great Britain and Ireland

  3   The United States

  4   All other markets

TABLE 44

PILKINGTON AND CONVENTION PLATE GLASS SALES
1925-7

| | m. sq. ft | | |
	Convention	Pilkington (including Maubeuge)	Ratio
(Pre-war)	81·7	19·6	4·17 : 1
1925	77	24·2	3·18 : 1
1926	93·3	23·5	3·97 : 1
1927	83·1	25·4	3·27 : 1

Source: PA PB97/126 TD2 Delloye File, Notes on Different Methods of Determining Relativity Between P.B. and C.I.G., 6 December 1928.

In France, Pilkington was not to sell in 1929 more than it had done yearly in 1926-8, but after 1929 this total could grow by $1\frac{1}{2}$ per cent per annum. The Convention guaranteed these sales. In the other European markets Pilkington could sell 39,000 sq. metres: 20,000 in Germany, 15,000 in Italy and 4,000 in the other three markets. The Convention, in return, was allowed to sell in Britain and Ireland in 1929-31 the average it had sold in 1925-7 plus 15,000 sq. metres. In and after 1932 this quantity could rise at the same pace as Pilkington's sales in France, $1\frac{1}{2}$ per cent per annum. Similarly, Pilkington gave the Convention guarantees for its sales in Great Britain and Ireland: the quotas fixed for 1931 and 1932, and 75 per cent of permissible sales thereafter. In the other two areas sales were fixed on a ratio basis: in the United States Pilkington and the Convention were each to sell in the same relative proportions as they had done in 1925-7, elsewhere in the same proportions as in 1925-8. Quarterly returns, certified by auditors, were to be exchanged. Prices, terms and conditions of sales were to be fixed so that both parties were placed on the same footing taking into account differences in transport costs and customs duties. 'They shall be such as to enable both parties to sell their proper shares in the various market groups through their normal channels on each market.' There were to be no restrictive agreements with customers from then onwards, and existing ones had to be reviewed if the aggrieved party insisted.

The building and extension of works and the opening of depots also featured in the agreement. Neither party was to open new glassworks in the territory of the other – Grimberghen was specifically mentioned – and new works opened within each party's own territory, or improvements made to existing works, were not to increase the permissible sales. In the case of plate glass concerns which might be built or operated in other territories, including the United States, the other party had to be offered equitable participation. If the offer were refused, the output would count towards the permissible sales of the party concerned. If existing works in these other territories should be acquired or controlled, the two parties were to confer 'and such adequate and equitable alteration shall be made in the present agreement as will maintain without material change the equilibrium between the parties ...' No new depots were to be opened in each other's territories, and – no doubt much to Pilkington's gratification – the Convention's Leeds depot was to be closed when the selling arrangements were working satisfactorily and, in any case, by the end of 1931.[103]

The signing of this industrial peace treaty aimed to put an end to years of disturbance in the plate glass trade, coinciding with the rationalisation of the previously highly individualistic Belgian glass industry,* helped to bring greater order to the trade, and so make the Convention's aims more realistic. The Convention, having almost got Pilkington into the fold before 1914 but lost it because of the war, now at last secured its full allegiance; but Pilkington, on its side, had in the meantime gained a larger share of the market in this branch of the industry, though not so large as it would have been had 1926, the year of the General Strike, not been a disappointing one; and the company was technically in a stronger bargaining position than it had been before. But at the back of this new alliance was Pilkington's continued attempts to secure a licence for the Libbey-Owens process. In a letter read to and agreed by Delloye just after the signing of the treaty, Pilkington put on paper a number of points which had been agreed between them. One of them read: 'If we should desire to acquire

---

*With the onset of the world depression, this soon went much farther. In 1931 the Belgian plate glass industry was grouped into two concerns: 1. Glaces de Charleroi, Glaces de Moustier-sur-Sambre and the Compagnie de Floreffe merged with Libbey-Owens Compagnie Internationale pour la Fabrication Mécanique du Verre to form Glaces et Verres (Glaver); and 2. Glaceries de Saint-Roch, Glaceries de Sainte-Marie d'Oignies and Glaces d'Auvelais joined to form Glaceries de la Sambre.[104]

from the Libbey-Owen [sic] Company a licence to operate their Glass Drawing process in Great Britain, the Convention will use its best endeavours to facilitate matters.'[105]

In the event, St Gobain was called upon for other services but not for this particular one. On 27 June 1929, only a few days before this letter was written, Cecil Pilkington reported to the Board about a visit he had just made to the Pittsburgh Plate Glass Company's sheet glass plants at Mount Vernon (Ohio) and Clarksburg (West Virginia), where the PPG was developing its own flat drawn process. He thought the prospects were promising and, in any case, as the Board minutes sadly lamented, there was 'no other process on the horizon so far as is known'.[106] An invention of an American of Russian origin named Slingluff, this process differed from the Fourcault and Libbey-Owens in one essential feature – the method of drawing the ribbon of glass from the tank – but was like the Fourcault machine in that it had a vertical lehr and was thus economical in the use of ground space. On Cecil Pilkington's advice, the Board agreed to start negotiations for a licence from PPG and, at the same time, also to spend about £10,000 to see if better results were likely to be obtained from its process with a different glassmaking mixture.[107] In October J.B. Watt and D. Railton sailed from Liverpool to study the process further,[108] and by the end of November 1929 Pilkington had decided to pay £2,000 for an 18-month option on it from the N.V. Hollandsche Maatschappij Voor de Vervaarding Van Glas, a Dutch company which was responsible for licensing the process in Europe for the PPG. This gave Pilkington the right to experiment with one machine. If the option were exercised, the licence would involve the company in expenditure of at least £50,000 in the installation of plant, engineering fees of £1,000 per machine and a royalty of ½d for each 10 sq. ft of glass cut and packed over a period of ten years.[109] Much development was still needed. Although the process had been operated at Mount Vernon since 1926 and Clarksburg since 1927,[110] Pilkington, having received J.B. Watt's full report in June 1930, took the view that it was still in an experimental stage. Little or no thin glass (15 oz) had apparently yet been made by it and it had a major defect: seam line, a line down the middle of the ribbon. (Watt later recalled that Cecil Pilkington had not noticed this on his visit and had he done so, would not have recommended the process to the Board.) The PPG product did, however, weather much better than Fourcault glass.[111]

In the further development that was needed, Pilkington did not operate in European isolation and here its new alliance proved helpful. St Gobain was very much involved in the N.V. Hollandsche Maatschappij Voor de Vervaarding Van Glas. It had its planning bureau at St Gobain's

Paris Headquarters. Lucien Deschamps, St Gobain's engineer, was working on the process at a factory of another licensee in Zeebrugge in July 1930,[112] and later at Porz am Rhein, near Cologne. Samples of glass and details of glassmaking mixtures passed between Deschamps and Watt, and a valuable technical liaison developed between them. The composition of the mixture gave trouble and the glass solidified too readily. Manufacture on the machine at No. 10 tank at St Helens had to be stopped for a time from June 1930 while this was put right.[113] But then the process seemed most promising. In February 1931 Pilkington decided to exercise its option and to install a four-machine production unit. The licence, dated 30 June 1931, granted Pilkington the exclusive use of the process in Britain provided it installed at least eight machines before 15 October 1932 and a further four by 15 October 1933; otherwise the licence woud be a non-exclusive one. Pilkington was, however, to be at liberty to allow Chances to have two of these machines if Chances wanted them.[114] By then, Watt reported to Paris, Pilkington had made 21 oz glass at speeds of 26 to 30 in. per minute with a manufacturing loss of only $12\frac{1}{2}$ per cent. It had also made thin (15 oz) and thick (32 oz) glass on the machine, which on one run had operated non-stop for 32 hours. 'There can be little doubt,' Watt concluded, 'that good edge control is the main secret in [the operation of] the process, not only from the point of view of breakage but also for flatness of the sheet and good cutting'.[115] At the beginning of March 1931 Austin Pilkington told the Joint Industrial Council that the process was as good as any then known. Although it was slightly more expensive to work than the Libbey-Owens, it made better glass. The fort-holding drawn cylinder machines at No. 6 tank were to go into production again to supply the market while the four new machines were being installed at No. 7[116] at a construction cost of about £44,500.[117] By October 1931, when the four-machine unit was about to come into use, Pilkington had arrived at a very satisfactory glassmaking mixture.[118] The new machines, which came into service on 10 November, did well, producing ribbons between 80 in. and 84 in. wide with breakage down to 5 or 6 per cent.[119] At the end of November the Board presented J. B. Watt with a lump sum payment of getting on for one-third of his annual salary, and Joseph Gaskell, Sheet Works engineer, with a smaller sum, in recognition of their special services to the company.[120] While, as will be seen in chapter 20, more new PPG machines were installed, some cylinder glass continued to be made at one tank for a little while longer. This tank was eventually put out on 13 May 1933.[121] At the end of that year the Empire Machine Co. went into voluntary liquidation.[122]

Pilkington was now able to hold its own once more in the sheet glass market; and in this branch, as in plate, further rationalisation was taking place in Belgium which reduced the most unsettling effects of unrestricted competition. The flat drawn processes drove even the more persistent hand blowers out of business in the latter 1920s, and the combined effect of continued pressure from the banks and the onset of world depression in 1930 reduced competition both among Fourcault manufacturers and between them and the Libbey-Owens proprietors. The former, who had (with one exception) tried to operate a Comptoir since 1927, not too successfully as we have seen, in 1930 all merged – 13 companies operating 17 works in which were 192 machines – to form the Union des Verreries Mécaniques Belges (U.V.M.B.) with a capital of 200 m. BF. The Union at once started to reduce manufacturing capacity and to run down stocks, and in 1932 an agreement was reached between the U.V.M.B. and Glaver (representing the Libbey-Owens interest) dividing the home and export markets of the two companies, 70 per cent of window glass sales going to the U.V.M.B. and 30 per cent to Glaver.[123]

The drawn cylinder process had been a disastrous failure in Canada and was, arguably, a very doubtful asset at St Helens. In the early stages it produced relatively small quantities of poor export quality glass; it did not become Pilkington's mainstay until 1926 and then usually ran at a loss. The best thing to be said for it is that when worked for longer hours, it enabled Pilkington to survive in sheet glass and to maintain the scale of its sales organisation, upon which its success in plate glass also depended. But if Pilkington had not taken up drawn cylinder in the first place, would it not have been driven at an earlier stage to adopt one of the flat drawn processes and improve it, thus producing glass of higher quality suitable for the home market?

Heavy capital expenditure without an equivalent increase in income had placed the company in a weaker financial position in the 1920s than it had been before 1914 and made it more dependent on borrowed money. It is true that the Bank of England loan of 1921 had been reduced to £89,000 by 1925 and that in that year the $6\frac{1}{2}$ per cent 'B' debenture stock of 1920, which then became redeemable, was renegotiated at 5 per cent. But, at the same time, with further investment being called for to finance the plate glass developments and the new drawn cylinder unit, and with more money needed to repay the rest of the Bank of England debt, Pilkington issued an additional £1,000,000 $5\frac{3}{4}$ per cent, 25-year debenture stock at £95 per cent to the Prudential Assurance Company Limited, to be repaid by means of a cumulative sinking fund.[124] The Board was very concerned that this loan should not entail the disclosure of any private business information. To quote the relevant minute:

The Directors have all along appreciated that they were paying more than would be necessary for public issue, but the firm attach such importance to secrecy that they decided to face the extra cost of private issue. The Directors felt it incumbent upon them to see that nothing is left undone to protect their interests in the matter of disclosure to outside parties of confidential information.[125]

The company's accounts, in any case, present difficulties of interpretation for this period, even to Pilkington's present-day accountants, the main difficulty being the different meanings of 'profit' depending upon what is charged against income before the balance is struck. The two tables below, however, the second of which continues the series of figures given in Tables 22 and 29, perhaps provide the most satisfactory financial overview of the company's far weaker position after 1926. The returns on capital employed in manufacturing were then much lower and so was

TABLE 45

RETURN ON CAPITAL EMPLOYED IN MANUFACTURING

1918–1931

Year	Capital Employed £000	Net Manufacturing Profit £000	Return %
1918	3,393	735	21·7
1919	3,788	648	17·1
1920	4,893	1,114	22·8
1921	5,477	234	4·3
15 months to March 1923	5,650	828	14·7
Year to March 1924	5,343	912	17·1
March 1925	5,296	943	17·8
March 1926	6,038	867	14·4
March 1927	6,141	649	10·6
March 1928	6,199	417	6·7
March 1929	6,324	552	8·7
March 1930	6,296	572	9·1
March 1931	5,990	135	2·3

Source: Pilkington Accounts

TABLE 46

DISPOSAL OF PROFIT IN THE YEARS 1914–1931

Year Ended	Adjusted Profit (Loss)	Directors' salaries, fees and expenses	Income Tax	Transfer to reserve for replacement of fixed assets	Debenture interest	Net Profit (Loss) (a)	Dividend and bonus on shares	% Dividend	Balance retained in Company (b)
1914	512,303	15,896	19,512	—	30,000	446,895	60,000	7½	386,895
1915	608,348	16,212	53,528	—	30,000	508,608	241,000	30	267,608
1916	616,883	16,841	121,165	—	30,000	448,877	182,250	22½	266,627
1917	668,939	17,646	117,275	—	30,000	504,018	202,500	25	301,518
1918	608,804	23,530	142,651	—	30,000	412,623	232,875	28¾	179,748
1919	658,203	23,803	216,097	—	30,000	388,303	208,575	17¾	179,728
1920	608,222	29,638	184,274	—	37,418	356,892	158,069	6	198,823
Dec 1921 1922	(176,623)	30,622	155,226	—	48,919	(411,390)	Nil	Nil	(411,390)
March 1923	689,531	31,682	154,488	—	62,271	441,090	231,420	7¼ (15 mths)	209,670
1924	775,552	33,783	165,902	—	49,912	525,955	191,520	6	334,435
1925	664,234	32,120	84,755	—	49,452	497,907	123,440	7	374,467
1926	658,290	30,914	79,129	—	82,588	465,659	175,560	5½	290,099
1927	509,195	30,874	97,207	—	87,040	294,074	159,600	5	134,474
1928	530,715	32,609	126,891	—	87,040	284,175	159,600	5	124,575
1929	571,332	36,045	124,569	—	87,040	323,678	191,520	6	131,158
1930	678,850	48,185	95,796	—	84,452	450,417	215,176	6½	235,241
1931	363,150	8,055	159,699	93,884	81,864	19,648	63,840	2	(44,192)

(a) Profit as shown in Profit and Loss Account
(b) From 1926 includes surplus found for redemption of debentures

Source: Pilkingtons Accounts

the balance retained for development. Debenture interest was higher because of the additional £1,000,000 issue to the Prudential, but this began to be reduced after 1929. By then, however, the company was again borrowing from the Bank of England. Overdraft facilities of £100,000, arranged in March 1928, were increased to £150,000 in May 1929.[126] By the end of 1929 shareholders' funds (shares, debentures and other long-term loans), which had just exceeded £6m nine years before, stood at £7,765,000. During the second half of the 1920s, however, satisfactory dividends continued to be paid on ordinary shares all held by the Pilkington family, at the rate of 5 or 5½ per cent per year, income tax (but not surtax) being paid by the company; and when better results were reported in 1928–9 and 1929–30, this was increased to 6 per cent and 6½ per cent respectively. The company's performance in the following year, however, was very much poorer. This was to lead to major changes in its management.

Chapter 19

Reorganisation in the 1930s

WE have already drawn attention (pp. 256-7) to the division between ownership and management which had occurred between 1894 and 1920. While all the shareholders were called upon to find the new capital needed for post-war development, particularly for the Doncaster works, this was the last major demand made upon them apart from the need to keep their capital tied up in Pilkington Brothers Limited. The responsibility for running the business and earning the dividends for the absentees as well as for themselves rested upon the shoulders of a few members, drawn, especially in the 1920s, from two of the four branches of the family. During the 1920s these men were not particularly well rewarded for their services; but at the end of 1929, a prosperous year, the Board decided that their salaries, which had been fixed in 1920 at various points on a scale rising by annual increments of £100 from £1,700 to £2,500 per year,[1] with a bonus (usually £1,500) if business was good – all free of income tax but not surtax – should be increased to £4,500, plus bonus rising from £1,000 to £2,000 according to trade results, with the same tax advantage. It was also then agreed that directors might retire from management at 63 if they wished to do so on a pension of £2,500 per year, income tax free, and *had* to retire at 68 unless the Board decided otherwise; and, if it did so, its decision had to be confirmed annually thereafter.[2]

This concern in 1929 over arrangements for directors' retirement is at first sight rather surprising, for none of the ruling triumvirate was yet very close even to the permissive retiring age of 63. The most senior, the chairman Austin Pilkington, would reach that age in 1934, Cozens-Hardy in 1936 and Cecil Pilkington in 1938. Family problems were, however, already weighing heavily upon Cecil Pilkington and, although he was only 54 in 1929, it was these which had caused the matter to be ventilated. He had a grown-up son whose health caused him concern, and his wife suffered from ill health and wished to move away from St Helens. To the list of third-generation Pilkington casualties by death and premature retirement, the company's able and experienced technical director must now be added; to the extent that he became a part-timer and went to live near Oxford. The Board agreed in October 1929 – as a six-month trial in the first instance – that he should be at St Helens from Monday to Thursday afternoon only and that, in compensation, his salary should be cut by half.[3] (When the six months were up, however, it was noted that he had spent longer at the works than had been expected,[4] but in the late summer of 1930 he spent much time in London while his son was being treated there.[5]) After his move south, he lived for a time at Scar Top, Boars Hill, while building himself a new house amid 30 acres of woodland nearby, to be called Blackthorn. He also owned a farm, Church Farm, Sunningwell, a mile away, where he was able to carry out various agricultural experiments as well as introduce the latest farming methods.[6]

The company's management problems did not, however, stop at the loss of a key director's services. Its whole management structure had changed little since the partnership days of the nineteenth century, despite the growing complexity of the business. In March 1927, Pilkington was employing 13,500 people; and even if the 2,000 coalminers and 672 employees at Maubeuge are excluded from this total, about 11,000 still remained.[7] Although top management was on the look-out for bright young men to encourage and promote, such as Russell Donald, who, after five years as assistant to J.E.Harrison in Canada from 1923, was brought to St Helens and in December 1930 was put in charge of the important Glasgow warehouse,* the company as a whole seems to have become rather departmentalised – and there was certainly a most fundamental gap between the Works and Sales – and within each department initiative and enterprise do not appear to have been fostered. Outside consultants, called in by Pilkington after 1931, drew attention to this departmental rigidity:

The Managers collectively do not form the Management. They are fully engaged with the responsibilities of their own respective departments, and there is no great amount of co-ordination between them. In general, they appear to perform their routine functions very satisfactorily; but the majority are men who have spent their lives in the service of the Firm, and many of them have

*He died suddenly in 1932.

M

spent a number of years in the same department either as Managers or previously as Clerks. A certain amount of stagnation is the natural outcome. The various departments are practically watertight, and there are few managers who have a knowledge of the details of any department other than their own.[8]

This criticism may have been too sweeping. Certainly the management took exception to it, treating it as the kind of shock report not infrequently produced by outside consultants after a short investigation. The company's misfortunes in the 1920s arose mainly from its commitment to an already obsolescent, and by 1930 nearly obsolete, method of making sheet glass, not to ineffective top management. Nevertheless we have already seen that the ruling triumvirate had their time fully occupied in dealing with all sorts of day-to-day detail, and it is likely that in such circumstances departmental stimulus may have been lacking in the middle and lower reaches. The chief executives no longer had sufficient time to devote to such matters and other managers, by long-standing partnership tradition used to acting on orders from above, did not have enough responsibility delegated to them.

The wave of mergers during the 1920s which swept together many British companies on a scale not to be witnessed again until the 1960s,[9] creating, *inter alia*, ICI, Unilever and four main-line railway companies (the largest of which, the LMS, employed 250,000 people), obliged businessmen to think more deeply about delegation of responsibility. Professor Chandler, an authority on the even more spectacular growth of business in the United States, has pointed out that in the case of these new giants which needed 'to plan and direct the use of resources to meet the short-term and long-term fluctuations and developments in the market ... trained personnel with manufacturing, marketing, engineering, scientific, and managerial skills often become even more valuable than warehouses, plant, offices, and other physical facilities'.[10] Accountants, in particular, came to play a larger part in management. At the Dunlop Rubber Co., for instance, F.R.M.De Paula, a former Professor of Accounting at the London School of Economics, became Controller of Finance in 1929 and developed a comprehensive system of internal audit, costing and forecasting. Francis D'Arcy Cooper, a former partner in the accounting firm of Cooper Brothers, succeeded the first Lord Leverhulme as vice-chairman of Lever Brothers and later became chairman of Unilever. In America, some of the largest industrial corporations were starting to devise divisional systems of management to control their multifunctional enterprises.[11] British businesses were not yet of this size and complexity. Pilkington, which still operated mainly in three factories at a single place,

concentrating on making flat glass alone and valuing its privacy too much
to be tempted to merge with any other concern, posed relatively straightforward management problems. These were nevertheless becoming
acute, and Cozens-Hardy and Geoffrey Pilkington realised this all the
more forcibly after attending meetings of Management Research Group
No. 1 in London.[12] This had been created in 1926 by Seebohm Rowntree
who, in addition to his well-known role as social investigator, was then
also labour director and chairman of Rowntrees of York. He brought
together senior executives from eleven large British companies not in
direct competition with one another (they included ICI, Lever Brothers,
AEC, Standard Telephones and Dunlop) and he himself chaired the
meetings.[13] They caused the two Pilkington directors to think further
about the company's management problems even though at the time they
could do little about them.

The position was complicated to some extent by the entry into the
business of other members of the fourth generation of the family who
joined Geoffrey Pilkington, much older than themselves. There were
four of these men and they each went through a three-year period of
probation before being considered for appointment as a sub-director.
They included two grandsons of Thomas Pilkington by two of his daughters, one of whom had married J.V.Phelps and the other an Anglican
clergyman, the Rev. (later Prebendary) L.J.Percival. Douglas Vandeleur
Phelps (b. 1904; educated at Harrow and Magdalen College, Oxford)
joined the company in 1927, and Lancelot Roger Percival (b. 1906;
educated at Eton and Trinity College, Oxford – he represented the
university at hurdles and Britain in the 1928 Olympic Games) in 1928.
Another arrival in 1927, who was to play a very important part in the history of the company, was Austin Pilkington's eldest son, William Henry
(the future Sir Harry, later Lord Pilkington) (b. 1905; educated at Rugby
and Magdalene College, Cambridge); and a grandson of second-genera-
tion William (Roby) Pilkington, William Lee Pilkington (b. 1905;
educated at Eton and Oxford) also entered the company that year. This
was a welcome infusion of new blood; the third generation was now
about to be strongly supplemented. Moreover, Cozens-Hardy's son, the
Hon. Herbert Arthur, known as Peter (b. 1907; educated at Winchester
and Worcester College, Oxford) was a trainee of J. and J. Colman Limited,
a family business with which the Cozens-Hardy had close links; he was to
gain experience with it, particularly in the United States, which would
serve him in good stead when he joined Pilkington. In May 1930, when
the progress of the others was being discussed, the Board agreed that,
should Peter Cozens-Hardy wish to join as a probationer at the end of his

training with Colmans, he would be accepted and, what was more, his probationary salary would take account of his earlier training.[14] All this potential strengthening of management with youth, vigour and new ideas was to the good; but superimposed upon a now obsolete partnership structure, it posed problems.

Having served his three-year probation, Douglas Phelps became a sub-director in June 1930. He was followed by Harry Pilkington in August and William Lee Pilkington in November.[15] Ronald Weeks, the bright young man from Cambridge who had become manager of the Cowley Hill works and a sub-director in 1920, moved up to full director in 1928.[16] He had already joined the Pilkington family by marrying, in 1922, Evelyn Elsie Haynes, a grandaughter of William (Roby) Pilkington.

In the summer of 1931 the old partnership structure, which had been creaking more and more audibly, was finally swept away, and with it went the company's chairman and his brother. Matters were brought to a head by Pilkington's poor trading results in the half-year ended 31 March 1931 and by the deteriorating national and international economic outlook. The writing down of its stocks of timber was responsible for turning meagre profit into loss. The return on capital employed in manufacturing had shrunk to next to nothing. The dividend on ordinary shares had been reduced to 2 per cent in the first half of 1930/1. For the year as a whole, even though the directors forwent most of their recently increased emoluments, the company had to dip into reserves. No dividend was paid on the second half of the year.[17] (Chance Brothers, by contrast, paid 5 per cent on its ordinaries in 1930 and 3 per cent in 1931; so the explanation is not that there was no profit then to be made out of flat glass.)[18]

The Pilkington decision to pass its half-yearly dividend was taken on 22 May 1931.[19] In view of the grim national – and international – economic outlook at that time, which threatened to get worse, swift strengthening of control in the company was becoming imperative. The immediate cause of the crisis was a confrontation in the directors' luncheon room at the end of June when Austin Pilkington had words with his brother Cecil. (According to Lord Pilkington, Cozens-Hardy seized his opportunity to slip out in order to avoid having to take sides.) The Board minutes chronicle the chain of events following this rift in the triumvirate and the drama involved.

At a meeting held on 30 June – not attended by two of the younger members of the family, Harry Pilkington and Douglas Phelps, who had nevertheless been present at another routine Board meeting earlier that day – Austin Pilkington explained the circumstances in which he had 'finally decided' to tender his resignation as company chairman. Cecil Pilkington also expressed his wish to resign, though he indicated his willingness to continue his connexion in an advisory capacity. The other directors present – Cozens-Hardy, Geoffrey, Guy and Norman Pilkington and Weeks together with Tunnock, sub-director and secretary – having expressed their regret, postponed further consideration of the matter.[20] This took place the next day with five of the six present, Norman Pilkington taking the chair. (Guy Pilkington was the absentee.) The letter they then sent to Austin Pilkington indicates that the effort of running the business without sufficient delegation of authority had at last proved too great for him and that his health was breaking down under the strain:

Your Co-Directors have considered the position arising from the decisions announced at yesterday's Board. We very greatly regret the position, but recognising the wide range you give to your duties as Chairman, and the strain which it is imposing on your health, we think it essential in the interests of the business that the Board should not ask you to reconsider your resignation as Chairman, but should ask you to take 6 months holiday. We also feel compelled to respect ACP's [*sic*] very strong wish to give up executive duties.

In the meantime we propose that the Board should elect a Chairman for a year and should endeavour to evolve a scheme of reorganisation of the Directors' work with a more close definition of their duties.

In this scheme they would wish to make the fullest use of the unrivalled knowledge of yourself on Sales, and ACP on technical matters, whilst in addition securing the benefit of your views at the Board.[21]

Austin Pilkington's dignified reply shows that he saw the need for reorganisation; but in the last two sentences there is clear evidence of the bitterness of the blow. He addressed his letter to his old friend and right-hand man, Tunnock, the company secretary:

I wish to thank my Co-Directors for their letter. I unreservedly accept their decision with regard to my resignation as Chairman and thank them for the considerate terms in which it is couched. I am grateful for the leave of extended absence.

I am glad that they are proceeding with the scheme outlined which I think will be to the advantage of the business.

With regard to myself, I can only say at this time that it would meet my own wishes if on my return it is still the wish of the Board. There are certain matters which I should like to attend to at the Office before going away. This, I think, can be done without causing embarrassment to my Co-Directors or members of the staff. It will only be for a week or so.[22]

In due course Austin Pilkington and his wife sailed to India, and in September the company decided to pay their fares.[23] Meanwhile the Board asked Cozens-Hardy to draw up a reorganisation scheme, and Norman Pilkington became the company's acting chairman.[24]

On 21 July Cozens-Hardy outlined the principles underlying his proposed administrative changes:

The problem, as I see it, is to evolve from our present somewhat haphazard way of working, a scheme or organisation which (i) will retain the close personal touch with the work and with the employees which has been characteristic of the firm, (ii) will ensure continuity of policy, (iii) will fit in with the personalities now concerned and be adaptable to probable future requirements.

Under present arrangements the Board collectively and through its Chairman concerns itself in a great many matters of comparative detail which, in view of the size to which the business has grown, tend to absorb a large part of its time, leaving too little time for proper consideration of broad questions of policy. It is believed that more effective use can be made of the services of Directors and Staff if a scheme is evolved under which greater responsibility for definite parts of the work is put on individual shoulders, whilst leaving control of all important matters of policy in the hands of the full Board.

He went on to propose that there should be an Executive Committee elected by the Board from its members and subject to confirmation by the shareholders, which should consist of active directors who were concerned with the day-to-day running of the business, each of whom would be allocated particular duties. This would free the full Board, which would also include retired directors, to consider policy matters at meetings which would be held not more than once every two months. Non-executive directors might also be invited to undertake special duties from time to time 'such as representing the Company on outside bodies, watching its interests on the Town Council, or assisting in external relations, in special negotiations, in technical matters or the like'. It was also proposed that people 'who in the opinion of the Board had rendered special service to the Company or its Associated Companies' should be made directors without share qualification but that there should not be more than two such directors in this category at any one time.[25]

These recommendations were discussed and approved. The first meeting of the new Executive Committee, with Cozens-Hardy in the chair, took place on 31 July. While it had been intended that the company should have a president (who might or might not preside over the Board but would certainly chair general meetings of shareholders) and Austin Pilkington had been told that this post was intended for him,[26] the post did not come into being at that time. Norman Pilkington remained chairman of the Board, as distinct from the Executive Committee, as night watchman until the end of 1931 when he was succeeded by Geoffrey Pilkington who was to hold that office until 1949.

Both Austin and Cecil Pilkington stayed on as non-executive directors, attended meetings of the full Board as elder statesmen and performed special duties for the company. Austin Pilkington, for instance, joined the Triplex (Northern) Board. He continued to live in the St Helens district and for another 20 years maintained his interest in local activities as well as, at a national level, in the London Missionary Society and the YMCA. When he reached the retiring age of 68 on 8 February 1939, the Pilkington Board unanimously agreed that he should be invited to serve for another 12 months[27] and this arrangement was continued on a year-to-year basis until, on his 80th birthday in 1951, he eventually retired. The respect in which he was then held is reflected in the Board minute which recorded his wish to retire:

Mr W.H. Pilkington [his son, who had succeeded to the company chairmanship in 1949] stressed to Mr R.A. Pilkington that this decision need not necessitate his abandoning his room in the Head Office, nor breaking off in any way his contacts at the office and the various works; his presence at the Lunch Board [where he would meet the executive directors] would always be welcomed, and any advice and guidance he might care to give the Board at any time would be most welcome.[28]

He died later that year.

Cecil Pilkington, four years younger than his brother, also undertook special duties, such as a business visit to the United States in 1932, and made the journey from Oxford to attend Board meetings at St Helens until November 1949. He retired in the following year though he agreed to be available for consultation as and when required.[29] He enjoyed living at Boars Hill and continued to interest himself in the problems of the farm nearby until his death in 1966 at the age of 91.

The two brothers were the outstanding Pilkingtons of their generation, though it will be recalled that it was a generation with more than its share of casualties through death or premature retirement. They had the misfortune of inheriting the drawn cylinder process, and the decision to build Doncaster had also been taken before Austin Pilkington's chairmanship. They found themselves pitchforked into additional responsibility by the retirement in 1920 at the age of 41 of Alan Douglas Pilkington, – he had been company secretary from 1912 to 1919 and was a major shareholder – mainly on the grounds of ill health. (He went on to live for

another 53 years.) More important, the chairman, Arthur Pilkington, had
died suddenly in the following year at the age of 50. Yet, judged by its
trading results, the company did well for most of the decade after the
readjustment to post-war conditions had been made in 1921–2. Only in
1930, when the world economic climate suddenly worsened, did the business run into real trouble. This coincided with the eclipse of the drawn
cylinder process but by then the triumvirate, having failed to develop its
own method of flat drawn manufacture, had secured the PPG process
and had come to terms with the continentals. What is more, as we shall see
in the next chapter, they had brought the company into the rapidly-
growing safety glass industry. Pilkington Brothers Limited then rested on
much firmer foundations than the business which they themselves had
inherited. But it was still a business organised as, and managed like, a
nineteenth-century partnership. That major managerial changes were
overdue in 1931, is beyond question.

Lord Cozens-Hardy, deviser of the reorganisation scheme and chairman of the Executive Committee, now came into his own, with Weeks
as his closest associate. The timing of his arrival to this top position was
very fortunate; he soon enjoyed advantages denied to his two predecessors.
Within months, devaluation of the pound strengthened Pilkington's
competitive position in home and foreign markets, and the flat drawn
process soon began to restore the company's position in sheet glass
manufacture. Although, as has been seen, Cozens-Hardy was a relatively
small shareholder, he now wielded more power than the chairman of the
company himself. At 58, he was the Executive's oldest family member
and he had also served on the Board longer than any of the other managing
directors. He was to remain chairman of the Executive until early in
1939 when he retired under the new rules at the age of 65. He then served
on the Board in a non-executive capacity until his death in 1956.

It will be recalled that Cozens-Hardy was by training an electrical
engineer. He had previously been concerned mainly with developments
at Cowley Hill and with international negotiations. He lacked Austin
Pilkington's mastery of the sales side of the business or Cecil's grasp of
glass technology as a whole. When he found himself suddenly sitting in
the seat of power, he had to acquaint himself with features of the company's activities about which he knew little or nothing; and he was not
good at grappling with a range of problems simultaneously. His practice
was to deal with one matter at a time.[30] The new form of organisation he
devised, however, suited his style. He was in his element when chairing a

meeting of specialists or when encouraging people with different personalities to work together. He himself took charge of the key departments which dealt with costs and financial matters. At that time Pilkington employed only one chartered accountant, P.L. Robson, another Allan Glen product. Cozens-Hardy soon engaged more.

The two non-share-qualified directors who joined the Executive were chosen to look after areas of the business on which they already possessed more expertise than any of the family managing directors. W.S. Tunnock had been a sub-director since 1920, was Secretary of the company, had come up on the Sales side and had been Austin Pilkington's right-hand man; now he took over the Sales and Commercial Departments as well as the Secretarial Department. And John Herbert Dickinson, (b. 1870) who, after ten years' legal practice in London, had joined the company in 1905 to help his father handle its legal business, now became director in charge of the Legal Department. The division of managerial responsibility proposed by Cozens-Hardy at the first meeting of the Executive on 31 July 1931 and subsequently adopted was as follows:

Grove Street Works (Sheet and Rolled Plate) and Timber Yard – G.R.(Guy) Pilkington (assisted by Douglas Phelps)

Cowley Hill and Doncaster Plate Glassworks – R.M. Weeks

Ravenhead Works (Cathedral and Miscellaneous) – Geoffrey Pilkington (assisted by R.K. Uhthoff)

Planning and Propaganda – Geoffrey Pilkington

Technical Services – R.M. Weeks (assisted by Douglas Phelps)

Sales and Commercial Departments – W.S. Tunnock (assisted by Harry Pilkington and W.L. Pilkington)

Financial Department, Accounts, Costs, Cash – Cozens-Hardy

Legal Department, Estate, Property, Patents – J.H. Dickinson

Secretarial Department – W.S. Tunnock (assisted by J.B. Finlay, who was to become Company Secretary in May 1932).[31]

It will be noted that, of the family members of the Executive, Norman Pilkington, for the time being chairman of the full Board, had no specified managerial responsibility, and that Guy Pilkington was allocated only one function (and that with an able assistant). There was then no separate Personnel Department. Alan Douglas Pilkington, who had resigned from the Board in 1920, now rejoined it but in a non-executive capacity. He, Austin and Cecil Pilkington were all among those present at a meeting on 28 October 1931 which approved the new arrangements in a formal agreement which made them retrospective to 1 August.[32]

The four Pilkington newcomers, three of whom had become

M*

sub-directors in 1930, had now to undergo a further period of trial and training before qualifying for the new Executive. Harry Pilkington and Douglas Phelps were not put on it until June 1934.[33] This period of trial was as searching as it was prolonged, and the managers of the departments or works in which they served made regular reports on their progress. This was no mere formality. William Lee Pilkington, for instance, who had also become a family probationer in 1927, was in 1933 offered 'a final trial for a period of one year'.[34] He did not succeed in satisfying his examiners and, despite later appeals, never joined the Executive. He eventually left the company and became a stockbroker.[35] The services of another family probationer, Raymond F. Pilkington who came for trial in 1934, were dispensed with two years later.[36] Others, however, did reach the high standards set. Roger Percival joined the Executive in September 1936, and Peter Cozens-Hardy – who started with Pilkington in 1932 having completed three years with Colmans – in 1937.[37] Lawrence Herbert Austin Pilkington, Austin's second son (b. in Colorado 1911; educated at Bromsgrove School and Magdalene College, Cambridge, where he read Chemistry – the second science graduate among the family trainees) began going through the usual hoops and over the usual hurdles in 1934 but did not reach the Executive until 1943.[38] Arthur Cope Pilkington, the younger son of Arthur Richard Pilkington, who also started with the company in 1934, had a more unusual background. Born in 1909 and educated at Charterhouse and the Royal Military College at Sandhurst, he had served for four years in the Coldstream Guards. He was also unusual in that he was a Roman Catholic. 'Various difficulties and objections were placed before him,' the minutes record, 'but he still requested that the Board should consider his application.' It was agreed that he should come in as a non-family trainee for a year in the first instance 'and it should be made clear to him at the outset that the question of his religion will not prejudice his interests so long as it does not interfere with the business'.[39] He did well, joined the family probation contest in 1935 and was sent as acting manager in South Africa at the beginning of 1939. After returning to the Guards during the war, he joined the Executive when it was over (he was to become its chairman in 1965).[40] No member of the Pilkington family joined the top management of the company after 1931 without having proved his worth in various departments of the business over a long period of time. Indeed, the view taken by the Executive was that, to provide the leadership required, these men had to show themselves abler and more dedicated than any of the company's other employees.

This prolonged and rigorous training meant, of course, that, the Executive was slow to benefit to the full from the necessary infusion of new blood, although successful family trainees did reach top management younger than promising men could do in non-family companies. Of the family trainees, only Harry Pilkington, Douglas Phelps, Roger Percival and Peter Cozens-Hardy found their way on to the Executive during the 1930s. There was also one further promotion of an older man from the ranks during this period. This was James Meikle, one of the Allan Glen's School arrivals just before 1914. His training as an electrical engineer endeared him to Cozens-Hardy who got to know him well at Cowley Hill. He became manager there in 1931, joined the Executive in March 1936 and succeeded Dickinson, who retired at 65 in 1937, as a non-share-qualified director on the Board.[41] Tunnock was also in the process of withdrawing from active management at this time, for his health was troubling him. He served on a part-time basis from the end of 1936, retired from the Executive in May 1938 and from the Board in 1940.[42] As Edward Alan Evans, who had been head of the Sales Department since 1925, also retired unexpectedly in 1935, at the age of 53, Harry Pilkington then suddenly found himself as the most senior executive on the commercial side of the business. He was then aged 30. The Executive also lost two of its family members. Guy Pilkington retired from it in July 1934, though he was assigned special salaried duties for the next three years. He handed over responsibility for the Grove Street works to Douglas Phelps[43] but continued to serve as a non-executive director until 1964, six years before his death. Norman Pilkington died in February 1935. Thus, although the change in the Executive had occurred only gradually during the 1930s, only three of its original seven members still remained at the beginning of 1939 when Cozens-Hardy himself was about to retire from it; and it now included four younger men.

Membership of the Executive Committee

August 1931	January 1939
Lord Cozens-Hardy (58)	Lord Cozens-Hardy (65)
Geoffrey Pilkington (46)	Geoffrey Pilkington (54)
Ronald Weeks (41)	Ronald Weeks (48)
J.H.Dickinson (61)	Peter Cozens-Hardy (31)
Guy Pilkington (50)	James Meikle (48)
Norman Pilkington (54)	Roger Percival (32)
W.S.Tunnock (54)	Douglas Phelps (34)
	Harry Pilkington (33)

The new *régime* soon began to consider methods of recruiting and training future senior managers. Here Management Research Group No. 1 again played a part. The schemes already used by ICI, Lever Brothers,

Standard Telephones and Rowntrees were discussed at a meeting attended by Cozens-Hardy and Weeks early in 1932. The Board agreed, on 16 March, to have a similar scheme drawn up.[44] In June the Executive considered a report on the subject written by Weeks.[45] This began by outlining the need and defining the problem:

The modern tendency of Industry to organise itself in large and complicated units is creating a demand for a new type of skilled administrator, not only in the central management of such units but also in a large number of subordinate and highly responsible positions. There is every indication that the complexity of 'big business' will increase, rather than diminish, in years to come and, in consequence, one of the problems which is confronting the Directors of large industrial concerns today is how to ensure an adequate supply of suitable material from which to fill administrative and executive vacancies as they arise in the future.

Unfortunately, there is no certain source from which to obtain this suitable material. The qualities required for Industrial Management are such that neither the schools nor the technical colleges – nor even the Universities – can unfailingly supply Industry with its requirements in this direction. Knowledge alone is not enough; character alone is not enough; what is required, in general, is character, inherent ability, a disciplined mind, and initiative.[46]

Weeks then proceeded to indicate the kind of entrants required to fill three different types of function:

1. The secretarial, legal and accountancy function. After five years professional training followed by five years practical experience, candidates for training would be about 27 years of age.
2. The manufacturing function. Here a university course in engineering or science was needed and/or an apprenticeship. 'A University training involves the study and knowledge of fundamental principles; it develops, cultivates and disciplines the mind; it broadens the outlook of the student; it produces the best type of trained intelligence. Thus, at the age of twenty-one or twenty-two, it is possible to obtain from the Universities or Technical Colleges, men who are eminently suitable for further training in the special business in which the company is involved, and it is concerned that this is the time when the Works Management personnel ought to be recruited'. [This, of course, was precisely Weeks' own route to Pilkington.]
3. The commercial function. 'So far as Buying is concerned, there is much to be said for having a University man whose studies have enabled him to think of commodities otherwise than in terms of quality, quantity and price only –

one who can bring to bear on his problems a knowledge of, it may be, physics and chemistry, geology or natural history. Such knowledge is not, of course, absolutely necessary, and it may be that the Public School or Secondary School boy, introduced to the organisation at the age of 17 and given a comprehensive training in several selected phases of the Company's activities will prove to be the better executive of the future.

So far as regards Selling, the boy who is introduced at the age of 17 and given opportunities to learn in the Works, the Warehouse, the Office and the Sales Field, everything there is to be known about the Company's products will have a much better chance of turning out to be a first-class salesman than the University man. One might qualify this statement in the case of Speciality lines for which Speciality salesmen are required [this is a clear reference to Vita glass; in 1929 Pilkington had applied to the Cambridge Appointments Board for graduates to help in marketing the new product[47]] but in general it may be said that higher education does not count for so much in a salesman as do personality and a thorough knowledge of the commodity being offered for sale.'

Finally, Weeks advocated the formation of a directors' personnel committee and a personnel department. The decision to act on this last recommendation was eventually taken in October 1934 – despite protests from Tunnock who believed that personnel should be the responsibility of the Secretary's Department – and Peter Cozens-Hardy was put in charge. The new department was not, however, to concern itself with appointments to higher managerial positions. These the directors kept in their own hands.[48]

No immediate action followed Weeks' other recommendations either. Instead, a committee consisting of Lord Cozens-Hardy, Tunnock and Weeks was formed to consider recruitment possibilities further.[49] It was not until the following year, 1933, that, having consulted the departmental and depot managers, the first trainees were accepted, almost all of them on the commercial side. A large house, Ingleholme, at Eccleston Park was acquired as a hostel and full board provided at 42s 6d per week for trainees who chose to live there, and for 45s or 50s, according to bedroom size, for other 'approved members of the staff'. A housekeeper having been engaged at £100 per year plus board, the hostel was opened in November 1933 with three trainees and eight other residents.[50] Of the first intake of seven trainees, one came from Oxford and one from Cambridge (D.H.Jupp) – both aged 22 and starting at £230 per year – and four came from within the company. One of these, G.E.Beer, who had arrived shortly before, attracted by the prospect of a traineeship, was to become in due course the Head of Group Personnel Services. New recruits were added each summer, but in 1937 Peter Cozens-Hardy had to report that the scheme was not coming up to expectation so far as the university trainees were concerned. Having been given insufficient responsibility during their training, they were losing their enthusiasm. Two had left, two more were thinking of doing so, and if this happened only three graduate trainees would remain. The real trouble was that the number of jobs on the Sales side at salaries of £500 or more – the salary figure after training mentioned in the recruiting publicity handed out to university appointments boards – was very limited. Commercial and works appointments were usually better paid; and of all the good managerial posts in the company which were to fall vacant by retirement, more than 60 per cent would not do so until between 1949 and 1955.[51] The trainee scheme had been embarked upon with the best of intentions but without sufficient thought about the timing of future vacancies. Consequently nobody was recruited in 1938 and only two men, both from the staff, in 1939. The scheme was nevertheless to provide the company with leaders who were, in due course, to play a notable part in its operations overseas: Jupp in Canada; J.H.Pemberton (a staff recruit in 1935) in Australia; O.J.Breakspear (a graduate from Cambridge in 1937) and L,O.Gallon (1939) in South Africa; and R.Robinson (1939) in New Zealand. None of the commercial trainees of the 1930s, however, reached Board level at St Helens.

While these efforts were being made to improve recruitment and training of top management, attention also began to be given to encouraging enterprise and initiative at other levels. Lord Cozens-Hardy was himself very interested in this, and he gave a talk on the subject to Management Research Group No. 1 at the Waldorf Hotel, London, in May 1932.[52] Having considered general bonus and particular merit schemes, he reached the conclusion that

the greatest of all staff incentives is the simplest and the most obvious, namely the prospect of promotion. There has probably never been an office boy who, at one time or another, has not dreamed of one day occupying the position of managing director, and in the well-regulated company there should be no reason why such a dream should not be fulfilled. The best results will be obtained from the staff who see dangling before them not carrots but plums.

In the subsequent discussion, he emphasised that he was thinking of incentives for all grades, starting with the foreman and 'quite low down on the clerical side ... there is something to be said for going down almost to the bottom'. Unfortunately the Executive chairman's ideals were far from the reality at St Helens. In the 1930s the ladder of promotion on the sales side, for junior staff as well as for trainees, was blocked by senior men far from retirement. A paper on the subject, written at the beginning of 1938, pointed out that this was making it difficult to train staff and was also causing some dissatisfaction among the clerks. 'The net result,' the paper went on, 'is that movement of the younger members of the Sales Staff is practically neglible . . . and the Staff is not getting the training experience . . . which it should.'[53]

At the meeting in 1932 addressed by Lord Cozens-Hardy, the chairman, Seebohm Rowntree, had linked budgetary control with the staff incentive schemes:

. . . At the beginning of the year the director of production will have a conference with each of his departmental managers and will take the items which they can control and say: 'What is a fair figure for those items during the year'. Thus together they will build up the departmental budget. Then a manager will feel: 'I have to get something whereby I can measure up results. If I get £50,000 for my expenses in this department and can carry it on for £45,000, that is £5,000 to my credit'.

The representatives of several of the companies present on that occasion reported that they already employed budgetary control. Pilkington soon followed suit. P.L.Robson, the company's accountant, who by then had three young chartered accountants assisting him,[54] produced a paper on the subject at the beginning of October 1932, based upon a lecture he had just heard from Professor De Paula about the budgetary system De Paula had introduced at Dunlop. The works quickly approved his proposals with certain modifications, and arrangements were made to introduce budgetary control, at Cowley Hill and Doncaster in the first instance, from 1 January 1933.[55] The growing influence of the Accountants Department was a particular feature of this period. Robson's standing was already high, for he had just saved the company a considerable amount of unnecessary taxation by changing the existing procedure of charging a fixed annual rate of depreciation on capital assets to charging the actual cost of replacement in a given financial year. The Inland Revenue made allowances for depreciation, and there was a large amount of dead wood that could then be written off at a stroke. This was of particular benefit to the company at a time of financial stringency.[56]

Various attempts were made to tighten up on work methods. Outside consultants were brought in to improve labour productivity in the warehouse, works and office. A Bedaux engineer visited St Helens at the beginning of November 1932, and the Board subsequently agreed to try out the Bedaux system 'so long as we are kept in the closest touch with every step taken by them so as to ensure that the interests of the company are being watched'.[57] The Joint Industrial Council agreed to trials in February 1933, but later that year Guy Pilkington reported a $9\frac{1}{2}$ per cent fall in output among glass cutters in one of the Sheet Works warehouses where the Bedaux system had been introduced. 'Some of the men have been very awkward,' he added, 'and have not given the System a fair trial.'[58] In the end, time study was taken over by one of Pilkington's own men, George McOnie. Yet another Allan Glen product, he had taken an engineering degree at Glasgow University and worked in the ship-building industry before joining the company in 1927. With the Bedaux Department renamed 'Mr McOnie's Department', a steep increase in sheet cutters' output was soon reported.[59] Indeed, he succeeded so well that in the following year the Executive told him to slow up a little at Sheet and Plate Works and concentrate his efforts elsewhere in the company.[60] He was soon to become works manager at Doncaster and later at Cowley Hill and eventually to join the Pilkington Board.

Investigations into Pilkington's office organisation were undertaken by the National Institute of Industrial Psychology, a body which had been set up after the war by Charles S. Myers, Director of the Experimental Psychology Laboratory at Cambridge University, and Henry J. Welch, a businessman. It aimed to apply psychological techniques to industry and commerce, to study business activity at the workplace by inspection and by confidential interview, and to concentrate particularly upon removing material handicaps which wasted human energy. The success of their recommendations they measured by the increased output per head which resulted from them.[61] After a two-day preliminary survey in December 1932, the N.I.I.P. sent one of its men to carry out a six-month study of the recruitment, selection and training of clerical staff at St Helens. This he did between mid-March and mid-September 1933 for an inclusive fee of £840.[62] The N.I.I.P. representative advised on selection procedures for the original intake of management trainees – whom he also intelligence-tested – and produced a report on the recruitment, training, remuneration and treatment of office staff.[63] In all, four reports were produced[64] and a small Methods Committee of three people was formed to pursue a few of their suggestions,[65] some of which claimed that labour could be saved if orders were copied and checked in a different way;[66] but in fact staff numbers at Head Office were higher when the investigator left than before his arrival. The Methods Committee itself was disbanded in February 1936.[67]

There were two other signs of the times, both of which have survived.

TABLE 47
CLERICAL STAFF AT HEAD OFFICE, 1928–32 AND 1933

Department	Average 5 years 1928–32	In Post 1 Jan. 1933	In Post 31 Dec. 1933
Secretarial	9	10	12
Accountants	23	15	16
Pensions		9	10
Home Sales and Travellers	134	140	153
Order	45	46	52
Export, incl. Canadian	59	51	53
Legal and Estate	6	6	9
Cost	47	50	49
Statistical	3	1	4
Ledger (Sales)	31	29	29
Bought Ledger	9	7	7
Export Ledger	5	5	5
Settlement	6	5	6
Package	19	17	17
Railway	12	11	11
Transport	6	5	5
Buying	21	18	19
Stationery and Printing	18	19	20
Cash	12	11	11
Caretakers	2	2	2
Telephones	5	6	6
Doorkeepers	11	11	11
Postal	13	13	14
Wages and Yard Wages	30	26	29
Manager's Office	7	8	10
Electrical	5	6	7
Drawing Office	14	13	15
Correspondence	7	9	7
Dental Surgery	2	2	2
			591
Architects			9
Trainees			7
Bedaux			6
Methods			3
	561	551	616

Source: PA PB258 Executive Committee Papers, 21 February 1934

A suggestion scheme (with rewards of 2s 6d – quickly raised to 5s) for suggested improvements which were accepted, was introduced on 15 May 1933.[68] It brought in 1,848 ideas in the first year, 10 per cent of which were adopted.[69] (One that was not was a suggestion that all staff should have a ten-minute break during the morning.[70]) The second new development was the formation of a Statistical and Intelligence Department to assemble information about the business and the glass trade in general which had previously been collected but on a less formal basis. Harry Ward, secretary of Research Group No. 1, collected details of procedures in other large businesses on Pilkington's behalf before the company set up its own organisation, with A. M. Burdon-Cooper in charge, at the beginning of 1937.[71]

Another development intended to increase efficiency, though by no means a new one in the 1930s, was the greater use by Pilkington of its own motor transport. Motor lorries had been used to take cases of glass to Liverpool just before 1914, but it was not until the end of the war that a fleet of vehicles – starting with two Sentinel steam wagons, one based on St Helens and the other on the Birmingham warehouse – was built up.[72] In 1934 an outside specialist was recruited to take charge of the Motor Transport Department and to reorganise it.[73] Two years later the company was operating 72 lorries either from St Helens or from its depots, and some of them already had frames on their near sides so that plate glass could be carried with a minimum of packing and handling. The geographical range of motor lorries was still limited, however, those from St Helens travelling only so far as Fleetwood, Burnley or Manchester or, to the west, along the North Wales coast to Llandudno. For longer journeys glass still went by rail. In 1932 the railway rate from St Helens to London was reduced from 35s per ton (plate glass) and 32s (sheet glass) to 30s for both, and the same terms were also obtained to London from Doncaster.[74] The service, moreover, was improved in that year as the manager concerned noted at the time:

The Railway Companies have made considerable improvements during the last few years in the delivery of traffic. Express goods trains run every night between important centres, and freight trains run to scheduled time just the same as passenger trains. With the advent of powerful locomotives, longer trains are run at higher speeds and many of the express goods trains which run nightly are fitted with vacuum brakes . . . Loaded wagons are placed on outward sidings at the Sheet Works and at Ravenhead Works at 6.15 p.m. each day for London, Nottingham, Glasgow, Birmingham etc., and arrive at their destination early the following morning.

Prior to 1932, wagons for London were conveyed to Warrington to connect with the train to London at that point. It was found that frequently wagons did not arrive in London until very late the day following despatch and too late for the packages to be delivered that day ... Since October 1932 a through train has run from the Ravenhead branch conveying all wagons for London and south of the Thames. Wagons arrive in London before 6 o'clock in the morning following despatch, which enables traffic from the London warehouse to be loaded on drays for delivery by 9 a.m. Wagons for south of the Thames usually arrive at the destination station the day but one after despatch.[75]

Even containers were already in use, provided by the railway company, to convey glass cells and shades.

By the early 1920s a number of major British companies, including Boots, Brunner Mond, Burroughs Wellcome, Courtaulds, Crosfield – and Pilkington's competitor Chance – had formed their own research and development departments. There was also collaboration between companies and research organisations in particular industries, or with universities.[76] Pilkington, however, continued for some time in its pre-war way. It gave financial support to the work of the Society of Glass Technology, set up during the First World War, and contributed £5,000 to the new building of the Department of Glass Technology at Sheffield University in 1937,[77] but it was afraid of working too closely with Sheffield because of the need for technical secrecy. Cecil Pilkington had even declined the Presidency of the Society on that score in 1926.[78] Each Pilkington factory had its own technical experts whose task was mainly to undertake analytical work and to assist managers in maintaining production and improving the efficiency of existing processes. Several able young science and engineering graduates had been recruited for these purposes, as we have seen. At Cowley Hill these men, and the development team working with them, had achieved important cost-reducing innovations in plate glass manufacture. In addition, Cecil Pilkington, as technical director, had assembled his own team after the war to conduct flat drawn experiments in sheet glass.[79] With his departure, however, any semblance of technical co-ordination disappeared just when Pilkington's processes were becoming much more capital intensive and therefore called for centralised research and development. The chairman of the new Executive, a technical man, realised that something needed to be done about this, and so did Weeks, the Cambridge science graduate.

In April 1933 the Executive decided to co-ordinate the activities of the engineering departments in the various works.[80] Later that year a Technical Committee (or Technical Conference as it came to be called) was set up, consisting of the works managers, with Weeks as its chairman and R. F. Taylor as its secretary. (Taylor was also responsible for patents, assisted by E. M. S. Wood, a recently-arrived Cambridge graduate in Mechanical Sciences who had already had experience in industry and was later to take over from him.) Reports of all technical investigations were to be sent by the departmental manager concerned to the works manager for summarising before being circulated, through the secretary, to the members of the committee in good time for each of its bi-monthly meetings. The intention, Weeks told the first of these in September 1933, was not merely to avoid duplicating experimental work but also to discuss plans common to the various factories and – most important – to institute fresh lines of investigation.[81] A subscription was taken out for two German glassmaking journals.[82]

While there is no doubt that the new committee achieved some success in surveying Pilkington's technical efforts as a whole, it did confine itself almost entirely to consideration of reports which came in via the works managers instead of trying to identify the most promising research projects, possibly because it was felt that further development at Cowley Hill – the twin grinder – was the most promising of all. So the works managers who formed the committee continued to interest themselves when they met in the same sorts of problems which had interested them previously in their own factories. In March 1934, for instance, the characteristics of sand from Pilkington's new sandfield at Billinge were discussed[83] and during the hot summer of that year there was much talk about deficient water supplies. This continued, meeting after meeting, until eventually a new and improved source of well water became available in the autumn of 1936.[84]

In the mid-1930s, at a time when British industry as a whole was spending much more on research – 422 concerns spent £1·7 m. in 1930; 566 of them were to spend £5·4 m. in 1938[85] – Pilkington at last took the decision to centralise and greatly extend its research activities. This decision coincided with further change in the company's administrative structure.

Greater concern with research was undoubtedly a response to ICI's marketing in 1935 of a transparent plastic and possible substitute for glass which it called Perspex, a result of its discovery of 'Resin M', polymethylmethacrylate.[86] The minutes of the Pilkington Executive in May 1934 and April 1935 mention meetings out of which emerged the suggestion (it is not clear from which side) that the two companies should collaborate, rather than compete, in the exploitation of the new product.[87]

Pilkington's proposals for its handling were, however, unacceptable to ICI; nevertheless, the Executive minuted:

they have given us a written undertaking that should their researches into the resin field lead them to a point where the product of that field is likely to become useful on a substantial scale as a substitute for flat glass generally, they will confer with us with a view to evolving a mutually satisfactory *modus vivendi*.[88]

ICI once again behaved with friendliness towards a major customer, as they had done in 1927 over the Libbey-Owens flat drawn licence, and agreement was soon reached. In November 1935, it was agreed to sell Perspex as a substitute for safety glass only through Triplex, and Triplex, in its turn, gave an undertaking not to manufacture synthetic resin.[89] This was followed, in June 1937, by an agreement between ICI and Pilkington, terminable at three years' notice after 31 December 1942, relating to sales of soda ash and flat transparent resins. If ICI sales of the latter exceeded 2,000 tons over four consecutive quarters (which Pilkington calculated to be the equivalent of 6 m. sq. ft of $\frac{1}{8}$ in. glass), Pilkington would have the right to call on ICI to form a joint company (51 per cent ICI and 49 per cent Pilkington) to market the product.[90] This was a very satisfactory outcome: it safeguarded Pilkington's short-run interests, and in the longer term Perspex was never to become a serious competitor to plate glass for glazing or motor car use (it scratched too easily and was not competitive on price). Although Perspex output reached the stipulated tonnage during the war, the joint company was not then formed, and in 1948, in the absence of competition between Perspex and plate glass, the 1937 agreement was cancelled.[91]

This amicable relationship with ICI did not, however, prevent Pilkington from taking greater interest in research in general and plastics in particular. In 1936 Triplex (Northern) Limited, in which Pilkington was a major shareholder, bought the plastics moulding concern of H.E. Ashdown (Birmingham) Limited at Perry Barr (which proved a very costly insurance policy);* and Pilkington also set up a Central Research Department,

---

*More capital was put into Ashdowns, but the business lost money and in 1938 it was taken over by Pilkington Brothers. Moulding was concentrated in accommodation leased at Eccleston from Triplex (Northern), leaving the other activities, such as estimating, design and sales, at Perry Barr. Losses continued. In May 1939 Urwick, Orr & Partners recommended selling, and it was decided to dispose of Perry Barr (which was done in July 1939) and to bring the remaining activities to Eccleston. Losses still continued, and in 1940 Pilkington tried to sell this encumbrance to British Industrial Plastics, but without success. Moulding ceased in 1957.

In 1937, Kenneth Horne, later to become famous as a broadcaster, was offered the post of Sales Manager at Ashdowns, but it was subsequently decided that he should remain in his

among the newly-recruited staff of which was C.F.Griffith, a plastics research chemist.[93] Later that year Lord Cozens-Hardy told the Board that Pilkington was proposing to enter plastics research 'on a large scale' and a year later doubts were expressed by the directors about whether the company was spending enough money in this direction. Pittsburgh Plate Glass and Libbey-Owens-Ford were said to be paying special attention to plastic containers and sheeting.[94]

Although, in the event, the new Research Department never had to devote much of its activity to plastics, it soon became quite well staffed to undertake analytical work and general research work on glass. Scientists were either brought in from the works—as was A.R.Wood, the Deputy Director, and others, such as Horace Cole, M.N.L.Leathwood, L.Woods and Dr W.B. Price, who were to devote the rest of their lives to research with the company—or were specially recruited from outside. So rapidly did the research team grow, in fact, that in 1939 efforts had to be made to keep the salary bill for research staff (excluding those engaged in analytical work) down to £10,000 per year.[95] The first director was Dr Harry Moore, formerly Director of the Scientific Instrument Research Association in London, who was brought to St Helens in 1936 at the handsome salary of £2,000 per year.[96] Specially-built research laboratories, costing about £44,000,[97] were opened by Sir William Bragg in October 1938. The Board, however, seemed to view the whole venture as an act of faith rather than as a sizeable investment which should be made to pay for itself:

The Directors were of the opinion that the establishment of Research Laboratories will prove to be of very great value to the Company, although the benefits may be neither immediate nor easily identifiable.[98]

The Executive, in forming a separate Research & Analytical Department, were at pains to lay down that 'the closest liaison will exist between the staffs of these Directors [R & A and T.D.], and a representative of the R & A Department will attend all meetings of the T.D. Department. The new building for the R & A Department will also include Laboratories for the T.D. Department.'[99] Unfortunately R & A and T.D. tended to go their own separate ways. The works managers did not take kindly to losing their scientists and looked askance at the new Director of Research

existing employment on the sales side of Triplex itself, where he was later to become Sales Director. The possibility of his coming to work for Pilkington was considered in 1939 and again in 1956. He was related to the Pilkingtons – his father, the well-known preacher Charles Sylvester Horne, had married Cozens-Hardy's sister – and was much liked by both Austin Pilkington, his uncle, and Harry Pilkington, his cousin, with whom he used to play energetic games of tennis before breakfast.[92]

who had been brought up from London at a high salary. By the new arrangements of 1936, Technical Development had its own Director (Meikle, now on the Executive) and its work was divided among ten specialist group committees dealing with particular matters such as refractories, melting, or grinding and polishing. R.F.Taylor was responsible for all the groups and their reports. This was a means of bringing more technical people into the decision-making process; these group reports, like those of the Director of the Research & Analytical Department, eventually found their way to the Technical Committee over which Weeks continued to preside. But the minutes of that committee down to the war do not suggest that any serious effort was being made to combine research and development. Indeed, on the contrary, the research department was soon complaining that its 'pure research work' was being held up by calls made on its time for what it termed 'service work'.[100]

The creation of the Research & Analytical Department and the Technical Department coincided with a further administrative reorganisation in which three other committees were formed which also, like the Technical Committee, reported to the Executive. These were important in that they, too, involved more senior managers in policy making. They were:

The Finance Committee, chaired by Lord Cozens-Hardy, and including, in addition to Weeks, Harry Pilkington and Peter Cozens-Hardy, the accountants, P.L.Robson and J.B.Bowden. The committee was to meet monthly and, according to the paper presented to the Executive at the time of its formation:

Its functions include the direction of the financial policy of P.B. Ltd and all subsidiary companies, and the issue of reports on progress and results achieved. Most of the executive responsibility in connection with these functions devolves upon the Accountants Department whose work includes the preparation of Manufacturing, Trading, and Profit & Loss Accounts and Balance Sheets, Budgets, Costs, Investment of Funds and Taxation. Other departments responsible to the Finance Committee, through the Chief Accountant, are the Cost, Tabulating, Cash, Bought Ledger, Home Sales Ledger, and Foreign Ledger, with the proviso that credit control is vested in the Sales Manager.

The Accountants Department will be responsible for the installation, as far as possible, of uniform systems of accounting and reporting by all subsidiary companies, and will revise the bookkeeping, financial and internal check systems at all home depots. It will furnish statistics and information relating to the Company's business to the newly-formed Statistical and Intelligence Dept. As regards Process Costs, etc., it will be the duty of the accountants employed at the various works to collaborate with the Accountants Department.

The operation of the Superannuation and Workmen's Pension Funds is also supervised by the Finance Committee, another of whose functions is the supervision of the Purchasing Department and the Stationery Department ... The Purchasing Controller will, as far as possible, purchase centrally for P.B. Ltd and its subsidiary and associated companies. Standard storekeeping methods will be introduced by him throughout the organisation and regular analyses of stocks prepared.

The Sales Committee including, in addition to Tunnock, Harry Pilkington and Arthur Pilkington, John Tilbury (manager of the Home and Export Department), R.Lyon and G.H.Mills. The committee met at least fortnightly:

to consider market prospects, commercial agreements, and prices, and to deal with sales questions and points of policy. Matters of importance which have arisen since the last meeting are reported and recorded. It secures collaboration with the various works, departments on production, sales budgets, qualities, despatches, etc., and links up the different sections whose managers and others are invited to attend when subjects are being discussed in which they are interested. It is proposed that a comprehensive survey of one depot is made at each meeting and the depot manager will be present. The same will be applied to one export market at each meeting.

The Personnel and Welfare Committee including, in addition to Phelps, Meikle and Peter Cozens-Hardy, R.K.Uhthoff and J.E.Stewart (Personnel and Welfare Manager). T.Appleton was to join the committee whenever labour questions were being discussed.[101]

New committees, new departments, and the general growth of the business during the 1930s placed more responsibilities on the shoulders of the company's Secretary, J.B.Finlay. J.Fraser Rigby became his assistant in 1938 and succeeded him when he left for a post in South Africa in the following year.[102] The growing numbers of staff also called for additional accommodation. Plans for a new head office were under consideration from the middle of 1933, and in the following year Herbert Rowse was invited to submit plans for a combined office and canteen block.[103] His proposals for a two-storey building to cost about £80,000, built out from the existing head office on a corner site, were accepted at the beginning of 1935 'with the reservation that the strictest economy should be observed whenever possible and, further, that safeguards should be adopted to prevent any tendency, after the new premises are available, to appoint additional staff to fill the surplus accommodation'.[104] A £32,000 tender for the canteen, to be completed in 12 months, was accepted in

April 1937,[105] and in September 1939, when £60,000 had been spent on this and the new offices, the expenditure of the remaining £20,000 was authorised to complete the scheme.[106] The Board's cautionary resolution of 1935 seems to have been heeded, for this pleasing, oval-shaped brick building, lined inside with Vitrolite and containing many walls of glass brick, managed to contain the swelling ranks of head office staff for over 20 years.

The new head office extension was symbolic of the changes of the 1930s, for the company then took on the appearance of a modern business. The centralisation of research and development paved the way for further technical progress after 1945. In the committees created senior managers were associated regularly and formally with members of the Board to hammer out new ideas and introduce new methods; the very ablest employees were admitted to the rank of director; the best of the locally recruited talent (still sought out and promoted) was supplemented by promising young men from elsewhere. The company's limited, nine-teenth-century structure evolved into a more complex and sophisticated organisation capable of extending its operation into new branches of glass manufacture and into glass processing in other parts of the world.

Chapter 20

New Developments at Home and Overseas

D URING the 1920s the motor trade became an important market for glass; but with more motor vehicles came more accidents in which flying glass was a serious hazard. Motorists were prepared to pay a little more to have their windscreens – and sometimes their other car windows as well – processed so that they would not splinter on impact. The production of safety glass became an important new branch of the industry.

John Crewe Wood, a Swindon solicitor, perceived so early as 1905 that a transparent laminate, such as celluloid, sandwiched between two thin pieces of glass would prevent the glass from shattering when subjected to a sudden shock. He took out a patent for the idea and specimens were exhibited by the Safety Motor Screen Co. Ltd at the Motor Show in 1906. The market for the product was, however, then very limited and the adhesive used to cement the glass to the celluloid does not appear to have been satisfactory. The company did not last long.[1]

A remarkable Frenchman, Edouard Benedictus, was more fortunate. Nephew of Théophile Gautier's daughter, he was trained at the School of Decorative Arts where his chief interest was theatrical décor; and, revealing considerable versatility, he also studied from 1900 at the Darmstadt School of Chemistry. On his return to Paris, he set up a laboratory where he carried out experiments in and after 1903. In 1909, having had his attention drawn to the dangers of flying glass in motor accidents, he recalled that, six years before, he had dropped a large, empty flask on his laboratory floor and it had not broken. This had aroused his curiosity at the time, and he had noticed from the label on the bottle that it had previously contained nitrocellulose. The liquid had long before evaporated leaving a dried residue which had held the bottle together. Benedictus now put this recollection to good use and soon was in a position to take out a number of world patents, the first of them dated August 1909.[2] The business which was set up to exploit these distinguished its product with a trade mark consisting of three large Xs, and the company called itself the Société du Verre TripleX. British rights were offered to anyone prepared to manufacture the product on this side of the Channel, and in June 1911 two of Benedictus's representatives called at St Helens in the hope of finding a licensee. The Pilkington directors were at first not unresponsive though they evidently did not see car windscreens as the main use for the new product. As they wrote at the time to G.H.Baillie, the London patent agent who acted for them: 'We, more to protect a product of ours (namely wired glass) than for any other reason, would prefer to get hold of the thing unless it is obviously worthless.'[3] Baillie, however, was not encouraging – there was, among other objections, the little matter of Wood's patent – and when, in August, the inventor's representatives put forward some fairly greedy financial proposals, Pilkington had no hesitation in instantly rejecting them.[4] Another option holder was touting the patent round in March 1912[5] but no takers could be found until, in July of that year, George Marius Delpech, a Kentish man and a pioneer motorist and aviator, who had recently had experience of splintered glass in a taxi-cab, went to Paris and signed an agreement to form an English Triplex Company. This he did, with General Sir Bindon Blood, GCB, RE(Retd), on 2 August. The public was slow to subscribe to 28,000 £1 shares out of an authorised total of 60,000 then offered for sale, but the little newcomer, having recruited an able engineer in Westcote Raymond Lyttleton, recently arrived from New Zealand, moved into vacant premises at 5 Hythe Road, Willesden, and was ready to start production before the year was out. Pilkington was not involved and, so long as it was free to import thin glass, Triplex did so from Bohemia and Belgium.[6] In January 1915, Pilkington was approached yet again, this time by Delpech, with the offer of 10,000 of the unissued shares. He was told that Pilkington was not interested because Triplex was over-capitalised, but that it might consider working the process. 'Mr A.C.Pilkington judged that though he [Delpech] was disappointed, he will return again to this suggestion within a week or two';[7] but return he did not.

Triplex became profitable during the war, thanks to government orders for goggles as well as for windscreens, and, on the strength of this wartime profit, raised fresh capital in 1919. But this was mis-spent and the company came for a time under the control of Hatry's British Glass Industries. In 1921 it was driven into the hands of the Official Receiver when the Bohemian Glass Company, its main supplier, pressed for payment. A second company, in which Delpech and Lyttleton were also involved, was created to keep the business going, and its assets were taken over by the Central and Western Corporation Ltd from which they were bought, in 1923, by Col. O. C. Clare, son of the company's stockbroker. A regular officer who had served in both the South African and First World Wars, he was then playing the market while living the life of a country gentleman and racehorse owner. He became chairman of Triplex. By this time business was improving as more cars came on to the roads and as the company was able to supply Triplex not only to garages for fitting into existing vehicles, the previous procedure, but also direct to the car makers themselves. By January 1924 Daimler, Riley, Lagonda, Rover and Fiat had all agreed to fit this safety glass as an optional extra, and by July Austin, Lanchester and Wolseley had followed suit. Triplex was now coming into direct competition with Pilkington-made glass in a growingly important market.[8] To Pilkington it was of particular importance in that, for windscreens at any rate, the distortion-free plate glass, the branch of manufacture in which the company excelled, was preferable to the cheaper sheet glass in the manufacture of which, as has been seen, the company was running into difficulties. A further attraction was that lamination, of course, required a greater square footage of glass – three times the windscreen size, it was estimated, when wastage and breakage were taken into account.[9] But it also called for *thin* plate. This was not a Pilkington speciality, although its newly-developed grinding and polishing plant provided a very promising means of making it.

At the end of 1925 the Pilkington Board, observing that Triplex had 'apparently engaged themselves to buy glass from Czechoslovakia and we have no intention of being kept out of what may be a growing trade [*sic*]' decided to approach the Triplex Company for a trial order of 5,000 sq. ft so as to be quite sure it could make the thinner plate glass.[10] The order then gained from Triplex led to closer association between the two companies and when, in November 1927, Pilkington heard that the Austin Motor Company was placing an order for 1·4m. sq. ft of Triplex – requiring over 4 m. sq. ft of glass – the Pilkington Board decided to quote a special price.[11] In the following month Pilkington bought 7,500 shares in Triplex but declined a seat on the board.[12] ICI started to stir. Mond, its chairman and joint managing director, was impressed by the way Triplex shares had risen. Since his company had interests in plastics and, as we have seen, had received an offer of the Libby-Owens glassmaking process, why did it not go into safety glass? ICI, however pursued its peaceful policy of not antagonising major customers.[13] Meanwhile Triplex grew fast. It built a second factory at Willesden in 1927 and acquired the former Baker Precision Works at King's Norton, Birmingham. With a floor space of 77,000 sq. ft, this was half as big again as the two Willesden works put together. In 1928 a further 18 acres were acquired at King's Norton for further expansion. By 1929 there were four Triplex factory units on the site.[14]

It was the Austin Motor Company's large order at the end of 1927 that gave rise to what came to be called the 'splinterless' boom. That company took the important decision to make Triplex safety glass windscreens a standard item in all its cars and also to use TSG in some of the other windows of its saloon models. In return it received preferential terms from Triplex – 6d per sq. ft less than any other customer apart from Morris – and a prior claim on the whole of King's Norton's output.[15] The agreement between the two companies, signed on 7 December 1927, was followed, on 25 January 1928, by a three-year agreement between Triplex and Pilkington whereby Triplex agreed to take at least 75 per cent of its plate glass from St Helens at a price 15 per cent below that quoted by Pilkington to any other safety glass manufacturer.[16] The preamble specifically stated that this was to compensate Pilkington for its loss of sales to the motor trade; from the time of its first major contract, that is to say, Triplex policy was to collaborate with its major supplier of plate glass rather than to antagonise it and run the risk of encouraging the suppliers of glass themselves to become safety glass manufacturers. Here the British glass industry took a different course from the American. In the United States the Pittsburgh Plate Glass Company had already joined forces with Dupont to manufacture laminated safety glass, and in 1931, when PPG bought out Dupont's interest, the Duplate Corporation became a PPG subsidiary. In the same year, Libbey-Owens-Ford bought out the American Triplex Company and cross-licensing arrangements were made with PPG. The two plate glass giants saw to it that only plate glass was used for safety glass manufacture in America.[17]

Morris Motors of Oxford, then the largest of Britain's car makers and responsible for a third of Britain's output in 1928,[18] were not prepared to look on idly while their great rival, Austin, gained an advantage over them. Morris himself left it until the very end of May 1928 before coming to terms with Triplex for the 1928/9 models and drove a hard bargain. He chose the cheaper Triplex sheet glass and then for only a quarter of his cars. Triplex lost money on the contract.[19] At the same time, operating through Westminster Bank Nominees, Morris took advantage of the issue of new shares to finance the expansion at King's Norton to secure a majority shareholding in the company. He bought a large block of shares in the middle of 1928 and later on in 1929 acquired a further 45,000. By December 1929 he held 114,000 altogether, Clare, the next largest share-holder, owning only 20,000.[20] All this was done with extreme secrecy, not even Clare being told of the anonymous purchaser's identity. Morris was represented by Graham Cunningham, the only person outside the bank aware of his identity. Cunningham was a 36-year old solicitor in the City firm of Parson, Lee and Company, and a specialist in industrial law. He quickly became a powerful figure in Triplex, was co-opted to the Board in April 1929 and in the following December became managing director. Morris, having secured his immediate objective and satisfied him-self that Triplex would not discriminate against his company, sold out gradually during the 1930s.[21] (Sir) Graham Cunningham, however, remained managing director of Triplex until 1960 and was also its chair-man from 1935 until 1961.

In retrospect, Pilkington itself would have done well to have gained control of Triplex, not in 1928/9 when Morris was doing so expensively at a time of high share prices but a few years earlier while the company was still small and before its great expansion. It was then already the leading safety glass manufacturer in Britain, and its position was to be greatly strengthened when, in February 1929, Lyttleton and Wilson filed the autoclave patent on its behalf.[22] (This device made possible a number of simultaneous laminations in the same vessel, thereby reducing production costs.) On the other hand, if Pilkington had gained control of Triplex before Triplex's rapid growth, it would have been involved in raising large amounts of capital to expand safety glass manufacture in and after 1927 when its own sheet glassworks had become unprofitable and was likely to need an injection of capital.

Despite these difficulties, Pilkington nevertheless seized the opportunity, in 1929, to collaborate more closely with Triplex by forming a joint sub-sidiary, Triplex (Northern) Ltd, to build and operate a safety glass factory at St Helens. Pilkington took the initiative in this matter[23] and the decision to do so came soon after the Board had been discussing the possibility of investing in a Canadian Triplex venture.[24] The aim was to pool the exper-tise of the two parents, and an essential part of the scheme was that Pilkington should find outlets for safety glass 'in new directions outside the motorcar trade'. Triplex (Northern) was also licensed to make Triplex elsewhere in the world, apart from those countries on the continent of Europe where licences had already been granted, and North and South America. This, as will be seen, was an important function of the new company and was understood to be so from the outset; indeed, the original intention had been to call it Imperial Triplex.[25] In planning the new factory, Pilkington persuaded its partner to think on a rather larger scale than had been originally intended, in terms of £100,000 capital rather than £50,000, and with a capacity of 1 m. sq. ft per year.[26] Pilkington was to provide 51 per cent of this capital and be responsible for the management. The new company was to be allowed 25 per cent of Triplex's UK market up to 1 m. sq. ft, but pricing policy was to remain with the main Triplex Board so far as home sales were concerned, there being joint consultation on exports.[27]

By July 1929 the details of the new factory, to be built on a green field site at Eccleston, St Helens, on Pilkington land just beyond the existing built-up area of the town, were under discussion and an initial expenditure of £30,000 was approved.[28] When the Triplex company, hard pressed with other heavy expenditure at King's Norton, was unable to meet its 49 per cent liability, Pilkington chose to advance a loan rather than take more Triplex shares;[29] and, at the same time, the company took the opportunity to try to discover more about the secret majority shareholder (which it failed to do) and his nominee on the Triplex Board.[30] The company also approached ICI to enlist its help in improving the quality of the celluloid interlayer supplied by British Xylonite which was more liable to discoloration than the product imported from Germany. ICI responded by setting up a technical committee composed of representatives from British Xylonite and Triplex, as well as Pilkington and themselves, to investigate this matter.[31] Better quality celluloid was obtained, though further progress in this direction had to await the introduction of cellulose acetate in 1936.[32]

The new works at Eccleston, designed in the drawing office at Cowley Hill and managed by Lewis Jex-Blake Forbes, an Edinburgh engineering graduate who had been working for Pilkington since 1921, with a staff also largely drawn from Cowley Hill, began to produce Triplex in April 1930.[33] By then, however, more safety glass was being made with cheaper sheet glass than with the more expensive plate upon which Pilkington depended. The 'splinterless' boom had given encouragement to other safety glass manufacturers, more than 20 of them altogether, including Protectoglass and British Indestructo, the Lancegaye Safety Glass Company (formed in 1928 from money won from backing a horse of that name), Safetex and Splintex.[34] Greater competition drove down prices as the world depression deepened and the motor manufacturers were keen to cut every penny they could from the cost of their popular models. Sheet Triplex cost 3s 6d per sq. ft to make; the plate glass variety more than twice as much.[35] While the Triplex company preferred to sell the more expensive product, the market demanded the cheaper, and if Triplex did not supply it, its rivals would. The Eccleston factory, therefore, produced at the outset mainly sheet Triplex; £2,346 of it in July 1930, for instance, and only £400 worth made from plate glass.[36] What was worse, since Pilkington was not yet making its own flat drawn glass, Belgian or Czechoslovakian sheet glass had to be used.[37]

The position changed from the end of 1931, however, when the PPG machines came into production at St Helens. By then, too, the remaining motor manufacturers who had not fitted safety glass windscreens were doing so in anticipation of government regulations making them compulsory in new cars, which came into force on 1 January 1932. (These regulations were to apply to all vehicles, including those made before 1932, from the beginning of 1937.)[38] Even more significant for Pilkington was the introduction of a new sort of safety glass which did not depend upon lamination and therefore did not discriminate so much against the more expensive plate glass. With this new process it now became possible to make a square foot of safety glass from little more than a square foot of thicker polished plate instead of from three times as much of thinner substance – with three times as much costly grinding and polishing. Pilkington's recent alliance with the continental Plate Glass Convention now paid an unexpected dividend.

It had long been known that glass could be made harder, or tempered, by quenching it in hot oil after it had just set; glass boiler gauges, for instance, were made in this way. But nobody had previously been able to toughen whole pieces of flat glass. This was now achieved by an invention patented by the Compagnies Réunis des Glaces at Verres Spéciaux du Nord de la France (Boussois) in 1928 and four others patented by St Gobain in 1929.

It consisted of heating pieces of flat glass, suspended by tongs from a carrying bar, in an electric furnace up to softening point, about 650°C. The glass was then removed from the furnace and both sides blown upon by jets of compressed air. The outer skin of the glass contracted quickly; the inside more slowly, glass being a poor conductor of heat. Then, as the inside tried to contract, it was resisted by the outer skin, now set hard. Two outside layers in compression were separated by an inner layer in tension. The resistance of the tempered (or toughened) glass to thermal or mechanical shock was four or five times greater than that of ordinary glass; and when the glass was eventually broken, it shattered into many small fragments the size of crystals. There were no jagged edges.

Cecil Pilkington discussed this *verre trempé* with the French during one of his visits to Maubeuge in September 1930 and the company decided, later that month, to secure the British rights to the process. This was achieved by the end of October and Triplex was informed.[39] In May 1931 Pilkington signed an agreement with the two French companies which gave it exclusive rights to make and sell tempered glass both in Britain and Ireland and in the British Commonwealth on payment of a ten per cent royalty.[40]

The new toughened safety glass, for which the trade mark 'Armourplate' was filed, not only gave Pilkington a product which it could itself sell outside the motor trade but also helped it in further negotiations with Triplex. That company's three-year agreement to take 75 per cent of its plate glass from Pilkington ran out in January 1931, and by then its total plate glass purchases were considerably less than they had been previously because of the large-scale switch to the cheaper Sheet Triplex. Toughened plate glass, however, was likely to sell at about the same price as this cheaper laminated product. In negotiating the new agreement Pilkington's aim, therefore, was to sub-licence toughened plate glass manufacture (which would ensure higher plate glass sales) in return for the new product being given a share of the total Triplex quota. By August 1931 these negotiations were moving towards a Triplex (Northern) concentration upon toughened glass, and Graham Cunningham suggested that this should be sold to the trade as Triplex Toughened.[41] Even closer collaboration was eventually reached in two separate agreements.

By the first of these, signed on 6 November 1931, Pilkington sublicensed Triplex (Northern) to make toughened glass on the same terms as it had itself received from the French on condition that it supplied all the glass which was used in the process and on the most favourable terms. Pilkington was to receive 3 per cent on the net sales of Triplex Toughened to the motor industry in all markets, and the parent Triplex company was to receive 3 per cent on laminated glass sold to its customers in the home market.[42] The second agreement, signed on the following day, this time between Pilkington and Triplex itself, set up a four-man sales committee (two from each side) which was to meet once every four weeks to decide the price and selling conditions of both toughened and laminated glass. Orders were to be allocated to Willesden, King's Norton and Eccleston 'as far as possible to suit their requirements'; Willesden and King's Norton were to concentrate upon laminated glass and Eccleston upon toughened. Export orders for both types of glass were to go to Eccleston, which was not to be deprived of orders for laminated glass until it was working to full capacity on toughened. All Triplex factories were to buy Pilkington glass so long as Pilkington could match foreign competitors on price and delivery. Finally, from 1 January 1932 all Triplex and Triplex (Northern) profits were to be divided in the proportion of two-thirds to Triplex and

N

one-third to Triplex (Northern).[43] This last arrangement did not prove very satisfactory, however, and from 1 July 1933 the previous market division was restored: three-quarters to Triplex and one-quarter to Triplex (Northern) but without the 1 m. sq. ft limit upon the latter's output.[44]

The launching of the new toughened glass on the British motor market was far from simple and straightforward. The stresses within the glass sometimes caused it to break with a frighteningly loud report even when stored within the stillness of a warehouse, far from any mechanical shocks. Scotland Yard turned it down initially, and Austin would fit it only in export models.[45] Morris Motors refused to accept it at all, considering it 'a dangerous material'. They feared that, if it continued to be sold as Triplex Toughened, it would discredit laminated Triplex itself.[46] The manufacturers took this advice and marketed it for the time being only as Armourplate. But by January 1933, by which time a more consistently stable product was produced and the critics had been satisfied about its safety, it was finally launched upon the market as Triplex Toughened, with its own brand mark stamped on the glass.[47] The product, commended by its cheapness, then soon established itself. In the middle of 1933 Triplex was granted a sub-licence to manufacture toughened glass at King's Norton[48] and there was talk of closing the laminated department at Eccleston.[49] A year later more toughened than laminated Triplex was being sold from the Triplex factories.[50] Eccleston, which had produced just over 67,000 sq. ft of toughened in the second half of 1932 (together with 111,121 sq. ft of Sheet Triplex and a mere 19,721 sq. ft of Plate Triplex), made 789,000 sq. ft of it in the first half of 1934 and 992,115 sq. ft in the second half of 1935. The manufacturing cost in the meantime had fallen from 3s 8½d to 2s 2d. The average selling price in 1934 and 1936 was a fraction over 3s.[51] Curved toughened glass also began to be manufactured at Eccleston as streamlining was introduced into car design.[52] As Table 48 shows, Pilkington's gain from toughened glass came from the growing sales of plate glass to safety glass factories and to the motor trade after the setback of 1930–2 rather than from the income derived from Triplex (Northern). The fall in plate glass sales in 1938, caused by the switch to thick drawn sheet glass as well as to the general downturn in industrial activity in the country as a whole, will be discussed later in the chapter.

Increasing motor industry demand for plate glass was of paramount importance to Pilkington during the 1930s, for sales to all other sources at home remained stationary at about 10 m. sq. ft per year, and exports, as will be seen from Table 34 on p. 251, moved gently downwards from 10 m. sq. ft to under 5 m. sq. ft. More foreign plate glass, however, was sold

TABLE 48

PILKINGTON INCOME FROM TRIPLEX (NORTHERN) SALES OF GLASS TO SAFETY GLASS MANUFACTURERS AND THE MOTOR TRADE, TOTAL HOME SALES AND IMPORTS OF PLATE AND SHEET GLASS, 1929–38

'000 sq. ft

	Pilkington income from Triplex (Northern)	Plate Glass			Sheet Glass		
		Sales to SGM and MT	Total Pilkington Home Sales	Imports	Sales to SGM and MT	Total Pilkington Home Sales	Imports
	£						
1929	nil	3,818	14,852	10,351	322	39,298	88,786
1930	nil	2,247	13,111	7,966	405	37,946	93,155
1931	nil	1,643	12,264	10,926	311	34,304	101,156
1932	nil	1,456	10,525	8,888	1,927	48,406	84,214
1933	nil	2,516	12,572	9,187	4,617	70,483	71,944
1934	24,352*	5,322	15,449	10,087	1,611	75,581	88,885
1935	16,542	7,139	17,434	11,165	1,453	75,744	90,093
1936	9,331	7,794	18,337	12,523	1,752	73,001	99,549
1937	10,441	8,438	19,088	12,081	2,161	84,977	94,881
1938	nil	4,681	13,949	9,692	3,884	88,571	78,639

*Includes repayment of capital

Source: Pilkington Statistical Department and Pilkington Accounts. The authorities' definition of imported plate glass was changed in 1935 to include certain categories of sheet glass. The figures given here for 1935–8 are those for plate glass imports only used in negotiations with the Convention in 1938–9.[53]

on the home market, despite the introduction of a ten per cent import duty in March 1932 (soon raised to 15 per cent).

Pilkington's failure to seize a larger share of the non-safety glass home market, as it was allowed to do by its agreement of 1929 with the Plate Glass Convention – it was free to exploit the British and Irish market but the continentals were subject to a sales quota – is explicable partly in terms of the guaranteed import quantum under that agreement and partly in terms of the gradual encroachment of thick drawn sheet, which will be considered presently. There was no question of the company not continuing to be technically very progressive and enterprising in plate glass. The continuous grinding and polishing machines were speeded up, and grinding and polishing costs were further reduced: from over 3d per sq. ft at the end of the 1920s to about $2\frac{1}{2}$d per sq. ft in the mid-30s.[*][54] Even more important, the company was developing a machine which would grind both sides of the ribbon of plate glass simultaneously. This was a vital stride forward towards continuous production, for the ribbon of glass, as it emerged from the annealing lehr, could be fed straight through the twin grinder. If a twin polisher could also be perfected, the process would be continuous throughout.

F.B. Waldron, Harris Griffin and their assistants at Cowley Hill were already at work on this development in the middle 1920s. On 6 August 1926 Cozens-Hardy, Weeks and LeMare watched a 48-inch ribbon of glass passing from the lehr at 15 inches per minute through two pairs of continuous grinding heads mounted on a rough framework. The experiment continued for 20 minutes without a break. It was considered promising and £1,000 was voted for more simple experiments,[56] followed in November 1927 by £10,500 for a further trial using eight double heads.[57] This machine began work on 29 October 1929 with 48-inch wide, 250-inch long strips of glass which were passed to and fro through it. It showed that glass could be produced which was remarkable for its parallel

*A Bicheroux machine was installed at Cowley Hill in 1930–1, at a cost of about £60,000, to deal with special orders for large sizes of plate glass. This was based on the old pot furnace and casting table principle but tipped the molten glass down a gradient through double rollers, 'allowing the plate to pass forward on to a moving car, cutting the plate while still soft, and transferring the individual plates in this way, by means of the travelling car, direct into the annealing furnace'. This important invention allowed the glass to be cast much more thinly and therefore economised in grinding and polishing. A longer lehr was used, and in it the rollers could be reversed, 'this to-and-fro movement being arranged to assist in maintaining a greater degree of uniformity of temperature in the region of the lehr occupied by such substantial lengths'. Pilkington had put in a Bicheroux machine just before the First World War but had subsequently given it up because it was not then a good commercial proposition. By the mid-1920s, however, it had been further developed, and the need for an improved method of making plate glass of sizes which the continuous process could not do, made it an attractive alternative to the former process.[55]

surfaces.[58] The problems to be surmounted before the machine could achieve good results over a long period were considerable, however, because the grinding heads were themselves being worn down all the time by the abrasives, and the lower ones had to support the glass as well as grind its lower surface. Sufficient progress had nevertheless been made with the twin grinder by 1932 for work to concentrate upon a twin polisher,[59] and in the following year the directors decided that the time had arrived to authorise a production machine. They voted £58,881 for a twin grinder to be built at Doncaster where final development work could be continued with least interference to production. This first commercial model processed a 60-inch ribbon through 14 pairs of grinding heads.[60] A machine was soon put in hand for Cowley Hill, too, this time to take a 100-inch ribbon. The Doncaster twin was started up on 31 March 1937 but gave some trouble and the sale of twin-ground plate glass did not begin until March 1938.[61] A satisfactory twin polisher was never developed, though experimental work continued until the later 1940s. The difficulty here was that there was no water to disperse the heat that was generated. The twin-ground glass therefore had to be polished, one side at a time, on continuous polishers as before.

The manufacture of plate glass was now almost, but not quite, a continuous process. The whole plant was a remarkable feat of engineering of which the company was exceptionally proud. Stretched out in a line of furnace, lehr and twin, it was no less than 1,400 ft long which, as contemporaries were not slow to observe, was 70 feet longer than the *Queen Mary*, the largest ship afloat. It was, however, expensive in space and energy. At first, in the months immediately before the war, the speeds at which it could be run did not reduce production costs. It did, however, make glass of unexcelled quality, for such remarkable parallel surfaces were hitherto unknown. It was a machine which foreign competitors wished to use and it strengthened Pilkington's hand in the world of industrial diplomacy.

In plate glass manufacture, as elsewhere, events in the United States had their effects in Europe. The American industry had flourished greatly during the 1920s because of intense demand from both the motor and building industries there. Between 1913 and 1929 American manufacturers of plate glass had doubled their output and increased their share of world production from a third to a half.[62] European exporters of plate glass, including Pilkington as we have seen, had been able to participate in this American boom; but between 1929 and 1932 American output of

1   Mixing Room
2   Furnace Hall
3   Gas Producers
4   Lehr
5   Tank Lehrs
6   Disc Grinding & Polishing
7   Matching Room
8   Continuous Grinding &
    Polishing
9   Rouge Plant
10 Warehouses & Stock
    Rooms
11 Bevelling Rooms
12 Silvering Rooms
13 Embossing Rooms
14 Toughening Dept.
15 Reservoirs
16 Power Station
17 Pot Rooms & Arches
18 Office
19 Garage
20 Maintenance & Stores
21 Laboratory
22 Canteen
23 Surgeries
24 Albert St. Lodge
25 City Rd. Lodge
26 Windle Sand Wash
27 Sand Lodges
28 Goliath Crane

N

L M.& S.RY.

Washway Lane

Liverpool Corporation Water Main

Allotments

Football Ground

Windle City

Plan 10 Pilkington Brothers Ltd Plate Works in 1938

cars tumbled from nearly four and a half to little more than one million per year and building activity fell away even more sharply.[63] By 1932 Belgian plate glass exports to the United States were only one-tenth of the volume they had been in 1928.[64] Meanwhile the American manufacturers sought to offset their reduced sales at home by increased exports; and the Pittsburgh Plate Glass Co.'s control of the Courcelles works in Belgium gave it added strength.

Courcelles was not prepared to collaborate with the Convention and was therefore shut out of most of the British market, for after Pilkington had reached agreement with the Convention, in June 1929, the British glass merchants were asked to sign fidelity agreements by which they promised, in return for preferential discounts, not to buy from any source apart from Pilkington or the Convention, and not to sell thick drawn sheet glass.[65] Most of the merchants gave this undertaking and the Belgians were not slow to appreciate what this would mean to them. De Longueville of the Union Commerciale des Glaceries Belges wrote to Pilkington in April 1930:

If Courcelles is limited in England, they will revert to Belgium and in all the export countries the portion they would sell . . . in England. . . You are not unaware that for the moment the quantities of orders received are diminishing instead of increasing and moreover Courcelles does not cease to work and takes orders in very many markets, with concessions more and more serious. Our Works will not be able to tolerate for long such a state of things.[66]

Pilkington's reply showed that the company realised the advisability of relaxing the fidelity agreements in order to allow Courcelles glass to be sold to former customers.[67] The need for the Convention to come to terms with the Americans themselves, now reduced to two main manufacturers, Pittsburgh Plate Glass and Libbey-Owens-Ford, was already becoming clear.

As the depression deepened and American exports became a matter for greater concern in Europe, the Convention manufacturers sought to strengthen their bargaining position. St Gobain already had interests with Saint-Roch in America at Blue Ridge, Kingsport, Tennessee, where sheet and rolled glasses were made from 1927 and polished plate from 1929; and it had also, with the Belgians, formed the Franklin Glass Corporation in 1927 as an import-export agency. In 1932 Franklin bought the bankrupt works of the Standard Plate Glass Co. at Butler, Pa. Pilkington, for its part, also had its contribution to make, for it had long-standing links with Pittsburgh Plate Glass, and the Americans appreciated its technical ascendancy in this branch of the industry: the Flow process came into the negotiations early in 1933, for instance.[68] The company was also well established commercially in Canada and, from his vantage point there, J.E.Harrison continued to act as informant and go-between.

In June 1933 discussions took place during a visit of the Americans to Europe, but a few months later the heavy export shipments from the United States were still causing serious concern.[69] In the following spring, Gentil (St Gobain), Poncelet (Glaver) and Cozens-Hardy, accompanied by Tunnock, went to America for further talks. Agreement between the American and European manufacturers was reached on 2 May 1934. They contracted to divide all exports of plate glass to markets outside the United States in the proportions of approximately 20 per cent to the Americans and 80 per cent to the Europeans. In Canada, however, thin glass for laminating was not to be counted in this total, and the Americans were to be allowed to sell there one-third of the combined European and American total. Courcelles was in future to collaborate with the Convention, machinery was to be set up for a regular exchange of statistics at monthly or other agreed intervals and, if either party failed to reach its quota, it was to be allowed to sell at a discount in order to make up all arrears. The agreement as a whole was to last until the end of 1938 and thereafter from year to year.[70] In fact, fears that it might contravene the American anti-trust laws led to the setting up of a Plate Glass Export Corporation (Pittsburgh, Libbey-Owens-Ford and Franklin) and the signing of a new agreement on the same terms with this body on 31 December 1935.[71]

The bringing into line of Courcelles was soon to be followed by the disposal and closure of Maubeuge. This was part of further rationalisation in continental Europe where production came to be concentrated in fewer, better-equipped works. By the mid-1930s, for instance, the two Belgian producers, Glaver and Glaceries de la Sambre, each operated only one factory.[72] Pilkington was also very dissatisfied with the way the 1929 agreement was working so far as the British market was concerned. The Convention was not selling its permitted quota in Britain and had to be compensated for this. Pilkington had already decided by October 1932 that, if it could obtain a more favourable settlement, it would, given adequate compensation, be prepared to part with Maubeuge, which it wholly owned.[73] In February 1933 the two parties reached a temporary agreement, with a new compensation clause, but it was to last for that year only 'or alternatively until the American question is settled'.[74] But later in 1934, after the treaty with the Americans had been signed, Pilkington was still no nearer a permanent settlement with the Convention. There was even talk of another *période de lutte*.[75]

Instead of offering to close Maubeuge, Pilkington now changed its tactics and went through the warlike motions of preparing to increase its manufacturing capacity there. It also brought into the negotiations a tank-made opal glass (this sort was still usually made from pots) known by the name of its American parent, Vitrolite. Pilkington had come to terms with Vitrolite in April 1932[76] and had then taken over its failing British licensee which had been making the product at Harlesden since 1925. A new British Vitrolite Company was set up, and plant was installed at Pilkington's Ravenhead and Doncaster works, production soon being concentrated at the latter.[77] Considerable publicity was gained for the new product when it was used to line the walls of the Mersey Tunnel, opened in 1934. In March of that year Pilkington decided that Vitrolite had profitable sales prospects in France and believed that from this the continentals 'might also conclude that our next step would be to manufacture Vitrolite at Maubeuge and that therefore their acquisition of Maubeuge would be more desirable'.[78] St Gobain was soon seeking a Vitrolite licence for France; and Pilkington took the opportunity to rattle its sabre rather more noisily by making arrangements for the installation at Maubeuge of a continuous grinder and a toughening plant. Some of the machinery for the grinder was actually sent there.[79]

This diplomatic pressure at last produced a result. Agreement for the sale of Maubeuge to St Gobain was signed on 24 May 1935 and the works were then closed. The first 30 per cent of Pilkington's 5,000 Maubeuge shares were sold for £300,000 on signature of the agreement. A further 50 per cent were to be sold in equal instalments on 1 April of the following four years at a price which would take account of any increased profits resulting from the sale of the Maubeuge quota and any change in the exchange rate of the franc. The remaining 20 per cent of the shares could be sold for cash in 1940 or 1941 unless Pilkington wished to hold on to them. (This timetable was subsequently speeded up.) In a supplemental agreement of the same date the two companies agreed not to build, or participate in, factories in each other's territories for 25 years nor, for 15, 'to take or support any aggressive or unfriendly action against the other'.[80] The new alliance was further cemented in 1937 when Pilkington licensed its twin grinder to St Gobain on very favourable terms: a non-exclusive licence for France and her territories and an exclusive licence for Germany, Italy, and Spain and territories for a lump sum of £80,000 (£20,000 of which went to Heuze) plus royalties of a farthing per sq. ft to be reduced by 25 per cent if a successful twin polisher should not be forthcoming.[81] No further licences of this important invention were issued until 1950.

In view of Pilkington's difficulty, despite its technical advantages, in increasing the volume of its home sales of plate glass except to the motor trade, its success in selling much more sheet glass than ever on the home market after 1933 (Table 36 p. 254) is tribute indeed to the effective way in which it exploited the new PPG machines – and exploited its diplomatic expertise. As the level of housebuilding rose to boom proportions after 1932[82], Pilkington was able to win a greater share of the market in the sheet glass needed to glaze these buildings. The volume of imports, more than twice Pilkington's home sales footage both just before 1914 and during the mid-1920s, later rising to a peak three times as high, fell back to only a third more by the mid-1930s; and in 1938, for the first time apart from the war years, more Pilkington than foreign sheet glass was sold in the United Kingdom. Pilkington, like British industry in general, came to depend much more on the home market. Exports never reached their pre-1914 heights, although they rose steadily in volume in the 1930s. Taken together, however, the home and export footage was greater than it had ever been.

These quantity sales were achieved in such a highly competitive situation only by aggressively cutting prices to the point where manufacturing profit was no higher than it had been when Pilkington had lower sales and a smaller share of the market. Indeed, as Table 49 shows, the company did not begin to turn loss into regular profit on its sheet glassmaking operations until after September 1934, and even this relatively modest return almost dwindled away in the year ended March 1938 when the sales volume reached new heights. In this respect, sheet glass manufacture contrasted sharply with plate which continued to sell steadily to the top end of the non-motor market (at the expense of encouraging lower-priced imports) but produced a much more satisfactory return. Even plate glass, however, was much less profitable in and after 1937 when, as will be seen shortly, thick drawn sheet was to become more widely used. Only cast glass, included here for comparison but to be considered later, reported increasing manufacturing profits at the end of the 1930s. This rather disappointing financial result from sheet glass was obtained despite the cutting of production costs on the PPG machines to about $1\frac{1}{2}$d per sq. ft by late 1934, and despite sustained efforts to reach agreement with foreign sheet glass manufacturers to curb shipments to Britain.

The four 94-inch PPG machines which, as we saw, came into use at No. 7 tank in November 1931, and the re-started pioneer at No. 10, were soon followed by nine others of the same width. By October 1932 annual capacity was over 58 m. sq. ft and plans were being made to put in four 132-inch machines, the largest in the world. (They subsequently proved fickle to handle and two of them were changed to 94-inch in 1935.)

TABLE 49
PILKINGTON MANUFACTURING PROFIT ON
SHEET, PLATE AND CAST GLASS MANUFACTURE
(EXCLUDING STOCK ADJUSTMENTS) 1931–9
£'000

Half Year Ended	Sheet	Plate	Cast
Sept 1931	− 36	180	60
Mar 1932	4	242	− 5
Sept 1932	− 40	114	47
Mar 1933	− 11	152	38
Sept 1933	− 3	135	44
Mar 1934	2	221	41
Sept 1934	− 52	195	49
Mar 1935	32	250	14
Sept 1935	61	224	58
Mar 1936	64	187	61
Sept 1936	74	155	81
Mar 1937	112	266	104
Sept 1937	12	161	91
Mar 1938	3	80	77
Sept 1938	52	124	104
Mar 1939	38	86	109
Sept 1939	19	181	166

Source: Pilkington Accounts

Chances did not take up the two machines offered them and, by October
1933, Pilkington, having installed more than the 12 required by the PPG
agreement, secured the exclusive British rights. Under J.B.Watt's* able
direction, the company considerably improved the process. It gained the
reputation of being its most efficient operator in Europe and it soon became
the largest user of PPG machinery outside the USA. By July 1934, thin,
1·2 mm, glass was being made frequently on an 80-inch machine;
Pilkington had, indeed, produced 120,000 sq. ft of it during the previous
week.[83] In that year Sheet Works at St Helens manufactured 75 m. sq. ft

*J.B.Watt, who had successfully introduced the PPG machines (pp. 314-315), was
appointed production manager and deputy general manager of Sheet Works in September
1935 at a salary of £1,500 per year. In 1938 he became a local director and was put in
charge of all sheet glass production as general manager at Sheet Works. He was to become a
sub-director in 1949 and a director in 1950. When he retired from the Executive Committee
in January 1961, he had served the company for 46½ years. He was to remain on the Board
for another ten in a non-executive capacity.

of glass of all substances. To this the Fourcault capacity of the Queenborough Works on the Isle of Sheppey in Kent had by then been added, raising the total Pilkington output by about 25 per cent.[84]

The Queenborough Works (see pp. 287, 310), closed in 1929, were restarted in October 1932 after extensive repairs and improvement and under the competent management of Octave Jacqmain. An experienced glassmaker then nearing his sixtieth birthday, he had previously supervised the erection of the Libbey-Owens plant at Moll in Belgium. F.P. Jones, the Canadian chairman of Queenborough's owners, Sheet Glass Limited, was in touch with Pilkington earlier that year about the possibility of reaching a marketing arrangement. The Executive Committee went further and agreed in April that the time had come to acquire Queenborough if reasonable terms could be reached.[85] Pilkington was talking to Jones in May,[86] and Jacqmain visited St Helens – to try to recruit labour as well as to visit the company – at the beginning of June.[87] These negotiations, however, then came to nothing; but Queenborough did not undercut St Helens in price when glass began to be made there again in October.[88] Sheet Glass Limited reported a loss of £75,000 on the calendar year and takeover negotiations were resumed in April 1933. This time agreement was soon reached. Pilkington agreed to go up to Jones's price, £260,000, and the works were acquired in the following month.[89] The new, wholly-owned subsidiary was controlled from St Helens and Pilkington in due course sent down its own manager to take charge. The cost of making glass on the six Fourcault machines there, 2·5d per sq. ft immediately after the takeover, had been reduced to 1·6d by the end of 1935.[90]

Pilkington acquired Queenborough before the factory had been able to establish itself and become a serious rival. The Belgian manufacturers, too, were now prepared to discuss the possibility of reducing competition in the British market, a policy which was strongly encouraged by the British government at that time. As will be seen from graph 12 on page 293, the bank-induced rationalisation of the Belgian sheet glass industry and the formation of its own selling agencies had resulted in a modest price rise in the British market during the worst of the depression, from the very low level reached in 1928–9. The emergence of the two Belgian window glassmaking groups, UVMB in 1930 and Glaver in 1932, their 70 : 30 world market-sharing agreement (p. 316) and the plate glassmaking connections of both of them – St Gobain had a stake, through Saint-Roch, in a number of UVMB companies, for instance, and Glaver was the product of a merger between three plate glass concerns and the Libbey-Owens Compagnie Internationale – gave Pilkington the chance to open negotiations.

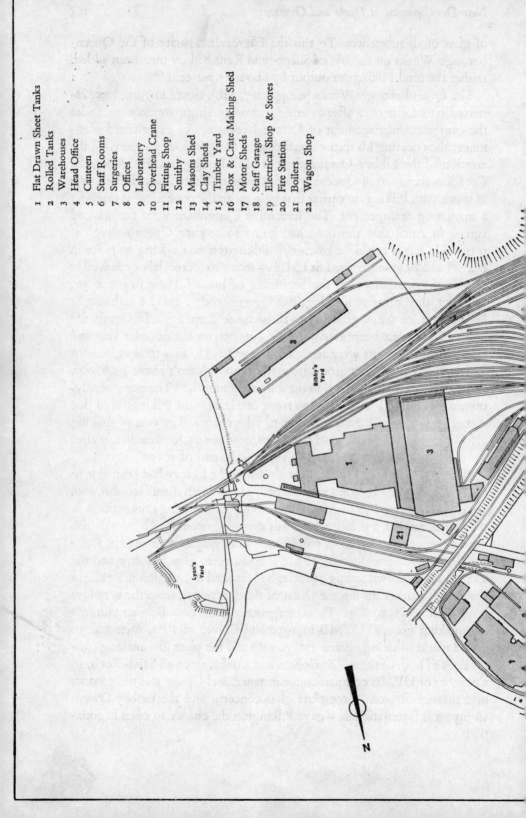

1 Flat Drawn Sheet Tanks
2 Rolled Tanks
3 Warehouses
4 Head Office
5 Canteen
6 Staff Rooms
7 Surgeries
8 Offices
9 Laboratory
10 Overhead Crane
11 Fitting Shop
12 Smithy
13 Masons Shed
14 Clay Sheds
15 Timber Yard
16 Box & Crate Making Shed
17 Motor Sheds
18 Staff Garage
19 Electrical Shop & Stores
20 Fire Station
21 Boilers
22 Wagon Shop

Bibby's Yard

Lyon's Yard

N

Plan 11 Pilkington Brothers Ltd Sheet and Rolled Works in 1936

Pilkington's Executive Committee started to jockey for position in September 1932 by deciding to obtain an immediate footing in as many export markets as possible and to increase its share of the home market.[91] In May 1933 the Executive agreed to use a forthcoming meeting of the Plate Glass Convention to inform the interested parties that Pilkington was to raise its sheet glass prices.[92] This overture apparently bore fruit, for the Executive was told in July that the continentals had increased their prices by 5 per cent.[93] From this beginning Cozens-Hardy pressed on farther. In September a letter was sent to Poncelet of Glaver asking for sheet glass sales talks 'because the present low prices prevent the manufacturers from making as much profit as they might otherwise do'. As a basis for discussion it was suggested that imports should be limited to 50 m. sq. ft per annum and prices put up in stages by 20 per cent.[94] A meeting took place in Brussels in October at which there was talk of trying to reach a world agreement regulating sheet glass sales, or, failing that, a partial agreement. Poncelet promised to keep Pilkington informed of endeavours then being made to form a European cartel.[95] Although such a grand design was premature, these negotiations did for the time being achieve positive results. Imports in 1933, at 72 m. sq. ft, were considerably lower than they had been in previous years, and Pilkington's home sales took a great leap upwards and almost reached that level; yet, as has been seen, the company was still not making money on its sheet glass. Worse was to follow, for the higher prices drew in imports from continental producers outside the major groups, notably Estonians, and, from February 1934, a newcomer in Belgium, the Verreries des Piges with six Fourcault machines.[96] Imports in that year were much higher and Pilkington's sheet glass manufacture plunged deeply into the red.

The company's reaction to this new challenge was to increase its diplomatic activity in order to secure the continentals' collaboration in cutting their exports to Britain of sheet glass, and particularly of thick drawn sheet. Cozens-Hardy, usually accompanied by Harry Pilkington and Tunnock, started a round of meetings in Paris on 26 May 1934 which took them during the following 12 months not only to Belgium but also to Cologne to confer with the German group and to Prague to meet representatives of the Bohemian Sheet Glass Corporation (Vitrea).[97] In January 1935 the Germans agreed to limit their exports to Britain to 1·1 m. sq. ft (calculated on the basis of 18 oz glass) for that year only, and Vitrea to 23·75 m. sq. ft reducing to 21 m. sq. ft, plus a further 1·5 m. sq. ft of thick drawn sheet. (The agreement with Vitrea subsequently brought in an Italian manufacturer.) In February a five-year agreement was reached with the two Belgian groups (decreasing from 55 m. sq. ft in 1935 to 46 m.

sq. ft in 1939) and this was followed by another with the French in April. The Estonians were in London at the beginning of that month trying to borrow money in return for promises about exports to Britain for the duration of the loan. Their efforts were fruitless; but an agreement was reached with the Russians in October. (The final session in Moscow lasted 11 hours during which time Cozens-Hardy and Tunnock received no refreshment at all apart from a glass of vodka and a caviare sandwich.)[98]

This painstakingly-created edifice soon collapsed, for the devaluation of the Belgian franc at the end of March 1935 gave fresh life to the Verreries des Piges and also encouraged a second Belgian outsider, Gobbe-Hocque-miller, to start manufacture in the following November.[99] The other Belgian manufacturers gave notice that they could only continue their agreement with Pilkington on a year-to-year basis[100] and in October 1936 they asked for its suspension for six months. (It was formally terminated at the beginning of 1939.)[101] During the 12 months from March 1937, Pilkington's sheet glass, which had been reasonably remunerative during the previous two years while Britain's economy was more prosperous and while the glass import agreements were in force, became hardly profitable at all. During 1938, however, when imports fell in response to these more depressed circumstances, Pilkington's profits on sheet glass recovered, somewhat helped, as we shall see, by the company's decision to sell thick drawn sheet; but in 1939 they were down again in the earlier part of the year and in July the Executive Committee considered the sheet glass position 'serious'.[102] Then the war came to the rescue.

Even the relatively profitable period down to the beginning of 1937 was a mixed blessing to Pilkington, for the smell of profit brought the threat of a rival concern operating within Britain itself; another Queenborough.

Pilkington learned, at the beginning of February 1937, that Dr Eckert, a German who (to quote Cozens-Hardy's somewhat partisan opinion of him) 'spent his time trying to obtain slight alterations to other people's patents and processes and palming them off on unsuspecting firms',[103] had put forward proposals to the Board of Trade to erect two small sheet glass factories in distressed areas, one at Blaydon on Tyne and the other at Merthyr Tydfil. His company was to be capitalised at £130,000 and the government was to advance £60,000 at 4 per cent in support of the venture as it was empowered to do by the Special Area legislation.[104] Pilkington was quite taken aback by this news, and Cozens-Hardy hurried down to London and got Tom Williamson, District Secretary of the National Union of General and Municipal Workers, out of a meeting at the Ministry of Labour to persuade him to bring his influence to bear upon the St Helens Labour MP. He then went on to make his own representations to Leslie Burgin, Parliamentary Secretary at the Board of Trade. There was no difficulty in showing that Pilkington had more than enough sheet glassmaking capacity to meet the existing home demand. The point was also made that 'such a scheme would seriously disturb the international marketing arrangements which have been secured by long and difficult negotiations'.[105] It transpired, however, that the government was so committed to having a glassworks in South Wales – the needs of the North East were apparently not so pressing – that the only condition under which it would consider withdrawing support for Eckert was if Pilkington itself were to build a factory there.[106] This the company very reluctantly agreed to do, at Pontypool not at Merthyr. For this Pilkington Brothers (South Wales) Limited was formed with a share capital of £150,000, wholly owned by Pilkington Brothers Limited. The Special Areas Reconstruction Association Limited advanced £40,000, covered by debentures. The factory, operating two PPG machines, started production at the end of September 1938.[107] Its manufacturing costs during the half year March–September 1939 were 1·9d per sq. ft.[108] Both Queenborough and Pontypool were then making substantial losses which were carried by Sheet Works at St Helens.[109]

The agreements of early 1935 with the continentals did achieve some success in checking the growth in imports of thick drawn sheet (TDS) glass which, because of its cheapness and improving quality, threatened Pilkington's increasing and profitable sales of plate glass for toughening. On the other hand, the agreement of the Belgian Fourcault manufacturers (now UVMB) with the plate glass makers, not to make TDS expired in 1934. Nevertheless, as will be seen from Table 48, Pilkington's profitable sales of plate glass for toughening went on rising until 1937. Sales of plate glass for other purposes through the trade were preserved by means of the fidelity agreements with the merchants themselves; later in 1935, 75 per cent of the Plate Glass Merchants Association's members had given an undertaking not to sell TDS in place of polished plate.[110] In 1937, however, when the 1935 agreements were breaking down, the Belgians rejected Pilkington's quota proposals. The company decided that the time had arrived to sell TDS itself, and in October it circularised the leading merchants accordingly.[111] It had then already decided to sell the product to Triplex for windscreens and asked that company if it could secure three-year contracts with the motor trade on the basis of 2s 6d per sq. ft for toughened plate and 2s per sq. ft for toughened TDS.[112] By October Eccleston was toughening smaller sizes with success, though larger ones were giving difficulty.[113] Pilkington toughened TDS was not to be sold for windscreens until July 1938.[114] As will be seen from Table 48, sales of plate glass to the motor trade were about 3 m. sq. ft lower in that year than they had been in 1936 and sales of toughened sheet only about 2 m. sq. ft higher. In the three half-years from September 1937 manufacturing profits on plate glass were much lower than they had previously been, even during the worst part of the depression.

The use of toughened plate glass in the British motor industry had been a great boon to Pilkington during the difficult years when the company had been weak in sheet glass manufacture. But this short-term advantage, important though it was, was gained at a longer-term cost. In all other countries, outside Britain and the Commonwealth, the plate glass industry had, by controlling the safety glass companies, insisted on their continuing to supply laminated safety glass for windscreens and using thin plate for the purpose. These countries continued to use large quantities of plate glass; in Britain the official recognition and successful promotion of the toughened product for larger windscreens during the early 1930s prepared the way for sales of TDS for this purpose. In 1938 sales of plate glass to the safety glass industry declined much more rapidly than did British car production.

On the other hand, however, new outlets for plate glass were beginning to appear. In 1937 Pilkington began experimental work on double-glazed units, a line of research already being pursued in the United States though apparently at that time with little success.[115] In November 1938 the recently-formed Sales Committee began to discuss the promotion of the product and at first adopted the policy of encouraging other concerns like Crittalls or Hopes to make the units rather than embarking upon large-scale commercial manufacture itself.[116] In the following year, on the very eve of the war, there is the first mention of Armourplate doors being ordered from Italy, where they had 'passed the luxury stage', for display at the Marine Engineering Exhibition. The sales committee decided to submit the Italian fittings to British brass manufacturers for competitive quotation with a view to making them widely available.[117] Meanwhile Geoffrey Pilkington, assisted by John Gloag of Pritchard, Wood and Partners, continued to advertise by Glass Age exhibitions and publications, and especially among architects, the uses and advantages of glass, particularly large and profitable panes of plate glass, for shops, offices and architect-designed houses. In 1937, 3,000 copies of a specially commissioned book about glass were ordered for distribution among architects and glass merchants. More general publicity was also embarked upon. In 1937, for instance, £3,000 was voted for the conversion of two LNER coaches for glass publicity purposes. This Glass Train not only mounted its own exhibition but also showed a film about Vitrolite, partly in colour, made at a cost of £1,350. In 1936–8 the total Pilkington advertising budget had reached about £20,000 per year.[118]

The sharp fall in Pilkington plate glass sales because of reduced motor trade demand had serious implications for its costly satellite at Doncaster, especially in view of Cowley Hill's increased efficiency. Some of Doncaster's spare space had been filled by leasing off part of the works in 1933 to Rockware,* a pressed glass syndicate specializing in containers, in which Pilkington had taken financial interest; but now the decline in plate glass sales raised new problems.

In the middle of 1938, the Executive received a paper which showed that Cowley Hill could meet nearly all the orders expected during the following 12 months. Meikle, the director responsible, urged that plate glass production at Doncaster should cease because output was out of all proportion to the capital sunk in the works.[120] In September, when it was clear that orders were to be even lower than expected, it was agreed to expedite these plans: in November 380 men had been paid off and about 220 still had to be given notice.[121] In May 1939 the decision was taken to end all grinding and polishing there within a few months.[122] Vitrolite production also stopped in 1940 and the factory, for the time being, concentrated upon munitions work and the manufacture of glass tubing.

Ravenhead, the other under-utilised factory, had been a cause of concern throughout the 1930s. Although cathedral glass was made there profitably, items produced by the miscellaneous department, such as wireless accumulators, shades, bullions and door stops, were not. Repeated inquests were held into its losses and repeated searches made for profitable lines which could be made there. Glass insulators were produced from 1932,[123] and glass bricks from 1936, the latter under licence first from Owens-Illinois and then also from the American Corning Glass Company, which caused Pilkington to take a financial stake in James Jobling & Co. Ltd of Sunderland, makers of Pyrex, who had a prior claim upon the Corning licence.[124] These additions helped to provide additional load for

---

*Cecil Pilkington had had a financial interest in the Rockware Syndicate Limited, which made pressed glass at Greenford, Middlesex, using up-to-date American methods. At the beginning of 1931, when the success of its PPG plant was not yet assured, Pilkington had told W.A. Bailey, the chairman of Rockware, that it intended to diversify into pressed glass. In the middle of 1932 the two companies had talks about the possibility of Pilkington producing this product on Rockware's behalf for sale in the north of England. It was eventually agreed, however, after considerable haggling over their price, that Pilkington should acquire 81,530 shares in the Rockware Syndicate which was to erect a pressed ware tank for bottles at Doncaster. Production began there, falteringly at first, early in 1934.[119]

the tank furnace to offset the fall in demand for accumulators, quite sharp in the early 1930s as more people bought all-mains wireless sets. The department, losing £6,000 or £7,000 a year in the later 1930s, was, however, carrying overheads nearly twice as large, and sales of glass bricks and insulators seemed promising. The directors therefore decided to keep an eye open for yet other promising products to add to the list.[125] Meanwhile it was decided to move white cathedral and prismatic glass elsewhere. Doncaster was considered but turned down in favour of Sheet Works at St Helens.[126]

Despite the Miscellaneous Department's losses, the manufacture of cathedral glass kept Ravenhead in overall surplus down to the war. The other cast glasses, rolled and wired, made at Grove Street, could also be relied upon to return a regular profit as will be seen from Table 50. The rising sales of wired glass reflected Pilkington's success in developing a new method of continuous production. This Double Flow process consisted of applying wire mesh on top of a molten ribbon of glass and a second ribbon on top of the wire, the whole sandwich then being passed through casting rollers. The new process was first used with diamond mesh in 1934,[127] shortly afterwards with hexagonal and finally with square (Georgian) mesh.[128]

Foreign competition was much weaker in cast glass than in either plate or sheet. In 1931–3, for instance, imports averaged only just over 6 m. sq. ft (most of it cathedral and figured rolled in which foreign sales amounted to about 30 per cent of the market) out of total cast glass sales in Britain of about 37 m. sq. ft. Of the British production sold at home, Pilkington was responsible for about 20 m. sq. ft and Chances for 11 m. sq. ft.[129] Since the First World War, the two companies had not competed on price and had made fidelity agreements with most of the larger British buyers.[130] Chances also had ties with St Gobain which, as has been seen (p. 205), had had a stake in their business since 1911. In October 1933 manufacturers in Belgium, Britain, France, Germany, Italy, Rumania and Spain attempted to regulate sales outside their own home markets on the basis of what had been sold between 1 January 1928 and 30 June 1933, but the attempt soon failed owing to outsider activity.[131] Individual agreements were reached in 1934, but not with the Belgians. So in September of that year the British were making plans to cut the price of some of their figured rolled patterns and were even thinking of exporting their glass to Belgium.[132] Imports rose to 10 m. sq. ft in each of the years 1934, 1935 and 1936 (Table 35, p. 252) but, apart from the half year ended March 1935, Pilkington continued to make a healthy profit from this branch of its business.

We have noticed (p. 294) that Chances, concerned about the lack of new

TABLE 50

PILKINGTON ROLLED AND WIRED GLASS OUTPUT, NET
SALES PROCEEDS AND MANUFACTURING PROFIT; AND
RAVENHEAD MANUFACTURING PROFIT, 1931–40

Half Year Ended	Output '000 sq ft		Net Sales Proceeds (£'000)	Manufacturing Profit (£'000)	Ravenhead Manufacturing Profit (£'000) whole year
	Rolled	Wired			
September 1931	1,393	3,333	150	60	
March 1932	5,985	5,424	137	− 5	52
September	3,310	2,124	126	47	
March 1933	2,853	2,578	144	38	73
September	3,105	3,478	130	44	
March 1934	2,877	3,614	127	41	1
September	5,038	4,408	160	49	
March 1935	4,160	6,663	149	14	33
September	2,090	4,785	154	58	
March 1936	2,927	5,306	172	61	33
September	4,063	4,378	186	81	
March 1937	4,532	5,587	227	104	74
September	6,476	8,464	254	91	
March 1938	8,353	6,302	231	77	63
September	3,884	7,618	240	104	
March 1939	4,569	6,866	238	109	13
September	2,069	8,408	290	166	
March 1940	2,614	12,094	385	225	− 11

Source: Pilkington Accounts

blood and capital, had discussed with Pilkington the possibility of amalgamation at the end of the war but that these talks had come to nothing.* Chances had continued to survive, despite their relatively modest size, thanks to the greater profitability of cast glass, and the business paid a good

*Even in November 1923, when the two companies were already collaborating on price in the rolled plate market and Austin Pilkington had occasion to visit Smethwick, (Sir) Hugh Chance found it worth recording in his private notebook: 'First member of his family to enter Works'.[133]

tax-free dividend: 10 per cent in 1925, 1926 and 1928, $7\frac{1}{2}$ per cent in 1927 and $9\frac{1}{2}$ per cent in 1929. This fell to 3 per cent in the trough of the depression, but rose again as business picked up, to $5\frac{1}{2}$ per cent in 1934 and to 9 per cent in 1935.[134] By then there was even more concern about the ageing family directorate and shortage of able younger members keen to enter the business. So the Board decided to take advantage of this growing prosperity to issue some preference shares to the public. Early in June 1935 Cozens-Hardy passed on the news to the Pilkington Executive that preference shares worth £100,000 were to be created, £60,000 of them to be treated as capitalised reserves and kept by the Chance family, and the remaining £40,000 to be issued to the public. (This would raise Chances' nominal capital value from £320,000 to £420,000.) The Pilkington Executive, disturbed about 'certain undesirable aspects of a public issue in connection with a glass manufacturing concern in this country' – that is to say, the publication of the company's financial affairs – decided to put in a bid for all the £40,000 preference shares.[135] (This Pilkington was in a good position to do, for, only a few days before, the company had received from St Gobain £300,000 on signature of the agreement to sell Maubeuge. Chances could hardly have chosen a more opportune moment to go partially public.) They, not surprisingly, were not prepared to sell privately, wanting to test the market. In the event, Pilkington bought as many shares as they could, but ended up with only 7,000.[136]

Further discussions took place on matters of common interest. In December there was a joint meeting of the two Boards in Birmingham at which it was decided to fix a quota for the sale of rolled glass in the British market.[137] In January 1936 this was agreed at 63 per cent to Pilkington and 37 per cent to Chances.[138] This closer collaboration led in due course to an arrangement whereby Pilkington took a large financial stake in the Smethwick company. At the end of May 1936 Pilkington agreed to buy 'at a valuation on some agreed basis' Chance ordinary shares to the nominal value of £100,000, nearly a quarter of the total.[139] It was also prepared subsequently to buy more if offered, up to £40,000 in any one year after 1938, at an agreed formula price. The shares were divided into 10s units. An offer by Pilkington in July of 40s a share for 200,000 of these was received by Walter Lucas Chance 'with some disappointment'; but, after a little telephoning, the two Boards settled for 41s.[140] The deal went through secretly, Pilkington buying in the name of Barbinder Executors Limited. (Barbinder was the telegraphic address of the London office of Cooper Brothers, Pilkington's auditors.) Two Pilkington directors joined Chances' Board. In October the senior managers involved were told of 'technical and commercial collaboration' between the two concerns[141] but it was hoped that the true state of affairs would not be revealed to the public at large until Pilkington had secured control by acquiring more than half the equity (a forlorn hope as it turned out). By May 1939 it had acquired 44 per cent, including some shares received from St Gobain as part payment for Maubeuge.[142] In this way the once important and resourceful rival gradually slipped, quietly and unnoticed, into Pilkington's grasp.

It brought with it interests in optical glass and glass fibres which Pilkington did not already have. Indeed, Pilkington had specifically turned down both of them a few years before.[143] Optical glass was a branch of the industry in which Chances had much experience, and the two companies joined forces in 1939 to start a wartime shadow plant, Umbroc, at Sheet Works, St Helens.[144]

Glass fibres were a relatively new departure. They had been made for the first time on an industrial scale in Hamburg just before 1914, and had been further developed in Germany, as a substitute for asbestos, during the First World War.[145] When, in 1930, Chances were looking for a new product to bring a little business to its under-employed rolled plate glassworks at Firhill, Glasgow, they sent Lindsay Forster, who was in charge there, to the continent to prospect. He recommended a glass silk process developed by Dr Pollak in Vienna.[146] In April 1930 the Chance Board decided to go up to £2,000 plus royalties for the exclusive British and British Empire patent rights. Glass silk production began at Glasgow in the following September.[147] The process turned out to be not very satisfactory. It consisted of heating cullet in a small electric furnace, from small holes in which pinpoints of molten glass oozed out. Each of these was picked up on the end of a glass rod, drawn out into a thread and attached to a drum, three feet in diameter, which was set revolving, thus drawing off a number of long, fine, glass filaments. After three or four hours running, the hanks of fibre were cut off and hung on racks. In this particular process, however, the threads were drawn out horizontally from the furnace, and every time one of them broke, the glass oozing from the hole would spread over the furnace wall unless the operator kept a particularly sharp watch. Moreover, the hole itself grew larger all the time and the fibre diameter consequently increased.[148] During the earlier 1930s an improved continuous filament process was developed by Owens-Illinois, using a platinum alloy melter and a small-diameter winding head.[149] Chances were already in touch with them about this in 1934 but did not finally negotiate a licence, on the basis of minimum royalty payments of £1,000 in the first year rising to £3,000 in the third, until April 1935.[150] The Glasgow works were extended and the new plant installed there in 1937.[151]

The Pilkington Executive realised the significance of this step, and in

June 1936, having noted that 'great possibilities were foreseen in this article', decided to lay claim to some of the field. They suggested that Pilkington should have the textile market, leaving bulk sales for insulation purposes to Chances.[152] A few months later, however, opinion had veered in favour of the setting up of a new company to exploit all uses of glass fibres.[153] In this company, Turner and Newall, who also made glass silk, were to be included as well as Pilkington and Chances. Pilkington's eagerness to make headway with the promising product was not concealed; but the director in charge of it at Chances wrote to one of his colleagues that he was 'not favourably disposed towards letting them divert us from our well considered policy. If they can get their way,' he added with some foresight, 'we shall see the factory at St Helens and the research rather drifting in the same direction . . .'[154] In this climate negotiations for the joint company proceeded slowly. It was not until January 1938 that agreement was reached on the basis of the three parties each putting up one-third of the £120,000 capital.[155] In the end, Turner and Newall decided not to participate as minority shareholders; but they were keen enough to offer to sell their glass fibres works and to become the new company's selling agents.[156]

Glass Fibres Limited was formed in July 1938, Pilkington putting up £59,000 and Chances £4,500 in cash for £1 shares. Out of this sum Chances were to be paid £37,800 in cash for the new Owens-Illinois plant. They were also to receive the balance of the shares (56,500) for the goodwill, plant and assets of the old process at Glasgow.[157] With 61,000 shares altogether, they became major shareholders in the new venture; but Pilkington, slowly taking them over, was soon to acquire control. The factory at St Helens was to materialise at the end of the war.

The growing ramification and increasing complexity of the Pilkington business – moving into new products, acquiring new companies, improving existing methods of production and developing new ones – underlines the crucial importance of the administrative reorganisation, the infusion of new blood at top management level and, through the new committee structure, the closer association of departmental heads with major policy decisions. This broadening and strengthening of the management structure was essential to the company's activities. In particular, it gave the directors more time to think about events abroad and to conduct international negotiations. Those concerned with attempts to stabilise markets, we have seen. Others concerned new inventions and their development. Some of these stemmed from the peace treaty signed with the continentals in

1929 which had made it possible to acquire the PPG process and the toughening patents. The later connection with Owens-Illinois (and Corning) was a prerequisite to the development of glass fibre manufacture as well as to the introduction of glass bricks.

This widening range of Pilkington's interest may be illustrated by the tally of companies in which Pilkington had acquired a financial stake by the end of 1936.[158] These included a number which have already been noticed: Rockware, Chances, Joblings and the N.V.Hollandsche Maatschappij Voor de Vervaarding Van Glas, shares in the latter having been acquired in 1935 in return for a major improvement made by Pilkington in the PPG process. It wholly owned: Sheet Glass Limited (Pilkington Brothers (South Wales) Limited was to follow shortly), The British Vitrolite Company Limited, the Anglo-Belgian Silver Sand Co. Limited, the Société Industrielle de Grimberghen (the threat of 1928 and still in existence on paper), St Helens Collieries Limited and the Greengate Brick and Tile Works Limited.*

Pilkington had also acquired in 1932 for £35,000 the important furniture and mirror manufacturing concern of O.C.Hawkes in Bromsgrove Street, Birmingham, with a sales turnover of £130,000 per year and then employing about 400 people, which had got into financial difficulties.† This, wrote Tunnock, was to prevent the business from falling into the hands of an outsider who 'would be a menace to our local friends and adverse to the plate glass manufacturers' interests'.[161] Pilkington also, with 51 per cent of the shares, controlled the Plymouth glass merchants' business, Newton & Andrewartha Limited. These it had acquired in 1936 on an approach from its chairman when the glass merchant parent, J.M.Newton, got into difficulties.[162]

There were also a number of subsidiary companies concerned with

---

*The brick and tile works, acquired in 1919 for the Garden Village scheme (p.397), were operated in conjunction with the colliery nearby. St Helens Collieries Limited was managed by A.J.A.Orchard. When he retired at the end of 1936, he was granted the very considerable pension of £1,500 per year 'in view of freedom from accidents and the time he has saved PB directors from colliery affairs'.[159]

†Pilkington had tried to save O.C.Hawkes from liquidation in February 1932 by taking up £5,000 second debentures in that company. In April Major H.T.Valentine was sent down from St Helens to help reorganise the works, but this bid to save the company from liquidation did not succeed. Pilkington acquired it on 17 November 1932 and Valentine became managing director. The business usually returned a small loss and in June 1939 the Executive agreed that the factory and office should be moved to Ravenhead, leaving only a small bevelling and silvering plant in Birmingham. In June 1940 it was decided to close down the whole business as and when those who worked for it could be found alternative employment within the Pilkington organisation.[160]

Pilkington's activities overseas. We have already noticed the setting up of Pilkington Brothers (Canada) Limited in 1922 (p. 296) with J.E. Harrison as proconsul responsible for that part of the Pilkington empire from the First World War to the end of the Second. It fell a little behind Australia as the company's most important export market for plate glass during the interwar period – each took about one-fifth of Pilkington's total plate glass exports – but remained by far its most important oversea customer for sheet, taking between a quarter and a third of the company's sheet glass exports, rising to a remarkable three-fifths to three-quarters between 1933 and 1939.

In Argentina, quite an important market for Pilkington plate glass at the end of the 1920s, Pilkington had a warehouse in Buenos Aires dating from 1907 (p. 210) and a second opened at Bahia Blanca in 1927.[163]

In Brazil, where John Thorpe had acquired land for a warehouse in Rio in 1918, Pilkington Brothers (Brazil) Limited was formed in 1922.[164] Joseph Brooks, who had gone to South America for Pilkington in 1908, became the company's agent in Rio in 1911, at Buenos Aires in 1914, and for South America as a whole from 1919 until his death in 1946. The Rio warehouse became unprofitable in the 1930s when Pilkington's exports to Brazil fell off. There was talk in 1933 and again in 1938 of disposing of it, but it was not finally sold until 1966.[165]

The fourth sales subsidiary abroad was Pilkington Brothers (China) Limited. Here J.L. Kimmins (younger brother of H.L. Kimmins who became export manager at St Helens) was the key figure. He had been sent on a mission to Japan so early as 1902–4. (Pilkington had participated in the first industrial fair there, at Osaka in 1903.) Sales to the East became more important during the First World War (Table 33 p. 246) and in 1920 Kimmins was sent to visit customers in Japan, China, the Straits Settlement and India. The upshot was that Pilkington decided to replace its commission agent in Bombay by a permanent representative. Kimmins went to the East again in 1922–3, and it was as a result of this second visit that Pilkington established a warehouse in Shanghai in collaboration with its former commission agents there, Scott Harding & Co. Ltd. Pilkington Brothers (China) Limited was registered in March 1924 with Kimmins in charge. One of his assistants, George Wilkinson, subsequently became Pilkington's resident representative in Japan from 1928 to 1935, when that agency was closed. A new warehouse was opened at Shanghai in 1933; but in the 1930s, business, particularly in the remunerative plate glass, was disappointing because of higher tariffs. In January 1937 it was decided to wind up the company. The depot was leased for a time and finally sold in 1946.[166]

The spread of safety glass manufacture also involved Pilkington in investment abroad in businesses to process, as well as to sell, glass. The first of these was in Canada where, as has been seen, Pilkington was considering a Canadian laminated glass venture early in 1929, shortly before it became major shareholder in Triplex (Northern) Limited. This came to nothing at the time, and the Duplate Safety Glass Co. of Canada was formed joint-ly by the American Duplate Corporation (from 1931 a PPG subsidiary) and Col. W.E.Phillips, a leading Ontario glass merchant and chief share-holder in W.E.Phillips & Co. Ltd, who was married to the daughter of R.S.McLaughlin, the wealthy president of General Motors' Canadian subsidiary. Among J.E.Harrison's letters to St Helens is one, written at the end of 1930, in which he comments upon Phillips's extravagance and the concern of his father-in-law who had been in the habit of giving his daughters a 'bunch of bonds' every year. 'There is much gossip at the moment about Mr R.S.McLaughlin being tired of furnishing funds to WEP,' Harrison noted, 'and I would not be greatly surprised if WEP became a negligible factor in the glass trade in the near future.'[167] Quite the reverse happened, however, and early in 1933 Phillips came to St Helens to discuss the possibility of Canadian Duplate obtaining from Pilkington (who held the exclusive rights for the British Commonwealth) a licence to make toughened glass in Canada.[168] An exclusive licence was signed on 21 November 1933, Pilkington receiving in payment 666 shares in Canadian Duplate which was also to pay a 10 per cent royalty on sales from 1934 to 1943.[169] There is later mention of an understanding between the signatories that all $\frac{1}{4}$-inch plate glass would be bought from Pilkington or the Con-vention and all $\frac{1}{8}$-inch (for laminating) from American sources.[170] In 1936, Canadian Duplate extended its manufacturing capacity by building a toughening plant at Windsor, Ont. for Chrysler. Pilkington and PPG each invested about $50,000 dollars in 5 per cent preference shares to finance this.[171] By then Pilkington owned about a third of the capital of Canadian Duplate which, in 1937, after another visit to St Helens from Phillips, was encouraged to exploit all glassmaking developments outside the flat glass field, including the manufacture of glass fibres.[172] Early in the following year Canadian Duplate and Pilkington (Canada) acquired W. E.Phillips & Co. for $700,000, Phillips's own services being retained at a salary of $17,500 per year plus 3 per cent of the profits, no doubt to the considerable satisfaction of his father-in-law.[173] Phillips became for a time a member of the Pilkington (Canada) Board.

This was by no means the end of the story, for in 1947 Col. Phillips decided to sell 85 per cent of his holding in Canadian Duplate and he offered this to Pilkington. The company unwisely declined these shares and Phillips offered them to the PPG who thereby became majority shareholders in the Canadian subsidiary. Phillips later joined the main PPG Board but always remained a good friend of St Helens.

In Australia, now Pilkington's most important plate glass export market, the company had even more at stake than in Canada and was obliged to put up its own safety glass plant in order to safeguard its plate glass supplies which were made through the merchants to the growing motor industry there. Indeed, there were to be two plants, one at Adelaide to cater for the General Motors Holden works and the other at Geelong, the old port about 60 miles south of Melbourne on Port Philip Bay, to supply Fords. These were both owned by Pilkington Brothers (Australia) Pty Limited (PB(A)), incorporated at Adelaide in April 1935 with 20,000 £1 shares.[174] In this the Australian Window Glass Co. (AWG) was soon to have a 49 per cent stake. The background to this important move, and the actual negotiations themselves, are of considerable significance and need to be considered in a little detail.

AWG had grown out of the bottlemaking activities of the Melbourne wholesale drug house of Felton, Grimwade & Co., first at Melbourne (dating back to 1872), then at Sydney (1904) and shortly afterwards at Adelaide. In 1915, after the takeover of rival works in Sydney, Australian Glass Manufacturers Pty Limited (AGM) was formed with Norton Grimwade as its chairman. It was soon to own further bottlemaking concerns in New Zealand and in Western Australia and to establish a virtual monopoly of bottlemaking throughout Australasia. From the early 1920s, AGM was run by a swashbuckling managing director, W. J. Smith, who had been born in Liverpool and taken to Australia as a very small child. Having served his time in the bottle trade and become a trade union leader in his teens, he had been appointed a works manager in his early twenties. He took AGM into crystal glass manufacture in 1924 and, having carefully monitored the progress of the Fourcault process in Europe, formed AWG, in which AGM held all the shares, in October 1929.[175] The Scullin government which came to office that very month granted to AWG a very high protective tariff in the following year so that it could establish this new infant industry, and further protection was subsequently given by the exchange rate moving in the Australian manufacturers' favour, the pound sterling at one time reaching a premium of 30 per cent.[176]

AWG, however, did not succeed in making any Fourcault glass until January 1932, and then it was poor in quality and insufficient in quantity. In May 1931 the company had been obliged to turn to figured rolled

glass, thus upsetting this market, too, in order to make a little money.[177]
There was a Tariff Board Enquiry, and the duty had to be reduced again
for a time so that more window glass could be imported, for stocks in
Australia were dwindling fast despite the depression.[178] AWG in the
meantime was encountering considerable financial difficulty: the launching
of the Fourcault process was a costly matter. Its capital had been written
down in December 1933 and the Grimwade financial interests, whose
abundant resources had kept it alive, were pressing Smith to abandon
window glass altogether.[179] In the middle of 1934 he came to Europe to
try to reach some agreement with the British and continental exporters
and, if possible, to try to persuade a few of them to put up some capital.
He found the Belgians very unco-operative, resolved to win back their lost
Australian customers at all cost. The Belgian government had refused to
take Australian meat unless the Australian market was reopened to Belgian
glass. When agreement was eventually reached, the pro-British Australian
government saw to it that the British exporter acquired larger shares of
imports than before. In these new circumstances Pilkington offered Smith
a licence to make toughened plate glass (which would, of course, have had
to be made with the imported product) but refused to put any money into
his company. He declined to take up the offer and returned to Australia
disappointed.[180] Once back there, he began an advertising campaign for
his own thick sheet safety glass which he marketed under the cinematic
trade name Tarzan Toughened. It was at this juncture, in December
1934, that Pilkington took the decisions to open its own toughening plant
and to form PB(A).[181] Negotiations with Smith were resumed early in
the following year.[182]

These developments were occurring at a time when Australia was on
the point of becoming more closely linked with Europe. Imperial Airways
had reached Singapore in 1932, but it was not until April 1935 that Qantas
completed the route through to Brisbane. During the 1920s, mail from
Britain had taken from five to seven weeks to arrive. Australia was then
still a very remote place, and it is clear from the correspondence of Harold
Mees, Pilkington's agent there, that on many occasions he felt that his
principals far away at home had little appreciation of the problems, or
possibilities, on the spot. As we have seen (p. 167), he had been sent in
1904 to cover the whole of the Australian market from Melbourne,
first on commission and then as a salaried agent. In 1922 he was given two
assistants. George Scott, recruited out of uniform at the end of the war to
help restart Maubeuge, moved to Perth but, within a year, was posted to
Sydney. His territory covered Tasmania and the whole continent of
Australia, apart from the city of Melbourne where Mees was helped in the

office by the second assistant, George Mills. From there Mees sent letters to St Helens warning his masters of the threatening activities of Smith, and even suggesting that they should agree to see Smith on one of his visits to England, but without avail.[183] Harry Pilkington visited Australia on business in 1930, the first member of the family to do so, and John Tilbury, then the export manager, joined him there for the beginning of the Tariff Board hearings early in 1931; but otherwise Mees had to rely on occasional visits home or correspondence – apart from telegrams – for his communication with the management. He developed an independence which became unacceptable to St Helens, refusing, for instance, to move the head office from Melbourne to Sydney. It was decided that the time had arrived for him to retire, though he was still seven years from the normal retiring age. Accordingly, in March 1932, he was summoned to Ceylon to meet Austin Pilkington, then on his six-months' leave after the 1931 reorganisation, to be told this. Percy Norbury, a Pilkington employee at St Helens from 1901 until 1923 when he became Pilkington agent first at Cape Town and then, from 1929, in New Zealand, was brought to Australia to take Mees' place. As Scott was moved to South Africa soon afterwards (Norman Mackenzie being brought from there to replace him), the Australian agency was headed by two men who were newcomers to the country when the Tariff Board hearings were resumed and when the negotiations with Smith began.

Norbury, however, received very clear, detailed and specific instructions through Tunnock from St Helens after the Australian toughening plant had been decided upon.[184] He was to offer preferential terms to General Motors Holden (the details of which were spelt out) and, when these had been agreed, he was to consult a first-class lawyer about the formation of the subsidiary company in which the Australian merchants were to be offered a share. (They declined it.) Details followed about the staff needed to man the new concern – about 30 people altogether – and a full architect's plan of the factory formerly used for making batteries in the Kilkenny suburb of Adelaide, which had been found by Norbury, was requested to allow experts at St Helens to plan the layout of the machinery. The first item, a double screen furnace, was ordered from Triplex (Northern) on 20 February and despatched to Australia on 20 March 1935. It was producing toughened glass in Adelaide in June.[185] Harry Glover was sent out as factory manager and he was followed by two technical experts. He and Norbury were, in an unfamiliar role as directors, present at the first meeting of PB(A), held at the offices of the company's solicitors, Fisher, Powers, Jeffries & Brebner, Epworth Building, 33 Pirie Street, Adelaide on 10 April.[186]

Meanwhile Smith, disturbed by this activity, had offered to use only Pilkington plate glass and a proportion of his own TDS if Pilkington would leave all toughening in Australia to him. Pilkington wired its counter-proposals to Norbury on 5 April:

1. We agree to offer AGM [sic] financial interest in new company up to 49 per cent capital we to control operations of company. New company to be free to manufacture all forms of safety glass including laminated and AGM not otherwise interest themselves in safety glass.

2. British Plate Glass to be toughened exclusively and Thick Sheet only considered in light of later experience. In event of Thick Sheet being later adopted, we would agree AGM supply subject to quality being suitable.

3. Smith to undertake not to manufacture Plate Glass or grind or polish Thick Sheet Glass.

4. As AGM will have considerable interest in sale of Plate Glass through new company, we would prefer they should agree not to import Plate Glass for resale.

5. AGM should agree not to export any flat glass and co-operate to enable British Manufacturers secure reasonable share of orders Figured Rolled and Rolled Plate.[187]

When Smith rejected these proposals, Head Office told Norbury to use them as a basis for further negotiation. He thereupon had two further long talks with Smith at the beginning of May at which Smith demanded for AWG equal participation in the new safety glass company and a commission on all plate glass sold to it. At this juncture Norbury recommended to St Helens that Pilkington should come to terms, for he believed that the AWG would soon succeed with its sheet glass plant and be grinding and polishing its product. It would thus 'eventually become the Pilkington Brothers of Australia'. 'It is our opinion,' he wrote 'that we have everything to lose (taking the long view) by adopting a policy of non-co-operation.'[188]

While Pilkington took AWG's threat very seriously, it did not favour supine surrender, especially since the favourable import quota had greatly strengthened its hand. The Board decided (i) to send F. B. Waldron to prospect secretly in both New Zealand and Australia for the best site at which to set up rival sheet glassworks if need be and (ii) to send its chairman, Cozens-Hardy, and Harry Pilkington to Sydney to negotiate with the ultimate aim of obtaining a stake in AGM and of safeguarding to Pilkington 'a proper proportion of the Australian market for our own products rather than the establishment of a rival factory'.[189]

Cozens-Hardy and his wife travelled by sea. Harry Pilkington used the newly-opened air service to Brisbane, and, as he travelled to Singapore by KLM, instead of Imperial Airways, claimed that his journey to Australia was faster than any passenger had achieved up to that time, apart from the fliers in the Melbourne air race the previous year.[190] He was able to visit some of the glass merchants to size up the situation before joining Cozens-Hardy in Adelaide for a meeting of the PB(A) Board on 2 November, at which it was decided to add a multiple body furnace to the plant and to extend the factory.[191] The party then left for Melbourne (where the Cozens-Hardys attended the Melbourne Gold Cup as guests of the Governor of Victoria) before going on to Sydney and their confrontation with Smith which began on 4 November.

Cozens-Hardy was soon able to report to St Helens, whose approval was sought at every stage, that Smith had not rejected out of hand any of Pilkington's proposals of 5 April; so, although Waldron had reported that 20 acres at Botany Bay would be the best glassmaking base, he was told to delay putting in a bid for the site.[192] Smith eventually agreed to a 49 per cent interest in PB(A) in return for AWG being given 5 per cent commission on all plate glass imported into Australia up to £300,000 and 2½ per cent thereafter. This involved American and Convention exporters as well as Pilkington, but Pilkington was prepared to take the risk of the others not sharing the cost in the knowledge that the whole matter could be settled when the Convention agreement came to be renegotiated in 1939 if not before. A quota agreement on rolled plate glass was also reached. This, too, involved the continentals as well as AWG and Pilkington.

Pilkington sold the 49 per cent stake in PB(A) to AWG at £2 per £1 share (thereby recouping almost all its original outlay) and Smith became a PB(A) director. The final agreement was signed at 11.40 a.m. on 23 November, apparently on board ship in Sydney Harbour 20 minutes before Cozens-Hardy sailed for home. His mission was not, however, quite completed, for he went ashore at Melbourne to have an important lunch with Edward Norton Grimwade, chairman of AGM, owner of the bottlemaking and other business concerns as well as AWG (and to be renamed, in 1939, Australian Consolidated Industries (ACI)). There the two men discussed the possibility of Pilkington acquiring an interest in this growingly powerful industrial empire by purchasing some AGM shares in the hands of the Felton Trust which, by court order, the Trust had been ordered to sell sometime during the next 25 years.[193] Grimwade agreed to this proposal, and on 10 March 1936 Pilkington bought from the Felton Trust 10,000 AGM shares at 85s 3d, 1s below the market price, at a total cost of £42,625.[194] Thus, after standing aloof from significant glassmaking developments in Australia for a decade or so, Pilkington had, after less than three weeks' hard bargaining, succeeded not only in maintaining control of its new subsidiary and in safeguarding its plate glass business but also in obtaining a foothold in the Australian company which controlled the growing glass industry in that country and was also diversifying into other branches of Australian industry.

The Australian safety glass business grew and prospered. By March 1937 the second factory, at Geelong, financed by a further £20,000 capital (51 per cent raised by Pilkington and 49 per cent by AWG) came into production, at first on an experimental scale,[195] to supply laminated glass to Fords nearby, who had previously imported this type of glass from Duplate Canada. The factory was soon extended and a toughening plant installed, a further £10,000 being added to the capital of PB(A), bringing it to £50,000 in all. J. Dennett, sent out from St Helens to start the laminating plant, remained in charge at Geelong until June 1939. Three other men came into PB(A) in these early days who were to play a notable part in its subsequent remarkable growth. E. R. Robertson, an Australian, began as an accountant at Geelong in November 1936 and became Accountant and Secretary of PB(A) from 1951; A. P. Gee, who had previously served in Paris and Maubeuge between 1927 and 1935, came from St Helens to take Harry Glover's place as manager at Adelaide and director of PB(A) in March 1937 when Glover was posted to South Africa; and Alf Burrell, eventually to be in charge of production at Geelong, started work there straight from Geelong Junior Technical High School in September 1938. A fourth man who arrived in Australia at this time bound for the Pilkington agency, but later to take charge of all Pilkington operations in Australia, was J. H. Pemberton, one of the commercial trainees who, as we saw in the previous chapter, was recruited from the staff at St Helens in 1935. In June 1937, he replaced Norman Mackenzie, who had a spell away from Australia back in St Helens between 1938 and 1946. The Melbourne office was closed in 1937 and Pemberton joined the staff at Sydney which then still consisted only of himself, Norbury and two typists. Norbury, who had borne the main burden of responsibility in Australia since 1932, fell ill in 1938 and felt obliged to resign in January 1939. George Scott was brought back from South Africa to take his place.

Pilkington's plate glass exports to Australia returned to over 1 million sq. ft per year in 1934–9, a level unknown since 1929; and its sheet glass exports, which had shrunk to next to nothing in 1931, 1933 and 1934, were also back again by 1936 to the magnitude of the later 1920s. To the profit on these large sales was added the remarkable financial success of the safety glass subsidiary. A trifling loss of £737 on the first half-year's working, to December 1935, was transformed into a profit of £5,280 on the second and a 5 per cent dividend was declared on the year. Thereafter PB(A) was able to pay higher dividends on its larger capital as its scale of operations grew: 10 per cent in 1936–7 and no less than 60 per cent in each of the years 1937–8 and 1938–9. By then the profit and loss appropriation account of this £50,000 company stood at the healthy figure of £55,125. The war years, with accompanying vicissitudes in the motor industry, were not so prosperous; but dividends of 45, 50, 30, 19 and 12½ per cent were returned between 1939–40 and 1943–4, by which time the appropriation account still stood at £36,000. Early in 1944, A.P. Gee calculated the return to Pilkington from PB(A) down to the end of 1943:

Royalty on toughened glass Adelaide	£56,874	2	10
Geelong	£15,307	7	0
Royalty on laminated glass Geelong	£20,664	0	5
Dividends paid to P.B. Limited	£72,420	0	0
English directors' fees	£2,250	0	0
Incidentals	£1,070	14	7
	£168,586	4	10[196]

This return was received from an investment of under £16,000 since, as we have seen, 49 per cent of the first 20,000 £1 shares were sold to AWG at £2 each and Pilkington subscribed only 51 per cent to the remaining 30,000. Even after Pilkington had passed the royalty payments on to its French licensors, this still remained a very remarkable return on capital for the first eight years of a new company's existence. And even more prosperous vistas lay ahead after the war.

While these events were taking place in Australia and causing Pilkington to think of itself very much more as an international company, it was also exploring the possibility of building or acquiring factories elsewhere abroad: a plate glassworks in Canada, for instance,[197] a toughening plant in India and in New Zealand,*[198] the Phoenicia Glassworks at Haifa,[199] and even, as a long shot, a works in China.[200] Only two such ventures came to anything, however. One of these was in South Africa and the other in Argentina.

*James Austin Pinnington succeeded Norbury as New Zealand Agent in 1932. He had started work for Pilkington as a boy in St Helens in 1910. He went to New Zealand in January 1925 as assistant to F.W. Butcher, having responsibility for the South Island. He was himself Pilkington's New Zealand Agent from 1932, assisted from the later 1940s by Leslie Gallon and from 1955 by Raymond Robinson. In 1961 the latter succeeded him.[201]

South Africa, which had previously not been such a good customer for plate glass as Canada and Australia, greatly increased its imports from Pilkington in 1934 and 1935 and was, indeed, taking a little more plate glass in those years even than Australia. A promising motor business was developing and the country possessed substantial glass merchants but not, as yet, a flat glass industry of any sort. In June 1933, H.A.Evans & Co., a large and old-established firm of glass merchants in Johannesburg showed an interest in a licence to process safety glass.[202] At the end of the following year the firm of G.A.Smith, Port Elizabeth (owned by Barney Dubb who had been, among other things, an ostrich feather farmer) approached Pilkington who were prepared to consider a licence to them together with the Plate Glass Bevelling and Silvering Company of Cape Town (owned by the Brodie family).[203] Pilkington agreed to form Armourplate Safety Glass (Pty) Limited with £15,000 capital, and on 31 December 1935 a non-exclusive licence was granted to it to manufacture toughened glass for sale in South Africa, Northern and Southern Rhodesia, South West Africa and Portuguese East Africa. The raising of the capital for the new venture took some time, however. The original idea had been to offer 49 per cent of the shares to the Dubbs, agreeing to negotiate later with the Brodies 'if and when the Ford Motor Company became interested in toughened glass for their cars'.[204] A little later, the plan was for the Dubbs and the Brodies to take up all but 2 per cent of the capital provided General Motors contracted for 150,000 sq. ft of toughened glass over the following three years.[205] On this understanding Scott, then Agent in South Africa, bought a suitable site for the plant at Port Elizabeth for £50.[206] But the negotiations switched to the Brodies and another concern, Griffiths, Blooman & Co., also owned by the Dubb family, and then became more protracted because they and the Brodies could not settle matters among themselves.[207] The final agreement, a complicated document by which the Dubbs and the Brodies were to receive some of Armourplate's earnings on certain sales and the two concerns were each to be represented on its Board, was not signed until October 1936 on the basis of Pilkington taking 10,000 of the 15,000 shares.[208] A second licence, to make laminated glass, was signed by the Brodies on behalf of the Shatterprufe Safety Glass Co. (Pty) Limited – a subsidiary of Plate Glass Bevelling and Silvering – on 31 December 1937.[209] The new factory at Port Elizabeth began production in 1936. Pilkington bought out Dubb in 1947 but continued to work closely with the Brodie family and with Maurie Lubner who joined their business.

Pilkington had been planning to enter glassmaking – not just glass processing – in the Argentine a few years before this. There had been negotiations in London and St Helens in June and July 1932 with Leon Fourvel Rigolleau, chief shareholder in Cristalerias Rigolleau, a bottle and pressed glass manufacturing business at Buenos Aires, founded in 1906 and re-equipped after 1918. Pilkington was to subscribe £125,000 for a controlling interest in a new company which would take this over, pay £75,000 in compensation and spend the remaining £50,000 on the building of a sheet glassworks, the first in that country.[210] F.B. Waldron was sent to the Argentine to conduct an on-the-spot survey. His report, considered by the directors in March 1933, was not very encouraging,[211] but the event that really killed the project was the need at that time to find £260,000 to purchase Queenborough and cash to invest in Rockware. One of these schemes had to be jettisoned, and it was agreed that it should be the South American project.[212]

When manufacturing in the Argentine was again discussed, early in 1935, it was initially to put down a small toughening furnace in part of Pilkington's underused warehouse in Buenos Aires. Production had started there by January 1936.[213] At about the same time St Gobain licensed an Argentinian company, Trevisi & Co., to make toughened glass, but Pilkington was able to persuade them not to manufacture and to confine their sales to buyers other than the main motor businesses.[214]

In May 1936 Pilkington decided that, in order to safeguard the market, a factory should be built in the Argentine for the manufacture of rolled plate glass in the first instance, and then sheet, to which the company's toughening operations, which were soon to outgrow its limited warehouse site, might also be transferred. 'The advantage to be derived from combining with the European manufacturers in such a venture was recognised', the minutes record, 'particularly if the St Gobain Co. appear as prime mover.'[215] Joseph Brooks was instructed to exercise an option on a site at Llavallol and, a little later, to sink a well there 'to convey the impression of impending activity.'[216] In April 1937 Vidrieria Argentina S.A. (VASA) was formed to finance the whole venture and F.B. Grant, then manager of the Queenborough works, was appointed general manager.[217] There was also further discussion about taking over Cristalerias Rigolleau, this time by an international consortium which would have included American as well as European manufacturers, but again this came to nothing.[218] The Belgians, responsible for over 60 per cent of sheet glass sales in the Argentine, resisted the introduction of sheet glass manufacture there before the war; but rolled plate glass began to be made on 24 November 1938.[219] The safety glass plant adjoined the factory but was wholly owned by Pilkington. Of the ordinary shares in VASA totalling 2 m. paper pesos, Pilkington held 33·5 per cent, St Gobain 31·7 per cent, Glaver/

Boussois 15·1 per cent, Chances 10·7 per cent and St Roch 6·8 per cent. Rigolleau held the remaining 2·2 per cent. A small shareholding had been intended for Vitrea but was not taken up because of Hitler's occupation of the Sudetenland. No single participant had control, though Pilkington would have 44·2 per cent after it secured control of Chances. By 1939 Pilkington had invested £77,000 in this venture.

Pilkington's performance during the 1930s is more difficult to assess than it was during the 1920s because its subsidiaries and interests in other companies make the parent company's statistics less indicative of Pilkington activities as a whole. Accounting methods became more sophisticated, too, and capital employed in manufacturing was more rigorously written down when appropriate. Table 51 (to be compared with Table 45 on p. 317) does, however, reflect the company's greater manufacturing efficiency following the successful introduction of the PPG process and further improvements in plate glassmaking; but the return on capital employed in manufacturing during the 1930s does not reach the 17 per cent and more of 1923–4 and 1924–5; and the high net profit of 1936–7 is not maintained partly because of the switch to thick drawn sheet and partly because of the less favourable economic climate.

TABLE 51

RETURN ON CAPITAL EMPLOYED IN MANUFACTURING
1932–40

Year Ended	Capital Employed £'000	Net Profit £'000	Return %
March 1932	6,283	327	5·2
March 1933	6,136	309	5·0
March 1934	6,186	403	6·5
March 1935	6,354	677	10·7
March 1936	6,343	695	10·9
March 1937	5,997	877	14·6
March 1938	6,160	773	12·5
March 1939	6,080	635	10·4
March 1940	5,835	727	12·4

Source: Pilkington Accounts

Table 52 (the sequel to Table 46 on p. 318) shows the greater profitability of the company in the mid-1930s and the much larger sums paid out in dividend and bonus to Pilkington family shareholders. The amount paid in income tax was also much greater in the second half of the decade.

TABLE 52
DISPOSAL OF PROFIT IN THE YEARS 1931-40 (£'s)

Year Ended	Adjusted Profit (Loss)	Directors' salaries fees and expenses	Income Tax	Transfer to reserve for replacement of fixed assets	Debenture interest	(a) Net Profit (Loss)	Dividend and bonus on shares	(b) Balance retained in Company
March 1931	363,150	8,055	159,699	93,884	81,864	19,648	63,840	(44,192)
March 1932	607,788	18,034	66,613	200,000	79,278	243,863	47,880	195,983
March 1933	476,693	10,836	45,037	200,000	77,150	143,670	159,600	(15,930)
March 1934	586,630	13,522	84,914	200,000	74,562	213,632	159,600	54,032
March 1935	872,710	29,535	118,255	202,630	71,974	450,316	270,087	180,229
March 1936	919,339	37,640	153,415	210,097	69,388	448,799	269,938	178,861
March 1937	1,140,660	42,727	249,509	203,697	69,914	574,813	297,609	277,204
March 1938	1,168,196	40,277	240,685	274,380	70,212	542,642	241,229	301,413
March 1939	821,108	17,368	242,827	215,739	67,626	277,458	129,064	148,394
March 1940	871,415	27,265	354,806	218,317	65,038	205,989	112,115	93,874

(a) Profit as shown in Profit and Loss Account
(b) From 1926 includes surplus found for redemption of debentures

This greater prosperity is reflected in the Board's concern, early in 1935, about outlets for its growing cash surplus. By May this had already reached £100,000 and there was the first instalment of £300,000 on Maubeuge to come. What was to be done with all this money?

The advisability of investment in established companies in this country, for example manufacturers of ornamental and table glassware, was discussed [by the Executive], and the suggestion was made that an outlet might be found by linking up with oil and paint manufacturers.[220]

The possibility of making loans for the reconstruction of shop fronts by a specially-created finance company was subsequently approved, only to be withdrawn again when the large shop fitters objected.[221] The need to invest this surplus cash was a further inducement to Pilkington to take shares in AGM, specifically mentioned as a possibility at that particular Board meeting in May 1935, and in the other glassmaking ventures at home and abroad which have been discussed.

Profit was ploughed back to strengthen the company rather than divided among the family shareholders who were prepared to forgo immediate gain to themselves in favour of longer-term advantage from which, if the business prospered, all stood to benefit, shareholders and employees alike. A few shareholders were, however, unhappy about having to dispose of their shares only to other family shareholders—if they could find any takers—at a mere £5 to £15 per £10 share (the exact price being fixed by the Board according to the year's profit) instead of being free to sell at least some of them in the open market for as much as they would fetch. During the summer and autumn of 1933 the Board considered ways whereby transferability could be made easier without the privacy of the company's accounts being endangered and its financial affairs becoming known to its business rivals. It was decided to explore the possibility of dividing the ordinary share capital into ordinary and preference shares in an agreed ratio, which would be more than 2 : 1. A holding company could then be formed, whose directors would be either Pilkington directors or ex-directors, to which those who wished could transfer their preference shares in return for its shares, which would be publicly marketable.[222] These plans took shape in the following year, and in September 1934 it was agreed that one-eighth of the ordinaries should be transformed into 6 per cent preference shares. Pilkington share capital thereafter consisting of 280,000 £10 ordinaries and 40,000 6 per cent preference shares which could be redeemed by the company. The change was made retrospective to 1 April 1934.[223] The further vital step, the setting up of the holding company with shares which could be marketed, does not,

THE TWIN GRINDER

63 View along the twin grinder at Cowley Hill Works, 1944.

64 Ribbon of glass passing between twin grinding heads.

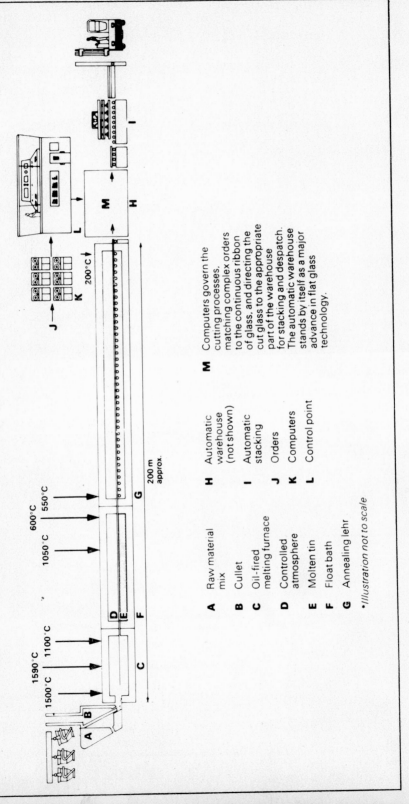

1590°C 1100°C
1500°C

1050°C
600°C 550°C

200°C

200 m approx.

A Raw material mix
B Cullet
C Oil-fired melting furnace
D Controlled atmosphere
E Molten tin
F Float bath
G Annealing lehr

H Automatic warehouse (not shown)
I Automatic stacking
J Orders
K Computers
L Control point

M Computers govern the cutting processes, matching complex orders to the continuous ribbon of glass, and directing the cut glass to the appropriate part of the warehouse for stacking and despatch. The automatic warehouse stands by itself as a major advance in flat glass technology.

*Illustration not to scale

65 THE FLOAT PROCESS

TABLE 53

HOLDERS OF ORDINARY AND PREFERENCE SHARES ON 30 JUNE 1939

Thomas Pilkington's Branch

	Ord	Pref
Alan Douglas	52,488	7,762
D.V.Phelps	537	63
Thomas	1,250	—
L.R.Percival	500	—
	54,775	7,825

Descendants of William Pilkington — William (Roby) Pilkington's Branch

	Ord	Pref
Exors. William Lee	8,887	1,269
Exors. George Herbert	6,521	931
Geoffrey Langton	9,975	1,425
	892	128
	20,174	2,882
R.M. Weeks	9,832	1,405
Kenneth Reginald	1,601	193
William Lee	2,905	415
Geoffrey Langton and R.M. Weeks jointly	2,625	375
William Lee and Kenneth Reginald jointly	2,888	412
Geoffrey Langton, D.V.Phelps and William Henry jointly	2,539	506
	3,000	—
	71,839	9,941

Descendants of William Pilkington — William Windle Pilkington's Branch

	Ord	Pref
Richard Austin	7,320	1,046
Alfred Cecil	22,391	3,663
Richard Austin and Alfred Cecil jointly	15,901	2,272
Alfred Cecil and Richard Austin jointly	5,457	780
William Henry	3,509	501
Alfred Cecil and William Henry jointly	8,365	1,195
	3,500	500
	875	125
Alfred Cecil and E.C.Arnold jointly	2,625	375
E.H.Cozens-Hardy	3,012	488
E.H.Cozens-Hardy and Geoffrey Langton jointly	875	125
H.A.Cozens-Hardy	488	12
	74,318	11,082

Descendants of Richard Pilkington — Richard Pilkington's Branch

	Ord	Pref
Guy Reginald	5,311	1,311
Lionel Edward	9,187	1,313
Lionel Edward and Guy Reginald jointly	16,813	2,687
	2,625	375
	1,750	250
	12,075	1,725
	4,594	656
Guy Reginald and Lionel Edward jointly	412	58
	411	59
	560	80
Richard Antony	18,130	2,590
Arthur Cope	1,000	—
	1,000	—
	73,868	11,104

Source: Pilkington Accounts

however, seem to have been taken, presumably because of the expense involved. The problem of transferability remained.

There was nevertheless as considerable a switch in shares within the family during the 1930s as there had been during the 1920s, although this time it was away from management; the retirement of Austin, Cecil and Guy Pilkington, the death of Norman Pilkington, and the formation of further family trusts mainly for death duty purposes, meant that the non-executive shareholders acquired a larger financial stake in the company.

Those family members actually running the business during the 1930s derived relatively little financial benefit as shareholders compared with the absentee shareholders. It would be going too far to say that the company was at that time becoming owned by absentees, just as a public company is, for some of the 'outside' family shareholders, notably Austin and Cecil Pilkington, attended meetings of the full Board and assisted the management by undertaking special assignments and joining the boards of subsidiary companies. Nevertheless, it would be mistaken to imagine that this successful family company, when it reached the fourth generation, was still owned by those who managed it. Large sums were indeed tied up in the family trusts and gifts to children before the testator's death but although some of the ex-managing directors declared substantial fortunes for probate purposes, none, apart from Geoffrey Pilkington and Lord Cozens-Hardy (fourth baron), whose deaths occurred after the company had gone public, left over £500,000.*

*Norman Pilkington (1935) £384,040 (£272,888); Austin Pilkington (1951) £168,436 (£161,629); E.H.Cozens-Hardy, third baron (1956) £58,801 (£21,430); R.M.Weeks (1960) £84,110 (£51,416); Cecil Pilkington (1966) £436,214 (£408,587); Guy Pilkington (1970) £459,476 (£364,447); Geoffrey Pilkington (1972) £820,684 (£769,800); H.A. Cozens-Hardy, fourth baron (1975) £789,546 (£736,487). The figures in brackets are the net totals.

Chapter 21

Labour Relations and Welfare Services, 1918–39

DESPITE the wage cuts and labour economies of these years and the transition from hand to machine production in the glass industry, Pilkington's labour relations were good. Having recognised the National Amalgamated Union of Labour (from 1924 part of the National Union of General and Municipal Workers), the company got on well with it and there was only one small strike throughout the period, of glass cutters at Doncaster at the end of the 1920s. Pilkington's glass workers were not at all involved in the nine-day General Strike of May 1926 and the NUGMW's District Secretary even promised, if need be, to use his influence with the railway unions to ensure that coal got through to keep the glassworks going at St Helens. (Pilkington's miners, of course, were on strike and remained out for most of the rest of that year.)[1]

At a time when the unemployment rate hardly ever fell below ten per cent of the insured labour force nationally and exceeded 26 per cent in the north-western area in the worst of the depression, jobs at a large and well-established company like Pilkington were at a premium, only won by ability and kept by deference and diligence. In March 1927, apart from its collieries employing about 2,000 men, the company was providing work for almost 9,000 people in St Helens (which, with their dependants, at that time probably accounted for more than a third of the town's population of just over 100,000 even when allowance is made for the considerable number of juveniles employed) and over 1,000 near Doncaster. This, however, was at the beginning of the switch from blown sheet glass and economies elsewhere. The number employed at the three factories in St Helens and at head office – that is to say, excluding Triplex (Northern) –

fell to about 7,000 in 1930 and to not much more than 6,000 in 1932 and 1933; but recovered to about 6,500 by 1934 and to 9,000 once more by 1937. By that date the total for the parent company and its home subsidiaries stood at over 13,000 and the weekly wage bill was £40,187.[2] Some of the employees made redundant benefited from Pilkington's pension scheme introduced in 1925, the displaced glassmakers were compensated from a special fund and, during the worst of the depression, the company supplemented the state unemployment benefit received by their employees who were temporarily laid off.[3] These efforts to alleviate distress helped to generate goodwill when directors and trade union representatives had their regular meetings to discuss matters of mutual concern in the St Helens Plate and Sheet Glass Joint Industrial Council.

The first such meeting, on 30 August 1918, was attended by four directors, Tom Williamson, the local trade union leader,[4] and six employees (Samuel Almond, Henry Briers, Thomas Davies, James Dolan, Peter Oakes, John Twist; a seventh, Alan Cunliffe, was absent on that occasion). Austin Pilkington was elected chairman, Tom Williamson vice-chairman and J.H.Dickinson, Pilkington's legal expert, secretary. This negotiating body, as we have seen, soon gained official recognition from the new Ministry of Labour as a district council[5] and as such continued to function successfully after the more imposing national bodies which were set up in other industries had faded away. Its procedure was formalised: movers and amenders of motions were to talk for not more than five minutes and supporting speakers for not more than three.[6] Its number was brought up to 18, nine from each side, Frederick Woodstock becoming the ninth employee representative.[7] Before the end of 1919, it was agreed by the JIC that all Pilkington workpeople should be encouraged to join the NAUL and that the following poster should be displayed:

NOTICE
St Helens Plate and Sheet Glass Industrial Council

For the information of Employees of Pilkington Brothers Limited, especially new employees, it is notified that as a result of a conference with their employees on 19th October 1917 the Firm have since that date discussed terms and conditions of employment with the Unions recognised by them.

For those in the Plate and Sheet Glass Industry, including all semi-skilled and unskilled workers, the recognized union is the National Amalgamated Union of Labour. It is the desire of the Council that it should be made plain that the Firm is in regular communication with this Union and quite approves of such employees becoming members of it.[8]

The period of euphoria immediately after the war saw the JIC in fine spirits discussing a grandiose scheme to build a garden city.[9] The directors, had been advised before the war by the company's surveyor that this would increase the value of some of its land. Other industrialists had already shown the way at Port Sunlight, Bournville and Earswick. Nearer home, Liverpool Garden Suburb had been started at Broad Green in February 1910. The Pilkington directors had tried to secure the manager of the latter, Frank Williams, as consultant but without success, and had then fallen back on their own Manchester architect, Isaac Taylor. Taylor, however, had caused them some alarm in the middle of 1913 by proposing a rather expensive scheme: 511 cottages, together with shops, on $45\frac{1}{2}$ acres of land at Ravenhead costing £181,000; and by the time his proposals had been scaled down to acceptable proportions, the war had postponed the whole venture.

It was revived in February 1918 in an even grander form than Taylor had contemplated. The new scheme envisaged building up to 4,000 houses and a school for 500 children on no less than 700 acres of the Eccleston Hall estate farther to the west of the town. Frederick Hopkinson, whose work on colliery villages near Doncaster had impressed some of the directors, submitted proposals. When these had been appraised by (Sir) Patrick Abercrombie, then Professor of Civic Design at Liverpool, and accepted by the Board, Hopkinson was invited to take charge of the actual building. A public utility company, Pilkington Garden Village Limited, was registered in October 1919 and the first sod was ceremonially cut on 6 November, in which month plans of the estate and details of the houses were put on view at the works for comment by foremen, foremen's wives and other possible residents. But building labour and materials were in very short supply and the work went ahead so slowly that in March 1920 the directors decided to dispense with Hopkinson's services and not to proceed beyond the 50 houses then being built on the slopes of Eccleston Hill, along Grange Drive and two other adjacent new roads driven a few hundred yards into the estate from the main road to Liverpool. (There were also 11 pairs of temporary wooden bungalows, built farther along the road itself. They were still occupied half a century later.) The company did suggest to the JIC, however, that if its employees wished to form a building society or another public utility society (Pilkington Garden Village Limited never issued any shares and went out of existence in January 1922) to finance a housing scheme of their own, it would sell land to them at the St Helens end of the estate, between the football ground in Knowsley Road and St Ann's Road, at the preferential rate of £100 per acre.[10] This offer, however, was not taken up.[11] Abercrombie's services were nevertheless retained and in 1923, when the building position had become easier, 31 houses were put up on this part of the estate, in Willow Road and Maple Grove. These were offered to employees for £350 each, £50 down and the balance of £300 payable, with interest, weekly over the following ten years.[12] Interwar housing in St Helens was to be supplied by private builders or the local council rather than by a Pilkington-supported garden city.

Pilkington did, however, build a garden village near Kirk Sandall to house the employees at its new factory, as it had done at Thorold in Canada. Abercrombie was responsible for the planning and T.H.Johnson, a Doncaster architect and land surveyor, for the building. 258 houses had been put up by March 1923 and 320 by April 1925, Pilkington spending more than £250,000 on the scheme. Although it then included sports fields, a cycle track, a public house, church hall, school and assembly hall, this constituted only part of the original Abercrombie/Johnson plan for a self-contained village built around its own central square. At Kirk Sandall, as at St Helens, there was a considerable gap between aspiration and achievement.

The heady and profitable later months of war also saw the introduction of a staff superannuation scheme. This was discussed in 1917 and came into force on 1 January 1918.[13] Employer and employee each contributed $2\frac{1}{2}$ per cent of salary to it, and this allowed a pension of up to two-thirds of annual salary after 40 years' service, those who joined after the age of 21 being allowed to make additional voluntary payments.[14] By the mid-30s one-third of the fund's income came from the latter. In order to make the scheme available to existing staff, 625 in number, the company in October 1919 set up a supplementary fund, with four directors as trustees, by an initial payment of £10,000 and half-yearly payments thereafter equal to the dividend on the 'A' shares less £250.[15] A further gain to the staff – and to foremen as well – was the staff bonus, depending on the half-yearly profits and paid for the first time early in 1920.[16]

After the bursting of the post-war boom later in 1920, the price of window glass collapsed (Graph 12, p. 293). The company returned a trading loss in 1921.

The JIC became the forum for the negotiation of a series of wage cuts[17] and the committee became a **most** useful channel whereby management was able to explain to the trade union representatives the difficulties with which it had to contend in competing with imported glass from Belgium, helped by lower labour costs in that country and exchange rates increasingly favourable to the Belgians. Another frequent item on the agenda was the employment of women and young persons on night work. The newly-formed International Labour Office of the League of Nations had recommended that the minimum age for such work should be raised from 14 to 16 and the British (but not the Belgian) government had, in 1920, introduced legislation which would implement this from July 1922. Trade unionists and management joined forces in an attempt to defer its operation until similar legislation was applied on the continent, and both Cecil Pilkington and Tom Williamson testified to this effect before the Commons committee. But to no avail.[18] The ILO's attempt to secure an interruption of working at weekends – difficult when processes were continuous – was a subsequent matter for concern. Again, the Pilkington JIC was prepared to agree but only if the continentals would.[19]

The compensation of glassmakers displaced by the switch from hand-blown glass to drawn cylinder came up for discussion at a financial meeting of the Pilkington Board in March 1923 when the chairman, Austin Pilkington, and his brother Cecil, the technical director, offered to set up a fund for the purpose out of their own pockets.[20] The JIC was told that it was to be managed by six trustees, including Tom Williamson.[21] Trade was then picking up, however, and no further action was taken at that time. Output of hand-blown glass did not begin to decline until after 1925 (Table 42, p. 303).

Having launched the staff superannuation scheme during the profitable period at the end of the war, the company took the opportunity of the next profitable phase to start a pension scheme for weekly wage earners over 21. The latter was considered by the Board in the summer and autumn of 1924 and came into force on 25 April 1925, having been accepted by an overwhelming vote of 3,662 to 165. (About 2,000 employees did not trouble to express a view.)[22] The company and employees over 21 were each to contribute 1s 2d per week (about $2\frac{1}{2}$ per cent of the average weekly wage), and this bought a pension of 20s 6d per week at 60 and 27s 9d at 63. This would be increased at age 70 by the non-contributory state pension of 10s. In fact, it was soon to be increased by that amount at 65, for within a few days of 25 April 1925, when the Pilkington scheme began, the government published its Widows, Orphans and Old Age Contributory Pensions Bill whereby, for an additional contribution of $4\frac{1}{2}$d per week from both employer and employee, the employee received 10s per week between 65 and 70 and this was not means-tested. So, for 1s $6\frac{1}{2}$d per week, Pilkington employees reaching the age of 65 qualified for a weekly pension of 37s 9d from the beginning of 1928 when state supplementary pensions began to be paid.[23]

The company had to subsidise these pensions much more heavily at first than it had the superannuation scheme, for 5,500 people were involved, not just 625. When the Board was making its plans, it estimated the cost of starting the scheme at a capital sum of £228,000 or £16,470 per year for 20 years.[24] That capital sum was soon to be raised to £297,000,[25] and T.S.Wason, who was manager of the Pensions Department from 1922 until 1948, subsequently put the annual cost at £24,000.[26]

The statistics collected for the pension scheme provide useful information about the size of the labour force at Pilkington's factories in 1925 (Table 54, p. 401). To these have been added figures for 1923 and 1927 derived from another source which, for 1927, also includes totals for Pilkington depots and agencies at home and abroad. These figures indicate that about a third of Pilkington's labour force at its works in St Helens, and a rather higher fraction at Doncaster, consisted of young people under 21. They also show increasing numbers at Ravenhead during the mid-1920s. At the time of the 1925 count the company employed 136 foremen in its various factories.

An early return sent in by Williamson to the Ministry of Labour in December 1919[27] – presumably excluding office staff – gives a total of 4,277 employees at Grove Street, 2,767 at Cowley Hill and 485 at Ravenhead, thus indicating (Table 54) that the labour force at Grove Street was reduced during the difficult years of the early 1920s while that at Cowley Hill and Ravenhead was increased. In 1919 the company employed 1,166 women (of whom 139 were described as semi-skilled and the rest unskilled) and 188 girls (60 of whom were semi-skilled). 750 of these women and girls worked at Grove Street, 514 at Cowley Hill and the remaining 90 at Ravenhead.* Of the male workers at Grove Street, 1,329 were skilled. Most of these were the experienced glassmakers for whose redeployment or retirement the company was beginning to make provision in 1923 and who were to need this help after 1925 when it concentrated first on drawn cylinder and then on flat drawn sheet glass. The former displaced the glass blowers and gatherers, the latter the flatteners as well.

The time had come to set up the special displaced glassmakers' compensation fund, and by deed of covenant dated 1 February 1927, Austin and Cecil Pilkington each agreed to pay into it £1,000 each half year for seven years. These payments began in March 1927 and continued until September 1933, and amounted to £28,000 in all. The fund was administered

---

*A Welfare Department, formed in 1920 and gradually increased in size, with branches in the various works, was concerned with the recruitment of, and was responsible for, female labour employed by the company. It also carried out sick visiting and ran a sewing room which made and repaired industrial clothing.

TABLE 54
SIZE OF PILKINGTON LABOUR FORCE
NOVEMBER 1923, JANUARY 1925 AND MARCH 1927

	November 1923	January 1925			March 1927	
	Hourly Paid	Aged 21–60	Over 60	Total over 21	Staff	Hourly Paid
Sheet and Rolled Plate Works, Grove Street	3,854	2,352	136	2,488	609*	3,596
Plate Works, Cowley Hill	2,971	1,789	135	1,924	138	3,108
Ravenhead	858	592	34	626	61	1,244
Doncaster		657	8	665	95	1,194
Greengate Brick and Tile Works		34	2	36	121	
Home Depots					428	
Collieries					2,009	
Canada					164	
Buenos Aires					38	
Rio de Janeiro					33	
Bahia Blanca					15	
USA					1	
China					4	
South Africa					1	
Australia					3	
New Zealand					2	
India					2	
France (Maubeuge)					672	
					Total	13,538

*Mostly Head Office staff

Source: PA PB139 Board minutes, 26 February 1925; PB258 Executive Committee Papers, 8 August 1969

by an advisory committee consisting of two directors (Guy and Geoffrey Pilkington), four members of Pilkington staff (R.K.Uhthoff, E.Bickerstaff, D.Molyneux and T.Railton) and T.Williamson. It was to be used for the assistance of glassmakers only. Those approaching pensionable age and with more than 20 years' service, if they were prematurely retired, were to receive the pension they would have received had they worked to 63, together with contributions to the supplementary state pension until they received this at 65. Other men who could be found work elsewhere in the company were to receive half the difference between what they had previously received and the current Yard Rate for unskilled men. This make-up pay was also to be given, together with up to £50 for sacrificing their claim to Pilkington's pension scheme, to those who left the company provided they did not work for another glass manufacturer.[28] The fund achieved its object of easing the transition from craft to machine glassmaking; but so successful was the company in finding alternative work for men who were not retired early, that demands upon it were growing much more slowly than its income by the latter part of the covenant period. In November 1932, it had a balance of £5,000.[29]

This fund, and the staff superannuation and employee pension schemes were the work of enlightened management. Introduced in periods of prosperity, they were a dividend to labour which, in the case of the pension schemes, involved considerable capital sums to launch and were not, like pay increases, at risk when trade worsened. At the same time, these schemes, were not entirely altruistic, for pension rights could be a powerful factor in maintaining and strengthening the recipient's loyalty to his employer. Pilkington came to believe that this was morally wrong and in the 1930s, unlike many other companies, favoured full transferability of pension rights.

Pilkington's employment statistics do not survive in sufficient detail to enable us to examine the effects that the redundancy or redeployment of the skilled sheet glassmakers had upon the distribution of the company's labour costs. Most of its employees, however, continued to do the same jobs as they had previously done, and in January 1933 the Executive compared a normal week's earnings of these people with those of 1914. Although the cost of living was then little more than 40 per cent above 1914, the pay for many jobs was over 100 per cent higher and for most of them over 80 per cent. (Labourers, the lowest paid, were receiving £2 2s 4d, 92 per cent higher.) Particularly worthy of note perhaps is the fact that while the range of pay on the almost extinct drawn cylinder process in 1933 was from £2 19s 6d to £4 0s 2d – 141 per cent and 100 per cent up on 1914 – the comparable range for the less skilled working on the new flat drawn process was from £2 11s 9d to £3 3s 4d.[30]

The Executive's creation of a Personnel Department in 1934 and its attempts during the 1930s to increase labour productivity in other branches of the business has already been mentioned in chapter 19. A 42½-hour week was introduced in August 1933 with the same intention. After a year's trial, during which output had grown more rapidly than the small increase in the number of employees, it was decided to prolong the arrangement.[31] At the same time the company kept an eye upon neighbouring employers' rates of pay. In 1934, for instance, this was done for its labourers, electricians, fitters and others who were found to have a higher hourly, but usually lower weekly, rate;[32] and in 1937, Pilkington, having put up its male clerical rate from 47s 6d to 50s at age 21 because the minimum labouring rate had been advanced to 48s 3d, was in touch with ICI about their clerical scales and was told that at almost all points Pilkington paid less. A general increase was then ordered.[33]

The third phase of interwar profitability, between 1934-5 and 1937-8, was accompanied by further fringe benefits for employees. Improved facilities for dental and medical inspection were provided in 1937 and 1938 respectively,[34] and in 1937 the company increased its contribution to the pension fund, then showing a healthy surplus, to allow one-third of a deceased member's pension to be paid to his widow.[35] The new canteen at Grove Street (p. 344) was built in 1937-8 at a cost of about £32,000.[36] Holidays with pay were extended to all employees in 1938, six days (to be taken between May and October) for those with 12 months' service, those with less receiving one day for each two-month period with the company and those with over 35 years' service to be entitled to nine working days.[37] (The latter had already been granted a week's holiday with pay in 1933.)[38] In 1938, too, family allowances of 5s per child had been introduced for families with more than three children under school age;[39] and a second annual Pilkington Scholarship was endowed, to be awarded on Higher School Certificate results to enable a boy from Cowley School, St Helens, to go up to Cambridge. (The first such annual scholarship had been given for the same purpose in 1926, being financed by the company for two out of three years and by Mr and Mrs Austin Pilkington personally in every third year.)[40] The company also continued to support its Recreation Club, well on the way to its centenary, and, in the winter months, its Lecture Section, started by T.S.Wason at the beginning of the 1920s.[41] In summer, the sports ground at Ruskin Drive was well supported and in 1938 it was allowed to have a bar; but only after the full Pilkington Board had discussed the matter. It was approved on an experimental basis and not without some wagging of heads.[42] Attitudes were changing, but not particularly fast.

Although Pilkington was progressive in its welfare schemes during this period, it was by no means a pioneer. Both Cadbury and Rowntree, for instance, had introduced contributory pensions for their wage earners in 1906, and in that year there were said to be already about nine such schemes in operation. The former went on to introduce pensions for widows in 1917 and the latter in 1923.[43] On the other hand, Pilkington was well ahead of some other major companies such as ICI, which brought in pensions only in 1937,[44] and Courtaulds, after 1940.[45] And the timing of its scheme, coming just before a period of redundancy, was just right. The displacement fund was a particularly worthy gesture, though it is remarkable that it came to be financed as a private venture by the chairman, a man, as we have seen, with a deep religious conviction, and his brother, and not, as would seem more appropriate, by the company itself.

So far as holidays with pay were concerned, Pilkington lagged farther behind the leaders in the field, for a number of firms had already been providing paid holidays for their wage earners before the nineteenth century was out and by 1925 1½ million manual workers took them under collective agreements with their employers. By 1938, when Pilkington introduced them, 7¾ million wage earners had holidays with pay. There were soon to be many more for, following the Amulree Committee's recommendation in that year that everyone should have a week's paid holiday, an Act was passed to encourage this.[46]

On Pilkington's wage levels it is much more difficult to reach a verdict. At the bottom end of the scale the company's rate for labourers in the early 1930s, £2 2s 4d per week, may be compared with an average labourer's wage at ICI of £2 10s[47] or with average industrial earnings of £3. On the other hand, Pilkington was very sensitive to any change there might be in local wage rates and there is no doubt that, like those in employment elsewhere, all its wage earners were far better off in real terms than they had been in 1914. At the other end of the scale, too, Pilkington executives seem to have been quite well rewarded, rising from £400/500 to £1500 or a little more just before the war for such people as the Chief Accountant or a Works Manager. Some particularly valued men earned even more than that: for instance, J.B.Watt was paid £2,000 a year when he became general manager of Sheet Works in 1938, F.B.Waldron £2,000 in 1939, and F.E.Slocombe, the manager at Doncaster who reached retiring age in 1938 after 51 years with the company, having risen from apprentice fitter and turner to local director, £2,500. (His retirement pension was fixed at the princely rate of £1,000 per year.)[48]

Relations with organised labour throughout these difficult years seem to have been remarkably good, despite the intractable hostility shown by the company to the unions before 1917. It was fortunate in having to deal almost entirely with one union, and Tom Williamson, the local organiser and old adversary of pre-war days – one of whose letters, the reader will recall, was thrown into the fire unopened by a director – was to prove an able and understanding negotiator. In 1938 when he was retiring and the directors heard that he was likely to be in straitened circumstances, they consulted the union's General Secretary to see whether it would be in order for the company to give to the collection being made by his fellow trade unionists. It not only contributed £50 but also quietly bought him an annuity worth 10s a week.[49]

Chapter 22

Epilogue, 1939–76

THE purpose of this book has been to set down, analyse and discuss, as fully as the surviving records permit, the history of Pilkington Brothers Limited and of British flat glass manufacture in its international context down to 1939. The time has not yet arrived to continue further in such detail, for from then onwards we are dealing with events involving people who are still alive. These events must remain to be considered *in extenso* by some future historian. It would be a mistake, however, to end without at least an outline of this most recent phase, for the company has, since the war, with the fourth generation of the Pilkington family in charge, enjoyed a more remarkable period of growth and change than during any previous 30-year period in its history, including the highly prosperous years before 1914. Exceptionally successful marketing policies for British-made glass were associated with a great extension abroad not only of processing but also of manufacturing. Pilkington is now a giant international concern in a sense that it never was in 1939 and its structural organisation has changed almost out of recognition to take account of this transformation. During the past decade, a very difficult one for the British economy and discouraging to business growth, the company has managed to maintain its momentum by the development of the float glass process, the most remarkable leap forward in the technology of this branch of the industry. In a surprisingly short time, this revolutionary development has superseded existing methods of making plate glass in all parts of the world, and its product is increasingly taking the place of sheet glass as well, the mechanical production of which was developed in such a laborious and time-consuming way between the early years of the century and the later 1920s. Pilkington, for the past half century well respected by its foreign competitors for its technical accomplishments and capability, has now become world leader in the technical field.

This epilogue chapter is necessary not only to give the reader some idea of this commercial and technical transformation but also to enable those who know the present-day company to relate it to the much more limited scale of its operations discussed in earlier chapters. We shall first of all attempt a brief survey of some of the main features of the post-war period and then look at one or two dominant themes.[1]

The increased demand for flat glass both for building and for the motor trade, which we noticed as an important feature of the interwar period even in the depression years, became much more pronounced after 1945 with full employment policies and higher levels of economic activity. Building was given high priority; and the number of cars and vans licensed in Britain, which had grown to 2 m. in the 20 years between the wars, increased by a further 12 m. or so in the 25 years after 1950. By the mid-1970s there were also getting on for 2 m. commercial vehicles. Such a rapid rate of expansion in the motor trade was typical of the more advanced countries of the world as they followed the United States into mass car ownership. Moreover, the pre-war trend towards greater glass usage per unit, both in buildings and in vehicles, was also sustained. Indeed, some of the tall post-war office blocks seem to consist of whole walls of glass stretching skywards.

By careful long-term planning, Pilkington managed to acquire a much larger share of this rapidly-growing trade. Without any increase in protection beyond the 15 per cent duty dating from the early 1930s, foreign imports of glass were reduced to a small share of the UK market – about ten per cent – for the first time, apart from the two wars, since the 1850s when, with the coming of free trade, the Belgians had first laid claim to a sizeable stake in it. And, at the same time, Pilkington's exports, so disappointing for most of the interwar period, regained their pre-1914 importance. After the war the company managed, for the first time in its history, to excel in both home and export markets simultaneously. Whereas in 1934–8 imports of flat glass were two and a half times the sterling value of exports, in 1956–65 exports were nearly three and a half times the value of imports.

This remarkable turnround was achieved at a time when, in addition to the opening of more safety glass processing plants overseas, which stimulated exports of raw glass from Britain, the company was also, either directly through its own subsidiaries or indirectly through associated companies, manufacturing more glass abroad in countries that had committed themselves to increased industrialisation, thereby reducing exports to these markets. By the 1970s Pilkington had important manufacturing or processing interests not only in Canada, Australia and South Africa but also in India, Ireland, New Zealand, Argentina, Mexico, Rhodesia, Sweden and Venezuela. In all, it then had more than 40 subsidiary and associated companies in 16 countries. The growth in the number of employees abroad, rather than at home, is the clearest indication of the increasing importance of these developments.

TABLE 55

PILKINGTON EMPLOYEES AT HOME AND ABROAD 1946-76

Date	UK	Overseas	Total
December 1946	15,332	667	15,909
December 1951	19,721	1,346	21,067
December 1956	20,302	3,121	24,423
September 1961	20,572	3,051	23,623
September 1966	23,515	6,155	29,670
September 1971	22,137	9,301	31,438
March 1976	19,900*	12,242	32,142*

*Provisional totals
Source: Pilkington Staff Records

The oversea figures underestimate Pilkington's total activity abroad to the extent that they do not include employees of associated companies; and all these labour statistics bear little relationship to total manufacturing activity in such an increasingly capital intensive industry. While the labour force doubled, sales grew more than 30-fold, a very remarkable growth in productivity even after the declining value of money over the period, (about five-fold) is taken into account.

This rapid increase in sales included not only income from the marketing of flat glass but also from the new products such as glass fibres, sold under the trade name of Fibreglass, the beginnings of which we noticed in Chapter 20, and optical and ophthalmic (spectacle) glass, in which Pilkington also became interested through its takeover of Chances. Indeed, by the mid-1960s Pilkington had developed a wider product range even than the major flat glass manufacturers in the United States. Since then new additions have been made in the optical field, such as the range of 'Reactolite' photochromic glasses, announced in 1973. 'Cemfil' fibres, the first glass fibre capable of reinforcing Portland cement, made

68 THE LAST BOARD MEETING AT GROVE STREET, 1964. *Back row, left to right;* J.A.Burns (sub-director), G.W.T.Bird, A.C.Pilkington, D.F.Pilkington, L.A.B. (Sir Alastair) Pilkington, A.M. (Sir Alan) Hudson Davies, Sir Humphrey Mynors, G.McOnie, Lord Cozens-Hardy, L.H.A.Pilkington.
Front row, left to right; D.V.Phelps, G.R.Pilkington, Sir Harry (Lord) Pilkington, G.L.Pilkington, J.B.Watt.

TABLE 56
FINANCIAL AND SALES STATISTICS, 1945/6–1975/6

£'000

	1945/6	1950/1	1955/6	1960/1	1965/6	1970/1	1975/6
Capital employed (incl. overdrafts)	7,508	17,012	28,781	48,776	92,778	174,322	401,421
Shareholders' equity	5,543	13,708	25,019	41,090	62,264	105,895	209,368
Borrowings – loans etc.	1,015	889	809	778	8,493	14,376	90,498
bank overdraft	—	360	—	207	6,969	20,802	15,946
Sales to outside customers	9,296	15,641	42,571	57,957	84,850	123,180	303,147
Group profit before tax	986	2,868	4,655	8,751	8,683	13,940	34,586
Group profit after tax	677	756	1,867	3,908	5,806	7,511	11,287
Dividends paid	293	348	573	729	2,046	*2,630	5,694
Profit retained	112	408	1,795	2,684	2,052	1,654	3,278
Licensing income	N/A	N/A	91	50	924	8,623	19,908

*In all years shown dividends were paid net of tax apart from 1971. For purposes of comparison the net of tax equivalent for 1971 has been given in the above table.

Source: Pilkington Accounts

its appearance in 1972. In safety glass, Triplex 'Hyviz', a colourless, electrically conducting heating film for demisting and defrosting purposes (1971) and, particularly, 'Triplex Ten Twenty', a great improvement in laminated windscreens (1973), were new product additions. Elsewhere in the company's operation, certain other products have been abandoned: Vitrolite (1968), glass blocks and high voltage insulators (1971) and television glassware (1976).

Rapid growth in flat glass would not have been possible had the two major threats of the later 1930s, Perspex and thick drawn sheet, eventually materialised. Perspex, as has been seen, lacked the hardness of glass, and after the war it became evident that, even when produced on a larger scale, it could still not compete with glass on price. Translucent plastic did, however, take some of the market for glass, particularly cast glass, in the horticultural trade and for roofing purposes generally, on account of its lighter weight which made lighter structures possible; but even in this case there was some compensation in that glass fibres were used to reinforce polyester sheet.

The threat from TDS was a much more serious matter, for sheet glass was not a branch of the industry in which Pilkington particularly excelled before the war and it was already draining profit from plate upon which the company depended so much. If, as seemed probable with further technical development, the quality of TDS would be improved, the costly plate glass process itself would be at risk. Here the float process came to the rescue and placed the company ahead of all its rivals. The world's growing dependence on float is reflected in the increasing licence income in the last line of Table 56. And a float plant, less costly to install than the inordinately expensive and cumbersome plate glass machinery, made it possible for Pilkington to manufacture high quality glass in markets which were not large enough to justify plate glass production.

This remarkable record of progress, though assisted by many encouraging economic circumstances, was not helped by other developments during the period. Co-operation in industry, blessed before the war as rationalisation, came increasingly to be criticised after it as being monopolistic and against the public interest. Higher taxation reduced the incentive to take business risks. For a family business, the level of death duties posed particular problems. With the much greater value of shares, the death of important holders involved the payment of much larger death duties; and so high was the level of taxation generally that shareholders could not afford to purchase shares in large quantities from other family shareholders. These fiscal problems eventually obliged the company to go public in 1970.

Yet, despite all these difficulties, Pilkington remained highly profitable and, as will be seen from Table 56, was still able to plough back very large sums into the development of the business. When, in the mid-1960s, the Monopolies Commission came to investigate the supply of flat glass, including safety glass, in the United Kingdom, it produced a report which was unique in positively welcoming the company's policies and in praising the way the family business had throughout used its monopoly position very responsibly and with great concern for the public interest:

Pilkington submits that throughout the world 'it is competition and the nature of large-scale, continuous, high quality manufacture that dictates the structure of the industry'; the company aims 'to be competitive and efficient – if this means that we become the only supplier, that would be an incidental result, but it is not the objective'.

We accept that the tendency towards national monopolies in flat glass is due mainly to the large capital investment required to lay down the most efficient and economical plant and to the fact that the maximum efficiency and savings of such plant can only be realised if it is producing for a very large market. As Pilkington itself has emphasised this is a consideration which does not affect only the consumers of flat glass in this country. Pilkington has established a very important export trade, which it could not maintain, much less increase, unless it were able to exploit to the full the potential economies of scale which are available to its competitors ...

We are satisfied that Pilkington is conscious of its responsibility, as a monopolist, to the public interest. This sense of responsibility may be associated to some extent with the long-established dominance of the Pilkington family within the business ...[2]

So far as the glass industry was concerned, the Second World War differed from the First in two respects: imports were reduced to negligible proportions within a very short period and air raid damage created a large demand for glass, the building material most vulnerable to bombing. 'It can be said with some justification', the company subsequently claimed, 'that London was twice reglazed, and at one period three million square feet of glass per week was sent to the London area.' This demand, in the absence of imports, more than compensated for the lack of new cars and new buildings. Pilkington home sales of sheet glass were 50 per cent higher in volume in 1941 than they had been in 1938, and they rose higher still in the subsequent years; and to meet urgent need, a special wartime product had to be made, known as rolled sheet – rolled plate made at speed and only slightly obscured. During the war the company was also able to increase its export trade to markets which could no longer be supplied from continental Europe. Again, it was sheet glass which benefited most: exports rose in 1941 to nearly three times their 1938 volume: and 1938 had been Pilkington's best pre-war year.

The company took advantage of lack of competition in the home market to rationalise selling and to lay longer-term plans aimed to ensure that, when international competition returned, British glass would compete so strongly on price, quality and delivery that the foreign product would not be able to regain its previous large share of the home market. One of the company's first actions was to alter the basis upon which sheet glass was sold so that prices were brought into line with costs. When glass had been hand blown, the larger sheets cost more to produce and fetched higher prices. With flat-drawn machine production, however, unit costs were lower on the larger stock sizes, for they required less cutting and handling per sq. ft; but the Belgians had continued to sell machine-made glass on the same basis as the hand-blown product, and, since they were then market leaders, Pilkington had no alternative but to follow suit. Given wartime freedom of manoeuvre, the company related price to cost. It also cut distribution costs by increasing loose load delivery of glass in stock sizes by motor lorry to large purchasers, thus avoiding packing, a method already introduced before the war. It was to depend very much more on road transport when the war was over, and on-site glazing by specialist glass dealers became increasingly common. These larger merchants, besides cutting to size from stock sizes, were also equipped to perform many other processing functions, such as silvering for mirror manufacture and edge working for shelves. They often had showrooms. In recognition of these greater commitments and higher overheads, they had traditionally received a larger discount on Pilkington's national price list (or tariff); but these discounts, which ranged up to 20 per cent or so, were so arranged that the highest discount level was relatively easy to achieve in terms of turnover. This encouraged the young and enterprising concerns and merchants in smaller towns. In the middle 1960s, 50 per cent of all glass was sold to merchants receiving the maximum discount and another 34 per cent to those who were within $7\frac{1}{2}$ per cent of it. The function of Pilkington's own depots, while remaining the centre of operations for the local sales force, was no longer to supply local services in competition with merchants selling foreign glass but to act as reserve stockists and to supply customers with whom the company retained direct accounts. In recognition of this changed role, all depots, with the exception of Glasgow, were closed during the 1970s and replaced by regional sales and service offices. At part of the Cowley Hill factory, known from 1953 as the City Road Works, Pilkington had its own plant for worked glass, for silvering and for the manufacture of items such as double glazed units and Armourplate (Armourfloat) doors.

In 1942, at Pilkington's suggestion, a meeting was held with English and Welsh glass merchants which led to the formation, at the end of that year, of the National Sheet Glass Merchants Association whose members pledged themselves to buy only from British manufacturers or from other producers who subsequently made agreements with the Association. Pilkington's own agreements with the continentals had been automatically cancelled with the war under the Trading With the Enemy Act and were not renewed when it was over. There was then a world shortage of glass and Pilkington took advantage of the high world price to profit as much as it could in export markets while keeping its home prices as low as possible, thus helping to keep domestic building costs down and make foreign imports uncompetitive. All the pre-war fidelity agreements with merchants, which had lapsed in 1939, were formally cancelled in 1950, and in 1957 all agreements between the company and the National Sheet Glass Merchants Association were themselves cancelled. The former Plate Glass Merchants Association (renamed in 1934 the Plate Glass Association and in 1964 – with the advent of float – the Flat Glass Association), membership of which overlaps with the NSGMA but is not so extensive, had discussions with Pilkington three or four times a year which ranged over all types of flat glass.

Since the war the trade has benefited from the Technical Sales and Service Department which the company set up in 1945. This has developed its own testing laboratory, an environmental section, an architectural information service (stemming from the more modest interwar beginnings already mentioned) and a section to extend the existing uses of Pilkington products and to develop and launch the new ones.

Increased sales called for greater output. A new five-machine sheet glass tank came into operation at St Helens at the end of 1946 and, at the insistence of the government, the next new tank, with four machines, was located at Pontypool. Increased output was also obtained by further improving the PPG process. One of the St Helens tanks, for instance, which produced 650,000 sq. ft per week when it first made PPG glass in the early 1930s, was making 1,150,000 sq. ft per week by 1954 and 1,800,000 sq. ft by the mid-1960s. Sheet glass was also made at Llavallol in the Argentine from 1941, Pilkington's first sheet glassmaking interest abroad since Thorold had been closed. (The company's financial stake in Vidrieria

Argentina S.A. was subsequently increased until it eventually came to own almost all the ordinary shares.) Other sheet glass factories were opened overseas: by Pilkington subsidiaries at Springs, near Johannesburg, (Pilkington Brothers (South Africa) Pty Ltd), and at Scarborough, a suburb of Toronto (both in 1951), and by the Hindusthan Development Corporation, with both Pilkington and Indian capital, at Asansol in Bengal (1954). (This became the Hindusthan-Pilkington Glass Works Limited in 1961 and was converted from Fourcault to PPG machines. Pilkington subsequently obtained a majority interest.) In 1963 a joint Pilkington-ACI company started to make sheet glass at Dandenong, Victoria; and Pilkington, through its New Zealand subsidiary (Pilkington Brothers (New Zealand) Ltd) formed in 1949, and ACI, acquired a glass-making concern which had tried to make sheet glass in New Zealand and had gone bankrupt in the process. The new concern, operating as New Zealand Window Glass Ltd, began to manufacture successfully at Whangerei, nearly 100 miles north of Auckland, in 1964. A year later in Mexico the parent company, with Fomento de Industria y Commercio SA, acquired a 35 per cent shareholding in both Vidrio Plano SA (VIPSA, which made sheet and rolled glass) and Vidrio Plano de Mexico (VIPLA-MEX, which made sheet and safety glass). In 1972 Pilkington and ACI re-organised their flat and safety interests in Australia in a new joint company, Pilkington-ACI Limited.

Safety glass output at home was greatly increased and Pilkington eventually acquired control of Triplex in 1965. (It became a wholly owned subsidiary in 1971). With Triplex also went Triplex Ireland, to which Triclover Safety Glass Limited was added in 1971. British Indestructo Glass, the largest other British safety glass manufacturer, was purchased by Triplex in 1967. A new safety glass factory was opened at Larkhall in Lanarkshire in 1965 to supply the new Scottish motor industry and in 1971 the Willesden works were closed. New Safety plants were added to the existing ones abroad: at Sao Paulo in Brazil (1946–1966); Lower Hutt in New Zealand (1952; controlled by Pilkington Brothers (New Zealand) Limited); at Villawood, near Sydney (1956); at Umtali in Rhodesia (1961); in South Africa at Springs (1966); at the new works at Struandale, Port Elizabeth (1973), and at a small toughening plant in Durban (1974). In 1973 Pilkington obtained a foothold in Venezuela by acquiring a 20 per cent shareholding in Vidrios Venezolanos Extra CA (VIVEX).

Fibreglass was another product which became increasingly important at home and was also made abroad. Chances' pre-war forebodings proved justified when Fibreglass Limited (as Glass Fibres came to be called) established its main centre of operations at Ravenhead, St Helens, in

preparation for the post-war building programme.* A completely new
factory for the manufacture of glass textiles and glass fibres for reinforced
glass plastics was established at Possilpark, Glasgow, in 1948. Manufacture
of the latter was later moved to Valley Road, Birkenhead, where an existing factory was bought and re-equipped in 1957. Reinforcements manufacture was moved to Wrexham in 1971. Possilpark and Valley Road
were subsequently closed.

Kitson's Insulations Limited, thermal insulation contractors and very
important customers of Fibreglass, were acquired in 1973, and a substantial stake in the insulation division of Bernard Hastie Limited (now Hastie
Insulation Limited) in 1976. Quite recently a new fibre insulation works
has been built at Pontyfelin in South Wales. (This has absorbed some of the
employees from Pontypool when those glassworks were closed down in
1975. The other works which Pilkington had acquired out of necessity
and not by design, at Queenborough in Kent, were closed in 1973.)

Fibreglass plants were also started abroad: at Llavallol in Argentina in
1940, at Springs in South Africa in 1954, and Thana in India in 1965
(Fibreglass Pilkington Limited). Fibreglass-Pilkington (Malaysia) (1970)
and Fibreglass Pilkington (Singapore) (1971) were merchanting companies whose function has been taken over since 1974 by Pilkington
(South East Asia) Pte Limited. Pilkington Glass (Nigeria) (1964) and
Pilkington Glass (Jamaica) (1972) are also merchanting concerns.

Optical glass manufacture, the other branch of the industry which came
to Pilkington with Chances, was made at the Umbroc shadow factory
in St Helens during the war. Since June 1957, optical and ophthalmic glass
has been further developed, using a continuous process licensed from the
American Corning Glass Company, at the specially-built Chance-
Pilkington Optical Works at St Asaph in North Wales. This factory has
become, *inter alia*, one of the largest producers of unpolished spectacle
glass blanks in Europe. In 1966 Pilkington and Perkin Elmer Limited,
subsidiary of the American Perkin Elmer Corporation, joined forces to
make advanced optical and electro-optical systems, also at St Asaph, and
the factory was opened a year later. (Pilkington acquired the Perkin Elmer
shareholding in 1973 and the subsidiary was re-named Pilkington P.E.
Limited.) The Michael Birch Group Limited, a holding company for a

*Pilkington acquired control of Chances in September 1945 and a large final purchase of
shares took place in March 1952. The rationalisation of the production and sales function of
the two businesses followed over the next five years or so. A further milestone was reached in
1976 when Spon Lane ceased to make rolled plate glass; but it remained in existence chiefly
as a producer of glass tubing for fluorescent and incandescent lamps and for electronic,
medical and pharmaceutical purposes. Further processing of tubing for syringes, etc., was
carried out at works in Malvern.

group of ophthalmic manufacturing opticians and manufacturers of microfilm equipment, was acquired in 1974. An attempt to expand further in this field by the taking over of UK Optical was referred to the Monopolies Commission in the summer of 1976.

All this restless growth, impressive enough in itself, was overshadowed from about 1960 onwards, by the advent of float glass – a fascinating and dramatic story which it is hoped will be the basis of a future history. For the present we shall confine ourselves to the main features of what was in fact a kind of mid-twentieth century adventure story, an advance into the world of science and technology which was, in some respects, the modern equivalent of expeditions across uncharted seas or into unknown continents in years gone by.

Both design and accident contributed to the original discovery and the element of good fortune, or serendipity as it is now sometimes called in this context, continued to be a feature of subsequent development right down to the point at which the new product became commercially profitable. From the end of the war, the company correctly diagnosed the grinding and polishing of plate glass as the part of its manufacturing operations which would most repay the further attention of Research and Development. To cast glass thicker than was needed and then grind off about a third of it, including the lustrous fire finish, then smooth it (to remove the worst grinding marks) and finally polish it, expending very large amounts of energy in the process, was clearly an extremely clumsy and costly way of making even a high quality product. Pilkington's twin grinder of the 1930s was only an improvement upon a process which was still grossly inefficient. Moreover, it was being increasingly challenged by the drawn sheet glass processes as they were further developed. The director chiefly responsible for plate glass production from 1939 was James Meikle, chairman of the Technical Committee – after the war renamed the Manufacturing Conference, representing a change of purpose and not merely a new title. He gave top priority to the discovery of ways of reducing, or even eliminating altogether, the cumbersome grinding and polishing machinery. More scientists and engineers were recruited with this aim chiefly in mind.

One of them, (Sir) Alastair Pilkington, who was to invent the float process, came to the company by a most remarkable accident, for he was not related to the St Helens family in any way. They heard of him through Sir Richard Pilkington, one of the family shareholders but not a director, who, having lost his parliamentary seat in the Labour landslide of 1945, turned his attention to his hobby of genealogy or, more specifically, tracing back the Pilkingtons' own family tree. This put him into touch with Col. Lionel Pilkington, a businessman in Reading. When it soon became clear that there was no traceable link between their respective ancestors, they got round to discussing the rising generation. Alastair Pilkington, Lionel's second son (b. 1920), having fought in the war and been taken prisoner, was then back at Cambridge completing his Mechanical Sciences Tripos and would, in getting on for two years' time, be looking for a job. Would Pilkington Brothers Limited be interested? Here, after all, was a promising experimental engineer in the making. Harry Pilkington and Douglas Phelps met Lionel Pilkington to learn more. It was, however, the next step in this strange sequence of events which was the most remarkable, for, as the Board minutes of 29 November 1945 relate, the company decided to offer the young man, if suitable, the most unusually generous conditions of service. The whole minute is worth quoting in full, not least for its rather ungrateful reprimand to Richard Pilkington for taking the initiative:

The Directors considered a report furnished by Col. Phelps of an interview which he and Mr W.H.Pilkington had had with Col. Lionel G.Pilkington on the subject of his second son, Alastair, joining the PB Organisation after completing his studies at University. The matter had arisen from an almost casual introduction by Mr Richard Pilkington. The Directors felt that it should be pointed out to Mr Richard Pilkington that the method of introduction was very irregular.

Mr L.G.Pilkington's branch of the family broke away at least 15 generations ago [i.e. as far back as the family tree went]. It was agreed that a member of the Pilkington Family, however remote, could be accepted only as a potential Family Director. After considerable discussion, the Board agreed that, in principle, they were prepared to open the door wider to really promising candidates.

Mr A.C.Pilkington [who, it will be recalled, had moved down to Boars Hill, near Oxford] pointed out that our business is largely in the North of England, that conditions of life in the North of England are very different from those in the South, and we must be very sure that a potential candidate brought up in the South understands and is willing to take on the obligation of living in the North, both for himself and his family.

It was also emphasised that the private nature of PB's business, which has had great advantages for both employers and workpeople, demands a high standard from the Directors, and in the political conditions of the future will probably do so to an even greater extent. If we are to throw the net wider, we must take applicants only of the very highest standard.

P

With regard to the particular case under discussion, it was considered that before any action in respect of Alastair Pilkington was taken, we should take steps to learn more about Col. L.G.Pilkington – in particular his business and family background. He is Managing Director of the Pulsometer Engineering Co., Reading, which Lord Cozens-Hardy pointed out was a small but old and well established company, he believed of Quaker origin.[3]

Enquiries about Lionel Pilkington evidently proved reassuring and in due course Harry Pilkington met Alastair in London. Alastair was brought up to St Helens to spend three days at the various works and to meet all the members of the Executive. In March 1947, the Board, having received favourable reports from the works managers and technical directors, were prepared to offer him a family traineeship and he started work at St Helens in the following August. He soon learned of the company's quest for an alternative to grinding and polishing and he also became involved in experimental work of various sorts both at Cowley Hill and, between 1949 and 1951, at Doncaster where he had been posted as production manager. Soon after his return to St Helens, in the middle of 1951, Meikle unexpectedly decided to retire on account of deafness and Alastair Pilkington found his promotion even further accelerated. He joined the Executive Committee at the beginning of 1953, aged 32. His experimental work was then sure of a hearing at the highest level; and he was a superb advocate.

He had started to attend the bi-monthly Manufacturing Conference in November 1951. At his second meeting, in January 1952, in connection with other experiments then taking place, he suggested the possibility of fire-finishing glass by floating it on a bath of molten tin in a neutral atmosphere. (Another experimental engineer, Kenneth Bickerstaff, had already tried tin as a conveyor of glass at about 600°C; but nobody had until then had the idea of using tin for fire finishing at about 1,000°C.) Very soon after this, Alastair Pilkington had his brainwave. Why not pass the molten glass from the tank, either as a rolled ribbon or directly, on to the bath of tin at 1,000°C, and float it frictionless down the bath through a temperature gradient falling to about 600°C at which temperature the ribbon of glass would be cool enough to be taken off on rollers without marking the surface? Tin was molten over a wide temperature range and, as its specific gravity was much greater than that of glass, it would be an admirable supporter for the ribbon. The lighter ribbon was likely to acquire strictly parallel surfaces as it floated down the bath. Here might be the way of making quality glass without grinding and polishing – and at a fraction of the cost.

Three pilot plants were used between 1952 and 1955 to explore these possibilities further. The first two were small (about 25 ft long and floating a ribbon 12-in. wide) costing under £10,000 each. The third was larger. It floated a 30-in. ribbon and cost about £30,000. These experiments were most promising and the provisional application for the first British patent in the float series was filed in December 1953 in the names of Alastair Pilkington and (much to his surprise) Kenneth Bickerstaff in respect of his work on tin as a conveyor. By mid-1955 the point had been reached at which the Executive had to decide whether or not to risk building a full-scale production plant.

The economic climate was then most encouraging. The British economy was enjoying its first post-war boom, and the world demand for glass, for use both in the rapidly-growing motor industry and in building, had reached famine proportions. The company's profits had risen sharply, and especially its profits on plate glass as grinding and polishing techniques were improved and both twin and continuous polisher were speeded up. Four other foreign manufacturers joined St Gobain as licensees of the twin between 1950 and 1954. The limited developments of the interwar years were now helping to provide the resources for the next, much more radical and far-reaching, change. The accident of a spell of economic prosperity coincided with the fruits of careful planning. Moreover, expected demand in three or four years' time was making imperative the installation of additional productive capacity. Was the company to go for float at an estimated fixed cost of £100,000 or £200,000 or to put down another long, inefficient grinding and polishing line at a cost of millions? The Board decided to take the risk and build the float plant.

Several serious setbacks followed and later caused great anxiety when no float glass was produced to provide the much-needed additional output. Already, in the autumn of 1955, it was discovered that only $\frac{1}{4}$-in. glass could be made by the new process; but – and again good fortune prevailed – that was the substance for which Pilkington happened to have the greatest sale; so that particular problem could be left aside for the time being while more urgent matters were tackled. Among these was a surface bloom which appeared when float glass was toughened. This was soon explained and the problem largely, and eventually wholly, cured. Worse still, when the production unit was started up at Cowley Hill in May 1957, all sorts of new difficulties revealed themselves which had not been experienced on the pilot plant and it was 20 January 1959 before the new product could be announced to the world. Not a square foot of saleable glass was produced for over 15 months after the start-up – and then as the result of another fortunate accident. Some good glass suddenly appeared in the centre of the ribbon. More experiments had to be carried out to discover why. With this knowledge the proportion of saleable glass was slowly increased. Much more development work lay ahead, including means of making float glass of substances other than ¼-in., quite essential before foreign manufacturers could be persuaded to take out licences. Huge losses had been sustained before the process began to make a profit – over £900,000 in the year ended 31 March 1959, for instance – but again fortune smiled on the company: these losses coincided with prosperous years and good trading profits met the development costs. A modest profit of £350,000 was made on float in 1960–1 but this became a loss again, because of further development work, in the next year. Only after 1962–3 did the new process become uninterruptedly profitable. It was in that financial year, too, that the first foreign licence was granted, to the Pittsburgh Plate Glass Co. Others soon followed. In 1976 21 manufacturers abroad were paying float royalties to Pilkington.

As float operating costs were reduced by further development, the new product not only replaced plate, which Pilkington stopped making in 1967, but also the thicker substances of sheet. More float lines were built at Cowley Hill and, with lower fixed and operating costs, the manufacture of quality glass also became possible abroad: in Canada (first float line 1967 and second 1970) in Mexico (1968) and in Australia (1974). A wholly-owned subsidiary began to make float in Sweden in 1976, and production is due to begin in South Africa in 1977.

Never before in its long history had flat glass manufacture witnessed such a rapid transformation. Alastair Pilkington became a Fellow of the Royal Society in 1969 and was knighted at the beginning of the following year.

Company growth at the post-1945 pace called for more than one change in the company's structure, and in more recent years reorganisation has become no longer an occasional large event but a continuing process. Only by devolution and the involvement of more people in decision-making was it possible to exercise control over a business which was not only growing in size but also in product range and geographical extent. Centralisation remained essential over such areas as allocation of financial resources and appointment of the highest management; but in general more authority was given to people on the spot, including, in the case of operations abroad, nationals of the countries concerned. To have undertaken these major administrative reforms at a time when so much else was happening in the business, required leadership and managerial ability of the highest order.

The major committees which reported to the Executive in the later 1930s – Finance, Sales, Personnel and Welfare, and Technical – continued to do so until the early 1950s when it was felt that a new structure was needed which delegated more responsibility to senior managers, thus leaving the Executive with more time for policy matters and planning. Accordingly, in 1954 the Executive Committee was transformed into a Group Executive below which were two management committees, one dealing with flat, and the other with pressed, glass, each having responsibility for production, sales, distribution, costs and prices of the products concerned subject to a limit of £10,000 on any one capital requisition. Both management committees included senior managers as well as directors. Subsidiary and associated companies also were to be managed by their own Boards 'with degrees of freedom varying from time to time as well as from company to company'. They reported, as appropriate, either to the Flat Glass Management Committee or the Group Executive. Each of the directors, as before, was to bear responsibility for a number of the company's main functions with senior executives in day-to-day control of departmental detail. (J.B.Watt and Alastair Pilkington, for instance, were the directors responsible for manufacturing, with the works managers in day-to-day charge.)

Within a year or two, with considerable further growth, it was felt that, despite the beneficial effects of these changes, more were needed if the directors were to be freed from detailed executive work. In an attempt to achieve this objective, from 1958 the Group Executive was advised by four committees (financial, commercial, technical and personnel) whose function was to pre-digest the more important matters coming up for its consideration. An enlarged Secretarial Department was to service the Boards, Management and Policy Committees, and UK subsidiaries. Physical form was given to these structural changes in 1964 when the Head Office staff were moved from Grove Street, where the company's headquarters had long outgrown the extensions of the later 1930s, to a new and imposing 12-storey, glass-clad office block in pleasant, landscaped surroundings at Ravenhead, quite near to what remained of the original plate glass factory of the 1770s which had first given St Helens its place in the glassmaking world. And, in recognition of Pilkington's greater commitment to science and technology, a large new research and development complex, situated in the country at Lathom, about ten miles from St Helens, was opened in 1961.

Further changes followed during the next decade until British-based activities had been divided into five main profit centres or product divisions: flat glass, safety glass, glass fibres, optical and spectacle glass, and

pressed glass, each with its own Board on none of which either the chairman of the company or chairman of the Group Executive sat, thereby
encouraging them to assert proper initiative and a measure of independence. In the mid-1960s outside directors of distinction, chosen entirely
for their personal qualities, were introduced to the main Pilkington
Board. In 1976, for instance, there were four such directors: a former Deputy Governor of the Bank of England; a former Chairman of the British
Iron and Steel Board and ex-director of a number of important companies;
a former Head of the Ministry of Health and Board of Inland Revenue;
and the former adviser to British Rail on industrial policy matters.
Besides serving on the main Board, these men also sat on one or more
functional, or line management, committees. This principle of bringing in
eminent men from outside the glass business was also applied to subsidiaries
overseas. Such partnership with local individuals and local interests has
worked most successfully.

These developments – and the policy of circulating annually to employees the chairman's review of the year's activities – occurred when it
was realised that the company would soon have to go public. The chairman, who felt particularly responsible for handling this matter, made it
clear that the company would never fail to undertake desirable expansion
on the grounds of shortage of money; and it will be seen from Table 56
that the company's borrowing, quite small before 1960, rose thereafter
despite rising royalties from float. Indeed, so early as 1960 the chairman
himself had decided that round about 1970 would be the earliest date at
which the company could go public and that it would be impossible to
postpone the move for long after that in view of the family's growing
difficulty in finding the money to buy shares from estates of deceased
shareholders and of the known feeling among a few shareholders that they,
like their predecessors of the 1930s, would like to have a wider market
so that they could obtain a higher price for their shares. 1970 was chosen
by the chairman as the earliest date because it was likely to be only about
then that float royalties would have started to reach appreciable proportions. To go public sooner would have been unfair to family shareholders;
to delay much beyond 1970 would have been unfair to public buyers.

It was eventually decided to go public at the chairman's earliest target
date, 1970. The decision was finally taken in January of that year and was
not reversed either following the disastrous and much-publicised strike in
April or after the further decline in stock market levels. (Shares fell to less
than half their price two years before.)

The strike, which cost the company £5 m. plus pay increases greater
than would otherwise then have been granted, was of a quite unexpected

kind. It began on a Friday afternoon at one works and by Monday had spread throughout almost all the others in the United Kingdom. It was the first such stoppage at Pilkington since the 1870s. Beginning as a trivial issue, it produced a number of claims – arising particularly out of a complex and rigid wage structure, and involving treasured differentials, which had been built up over time – and settled down much more as a dispute between the official National Union of General and Municipal Workers and a breakaway union which was taking the opportunity to try and establish itself. For much of the time the company was left helpless on the sidelines. After three weeks, most of the employees outside St Helens went back to work but at St Helens itself the strike dragged on for seven weeks altogether; and even then there was a brief, though quite ineffective, further strike six weeks later.

Despite this setback and the sagging stock market – and despite suggestions from the company's merchant bankers – it was nevertheless decided to proceed with the formation of the public company. (The market was so bad at the time that only 10 per cent of the shares were issued to the public in the first instance.) The view was taken that there would probably always be a time when the company's operations were in difficulty in some part of the world – two years after the 1970 strike, for instance, there was a 14-week stoppage at its plant in Canada – and in any case the public issue could not be delayed much longer. In the event, the effect of the change was not particularly marked, for the chairman had for some time preached, and acted upon, the principle that a large private company should be run as if it were a large public one. The directors' main fear was that, as a public company, they would have less control over its resources and would find it more difficult to formulate long-term policies. Would Pilkington so readily have taken the decision to build the float production plant in 1955 if it had been a public company and responsible to outside shareholders? Some of the directors who took that decision doubt this. Only a similarly costly plunge into the unknown (if it is possible to envisage the like of float again) would help us to arrive at an answer.

The men who controlled the destiny of the business during these years, an increasing though still quite small band of leaders, included people of unusual stature. Harry Pilkington – knighted in 1953 and granted a life peerage in 1968 – who was company chairman from 1949 to 1973 and then became its Honorary Life President, is undoubtedly the most remarkable of all the remarkable members of the family who have appeared in these pages.

We have noticed how each new generation of the family has had its impact upon the growth of the company, most successfully in the case of the second generation between about 1870 and 1914, much less so in the case of the depleted third generation which was in charge between the wars. The fourth generation, having undergone a more rigorous period of training than any of its predecessors, was already making its influence felt in the later 1930s, particularly in the persons of Harry Pilkington, who, as has been seen, found himself as the leading director on the sales side while still in his very early thirties, and Douglas Phelps, 15 months his senior in age though exact contemporary in terms of company service, who was concerned mainly with manufacturing. He became chairman of the Executive Committee in 1947, two years before Harry Pilkington became chairman of the company. From then on it was Douglas Phelps who was responsible for its day-to-day running while Harry Pilkington was concerned with taking the wider and longer views of its operations. The latter was especially involved in its rapid international growth. A great believer in going to talk to people on the spot and a compulsive traveller, he took some pride in noting the large number of miles he flew every year. He also represented the company in its relations with government and found himself rising in the hierarchy of the Federation of British Industries, eventually reaching its presidency in 1953–5, with which came his knighthood. He also became a director of the Bank of England in 1955. There followed two important chairmanships in quick succession – the Royal Commission on Doctors' and Dentists' Remuneration (1957–60), and the Committee on Broadcasting (1960–2) – which brought him much more into the public eye. Yet they did not seem to distract his active mind and energetic body from his heavy company responsibilities or his ceaseless travels.

Other members of the fourth generation took charge of specific functions within the company. As we noticed in chapter 19, Roger Percival and Peter Cozens-Hardy (who succeeded to the barony on his father's death in 1956) joined the Executive before the war, (Dr) Lawrence Pilkington during it, and Arthur Cope Pilkington on his return from the Guards when it was over. (He was to succeed Douglas Phelps as chairman of the Executive in 1965, and, with further company reorganisation, two years later became Executive vice-chairman (number two in the succession) until his retirement in 1971; he continued to radiate the spirit of confidence and goodwill, so important for morale, for which his predecessor, and the company's chairman, were renowned.) David Frost Pilkington, Guy Pilkington's third son, entered the business from the RNVR in 1947 and joined the Executive ten years later. With the arrival as a trainee in 1958 of Arthur Pilkington's son, Antony Richard (b. 1935), the first member of the fifth generation of the family entered the business. He was to join the General Board in 1972.

Other non-family directors were also introduced to the Executive, building upon the tradition started between the wars. John Tilbury, Home and Export Sales Manager, became a member of the Executive Committee from 1944 until his retirement in 1950, and J.B. Watt, who had developed the PPG process more successfully than anyone else outside America, followed him on to the Executive (1949–61) and served on the Board until 1971, taking over many of James Meikle's responsibilities after Meikle's early retirement. Other non-family directors were also promoted: (Sir) Alan Meredyth Hudson Davies, who had been recruited to take charge of Fibreglass, and George McOnie, whom we have already encountered at Pilkington in the 1930s as a specialist in works management. More non-family directors were added after 1960 as the pace of expansion quickened. One of the latter, George William Terence Bird, educated at Prescot Grammar School and Imperial College, London, who had entered the company as a technical assistant at Cowley Hill in 1935, succeeded Arthur Pilkington as Executive vice-chairman in 1971. Sir Alastair Pilkington himself became chairman of the company on Lord Pilkington's retirement from the chair two years later.

In his speech on the occasion of Lord Pilkington's retirement, Sir Alastair remarked that his distinguished predecessor, who had guided the company with such a sure hand and had gained the esteem of the industry throughout the world, had set both a good and a bad example: good because he was so active, creative and buoyant; bad because it would kill off most people who tried to follow in his footsteps too closely. A new generation, with a stronger non-Pilkington element in its top management, began to add its own particular stamp to the recently-formed public company as it moved on into what looks like being a new and quite distinct phase of its history.

Appendices

I

Wages lists for the weeks ending 12 and 19 May 1849

Crown Houses	Week ending 12 May 1849			Week ending 19 May 1849		
	£	s.	d.	£	s.	d.
W. Blanshard	2	17	9	2	17	9
W. Ashall	1	1	0	1	1	0
T. Fury	1	1	0	1	1	0
J. Pemberton		5	0		5	0
W. Hunter	1	0	10	1	4	11
His Son		8	11		11	1
R. Cooper	1	8	9½	1	14	4½
D. Dale	1	8	9½	1	14	4½
W. Jones		5	11		8	1
W. Clare	1	1	6	1	1	6
P. Cowens		8	7½		9	7½
F. Railton		8	11		11	1
T. Roughley		18	0		18	0
R. Henderson		9	7½		9	7½
W. H[enderson]		7	0½		5	7½
T. Ashall	1	4	10	1	4	10½
R. Pemberton		13	8		13	7
Glass d. 2 [sic]		8	9		8	9½
J. Farr		8	7½		8	7½
C. Sidney	1	1	0	1	1	0
J. Dobson	1	12	0½	1	17	8½
His Son		5	11		8	1
W. Brotherton	1	5	8½	1	10	2
W. Benson	1	12	0½	1	17	8½
W. Brown	1	12	0½	1	17	8½
J. Holt	1	12	0½	1	17	8½
W. Radcliffe	1	5	2	1	9	7
W. Hudspeth, senior	1	6	3½	1	14	6½

G.Lunt	1	3	1	1	7	2
J.Hussy		19	6		19	6
J.Cookson		15	0		15	0
—.Short				1	10	0
W.Short		15	0		15	0
G.S.J.Edmondson	1	10	0			
D.Edmondson		5	7½		7	1½
T.Dutton	1	2	8	1	2	8½
T.Henderson		5	7½		5	8½
J.Kenmore	1	11	3	1	11	10½
J.Atkinson	1	11	3	1	11	10½
J.Hall	1	2	8	1	2	8½
J.Lockhart	1	11	3	1	11	10½
T.L[ockhart]	1	12	1½	1	17	8½
D.L[ockhart]	1	0	11	1	3	1
Glass d. 3 [sic]		10	3		10	4½
G.Forber		10	11		13	1
W.Hewitt		13	4	1	1	7
E.Hazledon	1	5	2½	1	5	3
E.Vose		17	7½		17	7½
W.McConnell	1	7	11	1	8	6½
E.McMullen	1	10	7	1	15	7½
J.Gallagher	1	5	8½	1	10	2
J.Marsh [?J.Nash]	1	11	3	1	11	10½
G.Greaves	1	5	2	1	9	7
J.Phillips		18	9		18	9
W.Birchall	1	9	8	1	9	8
R.Catterall		19	6		19	6
J.Pinnington	1	1	0	1	1	0
H.Pownall	1	4	9½	1	4	11
T.Gregson	1	1	0	1	1	0
J.Holding	1	7	11	1	8	6½
E.H[olding]		6	11		9	1
C.H[olding]	1	4	7			
J.Holt	1	11	3	1	11	10½
R.Hudspeth	1	7	11	1	9	7
W.Milburn				1	5	3
T.Fildes				1	4	9
	£66	17	0	£73	12	0
Low & Helsby		9	0		13	6
H.Taylor	1	12	1	1	7	0
J.Appleton		15	0		16	6
W.Pownall		14	0		14	0
W.Livesley		13	0		13	0
B.Jones		13	0		10	0
J.Cownes		12	0		11	0

E. Risley	15	0		
W. Woodyer	11	6	12	0
W. Arnold	4	0	4	0
A. Spratt	1 0	0		
W. Hewitt	9	0	8	8
E. Lyon	5	7½		
W. Ewin	9	0	9	0
W. McCully	10	6	12	0
W. Robinson	10	6	8	6
M. Ford	5	0	5	0
J. Case	1 0	3	1 0	3
G. Pris	6	0		
J. Atherton	14	0	14	0
J. Mercer	4	0	14	0
S. Wilcox	10	0	10	10
H. Taylor	12	0	12	0
J. Burrows	17	6	12	6
J. Richardson	12	0	12	6
A. Back	12	0	14	6
P. Ashall	12	0	13	0
W. Patterson	13	6	14	2
J. Cole	10	0	10	0
E. Brownbill	10	0	5	10
J. Culshaw	10	0	10	0
W. Critchley	10	6	10	0
J. Mather	13	6	16	2½
A. Dixon	13	6	16	4½
W. Iveson	13	6	14	0
J. Peak	13	6	14	0
E. Atkinson	18	0	18	8
W. Morris	13	6	14	0
T. Boardman	10	0	10	0
J. Murfy [sic]	14	6	14	6
M. M[urphy]	14	7½	15	2
G. Sixmith	7	6		
E. Glover	19	6	12	0
E. Stanistreet	16	0	13	0
Clay Grinding	6	0		
E. Birchall	5	0	5	7½
J. Short	10	0	10	10
J. Hulme	12	0	10	0
W. Henderson	6	8	8	2
J. Benson	12	0	10	0
J. Parr	6	4	7	8
Glass prs.	9	2	9	1
J. Jameson			8	8
W. Dale			5	7½
N. Maxwell			8	7½

	£	s.	d.	£	s.	d.
J.Rea					10	0
A.Telford					9	0
W. Wills					11	0½
	£30	**16**	**9**	**£30**	**10**	**0**
French (or Sheet) Houses						
Gaspard and Son	4	3	0	3	10	0
C.Etheridge	2	17	9	2	11	1
E.Hall	2	14	10	2	7	8
Auguste	3	15	0	3	8	0
Ferdinand	2	18	0	2	11	6
Beck	3	6	6	3	3	6
Adam	3	18	0	3	16	6
Aikin				2	16	10
Geo.Dixon	1	0	2		8	0
Jno. Lockhart	1	18	4	1	1	9
Tattens		11	3	1	5	8
Raper		15	0	1	6	4
Thos. Mather	1	9	5	1	3	4
Thos. Carlisle	2	6	7	1	11	8
Jas. Tickle	3	10	0	3	18	7
Hypolite	4	4	0	4	4	0
Eugene	3	18	6	3	14	0
Geo. Fog	3	6	0	3	10	0
Zelere	3	5	6	3	9	0
W.Dixon	2	4	4	2	13	0
Merryfield	2	1	7	1	15	0
Jas. Rose	1	5	1	2	2	10
Jas. Grieves	3	2	6	2	15	0
L.André and L.Lourd				2	2	0
A.Hartley	2	0	0	2	0	0
J.Edmondson	2	0	0	2	0	0
Thos. Hudspeth	2	0	0	2	0	0
Jno. Taylor	1	16	7	1	9	10
T.Jones	2	4	2	2	0	0
J.Wright	1	17	4	1	11	2
Jno. Bibby	1	17	0	1	14	5
Jos. Owen	2	5	0	1	10	0
W.Edmondson	1	3	10	1	8	4
Wm. Owen	1	9	3	1	10	6
Wm. Scott	1	4	9	1	3	0
Frank Hodgson	1	5	0	1	5	0
John Scott		15	0	1	2	6
Rd. Glover	1	0	0	1	3	8
Joseph Scott	1	2	0		12	11

	£	s	d	£	s	d
Frederick Vose	1	10	0	1	5	0
J.Harper		18	0		18	0
T.Ryan	1	0	0		16	0
B.Jones		3	0		3	0
J.Brotherton		6	0		6	9
W.Gaskell		18	0		18	0
His Son		3	0		3	0
W. & G.Ashal		6	0		6	0
J. & W.Hunter		6	0		6	0
W.Glover	1	3	0	1	4	0
J.Anders					8	5
R.Vose		5	0		5	0
A.Broadhurst		18	0		18	0
T. & P.Anders		6	6		6	0
J.Cowens		3	0		3	0
W.Butler		3	0		3	0
J.Bridge		16	0		16	0
I.Frodsham		3	0		3	0
J.Battersby		3	0		3	0
J. & T.Roughley		7	3		7	6
J.Makin		3	0		3	0
W.Jones		3	0		3	0
C.Henderson	1	2	3	1	1	2
P.Henderson		3	0		3	0
R.Wilson		3	0		3	0
J. & C.Hodgson		6	0		6	0
R.Appleton		3	6		3	0
J.Kitchin		3	0		3	0
J.Matthews		3	0		3	0
J.Holland		3	0		3	0
H.Tickle		13	6		13	6
W.Tickle		8	3		8	3
S.Leyland		4	0		4	0
W.Monks		3	0		3	0
J.Raper		12	0		12	0
T.W.					3	0
J.Prescott		6	0		6	0
J.Meredith		8	9		9	3
T.Meredith		5	3		4	6
W.Meredith		3	0		3	0
S.Colville	1	12	9	1	11	2
J.Appleton	1	14	0	1	9	4
J.Nash		19	4		17	3
R.Thompson		13	5	1	4	5
His Son		3	0		3	0
B.Holt	1	3	11	1	4	8
W.Hall	1	3	11	1	4	8
J.Owen	1	1	0	1	1	0

T.Welsh	1	1	0	1	1	0
T.Rose	1	1	0	1	1	0
J.Edmondson		7	6		8	0
J.Holt	1	12	8	1	12	8
His Son		3	0		3	6
J.Wear		18	0		18	0
J.Baily	1	7	8	1	7	8
T.Travers		18	0		18	0
E.Vose		3	0		3	0
W.Mulvaney		13	5		13	0
F.Mulvaney		6	0		6	0
W.Mulvaney					3	0
R.M.Moss		3	0			
W.Moss		12	0		12	0
W.Yates						9
W.McCully					5	2
G.Lidiate		12	0		12	0
J.Dixon		14	2		19	10
R.Dixon		3	0		3	0
J.Edmondson		13	9		19	0
E.Ford		11	3		12	0
W.Milburn	1	5	2½			
J.Risley	1	2	6	1	2	6
E.Risley					15	0
W.Taylor		3	0		3	0
J.Barlow	1	1	0		19	0
W.Roughley		15	6		15	6
His Son		18	0		18	0
J.Roughley		15	0		15	0
R.Davis		18	0		18	0
R.Sudlow		10	11		11	6
A.Malcolm	1	4	2		7	11
J.Broadhurst		17	8		17	8
His Son		3	0		3	0
R.White		3	0		2	3
T.Unsworth		10	0		9	5
R.Unsworth		3	0			
T.Appleton		11	0		11	0
J.Appleton		3	0		3	0
M.Lyon		8	6		9	6
I.Lyon		3	0		3	0
D.Lockhart		3	0		3	0
J.Andrews		9	0			
J.Arnold		1	6		3	0
W.Hewitt		7	0		8	6
J.Hewitt		12	6		10	0
E.Hewitt		6	0		6	0
G.Hewitt		5	0		5	0

	£	s	d	£	s	d
T.Burdice		15	0		15	0
J.Taylor		13	2		15	0
E.Grayson		3	0		3	0
R.Hardman	1	6	10	1	4	5
E.Hazleden		3	0		3	0
P.Wright		19	6		19	6
S.Bate		12	6		11	0
J.Scott		6	0		6	0
I.T[aylor]		10	1		9	0
J.Taylor		3	0		3	0
J.Taylor		14	11	1	0	6
R.Lyon	1	1	0	1	1	0
His Son		8	4		8	0
R.Bate		3	0		3	0
T.Vose		12	1		15	0
E.Vose		3	0		3	0
J.Banks		12	1		10	0
L.Holland		3	0		3	0
T. & W.Greaves		5	9		5	6
J. & G.Phillips		6	0		6	0
Edward Holt					3	0
J.Andrews	1	8	8	1	8	8
His Son		7	0		9	7
J.Sherlock	1	1	0	1	1	0
W.Phillips	1	1	0	1	1	0
J.Case	1	1	0	1	1	0
His two Sons		5	0		5	0
		3	0		3	0
T.Holding	1	3	6	1	1	1
T.Case		18	0		18	0
His two Sons		6	0		6	0
3 Members of the Brogan Family		9	0		10	3
		7	0		10	7
		3	0		3	0
J.Critchley		11	1		10	8
B. & E.Holt		6	0		6	0
J.Molyneux		19	6		19	6
J.Frier		9	6		11	4
M.Dixon		3	0		3	0
W.Milburne		13	5			
J.Hudspeth		3	0		3	0
J.Livesly		18	0		18	0
J. & P.Marsden		6	0		6	0
R.Appleton		3	0			
Fines		6	0			
	£156	10	0	£156	9	4

Cutting Rooms, etc.	£	s.	d.	£	s.	d.
Mr William Pilkington, junr.	4	4	0	4	4	0
Henry Deacon	5	18	6	5	18	6
J.Varley	2	6	0	2	6	0
W.Ross	1	18	6	1	18	6
W.Johnson	1	10	0	1	10	0
W.Sothern	1	0	0	1	0	0
J.Fidler		13	6		13	6
W.Taylor		11	6½		11	6½
H.Johnson		11	6½		11	6½
Thomas Jenkins		16	0		16	0
J.Pagan	1	10	0	1	10	0
W.Holt & Co. [sic]	2	8	6	2	10	0
J.Alpas	1	0	0	1	3	4
W.Hardy		5	0		5	0
W.Banks		18	0		18	0
G.Houghton	1	2	6	1	2	6
H.Taylor	1	10	0		2	6
B.Getley		3	0	1	3	0
R.Haslom		5	3		8	3
W.Waterworth		4	9		5	6
Glass Polishers		1	5	2	5	0½
T.Webster		5	0		5	7½
W.Edmundson		18	0		18	0
W.Woodward		13	0		13	0
His Son		3	0		3	0
J.Smith		17	0		17	0
B.Appleton		18	0		18	0
J.Seddon		3	0		3	0
J.Prescot		3	0		2	10½
E.Lyon					5	0
B.Webster					1	6
J.Ford		6	0		5	9
H.Nash		3	0		2	10½
J.Bickerstaff		7	0		7	0
W.Ross		4	0		4	0
W.Holt, junior		2	10½		3	0
J.Houghton		2	10½		3	6
P.Holden		5	3		6	0
M.Seyer		9	0		8	7½
T.Rigby		9	0		9	4½
A.Holt		16	6		18	0
H.Arnot		18	0		18	0
M.Brogan & Co. [sic]	2	5	0	2	5	0
J.Vass		3	0		3	0
J.Dixon		12	0		12	0
W.Appleton		13	0		13	0
W.Maxwell	1	10	0	1	11	3

	£	s.	d.		£	s.	d.
J. Scott		3	0			3	0
Jno. King		18	0			18	0
	£44	**5**	**6**		**£46**	**1**	**1**

Joiners, etc.	£	s.	d.		£	s.	d.
W. Wharton	1	15	10		1	13	10
H. Hunter		16	6			19	6
Rd. King	1	1	0		1	5	4½
Jas. Houghton	1	0	0		1	4	2
J. Grayson		19	6		1	2	6
T. Clarkson		17	0		1	0	6½
Thos. Webster		18	0		1	0	3
M. Owen	1	1	0		1	6	3
H. Wharton	1	0	0		1	5	0
Richd. Atkinson		3	0			3	7½
Thos. Forshaw		7	0		1	5	4½
Thos. Colquitt	3	6	2½		3	5	3
Johnson	2	6	3		3	6	2
Isaac Vose	1	0	2		1	2	0
Jno. Vose	1	0	0		1	0	0
Will Vose, senior	1	11	3			16	8
Will Vose, junior	1	4	1		1	1	3
Jas. Bromilow		12	6		1	0	0
Jas. Vose	1	0	5			14	7
Thos. Woodward		18	8			16	4
W. Cooke		14	0			14	0
W. Wilson		4	8			4	8
J. Staples	1	11	0		1	7	0
J. Mather	1	7	8		1	3	8
His Son		3	10½			3	4½
J. Murray		19	3			15	9
P. Leigh		5	4			4	6
T. Glover	1	11	6½		1	3	8
H. Blundell	1	8	5		1	3	10
E. Evans	1	9	4		1	4	9
T. Latham	1	2	11		1	2	0
W. Greenholgh		17	4			16	0
T. Burrows	1	2	2		1	0	0
T. Bibby	1	2	9		1	1	0
J. Taylor		16	8		1	7	2
M. Dale		5	0				
J. Chapman	1	3	11½		1	8	1½
J. Blundell	1	2	6			14	0½
J. Gilday		6	0			14	0
A. Vass	1	5	0		1	8	1½
R. Young	1	1	6		1	5	4

	£	s.	d.		£	s.	d.
G.Evans	1	10	3			3	8
J.Burrows		13	0			12	6
J.Holland	1	2	0		1	2	0
A.Spratt					1	0	0
	£46	4	6		£47	7	10

Staining Room	£	s.	d.		£	s.	d.
R.Edmundson	2	2	0		2	2	0
W.Gardner	1	15	0		1	16	5½
W.Arthur		16	10½			18	0
J.M.Kethney	1	4	2		1	4	2
Myatt		10	10			12	1
Jas. Edmondson		14	0			12	0
W.Edmondson		8	8			7	0
Eliz.Edmondson		7	0			6	0
J.Hall		10	6			9	0
Eliz. Parr		6	3			6	3
M.Davidson		5	10			5	0
Ann Williamson		5	10			5	0
Mary Atkinson		5	10			5	0
Overtime		16	6				
	£10	9	3½		£9	7	11½

Summary of Totals	£	s.	d.		£	s.	d.
Crown Houses	66	17	0		73	12	0
	30	16	9		30	10	0
French (or Sheet) Houses	156	10	0		156	9	4
Cutting Rooms	44	5	6		46	1	1
Joiners	46	4	6		47	7	10
Staining Room	10	9	3½		9	7	11½
	£355	3	0½		£363	8	2½

2

Statement issued by Pilkingtons during the labour crisis of 1845

In order to prove our desire to terminate all disagreement and to cultivate to the utmost that mutual good will which has heretofore subsisted between ourselves and our workmen, we are induced to lay before them a plain statement of facts, from which we will leave it to their own good sense to decide, whether all parties are not likely to gain both present comfort and future profit, rather by arranging in a friendly manner anything in their present position which may seem capable of improvement, than by continuing a contest on the legality of a power never hitherto considered unjust, and which our workmen themselves have deliberately given us.

It is well known that RICHARD PEMBERTON entered into an Agreement to serve us for seven years. It is said by his advisers that this Agreement is bad in point of law. But whether good or bad, is he not bound as an honest man to keep his word with us? He had the benefit of the Agreement for a time, but then he shewed us letters from Dumbarton wishing him to become a Manager of works there. One object of the Agreement was to prevent a frequent change of hands, yet we consented to his leaving us in order to improve his circumstances, provided he prevented any loss to us by finding another blower equal to himself. He failed to do this, but offered us instead a sum of money, which we refused. He then absconded from our employ. To submit to this would have been to give the Dumbarton Company free permission to select and engage all our best men, just as it might suit their convenience. We therefore gave them notice, that if they employed PEMBERTON, they must either pay us £100 as a compensation, or expect us to bring an action against them. Could there be any injustice in this? PEMBERTON's Agreement with us was only a few months old, and we had paid £152 10s 0d for leave to engage his Father when his Agreement had only seven months to run. He did not return, however, and after waiting two months we felt ourselves obliged to send for him to Scotland, and, much against our inclination, to cause him to be committed to prison. From thence he has been discharged, not from any defect in the Agreement, which we are assured by most eminent Counsel cannot be set aside; but, because a single Judge considered the Justice's Warrant of Commitment informal.

Now it must be observed, that our real ground of complaint is not against our workmen, and scarcely against RICHARD PEMBERTON, but against the Dumbarton Company, If they interfere with our rights, may we not claim compensation? But it is said that the Agreement is bad in law. This we deny. But if it were, would not the law prevent many a workman from earning bread for himself and his family, at a time when his work perhaps hardly pays his employer? At such a time, the master hopes that under an Agreement, he may at a future day turn his workmen to good account, and the workman trusts to his master's liberality to advance his wages according to the times. The workman for a present benefit runs the risk of future loss, just as the tradesman often pays much more than the usual rate of interest for a sum of money, either to enable him to make still greater profits, or to prevent serious loss. The law allows it, and trade could not go on without it. It must be remembered too, that though at the present moment Crown Glass Makers are much sought after, there is great reason to fear that the introduction of Foreign Glass at a lower duty, and the increased production of other kinds of Glass, may shortly produce a very serious change for the worse, and we would ask, whether our workmen would rather run the risk of sharing adversity with strangers or with old acquaintances? If they have stood by us in the summer, may they not expect us to stand by them in the winter?

Though, as we have shewn, there is no injustice in the Contracts, yet when the question of Bounty or Binding Money was named to us, we did not refuse it as we might have done, on the grounds that our men were already bound, and that we had raised their wages considerably beyond the rates we had agreed to pay. But having heard that some were desirous of breaking their Contracts, and knowing that others who had formerly received Bounty Money had not completed their term of service, we proposed to give the whole sum asked for, not at once, but divided into annual payments to be made on each New-year's day during the several contracts. Many expressed themselves perfectly satisfied with this plan, none to our knowledge objected to it, and we considered the matter settled. If however the immediate payment of the sum in question would terminate all discontent, we are not disposed to withhold it from any who may apply for it.

It is true that in making this offer our motives may be doubted, and that it may be insinuated by those whose interest it is to keep alive ill feeling, that we doubt the validity of our Contracts. But we have to state that our rights have been unjustly assailed; that we will not yield them up to threats or intimidation; and that we are firmly resolved to maintain not only those rights, but also that proper discipline, obedience, and order in our Works which are one great object of the Contracts, and without which not only the Master but every good and steady Workman might suffer from the misconduct and irregularity of others. At the same time we have no animosity or ill feeling towards any one in our Works. It is our duty and our study, and we have always considered it our interest, to promote the happiness and welfare of all, and whatever grievances may be properly made known to us, we are most willing to redress them.

We trust these remarks will be received with the same good feeling by which they are dictated, – that all disputes may cease and be forgotten, – and that the harmony and tranquillity which we have always endeavoured to establish, may in future reign amongst us undisturbed.

RICHARD AND WILLIAM PILKINGTON

St Helens Crown Glass Works,
7 October, 1845.

PS It may perhaps be said that this address should have been issued earlier; we feared however that our motives might be misconstrued, and we hoped, that as we had been led to expect, our men would have laid their wishes before us. A season of affliction too has lately come upon us which absorbed almost our whole thoughts, but we have great satisfaction in acknowledging the good conduct and respectful demeanour observed by *all* our Workmen upon this occasion of general mourning and regret.

3

Bessemer's experiments with Glass, 1841–1851

Bessemer, that most prolific patentee, had been interested in glass for some years before 1847. In 1841 he had taken out a patent (in association with a man called Schonburg) for improving the manufacture of plate and flint glass[1] and at the end of that year the two inventors tried to interest the proprietors of the Ravenhead Plate Glassworks in this patent but without success.[2] Bessemer's fertile brain later turned its attention to the manufacture of window glass. The improvements he suggested in this field foreshadowed in several respects the later mechanisation of the industry. He proposed to pass a long sheet of glass ladled from the pots through two sets of rollers, the first set having a roughened surface to exert the necessary drawing effect and the second being either smooth or patterned according to the type of glass required. The lehr, placed next to this rolling machine, was to be in the form of an inclined plane down which the long sheet or sheets of glass could slide. When annealed, the glass was to be smoothed and polished by an endless belt 'charged with polishing material'. The lehr was not to be coal-fired but indirectly heated by hot air conveyed by cast iron pipes from the founding furnace 'after the practice in heating air for hot blast in the manufacture of iron'.[3]

Bessemer's ingenious suggestions attracted Robert Lucas Chance, who persuaded his firm to advance £250 for these experiments.[4] He later visited Baxter House, St Pancras, where Bessemer was working, in order to witness a demonstration of the rolling machine. Bessemer later claimed that on this occasion he drew a piece of glass seventy feet long and two and a half feet wide.[5] R.L.Chance was very impressed and decided to support Bessemer further. J.T.Chance, however, who was the firm's technical expert, was unpersuaded by Bessemer's preliminary experiments and refused to support the development of the patent, as did his father, William Chance. R.L.Chance and his son, Robert, were therefore left to support the venture on their own. They built and equipped works at Camden Town, partly for Bessemer's convenience and partly so that he should not have constant opportunity to observe what was being done at Spon Lane. The process, however, could not be satisfactorily developed. Bessemer became interested in other fields of research and in 1851 withdrew altogether from his association with the Chances. After further disappointments and delays, the whole project, a most costly failure, was finally abandoned in 1854. As Bontemps later commented:

'The whole system showed, unquestionably, immense mechanical ability but ... complete ignorance of the qualities inherent in the substance of glass.'[6]

4

Exports of Belgian window glass to Britain and the United States 1850–1913

The following figures, derived from each year's *Tableau Générale du Commerce avec les Pays Etrangers* (*Statistique de la Belgique*) show the relative importance of Britain and the United States as markets for Belgian window glass.

Year	Total Exports (kgs)	To Britain (kgs)	To the United States (kgs)
1850	11,672,300	1,812,540	3,429,234
1851	14,681,002	1,980,241	5,213,099
1852	16,443,568	1,865,896	4,948,538
1853	20,607,865	2,965,150	7,878,668
1854	27,261,609	4,306,675	11,112,534
1855	21,763,996	2,835,586	6,946,189
1856	24,303,458	3,056,073	7,819,029
1857	27,551,166	8,513,491	7,076,634
1858	22,634,377	4,912,032	6,032,627
1859	27,188,823	5,726,552	8,077,377
1860	30,227,965	5,469,406	9,868,672
1861	24,045,726	6,167,356	4,420,338
1862	25,616,910	7,459,588	3,084,442
1863	30,940,096	9,370,274	2,345,426
1864	35,501,712	10,972,019	6,151,775
1865	40,625,500	Details not available	
1866	41,584,103	14,800,157	11,891,138
1867	41,366,271	12,646,108	13,837,148
1868	38,678,083	16,370,666	6,369,425
1869	45,893,254	19,251,934	9,906,036
1870	40,847,233	18,098,478	8,167,166
1871	28,721,705	12,714,007	5,402,929
1872	23,963,568	11,080,802	1,695,256

1873	63,747,861	21,862,388	15,160,074
1874	80,649,334	25,385,960	17,608,240
1875	80,546,576	27,909,622	16,862,710
1876	74,668,468	30,820,145	9,985,220
1877	76,160,653	27,960,457	11,504,458
1878	78,134,823	33,518,731	9,440,314
1879	84,214,180	33,792,907	11,697,414
1880	93,430,744	32,250,567	26,687,139
1881	97,482,670	30,482,198	24,673,384
1882	97,061,079	30,315,334	24,055,675
1883	105,366,016	27,580,461	31,305,405
1884	110,429,066	30,130,403	35,537,945
1885	109,554,284	32,501,334	27,357,853
1886	107,849,996	30,420,877	27,705,097
1887	122,973,617	33,340,095	34,821,889
1888	130,783,734	34,347,920	39,115,838
1889	123,096,892	30,325,464	35,768,859
1890	129,460,725	31,144,210	38,254,777
1891	132,440,106	31,469,189	34,366,256
1892	134,254,750	30,655,563	34,033,022
1893	136,151,772	30,194,272	28,705,934
1894	136,384,483	39,242,026	26,733,177
1895	132,026,884	42,178,808	19,961,650
1896	153,476,414	48,474,269	23,219,431
1897	149,251,775	52,723,267	19,411,432
1898	154,300,287	58,785,687	21,456,178
1899	170,092,136	58,727,783	23,474,624
1900	133,201,083	46,626,930	16,752,340
1901	127,447,281	43,745,729	17,007,893
1902	171,370,275	59,896,030	24,796,583
1903	168,950,067	55,406,752	25,232,269
1904	118,298,868	40,049,278	12,725,051
1905	152,332,184	47,695,530	9,884,478
1906	212,041,397	59,932,027	13,542,562
1907	181,783,001	50,292,671	11,404,511
1908	155,711,414	48,023,977	7,528,393
1909	186,239,587	46,075,327	8,589,105
1910	213,507,116	46,869,009	12,022,891
1911	204,663,350	49,243,016	9,253,329
1912	217,265,095	53,757,151	8,115,372
1913	205,561,684	47,241,594	8,698,647

5

Extract from the Siemens' Furnace Patent Specification of 1870

'... Another part of the Invention has reference to an improved construction of and mode of working glass pots or tanks of glass furnaces. Heretofore the materials have been first charged into glass pots or tanks then melted down and then worked out completely, after which they have been recharged and the process repeated, thus entailing considerable loss of time through the intermittent nature of the work. Now the present improvement has for its object to render the process of glass making a more uniform and continuous one, and consists in constructing the glass pots or tanks with three separate compartments, in one of which the materials are introduced continuously or at short intervals, and from which the materials as they melt are caused to flow into the next compartment where the operation of melting is completed, and whence the glass flows into a third compartment where it is worked out continuously. To produce this circulation of the melted glass through the three compartments, advantage is taken of the gradually increasing specific gravity of the glass as it becomes more and more heated. Thus, when this invention is applied to glass pots the first compartment communicates with the second one through a small vertical passage into which the melting materials as they descend in the compartment by virtue of this increasing specific gravity enter through a hole at the lower end, and in rising up in the passage eventually flow over into the second compartment. Here as the melted glass accumulates, that portion thereof which has become most highly heated and is consequently in the most fluid and clarified condition again descends by virtue of its increasing specific gravity and finds its way through an aperture at the bottom of the third compartment in which it rises, and whence it is worked out in the usual manner. This latter compartment is provided with a cover having a working aperture as in ordinary glass pots.

In applying the Invention to tank furnaces the tank is divided in its length into three compartments by means of transverse partitions or bridges provided with air passages in communication with vertical air shafts for effecting a circulation of cold air through the same. Into the hindmost of the compartments the crude materials are introduced and as they melt they pass through the apertures at the bottom of the first bridge into vertical channels formed in the same in which the melted glass rises and then flows over the bridge into the second or middle compartment where the operation of melting is completed. Lastly the glass flows from this compartment through the apertures in the bottom of the second partition into the front or working compartment. The heated air and gas ports are arranged along each side of the tank so that the flames play across the same, thus allowing the requisite temperature to be maintained in each compartment by means of a regulated admission of the gas and air effected by making the ports of different dimensions. For this purpose also a division wall provided with air passages is carried right across the furnace at the hindmost partition, thereby entirely separating the heating chamber to the hindmost compartment from that of the other compartments, in which a greater heat is maintained. The gas and air ports are continued backwards through the brickwork of the furnace and are closed outside by means of slabs, by removing which the glass tank may be rendered accessible through such ports at any point of its length.'

6

Improvements in grinding and polishing techniques at Cowley Hill before 1914

When Cowley Hill Works were built during the period 1873–6, they incorporated the most up-to-date machinery for the manufacturing and processing of plate glass.

Grinding

The rough cast glass was laid in plaster on a fixed rectangular table and pegged. A further piece of glass was then fixed to the surface of a runner plate and sand and water fed between them. Increasingly finer grades of sand were fed onto the glass surface to remove surface irregularities. The runner plate had a circumlinear motion, motive power being provided by main shaft drive. When the glass was laid on its second side, it is probable that wet bench cloth rather than plaster of Paris was used. Grinding renders the glass surface flat, but not yet ready for polishing. It needs also to be smoothed.

Smoothing

The smoothing process was similar to that for grinding except that the abrasive was graded emery. Smoothing removed the final irregularities but left the surface of the glass opaque.

Polishing

The smoothed glass was laid in plaster and pegged on a rectangular table. The table moved on a track with a slow backward and forward motion. Astride the table, a pair of beams each carried several felt-clad polishing blocks. The blocks had a transverse reciprocating motion across the surface of the glass, driven by a crank from a line shaft. Grinding and smoothing a plate took about ten hours to complete and polishing seven.

Fixed circular tables, especially for polishing, were gradually introduced at other plate glass works though not at Cowley Hill where the use of rectangular benches continued with improvements to the existing machinery notably by W. W. Pilkington in the late 1870s. The first mention of 'discs' at Cowley Hill comes in the Plate Board minutes of September 1886 when 'Belgian discs' were discussed: 'These no doubt contribute to do away with smoothing and deal better with uneven glass'. It was decided to investigate further. A disc was ordered from Gilly near Charleroi, Belgium and was installed to grind and smooth by November 1887. Four more were in use by August 1888. For the most part the directors were pleased with the quantity and quality of the glass but breakage remained slightly higher than on the traditional benches.

In 1889 Pilkington began negotiations with Melchior Malevez in connection with his British patent 6028 of 1888. Malevez's major claim under this patent was that the circular table upon which the glass was laid was transportable, by truck, from the grinding apparatus platform to the polishing platform (which formed the second part of the patent) thereby obviating the need to re-lay the glass.

The 22-ft Malevez discs were installed at Cowley Hill in 1890. The rough cast glass was laid on the circular tables in plaster of Paris mixed to the consistency of fresh cream. It had a setting time of six minutes. After the glass had been lowered, a gang of men in clogs would 'swim the plate' or dance over it in perfect rhythm to oscillate the plate and bed it firmly. The table was then lifted by truck and manoeuvred under two circular iron-shod grinding runners of different diameters weighing about 20 tons, each carried on a fabricated steel superstructure beam and bearings so that the runners could revolve freely when fed with abrasive and lowered on to the working surface of the glass. When grinding was complete – smoothing had been virtually eliminated – the table with glass was moved to the polishing area. The main rectangular polishing frame was supported on each corner by four cranks and the main drive was given to the frame by two cranks in the middle of each side. Felt covered polishing blocks were carried on a segmented frame which in turn was carried on the main oscillating frame.

The hydraulic footstep seems to have been introduced in the late 1890s. With its introduction the table top/platform and truck became one unit which could be positioned over a 'mushroom' almost at ground level. The mushroom was carried on a vertical shaft and footstep bearing, and raised by a hydraulically operated ram which elevated the table above the rail tracks and locked, allowing the table to revolve freely. Drive to the table was taken from a line shaft. A table so adapted could be moved complete from one site to another by bogey to the transporter railway. In 1907 work was completed on the Extension Grinding Shed where 35 ft Malevez discs were installed, each of which could hold 963 sq. ft of glass.

7

Sheet, plate and rolled exports by markets, 1917–1945

Pilkington Sheet Glass Export Sales
1917–1945

				'000 sq. ft	
MARKET	1917	1918	1919	1920	1921
Australia	206	43	281	1,646	898
New Zealand	159	38	212	1,046	127
Canada	183	30	124	641	672
South Africa	604	212	955	1,208	217
India	3,399	1,480	3,422	3,044	1,230
Egypt and Sudan	156	101	227	275	68
Straits Settlements	34	7	8	8	10
Argentine	508	291	755	557	1,054
Brazil	179	18	239	953	566
USA	250	94	243	283	328
China	85	41	14	250	68
Japan	—	—	—	7	328
Denmark	199	23	752	484	333
France & Colonies	1,305	1,829	3,948	1,106	229
Holland	56	45	51	7	56
Italy	—	73	—	—	170
Norway	—	—	5	—	—
Sweden	—	1	2	—	11
Rest of Africa	—	—	—	—	353
Chile and Peru	30	1	39	78	82
Uruguay	53	—	3	7	4
Cent. & S. America	—	—	91	225	87
West Indies and Paraguay	193	47	—	—	40
Elsewhere	490	204	486	355	132
TOTAL	8,089	4,578	11,857	12,180	7,063

1923	1924	1925	1926	1927	1928	1929	1930
2,881	2,281	1,958	1,972	1,932	1,631	2,674	1,064
2,144	3,338	2,178	1,427	1,016	1,330	1,774	773
4,329	2,012	5,327	3,701	2,837	2,076	2,420	1,563
566	598	318	310	338	260	331	204
1,431	1,589	852	875	622	494	403	375
14	18	18	24	30	35	29	33
8	26	27	19	21	61	174	64
923	1,718	1,502	631	1,118	272	287	431
849	1,432	867	517	520	694	833	571
1,882	515	490	233	183	71	13	11
162	415	217	84	113	117	188	151
1,741	468	303	234	3	16	12	22
484	615	308	53	29	41	25	25
31	61	50	48	50	46	18	3
54	15	6	3	2	16	15	8
188	191	153	93	36	30	10	1
16	15	17	6	9	3	—	—
237	283	255	217	128	89	127	32
253	271	245	433	539	560	391	429
56	78	77	86	90	30	62	93
29	91	31	8	20	16	13	63
62	131	213	248	203	156	107	115
132	221	117	70	91	63	95	69
81	61	115	97	171	72	71	181
18,553	16,443	15,644	11,389	10,101	8,179	10,072	6,281

R

Pilkington Sheet Glass Export Sales 1917–1945 (cont.)

'000 sq. ft

MARKET	1931	1932	1933	1934	1935	1936
Australia	72	835	21	16	955	1,803
New Zealand	326	782	1,034	875	525	1,280
Canada	773	966	6,899	8,334	10,234	10,241
South Africa	192	98	381	381	354	545
India	227	263	275	227	231	128
Egypt and Sudan	9	17	12	10	15	16
Straits Settlements	35	6	12	23	9	37
Argentine	218	44	350	407	324	414
Brazil	244	209	527	229	99	121
USA	9	3	3	—	—	63
China	191	74	59	120	291	256
Japan	13	14	—	20	28	13
Denmark	9	15	29	131	353	330
France & Colonies	—	2	2	5	2	1
Holland	—	—	—	3	2	1
Italy	1	2	15	57	25	—
Norway	—	—	—	—	—	—
Sweden	16	10	9	4	1	2
Rest of Africa	184	156	179	229	202	279
Chile and Peru	33	10	75	19	35	43
Uruguay	5	1	12	10	20	15
Cent. & S. America	37	42	65	21	22	22
West Indies and Paraguay	51	58	65	49	36	40
Elsewhere	196	63	140	88	183	202
TOTAL	2,841	3,670	10,164	11,258	13,946	15,852

1938	*1939*	*1940*	*1941*	*1942*	*1943*	*1944*	*1945*
1,724	1,341	3,203	4,411	559	705	269	254
1,977	3,178	4,340	4,458	4,344	3,960	3,672	3,063
15,473	15,512	27,549	37,168	39,689	32,244	24,207	17,473
1,459	1,915	5,457	8,224	5,354	3,766	3,334	5,643
241	248	1,139	2,716	248	1,161	2,397	2,497
33	49	310	123	57	—	—	172
18	18	636	589	—	—	—	2
953	1,834	3,746	4,360	1,714	3,241	1,311	678
330	477	993	891	1,014	885	421	521
—	—	—	—	—	—	—	—
152	360	513	194	—	—	—	—
—	—	—	—	—	—	—	—
817	753	106	—	—	—	—	—
1	1	—	—	—	—	—	—
—	11	1	—	—	—	—	—
—	—	—	—	—	—	—	—
—	64	22	—	—	—	—	—
8	94	—	—	—	—	—	—
420	414	1,141	1,546	1,127	2,229	2,361	1,440
27	24	91	8	224	955	616	351
71	60	754	800	380	649	310	516
13	11	372	44	404	1,789	1,072	987
66	90	648	914	1,774	613	606	688
383	421	1,095	1,219	1,256	292	2,432	4,031
24,166	26,875	52,116	67,665	58,144	52,489	43,008	38,316

Pilkington Plate Glass Export Sales
1917–1945

'ooo sq. ft

MARKET	1917	1918	1919	1920	1921	1
Australia	235	278	182	284	438	I,
New Zealand	73	87	113	132	98	
Canada	84	140	47	406	395	I,
South Africa	220	248	133	220	173	
India	520	315	589	760	348	
Egypt & Sudan	24	22	18	48	33	
Straits Settlements	16	18	23	40	25	
Argentine	382	150	176	232	215	
Brazil	120	75	157	215	106	
Cuba	6	—	—	I	4	
USA	—	—	—	—	I	
China	260	137	281	417	271	
Japan	476	563	539	609	923	I,
Denmark	—	7	22	9	5	
France & Colonies	80	130	179	46	3	
Germany	—	—	—	—	—	
Holland	—	4	26	8	6	
Italy	—	—	—	—	2	
Norway	—	3	14	I	—	
Sweden	—	—	—	—	—	
Rest of Africa	—	—	—	—	20	
Chile & Peru	28	9	I	7	8	
Uruguay	—	—	—	—	I	
Cent. & S. America	—	—	—	—	7	
West Indies & Paraguay	19	10	5	10	7	
Portugal	29	22	8	I	—	
Elsewhere	28	6	21	13	21	
TOTAL	2,600	2,224	2,534	3,459	3,110	5

1923	1924	1925	1926	1927	1928	1929	1930
1,264	1,325	1,496	1,862	1,954	1,704	1,943	738
407	461	440	489	443	517	685	363
1,045	1,010	1,360	1,926	2,092	1,549	1,508	1,340
352	425	580	693	630	780	800	850
582	647	641	676	877	518	365	324
32	31	121	57	165	98	75	58
41	11	15	13	17	27	37	14
312	375	697	465	770	1,093	1,317	1,277
126	113	188	179	157	259	252	184
11	9	24	—	6	included in West Indies		
1,288	1,695	2,401	2,221	231	546	199	191
415	504	302	237	234	373	299	493
2,474	1,875	2,608	2,470	3,526	3,286	1,545	2,042
77	45	74	91	89	203	276	354
8	35	23	44	19	3,624	3,062	2,664
—	—	—	3	1	96	74	106
22	118	246	272	415	462	547	453
—	19	8	—	19	31	13	183
34	6	16	24	33	33	35	31
36	68	62	52	39	40	72	98
12	23	24	34	39	included with Elsewhere		
6	5	15	8	43	,,	,,	,,
1	4	2	1	9	,,	,,	,,
10	8	14	18	16	,,	,,	,,
11	10	11	18	22	,,	,,	,,
2	—	30	—	47	,,	,,	,,
21	9	13	32	39	472	570	559
8,589	8,831	11,411	11,885	11,932	15,711	13,674	12,322

Pilkington Plate Glass Export Sales 1917–1945 (cont.)

From 1935 Maubeuge figures are not included.
Some of these figures include 'Bought Glass'

'ooo sq. ft

MARKET	1931	1932	1933	1934	1935	1936	1
Australia	248	544	688	1,050	1,219	1,158	1,3
New Zealand	273	242	174	300	345	389	2
Canada	926	646	617	952	691	1,416	1,0
South Africa	890	543	890	1,227	1,453	1,365	1,2
India	192	246	259	260	259	202	2
Egypt & Sudan	51	54	71	66	72	56	
Straits Settlements	10	7	2	4	14	13	
Argentine	576	303	304	293	190	108	
Brazil	92	45	84	70	43	34	
Cuba	←————————————included in West Indies————————						
USA	143	26	4	5	—	—	
China	476	427	228	173	99	54	
Japan	2,017	1,194	740	564	302	121	
Denmark	345	245	168	242	143	137	
France & Colonies	2,658	2,449	2,418	2,197	Sale of Maubeuge 1935		
Germany	63	39	71	40	,, ,,	,,	,,
Holland	437	305	345	183	226	160	
Italy	159	148	128	103	68	—	
Norway	40	49	32	33	32	16	
Sweden	70	52	42	36	48	35	
Rest of Africa	included with Elsewhere						
Chile & Peru			,,	,,	,,		
Uruguay			,,	,,	,,		
Cent. & S. America			,,	,,	,,		
West Indies & Paraguay			,,	,,	,,		
Portugal			,,	,,	,,		
Elsewhere	434	360	292	212	242	310	
TOTAL	10,100	7,924	7,557	8,010	5,446	5,574	6,

1938	1939	1940	1941	1942	1943	1944	1945
1,129	1,078	1,921	3,592	1,133	901	1,444	2,640
209	223	370	492	425	365	583	493
999	735	960	1,045	625	599	573	812
936	1,191	947	1,935	1,091	411	450	739
150	148	179	353	70	87	275	520
66	53	22	5	10	3	—	11
13	12	23	54	—	—	—	—
267	530	521	762	1,396	441	545	886
33	47	29	16	22	80	61	76
←			included in West Indies				→
—	—	—	—	—	—	—	—
38	56	57	88	—	—	—	—
—	—	—	—	—	—	—	—
24	23	2	—	—	—	—	—
160	141	14	—	—	—	—	—
—	—	—	—	—	—	—	—
15	29	2	—	—	—	—	—
4	7	—	—	—	—	—	—
75	65	46	39	28	31	66	60
2	1	11	—	6	7	30	12
9	23	17	67	9	3	9	25
1	1	4	—	9	15	18	1
18	26	40	47	80	39	40	50
—	—	10	14	19	42	38	121
246	296	242	364	145	116	88	117
4,394	4,685	5,417	8,873	5,068	3,140	4,220	6,563

Pilkington Rolled, Wired and Cathedral Glass Export Sales 1917–1945

'000 sq. ft

MARKET	1917	1918	1919	1920	1921	1
France & Colonies	381	770	842	30	1	
Holland	11	—	15	20	9	
Spain	—	1	33	—	2	
Denmark	—	—	63	138	14	
Sweden	—	—	20	—	4	
Germany	—	—	—	—	—	
Isles of Mediterranean	—	—	8	4	13	
Portugal	9	14	14	37	11	
Norway	—	—	—	2	1	
Greece	—	—	—	10	—	
Palestine	—	7	8	7	—	
Australia	698	445	963	1,624	1,079	1,
Canada	246	192	594	883	599	1
New Zealand	305	121	229	607	426	
South Africa	107	49	181	335	193	
Rest of Africa	—	—	—	—	38	
USA	31	6	22	47	109	
Argentine	841	241	1,641	3,245	1,404	1
Brazil	483	123	609	1,011	518	
Chile & Peru	60	39	80	129	29	
Malaya	21	11	16	56	22	
Uruguay	—	—	2	37	5	
Cent. & S. America	—	—	3	24	25	
Cuba	42	12	31	125	13	
Dutch E. Indies	—	7	—	61	—	
China	190	122	252	802	138	
Japan	445	19	120	221	265	
India	205	110	378	635	336	
Egypt	74	58	124	154	43	
Isles of Pacific	—	—	—	—	—	
Persia & Afghanistan	—	—	—	—	—	
Siam	—	—	—	—	—	
West Indies	—	—	—	—	—	
Fiji	—	—	—	—	—	
War Office	—	—	—	—	—	
Elsewhere	39	6	14	3	6	
TOTAL	4,188	2,353	6,262	10,247	5,303	2

1923	1924	1925	1926	1927	1928	1929	1930
—	—	—	132	8	8	27	16
4	4	8	5	5	3	2	19
4	5	6	—	1	—	—	—
18	25	25	16	21	21	42	58
8	8	12	6	10	5	9	17
—	—	3	1	—	—	—	—
4	18	6	5	4	—	—	—
9	9	6	11	7	—	—	—
—	—	1	—	2	—	1	1
8	13	9	—	—	—	—	—
—	—	—	—	—	—	—	—
2,478	2,596	2,389	3,142	3,258	2,582	2,576	983
1,152	877	863	1,017	1,163	1,338	1,770	1,189
679	827	825	927	1,286	843	807	545
293	266	317	366	362	424	435	595
62	51	58	55	163	116	105	152
187	115	116	133	93	175	124	104
1,359	1,943	2,531	2,636	2,582	3,077	3,479	2,965
692	851	744	842	776	1,358	1,469	831
48	30	24	10	53	50	61	67
27	15	24	62	113	188	177	112
528	507	472	615	504	583	588	472
19	18	108	61	58	47	41	30
96	61	44	12	2	—	—	—
—	—	—	—	—	—	—	—
164	200	168	146	96	253	264	338
898	573	448	432	275	406	369	786
432	499	542	740	596	488	559	448
87	32	162	38	136	156	224	274
2	3	2	3	19	—	—	—
—	—	—	—	—	—	—	—
—	—	—	—	—	—	—	—
—	—	—	—	—	—	—	—
—	—	—	—	—	—	—	—
—	—	—	—	—	—	—	—
47	24	24	45	47	137	103	143
9,305	9,570	9,937	11,458	11,640	12,258	13,232	10,145

R*

Pilkington Rolled, Wired and Cathedral Glass Export Sales 1917–1945 (cont.)

'000 sq. ft

MARKET	1931	1932	1933	1934	1935	1936	19
France & Colonies	2	—	I	3	7	2	
Holland	7	6	2	I	I	—	
Spain	—	—	—	—	—	—	
Denmark	106	177	182	236	164	136	
Sweden	22	59	II	8	15	13	
Germany	—	—	—	—	—	—	
Isles of Mediterranean	—	—	—	—	—	—	
Portugal	—	—	—	—	—	—	
Norway	I	9	5	2	I	I	
Greece	—	—	—	—	—	—	
Palestine	—	—	—	—	—	—	
Australia	150	145	372	442	482	599	
Canada	809	456	530	582	507	759	I,
New Zealand	347	236	219	334	455	681	
South Africa	331	210	262	507	625	646	
Rest of Africa	41	26	36	41	53	46	
USA	49	35	27	31	18	21	
Argentine	1,798	1,188	1,129	1,149	1,410	1,572	I,
Brazil	426	413	763	527	387	467	
Chile & Peru	32	—	I	10	3	4	
Malaya	59	22	2	29	59	71	
Uruguay	440	263	266	77	488	26	
Cent. & S. America	8	4	12	30	8	6	
Cuba	—	—	—	—	—	—	
Dutch E. Indies	—	—	—	—	—	—	
China	337	564	562	293	245	70	
Japan	1,578	486	670	661	279	8	
India	445	345	241	248	238	203	
Egypt	231	178	244	523	406	184	
Isles of Pacific	—	—	—	—	—	—	
Persia & Afghanistan	—	—	—	—	—	—	
Siam	—	—	—	—	—	—	
West Indies	—	—	—	—	—	—	
Fiji	—	—	—	—	—	—	
War Office	—	—	—	—	—	—	
Elsewhere	66	43	56	164	138	101	
TOTAL	7,285	4,865	5,593	5,898	5,989	5,616	C

1938	*1939*	*1940*	*1941*	*1942*	*1943*	*1944*	*1945*
—	—	—	—	—	—	—	—
—	1	3	—	—	—	—	—
—	—	—	—	—	—	—	—
131	197	20	9	10	—	14	8
14	19	2	—	—	—	—	—
—	—	—	—	—	—	—	—
15	16	73	35	2	—	5	18
—	—	—	—	—	—	—	—
4	3	—	—	—	—	—	—
—	—	—	—	—	—	—	—
17	13	22	36	19	—	—	101
1,014	843	498	250	98	104	125	92
636	1,025	2,537	2,579	1,740	1,379	1,195	1,121
643	685	800	659	499	554	586	449
465	629	932	1,342	792	203	362	570
37	109	69	78	89	73	74	49
23	31	20	6	—	—	—	—
1,102	350	245	383	887	584	449	487
245	379	214	353	544	1,029	932	676
2	3	36	1	54	18	47	17
43	71	342	159	—	—	—	29
38	2	52	114	27	38	38	29
29	14	37	107	99	133	133	120
—	—	76	47	25	—	—	2
—	2	56	1,028	18	—	—	—
16	85	163	241	—	—	—	—
—	—	—	—	—	—	—	—
421	434	937	1,454	117	240	483	1,543
185	146	307	181	21	—	—	286
—	—	—	—	—	—	—	—
71	18	6	—	1	2	43	20
1	—	75	27	—	—	—	—
32	21	37	57	80	10	42	67
14	13	10	9	5	1	—	1
—	237	1,710	375	23	249	12	1
53	36	96	63	91	1	7	54
5,251	5,382	9,375	9,587	5,240	4,617	4,547	5,740

8

Biographical Notes on Directors of the Company

GEORGE WILLIAM TERENCE BIRD

Born 1914. Educated Prescot Grammar School and Imperial College of Science and Technology (London University) where he graduated with BSc (Physics) ARCS.

1935 joined Pilkington as technical assistant Cowley Hill Works; 1936 head of Triplex (Northern) Limited laboratory; 1940 moved to Sheet Works; 1945 manager Flat Drawn department, Sheet Works; 1954 production manager, Sheet Works; 1956 Sheet Works manager; 1960 sub-director; 1962 director. 1966–71 chairman, Flat Glass Division; 1965–71 director, Chance Brothers Limited. 1971 Executive vice-chairman.

Mr Bird is a member of the Manchester Business School Council (1971); Grants Advisory Committee of the Glass Manufacturers' Federation (1971); Manchester Business School Finances and General Purposes Committee (1972); CBI North-West Regional Council (1973); and the Merseyside Development Committee (1975).

DENIS CAIL

Born 1925. Educated Shrewsbury School and Cambridge. 1944–7 served as Engineer Officer in Royal Navy.

1947 joined Pilkington as technical assistant at Sheet Works; 1949 assistant flat drawn manager, Sheet Works; 1954 flat drawn manager, Sheet Works; 1961 assistant production manager, Sheet Works; 1966 production manager, Cowley Hill Works; 1968–74 Cowley Hill Works manager; 1974 production director, Flat Glass Division UK; 1975 director; and chairman-designate Optical Division.

Member Institution of Mechanical Engineers.

LORD COZENS-HARDY (THIRD BARON)

Edward Herbert, third Baron Cozens-Hardy of Letheringsett. Born 1873. Educated Rugby, he served a pupilage with Brush. 1898 went into partnership with Colonel O'Gorman as electrical consultants, O'Gorman and Cozens-Hardy.

1908 joined Pilkington as director. 1924 succeeded to title on death of his elder brother. Responsible for the re-organisation of 1931. 1931–9 chairman of Executive Committee. 1939 retired as executive director but remained on the Board in a non-executive capacity for the rest of his life.

He was a JP for Lancashire 1914–38 and Norfolk 1938–56, being chairman of the Standing Joint Committee for Lancashire for many years to 1938; Deputy Lieutenant for Lancashire 1919–38; chairman St Helens National Insurance Committee; 1923–4 president National Association of National Insurance Committees; first chairman Merseyside Hospital Council; 1933–5 chairman Liverpool Hospital Commission; chairman Liverpool Convalescent Hospital; chairman Huyton College for Girls; governor of Gresham's School, Holt. President and Steward of Royal Automobile Club, and Steward of Royal Aero Club from 1927.

He died in 1956.

LORD COZENS-HARDY (FOURTH BARON)

Herbert Arthur, fourth Baron Cozens-Hardy of Letheringsett. Born 1907. Educated Winchester and Worcester College, Oxford. Trainee with J. &J. Colman Limited, a business with which the Cozens-Hardy family had close connections. Knight of Justice of the order of Saint John of Jerusalem 1952. Succeeded to title on death of his father in 1956. OBE in New Years' Honours, 1966.

1932 joined Pilkington as a trainee. 1937 director. He took a close interest in welfare and personnel affairs. During second World War, organised Company's Civil Defence. 1967 retired executive director. 1971 retired as non-executive director.

Lord Cozens-Hardy was a Deputy Lieutenant of Lancashire 1953–74 and for Merseyside 1974; a Justice of the Peace 1939; chairman of the Prescot Magistrates 1953–74; and the Knowsley Magistrates 1974; chairman of the Lancashire Magistrates' Court Committee 1952–74; president

Lancashire Royal Agricultural Society 1959–63 and chairman 1965; chairman Huyton College School Committee 1958–75; life governor and member of Liverpool College 1952 and chairman of council 1962–75; vice-chairman of Policy Committee of Lancashire Police Authority; chairman St Helens Savings Committee 1950–60.

He was chairman of the St John Council for Lancashire 1947–75; commander of the St John's Ambulance for County Palatine of Lancaster before becoming Bailiff of Egle of the Order of St John in 1971; he was a member of the Executive Council of the Order.

Lord Cozens-Hardy was also president of the North-Western Association of Building Societies, the Prescot and St Helens Civic Societies; a trustee of the Civic Trust for the North-West; a lay member of the Liverpool Cathedral Finance Committee and member of the Cathedral Executive and Stained Glass Committees.

He died in 1975.

JOHN HERBERT DICKINSON

Born 1870. He spent ten years in legal practice in London.

1905 joined Pilkington to undertake general legal services and assist his father who was the Company's legal agent. 1914–8 mobilised with the 5th South Lancashire Battalion he won the MC and bar and was wounded at the Somme. 1931 director; 1937 retired.

As Secretary to the Sheet and Plate Glass Manufacturers' Association, he acted as adviser to the UK Employees' Delegation at the International Labour Conferences in 1924, 1933 and 1934 when matters related to the glass industry were discussed.

He died in 1958.

SIR ARNOLD FRANCE

Arnold William France, born 1911. Educated Bishop's Stortford College. 1929–40 worked for District Bank; 1940–43 war service; 1943 deputy economic and financial adviser to Minister of State in Middle East; 1945 HM Treasury; 1948 assistant secretary; 1952 under secretary; 1960 third secretary; 1963–4 deputy secretary Ministry of Health; 1964–8 permanent secretary Ministry of Health; 1968–73 chairman Board of Inland Revenue.

1973 joined Pilkington as non-executive director.

BARRIE HEATH

Born 1916. Educated at Wrekin College and Pembroke College, Cambridge where he read engineering. 1939–45 served as fighter pilot with 611 (County of Lancaster) Squadron, Royal Auxiliary Air Force, attaining rank of Wing Commander and being awarded DFC. He later served in the Middle East and in 1945 was on the Joint Planning Staff of the War Cabinet office. After the war he joined Hobourn Aero Components and 1950 Powell Duffryn Limited as director of their engineering subsidiaries.

1960 joined Triplex Safety Glass Limited; 1960–8 managing director; 1965–74 chairman; 1967 Pilkington executive director; 1967–74 chairman Safety Glass Division; 1967–74 director Fibreglass Limited and Glass Fibres Division and chairman 1971–4. In 1972 he joined the GKN Group as a non-executive director; 1973 appointed non-executive deputy chairman; 1975 GKN chairman. In 1974 he resigned his executive duties with Pilkington and its subsidiaries but remains a non-executive director on the general board.

Mr Heath is a long-standing member of the council of the Society of Motor Manufacturers and Traders and is a vice-president. He is a non-executive director of Smiths Industries Limited and of Barclays Bank UK (Management). He is a Freeman of the City of London and Liveryman of the Coachmaker and Coach Harness Makers' Company.

SIR ALAN HUDSON DAVIES

Alan Meredyth Hudson Davies. Born 1901. Educated Bancroft's School and King's College, Cambridge where he took a Natural Sciences Tripos. 1924 industrial investigator, National Institute of Industrial Psychology; 1928 assistant commercial manager, ICI, Billingham-on-Tees; 1933 H.P.Bulmer & Co. Ltd (1936 works director); 1941–6 chairman, Birmingham District Manpower Board (Ministry of Labour and National Service); 1945 OBE.

1946 joined Fibreglass Limited as managing director; 1951 Pilkington sub-director; 1952 Pilkington director; 1965–6 chairman, Pressed Glass Division; 1965–8 chairman, Fibreglass Limited; 1966 retired as Pilkington executive director; 1971 retired as Pilkington non-executive director. He was closely concerned with the setting up of the Glass Museum and the building of the new Head Office.

1960–1 he was national chairman of Institution of Works Managers; 1963–6 chairman of Ministry of Health Advisory Committee on Management Efficiency; 1967–74 chairman of Board of Governors of

United Liverpool Hospitals; 1950–71 member of Council of University of Liverpool; 1967–71 chairman of Appointments Board; Member of Council of Confederation of British Industry and British Institute of Management. Governor of Fircroft College, Birmingham. Trustee of the Bluecoat School, Liverpool. 1956 Silver Medal, Royal Society of Arts; 1966 CBE; 1974 honorary LLD (University of Liverpool); 1975 awarded a Knighthood for his work in the Health Service.

He died in 1975.

EDWARD THOMAS JUDGE

Born 1908. Educated St John's College, Cambridge where he read mechanical sciences. 1930 joined Dorman, Long & Co. Ltd; 1947 director; 1960 joint managing director; 1961–7 chairman and managing director; 1967 joined Reyrolle Parsons as director; 1969–74 chairman. Also a director of Dorman Long Vanderbijl Corporation Limited, South Africa; BPB Industries Limited; and The Zenith Electric Co. Limited. 1958 vice-president Iron and Steel Institute; 1965–7 president British Iron and Steel Federation; 1952–62 member North Eastern Electricity Board.

1968 joined Pilkington as general board director and director of Glass Fibres Division.

SOLOMON ELIJAH KAY

Born 1923. Educated Shanghai Public School; Dulwich College and Leeds University where he took a first-class honours in General Science. 1948 joined British Leather Manufacturers Research Association; 1949 research chemist Middlesex County Council.

1951 joined Pilkington as a technical assistant in silvering department, Plate Works; 1954 manager Silvering Room, City Road Works; 1957 deputy works manager, City Road Works; 1961 City Road Works Manager; 1965 technical manager Triplex Safety Glass; 1967 technical director Triplex Safety Glass; 1971 managing director Triplex Safety Glass Limited; 1972 director Triplex Holdings Limited; 1973 General Board and director Optical Division; 1974 chairman Triplex Safety Glass Limited; 1975 chairman Triplex Holdings Limited.

SIR NORMAN KIPPING

Norman Victor Kipping. Born 1901. Educated University College School and Birkbeck College, University of London. 1920–1 with GPO as junior engineer; 1921–6 International Western Electric Co.; 1926–42 Standard Telephones and Cables Limited, finishing as works manager; 1942–5 Head of Regional Division, Ministry of Production; 1945 Under Secretary, Board of Trade; 1946–65 Director-General of Federation of British Industries until retired on formation of Confederation of British Industries.

Director of British Overseas Fairs Limited from foundation in 1953, chairman 1958–66; FIEE, FIPE (chairman of Council 1940–1); chairman of the Council of University College School 1960–71. President of Consultative Council of Professional Management Organisations; President of Anglo-Finnish Society; past secretary Anglo-American Council on Productivity; past member of British Productivity Council, Dollar Exports Council, Export Council for Europe, British National Export Council, National Productivity Advisory Council, BBC Advisory Council and Fulton Committee of the Civil Service. He led missions for FBI to India, Japan and Nigeria and for HM Government to Zambia. Knighted 1946, KBE 1962, GCMC 1966. JP. Honorary Fellow, British Institute of Management (Elbourne Lecturer 1965), Hon. DSc Loughborough 1966. Commander Order of Danneborg (Denmark) 1948, Order of the Lion (Finland) 1959, Order of Merit of the Italian Republic 1962, Order of Vasa (Sweden) 1962.

Sir Norman joined Pilkington as a non-executive director in 1965 and retired 1973. He retired from the Pressed Glass Divisional Board and Planning Panel in 1975.

JOHN ALFRED STUART LEIGHTON LEIGHTON-BOYCE

Born 1917. Educated Allhallows School, Devon and New College, Oxford where he read History. 1936 joined Barclays Bank DCO. 1939–45 he served with Kings Royal Rifle Corps mainly in the Middle East. 1942 Associate Institute of Bankers; 1944 Associate Chartered Institute of Secretaries; 1945–50 Oxford University; 1951–66 The Chartered Bank.

1966 joined Pilkington as Group Treasurer; 1971 director; 1972–4 chairman Flat Glass Division UK; 1974 chairman Pressed Glass Division.

1973 director North Regional Board of National Westminster Bank.

GEORGE McONIE

Born 1903. Educated at Greenock Academy, Allan Glen's School, Glasgow and Glasgow University where he took an engineering degree. Seven years in the shipbuilding industry.

1927 joined Pilkington and was for several years primarily concerned with the introduction of methods of works control. 1937 Doncaster Works manager; 1938 Triplex (Northern) Limited Works manager; 1939 Ravenhead Works manager. 1941–3 seconded to War Office as Civil Adviser to the Director General of Army Equipment (General Weeks). 1945–52 Doncaster Works manager; 1949 local director; 1952–4 Cowley Hill Works manager; 1954 sub-director and member of Executive Committee. 1958 General Board director; 1961–8 director Chance Brothers Limited; 1965–8 chairman Chance Brothers Limited; 1965–8 chairman of Joint Industrial Council, Foreman's Council and Staff Council; 1966–8 first chairman of Pressed Glass Division. 1968 retired as executive director; 1969 retired as non-executive director; 1971 retired as Industrial Relations Consultant.

Mr McOnie has been a chairman of the North Western Branch of the Institution of Mechanical Engineers, a member of the Court of Cranfield Institute of Technology and chairman of the Providence Hospital, St Helens.

JAMES MEIKLE

Born 1890. Educated Allan Glen's School and Royal Technical College, Glasgow. He served with Allen Maclellan, Mayor and Coulson and with the electrical undertaking of Glasgow Corporation.

1914 joined Pilkington as electrical engineer; 1926 assistant works manager Doncaster; 1929 assistant works manager Cowley Hill; 1931 Cowley Hill Works manager; 1936 sub-director; 1937 director; 1939–51 production director. He was very much involved with industrial relations. 1951 retired as executive director; 1953 retired as non-executive director.

1939–51 chairman St Helens Group of Manufacturers.

He died in 1972.

SIR HUMPHREY MYNORS

Humphrey Charles Baskerville Mynors. Born 1903. Educated Marlborough and Corpus Christi, Cambridge. He was a fellow of Corpus Christi 1926–33. 1933 joined the Bank of England; 1949 director; 1954–64 deputy governor. 1964 created 1st baronet. 1968–9 chairman of Panel on Takeovers and Mergers; 1969–70 deputy chairman; 1964–74 chairman of Finance Corporation for Industry Limited; 1964–72 director of General Electric Company; 1964–74 director of Legal and General Assurance

Company; 1970–5 director H.P.Bulmer Limited; 1964–74 director of Imperial Tobacco Group. Hon. Fellow Corpus Christi 1953; Hon. DCL (Durham).

1964 joined Pilkington as non-executive director.

SIR LEONARD NEAL

Leonard Francis Neal. Born 1913. Educated London School of Economics, Trinity College, Cambridge.

Labour Manager, Esso, 1956; Employee Relations Manager, Fawley Refinery 1961; Labour Relations Adviser, Esso Europe Inc. Member of British Railways Board 1967–71. 1971–4 Chairman of Commission on Industrial Relations. Part-time professor of Industrial Relations UMIST.

1976 joined Pilkington as non-executive director.

LANCELOT ROGER PERCIVAL

Born 1906. Grandson of Thomas Pilkington. Educated at Eton and Trinity College, Oxford. He represented Oxford in the low hurdles and Great Britain in 400 metres hurdles event in 1928 Olympic Games.

1928 joined Pilkington working mainly on the commercial side. 1936 director. He joined the 5th South Lancashire Regiment in 1929 and was mobilised in 1939 serving throughout the war in Anti-Aircraft Command. He was awarded the MBE. He returned to Pilkington in 1945; 1954 first chairman Worked Glass Management Committee. Partly on account of his own athletic ability, he was always closely associated with the Recreation Club. His other interests included the Public Relations and Advertising Departments and the Glass Museum.

He was a JP for Lancashire 1952 and chairman of the St Helens Council of Social Service.

He died in 1964.

DOUGLAS VANDELEUR PHELPS

Born 1904. Grandson of Thomas Pilkington. Educated at Harrow and Magdalen College, Oxford, where he read Chemistry.

1927 joined Pilkington. 1934 director. 1939 mobilised with Territorial Army, he went to Staff College, Camberley in 1940 and served in staff appointments throughout the war in the United Kingdom and the War Office, Middle East and Italy. Chairman Executive Committee 1947–65; Joint Industrial Council, Maintenance Trades Council and the Staff

Council 1949–65. Chairman of Chance Brothers Limited 1950–60; Fibreglass Limited 1946–60. 1965 retired as executive director. 1973 retired as non-executive director.

He was a director of the Westminster Bank 1955–69 and of the northern board of the National Westminster after the merger with the National Provincial, having also been a director of the District Bank (a National Provincial subsidiary). 1947–51 he commanded the local Territorial Regiment and 1951–4 an Anti-Aircraft Brigade with the rank of Brigadier. He was appointed ADC to George VI and subsequently to the Queen. He was for many years vice-chairman of the West Lancashire Territorial and Auxiliary Forces Association.

JP St Helens 1937–54; chairman of the Bench 1956–64. A Deputy Lieutenant Lancashire 1953–74. Subsequently JP Norfolk from 1967 and Deputy Lieutenant of Norfolk from 1974. He was chairman of the National Health Executive Council for St Helens 1947–1964. He is now County President of the St John's Ambulance Brigade for Norfolk.

ALFRED CECIL PILKINGTON

Born 1875. Youngest son of William Windle Pilkington. Educated at Shrewsbury and Christ Church, Oxford where he read natural science.

1897 joined firm where he followed in his father's footsteps as the technical expert; 1898 sub-director; director. 1931 retired as executive director; 1950 retired as non-executive director.

He died in 1966.

ARTHUR COPE PILKINGTON

Born 1909. Younger son of Arthur Richard Pilkington. Educated at Charterhouse and Royal Military College, Sandhurst, serving for five years as a regular officer in the Coldstream Guards.

1934 joined Pilkington. After training at Head Office and Leeds Depot he became the Pilkington representative in South Africa in 1939 just before being recalled to the Coldstream Guards. He served throughout the war as a regimental officer and in north-west Europe in the Guards Armoured Brigade. In 1943 whilst on active service, he was appointed a Pilkington director. He was awarded the MC in 1945 and retired 1946 with the rank of major.

Returning to Pilkington in 1946 as commercial director responsible for exports, he travelled widely to all Pilkington export markets. Director of

Triplex (Northern) Limited 1946–65; director Fibreglass Limited 1950–64; director Chance Brothers 1950–8; director Triplex Holdings Limited 1956–71; director of Triplex Safety Glass 1958–65, chairman 1961–5.

Chairman of Group Executive 1965–7; executive vice-chairman of the Company and first chairman of the Co-ordinating Committee 1967–71. He retired as executive director in 1971.

ALAN DOUGLAS PILKINGTON

Born 1879. Younger son of Thomas Pilkington and Katherine Douglas. Educated Eton and Oxford. After death of his elder brother, Thomas (Boer War 1900), joined firm in 1903. Director 1904–19, non-executive director 1931–53. Secretary 1907–8 and 1912–19.

He formed a magnificent collection of water colours, largely of the old English School, the greater part of which he bequeathed to Eton College.

Died 1973, at the age of 94 having retired in 1919 mainly on the grounds of ill health.

ANTONY RICHARD PILKINGTON

Born 1935. Son of Arthur Cope Pilkington. Educated Ampleforth College and Trinity College, Cambridge where he read history. He spent his two years' national service in the Coldstream Guards where he was commissioned with the rank of lieutenant.

1959 joined Pilkington as trainee working in UK and export sales. 1967 Flat Glass Division Marketing Manager; 1968 Flat Glass Division director; 1969 Flat Glass deputy marketing director; 1970 head of Marketing Services Function; 1971 Flat Glass Marketing director; 1972 joint managing director, Flat Glass Division; UK general board director; 1974 chairman Flat Glass Division UK.

ARTHUR RICHARD PILKINGTON

Born 1871. Eldest son of Richard Pilkington. Educated Clifton.

1892 joined Pilkington; 1894 director. Having gained experience on the technical side he moved into the commercial field. 1914–21 chairman of the Company.

He was a major in the 5th South Lancashire Battalion 1896–1904; JP 1902–21; member of St Helens County Borough Council 1906–9; and warden of St Helens Parish Church. County Magistrate 1917.

He died in 1921.

DAVID FROST PILKINGTON

Born 1925. Third son of Guy Reginald Pilkington. Educated Upper Canada College, Toronto and Trinity College, Cambridge where he obtained an honours degree in engineering. 1945–7 he served in the RNVR and on demobilisation held the rank of sub-lieutenant.

1947 joined Pilkington as technical assistant at Doncaster Works; 1953–6 Pontypool Works Manager; 1957 sub-director; 1959 director; 1958–61 director of Chance Brothers Limited; 1964–8 director of Triplex Safety Glass Company Limited; 1968 chairman of all the central negotiating and consultative councils; director responsible for Management Services Function; 1970 Personnel director.

He is a member of the Institution of Works Managers and Institution of Mechanical Engineers. 1968 elected Fellow of Institute of Directors; 1968–75 director of Merseyside Industrial Therapy Services Limited. He serves on the Family Practitioners Committee, Area Health Authority. 1973 director of The Guy Pilkington Memorial Home Limited; 1975 chairman of World Friendship House.

ERNEST SINCLAIR PILKINGTON

Eldest son of Richard Pilkington and Louisa Sinclair. Born 1869. Educated Clifton and Oxford. Joined firm as director 1894. Went to South Africa in Imperial Yeomanry and did not return to active work in the firm. Remained director to 1914.

He died in 1932.

GEOFFREY LANGTON PILKINGTON

Born 1885. Son of George Herbert Pilkington. Educated at Eton and Magdalen College, Oxford.

1909 joined the firm as trainee director; 1910 sub-director. Having joined the Lancashire Hussars in 1911 he served during the first World War in England and Egypt until 1916 when he transferred to Royal Flying Corps. 1919 director; 1932–49 chairman of the Company; 1939–45 acting chairman Executive Committee; 1939–47 chairman Executive Committee. 1964 retired as non-executive director.

He raised and commanded (from 1937) the 611 (West Lancs) Squadron, Royal Auxiliary Air Force and was mobilised in 1939, command of which however, in view of his age, he handed over becoming ultimately its honorary Air Commodore.

1945 Deputy Lieutenant of Lancashire; chairman St Helens National Savings. President of Royal Horticultural Society and in 1960 received Victoria Medal of Horticulture.

He died in 1972.

GEORGE HERBERT PILKINGTON

Born 1858. Second son of William (Roby) and Elizabeth Lee Watson. Educated at Harrow.

Joined the firm in 1877; partner 1884. Retired from active management 1907 but returned World War I.

Sub-lieutenant 4th Royal Lancashire Hussars.

He died in 1931.

GUY REGINALD PILKINGTON

Born 1881. Youngest son of Richard Pilkington. Educated at Clifton and Trinity College, Cambridge. Spent some years at Richard Evans Colliery, Haydock in which his father was a shareholder.

1909 joined the firm; sub-director 1910. 1914 mobilised with Territorial Forces and went to France in 1915. He won the DSO in 1917 and was severely wounded. After the war he returned to the Company becoming a director in 1919. He was particularly involved with Sheet Works. 1937 retired as executive director, and as a non-executive director in 1964.

He rejoined the Territorial Association after the first World War and commanded the 5th South Lancashires 1928–34. He served on the Town Council 1916–67 being an alderman from 1947; 1967 Freeman of St Helens. A St Helens JP 1934–56, he was chairman of the Bench 1954–6. He was president of the St Helens YMCA and a member of the National Council of YMCAs.

He died in 1970.

HENRY WILLIAM PILKINGTON

Born 1871. Elder twin son (twin Richard Austin) of William Windle and Louisa Salter. Educated Shrewsbury and Oxford. Joined the firm 1894 as director. Retired with lung trouble.

He died in 1902.

SIR ALASTAIR PILKINGTON

Lionel Alexander Bethune (Alastair) Pilkington. Born 1920. Educated at Sherbourne School and Trinity College, Cambridge. He was commissioned in the Supplementary Reserve of the Royal Artillery in 1938 and had to leave Cambridge when he was posted to Egypt a week before war was declared. He fought in the Desert, Greek and Crete Campaigns, and having been taken a prisoner after the fall of Crete he spent the rest of the war in Germany. On his return to Cambridge after the war, he completed his Mechanical Science degree and won Blues for tennis, squash, fives and in 1947 was Fives Amateur Champion in England.

He joined Pilkington in 1947 as technical officer. 1950–1 Production manager and Deputy Works manager, Doncaster. 1951 assistant to technical director. 1953 sub-director and member of Executive Committee. 1955 director. 1971–3 deputy chairman of the Group. 1973 Chairman of the Group.

Sir Alastair has received a number of honours for his work on the invention and development of Float glass including Royal Society Mullard Award 1968; honorary degree (Doctor of Technology) Loughborough University of Technology 1968; Fellow of the Royal Society 1969; Fellow of University of Manchester Institute of Science and Technology 1969; John Scott Award from Board of Directors of City Trusts, City of Philadelphia 1969. He received a knighthood in the 1970 New Year's Honours; member of Central Advisory Council for Science and Technology 1970; Wilhelm Exner medal from Austrian Trade Association 1970; honorary degree (Doctor of Engineering), Liverpool University 1971; member of the Council of Liverpool University 1969; member of Management Committee of Royal Liverpool Philharmonic Society 1960; Fellow British Institute of Management 1971; Carborundum Award of Excellence 1972; a Governor, Administrative Staff College, Henley 1973; part-time director British Rail 1973; and director of the Bank of England 1974; Fellow of Imperial College of Science and Technology 1974. Fellow Royal Society of Arts 1975.

RICHARD PILKINGTON

Born 1841. Second son of Richard Pilkington and Ann Evans. Joined works 1858–9. Partner 1863. Directed sales. Managing director Richard Evans & Co. Ltd. Chairman St Helens Collieries.

He was chairman Cowley Middle Schools and involved in Victoria Park, Queens Park and Parr Recreation Ground. Supported St Helens

Hospital, St Johns Ambulance, YMCA, Masonic and Friendly Societies. He was a member of the Congregational Church.

St Helens Town Councillor 1873–1908. Mayor 1881, 1896–8. Alderman 1889. Freeman 1897. County Magistrate 1876, Borough Magistrate 1882. Liberal but became Conservative after Gladstone's Home Rule Bill. President St Helens Conservative and Unionist Association. Conservative MP (Newton) bye-election 1899, general election 1900 (-06). CB 1905. 1862 joined 47th Lancashire Rifle Volunteers (5th Battalion South Lancashire Regiment). Colonel 1902–8. Volunteer officers decoration 1889.

He died in 1908.

RICHARD AUSTIN PILKINGTON

Born 1871. Younger twin son of William Windle Pilkington. Educated Shrewsbury and Christ Church, Oxford.

Joined Pilkington direct from Oxford becoming a sub-director in 1894; director. From 1907 he suffered severe illness and was advised to live abroad, taking his family to Colorado USA. He attended board meetings during the summer of 1912 returning full-time 1914. War service in 5th South Lancashire Battalion; chairman of the Company 1921–31; 1931 retired as executive director; 1951 retired as non-executive director. He was always particularly involved on the sales side of the Company.

1897–1908 member St Helens Libraries Committee; 1908 member Cowley School Governors; 1900–43 JP; chairman of the Licensing Justices; 1921–43 member St Helens Town Council; 1917 member of Education Committee, 1921–43 chairman.

His work for the Liberal Party dates from the 1920s. He was President of the St Helens Liberal Association 1933–6 and 1948–51, a member of the National Liberal Council from 1937, and of the Lancashire Cheshire and North West Liberal Association.

He was involved with the work of the YMCA in St Helens for over 50 years being a member of committees from 1893 and president from 1915. He was also involved with Lancashire and Cheshire Divisional Council and the National Council 1932–46, being National Treasurer 1940–6. He was made a Life Member of the YMCA in 1946.

He died in 1951.

THOMAS PILKINGTON

Born 1835. Third son of William Pilkington and Elizabeth Charlotte Boyes. Educated privately. Joined the firm in 1853. Partner from 1863.

Directed commercial business. Chairman of the Company 1894–8. Consultative director from 1898 when he retired to Hereford. After the death of his eldest son (Thomas Douglas Pilkington) in 1900 in the Boer War he divided his time between Caithness and London (and later Bournemouth). County Magistrate 1868. Deputy Lieutenant of Caithness.

He died in 1925.

LAWRENCE HERBERT AUSTIN PILKINGTON

Born 1911 in Colorado, USA. Second son of Richard Austin Pilkington. Educated at Bromsgrove School and Magdalene College, Cambridge where he read Natural Sciences. He spent some time as a technical trainee with the Grenfell Mission in Labrador.

1935 joined Pilkington; 1937–9 Queenborough Works manager; 1940 sub-director; 1943 director. He was primarily involved in the manufacturing side of the business, his particular interests having been the development of the research organisation. 1967–75 director and chairman of Optical Division; 1970–4 chairman of Pressed Glass Division. He retired as executive director in 1974.

He was chairman of Glass Delegacy 1949–54; chairman Glass Industry Research Association 1954–8; chairman British Coal Utilisation Research Association 1963–8; member Society of Acoustic Technology 1963–73; member of Building Research Board 1958–62; member of Wilson Committee on Noise 1960–3; president Society of Glass Technology 1960–4; member of Council of Sheffield University; chairman North West England Advisory Committee for Civil Aviation 1968–72.

He was awarded CBE 1964 and has received honorary degrees from Sheffield 1956; and Salford (DSc).

He was appointed a Lancashire JP in 1942.

LORD PILKINGTON

William Henry Pilkington. Born 1905. Eldest son of Richard Austin Pilkington. Educated at Rugby and Magdalene College, Cambridge.

Joined the Company in 1927 and associated with the sales side of the business. 1930 sub-director; 1934 director. Director of Triplex Holdings Limited, Pilkington Brothers Canada Limited (chairman 1939–75), Pilkington Brothers (Australia) Limited, Hindusthan-Pilkington Glass Works, Viplamex and other subsidiary and associated company boards. 1949–73 chairman of the Company. 1973 Honorary Life President and non-executive director. He was knighted in 1953 and became a Life Peer in the New Year's Honours, 1968.

Outside the Company, Lord Pilkington was a member of the British Productivity Council 1952–63; member of the Dollar Export Council; chairman of the National Council of Building Material Producers 1944–52, and president 1955–60; president of the Federation of British Industries 1953–5; president of the Council of European Industrial Federations 1954–7; director of Bank of England 1955–72; chairman of National Council on Education for Industry and Commerce 1956–66; first Chancellor of Loughborough University of Technology 1966; president of both British Plastics Federation 1972–4 and British Shippers' Council 1971–4; director Business International Corporation, New York; chairman of North West Regional Management Centre 1974; and president Management Research Groups 1974.

He undertook a variety of special appointments for HM Government including Report on the investigation into methods and costs of school buildings 1952; chairman of Committee to set up National Industrial Fuel Efficiency Service 1953; member Crichel Down Enquiry 1954; chairman of Royal Commission on Doctors' and Dentists' Remuneration 1957–60; chairman of the Committee on Broadcasting 1960–2; chairman of Economic Development Committee for the Chemical Industry 1968–72; and chairman of the National Council for Education for Industry and Commerce concerned with a wide range of reports on educational subjects.

Lord Pilkington has been awarded honorary degrees by the Universities of Manchester 1959, Liverpool 1963, Loughborough University of Technology 1966 and Kent at Canterbury 1968. He is a Fellow of the Royal Society of Arts, British Institute of Management and of the Institute of Building.

Locally, Lord Pilkington has been a JP since 1937. He became Freeman of St Helens 1968; Deputy Lieutenant of Lancashire 1968; and Vice Lord Lieutenant of Merseyside 1974. He is president of the South Lancashire Branch of the Magistrates Association. Other local activities include the YMCA, hospital committees and other social work. He is president of St Helens YMCA, St Helens Rugby League Football Club, St Helens Amateur Operatic Society and Grange Park Golf Club and a governor of St Helens College of Technology.

WILLIAM LEE PILKINGTON

Born 1857. Eldest son of William (Roby) Pilkington and Elizabeth Lee Watson. Educated Harrow and Christ Church, Oxford. c1876 joined the firm. 1885 partner. 1892–4 patents for corrugated rolled glass. Retired from active management 1907 but returned 1914–8.

1887 Borough Magistrate; 1892 County Magistrate. President St Helens Conservative and Unionist Association. 1911 Deputy Lieutenant of Lancashire. 1876 joined 4th Royal Lancashire Regiment. Colonel Lancashire Hussars.

He died in 1919.

WILLIAM NORMAN PILKINGTON

Born 1877. Second son of Richard Pilkington. Educated Clifton and Trinity College, Cambridge, where he captained Rugby Football XV, played in international matches and was first string in 100 yards relay against Oxford in 1897 and 1898.

1900 joined Pilkington; 1905 director; 1914–8 served in Prince of Wales Volunteers being awarded DSO and bar; 1919 rejoined the Company; July–December 1931 chairman of the Company; director until his death.

He joined the Prince of Wales Volunteers in 1900; major 1912; lieutenant colonel 1920; commanded Battalion 1920–8. Member of the St Helens Council 1906–35; member and chairman of Rainford Urban District Council to 1935; County JP 1932; director of the St Helens and District Reporter. He was president of the St Helens YMCA and a member of the National Council. He took a deep interest in the work of the Church of England in both St Helens and Rainford.

He died in 1935.

WILLIAM (ROBY*) PILKINGTON

Born 1827. Eldest son of William Pilkington and Elizabeth Charlotte Boyes. Educated Edgbaston Preparatory School and Croft Rectory Establishment. Joined works 1844. Partner 1853. Superintendent of factory. After retirement of uncle and father, became senior partner and director.

A member of Church of England, he presented organs to Sutton Parish Church 1865 and St Marks, Cowley Hill 1889. Encouraged recreational activities and the building of Sutton National Schools.

He was involved in negotiations for the incorporation of St Helens (1868) and acted as returning officer.

Chairman, St Helens Conservative Association from 1808 and South

West Lancashire Conservative Association from 1885. He refused to stand as MP. JP 1859. Deputy Lieutenant of Lancashire 1887.

He died in 1903.

* Known as 'Sutton Bill' or 'Roby Will' to differentiate from his cousin, William Windle Pilkington.

WILLIAM WINDLE PILKINGTON

Born 1839. Eldest son of Richard Pilkington and Ann Evans. Educated Bruce Castle, Tottenham. Joined firm 1857; partner 1863. Technical director of the Company. Chairman of the Company 1898–1914; director of Clifton and Kearsley Colliery.

A member of the Congregational Church and chairman of Lancashire Congregational Union. Helped to found Ragged School. Supported YMCA, St Helens Hospital and St Helens and District Nursing Association.

St Helens Town Councillor 1870–90. Mayor 1901–2. Alderman 1903. Freeman 1905. County Magistrate 1869; Borough Magistrate 1882; Deputy Lieutenant of Lancashire 1908. Joined 47th Lancashire Rifle Volunteers 1860 (later 5th Battalion South Lancashire Regiment). Colonel St Helens Division 1889–1902.

He died in 1914 at Cannes.

ROWLAND STANLEY ROBERSON

Born 1918. Educated Bromsgrove County High School and Birmingham Central Technical College. 1939–46 war service. Demobilised with the rank of major. MBE.

1946 joined Technical Development Department, Sheet Works; 1951 went to Canada as managing director Pilkington Glass Manufacturing Company and acting works manager Central Works, Scarborough; 1956–61 works manager and director Pilkington Brothers (South Wales) Limited; 1961–5 general manager Sheet Works; 1965–6 works manager Cowley Hill; 1966 general manager Float Glass and Flat Glass divisional director; 1967 managing director, Flat Glass Division; 1970 General Board director.

Member of South West Lancashire Productivity Association 1961–72 and chairman 1964–72. Mr Roberson was awarded OBE in New Year's Honours 1972.

He died in 1972.

JOHN TILBURY

Born 1887. Apprenticed to London and North Western Railway. He served in the RE (Royal Transport Establishment) during first World War being mentioned in despatches and commissioned in 1916.

1919 joined Pilkington as manager of Transport Department; 1922 manager Railway Department; 1924 transferred to Home Sales; 1928 Export manager; 1935 Home and Export manager; 1938 sub-director; 1944 director; 1950 retired.

He died in 1963.

WILLIAM STUART TUNNOCK

Born 1877. Educated at Glasgow High School.

1891 joined Pilkington at Glasgow depot where his father was Scottish agent; 1909 northern Scotland traveller based at Aberdeen; 1910-2 Glasgow agent; 1912-3 Export department, St Helens; 1913-4 in Canada in connection with setting up Thorold Works. 1915 visited New Zealand; 1919-32 secretary to the Company; 1920 sub-director; 1931 director; 1938 became non-executive director; 1940 retired.

He died in 1947.

LESLIE NEWTON WALL

Born 1916. Educated at Oldham Hulme Grammar School and articled to firm of Manchester solicitors. During the second World War he served in France, the Middle East, Aegean Islands and India. He was demobilised with the rank of major, becoming a solicitor in private practice.

1956 joined Pilkington as assistant to Company solicitor; 1965 legal adviser; 1967 deputy chairman Pressed Glass Division; 1968-70 chairman Pressed Glass Division; 1970 director; 1974 chairman of Glass Fibre Division and Fibreglass Limited.

JAMES BONAR WATT

Born 1896. Educated Allan Glen's School, Glasgow.

1914 joined Pilkington at Sheet Works going soon afterwards to Canada. He served in France with the Canadian Artillery and returned to the Company at Thorold Works in Canada after the war. 1923 returned to St Helens to take charge of drawn cylinder process at Sheet Works; 1929-30 in charge of first PPG flat drawn trials; 1934 Sheet Works production manager and deputy works manager; 1936 Sheet Works manager; 1938 local director; 1949 sub-director; 1950 director; 1953 production director and responsible for all industrial relations; 1961 retired as executive director; 1971 retired as non-executive director.

Mr Watt was chairman of the St Helens Group of Manufacturers 1951–60 and a part-time member of the North Western Gas Board 1955–66.

LORD WEEKS

Ronald Morce Weeks, first Baron Weeks of Ryton. Born 1890. Educated Charterhouse and Caius College, Cambridge where he was captain of University Football XI.

1912 joined Pilkington as technical trainee. 1914–9 served with Prince of Wales' Volunteer Territorial Forces and Rifle Brigade being mentioned in despatches three times and won DSO, MC and Bar. 1919 rejoined the firm; 1920 Cowley Hill Works manager; 1921 sub-director; 1928 director; 1939 briefly chairman of Executive Committee. 1945 Sir Ronald retired as executive director but remained a non-executive director until his death.

1934–8 commanded 5th Battalion South Lancashire Regiment; 1939 general staff officer 66th (Territorial) Division; 1940 Brigadier General Staff at GHQ, Home Forces; 1941 Director-General of Army Equipment; Major General; 1941 deputy chief of Imperial General Staff as Lieutenant General with seat on the army council; 1943 KCB; 1945 deputy military governor and Chief of Staff, British Zone Control Commission for Germany. 1956 created first Baron Weeks of Ryton.

He became a director of Vickers Limited becoming chairman 1948–56; also director of English Steel Corporation; Palmers Hebburn & Co. Ltd; Associated Electrical Industries; Royal Exchange Assurance; Hudson Bay Company; and Westminster Bank (to 1957). 1957 he succeeded Lord Bruce of Melbourne as chairman of the Finance Corporation for Industry.

His other activities included directorship of Remploy Limited; vice-chairmanship of King George's Memorial Trust Fund; chairmanship of National Advisory Council of Education for Industry and Commerce. He was president of the British Scientific Instrument Research Association. He was an honorary fellow of Caius College, Cambridge, chairman of Governing Body of Charterhouse and honorary LLD of Liverpool University.

He died in 1960.

ABBREVIATIONS USED IN ENDNOTES

PA	Pilkington Archives
L.R.O.	Lancashire Record Office
P.R.O.	Public Record Office
J.S.G.T.	*Journal of the Society of Glass Technology*
H.M.C.	Historical Manuscripts Commission
Cal.S.P.D.	*Calendar State Papers Domestic*
S.P.D.	State Papers Domestic
D.N.B.	*Dictionary of National Biography*
Customs	Records of HM Customs and Excise

Other abbreviations, if not self evident, refer to full titles cited in the preceding notes within the same chapter.

London is taken as the place of publication of all printed material unless otherwise stated.

NOTE ON THE PILKINGTON ARCHIVES

All the records prefixed PA are to be found at the Group Archives and Records Service, Pilkington Brothers Limited, St Helens, Merseyside, WA10 3TT. The major collections have the following prefixes:

PB   The records of Pilkington Brothers Limited and its predecessors from 1826.

ZZ   The records of Chance Brothers Limited, Birmingham.

BPG The records of the British Cast Plate Glass Company, Ravenhead.

PILKINGTONS and PILKINGTON

It is now customary to describe the company as Pilkington. The singular form of the name has normally been used in this book from 1894 when the partnership became a limited company.

s

I

THE HISTORICAL
BACKGROUND

1 J.U.Nef, *The Rise of the British Coal Industry* (1932), I, 359.

2 S.E.Winbolt, *Wealden Glass* (Hove 1933), 53; see also the same writer's contributions in *J.G.S.T.* vols. XVI (1932) and XX (1936); and G.Kenyon, *The Glass Industry of the Weald* (Leicester 1967).

3 PA BPG5 Minutes of the British Plate Glass Company, 12 April 1815. Local sand was, of course, used for grinding.

4 Kurgliga Biblioteket, Stockholm, MS. M.260. J.L.Robsahms dagbok over en resa i England, 1761. I owe this reference to Prof. M.W.Flinn.

5 23 Eliz. cap. 5. For a recent discussion of this subject see G.Hammersley, 'The Crown Woods and Their Exploitation in the Sixteenth and Seventeenth Centuries', *Bulletin of the Institute of Historical Research, 30* (1957), 148 *seq.*

6 William Hyde Price, *The English Patents of Monopoly* (Cambridge, Mass. 1906), 107–8.

7 Rhys Jenkins, 'The Reverberatory Furnace with Coal Fuel, 1612–1712', *Transactions of the Newcomen Society*, XIV (1933–4), 68.

8 T.S.Ashton, *Iron and Steel in the Industrial Revolution* (Manchester 1924), 10.

9 S.P.D., Jas I, Vol. 162, No. 64 (16 April 1624), cited in Albert Hartshorne, *Old English Glasses* (1897), 424; debate in the House of Commons, 7 May 1621, Notestein, Relf and Simpson, *Commons Debates 1621,* (New Haven 1935), III, 196.

10 Simon Sturtevant, *Metallica* (dated 22 May 1612) in *Dud Dudley's Metallum Martis* ed. Bagnall (Wolverhampton 1854), 8; *The Loseley Manuscripts* ed. Alfred John Kempe (1836), 493.

11 Part of the following account is a version of Warren C.Scoville's observations on the glasshouse *à l'anglaise* in his volume *Capitalism and French Glassmaking 1640–1789* (University of California Publications in Economics 1950), 41–2. For wood-fired furnace designs, *ibid.*, 37–8, and Georgius Agricola, *De Re Metallica* (1556), translated by Herbert Clark Hoover and Lou Henry Hoover (1912), 584 *et seq.*

12 D.R.Guttery, *From Broad Glass to Cut Crystal* (1956), 38.

13 S.P.D., 27 and 28 July 1610, cited in Price, *op. cit.*, 71.

14 Nef, *op. cit.*, I, 222; Scoville, *op. cit.*, 42.

15 D.W.Crossley, 'The Performance of the Glass Industry in Sixteenth Century England', *Economic History Review*, XXV (1972), No. 3. Eleanor S.Godfrey, *The Development of English Glassmaking 1560–1640* (Chapel Hill 1975) came out too late for the revision of this chapter.

16 H.S.Glazebrook, *Collections for a Genealogy of the Noble Families of De Hennezel, etc.* (privately printed 1872). For increased taxes and irksome restrictions inside Lorraine, see E.Graham Clark, 'Glassmaking in Lorraine', *J.S.G.T.* xv (1931), 111–3.

17 S.E.Wimbolt, *op. cit.*, L.F.Salzman, *English Industries in the Middle Ages* (Oxford 1923), 183–6; M.S.Giuseppi in the *Victoria County History of Surrey*, II, 298.

18 MSS. of Rye Corporation, 1579, 1581 (*H.M.C.*, 13th Report, Appendix Part IV, 62–3, 75–6); *Cal. S.P.D.*, 25 April 1574; *Victoria County History of Surrey*, II, 298.

19 Hartshorne, *op. cit.*, 424.

20 Longe to Burghley, 3 October 1589 (Lansdowne MSS. 59/75, transcribed in Hartshorne, *op. cit.*, 402).

21 Alford Papers transcribed in Notestein, Relf and Simpson, *op. cit.*, 543.

22 *Registre de l'Eglise Wallone de Southampton* (Publications of the Huguenot Society, vol. IV) contains references to Buckholt glassmakers, and Hartshorne, *op. cit.*, 171–2, a report on excavations. For glassmaking on the North Staffordshire-Shropshire border, see T. Pape, 'Medieval Glassworkers in North Staffordshire', *Transactions of the North Staffordshire Field Club*, LXVIII (1933–4), 74–121; and D.W.Crossley, 'Glassmaking in Bagot's Park, Staffordshire in the Sixteenth Century', *Post-Medieval Archaeology*, I (1967).

23 Newent Parish Registers, 1599 and 1601, cited by A.W.Cornelius Hannen, 'Glassmaking', *Scottish Antiquary*, VII, 151; J. Stuart Daniels, *The Woodchester Glass House* (Gloucester 1950).

24 For this proclamation, see Hartshorne, *op. cit.*, 413–4.

25 New Letters Patent were issued on 19 January 1614–5, granting a monopoly of the use of the new furnace to Thomas Percival and nine others, mostly courtiers.

26 *D.N.B.* summarizes most of the known facts about Mansell.

27 James Howell, *Epistolae Ho-Elianae* (5th ed. 1678), 68.

28 *Loseley Manuscripts*, 493.

29 S.P.D., Jas. I, Vol. 162, No. 63, transcribed by Hartshorne, *op. cit.*, 426–30.

30 Sturtevant, *Metallica*, 110. The Scots at this time were very touchy about this export of their coal to what was, apart from the union of thrones, a foreign land. The matter was raised before the Scottish Privy Council (*Register of the Privy Council of Scotland* ed. Masson, X, 277, 372, 382–3). The same source also contains useful information about the Scottish glass patent and the glasshouse at Wemyss, the rivalry of which was a constant worry to Mansell in the earlier years of his patent (XI, 138–9; XII, 374, 428, 439–40, 451–2, 772).

31 The following is based upon Mansell's own account, written in 1624 (S.P.D., Jas. I, Vol. 162, No. 63, printed in Hartshorne, *op. cit.*, 427).

32 In December 1615, an agreement was made between Sir Percival Willoughby and Sir Robert Mansell whereby Willoughby leased to Mansell a great barn at Wollaton for seven years with dwelling house and garden adjoining them in the occupation of Jacob Henzey and John Squire, two glassmakers. He also contracted to deliver at the barn as much coal as Mansell's workmen should require to use in the two glassworks lately erected in the barn. On 23 July 1617, arrangements were being made to build a glasshouse and furnace near the coalpits at Awsworth. (H.M.C., MSS. of Lord Middleton, 69, 499–500.) It is difficult to know whether either of these ventures was connected with Mansell's main effort or whether they were merely smaller furnaces, intended to supply a local market. The first coal-fired 'glassworks', housed in a barn, was obviously a very makeshift affair. The second one, where both glasshouse and furnace were to be specially built, may have borne a closer resemblance to the new model.

33 S.P.D., Chas. I, Vol. 282, No. 99, transcribed in Hartshorne, *op. cit.*, 432. Some glass had been exported from Newcastle at the end of the sixteenth century in very small quantities and the suggestion has been made that this was in the form of bottles. Whether they had been made in Newcastle itself, is not clear. (Nef, *op. cit.*, I, 180; Alexander Nesbitt, *Notes on the History of Glass-making*, privately printed 1869, 128.)

34 Nef, *op. cit.*, I, 25.

35 Newcastle Reference Library, details of the parish register of All Saints, Newcastle. Edward Hensey, described as servant to Sir Robert Mansfield, was buried on 11 February 1617/8. Other references to glassmakers occur on 8 July 1619, 1 January 1620 and 15 October 1620.

36 S.P.D., Jas. I, Vol. 162, No. 63, cited in Hartshorne, *op. cit.*, 430.

37 *Ibid.*, 427. An agreement dated 1678 gave glassmakers permission to dig clay at Bichfield, Northumberland (*Proceedings of the Society of Antiquaries of Newcastle-upon-Tyne*, I, new series (1884) 127). This may have been the neighbourhood where Mansell obtained his clay. On the other hand, leases of glasshouses in Newcastle itself, dated 7 June 1658 and 20 October 1679, include the right to dig clay (Tyne and Wear County Archives, 43/2/50; and 46/2/50).

38 S.P.D., Jas. I, Vol. 162, No. 63, cited in Hartshorne, *op. cit.*, 430.

39 *Cal. S.P.D.*, Chas. I, 15 September 1640; T.S. Willan, *The English Coasting Trade, 1600–1750* (Manchester 1938), 98–9.

40 *Journals of the House of Commons*, II, 523, 529, 530, 596, (12 and 15 April, 31 May 1642); Price, *op. cit.*, 78.

41 *Extracts from the Newcastle-upon-Tyne Minute Book 1639–56* (Newcastle 1920), 54, 74–5. For the site of Mansell's glasshouses, recital in lease dated 7 June 1758, Tyne and Wear County Archives, 43/2/50.

42 *Chorographia or a Survey of Newcastle-upon-Tyne, 1649* (reprinted Newcastle 1818) 40.

43 Thomas Salmon, *South Shields, Its Past, Present and Future* (South Shields 1856), 21.

44 The Rev. C.E. Adamson, 'John Dagnia of South Shields, Glassmaker', *Proceedings of the Society of Antiquaries of Newcastle-upon-Tyne*, New Series, VI (1894), 163.

45 P.R.O., Chancery Records C5.284/96. Bill from Zachariah Tizack of Howden Pans, broad glassmaker, dated 28 February 1697/8.

46 Guttery, *op. cit.*, particularly chapter 5.

47 *The City and County Purchaser's and Builder's Dictionary or the Complete Builder's Guide* originally written by Richard Neve (3rd ed. 1736) *sub* Glass.

48 *Craftsman*, 30 April 1743, quoted in Francis Buckley, 'Glasshouses on the Tyne in the Eighteenth Century', *J.S.G.T.*, X (1926), 43. Isaac Cookson was living at Newcastle when his father, William Cookson of Penrith, drew up his will prior to his death in 1712 (*Newcastle Daily Chronicle*, 20 May 1897). For eye witness accounts of the Newcastle glasshouses, see Basil Cozens-Hardy (ed.), *The Diary of Silas Neville*,

1767–1788 (1950), 158, and B. Faujas de Saint Fond, *A Journey Through England and Scotland to the Hebrides in 1784* (Glasgow, 2 vols 1907), I, 133.

49 13th Report of the Commissioners of Excise Inquiry (Glass), 1835, [15] XXXI, Appendix 7.

50 *Ibid.*, Appendix 23.

51 S.P.D., Jas I, Vol. 162, No. 63, cited in Hartshorne, *op. cit.*, 431.

52 Thomas May, 'On the Altar and Other Relics Found during Recent Excavations (1895–6) on the site of the Roman Station at Wilderspool', *Transactions of the Historic Society of Lancashire and Cheshire*, XLVIII (1897), 16–17.

53 L.R. Salzman, *English Industries of the Middle Ages* (Oxford 1923), 186; Maurice H. Ridgway and George B. Leach, 'Further Notes on the Glasshouse site at Kingswood, Delamere, Cheshire', *Chester Archaeological Society Journal*, XXXVII, Part I (1948), 133–40; Maurice H. Ridgway, 'Coloured Glass in Cheshire', *Transactions of the Lancashire and Cheshire Antiquarian Society*, LIX (1947), 41–84, LX (1948), 56–85.

54 J.A. Twemlow, *Liverpool Town Books* (Liverpool 1918), II, 549–51, 708, 789, 974; *The House and Farm Accounts of the Shuttleworths of Gawthorpe Hall, 1582–1621*, Chetham Society, old series. 35 (1856); L.R.O., Quarter Sessions Records (Recognizances).

55 The Register was printed by the Lancashire Parish Register Society in 1902. I am grateful to the late F.A. Bailey for drawing my attention to this source.

56 Ruth Hurst Vose, 'Bickerstaffe and Haughton Green Excavations', *Annales du 5ᵉ Congrès de l'Association Internationale pour l'Histoire du Verre* (Liège, Musée de Verre 1972), 137–9.

57 J.P. Earwaker, *East Cheshire Past and Present* (1877), I, 405–6n.

58 Vose, *op. cit.*, 139 *seq*. See also *The Denton Glass Excavation* (North West Museums and Art Gallery Service and Pilkington Glass Museum (n.d.) and *J.G.S.T.*, XII (1970).

59 For information concerning Shirdley Hill sand, P.G.H. Boswell, *A Memoir of British Resources of Sands and Rocks Used in Glass-Making* (1918), 64, and the same author's paper on 'British Glass-Sands: Their

Location and Characteristics', *J.S.G.T.*
I (1917), 20–4. A map showing the geographical extent of this sand is to be found in
Wilfred Smith, *A Physical Survey of Merseyside* (Liverpool 1946), 23.
60 Thomas Baines, *History of the Commerce and Town of Liverpool* (1852), 715.
61 Evidence of Thomas Holt to the Committee of the Whole House on Orders in
Council 1812 [210] III, 292. The glass industry at Bristol appears to have grown up in
much the same way. A historian of the port wrote in the early 1790s that 'The call for
window glass at home, at Bath and in the Towns about Bristol; in the Western
Counties, Wales, and from North to South wherever Bristol Trade extends, and the
great quantities sent to America, employ several houses for this article'. (Quoted by
Professor MacInnes in *The Trade Winds*, ed. Parkinson, (1948), 65.)
62 Pearce Davis, *The Development of the American Glass Industry* (Cambridge, Mass.
1949), chapters 3 and 4.
63 *A Collection of Letters for the Improvement of Husbandry and Trade* (ed. Houghton), No.
198, 15 May 1696. This list appears to have been connected with the recently introduced
excise duty on glass. It has been reproduced by J.N.L.Baker in *A Historical Geography of
England Before AD 1800* (ed. Darby) (Cambridge 1936), 420.
64 I am indebted to my friend Mr S.A. Harris of Liverpool for this information.
65 Liverpool Town Books, 23 October 1721; Chadwick's Map of Liverpool (1725);
George Skene's observations of 1729, published in *The Miscellany of the Spalding Club*
(Aberdeen 1940), II, 132; Francis Buckley, 'Old Lancashire Glasshouses', *J.S.G.T.*, XIII
(September 1929); C.P.Hampson, 'History of Glass-making in Lancashire', *Transactions
of the Lancashire and Cheshire Antiquarian Society*, XLVIII (1932), 70–1. It seems unlikely that glassmaking was carried on in
Liverpool on any scale before the middle of 1724, when St Nicholas's Church registers
first begin to include glassmakers. (Transcripts at L.R.O.)
66 J.R.Harris, 'Origins of the St Helens Glass Industry', *Northern History*, III (1968).
67 L.R.O., transcripts of Warrington Registers.

68 *St James's Evening Post*, 12–14 December 1745, quoted in R.C.Jarvis, 'The Rebellion
of 1745. The Passage Through Lancashire from Contemporary News-Sheets', *Transactions of the Lancashire and Cheshire Antiquarian Society*, LVI (1941–2), 144.
69 King's College, Cambridge, MS PC 2/132. Survey of the Manor of Prescot, 1721.
Quoted in a paper on 'Early Glassmaking in Prescot', read to the Prescot Historic
Society in 1946 by Mrs R.H.Hughes, the manuscript of which is in the possession of
the Society. I am also indebted to the late F.A.Bailey for information about glassmaking in Prescot.
70 *Craftsman*, 22 June 1734, quoted in Buckley, *J.S.G.T.*, *13* (1929), 239.
71 *Selections from the Diary of Nicholas Blundell* ed. T.Ellison Gibson (Liverpool
1895), 153–4,
72 *The Travels Through England of Dr Richard Pococke* ed. J.J.Cartwright (Camden
Society 1888. New Series 42, 209, *sub* 12 June 1751).
73 King's College, Cambridge, MS. PC 2/132 quoted in Mrs Hughes's paper.
74 *The Great Diurnal of Nicholas Blundell of Little Crosby* (eds) F.Tyler and J.J.Bagley
(Record Society of Lancashire and Cheshire 1972), III, 48 and 122.
75 It is impossible to say to what extent the local clays were used at this time. Clay was
certainly an ingredient used in bottle-making. It may have been used for pot
making, though it must have been very inferior to Stourbridge clay. Yet it must be
remembered that local clays were used for this purpose quite frequently. One of the
advantages of a glasshouse at Maryport, for instance, so late as 1760 was that clay for
making pots could be found within two miles (*Newcastle Journal*, 5 July 1760,
quoted in Francis Buckley, 'Cumberland Glasshouses', *J.S.G.T.* x, 385). The St
Helens clays were specifically mentioned as a bargaining point in an agreement of 29
September 1779, between John Mackay of Ravenhead and three men who were about
to establish a copper works on Mackay's estate. They were to be supplied with 'all
such Fire Clay as they may want and have occasion to make use of it at their ...
Smelting and Refinery Works'. (L.R.O.

Gerard Papers, DDGe (M) 830.) I am indebted to Prof. J.R.Harris for this reference. For use of local clay at the Ravenhead works early in the nineteenth century see below n. 133.

76 J.N.L.Baker in his chapter on 'England in the Seventeenth Century' in *An Historical Geography of England Before 1800* (ed. Darby) (Cambridge 1936), 419, observed that the most important glassmaking centres, with the exception of London, were situated near to salt workings.

77 T.C.Barker, 'Lancashire Coal, Cheshire Salt and the Rise of Liverpool', *Transactions of the Lancashire and Cheshire Historic Society, 103* (1951), 83–101.

78 Notestein, Relf and Simpson, *op. cit.*, II, 366; S.P.D., Jas, I, Vol. 162, No. 63, cited in Hartshorne, *op. cit.*, 428, 430.

79 *The Plate Glass Book* by a Glass-house Clerk (1757), XXIV.

80 *A New and Complete Dictionary of Arts and Sciences* by a Society of Gentlemen (1754), 1442.

81 J.R.Harris, 'St. Gobain and Ravenhead', in Barrie M. Ratcliffe (Ed.) *Great Britain and her World* (Manchester 1975), 15–16; Scoville, *op. cit.*, 28–32, 39–41, 47n. 25.

82 Harris, 'St Gobain' which includes much information about that factory. An account is also to be found in *The Universal Dictionary of Trade and Commerce from the French of the celebrated Monsieur Savary . . . With Additions and Improvements by Malachy Postlethwayt Esq* (1751) *sub.* Glass.

83 British Patent 268 of 1691.

84 *Cal. S.P.D.*, May 1690–October 1691, 537, 540.

85 *London Gazette*, 6 June 1692, quoted in Francis Buckley, *The Glass Trade in England in the Seventeenth Century* (1914), 46.

86 *Post Man*, 13 February 1700/1, quoted *ibid.*, 59.

87 Guildhall Library, Broadsides 13/49, 50. *The Case of Mr Gumley and his Partners, Proprietors of a Glasshouse over against Hungerford Market* (1706); *The Answer of the Proprietors of the Bear Garden Glasshouse to the Case of Mr John Gumley and Partners* (1706).

88 This section is based upon the evidence given by various witnesses to the House of Commons on the bill for the incorporation

of the British Cast Plate Glass Manufacturers, 24 February 1773 (*Journals of the House of Commons*, XXXIV). A correspondent described methods of blowing, *casting*, grinding and polishing plate glass at Southwark in the *Universal Magazine*, November 1747, and June 1748.

89 When the Bill was first introduced into the Commons by Herbert Mackworth on 25 January 1773, it aroused much oppositon and was said to introduce a dangerous precedent. The Attorney General thought that it 'contradicted every rule of justice, of legal compensation and every established notion of trade and commerce' (*The History Debates and Proceedings of Both Houses of Parliament*, VII, 420).

90 The best kinds of barilla consisted of ashes of a plant of the goosefoot family, *salsola sativa*, extensively grown in Spain, Sicily and Teneriffe and contained about 20% alkali (C.T.Kingzett, *The History, Products and Processes of the Alkali Trade* (1877), 70). Scottish and Irish kelp, the ash of seaweed, contained 10% alkali.

91 Harris, 'St Gobain'.

92 British Patent 760 of 1761.

93 T.C.Barker and J.R.Harris, *A Merseyside Town in the Industrial Revolution* (Liverpool 1954), 35.

94 PA PB147/15 and 16 Ravenhead deeds.

95 *Gore's General Advertiser*, 24 May 1771, cited in Barker and Harris, *op. cit.*, 44.

96 L.R.O., Gerard Papers, DDGe (M) 830; J.R.Harris, *The Copper King* (Liverpool 1954), 37–8.

97 The proprietors mentioned in the petition to Parliament of 25 January 1773, were: Charles Fitzroy, the Honourable Robert Digby, Peregrine Cust, Thomas Dundas, John Mackay, Philip Affleck, Henry Dagge, James Bourdieu, Angus Mackay, Henry Hastings, Ranald Macdonald and Samuel Chollett. General Sir James Affleck later claimed that 'the concern itself originated with my family' (PA BPG5, 20 May 1829). For Philip Affleck and Robert Digby see the *DNB*.

98 David Garrick of Hampton, Middlesex, lent Mackay £12,000 on 2 and 3 July 1776 (PA PB147/15 and 16 Ravenhead deeds).

99 James Christie in his evidence to the House of Commons Committee was reported to have said that 'a large quantity of such crates would be exported to the East Indies and elsewhere, though at present he knows of no exportation from England while a very considerable one is carried on from France'. It would be tempting to see in the promotion of the new firm the hand of the East India interest wishing to deny the French East India company an advantage they possessed through the St Gobain works.

100 Harris, 'St Gobain', 36–7.

101 13 Geo. III cap. 38.

102 PA BR1, Richard Bright to his father, 7 May 1773; PA BPG5, 22 April 1829. For an interesting account of the works, see *An Illustrated Itinerary of the County of Lancaster* (1842), 89–99.

103 Customs, Communication from John Grant of Waltham Place, 3 May 1793, Treasury and Excise Papers, Customs 48/26, 240.

104 Scoville, *op. cit.*, 81–2.

105 The grave is to be found in the old burial ground, Windleshaw, St Helens. His will, dated 17 November 1787, with a codicil dated 28 November, was proved on 17 April 1788, at Chester. He signed himself G. La Bruyère. His executors were Rev. Joseph Emmott of Fazakerley, Thomas West of Croppers Hill and George Mackay of Ravenhead.

106 PA GR2 Graux de la Bruyère, Articles of Association with British Cast Plate Glass Company, 25 March 1776. The agreement also specified that Graux should receive £400 for his services to the company up to that date.

107 Harris, 'St Gobain', 40–1.

108 Customs, Treasury and Excise, Customs 48/26, 240.

109 George Mackay (see above p.23) reported to the House of Commons (*Journals* XL 806–7, 7 April 1785) that they had only been able to reduce the level of waste 'in cases where wood alone had been constantly burnt, which on account of the expense, the company cannot afford to do'. He added, however, that the saving was not great. The chief causes of waste he mentioned were: more frequent breakage of the pots because of the great heat; ladling from the furnace to the cuvettes; metal adhering to the bottom and sides of the cuvette; metal forced over the end of the table by the roller; and unevenness and losses in squaring.

110 Joseph Black to Alexander Black, 20 March 1783, quoted in Douglas McKie and David Kennedy, 'On some letters of Joseph Black and others', *Annals of Science 16* (1960), 139. This paragraph is based on this source. For Joseph Black see the *DNB;* and A.E.Musson and Eric Robinson, *Science and Technology in the Industrial Revolution* (Manchester 1969), 5–7.

111 An attempt was made to tax the French glass industry during the American war in 1781. But the proprietors of St Gobain appealed and were allowed to compound for 150,000 livres a year from which the amount of glass provided for the use of the royal palaces and the amount exported were to be deducted (Evidence of Alexander Black, 18 June 1784, *Journals of the House of Commons*, XL, 223).

112 17 Geo. III cap. 39. The duty was raised from 9s 4d to 18s 8d.

113 Customs, Treasury and Excise Papers, Customs 48/19, 455–6, 12 February 1779.

114 *Ibid.* (Memorial: Proprietors to Commissioners dated 26 April 1779), Customs 48/19, 482.

115 *Journals of the House of Commons*, XL, 226.

116 *Ibid.*, 806.

117 27 Geo. III cap. 28. This Act was related to the Eden Treaty of 1786.

118 Customs, Treasury and Excise Papers, Customs 48/26, 237.

119 Customs, Treasury and Excise Papers, 48/26, 240.

120 Birmingham Reference Library, Correspondence in the Boulton and Watt Collection.

121 PA BPG5 Minutes, 19 April 1809.

122 PA BPG1 *A Correct State and Estimate of the Stock and Premises of the British Plate Glass Company* (n.d.), 15.

123 *Journal of the House of Commons* XLIX, 349, 413, 467 and 570, House of Lords Record Office, Parchment Collection, MS bill of 9 May 1794.

124 PA PB147/31 Ravenhead deeds. Indenture of 30 September 1794 between the Governor and Company and Thomas Oakes.

125 *Journals of the House of Commons* LIII, 288; 38 Geo. III cap. 90. Unlike the previous Act of 1773, this Act is not generally available in print but the original document can be consulted at the House of Lords Record Office. It names the following as Governor and Company of the British Plate Glass Manufacturers: Philip Affleck, Paul Benfield, Walter Boyd, John Grant, Henry Grant, Thomas Oakes, Philip Stowey, the Rt Hon. Thomas Lord Dundas, Sir John Call, Bart, Robert Digby, William Mills, John Pybus, Robert Sherbourne, John Burnall, Henry Errington, James Affleck and Alexander Aubert. For Boyd and Benfield, see S.R.Cope, *The History of Boyd, Benfield and Co.* (London Ph.D. Thesis 1947).

126 PA BPG5 Minutes, 22 April 1829. Letter from Robert Sherbourne dated 20 April 1829.

127 *Ibid.*, 19 April 1809.

128 PA PB147/31.

129 Miss Pemberton's research into the origins of the British Cast Plate Glass Company and its promoters will be presented as an MA thesis at the University of Liverpool during 1976.

130 PA BPG5 Minutes 19 April 1809.

131 Customs, Treasury and Excise Papers (Memorial from the British Plate Glass Manufacturers dated 15 October 1801), Customs 48/35, 263–4.

132 Customs, Treasury and Excise Papers, Customs 48/26, 422–4 (February 1794); 34 Geo. III cap. 27.

133 PA BPG5 Minutes, 12 April 1815. Sherbourne also used local clay to some extent as well as that from Stourbridge. In 1809, for instance, £511 was spent on Stourbridge clay and £874 on furnace bricks made of Stourbridge clay. In addition, £67 was spent on Whiston clay. In 1811, £202 was spent on Rainford clay and in 1813 £190 on Rainford and Whiston clay.

134 PA BPG5 Minutes, 19 April 1809.

135 The information in this paragraph is taken from the minute books (PA BPG5–7) and account book (PA BPG1).

136 *Gore's General Advertiser*, 29 April 1790.

137 Henry Saladin quoted in Harris, 'St Gobain', 59.

138 PA PB147/35 Abstract of title.

139 L.R.O., Land Tax Returns (Sutton Township), 1781. John Mackay was also

partner in a glass enamelling business in Liverpool (P.R.O., P.L.6/88/42).

140 *Journals of the House of Commons*, XL, 806; Boulton and Watt Papers (Birmingham).

141 *Gore's General Advertiser*, 19 April 1792; Buckley, 'Old Lancashire Glasshouses', 240.

142 Barker and Harris, *op. cit.*, 110.

143 A marble slab was originally used and marver is the anglicization of the French for marble, *marbre*.

144 Believed to be the anglicization of *pontil*.

145 There has been a change in the meaning of this word. At the time of which we are writing, flashing was the name given to the process of rotating the piece of glass on the end of the punty. The term is now used to mean the applying of a thin layer of an opaque or coloured glass to a clear glass while both glasses are in a molten condition.

146 The earliest reference to crown glass in the *OED* is 1706. William Henry Bowles in his *History of the Vauxhall and Ratcliff Glass Houses and their owners 1670–1800* (privately printed 1926), 14, suggests that Normandy glass came to be called crown glass because his ancestor John Bowles who made it at the Bear Garden Glasshouse, Southwark, in the late seventeenth century and marketed it successfully – and probably in a higher quality form – stamped his product with a crown.

147 Anthony Becku to Sir William Cecil (Lansdowne MSS. 59/76 quoted in R.H. Tawney and Eileen Power, *Tudor Economic Documents*, (1924), I, 306).

148 *Cal. S.P.D.William and Mary*, 1694–5, 5 January 1693/4.

149 *Collections of Letters for the Improvement of Husbandry and Trade*, 15 May 1696.

150 13th Report of the Commissioners of Excise Inquiry (Glass), 1835 [15] XXXI, Appendix 23. Evidence of Thomas Dunn, 4 November 1833.

151 PA PB147 Lease from Millicent Fraser and John Gladstone to Bell, 5 October 1822; Customs, Excise Trials, Customs 103/131.

152 T.C.Barker, *Pilkington Brothers and the Glass Industry* (1960), 22. This paragraph and the next are based upon this source where fuller details of the family background are given together with full documentation.

153 About a dozen firms in England

distilled what were known as Plain British Spirits. These were sold to rectifiers of whom there were 108 in England in 1832. Of these firms there were seven in Liverpool, nine in Manchester, one in Bolton, one in Warrington besides William Pilkington and Sons at St Helens. The rectifiers redistilled the Plain British Spirits and compounded them with certain herbs, berries and seeds to add flavour (7th Report from the Commissioners of Excise Inquiry (British Spirits) 1834 [7] xxv, 29, 234–6; article on Messrs Octavius Smith and Co's distillery in the *Penny Magazine*, xi, 303–4).

154 *St Helens Newspaper*, 21 September 1872; petition 23 December 1825.

155 6 Geo. iv cap. 80. The duty was reduced from 10/6 per wine gallon to 7/- per imperial gallon, equivalent to 5/10 per wine gallon (Hansard's Parliamentary Debates, new spirits, xii, cols. 133–4, 22 April 1825).

2

AN UNPROMISING
START

1 Parliamentary Return 1830/1 [124] xi.

2 PA BPG5 Minutes, 10 May 1826.

3 T.C.Barker and J.R.Harris, *A Merseyside Town in the Industrial Revolution* (Liverpool 1954), 197–200, 203.

4 L.R.O., will of William Pilkington proved at Chester, 4 April 1832.

5 L.R.O. Cross Papers, DDCS 37/20. Lease dated 26 December 1826. It was to take effect from 2 February 1827, and to last for 13 years.

6 L.R.O., will proved at Chester, 4 April 1832.

7 For these activities, see Barker and Harris, *op. cit.*, 181 *et seq.*

8 Abstract of title St Helens Crown Glass 1870. (Pilkington Legal Deeds Bundle 1e).

9 *Ibid.*

10 *Ibid.*

11 PA PB141/5 draft articles written in a copper-plate hand and dated 18 May. A careful search has failed to reveal the final signed articles of co-partnership.

12 *St Helens Newspaper*, *St Helens Standard*, 21 September 1872.

13 This was stated as a fact by Abraham Hartley, a glassmaker at the works from 1836, in an interview published in the *St Helens Lantern*, 3 January 1889.

14 According to a note in William Pilkington's handwriting, the initial cost of the first house and the price of the land totalled £9,189 9s 4d. (PA PB141/23). The dimensions of the cone are given on a plan of the works, 1856.

15 See above, Chapter 1; note 145.

16 Interview with William (Roby) Pilkington, *St Helens Lantern*, 7 June 1888.

17 *St Helens Newspaper*, 21 September 1872. According to the census returns for 1851 at the Public Record Office (H.O. 107/2195) Kenmore, then aged 54, was born at Midford, Northumberland, and his wife came from Scotland. Their daughter (22) was born in St Helens.

18 Henry Deacon, *The Manufacture of Blown Window Glass* (Liverpool 1855), 17.

19 For wages list see appendix 1; for list of cottage occupants see PA PB139 loose papers in Board minutes.

20 The following account is based upon Exchequer Records at the Public Record Office, E. 159/733/Mich. 8 Geo iv, m. 299; Excise Trials at H.M. Customs and Excise, Customs 103/132–142, 16 February, 25 April, 14 and 21 June, 29 November 1828 and 7 May 1830; and a leading article in the *Liverpool Mercury*, 16 January 1829.

21 Indenture 21 and 22 December 1827, cited in Abstract of Title.

22 Indenture 1 and 2 May 1828, cited in Abstract of Title.

23 *London Gazette*, 22 April 1828.

24 *Liverpool Mercury*, 19 January 1838. Bell's will, dated 29 April 1836, and proved at Chester, 21 May 1838, was sworn at less than £600. Thomas Bell, described in the 1841 census return as having been born in Lancashire, was not mentioned at all in the will.

25 *St Helens Newspaper*, *St Helens Standard*, 21 September 1872.

26 PA PB141/33 Note in William Pilkington's hand upon a list of production figures, 1827–40.

27 Bromilow Papers, Black Park, Chirk. Adam Bromilow to James Bromilow, June 27 1829. I am grateful to Col. H.A.Bromilow for permission to consult this correspondence.

28 Abstract of Title. Indenture of 2 and 3 February 1829.

29 When Richard Pilkington was formally admitted to the partnership in 1835, it was stated that half of William Pilkington's interest was held in trust for his elder brother. The correspondence between the two in 1831 makes it clear that Richard Pilkington was already actively engaged at the works at that time. (PA PB184).

30 PA PI3/1/1.

31 *The Annual Register's* obituary of Peter Greenall (1845, 296–7) states that he himself was a partner in Parr's 'in which he had acquired a large fortune', but there is no confirmation from any other source of this assertion.

32 J.F.Chance, *A History of the Firm of Chance Brothers & Co.* (privately printed 1919), 1–3; J.F.Chance, *Chance of Bromsgrove and Birmingham* (privately printed 1892); W.H.S.Chance, 'A family business – the early years', paper to Worcestershire Archaeological Society, November 1973.

33 Lucas had previously been a member of a bottlemaking firm in Bristol. His father, a cooper, had gone there from Hanbury in Worcestershire. The Lucases probably knew the Chances who lived nearby, at Bromsgrove. They had lived there since the fifteenth century. For the history of Nailsea see A.C. Powell, 'Glassmaking in Bristol', *Transactions of the Bristol and Gloucestershire Archaeological Society*, XLVII, 252 *et seq.*; Keith Vincent, *Nailsea Glass* (1975); and various articles by Sir Hugh Chance, particularly 'The Nailsea Glassworks', *Studies in Glass History and Design* papers read to Committee B sessions at Eighth International Congress on Glass, London, July 1968, ed. R.J.Charleston (Society of Glass Technology, University of Sheffield 1968).

3

THE COLLAPSE OF A COMPETITOR AND THE STRUGGLE FOR SURVIVAL

1 Thirteenth Report of the Commissioners of Excise Inquiry (Glass), 1835, 29.

2 J.F.Chance, *A History of the Firm of Chance Brothers & Co.* (privately printed 1919), 55.

3 Unless otherwise stated, this account is based upon Customs, Treasury and Excise papers, T.E. 1432 (Mackay, West & Co.), Register of Treasury Papers 1828–30; and Supplementary Statement and Proofs on the Part of the Petitioners (n.d.) among the Cross Papers at the L.R.O. (DDCS).

4 Thirteenth Report of the Commissioners of Excise Inquiry (Glass), 1835, 94.

5 L.R.O., Cross Papers DDCS 14/59, J.U. West to William Rowson, 25 September 1833.

6 *Gore's General Advertiser*, 14 January 1830.

7 L.R.O., Cross Papers, DDCS 14/30.

8 Thirteenth Report of the Commissioners of Excise Inquiry (Glass), 133. Evidence of Robert Lucas Chance; Bromilow Papers, Black Park, Chirk, letters from General Gascoyne, 14 October 1832, 1 March 1833; James Bromilow to General Gascoyne, 29 October 1832.

9 L.R.O., Cross Papers, Mackay, West and Co.'s Arbitration. King's Bench, Michaelmas 1834.

10 L.R.O., Cross Papers, DDCS 14/68.

11 *Wigan Gazette*, 8 October 1836.

12 L.R.O., Cross Papers, draft Deed for Settling Disputes, 23 January 1837.

13 The fiat of Bankruptcy was dated 28 September 1837.

14 See p. 104.

15 J.F.Chance, *op. cit.*; Customs, Excise and Treasury Papers, T.E. 5010 (memorial of William Chance, 1 February 1832).

16 John C.Logan, 'The Dumbarton Glass Works Company: a study in entrepreneurship', *Business History*, XIV (1972), 61–81; *id.*, 'The Operation of a Glassworks in the Industrial Revolution', *Industrial Archaeology*, 9, (1972), 177–87; *id.*, *The Dumbarton Glass Work Company* (M.Litt., University of Strathclyde 1970); *The New Statistical Account of Scotland*, VIII (1845), 9–11, 49–50. I am indebted to Miss Aileen Grierson of the Vale of Lever Academy, for allowing me to see her thesis on the history of Dumbarton and for making enquiries on my behalf. The reference to John Hartley is in *The Alderman*, 7 July 1877 (Copy in PA ZZ16).

17 Notestein, Relf and Simpson, *Commons Debates* 1621, VII, 547.

18 Agreement between the Glass-sellers' Company and various glassmakers, 1 September 1684 (MS. 5556 at Guildhall Library, London).

19 W.H.B.Court, *The Rise of the Midland Industries* 1600–1838 (Oxford 1938), 124–6.

20 See p. 10.

21 Quarto notebook containing details of correspondence and meetings during the 1780s. This was in the possession of Mr Guy L.Chater of the old-established firm of Joseph Chater and Sons, who kindly permitted me to look at it.

22 The following account is based on the Crown (after 1845 Crown and Sheet) Glass Manufacturers' Association minutes in the Pilkington Archives PB165 (Pilkington notes and minutes 1829–65) and ZZ45/8 (Chance minutes 1827–46).

23 PA ZZ45/8, 19 September 1828.

24 PA PB184, William Pilkington to Richard Pilkington, 3 November 1834.

25 In January and February 1836, several manufacturers met to consider the complaint of Mr Bower of Hunslet, but refused to take any decision until Mr Bower himself attended to substantiate his claims.

26 There was a meeting of the Lancashire manufacturers only on 15 December 1832 at Warrington. They fixed a minimum price for the sale of squares, PA PB165.

27 PA PB184, William Pilkington to Richard Pilkington, 29 April 1831.

28 Joseph Chater & Sons. Letter from J.W. Bell, 23 January 1828.

29 PA PB184, William Pilkington to Richard Pilkington, 23 April 1831.

30 William Richardson & Company were proprietors of the North Tyne Manufactory, Newcastle. Their works were opened about 1825. (Petition dated 29 September 1825, Tyne and Wear County Archives, 11/21/49.)

31 PA PB184, William Pilkington to Richard Pilkington, 29 April 1831.

32 PA PB184, William Pilkington to Richard Pilkington, 4 August 1834.

33 *Ibid.*

34 PA PB184, William Pilkington to Richard Pilkington, 3 November 1834.

35 PA PB184, William Pilkington to Richard Pilkington, 18 December 1838.

36 William Pilkington's eldest daughter, Mary, married Henry Chater in 1850.

37 PA PB184, William Pilkington to Richard Pilkington, 15 September 1834.

38 PA PB184, William Pilkington to Richard Pilkington, 8 December 1838.

39 These figures are taken from a list of production figures drawn up by William Pilkington in about 1840 (PA PB141/33).

40 R.C.O.Matthews, *A Study in Trade-Cycle History: Economic Fluctuations in Great Britain* 1833–1842 (Cambridge 1954), 115.

41 Reference is made to this second house by William Pilkington in a letter dated 3 November 1834 (PA PB184).

42 The figures from this and the following paragraph are from lists drawn up by William Pilkington about 1836 and 1840 (PA PB141/23,33).

43 PA PI3/1/2 William Pilkington & Sons ledgers.

44 Thomas Pilkington formally retired from the partnership on 28 June 1836 (*London Gazette*, 8 July 1836).

45 PA PB139 Board minutes, 8 and 14 December 1880 and 23 May 1882.

46 PA PI3, letter from William Pilkington 8 March 1836. The recipient is not known.

47 PA PI3/1/1 William Pilkington & Sons cashbook.

48 See p. 94.

49 Greenall, Whitley & Co. Ltd., St Helens Rent Book; the Cross Papers at L.R.O. contain letters about Millbrook House written by William Pilkington in 1836 and 1850.

4
THE INTRODUCTION
OF A NEW TECHNIQUE

1 See p. 25.

2 *Official Descriptive and Illustrated Catalogue of the Great Exhibition of the Works of Industry of all Nations*, 1851 (1852), 525; G.Bontemps, *Guide du Verrier* (Paris 1868), 231–3; Warren C.Scoville, *Capitalism and French Glassmaking* 1640–1789 (University of California Studies in Economics 1950), 8–9.

3 Samuel Parkes, *Chemical Essays* (1815), III, 446.

4 Although diamonds came into general use in England, the Belgians always employed splitting irons (PA ZZ9/30, Report on Belgian and French glassworks in 1859). The diamond cuts had to be made inside the cylinder.

5 Customs, Treasury and Excise Papers, 27 January 1758 (Crown and green glass. Customs 48/16, 125 and 423).

6 17 Geo. III cap. 39, sec. 26.

7 D.R.Guttery, *From Broad Glass to Cut Crystal: A History of the Stourbridge Glass Industry* (1956), 96.

8 *Ibid.*, 98–9.

9 British Patent 2812 of 1805.

10 13th Report of the Excise Commissioners Inquiry (Glass), appendix p. 95.

11 There were, in fact, two payments on production as well as the annual fee for each glasshouse. There was (1) a payment per pound for all glass melted calculated on the internal dimensions of each pot and the surface level of the molten glass within it, and (2) a payment per pound on the excess of manufactured glass over 40 per cent (or later 50 per cent) of the calculated weight of molten glass. There were certain allowances for glass loss in manufacture. H.J.Powell, *Glassmaking in England* (Cambridge 1923), 154–5.

12 Customs, Treasury and Excise Papers. T.E. 9651 Memorial submitted by manufacturers of window glass, 1830.

13 Customs, Treasury and Excise Papers. T.E. 5010. Memorial from Chance and Hartley's, 6 June 1835. Register of Treasury Papers 1833–5.

14 Customs, Treasury and Excise Papers. T.E. 5010 (see above); J.F.Chance, *A History of the Firm of Chance Brothers & Co.* (privately printed 1919), 6.

15 Customs, Treasury and Excise Papers. T.E. 5010 (see above).

16 *Ibid.*, Memorial dated 6 June 1835.

17 *Ibid.*, letter from Gervase Oldham at Stourbridge, 19 May 1832.

18 J.F.Chance, *op. cit.*, 5–6; speech by James Hartley reported in a supplement to the *Sunderland Times*, 6 November 1866; Bontemps, *op. cit.*, 375.

19 J.F.Chance, *op. cit.*, 6.

20 PA ZZ5 Board minutes, 15 October 1855. For exports to North America between 1837 and 1843, see Parliamentary Return, 1844 [200] XLV.

21 5 & 6 Wm. IV cap. 77, sec. 5; 1 & 2 Vict. cap. 44.

22 J.F.Chance, *op. cit.*, 26.

23 British Patent 7177 of 1836.

24 PA ZZ5 Board minutes, 29 December 1837.

25 British Patent 7618 of 1838.

26 56 Geo. III cap. 8, sec. 6; 13th Report of the Excise Commissioners Inquiry (Glass), 6, 29, 133.

27 PA ZZ7/26, J.T.Chance to W.Chance junior.

28 *Leeds Intelligencer* quoted by the *Mechanics Magazine*, XXXII (1839/40), 192; J.F.Chance, *op. cit.*, 7.

29 PA ZZ7/26, J.T.Chance to Wren & Bennett, 12 May 1840.

30 PA ZZ7/26, J.T.Chance to A.B.Goss, 5 September 1840.

31 PA ZZ7/26, J.T.Chance to Messrs Clough, 24 September 1839.

32 PA ZZ7/26, J.T.Chance to William Chance, 28 January 1841; ZZ11 Tariff, 7 April 1841.

33 J.F.Chance, *op. cit.*, 20–1.

34 Printed statement from Wear Glassworks, Sunderland, on proposed glass duties, 1841, in scrapbook kept by James Hartley or J.J.Kayll. This scrapbook was consulted with the permission of the late Leslie Brett, former Secretary of Plate Glass Merchants' Association, London; Customs, Treasury and Excise Papers, T.E. 7653. Memorial of window glass manufacturers, received February 1839. Register of Treasury Papers 1837–9.

35 *St Helens Lantern*, 3 January 1889.

36 P.R.O., H.O. 107/516.

37 This inscription is reproduced in the *St Helens Lantern*, Christmas edition, 1888.

38 PA ZZ7/26, J.T.Chance to Wren & Bennett, 14 September 1842.

39 PA ZZ5 Board minutes, 8 March 1843.

40 PA ZZ7/26, J.T.Chance to Wren & Bennett, 14 September 1842.

41 PA BPG5 Minutes, 27 July 1842.

42 PA ZZ7/26, J.T.Chance to Wren & Bennett, 24 March 1846.

43 PA ZZ18/8 Letter 13, Edward Johnson to Chance Brothers, 5 May 1843.

44 This matter has been carefully scrutinized in an unpublished paper entitled 'Innovation Unrewarded' by Mr T.V.Jackson of Pilkington Patents Department.

45 For the general background to Deacon's life, see J.Fenwick Allen's memoir in the *Chemical Trade Journal*, 18 September

1889, later printed in that writer's *Some Founders of the Chemical Industry*.

46 PA PB141/22.

47 British Patent 10,686 of 1845.

48 *Artizan*, 1 September 1864.

49 British Patent 9815 of 1843.

50 British Patent 11,384 of 1846.

51 J.F.Chance, *op. cit.*, 31–2.

52 See p. 88.

5

GROWTH DURING A
DEPRESSION

1 H.A.Shannon, 'Bricks – A Trade Index, 1785–1849', *Economica*, 1934, 304; R.C.O. Matthews, *A Study in Trade-Cycle History* (Cambridge 1954), 116.

2 PA PB184, William Pilkington to Richard Pilkington.

3 Minutes of the Manufacturers' Association in PA PB165 & ZZ45/8. Much of this section is based on this source.

4 For plus see pp. 90–91.

5 PA PB184, William Pilkington to Richard Pilkington.

6 PA PB165 Meeting 25 and 26 August 1841.

7 PA PB141/21, 33.

8 PA PB184, William Pilkington to Richard Pilkington.

9 PA PB141/2 Bank books. Account with Parr, Lyon's Bank, Warrington.

10 Pilkington Legal Deeds Sheet works, Bundle 1E.

11 Stanley D.Chapman, 'Working Capital in the British Cotton Industry, 1770–1850', paper read at the Ealing Technical College Business History Seminar, 2 May 1975.

12 Pilkington Legal Deeds Sheet works Bundle 1E.

13 *Liverpool Mercury*, 19 September 1845; *Manchester Guardian* & *Manchester Courier*, 20 September 1845; *Annual Register*, 1845, 296–7.

14 For a survey of the relevant legislation, see the Thirteenth Report of the Excise Commissioners Inquiry (Glass), 3–10; Stephen Dowell, *A History of Taxation and Taxes in England* (4 vols. 1884), III,

194–203; W.R. Ward, 'The Administration of the Window and Assessed Taxes, 1696–1798', *English Historical Review*, LXVII (1952), 522–542.

15 Thirteenth Report of the Excise Commissioners Inquiry, 138.

16 *The Economist*, 19 July 1845.

17 Thirteenth Report of the Excise Commissioners Inquiry, 137–8.

18 See p. 119.

19 PA ZZ5 Minutes, 22 October 1833.

20 Customs, Treasury and Excise papers T.E. 9651. Memorial from Chance Brothers & Co., 24 February 1842. Register of Treasury Papers 1839–42.

21 A.P.Wadsworth and J.deL.Mann, *The Cotton Trade and Industrial Lancashire* (Manchester 1931), 489.

22 Peter Drinkwater to Boulton and Watt, 3 April 1789, cited in W.H.Chaloner, 'Robert Owen, Peter Drinkwater and the Early Factory System in Manchester', *Bulletin of the John Ryland Library*, 37 (1954), 89.

23 Return 1831 [124] XI; 1841 [303] XXIV; G.R.Porter, *Progress of the Nation* (1847), 537.

24 Return 1846 [223] XXV.

25 See, in particular, the essays published in Stanley D.Chapman (ed.), *The History of Working-class Housing* (Newton Abbot 1971). An important early essay in this field is Professor W.G.Rimmer's paper on 'Working Men's Cottages in Leeds, 1770–1840', *Publications of the Thoresby Society*, Miscellany, Vol. 13, Part 3.

26 This paragraph owes much to discussion with Professor W.Ashworth. I am also grateful to Miss V.Hole, of the Building Research Station, for helpful advice.

27 *The Times*, 14 April 1845; return of window duty, 1846 [223] XXV.

28 8 & 9 Vict. cap. 6.

29 Return of the Reduction of the Excise Department . . . together with Information . . . respecting the Effects produced by the Repeal of the Duty on the manufacture of Glass, 1846 [109] XLIV.

30 7 & 8 Vict. cap. 84.

31 *The Builder*, 11 January 1845.

32 PA ZZ26/37, R.L.Chance to J.T.Chance, 8 July 1845.

33 Return 1846 [109], XLIV.

6

A LABOUR CRISIS

1 For the introduction of gatherers in sheet glass manufacture, see G.Bontemps, *Guide du Verrier* (Paris 1868), 117, 273–5; J.F. Chance, *A History of the Firm of Chance Brothers and Co.* (1919), 33.

2 L.R.O., Cross Papers. Cases arising from the disputed contracts at the St Helens Crown Glass Works, 1845–6.

3 Lecture by James Hartley, *The Journal of the Society of Arts*, 17 February 1854.

4 *Rules and Regulations of the British Crown Glass Makers' Society Agreed Upon at a General Meeting of Delegates from Spon Lane, Smethwick, Birmingham, St Helens, Old Swan, Eccleston and Newton Glass Works* (Birmingham 1846). A copy is deposited in PA BR2.

5 See Appendix 1.

6 L.R.O., Cross Papers, William Pilkington to Rowson and Cross, 27 November 1845.

7 Interview with Thomas Gerard, *St Helens Lantern*, 3 January 1889.

8 *St Helens Lantern*, 7 June 1888. See also p. 127.

9 PA ZZ26/37, R.L.Chance junr to R.L. Chance, 23 July 1845. This letter is included in a copy letter series dated 19 July 1845.

10 L.R.O., Cross Papers.

11 PA ZZ39, translation of a letter from Georges Bontemps to R.L.Chance, 2 January 1845.

12 Parliamentary Return, 1846 [109] XLIV.

13 *Ibid.*

14 This and subsequent paragraphs dealing with the labour difficulties of the firm in 1845 and 1846 are based upon a mass of documents discovered at the office of Henry Cross & Son, successors to Rowson and Cross who were the firm's solicitors at this time. These documents now form part of the Cross Papers, L.R.O., DDCS.

15 I owe this information to Miss Aileen Grierson of the Vale of Leven Academy.

16 By 4 Geo. IV, cap. 34, sec. 3.

17 See Appendix 2.

18 For these Birmingham works, see J.F. Chance, *op. cit.*, 61–2.

19 See p. 87.

20 L.R.O., Cross Papers. William Pilkington to William Cross, 3 September 1845.

21 Appendix to the Fourth Report of the Children's Employment Commission, 1865 [8357] XX, 276.

22 'A Day at a Glass Factory', *Penny Magazine*, 29 June 1844. This account of Cooksons' works in South Shields and Newcastle contains one of the best descriptions of window glassmaking at that time.

23 The agreements of 1839 and 1845, both printed, are among the Cross Papers at the L.R.O. That of 1833, in William Pilkington's handwriting, is at Pilkington, PB141/7.

24 L.R.O., Cross Papers.

25 These are reproduced as Appendix 1.

26 L.R.O., Cross Papers.

27 *Ibid.*

28 Royal Society of Arts, *Abstract of Proceedings*, 14 and 21 April, 9 June 1847.

29 T.C.Barker and J.R.Harris, *A Merseyside Town in the Industrial Revolution* (Liverpool 1954), 258–63.

30 H.Logan, 'Early Days of the Recs. Club', PA PB234 *Cullet*, January 1929.

31 Both William (Roby) and Thomas Pilkington played for a St Helens side in a match against an All England XI in May 1853 (*Wigan Times*, 13 May 1853).

32 Appendix to the Fourth Report of the Children's Employment Commission, 1865, 274. Evidence of William Pilkington.

33 *Liverpool Mercury*, 23 July 1850.

34 *Liverpool Mercury*, 23 January 1849.

35 Henry Deacon, 'The Manufacture of Blown Window Glass', lecture to the Architectural and Archaeological Society of Liverpool, 1851, quoted in 'The St Helens Crown Glass Works School', by R.C. Liggett, unpublished MS (1972) PA 72/36.

36 Appendix to the Fourth Report of the Children's Employment Commission, 1865, 275.

37 *The Builder*, 5 April 1851. According to a resolution of the Board on 17 March 1864, these fines were from that date onwards to be returned after a lapse of time in cases of good conduct.

38 Second Report of the Children's Employment Commission, 1843, b. 55. Evidence of Thomas Percival, manager of Messrs Molyneux and Well, Flint Glass Manufacturers, Manchester.

39 Third Report of the Children's Employment Commission, 1864, 191.

40 *Liverpool Mercury*, 21 May 1847.

41 See, for instance, the testimony of John Blundell, *Cullet*, July 1931; and *ibid.* April 1932.

42 Mrs Boyes subsequently married Richard Fildes, the leading grocer and draper in the town, himself a widower. Her previous husband, who had died, had been a captain in the Royal Navy.

43 According to addresses printed in the *Proceedings of the Institution of Mechanical Engineers*, he was living in various parts of London between 1864–6, at Darlington until 1869 and at Birmingham until 1872. His name does not appear in the *Proceedings* after this. He died in 1894.

44 List of students at the Royal College of Chemistry, evidence to the Royal Commission on Scientific Instruction, 1872 [C. 536] xxv, 359.

45 Obituary, *St Helens Newspaper*, 20 March 1914. This school founded in Birmingham by Thomas Wright Hill, was developed by his sons Rowland and Matthew Davenport (the criminal law reformer). It was moved from Hazelwood, near Birmingham, to Tottenham in 1827. For information about the curriculum and method of training, see R.L.Archer, *Secondary Education in the Nineteenth Century* (Cambridge 1921), 90–6.

46 Katherine Chorley in her book *Manchester Made Them* (1950), 128–134, has much to say in praise of Lawrence Pilkington, a neighbour of hers in her youth. For Alfred Pilkington's obituary, see *St Helens Newspaper*, 12 December 1896, and for Margaret Pilkington's *The Guardian*, 5 August 1974.

47 Recollections of James Marsh, Richard Pilkington's successor as superintendent, *St Helens Newspaper*, 3 May 1890.

7
THE REMOVAL OF
BRITISH COMPETITORS

1 *Journal of the Society of Arts*, 17 February 1854.

2 Henry Chance, 'On the Manufacture of Crown and Sheet Glass', *Journal of the Society of Arts*, 15 February 1856; Walter Lucas Chance in J.F.Chance, *A History of the Firm of Chance Brothers & Co.* (privately printed 1919), 277.

3 Warrington Public Library. Rate books.

4 P.R.O. C.101/5393 and 5394. I am grateful to Mr J.M.Hemphill for drawing my attention to these papers among the Chancery Master's Exhibits.

5 The leading shareholders were: George Bennett of Liverpool, wine merchant, who held 423 shares; John Blakeway Tipton, of Birkenhead, merchant, who held 277 shares; Oswald Airey, of Liverpool, chemist, who held 213 shares; Arthur Latham of Liverpool, merchant, who held 155 shares; John Sothern of Liverpool, merchant, who held 150 shares; Robert Falk of Cleveland Square, Liverpool, and Thomas Corlett of the North and South Wales Bank, who each held 130 shares; William Crosfield, wholesale grocer – also described as 'original proprietor' – who held 122 shares; and Andrew Kurtz, the manufacturing chemist of Liverpool, who held 100 shares (P.R.O. C.101/5393). William Crosfield had been trained by his brother Joseph, founder of the Warrington soapworks, before joining two other older brothers, George and John, in their Liverpool wholesale grocery business, George Crosfield & Co. In 1843–4 George Crosfield's son Joseph, became a founder partner in Harrisons and Crosfield, the well-known wholesale tea and coffee merchants. A.E.Musson, *Enterprise in soap and chemicals. Joseph Crosfield and Sons Limited, 1815–1965* (Manchester 1965), 19–20.

6 See p. 6. For obituaries of Isaac Cookson, see *Annual Register* and *Gentleman's Magazine*, 1851.

7 PA ZZ26/37, postscript in a letter written by R.L.Chance to James Chance, 31 July 1845. For a full account of this factory, see 'A Day at a Glass Factory', *Penny Magazine*, 29 June 1844.

8 L.R.O. Cross Papers. Richard Shortridge to William Pilkington, 15 November 1845.

9 I am much indebted to Professor F.M.L. Thompson who has placed at my disposal this information from the Ridley family diary at Blagdon Hall, Seaton Burn.

10 Thomas Salmon, *South Shields, Its Past, Present and Future* (South Shields 1856), 22.

11 Quoted in *The Builder*, 21 April 1849.

12 George B.Hodgson, *The History of South Shields* (Newcastle 1924), 246; J.Collingwood Bruce, *A Handbook to Newcastle-on-Tyne* (1863), 258. (The latter acknowledged the assistance of Hartley and Swinburne in compiling the handbook.)

13 *Report of the 32nd Meeting of the British Association held at Newcastle-upon-Tyne in August and September, 1863* (1864), 56.

14 *Newcastle Journal*, 25 May 1886.

15 British Patent 11,891 of 1847; report of Hartley *v.* Hadland, *Sunderland Times*, 28 February 1852. PA ZZ30/10, Mr Kayll's notes re Patent Rolled Plate, 30 October 1880.

16 J.F.Chance, *op. cit.* 52–3; Henry Chance, 'On the Manufacture of Crown and Sheet Glass', *Journal of the Society of Arts*, 15 February 1856; C.R.Fay, *Palace of Industry 1851* (Cambridge 1951), 16. Chances had already supplied glass to Paxton for Chatsworth Observatory (see p. 63).

17 *Journal of the Society of Arts*, 17 February 1854.

18 Raymond McGrath and A.C.Frost, *Glass in Architecture and Decoration* (2nd ed. 1961), 152 and 247.

19 James Hartley to William (Roby) Pilkington, December 1854. This letter was sent on to Chances and is printed in J.F. Chance, *op. cit.*, 78.

20 J.F.Chance, *op. cit.*, 78.

21 PA ZZ30/10.

22 PA PB165/3 Manufacturers' Association minutes, 28 February and 5 March 1845; *Gore's Directory*, 1845; plan of Old Swan Glassworks, 1851, in P.R.O. C101/5393.

23 The agreement of 7 April 1845 is recited in the conveyance of 31 August 1846 (Pilkington Legal Deeds Bundle 31 (old deeds)). Hadland had also acquired Bell's Flint Glass Works at Ravenhead and made bottles there for a short time before the works were sold in 1846 (Pilkington Legal Deeds Bundle 14/3, Abstract of title John and Edward Cannington 1876).

24 Mortgage, 24 February 1847 (Pilkington Legal Deeds Bundle 31 (old deeds)).

25 St Helens Improvement Commission Rate Books, Local History Archive Collection, Gamble Institute, St Helens.

26 *Sunderland Times*, 28 February 1852;

Sunderland Herald, 5 March 1852 (copies in Pilkington Archives).

27 J.F.Chance, *op. cit.*, 78*n*; schedule dealing with the Eccleston Crown Glassworks.

28 Appendix to the Fourth Report of the Children's Employment Commission, 1865, 275; agreement between Hartley and Pilkingtons. PA SD22.

29 J.F.Chance, *op. cit.*, 79.

30 Walter Lucas Chance in J.F.Chance, *op. cit.*, 278.

31 J.F.Chance, *op. cit.*, 46.

32 PA ZZ21/42, William Pilkington to R.L.Chance, 23 June 1855.

33 John Henry Lane, *Newton-in-Makerfield: its history* (Newton 1914–6) ii, 163–4; PA ZZ24/49, John Reynell to William Chance, 26 July 1833.

34 PA ZZ31/42, William Pilkington to R.L.Chance, 23 June 1855.

35 *Ibid*; and note on Newton Glassworks.

36 *Ibid*.

37 *Ibid.*, Robert Gardner to Chance Brothers Ltd, 12 March 1855.

38 *Ibid.*, William Pilkington to R.L.Chance, 23 June 1855.

39 *Ibid.*, Memorandum of agreement between Robert Gardner and William Pilkington, 4 July 1855.

40 *Ibid*.

41 *Ibid.*, Memorandum made by Mr Swinburne at Sunderland, 13 July 1855. There is no further evidence of the Bristol company's co-operation.

42 *Ibid.*, James Hartley to R.L.Chance, 30 January 1856.

43 *Ibid.*, James Hartley to J.T.Chance, 23 July 1856.

44 Information from Sir Hugh Chance and others (see PA PB97/109) and PA RE2 *sub* William Owen.

45 Joshua Bower, born in 1773, the founder of this firm, started work as a carpenter and in the Leeds Directory of 1817 is described as 'ironmonger, joiner and builder and crown glass manufacturer'. In later life, besides being a considerable glassmaker, he became one of the largest toll farmers in England and at one time is said to have possessed nearly all the tolls between Leeds and London together with some in Wiltshire, Cumbria, East Yorkshire, Lincolnshire and elsewhere. He also owned coal mines.

He died at Hunslet on 7 September 1835, leaving his son, also named Joshua, to continue his window glass business until 1860 R.V.Taylor, *The Biographia Leodiensis* (1865), 455–6; K.A.McMahon, 'Roads and Turnpike Trusts in East Yorkshire', *East Yorkshire History Society* (1964); L.A. Williams, *Road Transport in Cumbria in the Nineteenth Century* (1975), 63. William Albert, *The Turnpike Road System in England 1663–1840* (1972), 86n notes that Bower Senior left an estate valued at £14,000, not £100,000 as recorded by Taylor.

46 PA ZZ28/4 Deed of arrangement and covenant not to carry on glass trade during a period of 14 years, 31 May 1861.

47 PA ZZ24/46 Prospectus of Albion Glass Co. Ltd. 10,000 shares were to be issued at £1 each. R.T.Wolstenholme was named as the Secretary, and directors had still to be appointed. Dated about 1861.

48 Henry Chance, 'On the Manufacture of Plate, Crown and Sheet Glass', in *The Resources, Products and Industrial History of Birmingham and the Midland Hardware District*, ed. Samuel Timmins (1866), 149.

49 'The "piece" is "blocked" and blown as if for sheet, until it would be ready for opening, but the closed end forms the top of the shade, and the workman's object is to give it an agreeable form. He manages this by heating it, and allowing it to cup in, again heating when the sides become more softened, and then, according to circumstances, blowing out the depression with the end more or less elevated or hung down. By these means he destroys the pointed form resulting from the swinging, and, according to his skill, gives a more or less elegant curve to the "top". The "cap" is then removed and the open end of the "shade" squared in the same way as the cylinders.' (Henry Deacon *The Manufacture of Blown Window Glass* (1851), 79–80.)

50 *Ibid.*

51 A copy of this book is preserved among the firm's archives. There is also one in the Bodleian Library, Oxford.

52 See one of Henry Peet's editorial notes in his *Liverpool in the Reign of Queen Anne 1705 and 1708* (Liverpool 1908), appendix p. 128.

53 Legal deeds at Pilkington.

54 Lecture of R.B.Edmundson, published in *The Builder*, 8 April 1854; Appendix 2.

55 PA BPG5 Minutes 10 and 24 January 1844; *Manchester Guardian*, 14 February 1844.

56 PA WH1 Notebook of Robert Whyte. We have based the following paragraph on this source unless otherwise stated.

57 L.R.O., Tithe award (Windle).

58 *Liverpool Mercury*, 8 September 1854.

59 *St Helens Intelligencer*, 12 July 1856.

60 *Liverpool Mercury*, 11 October 1844.

61 Customs, T.E. 4168. Register of Treasury Papers 1833–5. This enquiry was occasioned by an attempt to sell New South Wales sand in this country.

62 See, for instance, PA PB139 Board minutes, 2 and 15 April, 23 July, 11 August, and 1 September 1869 (Windle); 2 March 1871 (Carr Mill and Moss Bank); 19 February 1874 (Eccleston and Rainford); 30 October 1879 (Rainford).

63 *Report of the Royal Commission on Noxious Vapours*, 1878 [C. 2159] XLIV. Evidence of William Windle Pilkington, q.11,080.

64 British Patent No. 8,000 of 1839.

65 L.R.O., DDCS 14/101. William Pilkington to Rowson and Cross, 2 May 1845.

66 T.C.Barker and J.R.Harris, *A Merseyside Town in the Industrial Revolution* (Liverpool 1954), 342–3.

67 John Fenwick Allen, *Some Founders of the Chemical Industry* (Manchester 1906; 2nd ed. 1907). These memoirs had previously appeared in the *Chemical Trade Journal* of 1889 and 1890. The article on Henry Deacon was published in the issue of 18 September 1889.

68 D.W.F.Hardie and R.Dickinson, 'Gaskell-Deacon 1853–1953', *General Chemical Division News*, ICI Ltd, August 1953.

69 L.R.O., Cross Papers. Deed of Dissolution of the Pilkington-Deacon Partnership, 15 June 1855. The following paragraph is also based on this source.

70 Patent of William Gossage (422 of 21 February 1854) and patent of J.H.Johnson (1504 of 8 July 1854).

71 L.R.O., Cross Papers, William Pilkington to William Cross, 2 June 1855.

72 Article by John Blundell, *Cullet*, July 1931.

73 D.W.F.Hardie, *A History of the Chemical*

Industry in Widnes (ICI General Chemical Division 1950), 61.

74 PA PB139 Board minutes, 9, 16 March, 22 June 1865.

75 First Report of the Rivers Pollution Commission, 1870 [C.109] XLIV, col. II, 132.

8

COMPETITION FROM
BELGIUM AND CONSOLIDATION
AT ST HELENS

1 V. Lefebvre, *La Verrerie à Vitres et Les Verriers de Belgique depuis le XVe Siècle* (Publications de l'Université de Travail de Hainaut 1938), 48. For a comprehensive bibliography of writings on the Belgian glass industry, see R. Chambon, *L'Histoire de la Verrerie en Belgique* (Brussels 1955), 261–81.

2 *Statistique Générale de la Belgique, Exposé de la Situation du Royaume, 1851–60* (Brussels 1865), 138.

3 James Frederick Chance, *A History of the Firm of Chance Brothers & Co.* (Privately printed 1919), 32.

4 Report from Lord Howard de Walden. Correspondence with Her Majesty's Missions Abroad Regarding Industrial Questions and Trades Unions, 1867 [3892], LXX, 5–6.

5 Customs, Treasury and Excise Papers. T.E. 5263. Memorial dated 2 March 1837. Register of Treasury Papers 1835–7.

6 Customs, Treasury and Excise Papers. T.E. 9651. Memorial dated 15 April 1841. Register of Treasury Papers 1839–42.

7 Customs, Treasury and Excise Papers. T.E. 9651. Memorial from Chance Brothers and Co. dated 24 February 1842. Register of Treasury Papers 1839–42.

8 Customs Tariffs of the United Kingdom from 1800 to 1897, 1898 [C.8706] LXXXV.

9 For the details, see appendix 4.

10 Henry Chance, 'On the Manufacture of Plate, Crown and Sheet Glass', in *The Resources, Products and Industrial History of Birmingham and the Midland Hardware District*, ed. Samuel Timmins (1866), 150.

11 The Association then had a London office. It was first situated at 14 Old Jewry Chambers and later at Adelaide Chambers, 52 Gracechurch Street.

12 PA PB139 Board minutes, 21 September 1865.

13 *Ibid.*, 9 February 1866.

14 PA ZZ49/M13, R.L. Chance to Richard Pilkington, 30 August 1877.

15 J.F. Chance, *op. cit*, 94.

16 *Ibid.*, 283.

17 PA PB165 Minutes of the Manufacturers' Association, 5 April 1865. The minutes of this meeting and those of 13–14 December 1865 and 27 September 1866, are the only ones after 1845 which remain at Pilkington.

18 PA PB139 Board minutes, 15 October 1866.

19 *The Brierley Hill Advertiser*, 30 November 1872 and 5 June 1873; *Birmingham Daily Gazette*, 12 November 1872. Bowen was to fail for a third time in 1872.

20 J.F. Chance, *op. cit.*, 106–7.

21 *Proceedings of the Institution of Mechanical Engineers*, 1863, 268–80.

22 See Ch. 6 note 43.

23 PA PB139 Board minutes, 17 and 24 May, 14 June, 14 November and 20 December 1866; Windle Pilkington took out 34 patents between 1869 and 1913. They were:

2959 of 1869 – improving melting furnace.
2201 of 1870 – blowing (provisional only).
3382 of 1870 – opening cylinder (provisional only).
 207 of 1871 – blowing machine.
2434 of 1879 – apparatus for grinding and smoothing plate.
3823 of 1879 – movable pot crane.
4041 of 1879 – apparatus for grinding plate.
 26 of 1880 – annealing plate glass.
1154 of 1880 – apparatus for grinding plate glass.
5748 of 1886 – apparatus for grinding plate glass.
 927 of 1890 – annealing kilns.
17204 of 1890 – annealing kilns.
1222 of 1891 – forming sheets.
6525 of 1891 – improved apparatus for rolling.
10661 of 1891 – annealing kilns.
19441 of 1891 – forming sheets.
21181 of 1891 – melting and firing plate glass.
4542 of 1893 – hollow articles in blown glass.
4543 of 1893 – reflectors.
9554 of 1893 – wired glass.

15719 of 1893 – lanterns for lamps.

3903 of 1899 – rolling machinery.

10671 of 1899 (with William Ormanby) – utilization of waste sand.

17120 of 1900 – manufacture of fire bricks.

7930 of 1902 – blowing and moulding of cylinders.

3750 of 1903 – improvements in wired glass.

22520 of 1905 – improvement on Clark (flat drawn).

5879 of 1907 – modification of 1905.

14283 of 1910 – drawn cylinder improvements.

16064 of 1910 – drawn cylinder improvements.

20141 of 1910 – drawn cylinder improvements.

27280 of 1910 – annealing.

9244 of 1911 – drawn cylinder improvements.

15290 of 1913 – pot handling gear.

24 C. William Siemens, 'On a New Construction of Furnace, Particularly Applicable Where Intense Heat is Required', *Proceedings of the Institution of Mechanical Engineers,* 1857, 103–11.

25 *Ibid.* British Patents 2861 of 1856 and 1320 of 1857.

26 C. William Siemens, 'On a Regenerative Gas Furnace as Applied to Glasshouses, Puddling, Heating, etc.', *Proceedings of the Institution of Mechanical Engineers,* 1862, 22.

27 British Patent 167 of 1861.

28 Siemens, 'Regenerative Gas Furnace', 29; J.F.Chance, *op. cit.,* 86.

29 The following is based on the Pilkington Board minutes, PA PB139.

30 For Crossley see T.C.Barker and J.R. Harris, *A Merseyside Town in the Industrial Revolution* (Liverpool 1954), 362.

31 PA ZZ46/JHC letterbook.

32 Appendix to the Fourth Report of the Children's Employment Commission, 1865, 275.

33 See p. 111.

34 Appendix to the Fourth Report of the Children's Employment Commission, 1865, 275.

35 PA PB139 Board minutes, 21 March 1867.

36 *Ibid.,* 10 July 1872.

37 For the transport monopoly, its rates, and the Act of 1864, see T.C.Barker and J.R.Harris, *op. cit.,* 342–3, 351.

38 *A Brief History of Efforts Made by Traders in the St Helens and Widnes Districts in Connection with the Retention and Continuation of the Special Rates First Authorised Under the St Helens Canal and Railway Act of 1864* (booklet issued by the Association in February 1950).

39 PA SD1 Memorandum of agreement made 31 March 1865.

40 *Ibid.*

41 *St Helens Standard,* 20 February 1869.

42 Obituaries are to be found in the *St Helens Standard* and *St Helens Newspaper* on 1 January 1870 and 21 September 1872.

9

EXPANSION ONCE MORE

1 PA PB139 Board minutes, 6 November 1891.

2 *Ibid.,* 21 January, 2 April 1869; 19 October, 9 November, 8 December 1870; 4 January 1883; 7 December 1891. See below p. 162.

3 *Ibid.,* 10 and 25 June 1869; 12 and 27 July, 25 August 1871; 31 May, 6 and 13 June, 10 July, 23 August 1872.

4 *Ibid.,* 13 May, 25 June 1869; 23 March 1870.

5 *Ibid.,* 8 December 1870; 23 February, 19 October 1871; 4 January 1872; British Patent 207 of 1871.

6 Report of Cannington *v.* Nuttall, *The Sunderland Times,* 7 December 1869. Mr H.A.Oakley of United Glass Ltd kindly presented a copy of this cutting to Pilkington Archives.

7 *Ibid.*

8 PA PB139 Board minutes, 21 May, 19 October 1868; 28 July, 11 and 18 August; 1 and 27 October, 10 and 17 November 1869.

9 British Patents 1513 of 1870; 2152 and 3478 of 1872.

10 The Siemens' knowledge of the behaviour of glass was derived from practical experiment rather than from theory. They believed, for instance, that the specific gravity of glass increased with its temperature. See the extract from the 1870 patent specification printed as appendix 5.

11 PA PB234 *Cullet*, January 1934, interview with James Taylor. James Taylor, the son of Henry Taylor, for many years manager of Pilkingtons' sheet glass warehouse, became the father of Sir Hugh Taylor, Professor of Physical Chemistry at Princeton.

12 PA ZZ20/2, Statement by Sample, a Pilkingtons' teaser who applied for a job at Spon Lane.

13 Information given by Cecil Pilkington to Mr D.F.Pilkington in conversations during 1962 and 1963.

14 PA ZZ20/2, Statement by Sample, 31 August 1876.

15 *Ibid.*, Statement by Thomas May, 13 February 1877.

16 *Ibid.*, Statement by Matthew P. Elliot, 7 May 1877.

17 *Ibid.*, C.W.Siemens to Chance Brothers, 29 October 1875.

18 *Ibid.*, Henry Chance to James Chance, 2 February 1877.

19 PA. Old memorandum book 7 February 1874.

20 *Ibid.*, 4 March 1878.

21 PA ZZ20/2, Statement by Thomas May.

22 *Ibid.*, Statement by Sample.

23 *Ibid.*, Dated 24 June 1876.

24 *Ibid.*, and Statement by Matthew P. Elliot.

25 *Ibid.*, Statement by Sample.

26 These sites were then occupied by the Bridgewater Chemical Works (advertised for auction in the *St Helens Newspaper*, 3 May 1884) and Forster's Navigation Boiler Works. Between the two lay Todds' St Helens Ironworks, the site of which was acquired by Pilkington in 1896.

27 PA PB139 Board minutes, 27 June 1878.

28 Pearce Davis, *The Development of the American Glass Industry* (Cambridge, Mass. 1949) 122.

29 PA ZZ20/2, Statement of Alexander Makin; PB139 12 March 1889; 14 April, 15 and 22 September 1891; 29 March 1892; PB149 Plate board minutes, 21 May 1891.

30 J.F.Chance, *A History of the Firm of Chance Brothers & Co.* (privately printed 1919), 128. See also pp. 117–8. I am also grateful to Sir Hugh Chance for information on this subject.

31 PA PB139, 17 April 1894; 12 March 1895 and 25 November 1897.

32 Under Lee Pilkington's patents, 15,162 of 1892, and 15,792 of 1894.

33 Pilkington Deeds Sheet Works bundle 18; PA PB139, 6 February 1873, 28 May 1875, 24 September 1875.

34 R.Chambon, *L'Histoire de la Verrerie en Belgique* (Brussels 1955), 181.

35 British Trade and Navigation Returns. Belgian trade figures show a considerable fall in window glass exports to Britain in 1871 and 1872. (See appendix 4).

36 J.F.Chance, *op. cit.*, 127.

37 *Ibid.*, 279.

38 *Ibid.*, 106–110.

39 PA ZZ49 Letter book M13, R.L. Chance to J.J.Kayll.

40 *Ibid.*, R.L.Chance to Gwilliam, 25 January 1878.

41 *Ibid.*, R.L.Chance to J.J.Kayll, 29 January 1879.

42 PA ZZ23/42, Richard Pilkington to Chance Brothers, 19 June 1880.

43 Mattesons' Wearmouth Glassworks was turned into a public company, 200 shares were issued and £100 called up on each. On 31 December 1875 (presumably this was very soon after the public company had been formed) T.G.Matteson owned 15 shares. All but one of the other shareholders – Ephraim Sadler of Eccles, near Manchester – came from Sunderland. They were: J.Fawcett, T.Gibson, and Rd.Lewis, shipowners; W.Moore, gentleman; and R. Preston, slate merchant. (MS. notes in scrapbook kept at Hartleys, in 1958 in the possession of the late Secretary of the Plate Glass Merchants' Association.) It is not clear when glass ceased to be made at this factory. Its closing is reported in the Pilkington Board minutes on 27 June 1878, but there is also a later reference, on 29 February 1882, which shows that it was then in operation again. PA PB139.

44 PA ZZ30/10, Mr. Kayll's notes re Patent Rolled Plate, 30 October 1880.

45 PA ZZ30, John J.Kayll to John H. Chance, 1 October 1874.

46 PA ZZ30/10. The prospectus is printed, but the names of the directors, manager, bankers, solicitors and secretary do not appear on it.

47 Article on James Hartley in a series on Commercial and Industrial Pioneers (news

cuttings at Newcastle Reference Library, 11257: source not stated). The rest of this paragraph was based upon newscuttings in the possession of the late Secretary of the former Plate Glass Merchants' Association and information provided by Sunderland Public Library.

48 William Waples, 'Glassmaking and glazing', a short manuscript written by a Sunderland man in 1952. Kayll's son was a glass merchant in Leeds trading as Kayll and Co. from at least 1882. PA ZZ30/10, John Kayll to Chance, 4 November 1914.

49 *The Times*, 22 May 1901.

50 For St Gobain's interest in the Stolberg factory, see Rondo E.Cameron, 'Some French Contributors to the Industrial Development of Germany, 1840–70', *Journal of Economic History* XVI, No. 3, September 1956, 307–8.

51 Joseph D.Weeks, Report on the Manufacture of Glass in *Report on the Manufacturers of the United States at the Tenth Census* (1 June 1880), 73. The information in this paragraph is based on this source unless otherwise stated.

52 *Statistique Générale de la Belgique, Exposé de la Situation du Royaume, 1841–50* (Brussels 1852), section IV, 140; companion volume covering 1851–60 (Brussels 1865), III, 140; companion volume covering 1876–1900 (Brussels 1902), 299. R.Chambon, *L'Histoire de la Verrerie en Belgique* (Brussels 1955), 174, 178, 182.

53 The Thames Plate Glass Company was in liquidation by 1874 when a new company (Thames Plate Glass Company 1874 Ltd) was launched with R.W.Swinburne from the Tyne Co. and chairman of the Plate Glass Manufacturers' Association as a director. (PA PB232 Cuttings 1861–81.) Nothing further is known of this venture.

54 For these factories, see T.C.Barker and J.R.Harris, *A Merseyside Town in the Industrial Revolution* (Liverpool 1954), 216–221, 361–363.

55 L.J.McDonald, 'Ravenhead: the first cast plate glass company', *Studies in Glass History and Design* papers read to Committee B Sessions, Eighth International Congress on Glass (July 1968), 31.

56 William Pilkington in *The St Helens Newspaper*, 13 July 1867.

57 PA PB147/104 Ravenhead deeds.

58 Evidence of John Crossley to the Royal Commission on Noxious Vapours, 1878 [2159], XLIV, q. 10,997.

59 PA PB139 Board minutes, 9 May 1863. It was then rumoured that Hartleys intended to make plate glass, but Pilkingtons did not credit this report 'especially as we are bound by agreement not to make plate (Chance, Hartley and ourselves)'.

60 PA PB174 Final accounts.

61 PA PB139 Board minutes, 20 March, 3 July and 2 October 1873.

62 PA PB149 Plate board minutes, 28 April 1875.

63 *Ibid.*, 19 April 1876.

64 *Ibid.*, 28 March 1876 *et seq.*

65 Since W.T.Pearce and F.J.Hawkins were witnesses to the new partnership agreement it would seem that Richard Pilkington mis-spelt the name of his cousin's lawyer.

66 PA PI4/1/5. I have re-punctuated this letter.

67 PA SD2.

68 Walter Lazenby, *Thrice Happy Place. The Story of Ormskirk Street Congregational Church, St Helens* (privately printed by the church 1975).

69 PA PB234 *Cullet,* July 1932.

70 PA PB139 Board minutes 8, 22 and 28 March and 14 November 1877.

71 British Patent 3823 of 1879.

72 British Patent 4041 of 1879.

73 British Patent 1154 of 1880.

74 British Patent 26 of 1880. There is no doubt that these last three patents were used by the firm, for J.H.Dickinson refers in his diary to payments of royalties to Windle Pilkington for them.

75 British Patent 5748 of 1886.

76 PA PB149 Plate board minutes, 28 September 1886 *et seq.*

77 British Patent 6028 of 1888.

78 PA PB149 Plate board minutes, 7 November 1889.

79 *Ibid.*, 13 November 1890.

80 For Windle Pilkington's patents, see, Ch. 8, note 23. Although the results of these experiments were not unsatisfactory, the lehr had to be built of an awkward shape because (according to F.E.Slocombe) the existing buildings could not be removed without great cost. The firm was unwilling

to incur this additional expenditure and the whole scheme had to be dropped.

81 J.F.Chance, *op. cit.*, 106, 108–110.

82 For the background to the glass industry in America, see Pearce Davis, *The Development of the American Glass Industry* (Harvard 1949) and Warren C.Scoville, *Revolution in Glassmaking* (Harvard 1948).

83 US Tariff Commission, Report No. 123 (second ser.). Flat Glass and Related Glass Products (1937), 82. *Glass Manual* (1946) section A2, 3–5.

84 US Census Reports, 1900, Vol. IX, 964.

85 For the rates, see US Tariff Commission, *op. cit.*, 97.

86 Report of the British Tariff Commission (1907), Vol. VI, table 12.

87 These figures are derived from each year's *Tableau de Commerce avec les Pays Etrangers* (*Statistique de la Belgique*).

88 George B.Hodgson, *The History of South Shields* (Newcastle 1924), 246.

89 *St Helens Newspaper*, 26 December 1891, 6 February and 15 October 1892. PA PB149 Plate board minutes, 4 February 1892. According to Hudson A.Binney, manager at Sutton Oak, in a statement published in the *St Helens Newspaper*, 27 November 1903, the Pocket Nook works ceased to make plate glass about five years before that date. Rolled plate was, however, made there until the company went into liquidation in 1904. (PA ZZ53 Letter book M18, K.A.Macaulay to Glasgow Plate Glass Co. 26 March 1897, to Richard Pilkington, 30 January 1904, and to George Crowther, 8 April 1904).

90 PA PB149 Plate board minutes, 5 January 1893 and 31 March 1896.

91 PA PB139 Board minutes, 13 March 1901.

92 *St Helens Newspaper*, 29 May, 12 and 26 June 1903, and Sutton deeds at Pilkington; PA PB139 Board minutes, 1 November 1902. Only 300 people were employed at this time compared with 1,500 in 1889.

93 PA PB139 Board minutes, 10 and 15 July 1905.

94 PA PB97 Libbey Owens (General) 1920–38. Typed extract from diary kept by Edward Ford during a trip to Europe made with Mr John Pitcairn in 1893 (in possession of Libbey-Owens-Ford, Toledo, Ohio).

95 PA PB174 Final accounts.

96 PA PB139 Board minutes, 3 June 1901.

97 PA PB174 Final accounts.

98 PA ZZ38 General meeting book.

99 PA ZZ58 St Gobain 1894–1922. Agreement dated 16 June 1892.

100 PA PB139 Board minutes, 23 December 1890; 19 November 1891, 18 February 1892, 20 December 1894, 15 December 1898, 2 May 1899; PB149 Plate board minutes, 5 February 1891.

101 PA PB139 Board minutes, 19 December 1900, 17 September and 24 December 1901, 14 January 1902, 20 January and 19 May 1903, 4 October 1904, 10 September 1906, 14 May 1907, 17 June 1908.

102 *Ibid.*, 3 April and 12 June 1883, 12 May 13 and 17 November and 22 December 1885; PB138 Mr Dickinson's office diary for opening 31 October/1 November 1887; for information on J.Medland and Henry Taylor and their other works see Nicholas Pevsner *South Lancashire* (in the Buildings of England series) (1969).

103 PA PB139 Board minutes, 30 January 1868, 5 March 1875, 20 December 1884; Pilkington deeds.

104 PA PB139 Board minutes, 4 and 5 March 1875, 3 March and 27 June 1876, 22 and 29 January 1889.

105 PA PB185 Canadian papers 1836–8.

106 PA NA1 Photographs sent by Australian agency.

107 PA PB139 Board minutes.

108 PA PB1/282 Canadian Import Duty Case, 12 July 1893.

109 Pilkingtons' pioneer representative in this market was a man called Dickinson.

110 Information from Pilkington's Export Sales Department; correspondence in the possession of Mr Hugh Salmond of James Hetley & Co.; PA PB139 Board minutes, 10 and 16 January 1868, 31 July 1873, 12 December 1878, 14 February, 2 April, 29 May, 12 September 1879, 31 August and 19 September 1882, 16 January 1883, 10 January and 3 April 1888, 2 May 1899; PB 149 Plate board minutes, 7 June 1883.

111 C.A.Cooke, *Corporation Trust and Company* (Manchester 1950), 181.

112 A copy of this letter will be found in J.H.Dickinson's diary PA PB138.

113 PA SDL1 Agreement dated 5 July 1894.

10

LABOUR RELATIONS AND WELFARE
SERVICES IN THE LATER YEARS OF
THE NINETEENTH CENTURY

1 PA PB234 *Cullet*, October 1933; *Sir James Sexton, Agitator* (1936), 27–8.
2 PA PB139 Board minutes, 2 July 1869.
3 *Ibid.*, 23 March 1870.
4 *Ibid.*, 6, 13 and 20 April, 9 November, 22 December 1870, 2 November 1877; *Liverpool Courier*, 11 May 1870; *St Helens Newspaper*, 16 July and 15 October 1870; *Liverpool Mercury*, 9 August 1878.
5 PA ZZ21/34 *Rules of the St Helens Sheet Glassmakers' Association* (St Helens 1874).
6 *Ibid.* This information is included in the minutes of a conference held at the White Lion Inn, Church Street, St Helens, from 4–9 May 1874, printed in this volume.
7 Letter in PB139 Board minutes volume 1870–3.
8 PA PB 139 Board minutes, 20 April 1876.
9 *Ibid.*, 12 January 1872.
10 PA PB149 Plate board minutes, 15 September 1881.
11 PA PB137/48 Contracts of 1878.
12 See above, p. 91.
13 PA PB139 Board minutes, 28 May 1875, 22 November 1877, 5 March 1878.
14 *Ibid.*, 15 August 1878.
15 *Ibid.*, 7, 12 and 21 November 1878, 29 January, 19 June, 4 November 1879; PB137/48; *St Helens Newspaper*, 10 August, 9 November 1878; *Birmingham Daily Mail*, 9 November 1878; J.F.Chance, *A History of the Firm of Chance Brothers & Co.* (privately printed 1919), 116; information from George Blake. The bonus lists still preserved, show that one employee was still benefiting from his action 42 years later, in 1920.
16 PA PB139 Board minutes, 5 March, 29 April, 6 July, 28 December 1880, 1 March 1881.
17 Henry Pelling, 'The Knights of Labor in Britain, 1880–1901', *Economic History Review*, Vol. IX No. 2 (December 1956), 313–331. This article draws upon the Knights of Labor Papers now at the Library of the Catholic University of America. This and the next two paragraphs are based entirely on this source unless otherwise stated. For another discussion of the activities of the Knights of Labor among American window glass workers, see Charlotte Erickson, *American Industry and the European Immigrant, 1860–85* (Cambridge, Mass. 1957), Chapter 8.
18 V.Lefebvre, *La Verrerie à Vitres et Les Verriers de Belgique depuis le XVᵉ Siècle* (Hainaut 1938), 63.
19 *Ibid.*, British Parliamentary Paper, 1888 [C.5269] XCVIII, 20.
20 *St Helens Newspaper*, 21 June 1884.
21 *Ibid.*, 28 June 1884.
22 PA PB139 Board minutes, 9 July 1884.
23 This was stated in a case of alleged assault and intimidation, reported in the *St Helens Newspaper*, 1 August 1885.
24 *St Helens Newspaper*, 28 February 1885.
25 PA PB138 J.H.Dickinson's diary, 5 April, 1888.
26 *St Helens Newspaper*, 22 June 1889.
27 PA PB149 Plate board minutes, 20 March 1890.
28 *St Helens Newspaper*, 28 June, 6 September and 8 November 1890.
29 PA RE2 Statement of W.J.Fillingham.
30 PA PB138 J.H.Dickinson's diary, 18 December 1890.
31 *St Helens Newspaper*, 11 and 18 October 1890.
32 *St Helens Newspaper*, 26 September 1891.
33 *St Helens Newspaper*, 4 May 1895.
34 H.Logan, 'Early Days of the Recs Club', PA PB234 *Cullet*, January 1929; PB139 Board minutes, 2 November 1898 and 22 January 1901.
35 PA PB234 *Cullet*, Spring 1952. T.C. Barker, 'Early Sports Clubs at St Helens'.
36 *St Helens Newspaper*, 4 April 1891.
37 *Prescot Reporter*, 14 May 1887; *St Helens Newspaper*, 21 May 1887; John Kerr in *Cullet*, July 1932.
38 Reminiscences of John Edmundson printed in *Now Thus Now Thus* (1926).
39 R.C.Liggett, 'The St Helens Crown Glass Works School', MS 1972 (PA I72/36).
40 Sheet works deeds; *Liverpool Daily Post*, 18 April 1891; PA RE2 Information from Charles Green; PB139 Board minutes, 30 December 1874, 17 April and 1 May 1888; 7 January 1890.
41 PA PB139 Board minutes, 27 October 1881, 3 and 10 January, 11 and 18 April,

2 May 1882; 7 February 1888, 29 January 1889, 8 March, 19 April 1898, 18 and 31 January, 8, 10 and 21 February and 7 March 1905.

42 *Ibid.*, 29 September 1886.

43 Note in PA PB139 Board minutes volume 1891–1900.

44 Joseph Stamper, *So Long Ago* (1960).

45 PA PB139 Board minutes, 26 June 1868.

II
COLLIERY AFFAIRS

1 *St Helens Weekly News*, 10 August 1861. The St Helens Colliery is not listed in a local directory of 1858.

2 PA PB139 Board minutes, 12 March 1863.

3 *Ibid.*, 8 January 1863. For this Association, see T.C.Barker and J.R.Harris, *A Merseyside Town in the Industrial Revolution* (Liverpool 1954), 248.

4 PA PB139 Board minutes, 24 December 1863.

5 *Ibid.*, 17 March 1864.

6 *Ibid.*, 2 September 1864.

7 *Ibid.*, 25 May 1865; 15 November 1866.

8 PA PB232 Newscuttings, miscellaneous, 30 March 1867.

9 *Ibid.*

10 *Ibid.*, for Princess Alexandra's visit to Ravenhead, see the *St Helens Standard*, 4 November 1865.

11 PA PB139 Board minutes, 25 January 1866; obituary notice, *St Helens Newspaper*, 20 February 1903.

12 PA PB139 Board minutes, 17 May 1866.

13 *St Helens Newspaper*, 20 February 1903.

14 W.Hopton, *Conversation on Mines* (Manchester, 8th edition 1886), 325–6.

15 PA PB139 Board minutes, 14 September 1870.

16 A third and larger concern, that of Bournes and Robinson, was also involved in the earlier negotiations, but withdrew after disagreement about the price at which their pits would have been taken over. PA PB139 Board minutes, 22 October 1868; 24 October and 22 November 1872; 27 February 1873.

17 PA S53 Minutes of the Ravenhead Colliery Co., 11 February and 14 December 1869.

18 *Ibid.*, 19 March, 15 May, 24 July and 20 November 1873.

19 Bromilow, Haddock and Co. were incorporated under the Companies Act of 5 September 1871, with a capital of £100,000 in £100 shares (*Mining Journal*, 16 September 1871).

20 When these coals were first put up for auction in 1848, they were said to lay under 1,100 acres of ground and to be worth £52,800. Portions of these mines were then leased to Bromilow, Haddock and Co. The coalmines were, however, not disposed of in 1848 nor at later auctions in 1852 and 1859. (Sale catalogues among the Cross Papers at the Lancashire Record Office.)

21 PA S53 Minutes of the Ravenhead Colliery Co., 24 October 1872.

22 *Colliery Guardian*, 4 February 1876.

23 PA PB139 Board minutes, 7 May 1872, 5 August 1880.

24 Printed notice of meeting.

25 *Colliery Guardian*, 4 August 1876; *St Helens Newspaper*, 29 July 1876.

26 PA S53 Minutes of the Ravenhead Colliery Co., 21 March 1872.

27 PA PB139 Board minutes, 5 January 1865.

28 *Ibid.*, 15 March 1867.

29 *Ibid.*, 5 April 1867.

30 *Ibid.*, 20 April 1876.

12
1900–1914
(i) EUROPEAN INFLUENCES:
COMPETITION IN SHEET GLASS, COLLABORATION AND INDUSTRIAL DIPLOMACY IN ROLLED AND POLISHED PLATE

1 Raymond Chambon, *L'Histoire de la Verrerie en Belgique du IIme Siècle à Nos Jours* (Brussels 1955), 192.

2 Report of the British Vice-Consul at Charleroi and of the British Consul-General at Brussels in Consular Report (Belgium), 1905 [Cd. 2682], XXX, 5, 30.

3 Chambon, *op. cit.*, 195.
4 Pearce Davis, *The Development of the American Glass Industry* (Cambridge, Mass. 1949), 175–80.
5 *The Times*, 15 August 1901. For other despatches on this subject see the issues of 10 and 21 August, 7 and 10 September and 1 October.
6 Consular Report (Belgium) 1907 [Cd. 3727] XLI, 39–41.
7 Consular Report (Belgium) 1906 [Cd. 2682] CXXII, 38.
8 Consular Report (Belgium) 1908 [Cd. 3727] CIX, 32.
9 Consular Report (Belgium) 1910 [Cd. 4962] XCVI, 21.
10 H. de Ninal, 'L'Industrie du Verre à Vitres en Belgique et la Crise Actuelle', *Revue Economique Internationale,* June 1904.
11 *Tricentenary History of St Gobain* (privately printed 1965), 82–3.
12 PA ZZ58 St Gobain 1894–1912, E.F. Chance's report of a meeting with Delloye, 9 July 1903.
13 PA ZZ43/23 Rolled Plate agreement 1904. The continental signatories were St Gobain; La Compagnie des Glaces et Verres Spéciaux du Nord à Jeumont; La Compagnie des Glaces et Verres Spéciaux de France à Boussois; La Société des Glaces de Charleroi à Roux; Glas und Spiegel Manufactur A.G. Schalke, Gelsenkirchen; Gebr. Mullensiefen, Cregeldanz; Glashütte vorm. Gebr. Seigevart A.G., Stolberg; Schlesische Spiegelglas Manufactur Carl Tielsch, Altwasser, Silesia; Engels, Bilin (Bohemia); La Société Anonyme des Glaceries et Charbonnage de Bohème. See also ZZ69, Minutes of a meeting at Liverpool, 20 October 1904.
14 See below, p. 198.
15 PA PB97 126 IPGC 1910–14, Delloye to Pilkington, 7 December 1910 recalling these arrangements.
16 PA ZZ54, Manufacturers' letters on Continental Agreement, K.A. Macaulay to Pilkington, 14, 17 and 23 January 1905.
17 PA ZZ58 St Gobain 1894–1912, E.F. Chance's report on a meeting with Delloye, 9 July 1903.
18 PA ZZ22A, Letter to Walter L. Chance, 15 April 1905; PB 139 Board minutes, 10 July 1915.

19 PA ZZ69/24, R.A. Pilkington to K.A. Macaulay, 25 January 1906.
20 PA ZZ58, E.F. Chance's meeting with Delloye, 7 January 1906.
21 PA ZZ69/24, K.A. Macaulay's notes on meeting, 10 March 1906. For Gobbe and Fourcault, see Chambon, *op. cit.*, 194.
22 PA ZZ69/24, RAP to KAM, 7 March 1906.
23 *Ibid.*, Despret to KAM, 15 March 1906.
24 *Ibid.*, enclosure sent by RAP to KAM, 5 December 1906.
25 PA ZZ39 Turner's Works, Richard Pilkington to KAM, 5 April 1907; Minutes of meeting, 6 June, 1907.
26 *Ibid.*, 10 August 1907; ZZ54 KAM to RP, 12 August 1907.
27 PA ZZ39, Arthur R. Pilkington to KAM, 20 February and 6 March 1909; notes of meetings, 10 February and 8 March 1909.
28 PA ZZ59 St Gobain 1898–1912.
29 *Tricentenary History, op. cit.*, 87 et seq. There is a convenient map showing St Gobain's possessions (chemical as well as glass) in 1914 on p. 97.
30 Chambon, *op. cit.*, 196.
31 PA PB97/126 TD18, 'Plate Glass Production Conference Notes, November 1906'. meeting at Euston Hotel, 2 July 1908.
32 *Ibid.*, note dated 12 November 1912.
33 U.S. Census of 1900, Vol. IX, 962–3; Pearce Davis, *op. cit.*, 251.
34 PA AC4, Memorandum by D.F. Pilkington on conversations with Cecil Pilkington at his home in Oxford in 1962 and 1963.
35 Information from Cecil Pilkington; PA PB149 Plate Board minutes, 2 December 1901, 29 September 1903, 17 November 1904; PB139 Board minutes, 9 August 1904.
36 Information from E.B. LeMare.
37 PA PB149 Plate Board minutes, 13 December 1905, 22 February and 29 August 1907, 7 May 1908 and 23 September 1909.
38 PA PB97/126 TD18, 'Plate Glass Production Conference Notes, November 1906', note dated 12 November 1912.
39 PA PB139 Board minutes, 8 April and 17 November 1881.
40 *Ibid.*, 10 December 1885; 6 May 1886.
41 *Ibid.*, 31 January, 18 and 25 April 1899, 7 March 1905; PB149 Plate Board minutes, 6 October 1902 and 31 March 1904.

42 PA PB139 Board minutes, 5 December 1911.

43 *Ibid.*, 22 October and 4 November 1913; British patents 156,919 and 156,920 (October 1919–January 1921); information from F.B.Waldron.

44 J.F.Chance, *A History of the Firm of Chance Brothers & Co.* (privately printed 1919), 132; C.A.Oakley (ed), *Scottish Industry* (The Scottish Council 1953), 282; PA ZZ58, notes of Chances' meeting with Delloye, 25 February 1911.

45 *Ibid.*, E.F.Chance to Delloye, 23 January 1911.

46 *Ibid.*, notes of meeting with Delloye, 25 February 1911.

47 *Ibid.*, note by WHS (Sir Hugh) Chance, 'Relations with St Gobain Co.', 21 January 1925.

48 PA PB97/126, IPGC 1910–14, Delloye to Pilkington, 2 December 1911 and 5 April 1912.

49 *Ibid.*, Delloye to Pilkington, 24 July 1912.

50 *Ibid.*, WWP to Delloye, 3 August 1912.

51 *Ibid.*, Delloye to Pilkington, 5 August 1912.

52 *The Times*, 5 December 1912 and 20 January 1913.

53 PA PB97/126 IPGC 1910–14, Delloye to Pilkington, 25 March 1913.

54 *Ibid.*, information about Spiegelglasfabrick Reisholz obtained from Hamburg and dated 17 April 1914. In retaliation the Convention started a bottle-making factory at Dorsten in Westphalia to the capital of which Pilkington subscribed (see page 239); but it was not equipped with the latest, Owens machinery.

13
1900–1914
(ii) NORTH AMERICAN INFLUENCES: CANADA, THE MAIN EXPORT MARKET AND BRIDGEHEAD TO NEW UNITED STATES TECHNOLOGY

1 PA PB1/434, Richard Pilkington to the Canadian Minister and Minister of Customs, 2 July 1904.

2 Report of the British Tariff Commission, Vol. 6 (1907) para. 19 and table 12.

3 PA PB139 Board minutes, 11 April 1905,

4 June 1907, 10 August and 18 September 1908.

4 PA PB174, Pilkington Final Accounts; PB258, Report to Executive Committee, 18 January 1933.

5 British Patents 10,584 and 11,373 of 1906. Hyde came to Pilkingtons in 1898, having been previously employed in the engineer's department of the Great Northern Railway.

6 Michael Sanderson, *The Universities and British Industry, 1870–1914* (1972), 21.

7 *Ibid.*, 83–4.

8 For Alfred and John Hopkinson, see *The Dictionary of National Biography*, and for the Hopkinson-Pilkington circle at Alderley Edge, see Katharine Chorley (Edward Hopkinson's daughter), *Manchester Made Them* (1950), especially pages 128–9.

9 PA PB139 Board minutes, 6 November 1907.

10 British Patent 489 of 1857.

11 PA ZZ54, Letter book Macaulay 1898–1905, KAM to Delloye, 26 May 1905.

12 PA PB139 Board minutes, 24 September and December 1903, 26 April 1904, 23 July and 18 August 1905 and 8 August 1907.

13 PA PB97/126, Lucien Delloye 1908–1913, meeting with Delloye in Paris, 29 October 1913; Raymond Chambon *L'Histoirie de la Verrerie en Belgique* (Brussels 1955), 199.

14 Pearce Davis, *The Development of the American Glass Industry* (Cambridge, Mass. 1949), 184; PA PB1/462, John Thorpe to Pilkington, 3 September 1909, M.K.McMullin to Pilkington, 27 November 1909. McMullin's letter contains a valuable summary of all the experiments to make machine-made glass then taking place in the USA.

15 Davis, *op. cit.*, 176.

16 PA PB139 Board minutes, 23 June and 24 September 1903.

17 Warren C.Scoville, *Revolution in Glassmaking* (Cambridge, Mass. 1948), 190; Davis *op. cit.*, 182–4.

18 PA PB139 Board minutes; statement to employees, 22 June 1909.

19 PA PB1/434, John Thorpe to Pilkington, 5 December 1905.

20 *Ibid.*, 5 September 1905.

21 *Ibid.*, F.B.Bamford, Montreal, to Pilkington, 5 November 1905.

22 PA S4/1, Secretary, Window Glass

Machine Company of Canada to A.K. Goodman.

23 *Ibid.*, Articles of Agreement between Municipal Corporation of the Village of Cayuga and the Window Glass Machine Company of Canada, 3 October 1905.

24 PA PB1/434, McConnell to Baylis, 18 June 1906; S54/1, Company Secretary to Goodman, 28 January 1907.

25 PA BP1/282, Baylis to Pilkington, 15 February 1907.

26 PA PB1/430, John Thorpe to Pilkington, 20 November 1905.

27 PA PB1/282, F.Baylis, Toronto to F. Bamford, Montreal, 19 December 1905.

28 *Ibid.*, Petition signed by Arthur R. Pilkington on behalf of Pilkington Brothers Limited, to the Canadian Prime Minister, Minister of Trade and Commerce, and the Trade Commissioners, 26 October 1906.

29 7 Ed. VII, cap. XXIX.

30 Davis, *op. cit.*, 116–7. For statistics concerning the speed of drawn cylinder machines in the United States, see Harry Jerome, *Mechanism in Industry* (New York 1934), 100.

31 PA PB139 Board minutes: statement to employees, 22 June 1909.

32 *Ibid.*, 18 May 1909.

33 PA PB1/462, W.W.Pilkington to E.H. Cozens-Hardy, 7 October 1909.

34 British Patents 14,283, 16,064 and 20,141 of 1910 and 9,244 of 1911.

35 H.R.Hilton, manager of the Allegheny Window Glass Company in *The Glass Industry as Affected by the War* (U.S. Tariff Commission 1918), 87.

36 PA PB1/462, Delloye to Pilkington, 30 August 1909. My italics.

37 *Ibid.*, McMullin to Pilkington, 31 May 1910.

38 *Ibid.*, J.Thorpe to Pilkington, 3 September 1909.

39 *Ibid.*, Letter to McMullin, 25 October 1909. Minor changes have been made in cases of obvious mistranslation where this affects the comprehension of the letter.

40 *Ibid.*, E.H.Cozens-Hardy to McMullin, 30 October 1909.

41 PA PB1/434, J.Thorpe to Pilkington, 19 December 1905.

42 PA PB1/462, Typed extracts from *National Glass Budget*, 30 April 1910.

43 PA PB26, Draft supplementary agreement.

44 PA PB1/282, Baylis to Pilkington, 15 February 1907.

45 PA S32.

46 Details about the factory's leaking roof, complaints of Cayuga local authority (disappointed at the company's failure to keep its side of the land bargain and provide employment) and enquiries from alternative users will be found in the correspondence of A.K.Goodman, partner in a firm of solicitors in Cayuga and director of the Window Glass Machine Company of Canada Limited, who dealt with the day to day matters on the spot (PA S3).

47 PA PB139 Board minutes.

48 PA PB1/462, E.H.Cozens-Hardy to T.H.Given, Empire Machine Company, 26 August 1911.

49 *Ibid.*, Pilkington to McMullin, 3 October 1911.

50 PA PB30, Directors' attendance register.

51 PA S2, Austin Pilkington to F.Baylis, 24 October and 17 November 1909.

52 *Ibid.*, Baylis to Austin Pilkington, 22 January 1912.

53 *Ibid.*, Baylis to Austin Pilkington, 10 April 1901.

54 *Ibid.*, Austin Pilkington to Baylis, 14 April 1911.

55 *Ibid.*, Austin Pilkington to Baylis, 20 June 1910.

56 *Ibid.*, R.A.Wenham to Austin Pilkington, 15 August 1911.

57 *Ibid.*, Austin Pilkington to Baylis, 17 February 1912.

58 *Ibid.*, Baylis to Pilkington, St Helens, 18 December 1911.

59 PA S2, Pilkington, St Helens to Pilkington, Montreal, 20 January 1912.

60 PA PB1/462, Austin Pilkington to Baylis, 5 January 1911.

61 *Ibid.*, Austin Pilkington to Baylis, 25 November 1910.

62 *Ibid.*, Austin Pilkington to Baylis, 28 January 1911.

63 *Ibid.*, Thynne to Austin Pilkington, 26 October 1911.

64 PA S2, R.A.Pilkington to Baylis, 6 June 1912; Wenham to Baylis, 10 July 1912.

65 PA PB1/462, Pilkington to J.E.Harrison, 10 October 1912.

66 PA S4, Austin Pilkington to Baylis, 24 November 1911.

67 PA S1, date undecipherable but between 15 and 18 January 1912 and written to Austin Pilkington.

68 PA S4, Austin Pilkington to Baylis, 24 November 1911.

69 PA S1, 5 October 1912; Baylis's report to St Helens of the same date.

70 PA PB1/625, R.F.Taylor's reports 1912, Austin Pilkington to Windle Pilkington, written from Niagara Falls, 4 November 1912.

71 PA PB35 (Austin Pilkington's Press Copy Letter Book), 22 January. 29 February, 6 March, 9 April and 19 November 1912, 25 March and 16 May 1913.

72 PA PB284 Pilkingtons in Canada MS, 1959.

73 PA PB1/13, R.F.Taylor to Pilkington, 26 June 1913.

74 PA PB1/36, Letters from Joseph C. Clare, 9 May 1914.

75 PA PB1/39, R.F.Taylor to Austin Pilkington, 12 September 1914.

76 PA PB1/33, A.C.Pilkington to R.F. Taylor, 3 November 1915.

77 PA PB236 Thorold Accounts; and PB237 Pilkington Brothers (Canada) Limited Accounts.

78 PA PB35, Austin Pilkington to W. Norman Pilkington, 24 October 1913.

79 *Ibid.*, Austin Pilkington to W.S. Tunnock, 30 November 1913.

80 *Ibid.*, Austin Pilkington to W.S. Tunnock, 6 December 1913.

81 PA S3, A.K.Goodman to C.D.Nevill, 19 October 1914.

14
1900–14
(iii) LABOUR AND CAPITAL

1 Pearce Davis, *The Development of the American Glass Industry* (Cambridge, Mass. 1949), 183.

2 *Ibid.*, 183–4.

3 T.C.Barker and J.R.Harris, *A Merseyside Town in the Industrial Revolution* (Liverpool 1954, repr. 1959), 460.

4 *St Helens Newspaper*, 7 June 1904, quoted in Alan Wild, 'The Origins of the National Union of General and Municipal Workers at Pilkington Brothers, St Helens' (University of Warwick MA thesis 1974), 51. I have turned reported into direct speech. For a study of the new winds which were blowing in Lancashire politics at this time, see P.F.Clarke, *Lancashire and the New Liberalism* (Cambridge 1971).

5 Wild, *op. cit.*, 21–3, 25, 44.

6 *Ibid.*, 51.

7 *Ibid.*, 22, 27, quoting *St Helens Newspaper*, 13 May 1904 and 15 May 1906.

8 PA PB120 Glassmakers' Deputation Book.

9 *Ibid.*

10 *Ibid.*, 21 March 1907.

11 *Ibid.*, 26 October 1911.

12 Wild, *op. cit.*, 28–30, 41–2.

13 Christ Church, Oxford, Salisbury Papers. Letter from Henry Seton-Karr to Lord Salisbury, 21 July 1889, 16 and 29 July 1892. I am grateful to the present Lord Salisbury for permission to quote from these letters and to my friend Dr J.F.A. Mason for drawing my attention to them.

14 PA PB139 Board minutes, 22 June 1909.

15 *Ibid.*, 30 December 1912.

16 PA RE2, Information from J.Tabern.

17 PA PB139 Board minutes, 15 January 1907.

18 Harold Penrose, *British Aviation: The Pioneer Years, 1903–14* (1967), 196, 528, 580; the Sir John Betjeman reference will be found in his *Collected Poems* (1974), 283.

19 Michael Sanderson, *The Universities and British Industry, 1870–1914* (1972), 57–8.

20 P.L.Payne, 'The Emergence of the Large-Scale Company in Great Britain, 1870–1914', *Economic History Review*, December 1967.

21 For their obituaries, see the *St Helens Newspaper* and *St Helens Reporter*, 17 April 1903 (William (Roby)); 20 March 1914 (William Windle); 22 May 1925 (Thomas). Richard's appeared in the *St Helens Newspaper* only on 13 March 1908.

15
THE FIRST WORLD WAR

1 PA PB97/127 TD1, T.R.Willis (Paris) to Pilkington, 12 June 1915; George van

Vorstenburg (Amsterdam) to Pilkington by wire, 15 January 1919.

2 *Ibid.*, T.R.Willis (Paris) to Pilkington, 10 July 1916.

3 *Ibid.*, 4 September 1916.

4 *Ibid.*, 21 March 1917.

5 PA PB139 Board minutes, 3 June, 21 September 1915; 21 March, 8 May 1917; 31 August 1920; J.R.Kerr, 'Orthopaedics in Relation to Manpower', *Engineering*, January 1919; Joseph A.Rae (ed.), *The History of Allan Glen's School 1853–1953* (Glasgow 1953), 69–70. Most of this information is contained in a paper on the Pilkington Special Hospital written by Mr Graeme Garvey of the Pilkington Group Archives staff to whom my thanks are due.

6 Pilkington Central Statistics.

7 PA PB97/127 TD10, Pilkington to T.R.Willis (Paris), 22 March 1919.

8 PA PB139 Board minutes, 20 March 1916.

9 Alan Wild, 'The Origins of the National Union of General and Municipal Workers at Pilkington Brothers, St Helens' (University of Warwick MA thesis 1974), 72.

10 N.A.U.L. Third Quarterly Report, 1917, 92, quoted in Wild, *op. cit.*, 73.

11 PA PB139 Board minutes, 28 February 1918.

12 P.R.O. LAB2/714/12030/2, quoted in Wild, *op. cit.*, 75.

13 P.R.O. LAB2/714/12030/6, quoted in Wild, *op. cit.*, 77.

16
THE INTERWAR YEARS: AN INTRODUCTORY SURVEY

1 These figures are conveniently collected in B.R.Mitchell and Phyllis Deane, *Abstract of British Historical Studies* (Cambridge 1962), 239.

2 *Ibid.*, 230.

3 Society of Motor Manufacturers and Traders, *The Motor Industry of Great Britain* (1938), 47, 51.

17
FORWARD WITH PLATE

1 J.A.Dowie, '1919–20 is in Need of Attention', *Economic History Review*, August 1975.

2 D.C.Coleman, *Courtaulds. An Economic and Social History* (2 vols. Oxford 1969), II, 153.

3 C.H.Wilson, *History of Unilever* (2 vols. 1954), I, appendix 3.

4 J.F.Chance, *A History of the Firm of Chance Brothers and Co.* (privately printed 1919), 123–4.

5 PA PB97/126 1922 file.

6 See above, page 239.

7 PA PB139 Board minutes, 31 August 1920.

8 *Ibid.*

9 PA PB30.

10 PA PB260 Executive Committee minutes, 24 February, 12 July 1937, 11 January 1950.

11 Coleman, *op. cit.*, II, 211–2; Asa Briggs, *A Study of the Works of Seebohm Rowntree, 1871–1954* (1961).

12 For McGowan's remarkable career at ICI see W.J.Reader, *Imperial Chemical Industries. A History*, II (1975).

13 PA PB139 Board minutes, 20 January 1919.

14 *Ibid.*, 10 April 1919.

15 *Ibid.*, 28 August 1919.

16 PA RE2 Information from F.B.Waldron and H.Swift.

17 PA PB139 Board minutes, 18 February, 23 August 1921; PB174 Pilkington Accounts.

18 PB97/102, J.E.Harrison file, R.A.Pilkington to J.E.Harrison, 25 May 1922.

19 PB97/127 TD1, L.Delloye to Pilkington, 27 March 1916.

20 *Ibid.*, T.R.Willis to Pilkington, 10 July 1917.

21 *Ibid.*, 5 November 1917.

22 PA PB97/127 TD10, Delloye to R.A. Pilkington, 30 November 1918.

23 PA PB97/127 TD1, R.A.Pilkington to Delloye, 24 October 1918.

24 *Ibid.*, Interview in Paris, 23 October 1918.

25 PA PB139 Board minutes, 19 July 1914.

26 *Ibid.*, Notes on meeting with Delloye, 12 March 1919.

27 *Ibid.*, Interview with Delloye, 15 July 1919; Delloye to Pilkington, 18 October 1919.

28 PA PB97/126 TD2, 'Notes as to the different methods of determining relativity between P.B. and CIG', 6 December 1928.

29 PA PB97/127 TD1, Notes on meeting with Delloye, 12 March 1919.

30 *Ibid.*, Delloye to Pilkington, 20 September 1919.

31 *Ibid.*, Arthur Pilkington to L.Delloye, 7 October 1919.

32 *Ibid.*, Notes on meeting in London, 31 October 1919.

33 *Ibid.*, C.H.Frérichs to Pilkington, 20 November 1919; A.R.Pilkington to C. H. Frérichs, 1 December 1919.

34 PA ZZ22/38, Chances' report on visit to Paris, 9 January 1920.

35 PA PB97/127 TD1, Notes on meeting in Paris, 14 February 1920.

36 Raymond Chambon, *L'Histoire de la Verrerie en Belgique du IIme Siècle à Nos Jours* (Brussels 1955), 205.

37 PA PB97/127 TD1, Pilkington to Delloye, 1 April 1921.

38 *Ibid.*, 15 October 1921. Cecil Pilkington had not been impressed by the glass which had begun to be cast there in May 1921, and Weeks thought the metal only moderate in September 1922; but Cecil Pilkington in July of the following year reported that quality was slowly improving (PA PB97/126 ACP File, 1921-1933, A.C.Pilkington to R.A.Pilkington, 5 May 1921, 18 July 1923, R.M.Weeks to A.C.Pilkington, 6 September 1932).

39 PA PB97/127 TD1, Pilkington to Delloye, 19 June 1923; Delloye to Pilkington, 13 July 1923; visit of Delloye to Maubeuge, 25 July 1923; R.A.Pilkington to Delloye, 14 August 1923.

40 *Ibid.*, Notes on meeting with Delloye, 12 March 1919.

41 See Appendix 6.

42 PA PB279, F.B.Waldron to Cozens-Hardy, 8 September 1917.

43 *Ibid.*, Cozens-Hardy to Waldron, 27 September 1917.

44 British Patent, 154,661.

45 PA PB139 Board minutes, 21 November 1919.

46 PA PB53 Cowley Hill Board minutes, 7 February 1921; RE2 information from J.H. Griffin.

47 See above, pages 158-9.

48 PA PB97/97, Correspondence with Edward Ford Glass Co., R.A.Pilkington to R.F.Taylor, 3 November 1919.

49 *Ibid.*, R.F.Taylor, 3 November 1919.

50 *Ibid.*, R.A.Pilkington to R.F.Taylor, 19 January 1920. For sucker pads see above, pages 202-3.

51 Ford Archives, Detroit. Paper read by C.W.Avery to the American Society of Mechanical Engineers at Detroit, 3 May 1929.

52 Ford Archives, Detroit. Speech by C.W. Avery at the Dearborn Inn, 19 December 1944, 1. Allan Nevins and Frank Ernest Hill, *Ford: The Times, The Man, The Company,* 1 (New York 1954), 474-5.

53 Ford Archives, Detroit, Oral History Section, Reminiscences of W.C.Klann, 1953.

54 Nevins and Hill, *op. cit.*, II (New York 1957), 230-1.

55 Klann, *op. cit.*

56 Ford Archives, Accession 285, Box 9. Edward Donner to Henry Ford, 20 January 1921.

57 Avery, *op. cit.* (note 51).

58 Avery, *op. cit.* (note 52).

59 PA PB97/97, Edward Ford Glass Co. File, R.F.Taylor's report, April 1922. According to Klann, 'a fellow from England', whose name he could not remember, came to their aid at that time; but this seems to be a confusion with the help later given by Pilkington. If anyone went to Detroit from England in 1921, he was not from Pilkington which was totally unaware of these developments until the appearance of the *Glassworker* article. It should be recalled that Klann was only intimately connected with the new process for one year.

60 *Ibid.*, R.F.Taylor's report, April 1922.

61 *Ibid.*, F.B.Waldron, 'Ford Motor Company's Glass Plant', n.d. but obviously April 1922. The statement by Nevins and Hill (*op. cit.*, II, 231) that the plant was in November 1921 'turning out an excellent product on an assembly line plan' suggests that it was much more highly developed than was the case.

62 PA PB97/97, R.F.Taylor's report, April 1922.

63 *Ibid.*, R.A.Pilkington to George R. Ford, 14 March 1922.

64 *Ibid.*, R.F.Taylor's report.

65 Avery, *loc. cit.*

66 PA PB97/97 Edward Ford Glass Co, file, F.B.Waldron to E.H.Cozens-Hardy, 20 April 1922. The rest of this account is based upon the Taylor and Waldron reports and information from this letter.
67 *Ibid.*, Waldron to Goodwillie, 6 June 1922.
68 *Ibid.*, Whittemore, Hulbert, Whittemore and Belknap to Pilkington, 5 April 1922; R.F.Taylor's report.
69 *Ibid.*, Waldron to Cozens-Hardy, 20 April 1922.
70 PA RE2, Record kept by J.H.Griffin.
71 *Ibid.*, Transcript of interview with E.B.LeMare.
72 *Ibid.*, Transcript of interview with J.Gaskell.
73 PA PB97/96 Ford Motor Company file, R.A.Pilkington to Edsel B.Ford, 29 November 1922.
74 *Ibid.*, R.A.Pilkington to Avery, 15 December 1922.
75 *Ibid.*, Griffin to Pilkington, 20 March 1923.
76 *Ibid.*, Avery to Pilkington, 23 March 1923.
77 *Ibid.*, A.C.Pilkington to Avery, 6 October 1923; 17 April 1925.
78 Details in the paragraph concerning the grinder are from the Griffin record PA RE2, and concerning the tanks from a summary contained in PB97/96 Ford Motor Co. file and PB149 Cowley Hill Board minutes, 5 February, 31 May 1923; 1 July 1924.
79 PA PB97/96 Summary in Ford Motor Co. file
80 PA RE2 Transcript of interview with J.Tabern.
81 PA PB139 Board minutes, 16 March 1927.
82 PA PB139 Board minutes, 17 June, 2 July 1924.
83 For the arguments leading to the termination of the agreement with Ford, see R.F.Taylor's notes on his visit to Detroit at the end of February 1925 (PA PB97/96 Ford Motor Co. file). See also PB139 Board minutes, 3 November 1925.
84 PA PB97/97 Edward Ford Glass Co. file, Goodwillie to Waldron, 14 December 1922; PB97/126 ACP 1922 file, R.A.Pilkington to A.C.Pilkington, 21 November 1922.
85 *Ibid.*, R.F.Taylor's notes, 20 March, July 1923.
86 *Ibid.*, Notes on visit of Messrs Goodwillie and Bowers to Doncaster and St Helens, 24 and 25 November 1925.
87 PA PB149 Cowley Hill Board minutes, 19 November 1920.
88 PA PB97/127, Heuze 1922–23, R.A.Pilkington's handwritten note of meeting with Heuze at Maubeuge, 12 March 1922.
89 *Ibid.*, Heuze to Pilkington, 23 December 1922; PB1/1436, Heuze to Pilkington, 30 January 1923.
90 PA PB285/3, Agreement between Pilkington and Heuze, Malevez and Simon Réunis, 15 February 1923.
91 PA PB97/127, Heuze 1922–23, R.A. Pilkington to Heuze, 6 April 1923.
92 PA PB1/1436, Heuze to Pilkington, 31 July 1923; PB254/4, Agreement with CIG, 25 January 1924.
93 PA RE2, Transcript of interview with J.H.Griffin.
94 PA PB1/1467, Copies of correspondence with the National Plate Glass Company, Heuze to Eckenrode, 13 October 1927.
95 Copies of correspondence with the National Plate Glass Company (PA PB1/1467) and with the Edward Ford Glass Company (PB1/1466); Agreement with the Libbey-Owens-Ford Glass Company, 30 June 1930.
96 PA PB280 Private Ledgers.

18

BACKWARD WITH SHEET

1 Warren C.Scoville, *Revolution in Glassmaking* (Cambridge, Mass. 1948), 126. For a detailed account of the two processes, see W.E.S.Turner 'Machinery and Methods of Manufacture of Sheet Glass', *Proceedings of the Institution of Mechanical Engineers*, December 1930, 1077–1095.
2 *Ibid.*, 127–8.
3 PA PB97/96 Libbey-Owens File 1, Letter to A.C.Pilkington, 28 December 1918.
4 *Ibid.*, Account of Charleston Factory.
5 *Ibid.*, Notes on Long Factory.
6 *Ibid.*, R.A.Pilkington, William Penn Hotel, Pittsburgh to E.D.Libbey.
7 *Ibid.*, Taylor to R.A.Pilkington, 3 March 1919.

8 *Ibid.*, Taylor's report on the second visit on 8 July 1919, dated 22 July.

9 *Ibid.*, Cozens-Hardy to Libbey-Owens Sheet Glass Co., 8 September 1919.

10 *Ibid.*, Taylor's report, 22 July 1919; W.L. Munro to A.C.Pilkington, 21 August 1919.

11 *Ibid.*, Taylor to A.C.Pilkington, 2 September 1919.

12 *Ibid.*, Taylor to Pilkington, 16 December 1919.

13 PA PB97/96 Libbey-Owens File 1, Pilkington to M.Lardinois, 18 June 1919.

14 PA PB97/97 Libbey-Owens-Ford File 1920–38, Pilkington to L–O, 20 October 1919.

15 Scoville, *op. cit.*, 128–9.

16 PA PB97/96 Libbey-Owens File 1, Taylor to Pilkington, 18 February 1920.

17 *Ibid.*, R.F.Taylor's report on visit to Long Factory, 11 February 1920.

18 PA PB97/97 Libbey-Owens-Ford File 1920–38, letter to Delloye, 25 March 1920; interview with Delloye, 1 April 1920; letter from R.A.Pilkington to Chance, 5 April 1920.

19 *Ibid.*, F.C.Gordon to R.A.Pilkington, 6 November; note of meeting with Delloye, 13 November; *Manchester Guardian Commercial*, 25 November 1920.

20 PA PB97/96 Libbey-Owens File 2, Particulars about the Compagnie Internationale *c.* 1926; extract from *The Glassworker*, 15 December 1923.

21 *Ibid.*, anonymous note headed Libbey-Owens, Moll.

22 PA PB97/96 Libbey-Owens File 1, Pilkington, Montreal, to J.E.Harrison, St Catharine's, 4 November 1920; J.E.Harrison to Pilkington, 4, 13 and 27 November; *Hardware and Metal*, 13 November 1920.

23 PA PB97/96 Libbey-Owens File 2, Pilkington to J.E.Harrison, 14 December 1921; J.E.Harrison to W.S.Tunnock, 3 July 1922; F.B.Gerard to Pilkington, 23 March 1923; Libbey-Owens sixth annual report, December 1923.

24 *Ibid.*, Monro to J.E.Harrison, 20 June 1922.

25 Raymond Chambon, *L'Histoire de la Verrerie en Belgique du IIeme Siècle á Nos Jours* (Brussels 1955), 200.

26 British Patent 182,805 of 1923. Further improvements were specified in British Patent 212,545 of 1924.

27 PA PB97/96 Libbey-Owens File 1, A.C. Pilkington to R.F.Taylor, 3 November 1919.

28 PA Ford Motor Company File, A.C. Pilkington to R.A.Pilkington, 16 November 1922.

29 PA PB139 Board minutes, 17 May 1923.

30 *Ibid.*, 16 April 1924.

31 PA AC4, A.C.Pilkington in conversation with D.F.Pilkington, March 1962 and July 1963.

32 PA PB139 Board minutes, 16 August 1921.

33 PA PB192 Minutes of the Joint Industrial Council, 5 March 1926.

34 PA ZZ30 Chance Brothers correspondence on closer contact with Pilkington, especially letters from E.F.Chance to G.F. Chance, 12 October 1917 and 22 April 1920.

35 PA PB97/103, Thorold Board minutes, 24 January, 7 February, 17 and 22 April, 2 and 9 May 1919.

36 PA PB97/102 J.E.Harrison File 1920–6, R.A.Pilkington to J.E.Harrison, 23 February 1922.

37 *Ibid.*, R.A.Pilkington to J.E.Harrison, 1 September 1922.

38 *Ibid.*, W.S.Tunnock to J.E.Harrison, 8 September 1922.

39 PA PB97/127 ACP 1922 file, R.A.Pilkington (Pittsburgh) to A.C.Pilkington, 21 November 1922.

40 PA PB97/102 J.E.Harrison File 1920–6, J.E.Harrison to Pilkington Brothers Limited, 14 January, 11 March, A.C.Pilkington to J.E.Harrison, 25 March, 3 April 1924.

41 *Ibid.*, J.E.Harrison to R.A.Pilkington, 5 November 1924.

42 *Ibid.*, Pilkington to J.E.Harrison, 7 May 1926; W.S.Tunnock to J.E.Harrison, 30 July 1926; PB97/103 Thorold Factory file, J.E.Harrison to Pilkington, 30 November 1926; PB139 Board minutes, 9 July and 26 November 1926.

43 PA PB97/103 Thorold Factory file, S.J. Andrews to Pilkington, 8 April 1931; notice of sale (undated) which gives an illustration of the factory and basic details.

44 PA PB139 Board minutes, 26 November 1931.

45 PA PB97/103 J.E.Harrison file 1930–3, J.E.Harrison to Agents, 12 January 1932.

46 PA PB257 Return to the Executive Committee, 18 January 1933.

47 PA PB97/103 J.E.Harrison file, 1930–3, internal note 8 November 1932.

48 PA PB139 Board minutes, 27 November 1924.

49 Scoville, *op. cit.*, 193n.

50 PA PB177 Depot Managers' Conferences. R.A.Pilkington's report to the 8th Conference, 24 February 1926.

51 PA LE1 J.Leathwaite's notebook, 23 March 1927.

52 R.F.Taylor in the discussion held in London after W.E.S.Turner's paper on 'Machinery and Methods of Manufacture of Sheet Glass', *Proceedings of the Institution of Mechanical Engineers,* December 1930, 1116–7.

53 PA PB139 Board minutes, 24 October and 20 November 1924.

54 PA PB97/126 A.C.Pilkington file, W.S.Tunnock to A.C.Pilkington, 12 August 1925, reporting the visit of Dreyfuss of Semon Bache.

55 Turner, *op. cit.*, 1097, 1099.

56 PA PB97/103 PB Canada 1927–8, J.E. Harrison to Pilkington 17 May 1927.

57 Chambon, *op. cit.*, 208; PA PB97/97 Edward Ford file, notes on visit of Goodwillie Bowers to Doncaster and St Helens in November 1925; PA PB97/126, R.A. Pilkington's notes on meeting with L. Delloye, n.d. but from internal evidence probably 5 January 1927.

58 Chambon, *op. cit.*, 208.

59 PA PB97/126 TD11, F.C.Gordon (Paris) to R.A.Pilkington, 16 February 1927; A.C. Pilkington to L.Delloye, 17 February 1927.

60 PA PB192 Minutes of the Joint Industrial Council, 6 December 1926.

61 *Ibid.*, 5 March 1926.

62 *Ibid.*, 27 May 1926, 15 June 1928.

63 PA ZZ22/38, Report by W.L.Chance of visit to Paris, 25 October 1926.

64 *Ibid.*, 22 March 1927; PA PB285/9 Agreement 20 October 1927; F.E.Lamplough, 'The Properties and Applications of "Vita" Glass', a paper to the Royal Society of Arts summarised in *Glass*, August 1929.

65 PA PB139 Board minutes, 24 March 1924.

66 *Ibid.*, 20 February 1928.

67 *Ibid.*, 30 January 1929.

68 *Ibid.*, 24 December 1929, 23 May 1930.

69 PA PB261 Executive Committee minutes, 3 May 1931.

70 *Ibid.*, 9 February 1937.

71 PA PB97/126 TD2, R.A.Pilkington to L.Delloye, 18 September 1926; R.A. Pilkington to F.C.Gordon (Paris), 20 September 1926; PB97/126, A.C.Pilkington correspondence, R.A.Pilkington to A.C. Pilkington, 28 August 1926.

72 R.S.Sayers, 'The Return to Gold, 1925' in L.S.Pressnell (ed), *Studies in the Industrial Revolution* (1960), 322.

73 PA PB97/126 TD2, note of meeting, 5 January 1927.

74 PA PB97/103 PB (Canada) Limited 1926–30, R.A.Pilkington to J.E.Harrison, 22 April 1927.

75 PA PB97/126 TD 2, note on meeting, 2 May 1927.

76 W.J.Reader, *Imperial Chemical Industries: A History*, I (1970), 55, II (1975), 23.

77 *Ibid.*, II, 6.

78 PA PB97/96 Libbey-Owens file II, B.E.Todhunter to Pilkington, 14 March 1927; note of meeting with Schmettau, 29 April 1927.

79 *Ibid.*, Notes of meetings, 29 April, 4 May, 17, 18 and 20 June 1927.

80 Chambon, *op. cit.*, 210.

81 PA PB97/96 Libbey-Owens file II, *Echo de Bourse*, 29 December 1927; Todhunter to R.A.Pilkington, 2 January 1928; translation of note concerning the agreement dated January 1928. The original agreement was in fact a provisional one dated 24 December 1927. A copy of the final agreement with Libbey-Owens, which was to run from 1 July 1928 to 31 December 1960, will be found in CIG Agreements file, PB285/16.

82 PA PB97/96 Libbey-Owens II, extract from letter from Mutuelle Solvay, 9 January 1928.

83 PA PB97/126 TD2, note on meeting in Paris, 24 June 1927.

84 PA PB97/96 Libbey-Owens file II, note of meeting, 31 August 1927.

85 *Ibid.*, note of meeting, 28 October 1927.

86 *Ibid.*, Cozens-Hardy to A.C.Pilkington, 5 September 1927.

87 PA PB97/126 A.C.Pilkington file, A.C. Pilkington (San Martino di Castrozza) to R.A.Pilkington, 5 September 1927.

88 PA PB97/96 Libbey Owens file II, R.A.Pilkington to Todhunter, 2 July 1928.

89 *Ibid.*, Note of Cozens-Hardy's interview

with Todhunter, 26 July 1928; Todhunter to E.J.Solvay, 26 July 1928.
90 PA PB139 Board minutes, 12 March and 4 June 1928.
91 PA PB97/127 AHMS file II, A.C.Pilkington to C.Heuze, 15 March 1928.
92 PA PB283, Typescript summary concerning the Queenborough works, 9 March 1928.
93 PA PB139 Board minutes, 17 November 1927.
94 *Ibid.*, 29 November 1928.
95 *Ibid.*, 7 February 1929.
96 Chambon, *op. cit.*, 210–11.
97 *Ibid.*, 211
98 PA PB97/126 TD2, A.C.Pilkington (Grasse) to R.A.Pilkington (n.d. but probably August 1928). A third 20-pot furnace had been installed at Maubeuge in 1927 (statement by Theo. Parry).
99 PA PB97/119, Grimberghen file 1929-32, J.Dickinson to Jeffes, 10 January 1929. The company was announced in the *Moniteur Belge*, 28 December 1928.
100 *Ibid.*, Delloye to Pilkington, 10 October 1928; W.N.Pilkington to Delloye, 19 October 1928.
101 PA PB97/126 TD2, Delloye to Pilkington, 1 June 1927.
102 *Ibid.*, Notes on Different Methods of Determining Relativity between Pilkington and CIG, 6 December 1928. These gave 1·25 m. sq. ft as the approximate pre-war output of Maubeuge but then calculated the Convention : Pilkington plus Maubeuge ratio as 4·05:1, which is obviously incorrect.
103 PA PB285/16, Agreement dated 1 June 1929, revised, rearranged and signed by Frérichs and Cozens-Hardy on 3 July 1929.
104 Chambon, *op. cit.*, 217–8.
105 PA PB97/130 CIG file, Pilkington to Delloye, 11 July 1929, upon which Cozens-Hardy has written: 'Read to Delloye, Frérichs and Lemoine and accepted by them.'
106 PA PB139 Board minutes, 27 June 1929.
107 *Ibid.*
108 PA PB97/103 Pilkington Brothers (Canada) Limited, General file 1926-30, W.S.Tunnock to J.E.Harrison, 18 October 1929; J.E.Harrison to W.S.Tunnock, 29 October 1929.
109 PA PB139 Board minutes, 28 November 1929.

110 *Glass Manual* (1946), section A2-12 (a copy is deposited in the Pilkington Archives).
111 PA PB139 Board minutes, 28 June 1930; information from Mr Watt.
112 PA PB97/129 Hollandsche Maatschappij file, L.Deschamps (Zeebrugge) to J.B.Watt, 16 July 1930.
113 A number of these letters have survived in the Maatschappij file (*ibid.*) Information concerning the PPG machine at St Helens is from J.B.Watt.
114 PA PB139 Board minutes, 19 February 1931; PA PB285/32 Agreement, 30 June 1931.
115 PA PB97/129 Hollandsche Maatschappij file, J.B.Watt to Bureau d'Etudes de la Hollandsche, Paris, 13 February 1931.
116 PA PB192 Joint Industrial Council minutes, 3 March 1931.
117 PA PB139 Board minutes, 27 May 1931.
118 PA PB97/129 Hollandsche Maatschappij file 1930-3, J.B.Watt to A.C.Pilkington, 7 October 1931.
119 *Ibid.*, J.B.Watt to L.Deschamps, 25 January 1932; information from J.B.Watt.
120 PA PB139 Board minutes, 27 November 1931.
121 PA PB234 *Cullet*, July 1933, 50; PB260 Executive Committee minutes, 17 May 1933.
122 *Ibid.*, 6 December 1933.
123 Chambon, *op. cit.*, 217–8.
124 PA PB139 Board minutes, 20 October 1924, 9 December 1926.
125 *Ibid.*, 12 December 1924.
126 *Ibid.*, 15 March 1928, 1 May 1929.

19

REORGANIZATION IN
THE 1930S

1 PA PB139 Board minutes, 15 April 1920.
2 *Ibid.*, 4 December 1929, minutes of shareholders' meeting, 9 December 1929.
3 PA PB139 Board minutes, 15 October 1929.
4 *Ibid.*, 4 April 1930.
5 PA PB97/126 A.C.Pilkington file, R.A. Pilkington to A.C.Pilkington, 8 August, 27 September 1930, A.C.Pilkington to R.A.Pilkington, 9 August 1930.
6 Information from Arnold Pilkington.
7 See Table 54, p 401.

8 PA NI2 First interim report of the National Institute of Industrial Psychology, 5 May 1933, 2–3 (see note 64, below).

9 Leslie Hannah, 'Managerial Innovation and the Rise of the Large-Scale Company in Interwar Britain', *Economic History Review*, May 1974. The rest of this paragraph is based mainly upon this source.

10 Alfred D. Chandler, Jr., *Strategy and Structure* (Cambridge, Mass. 1962), 383.

11 *Ibid.*, 342 *seq.*

12 Information from P.L. Robson.

13 Asa Briggs, *Seebohm Rowntree, 1831–1954* (1961), 177, 272–4.

14 PA PB139 Board minutes, 2 May 1930.

15 *Ibid.*, 25 June, 7 August, 1 December 1930.

16 *Ibid.*, 1 March 1928.

17 *Ibid.*, 22 May 1931.

18 PA ZZ72 Chance Brothers General Meeting Book, 1889–1938.

19 PA PB139 Board minutes.

20 *Ibid.*, 30 June 1931.

21 *Ibid.*, 1 July 1931.

22 *Ibid.*, 4 July 1931.

23 PA PB260 Executive Committee minutes, 9 September 1931.

24 PA PB139 Board minutes, 4 July 1931.

25 *Ibid.*, 21 July 1931 upon which all the previous part of this paragraph is based.

26 *Ibid.*, 4 July 1931.

27 *Ibid.*, 26 January 1939.

28 *Ibid.*, 25 January 1951.

29 PA PB260 Executive Committee minutes, 17 December 1932; PB139 Board minutes, 28 September 1950.

30 Information from P.L. Robson.

31 PA PB260 Executive Committee minutes 31 July 1931; PB139 Board minutes, 26 May 1932.

32 PA PB139 Board minutes, 28 October 1931.

33 *Ibid.*, 1 June 1934.

34 *Ibid.*

35 *Ibid.*, 1 June 1934; 28 May, 25 July 1935, 24 September 1936, 31 May 1937, 26 January 1939.

36 *Ibid.*, 27 September 1934, 24 September 1936; PB260 Executive Committee minutes, 3 October 1934, 22 May, 4 September, 28 November 1935, 14 October 1936.

37 PA PB139 Board minutes, 24 September 1936, 31 May 1937.

38 PA PB260 Executive Committee minutes, 3 October 1934; PB139 Board minutes 27 May 1943.

39 *Ibid.*, 1 June 1934.

40 PA PB260 Executive Committee minutes, 4 September 1935, 1 December 1938; PB139 Board minutes, 29 November 1945, 31 January, 28 March 1946, 30 January 1947.

41 PA PB260 Executive Committee minutes, 2 September 1931; PB139 Board minutes, 26 March 1936, 31 May 1937.

42 PA PB139 Board minutes, 26 November 1936, 26 May 1938.

43 *Ibid.*, 1 June 1934, 21 July 1937.

44 *Ibid.*, 16 March 1932.

45 PA PB260 Executive Committee minutes, 15 June 1932.

46 PA PB258 Executive Committee papers, 15 June 1932.

47 Michael Sanderson, *The Universities and British Industry, 1850–1970* (1972), 248.

48 PA PB139 Board minutes, 27 September 1934; PB260 Executive Committee minutes, 4 October 1934.

49 *Ibid.*, 15 June 1932.

50 *Ibid.*, 7 December 1932, 4, 18 January, 21 February, 26 April, 8, 17 May, 21 July, 6 September, 15 November 1933; PB139 Board minutes, 26 January 1933.

51 PA PB258 Executive Committee papers, 14 April 1937.

52 Management Research Group No. 1, Report on Meeting, 5 April 1932. I am grateful to Mr Harry Ward of 4 Lindsay Close, Epsom, for a sight of this document in his possession.

53 PA PB258 Executive Committee papers, 12 January 1938.

54 *Ibid.*, 15 June 1932, Notes regarding Staff Training as it affects the Accountants' Department.

55 *Ibid.*, 2 November 1932, P.L. Robson, 'Budgetary Control', 3 October 1932; PB260 Executive Committee minutes, 7 December 1932.

56 Information from P.L. Robson.

57 PA PB260 Executive Committee minutes, 2 November 1932; PB139 Board minutes, 1 December 1932.

58 PA PB192 Minutes of the Joint Industrial Council, 20 February 1933; PB139 Board minutes, 28 September 1933.

T*

59 PA PB260 Executive Committee minutes, 8 June 1933, 7, 21 February 1934; PB139 Board minutes, 25 January, 25 March 1934.

60 PA PB260 Executive Committee minutes, 19 June 1935.

61 C.B.Frisby, 'The Development of Industrial Psychology at the NIIP', *Occupational Psychology*, 1971, 33–7.

62 PA PB260 Executive Committee minutes, 16 November 1932, 4 January 1933.

63 PA PB182 National Institute of Industrial Psychology (NIIP), Second and Third Reports.

64 PA NI2 NIIP First Interim Report recommending Methods Department, 5 May 1933; Second Interim Report on recruitment, 1 June 1933; PB182 Third Report on recruitment and conditions of service for clerical staff, 9 September 1933; Fourth and Final Report in two parts dated 3 September and 6 October 1933.

65 PA PB260 Executive Committee minutes, 21 June and 5 July 1933.

66 PA PB182 NIIP Fourth and Final Report; PB260 Executive Committee minutes, 15 June 1935.

67 *Ibid.*, 5, 26 February 1936.

68 *Ibid.*, 25 January, 8 February, 26 April, 5 July 1933.

69 *Ibid.*, 16 May 1934.

70 *Ibid.*, 18 October 1933.

71 *Ibid.*, 16 September, 28 October 1936; PB295/1104 File 112, 1936–8, circular from Harry Ward, 9 November 1936.

72 PA PB139 Board minutes, 9 October 1918.

73 PA PB260 Executive Committee minutes, 7 February, 7 March 1934.

74 *Ibid.*, 6, 20 January 1932.

75 J.Moss, J.A.Baker and J.W.Pattinson, 'Transport, Rail and Water' in *Some Aspects of the Organisation* (privately printed by the company 1936).

76 Sanderson, *op. cit.*, 245; Michael Sanderson, 'Research and the Firm in British Industry, 1919–39', *Science Studies II*, 1972, 107–151.

77 PA PB260 Executive Committee minutes, 24 June 1936, 24 March 1937.

78 PA PB139 Board minutes, 12 February 1926.

79 PA PB139 Board minutes, 4 February, 9 April 1920.

80 PA PB260 Executive Committee minutes, 26 April 1933.

81 PA PB217 Minutes of the Technical Committee, 21 September 1933.

82 *Ibid.*, 27 November 1933.

83 *Ibid.*, 16 March 1934.

84 *Ibid.*, 23 July, 20 September, 22 November 1934, 23 January 1935, 17 September, 16 November 1936.

85 Sanderson, *The Universities and British Industry*, 1850–1970 (1972), 245.

86 W.J.Reader, *Imperial Chemical Industries: A History*, II (1975), 346.

87 PA PB260 Executive Committee minutes, 1 May 1934; 16 April 1935.

88 *Ibid.*, 4 September 1935.

89 Reader, *op. cit.*, II, 346; PB260 Executive Committee minutes, 25 September 1935.

90 Reader, *op. cit.*, II, 346; PB260 Executive Committee minutes, 28 April, 23 June 1937.

91 ICI Records, Board minutes no. 12,222; supporting papers 20 May 1948.

92 PA PB260 Executive Committee minutes, 18 March, 1 and 17 April, 22 May, 15 December 1936, 23 June, 1 September 1937, 23 February, 1 June (with supporting papers), 26 October, 9 November 1938, 1 February, 14, 26 April, 24 May, 7, 21 June, 4, 19 July 1939, 4 April, 1 May, 12 June 1940; Norman Hackforth, *Solo for Horne* (1976), 17, 21, 23, 84.

93 PA PB260 Executive Committee minutes, 23 June 1937.

94 PA PB139 Board minutes, 30 September 1937; PB260 Executive Committee minutes, 12 September 1938; PB217 Technical Committee minutes, 9 September 1938.

95 PA PB260 Executive Committee minutes, 17 April 1939.

96 *Ibid.*, 22 October 1936.

97 *Ibid.*, 23 February 1938.

98 PA PB139 Board minutes, 28 January 1937.

99 PA PB258 Executive Committee papers, 14 October 1936.

100 PA PB217 Technical Committee minutes, 17 November 1938.

101 PA PB258 Executive Committee papers, 14 October 1936.

102 PA PB260 Executive Committee minutes, 1 June 1938, 28 September 1939.

103 PA PB139 Board minutes, 27 July 1933, 27 September 1934.
104 *Ibid.*, 9 January 1935.
105 PA PB260 Executive Committee minutes, 19 April 1937.
106 PA PB139 Board minutes, 4 September 1939.

20
NEW DEVELOPMENTS AT
HOME AND OVERSEAS

1 Hugh Barty-King, *To See Through a Glass Safely. The Triplex Story, 1912–72* (unpublished MS.), 7–9.
2 PA PB1/1609 Triplex: Benedictus Patent 1911–29; Barty-King, *op. cit.*, 5–6.
3 PA PB1/1609 Triplex: Benedictus Patent 1911–29, Rivet to Pilkington, 13 June 1911, Pilkington to G.H.Baillie, 16 June 1911. Baillie, who acted as Pilkington's London patent agent until the 1930s, was to become widely known as a leading authority upon the history of clock- and watch-making.
4 *Ibid.*, G.H.Baillie's report, 19 June 1911, E.A.Maund to Pilkington, 23 August 1911, Pilkington to Maund, 24 August 1911.
5 *Ibid.*, J.S.Hitchcock to Pilkington, 30 March 1912.
6 Barty-King, *op. cit.*, 23–31, 35.
7 PA PB1/1609 Triplex: Benedictus Patent 1911–29, Visit of Delpech, 28 January 1915.
8 This paragraph is based upon Barty-King, *op. cit.*, 40–65.
9 PA PB97/122 Triplex Safety Glass Co. 1927–30, R.M.Weeks to R.A.Pilkington, 13 September 1929.
10 PA PB139 Board minutes (Cowley Hill Works), 1 December 1925.
11 *Ibid.*, 16 November 1927.
12 PA PB97/122 Triplex Safety Glass Co. 1927–30, Clare to R.A.Pilkington, 20, 21 December 1927; Barty-King, *op. cit.*, 80.
13 ICI Archives, EC SP 2/2/27, 12/2/27, 5/3/28, Papers by Mond. I owe these references to Dr W.J.Reader.
14 Barty-King, *op. cit.*, 73–5, 86; PA PB97/122 Triplex Safety Glass Co. 1927–30, R.A.Pilkington to C.E.Fletcher (Cooper Brothers), 17 July 1929.
15 PA PB2 Triplex Patents, Triplex agreement with Austin, 7 December 1927.
16 PA PB285/T3 Pilkington agreement with Triplex, 25 January 1928.
17 Article on PPG in *Glass Manual* (1946); PA PB97/103 J.E.Harrison File, 1930–3, Cutting from *New York Journal of Commerce*, 19 December 1931, J.E.Harrison to Pilkington, 4 December 1931; PB97/97 LOF file, Sands, de Rhom and Co.'s report in LOF, 8 January 1934.
18 P.W.S.Andrews and Elizabeth Brunner, *The Life of Lord Nuffield* (Oxford 1955), 185.
19 Barty-King, *op. cit.*, 84, 88, 106; PA PB97/122 Triplex Safety Glass Co. 1927–30, Clare to R.A.Pilkington, 8 June 1928. Clare reported to Pilkington (*ibid.*, 21 December 1927) that in an effort to secure the Morris contract Delpech had taken a passage on a sailing of the *Aquitania* on which it was known that Morris was travelling. The Vice-President of the American Triplex Company in New York, with whom Morris was to be staying, had also been lobbied.
20 Barty-King, *op. cit.*, 92, 102–3; PA PB 97/122 Triplex Safety Glass Co. 1927–30, Clare to R.A.Pilkington, 10 December 1929.
21 *Ibid.*, Barty-King, *op. cit.*, 92, 104, 118.
22 *Ibid.*, 92, 104, 118.
23 PA PB 139 Board minutes, 7 February 1929.
24 *Ibid.*, 28 November 1928.
25 PA PB97/122 Triplex Safety Glass Co. 1927–30, R.A.Pilkington to Clare, 22 February 1929; R.A.Pilkington to Delpech, 8 March 1929; PB139 Board minutes, 27 June 1929.
26 PA PB97/122 Triplex Safety Glass Co. 1927–30, Minutes of meeting held in London 1 July 1929, R.A.Pilkington's notes of meeting with Clare, 10 July 1929.
27 PA PB285/T5 Licence from Triplex to Triplex (Northern), 8 October 1929.
28 PA PB139 Board minutes, 9 July 1929; PB97/122 Triplex Safety Glass Co. 1927–30, Minutes of meeting held in London, 1 July 1929.
29 PA PB139 Board minutes, 2 August 1929; PB97/122 Triplex Safety Glass Co., 1927–30, R.M.Weeks to R.A.Pilkington, 13 September 1929.
30 PA PB97/122 Triplex Safety Glass Co. 1927–30, R.A.Pilkington to C.E.Fletcher (Cooper Brothers), 17 July 1929.

31 *Ibid.*, R.A.Pilkington to Clare, 9 August 1929, Clare to R.A.Pilkington, 15 August 1929, R.M.Weeks to Clare, 16 August 1929, interview with Andreae of Triplex, 20 August 1929, Graham Cunningham to Pilkington, 14 February, 3 March 1930, Weeks to Cunningham, 19 February 1930; W.J.Reader, *Imperial Chemical Industries. A History*, II (1975), 341–2.

32 *The Times*, 5 December 1931 (cutting in PA PB97/122 Triplex 1924–32); PB97/124 Meetings of Directors of Triplex (Northern), 18 February 1934.

33 Notes by L.J.-B.Forbes.

34 P.Lesley Cook, *Effects of Mergers* (1958), 328; Barty-King, *op. cit.*, 123, 164.

35 PA PB97/122 Triplex Safety Glass Co. 1927–30 R.M.Weeks to R.A.Pilkington, 13 September 1929.

36 Barty-King, *op. cit.*, 125.

37 *Ibid.*, 124.

38 The Motor Vehicles (Construction and Use) Regulations 1931. S.R. & O. Number 4. The Minister of Transport was empowered to bring in these regulations by the Road Traffic Act, 1930.

39 PA PB139 Board minutes, 4 and 16 September 1930; PB97/122 Triplex Safety Glass Co. 1924–32, Meeting between Cozens-Hardy and Graham Cunningham in Paris, 30 October 1930.

40 PA PB285/T6, Agreement dated 8 May 1931.

41 PA PB97/122 Triplex Safety Glass Co. 1924–32, Meeting 20 August 1931.

42 PA PB285/T7, Agreement between Pilkington and Triplex (Northern), 6 November 1931.

43 PA PB285/T8, Agreement between Pilkington and Triplex Safety Glass Co., 7 November 1931.

44 PA PB285/T11, Agreement between Triplex Safety Glass, Triplex (Northern) and Pilkington, 28 July 1933.

45 PA PB97/122 Triplex Safety Glass Co. 1932–35, Delpech to Cozens-Hardy, 11 March 1932; Pilkington to Delpech, 2 March 1932.

46 *Ibid.*, Interview at Morris Motors, 15 February 1932.

47 *Ibid.*, Meeting 18 February 1932; Barty-King, *op. cit.*, 156.

48 PA PB285/T9, Licence dated 28 July 1933; Barty-King, *op. cit.*, 162.

49 PA PB260 Executive Committee minutes, 21 June 1933.

50 Barty-King, *op. cit.*, 163.

51 PA PB97/124 Meetings of Triplex (Northern) Directors, 10 February 1933, 30 April 1935, 4 February 1936.

52 PA PB285/T139 Licence from Pilkington to Triplex (Northern), 28 October 1935; PB97/124 Minutes of meetings of Triplex (Northern) Directors, 25 June, 5 September 1935.

53 PA PB97/131 CIG file, Frérichs to Cozens-Hardy, 23 July 1938, Cozens-Hardy to Frérichs, 27 July 1938, Statistical table, 26 April 1939.

54 PA PB97/133 Minutes of Plate Glass Conference, 12 February, 23 September 1937; PB174 Pilkington accounts.

55 W.E.S.Turner, paper on 'Machinery and Methods of Sheet Glass', and R.F.Taylor's comments upon it, *Proceedings of the Institution of Mechanical Engineers*, December 1930, 1109–12, 1116, 1121; PA PB97/126 International Convention file, Delloye to Pilkington, 23 July, 10 October, 11 November 1913, Pilkington to Delloye, 17 October, 13 November 1913; PB139 Board minutes, 1 May 1929, 20 January, 4 April, 7 August, 16 October 1930; PB260 Executive Committee minutes, 9 September, 28 October 1931, 6 January 1932.

56 PA PB139 Board minutes, 4 June, 7 December 1926; RE2 interview with J.Harris Griffin.

57 PA PB139 Board minutes, 16 November 1927; RE2 interview with J.Harris Griffin.

58 *Ibid.*

59 PA PB139 Board minutes, 26 July, 27 September 1932.

60 PA PB260 Executive Committee minutes, 5 April, 8 June 1933; RE2 interview J.Harris Griffin.

61 PA PB260 Executive Committee minutes, 2 July 1936; PB258 Executive committee papers, 2 December 1936, 13 January, 14 April, 28 April, 19 May, 23 June, 11, 27 October, 10 November, 8 and 22 December 1937, 2 February 1938.

62 Raymond Chambon, *L'Histoire de la Verrerie en Belgique du IIᵉᵐᵉ Siècle à Nos Jours* (Brussels 1955), 224.

63 *Historical Statistics of the United States* (Washington 1960), 363, 462.

64 Chambon, *op. cit.*, 221.

65 PA PB97/128 Correspondence with Union Commerciale Glaceries Belges, Premiums and Arrangements for 1930.

66 *Ibid.*, de Longueville to Pilkington, 19 April 1930.

67 *Ibid.*, Pilkington to de Longueville, 22 April 1930.

68 PA PB260 Executive Committee minutes, 4 January 1933.

69 *Ibid.*, 18 October 1933.

70 PA PB253/80, Agreement of 2 May 1934.

71 *Ibid.*, Agreement of 31 December 1935.

72 Chambon, *op. cit.*, 224.

73 PA PB260 Executive Committee minutes, 19 October 1932.

74 *Ibid.*, 21 February 1933.

75 *Ibid.*, 7 November 1934.

76 PA PB285/38, Agreement dated 23 April 1932.

77 PA PB139 Board minutes, 20 January 1930; PB258 Executive Committee papers, 20 January 1932; PB260 Executive Committee minutes, 20 January, 6 and 20 April, 4 May, 1, 10, 15 and 28 June, 19 October, 2 November 1932, 21 February, 1 March and 30 November 1933.

78 *Ibid.*, 22 March 1934.

79 PA PB260 Executive Committee minutes, 20 September, 3, 17 October 1934, 6 February 1935.

80 PA PB285/63 Agreement between St Gobain and Pilkington, 24 May 1935.

81 PA PB285/136 Licence agreement with St Gobain for Twin, 20 October 1937.

82 See Graph 11 and H.W. Richardson, *Economic Recovery in Britain*, 1932–39 (1967), 154–5.

83 PA PB97/129, N.V. Hollandsche Maatschappij, J.B. Watt to Deschamps, 11 July 1934.

84 This paragraph is based upon information from J.B. Watt; PA PB260 Executive Committee minutes, 22 September, 19 October, 16 November and 7 December 1932, 4 January and 1 November 1933, 31 July 1935; PB174 Pilkington accounts.

85 PA PB260 Executive Committee minutes, 20 April 1932.

86 *Ibid.*, 4 May 1932.

87 *Ibid.*, 1 June 1932.

88 PA PB139 Board minutes, 26 July, 27 September and 1 December 1932.

89 PA PB260 Executive Committee minutes, 21 February, 5, 7, 12 and 26 April, 1933; PB139 Board minutes, 25 May 1933. The capital of Sheet Glass Limited consisted of 300,000, 1s. fully-paid ordinary shares and 135,000 7 per cent preference shares.

90 PA PB174 Pilkington accounts.

91 PA PB260 Executive Committee minutes, 22 September 1932.

92 PA PB139 Board minutes, 25 May 1933.

93 PA PB260 Executive Committee minutes, 5 July 1933.

94 *Ibid.*, 6 September 1933.

95 *Ibid.*, 18 October 1933.

96 Chambon, *op. cit.*, 223.

97 PA PB296/1185 contains notes of most of these meetings.

98 *Ibid.*, Meetings in Paris, 14 February 1935 and in London 1 April 1935; PB139 Board minutes, 28 November 1934, 21, 31 January 1935; PB260 Executive Committee minutes, 20 February, 4 September, 11 October 1935; Pilkington reply to Monopolies Commission Questionnaire (1966), 24; PB97/126 TD2, 16 March 1936.

99 Chambon, *op. cit.*, 223.

100 PA PB260 Executive Committee minutes, 23 September 1935.

101 *Ibid.*, 22 October 1936; PB186 Sales Committee minutes, 10 January 1939.

102 PA PB139 Board minutes, 20 July 1939.

103 PA PB260 Executive Committee papers, 9 February 1937.

104 *Ibid.*

105 *Ibid.*, PB139 Board minutes, 13 February 1937.

106 *Ibid.*, 13 February 1937.

107 PA PB260 Executive Committee minutes, 9 March 1937, 29 September 1938.

108 PA PB174 Pilkington accounts.

109 PA PB139 Board minutes, 20 July 1939.

110 PA PB260 Executive Committee minutes, 6 November 1935.

111 PA PB139 Board minutes, 30 September 1937; PB296/1185 Thick Drawn Sheet Glass Circulars, 23 October 1937.

112 PA PB139 Board minutes, 21 July 1937.

113 PA PB260 Executive Committee minutes, 11 October 1937.

114 *Ibid.*, 27 April 1938.

115 PA PB260 Executive Committee minutes, 9 February, 27 October 1937; PB258 Executive Committee papers, 24 February 1937.
116 PA PB186 Sales Committee minutes, 7, 21 November, 5 December 1938.
117 *Ibid.*, 9 August 1939.
118 PA PB258 Executive Committee papers, 1 September 1937; Executive Committee minutes, 21 June 1933, 1 April, 15 July 1936, 9 February, 9, 24 March 1937 6 April 1938; *Glass*, October, November 1937; the specially commissioned book, A.C.Frost and R.McGrath, *Glass in Architecture and Decoration*, was published by the Architectural Press in 1937 (rev. ed. 1961).
119 PA PB139 Board minutes, 26 July, 1 December 1932, 26 January, 23 March, 25 May, 27 July 1933, 22 March 1934; PB260 Executive Committee minutes, 1, 13, 22 March, 12 April, 1 November 1933; PB285/44 Agreement between Bailey Holding Company Limited and Pilkington concerning Rockware shares; 'The Rockware Story', *Glass*, January 1969.
120 PA PB260 Executive Committee minutes, 22 June 1938 (and supporting paper dated 18 June) and 13 July 1938.
121 *Ibid.*, 3 September, 9 November 1938.
122 PA PB218 Technical Committee minutes, 18 May 1939.
123 PA PB97/103 P.M.Hogg and E.B. LeMare visited America in the summer of 1930 to get ideas from Kahns about the manufacture of insulators (PB139 Board minutes, 2 May 1930; PB97/103 PB (Canada) Limited General 1926–30, R.A. Pilkington to J.E.Harrison, 20 May 1930, J.E.Harrison to R.A.Pilkington, 12 June 1930). Negotiations, conducted with M. Brudo, led to an agreement dated 16 November 1932 with S.A.Souchon Neuvesel and four other French companies (PB139 Board minutes, 26 May, 1 December 1932; PB260 Executive Committee minutes, 10 June, 2 November 1932; PB285/40, Précis of insulator licence with Société Anonyme des Verreries Souchon-Neuvesel, 16 November 1932). It was not until January 1937, however, that the Miscellaneous Department could report that it was 'within sight . . . of having a

complete range of insulators of first-class quality to market' (PB258 Executive Committee papers, 13 January 1937).
124 PA PB260 Executive Committee minutes, 6 March, 6 November 1935, 1, 22 April, 4 May, 24 June, 15 July, 16 September, 14, 22 October, 11 November, 15 December 1936, 27 October 1937; PB139 Board minutes, 24 September 1936; PB258 Executive Committee papers, 2 December 1936; PB285/93, Glass Brick licence with the Owens-Illinois Glass Company, 31 July 1936.
125 PA PB258 Executive Committee papers, 13 January 1937; PB260 Executive Committee minutes, 26 October, 5 December 1938.
126 *Ibid.*, 22 June, 13 July, 5 September 1938.
127 PA PB139 Board minutes, 22 March, 28 November 1934.
128 PA PB260 Executive Committee minutes, 6 March 1935.
129 PA PB295/1100, Memorandum on Cast Glass, PB and CB (Home Market), 18 December 1935; Table 35, p. 252.
130 Pilkington Replies to Monopolies Commission (1966), 45.
131 PA PB260 Executive Committee minutes, 1 November 1933, 5 September 1934.
132 *Ibid.*, 5 July, 3 October, 7 November 1934.
133 PA ZZ72, Note added in 1923.
134 PA ZZ43/6 Chance accounts.
135 PA PB260 Executive Committee minutes, 3 June 1935.
136 *Ibid.*, 19 June, 3, 31 July 1935.
137 PA ZZ5 Chance Board minutes, 20 December 1935.
138 PA PB139 Board minutes, 23 January 1936.
139 *Ibid.*, 28/29 May 1936.
140 *Ibid.*, 23 July 1936; PB285/97 Pilkington and Chance agreement concerning shares, 10 September 1936.
141 PA PB260 Executive Committee minutes, 14 October 1936.
142 *Ibid.*, 27 October 1937, 13 July 1938, 24 May 1939; PB139 Board minutes, 25 May 1939.
143 PA ZZ5 Chance Board minutes, 18 February 1931, 5 September 1933; PB139

Board minutes, 28 September 1933; PB260 Executive Committee minutes, 17 February 1932.

144 James Frederick Chance, *A History of the Firm of Chance Brothers and Co.* (privately printed 1919), 171–186.

145 For the technical development of glass fibres, see a series of articles in *Monthly Bulletin for the Glass Industry*, 1965–6.

146 PA ZZ45, Note by Sir Hugh Chance on the Firhill Glassworks, February 1964.

147 PA ZZ5 Chance Board minutes, 10 April 1930; ZZ136 Managing Directors' Committee minute book, 24 September 1930.

148 *Monthly Bulletin for the Glass Industry,* 1965–6.

149 *Ibid.*

150 PA ZZ5, Chance Board minutes, 19 July 1934; 9 April 1936.

151 PA ZZ45 Sir Hugh Chance, Note on Firhill.

152 PA PB260 Executive Committee minutes, 24 June 1936.

153 *Ibid.*, 14 October 1936.

154 PA ZZ61 Glass Fibres Limited, A.L.F. to W.H.S.Chance, 24 November 1937.

155 PA PB260 Executive Committee minutes, 12 January 1938.

156 *Ibid.*, 13 July 1938.

157 *Ibid.*, PB285/155 Pilkington and Chance agreement concerning glass fibres, 28 July 1938.

158 PA PB258 Executive Committee papers, 11 November 1936.

159 PA PB260 Executive Committee minutes, 26 November 1936.

160 PA PB260 Executive Committee minutes, 3 February, 6, 20 April, 21 November 1932, 21 June 1939, 12 June 1940; PB97/116 O.C.Hawkes file, especially Valentine to Tunnock, 15 August 1932 and Notes on the Business, 28 October 1932.

161 PA PB97/116, O.C.Hawkes File, Tunnock to Cozens-Hardy, 20 August 1932.

162 PA PB97/126 Andrewartha Limited 1929–40.

163 PA PB1/1361 Bahia Blanca depot 1924–57.

164 PA PB97/88 Pilkington Brothers (Brazil) file, 1922.

165 PA PB292 Correspondence with J.Thorpe concerning purchase of land for Rio warehouse 1917–1918; PB139 Board minutes, 25 May 1933; PB260 Executive Committee minutes, 26 October, 9 November 1938; 25 January 1939.

166 PA RE1 J.L.Kimmins reminiscences; S54 Copy of Pilkington Brothers (China) Limited minutes; PB97/126, Pilkington Brothers (China) Limited files 1920–32, 1932–46; PB260 Executive Committee minutes, 16 November 1932, 20 January 1937, 26 June 1940.

167 PA PB97/103, J.E.Harrison (Canada) file, 1930–3, J.E.Harrison to W.S.Tunnock, 12 December 1930; for Col. McLaughlin see obituary in *The Times,* 7 January 1972.

168 PA PB260 Executive Committee minutes, 1, 13 March, 21 June 1933.

169 PA PB285/49 Licence dated 21 November 1933.

170 PA PB258 Executive Committee papers, 14 April 1933 (Sales Committee).

171 PA PB260 Executive Committee minutes, 23 January 1936.

172 *Ibid.*, 29 April 1937.

173 PA PB139 Board minutes, 19 January 1938.

174 PA PB97/106, Pilkington Brothers (Australia) – Company formation, Minutes of first meeting, 10 April 1935.

175 J.R.Poynter, *Russell Grimwade* (Melbourne 1967), 23–7, 83–5, 118–9, 135–6, 176–8; PB97/106, Australian Glass Manufacturers (AGM) file, Correspondence, Copy of R.G.Dunn's Report on AWG, 12 September 1935. I have written at greater length about these matters in *Pilkington in Australia, 1920–45,* a 25-page duplicated monograph (Pilkington Group Archives and Records Service 1969). In addition to the sources cited, I owe much information to the participants in the events here described, notably A.P.Gee, Norman MacKenzie, Percy Norbury, George Scott, J.H.Pemberton and W.J.Smith himself (b. 1882) whom I met in Sydney at the end of 1968.

176 PA PB294/237 Australian Customs Tariff, Statements and Correspondence.

177 Evidence of W.J.Smith to the Commonwealth Tariff Board, 18 May 1931, 10 June 1932.

178 *Commonwealth Tariff Board's Report on Plain Clear Sheet Glass,* August 1932.

179 PA PB97/106 Dunn's Report on AWG.

180 PA PB97/106 AGM Correspondence, Meetings with Smith in London, 4 July, 27 August 1934; PB260 Executive Committee minutes, 26 July, 5 September, 3 October 1934.

181 *Ibid.*, 19 December 1934.

182 *Ibid.*

183 *Ibid.*

184 PA PB97/106 Pilkington Brothers (Australia) Company formation.

185 PA PB97/124 Minutes of Meetings of Triplex (Northern) Limited, 30 April 1935; PB260 Executive Committee minutes, 19 June 1935.

186 PA PB97/106 PB(A) Company formation file.

187 PA PB97/106 AGM Correspondence, telegram 5 April 1935.

188 *Ibid.*, Norbury to Pilkington, 3 May 1935.

189 PA PB139 Board minutes, 25 July 1935.

190 PA PB234 *Cullet*, Supplement April 1936, W.H.Pilkington, 'Leaves From Diary'.

191 PA PB97/106 AGM Correspondence, W.H.Pilkington (Wellington, NZ) to Cozens-Hardy, 10 October 1935; Pilkington Brothers (Australia) minutes, 2 November 1935 (in Australia).

192 PA PB97/106 AGM Correspondence, which includes copies of exchanges of cables at this time. Waldron later produced a full report on 'Conditions for Glassmaking in Australia', dated 20 January 1936, which is to be found in PB97/106 Pilkington Brothers (Australia).

193 PA PB97/106 AGM Correspondence 1926–36, Cozens-Hardy to Weeks, 1 December 1935; PB139 Pilkington Board minutes, 23 January 1936; PB97/106 AGM Correspondence 1935–8, Cable to Sydney, 21, 30 January, 7 February 1936, Cozens-Hardy to A.C.Pilkington, 25 February 1936.

194 *Ibid.*, Pilkington to Norbury, 12 March 1936, AGM to Pilkington, 5 March 1936.

195 Pilkington Brothers (Australia) minutes, 2 March 1937 (in Australia).

196 *Ibid.*, 21 March 1944.

197 PA PB139 Board minutes, 23 January 1936; PB260 Executive Committee minutes, 22 April, 15 July 1936. J.B.Watt visited Canada to investigate these possibilities.

198 *Ibid.*, 22 January, 18 March, 24 June 1936, 4, 19 July, 18 August, 1939; PB186 Sales Committee minutes, 20 March, 26 June 1939.

199 PA PB139 Board minutes, 26 November 1936; PB260 Executive Committee minutes, 15 December 1936, 13 January, 9 February, 19 May 1937.

200 PA PB139 Board minutes, 28 November 1935.

201 For further details, see my *Pilkington in New Zealand, 1900–45* (Pilkington Group Archives and Records Service 1969).

202 PA PB260 Executive Committee minutes, 21 June 1933.

203 *Ibid.*, 19 December 1934.

204 *Ibid.*, 19 June 1935.

205 *Ibid.*, 3 July 1935.

206 *Ibid.*, 23 July 1935.

207 *Ibid.*, 23 October 1935, 26 February, 18 March, 1 April, 4, 22 May, 14 October 1936.

208 PA PB285/99, 3 October 1936.

209 PA PB285/T16A, Licence dated 31 December 1937.

210 PA PB139 Board minutes, 26 July 1932; PB260 Executive Committee minutes, 28 June, 7, 11, 20 July 1932.

211 PA PB260 Executive Committee minutes, 22 March 1933.

212 PA PB139 Board minutes, 19 April 1933.

213 PA PB260 Executive Committee minutes, 20 February, 19 June, 3 July 1935, 8 January 1936.

214 *Ibid.*, 18 December 1935; 18 March, 22 May 1936.

215 PA PB139 Board minutes, 23 January 1936; PB260 Executive Committee minutes, 13 January 1937. In September 1937, the Executive agreed to send the second toughening furnace to Llavallol and a third was to be put in hand (*ibid.*, 1 September 1937).

216 PA PB139 Board minutes, 28/9 May 1936; PB260 Executive Committee minutes, 23 July, 14 October 1936.

217 *Ibid.*, 24 March, 14 April 1937.

218 PA PB97/81 Rigolleau file, for details of these negotiations which petered out at the end of 1937.

219 PA PB139 Board minutes, 24 November 1938. (Telegram received that day.)

220 *Ibid.*, 28 May 1935.
221 *Ibid.*, 28 November 1935, 18 March 1936.
222 *Ibid.*, 27 July, 28 September, 30 November 1933.
223 *Ibid.*, 26 July, 27 September 1934.

21

LABOUR RELATIONS AND
WELFARE SERVICES, 1918-39

1 D.E.Baines and R.Bean, 'The General Strike on Merseyside' in J.R.Harris (ed.), *Liverpool and Merseyside* (1969), 253; PA PB192 Joint Industrial Council (JIC) minutes, 6 December 1926. For an interesting, if brief, account of the General Strike at St Helens which was confined almost entirely to the coalmining and transport industries (and particularly the tramways), see Bob Davies's contribution to Jeffrey Skelly (ed.), *The General Strike, 1926* (1976), 330-9.
2 For 1927 statistics, see Table 54. Those for 1930-4 will be found in PA PB260 Executive Committee Papers, 20 March 1935 and for 1937 in PB139 Board minutes, 19 January 1938.
3 T.S.Wason, 'Superannuation and Pension Funds' in *Some Aspects of the Organisation* (Pilkington Brothers Limited, rev. ed. December 1936), 153.
4 Thomas Williamson (1867-1954) worked 'half-time' at Pilkington's Sheet Works before emigrating to Argentina (at 20) where he remained for about seven years; Vice-Chairman JIC 1918-38; NAUL official delegate 1905-24; NUGMW Liverpool district secretary 1924-37. See *Cullet* No. 42, 17 (1939) and H.A.Clegg, *General Union in a Changing Society* (1964).
5 PA PB192 JIC minutes, 30 August, 5 November 1918.
6 *Ibid.*, 3 December 1918.
7 *Ibid.*, 1 April 1919.
8 *Ibid.*, 12 December 1919.
9 This and the succeeding paragraphs are based upon 'Pilkington Brothers' Garden Village Ventures: The End of the Garden City/Suburb Movement', a manuscript written by Barbara R.Penny of the Austra-

lian National University in January 1976 and based upon PA PB1/422 Public Utility Society 1919-25; PB1/491 Pilkington Garden Village Limited 1921-3; PB1/502 Eccleston Hall Estate Garden Village 1919-41; PB1/826 Doncaster Housing; PB1/852 Eccleston Housing; PB1/853 Eccleston Hall Estate Garden City 1917-21; PB1/851 Ravenhead Estate and Garden suburb 1905-14; PB1/1280 Kirk Sandall Village Schemes. I am most grateful to Mrs Penny for sending me an advance copy of this work. For the garden city movement more generally, see William Ashworth, *The Genesis of Modern British Town Planning* (1954), ch. 5.
10 PA PB192 JIC minutes, 15 April 1920.
11 *Ibid.*, 8 November 1920.
12 *Ibid.*, 11 October 1923.
13 PA PB139 Board minutes, 10 August, 18 December 1917.
14 T.S.Wason, *op. cit.* 136 seq.
15 *Ibid.*, 140; PA PB139 Board minutes, 23 October 1919.
16 *Ibid.*, 27 February 1920.
17 For details, see Alan Wild, 'The Origins of the National Union of General and Municipal Workers at Pilkington Brothers, St Helens' (University of Warwick MA thesis 1974), 93-104.
18 PA PB192 JIC minutes, 7 June, 8 November 1920, 19 January 1921, 31 March, 5 July 1922.
19 *Ibid.*, 2 May, 29 November 1923, 14 July 1924, 2 February, 21 April 1925.
20 PA PB139 Board minutes, 13 March 1923.
21 PA PB192 JIC minutes, 2 May 1923.
22 PA PB139 Board minutes, 28 July, 20 October 1924; PB192 JIC minutes, 11 June, 3, 11 November 1924; 2 February 1925.
23 Wason, *op. cit.* For supplementary state pensions, see Bentley B.Gilbert, *British Social Policy, 1914-1939* (1970), 244-251.
24 PA PB139 Board minutes, 20 October 1924.
25 *Ibid.*, 26 February 1925.
26 Wason, *op. cit.*, 150.
27 PRO, LAB 2/714/12579/9A cited in Wild, *op. cit.*, 35.
28 PA PB139 Board minutes, 22 December 1926.
29 PA PB258 Executive Committee papers, 2 November 1932.

30 *Ibid.*, 25 January 1933.

31 PA PB260 Executive Committee minutes, 13, 22 March, 26 April, 21 July, 16 August 6, 20 September 1933; PB139 Board minutes, 25 January, 27 September 1934.

32 PA PB258 Executive Committee papers, 16 May 1934.

33 PA PB260 Executive Committee minutes, 24 February 1937; PB258 Executive Committee papers and PB260 Executive Committee minutes, 1 September 1937.

34 PA PB192 JIC minutes, 14 July 1936.

35 *Ibid.*, 8 February 1937.

36 PA PB260 Executive Committee minutes, 14 April 1937.

37 PA PB258 Executive Committee papers, 2 February 1938.

38 PA PB260 Executive Committee minutes, 4 October 1933.

39 *Ibid.*, 27 October 1937; PB139 Board minutes, 19 January 1938. *Glass*, January 1938.

40 PA PB139 Board minutes, 12 February 1926; PB260 Executive Committee minutes, 23 June 1927.

41 PA PB234 *Cullet News*, May 1964.

42 PA PB258 Executive Committee papers, 23 February 1938; PB139 Board minutes, 24 March 1938.

43 Iolo A. Williams, *The Firm of Cadbury, 1831-1931* (1931), 156, 160; Asa Briggs, *A Study of the Work of Seebohm Rowntree* (1961), 100-1.

44 W. J. Reader, *Imperial Chemical Industries: A History*, II (1975), 69.

45 D. C. Coleman, *Courtaulds* II (Oxford 1969), 448.

46 J. A. R. Pimlott, *The Englishman's Holiday* (1947), 155, 214, 219-221.

47 Reader, *op. cit.*, 68.

48 PA PB260 Executive Committee minutes, 23 June 1937, 26 May 1938 (Watt), 5 September 1938 (Slocombe), 7 June 1939 (Waldron).

49 *Ibid.*, 19 January, 2 February, 24 March 1938. Williamson's nephew, also named Thomas, was to become General Secretary of the National Union of General and Municipal Workers between 1946 and 1961 and then a life peer in the following year.

22
EPILOGUE, 1939-76

1 This chapter is based upon information from the Pilkington Accounts and Personnel Departments, the company's replies to questions from the Monopolies Commission (1966) and private communications.

2 Monopolies Commission: Report on the Supply of Flat Glass (1968), para. 301, 302, 304.

3 PA PB139 Board minutes, 29 November 1945. My italics.

APPENDIX 3
BESSEMER'S EXPERIMENTS WITH GLASS 1841-51

1 British Patent 9100 of 1841.

2 PA BPG5 Minutes, 27 October, 10 and 24 November 1841.

3 British Patents, 11,317 of 1846 and 11,794 of 1847.

4 This account is based upon J. F. Chance, *A History of the Firm of Chance Brothers & Co.* (privately printed 1919), 64-77.

5 Sir Henry Bessemer, *An Autobiography* (1905), 113-5.

6 Cited in Chance, *op. cit.*, 72.

Index

This index contains references to the text, appendices, and footnotes where these introduce additional material of an informative kind; purely bibliographical notes are not indexed.

Index prepared by Brenda Hall, M.A., Registered Indexer.

U*

294 C